THE
LATINO EXPERIENCE
IN U.S. HISTORY

CONSULTANTS

Pedro A. Cabán
Rutgers University

Bárbara Cruz
University of South Florida

José Carrasco
San Jose State University

Juan García
University of Arizona

GLOBE FEARON
EDUCATIONAL PUBLISHER
PARAMUS, NEW JERSEY

Paramount Publishing

ABOUT THE COVER

Illustrator Cindy Wrobel combined symbols and imagery from the root cultures of Latin America and from present-day Latino communities to create the cover design for *The Latino Experience in U.S. History.* Her design integrates these elements using vibrant colors that express the vitality, spirit, and diversity of Latino communities in the United States.

Executive Editor: Stephen Lewin

Project Editor: Dan Zinkus

Editors: Helene Avraham, Mindy DePalma, Francie Holder, Robert Rahtz, Kirsten Richert

Editorial Consultant: Deborah A. Parks

Literature Consultant: Angela M. Aguirre, Ph.D., Chairperson Department of Languages and Cultures, William Paterson College of New Jersey

Production Editor: June Bodansky

Production Manager: Penny Gibson

Production Supervisors: Walt Niedner, Nicole Cypher

Senior Product Manager: Elmer Ildefonso

Art Director: Nancy Sharkey

Electronic Interior Design and Production: Siren Design, Inc.

Maps: Mapping Specialists Limited

Photo Research: Omni-Photo Communications, Inc.

Cover Design and Illustration: Cindy Wrobel

Art Insert: Carol Anson

Printed in the United States of America.   1 2 3 4 5 6 7 8 9 10   98 97 96 95 94 93

ISBN: 0-835-90641-8

GLOBE FEARON
EDUCATIONAL PUBLISHER
PARAMUS, NEW JERSEY

Paramount Publishing

CONSULTANTS

Pedro A. Cabán is Associate Professor of Political Science and Chairperson of the Department of Puerto Rican and Hispanic Caribbean Studies at Rutgers University. He received his Ph.D. from Columbia University and has written and published on Puerto Rico's political economy and on multiculturalism in higher education.

José Carrasco is Chairperson of the Mexican American Studies Department at San Jose State University. He received his Ph.D. in Sociology of Education from Stanford University. He has worked in the social sciences with an emphasis on Mexican American Studies.

Bárbara Cruz is Assistant Professor of Social Science Education at the University of South Florida. She received her Ph.D. in Curriculum and Instruction from Florida International University. She has actively promoted both Latin American studies and global and multicultural studies at the secondary level of education.

Juan García is an Associate Professor of History and the Director of the University Teaching Center at the University of Arizona. He received his Ph.D. from the University of Notre Dame. The focus of his research is Mexican and Mexican American history, U.S. history, and ethnic studies.

REVIEWERS

Estella Acosta
Multicultual Education
Director
Orange County
Long Beach, California

John Arevalo
Social Studies Teacher
Harlendale High School
San Antonio, Texas

Theodore Bueno
Foreign Language,
Bilingual Education,
Red Program Administrator
and District Coordinator
Pueblo City School
District 60
Pueblo, Colorado

Mary García
Dean of Instruction
Pershing Middle School
Houston, Texas

Pilar de García
Bilingual Specialist
Albuquerque, New Mexico

Delores Gonzales Engelskirchen
District Superintendent
Chicago, Illinois

Lydia Hernández
Instructional Specialist
Cultural Heritage Center
Dallas, Texas

José E. Lebrón
Principal
Julia de Burgos
Middle School
Philadelphia, Pennsylvania

Albert Moreno
Bilingual Education
San Jose USD
San Jose ,California

Carrie Page
Social Studies Teacher
Sly Junior High School
Tampa, Florida

Manuel N. Ponce
Director of Mexican
American Education
Commission for Los
Angelels Unified School
District
Los Angeles, California

Carmen Idalia Sánchez
Assistant Principal of Social
Studies
South Bronx High School
Bronx, New York

Frank de Varona
Superintendent
Dade County Public
Schools, Region I
Hialeah, Florida

TABLE OF CONTENTS

◆ Unit 1

Spain in the Americas (1000–1700s)   2

THE BIG PICTURE   3

Chapter 1	**Face to Face in the Americas (1492–1540s)**	**10**
1	A Meeting in the Caribbean	11
2	Resistance and Conquest	13
3	Experiment in Empire Building	15
4	Out of Africa	17

Chapter 2	**Struggle for an Empire (1500–1525)**	**22**
1	Seeking Adventure and Gold	23
2	Marching to Tenochtitlán	25
3	Toppling an Empire	29

Chapter 3	**New Ways of Life (1521–1650s)**	**34**
1	Extending Spain's Reach	35
2	New Religious Voices	37
3	The Columbian Exchange	38
4	A Center of Spanish Culture	40

Latino Heritage: Sor Juana   40

Chapter 4	**Reaching Out From the Caribbean (1513–1695)**	**46**
1	La Florida	47
2	Outposts of Empire	48

Chapter 5	**The Spanish Borderlands (1536–1784)**	**54**
1	The Kingdom of New Mexico	55
2	Across the Rio Grande	58
3	Along the Pacific Coast	61

◆ Unit 2

Toward Independence (1763–1840s)   66

THE BIG PICTURE   67

Chapter 6	**The Spanish and the American Revolution (1763–1783)**	**74**
1	Supplying the Patriot Side	75
2	Joining the Fight	77
3	The First Cattle Drives	80

Chapter 7	**The Road to Independence (1783–1830)**	**84**
1	Challenges in the North	85
2	Independence for Mexico	88
3	Changes in Spanish America	89
Chapter 8	**Life in the Mexican Borderlands (1820s–1840s)**	**94**
1	Life in New Mexico	95
2	Life in Mexican California	98
3	Changing Ways in Texas	100

Latino Heritage: Ignacio Rodríguez Galván   **97**

◆ Unit 3

A Time of Upheaval (1830–1870)

A Time of Upheaval (1830–1870)		104
THE BIG PICTURE		**105**
Chapter 9	**Revolt in Texas (1820s–1836)**	**112**
1	A Time of Unrest	113
2	Alarms in Texas	114
3	Texas Gains Independence	117
Chapter 10	**War Between the United States and Mexico (1838–1848)**	**122**
1	Background to War	123
2	Mexico and the United States at War	126
3	Aftermath of War	128
Chapter 11	**Foreigners in Their Own Land (1848–1870s)**	**132**
1	Living Under a New Flag	133
2	Land Claims and Courts	135
3	Looking for Justice	137

Latino Heritage: *El Carroferril*   **138**

◆ Unit 4

A Time of Growth (1860–1920s)

A Time of Growth (1860–1920s)		142
THE BIG PICTURE		**143**
Chapter 12	**Latinos in the U.S. Civil War (1861–1865)**	**150**
1	The Civil War in the U.S. Southwest	151
2	Fighters for Two Flags	154

Chapter 13	**A Changing World (1860s–1912)**	**160**
1	New Spanish Immigration	161
2	Newcomers from Puerto Rico and Cuba	162
3	New Mexico	166
Chapter 14	**The Cuban-Spanish-American War (1868–1898)**	**172**
1	Background to Revolution	173
2	The War of 1895	174
3	Uncertain Victory	179
Latino Heritage: José Martí		**176**
Chapter 15	**Puerto Rico and Cuba Under United States Control (1898–1920s)**	**184**
1	The United States and Puerto Rico	185
2	The Republic of Cuba	188

◆ Unit 5

Changes in a New Century (1900–1945)

		194
THE BIG PICTURE		**195**
Chapter 16	**The Mexican Revolution and New Patterns of Immigration (1900–1920)**	**202**
1	Background to Revolution	203
2	A Long Struggle	204
3	North from Mexico	206
Chapter 17	**Latinos and World War I (1914–1920)**	**212**
1	Going to War	213
2	Growing Immigration	214
3	Moving North	219
Latino Heritage: *Registro de 1918*		**221**
Chapter 18	**From Boom to Depression (1920–1940)**	**224**
1	Boom Times of the 1920s	225
2	Hard Times and the New Deal	227
3	Organizing for Strength	231
Chapter 19	**Latinos and World War II (1941–1945)**	**236**
1	Latinos in the Armed Forces	237
2	The Home Front	239
3	Facing Prejudice	242

The Artists' View Follows Page 244.

◆ Unit 6

A Changing Postwar World (1945–1980)   248

THE BIG PICTURE   249

Chapter 20   The Great Migration from Puerto Rico (1945–1980)   256
      1   A New Form of Government   257
      2   Meeting New Challenges   260
      3   Lending a Helping Hand   262

Latino Heritage: Luis Palés Matos   263

Chapter 21   New Arrivals from the Caribbean (1945–1970s)   268
      1   Upheaval in Cuba   269
      2   A Growing Cuban Presence   273
      3   Turmoil in the Dominican Republic   277

Chapter 22   The Struggle for Equal Rights (1950s–1970s)   282
      1   *La Causa*   283
      2   A Time for Action   287

Chapter 23   New Immigrants from Central and South America (1950s–1970s)   296
      1   Struggle for Democracy in Central America   297
      2   New Voices from South America   299

Chapter 24   A Growing Voice (1945–1980)   304
      1   New Cultural Perspectives   305
      2   Reshaping Popular Culture   315
                 GALLERY OF LATINO WRITERS   308
                 GALLERY OF LATINO ARTISTS   310
                 GALLERY OF LATINO PERFORMING ARTISTS   312

◆ Unit 7

Latinos Today (1980–Present)   320

THE BIG PICTURE   321

Chapter 25   Mexican Americans Today (1980– Present)   328
      1   A Tale of Three Cities   329
      2   The Lure of *El Norte*   332

Chapter 26   Puerto Ricans Today (1980–Present)   338
      1   On the Mainland   339
      2   Ties to the Home Island   343

Chapter 27		**Cuban Americans Today (1980–Present)**	**348**
	1	New Waves of Refugees	349
	2	A Strong Cuban American Presence	352
Chapter 28		**Central Americans and Dominicans Today (1980–Present)**	**358**
	1	Leaving Central America	359
	2	A Growing Central American Presence	360
	3	Dominicans in the United States	362
Chapter 29		**South Americans in the United States Today (1980–Present)**	**368**
	1	The Lure of Freedom	369
	2	Building New Lives	371
Chapter 30		**Toward a New Century (1980–Present)**	**376**
	1	Latinos in the 1990s	377
	2	The Growing Reach of Latino Culture	381

Latino Heritage: Naomi Lockwood Barletta — **382**

GALLERY OF LATINO ENTREPRENEURS — **384**

GALLERY OF LATINO SCIENTISTS — **386**

Pronunciation Guide — **397**

Glossary — **398**

Sources — **403**

Index — **408**

Galleries

Gallery of Latino Writers	**308**	Octavio Medellín	311
Julia Alvarez	308	César Pelli	311
Sandra Cisneros	308	Pedro Pérez	311
Roberto Fernández	308	**Gallery of Latino Performing Artists**	**312**
Isaac Goldemberg	308	Martina Arroya	312
Nicholasa Mohr	309	Julio Bocco	312
Heberto Padilla	309	Joan Baez	312
Luis Valdez	309	Pablo Casals	312
Rima de Vallbona	309	Celia Cruz	313
Gallery of Latino Artists	**310**	Horacio Gutiérrez	313
Judith Baca	310	Tito Puente	313
Barbara Carrasco	310	Carlos Santana	313
George Febres	310	**Gallery of Latino Entrepreneurs**	**384**
Alberto Insua	310	Deborah Aguiar-Vélez	384
Antonio Martorell	311	Carlos José Arboleya	384

Nancy E. Archuleta	384	Angeles Alvariño de Leira	386
Oscar de la Renta	384	Teresa Bernárdez	386
Roberto C. Goizueta	385	Graciela Candelas	386
Luis Nogales	385	Francisco Dallmeier	387
Katherine Ortega	385	José Méndez	387
Joseph A. Unanue	385	Víctor Pérez-Méndez	387
Gallery of Latino Scientists	**386**	Pedro Antonio Sánchez	387
Luis Walter Alvarez	386		

Incorporated Biographies

Juan Garrido	15	Emiliano Zapata	205
Cuauhtémoc	31	Octaviano A. Larrazolo	218
Juana Inés de la Cruz	41	Luisa Moreno	232
Pedro Menéndez de Avilés	48	Carlos E. Castañeda	240
Angelina	59	Luis Muñoz Marín	257
Bernardo de Gálvez	76	Mercedes Cubria	274
Leona Vicario	88	Dolores Huerta	286
Manuel Armijo	96	Fernando Alegría	301
Antonio López de Santa Anna	114	Roberto Clemente	317
Juan Nepomuceno Cortina	139	Gloria Molina	331
Manuel Chaves	153	Nydia Velázquez	341
Vicente Martínez Ybor	165	Xavier Suárez	354
Paulina Pedroso	176	Rubén Blades	362
Luis Muñoz Rivera	186	Jaime Escalante	372
Carlos Juan Finlay	188	Henry Cisneros	383

Focus On

Rethinking Columbus Day	20	A Latino Astronaut	158
Rediscovering Aztlan	32	La Placita	170
The Gift of Maize	44	Guantánamo Bay	182
Cubans in Miami	52	El Morro	192
The Jémez Feast	64	Artists of the Revolution	210
The Heritage of New Orleans	82	Mutual Aid in Santa Barbara	222
The End of Slavery in South America	92	Basques of the United States	234
A Master Carver	102	The *Pachuco* Image	246
Tejano Place Names	120	Religious Diversity	266
Old Los Angeles	130	Latino Jews	280
El Clamor Público	140	A Changing Role for Latinas	294

The Tango   302

A Voice for Latino Writers   318

Border Jumpers   336

Puerto Rican Dance   346

The *Calle Ocho* Festival   356

The National Pastime   366

Honoring Latin American Heroes   374

Se Habla Español   390

Building Skills

Interpreting Primary Sources   21

Developing Empathy   33

Identifying a Point of View   45

Interpreting a Historical Map   53

Forming Inferences   65

Recognizing Relevant Information   83

Skimming and Scanning   93

Main Ideas and Details   103

Distinguishing Fact from Opinion   121

Stating the Main Idea in Your Own Words   131

Main Ideas in a Chapter Section   141

Stating an Implied Topic Sentence   159

Recognizing a Generalization   171

Recognizing a Generalization   183

Making a Generalization   193

Primary and Secondary Sources   211

Interpreting a Primary Source   223

Classifying Information   235

Drawing Conclusions   247

Interpreting Historical Statistics   267

Drawing Conclusions   281

Identifying Point of View in Poetry   295

Recognizing Propaganda   303

Understanding Points of View   319

Identifying Valid Generalization   337

Forming Generalizations Based Upon a Population Pyramid   347

Generalizing from a Primary Source   357

Analyzing Oral History   367

Interpreting a News Story   375

Identifying Trends   391

Maps

Early Native American Civilizations   6

Early Spanish Explorers   14

Spanish Empire in the Americas About 1600   43

Spanish Settlements in Florida and the Caribbean   50

Spanish Harbor Defenses in the Caribbean, 1695   53

Spanish Settlements in the Southwest   57

Spanish Settlements in California   63

Spanish Contributions in the American Revolution   78

Independence for Latin America   90

Mexico's Northern Frontier, 1822   108

Texas Revolt, 1835–1836   119

War Between the United States and Mexico, 1846–1848   125

The United States Gains Spanish and Mexican Lands   129

The Civil War in New Mexico, 1862   152

Cuban-Spanish-American War, 1895–1898   180

The Mexican Revolution and Mexican Migration to the United States   208

The Caribbean During the 1960s and 1970s   273

Conflict in Central America   300

Latino Population in the United States Today   325

The United States Today   392

Nations of the World   394

Latin America   396

Charts, Graphs, and Timelines

Unit 1 Timeline	4–5
Unit 2 Timeline	68–69
Unit 3 Timeline	106–107
Unit 4 Timeline	144–145
Unit 5 Timeline	196–197
World War I Honor Roll	215
Changes in the Lives of Latinos During the 1920s and 1930s	235
World War II Honor Roll	238
Unit 6 Timeline	250–251
Puerto Ricans in New York City and on the Mainland, 1950–1970	262
Unit 7 Timeline	322–323

Countries of Origin of Applicants for Amnesty, 1986–1988	334
Puerto Rican Population Distribution	340
Population of Children at Centro Mater, 1993	357
A Profile of Latinos Today	
U.S. Population, 1980–1990	378
Pouplation Projection, 1980–2020	378
States with the Largest Latino Populations	378
Latinos by Ethnic Group	379
Age Distribution of Latinos and Latinas	379
Selected Characteristics of Latino Families	379
Latinos and Latinas in the Labor Force	379
Latino Population in the United States, 1950–2010	391

ABOUT THE LATINO EXPERIENCE IN U.S. HISTORY

The book you are holding contains a very special story. It is the story of Latinos in the history of the United States. That story is older than the United States and any of the nations of Latin America. The story is also a very rich and personal one, reflecting the diversity of the Latino people. This book marks the first time that this story has been written especially for students.

This book is a *story* of the Latino experience, of people who shaped our history. It is told, as much as possible, in first-hand accounts of the people who lived it. Information from letters, diaries, official records, and interviews is combined with the latest available research to create a dramatic narrative of that Latino experience.

Latinos come from many countries and many cultures. This book recognizes that diversity. However, it also points out the backgrounds and experiences that different Latino people share. The focus of the book is the story of Latinos in the United States. The authors, however, realize that strong ties bind Latinos to their home countries and cultures. As a result, the text also describes events in Latin America. The impact of these events on this nation's history or on the lives of its Latino residents is part of the story.

The pages that you are about to read are filled with excitement. On them, bravery, endurance, struggle against incredible odds, suffering, and heroism all play their parts. The story they contain has been left out of U.S. history books for far too long a time. If this book helps awaken an awareness and an appreciation of that story, then it will have accomplished its mission.

Pedro Cabán

Juan García

José Carrasco

Bárbara Cruz

ABOUT THE
TERMS USED IN
THIS BOOK

The title of this book is *The Latino Experience in U.S. History.* We have used the words *Latino* and *Latina* to describe people in the United States whose roots lie in Spanish-speaking lands south of the United States. This territory includes Mexico, the nations of Central and South America, and many Caribbean islands.

Another word that is often used instead of *Latino* is *Hispanic.* That word is sometimes used in this text. When Hispanic is used here, the authors are highlighting connections with Spain rather than with the new cultures that developed in the Americas.

Other terms used in the book include *tejano, nuevomexicano,* and *californio.* These terms refer to people of Spanish-speaking descent who lived in lands now part of the United States but were once controlled by Spain and Mexico. The terms *Chicano* and *Chicana* are also used at times to describe U.S. residents of Mexican ancestry.

With all these terms—*Latino, Chicano, tejano, nuevomexicano, californio*—the authors have followed standard Spanish usage. Thus, *Latinos* generally refers to both males and females. When the authors are writing specifically about a woman or women from Spanish-speaking lands they would use *Latina* or *Latinas.*

The authors also frequently use the terms *Anglo* or *Anglos.* The words originally referred to English settlers in North America. They have come to mean any white U.S. resident of non-Latino descent.

U N I T

1

SPAIN IN THE AMERICAS
(1000–1700s)

Maya carving from the 600s AD

Chapter

1 Face to Face in
the Americas
(1492–1540s)

2 Struggle for an Empire
(1500–1525)

3 New Ways of Life
(1521–1650s)

4 Reaching Out From the Caribbean
(1513–1695)

5 The Spanish Borderlands
(1536–1784)

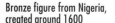

Bronze figure from Nigeria,
created around 1600

European sailors used astrolabe to navigate.

Unit 1 describes how three different groups of peoples—Native Americans, Africans, and Europeans—met in the Americas. By 1492, when the first Spanish ships arrived in the Americas, the peoples of these groups had developed distinctive **cultures**, or ways of life. As you will see, the collision of those cultures created a new culture in the Americas that combined elements of all three.

Peopling the Americas. About 2 million years ago, massive sheets of ice, called **glaciers** (GLAY-shuhrs), covered much of North America and Asia. Areas that had been under water had become dry land when the glaciers were created. One such dry area was a narrow land bridge that joined present-day Siberia, in Asia, with Alaska, in North America.

Over this bridge wandered a band of Asians who were following the trail of animals that provided most of their food. Dressed in animal skins and armed with stone-tipped spears, these new arrivals from Asia were the first of many humans to settle in the Americas. They were the ancestors of the people we call Native Americans.

This first **migration**—movement of a group from one place to another—may have occurred more than 30,000 years ago. Other such migrations followed from Asia to North America until rising seas covered the land bridge about 10,000 years ago.

Native Americans. Over time, the peoples from Asia spread east and south and made their homes over a wide area of the Americas. As Native Americans, some remained **nomads.** Many, like the Lakota of the Great Plains, wandered from place to place to hunt and gather food.

Peoples who drifted to warmer climates found ways to grow their own food and settled down. They farmed and grew crops of corn, squash, beans, and tomatoes. Over a long period of time, these people learned how to grow more than they and their families needed to **subsist,** or live on. They traded their **surplus**, or extra, crops with nonfarmers or with people who had different crops to trade. The Maya of the Yucatán Peninsula in what is now Mexico were farmers and traders.

Enormous Empires. In Mexico and Central and South America, farming peoples developed a number of great civilizations. In the dense forests of present-day Guatemala and the Yucatán (yoo-kah-TAHN) Peninsula of Mexico, one of these people, the Maya, carved out impressive cities. Their cities were religious centers. At the heart of each city stood a stone **pyramid** (PIHR-uh-mihd)—a huge building with a square base and sloping triangular sides. At the top of each pyramid was a richly decorated temple where priests worshiped the Maya's many gods and goddesses. They created systems of numbers

---

Voices of the Times

They came in battle array, as conquerors, and the dust rose in whirlwinds on the roads, their spears glinted in the sun, and their (banners) fluttered like bats.

— An Aztec describing the Spanish
arriving in the Valley of Mexico, 1519

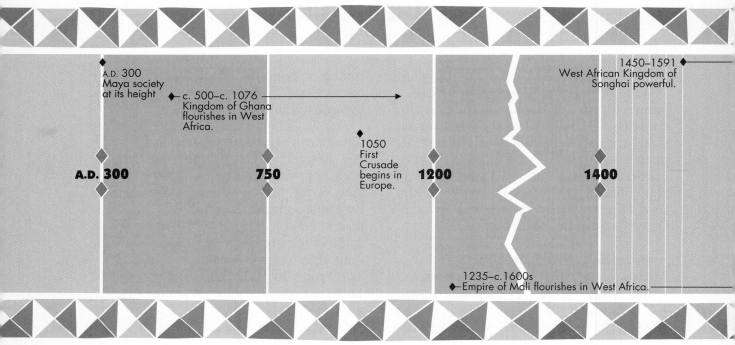

A.D. 300
Maya society
at its height

c. 500–c. 1076
Kingdom of Ghana
flourishes in West
Africa.

1050
First
Crusade
begins in
Europe.

1450–1591
West African Kingdom of
Songhai powerful.

A.D. 300　　　　**750**　　　　**1200**　　　　**1400**

1235–c.1600s
Empire of Mali flourishes in West Africa.

and of picture-writing. The Maya also invented a 365-day calendar more accurate than the one then used in Europe.

The Maya society of priests, nobles, peasant farmers, and slaves reached its peak between A.D. 300 and 900. Then, for some unknown reason, this society began to decline.

North of the Maya was another great early American civilization, that of the Aztec. From their remarkable island capital of Tenochtitlán (teh-nohch-tee-TLAHN), the Aztec ruled an empire covering most of Mexico. Aztec wealth came from trade and from the **tribute,** or payments, they forced conquered peoples to pay them. With this wealth, the Aztec built great pyramids like those of the Maya. But their harsh rule earned the Aztec the hatred of the people they conquered. As you will read, Aztec power came to an end when the Spanish invaded their land in the early 1500s (see page 25).

Another great American civilization was built high in the Andes Mountains of present-day Peru. There, the Inca ruled an empire of 16 million people. The Inca empire reached its peak in about 1500, just a short time before the Spanish invaded.

Peoples of the Southwest. Within 50 years of their arrival in the Americas, the Spanish had pushed into the deserts of what is now the southwestern United States. There, several ancient peoples had once flourished. One of these, the Mogollon (muhg-EE-ohn), got their food by farming and hunting.

Another ancient farming people of what is now the southwestern United States, the Hohokam (HOH-hoh-kuhm), were farmers who raised their crops in the dry lands by building irrigation ditches. These ditches brought water from the rivers of present-day Arizona to the Hohokam's fields of corn, squash, and beans.

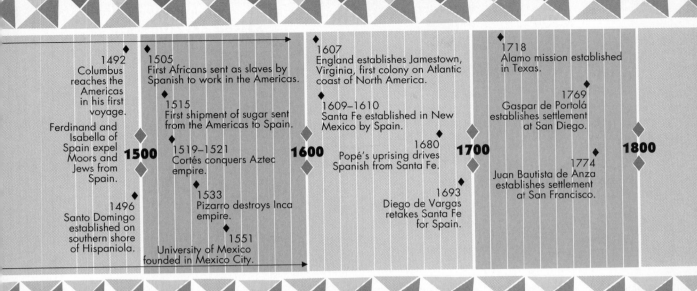

1492 Columbus reaches the Americas in his first voyage.

Ferdinand and Isabella of Spain expel Moors and Jews from Spain.

1496 Santo Domingo established on southern shore of Hispaniola.

1505 First Africans sent as slaves by Spanish to work in the Americas.

1515 First shipment of sugar sent from the Americas to Spain.

1500

1519–1521 Cortés conquers Aztec empire.

1533 Pizarro destroys Inca empire.

1551 University of Mexico founded in Mexico City.

1607 England establishes Jamestown, Virginia, first colony on Atlantic coast of North America.

1609–1610 Santa Fe established in New Mexico by Spain.

1600

1680 Popé's uprising drives Spanish from Santa Fe.

1693 Diego de Vargas retakes Santa Fe for Spain.

1718 Alamo mission established in Texas.

1769 Gaspar de Portolá establishes settlement at San Diego.

1700

1774 Juan Bautista de Anza establishes settlement at San Francisco.

1800

Many of the present-day Native Americans of the U.S. Southwest are the descendants of another people called the Anasazi (ahn-uh-SAHZ-ee). Like the Hohokam, they used irrigation to water their crops. The Anasazi built elaborate stone apartment houses on the steep sides of cliffs. Some structures were several stories high, with as many as 800 rooms.

In about 1300, the Anasazi scattered to other parts of the Southwest. The descendants of the Anasazi, among them the Hopi (HOH-pee) and the Zuñi (ZOON-yee), lived in villages of **adobe** (uh-DOH-bee) houses. Adobe is sunbaked brick made of clay and straw. The Spanish called these people the **pueblos,** after the Spanish word for village. These peoples were farmers. They also made beautiful pottery, baskets, and blankets and conducted religious ceremonies in underground chambers that were called **kivas** (KEE-vuhs).

In about 1500, the pueblo people were frequently attacked by the nomadic Navajo and the Apache who raided them for food. In time, though, the Navajos learned how to farm from the pueblos and also became sheepherders. The Apaches hunted for most of their food.

East of the Mississippi. Spanish explorers of the early 1500s also visited the Mississippi Valley and the lands of what is now the southeastern United States. One striking feature of the region that can be seen even today is huge earthen mounds in the shape of animals. These mounds were burial places built by early Native Americans. The Mound Builders lived in an area that stretched from the Mississippi River eastward for hundreds of miles, reaching almost to the Atlantic coast. Groups of Mound Builders lived in this region from about 2,800 years ago to as late as the 1700s.

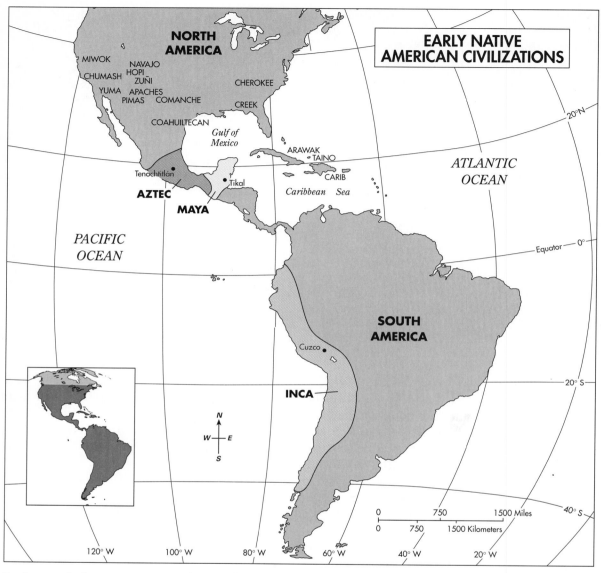

EARLY NATIVE AMERICAN CIVILIZATIONS

By the time the first Europeans landed in the Americas, Native Americans had created a wide variety of cultures. Why were their ways of life so different?

One group of Mound Builders, the Mississippians, built hundreds of villages with earthen mounds in the shapes of animals. From the peoples of what is now the U.S. Southwest, the Mississippians learned how to raise corn, beans, and squash. Although the Mississippians had vanished by about 1500, the Europeans met some of their descendants, the Cherokee, the Natchez, and the Creek.

African Homeland. The early peoples of the Americas are one group of ancestors of the people we now call Latinos. Another group came from Africa.

6

Africa was the home of one of the earliest and greatest civilizations of the world. Beginning in about 3500 B.C., along the Nile River, the Egyptians erected soaring stone pyramids as tombs for their rulers. They developed a system of writing and made important advances in mathematics and medicine.

African Empires of Gold. Wealth of another kind developed in Africa long after the great Egyptian civilization. Far to the west of Egypt, three grand kingdoms arose and fell between A.D. 500 and about 1600. West Africa was the homeland of most of the Africans who would be brought to the Americas.

The first kingdom was Ghana, which dated from about 500 to the early 1200s. The name of the empire, *Ghana,* itself meant gold. The ruler of Ghana was called "king of gold," and he wore a tall golden cap. Ghana's king was so rich that he could support an army of 200,000—the largest in the world at that time.

Next, beginning in the early 1200s and lasting until about 1450, came the empire of Mali. As large as Western Europe, Mali was even wealthier than Ghana. During the rule of Mali's famous king, Mansa Musa (MAHN-suh MOO-suh), the city of Timbuktu (tim-buk-TOO) became a major center of learning.

Finally, there was Songhai (sahng-HY), which flourished from 1450 to about 1600. Songhai was even larger than Mali, at its greatest extent covering most of West Africa. Its wise ruler, Askia Muhammad (AHS-kee-uh moo-HAM-uhd), set up a good government and fair taxation.

The wealth of these West African kingdoms depended on trade. Ghana, for example, was located on the trade route between a gold region to the south and the salt regions of North Africa. The people of West Africa depended on salt in their food to replace body salts lost in the terrible heat of the region. The people also used salt to keep food from spoiling.

The rulers of the empires kept tight control over trade. They collected taxes—paid in gold—on all trade goods passing through their lands. Ideas also moved along the trade routes. For example, from North Africa to the West African kingdoms came **Islam,** a religion based on the teachings of Muhammad.

The Slave Trade. Human merchandise also moved along the trade routes. In Africa, as in other parts of the world, such as Greece and Rome, **slavery,** or the system of owning people, went back hundreds of years. Usually, enslaved people were those captured by the Africans in wars. Working as farm laborers and servants, slaves were often able to purchase their freedom after a time.

In 1502, however, a Portuguese ship from Europe landed on the coast of West Africa. Slavery then underwent a drastic change. That ship carried away Africans as slaves to another land. They were the first of many millions who were taken from their homes and brought to the Americas over the next three hundred years. There, they and their descendants faced a lifetime of cruel bondage.

Widening Horizons for Europeans. Great changes within Europe brought the Europeans into contact with the West Africans and, later, the Native Americans. Before 1095, most Europeans knew little of the world beyond their own communities. In that year, however, European armies set out on the **Crusades.**

The Crusades were a series of religious wars aimed at winning back the Holy Land (modern-day Israel), sacred to Christians as the birthplace of Jesus. That land was ruled by the Arabs, who were **Muslims,** as people who practiced the religion of Islam were called. The Crusaders were not successful. The Holy Land remained in Muslim hands.

But important changes resulted from the Crusaders' contact with the Arabs. Europeans developed a taste for the products of the region. They wanted to buy spices, delicate porcelain dishes, and beautiful silks from India, China, and the Spice Islands of the Indies.

In those days, Arab traders brought these goods from Asia by a long, difficult overland route to ports along the Mediterranean. There they were met by Italian merchants, who then traded the goods in the rest of Europe.

Some Europeans wanted to bypass the Arab-Italian control of this trade. They started searching for new sea routes to Asia. One possible route lay around the southern tip of Africa, into the Indian Ocean. From there, ships might sail to India, China, and the Spice Islands. In 1488, a Portuguese sailor, Bartholomeu Dias (DEE-uhsh), managed to sail around the southern tip of Africa. Then, in 1498, Vasco da Gama (deh GAM-uh), another Portuguese, sailed all the way to India. The Portuguese now had a direct route to goods from Asia.

A New Spanish Nation. Other Europeans envied Portugal's success, especially the rulers of neighboring Spain. Since the 700s, a Muslim people called the Moors had controlled much of Spain.

Beginning in the 1000s, the Christians began *la Reconquista* (lah reh-cohn-KEES-tah), a reconquest, to win back the country from the Muslims. After many years of fighting, two Spanish rulers, King Ferdinand and Queen Isabella, drove out the last of the Moors in 1492. Determined to make all the people of Spain Christians, the rulers also expelled the Jews who lived in Spain. Spain was now a single nation under one crown and with one religion.

Ferdinand and Isabella were now in a position to approve the plans of an Italian sea captain named Christopher Columbus. Columbus had been begging them for six years to finance a wild scheme. He wanted to reach Asia by sailing west across the Atlantic. At the time, no one, including Columbus, realized that two continents and many thousands of miles lay between Europe and Asia.

On August 3, 1492, with the backing of the Spanish monarchs, Columbus set out on his historic voyage. Three months later, his three tiny ships landed at the island he named San Salvador (see page 11). Columbus's arrival in the Americas proved to be a turning point in world history.

Race for Colonies. Columbus returned to Europe with exaggerated reports of the riches he expected to find. The news rocked Europe. Fearing that Spain would cheat it out of lands it was about to claim, Portugal almost declared war. Instead, the two nations agreed to have the Pope, the head of the Roman Catholic Church, settle their dispute. Under the settlement, Spain claimed all of North America and most of South America. Only a part of eastern South America, later known as Brazil, went to Portugal.

France and England refused to accept this plan. They soon sent explorers of their own to the Americas. But until the early 1600s, neither France nor England was strong enough to start any **colonies,** or permanent settlements, in the Americas.

Spain, however, lost no time in taking advantage of its claim to the Americas.

Eager for gold and glory, Spanish **conquistadors** (kahn-KEES-tuh-dohrs), or conquerors, set out. Hernán Cortés (kohr-TES) crushed the Aztec empire in Mexico, while Francisco Pizarro (pih-ZAHR-oh) toppled the Inca empire of South America. To the north, other conquistadors laid claim to much of the present-day United States, including Florida, Arizona, New Mexico, Texas, and California. As Spanish ships returned from the Americas, loaded with gold and silver, Spain's empire became the envy of Europe.

Determined to share in the loot, English **sea dogs,** or pirates, swooped down on Spanish treasure ships, sinking them and carrying off their valuable cargoes. Spain finally sent a huge fleet, or **armada**, of 68 ships and 60,000 soldiers to punish England in 1588. But English ships pounded the Spanish Armada severely, and a violent storm finished off the attackers. This victory paved the way for the English to build colonies in North America.

Beginning in 1607, England eventually established a string of 13 colonies along the Atlantic coast. About the same time, France gained a foothold in Canada. That foothold expanded to include all the land from the mouth of the St. Lawrence River west to the Rocky Mountains and south to the Gulf of Mexico.

New World Rivalries. Spain, England, and France kept claiming more territory in the Americas. England and France engaged in an especially fierce rivalry. Beginning in the late 1600s and continuing into the 1700s, they fought four separate wars that included fighting in the colonies.

While England, France, and Spain battled for the Americas, few thought about the people already living there. The Europeans had little concern for the Native Americans whose lands they seized. Few

The mighty Spanish Armada, tightly grouped at the top left, was destroyed in a famous 1588 battle.

wondered how the Africans brought to the Americas in chains felt about the loss of their liberty. Nor did the Europeans consider that the colonists themselves might not always see eye to eye with the people in their home countries.

As far as the Europeans were concerned, colonies existed for the benefit of the home countries. The colonies were to supply raw materials, gold and silver, and markets for goods. But after 1763, when the final war for empire between France and England ended, the European powers were forced to pay more attention to the people who lived in the American lands they ruled.

Taking Another Look

1. How did the Native American cultures of Mexico and Central and South America differ from those of what is now the southwestern United States?

2. How did the kingdoms of West Africa get their wealth?

3. Why was Spain in a position in 1492 to back Columbus?

4. **Critical Thinking** Why might the Europeans living in the colonies have a different idea about the purpose of colonies than people living in the home countries?

The first meeting of two worlds. An old European print shows Columbus meeting "Indians" who give him gifts of gold and other treasures. How would the search for gold affect the history of the Americas?

CHAPTER 1

Face to Face in the Americas

(1492–1540s)

SECTIONS

1 A Meeting in the Caribbean

2 Resistance and Conquest

3 Experiment in Empire Building

4 Out of Africa

THINKING ABOUT THE CHAPTER

How did the arrival of the Spanish in the Caribbean affect the course of world history?

The sailors of Palos (PAH-lohs), a shipbuilding port on the southern edge of Spain, prided themselves on their skill and courage. They braved wind and waves to pick up cargoes of pepper and enslaved peoples from the western coast of Africa. Many carried scars from naval battles with Spain's chief rival, Portugal. Now, in May 1492, a white-haired Italian sea captain had come to Palos and asked them to take part in a daring adventure. He wanted them to join him on a voyage west across the uncharted waters of the Atlantic, a route he promised would bring them to the riches of Asia.

The Italian, Christopher Columbus, carried a letter of support from the Spanish king and queen. But few sailors wanted to risk the unknown with a foreign sea captain. "Sea voyages are always uncertain," worried one sailor. "It's a voyage never before attempted," added another. So no one signed up.

Help finally appeared in the form of Martín Alonso Pinzón (ah-LOHN-soh peen-SOHN), one of the best sea captains in Palos. Martín Alonso Pinzón listened closely to Columbus's plan. Impressed with Columbus's knowledge of the sea, he agreed to serve as captain on one of Columbus's three vessels. His brother, Vicente Yañez Pinzón (YAH-nyes peen-SOHN), would command a second ship.

The reputations of the brothers convinced Spanish sailors to sign up for the adventure. In all, 84 Spaniards, 4 Italians, 1 Portuguese, and 1 African agreed to serve on the *Santa María,* the *Pinta,* and the *Niña.* By August 1492, Columbus, the brothers, their ships and crews were ready for a voyage that would change world history. This chapter tells the story of Spain's arrival in the Americas.

1 A MEETING IN THE CARIBBEAN
◆ What were the first contacts between
◆ Spanish and Native Americans like?

On the evening of October 11, 1492, from the deck of the *Santa María,* Columbus saw a light in the darkness ahead. It "looked like a little wax candle bobbing up and down." He pointed it out to one sailor, who saw it, too. But other sailors saw nothing. Columbus ordered, "[Keep] a sharp lookout. . . . [W]atch for land." He then added, "To him who first sings out . . . land, . . . a silk [jacket]."

Throughout the night, Juan Rodríguez Bermejo (roh-DREE-ges behr-MEH-hoh) perched high above the deck of the *Pinta.* Sometime around "two hours after midnight," he saw a mass of dark rocks against a whitish sand dune. "*Tierre! Tierre!*" he

cried. "Land! Land!" Another sailor fired a cannon to wake the crews on the *Niña* and the *Santa María.* Sailors on the three ships lowered sails, dropped anchor, and awaited daylight.

Meeting of Two Worlds. At dawn, Europeans and Native Americans first sighted each other. Standing on the beach were a group of people who called themselves Taino (TEYE-noh), or "gentle ones." Rowboats brought the Europeans, armed with guns, to the shore for a closer look at the Taino. Columbus wrote his first impressions in his diary:

This woodcut from 1493 shows how Europeans thought of the islands just "discovered" by Columbus. What is wrong with the woodcut?

1492	Columbus's first voyage to the Americas.
1493	Native Americans attack Columbus's crew at St. Croix.
1505	First group of African slaves sent to Hispaniola.
1508	Ponce de León takes control of Puerto Rico.
1511	Montesinos speaks out against the *encomienda* system.
1515	First shipments of sugar sent to Europe from Hispaniola.
1517	*Asiento* for 4,000 African slaves approved by Spain.
1542	*Encomienda* system ended.

They are very well-built people, with handsome bodies and very fine faces. . . . Their eyes are large and very pretty and their skin is the color of . . . sunburned peasants.

The startled Taino watched as the armor-clad strangers stepped onto their island, which they called Guanahaní (gwah-nah-ah-NEE). In words the Taino did not understand, the strangers renamed the island San Salvador, or "Holy Savior." The strangers also took possession of the island in the name of Spain. Although nobody knew it at the time, the Spanish conquest of the Americas had begun.

In the days that followed, word of the strangers spread among the Native Americans. "Come see the men from Heaven," said messengers, "bring them food and drink." The Spanish quickly noted that the Taino had no iron weapons. In his diary, Columbus wrote that they might easily be made *captivos* (kahp-TEE-vohs), or

slaves. That entry gave a hint of the dark days ahead for the peoples of the Caribbean.

"How Great Is the Diversity." Columbus's ships soon left Guanahaní. For 96 days, they sailed around what is now called the Caribbean Sea. Columbus gave Spanish names to the islands and other geographic features he saw, even though the Native Americans had long before named them. For example, Puerto Rico was called Boriquen by the Taino.

Columbus also took careful notes on plant and animal life. "How great is the diversity," he exclaimed. But Columbus ran into trouble when he tried to identify species, many of which were unknown in Europe. "I don't recognize them," he wrote, "which gives me much grief."

Despite such confusion, Columbus believed he had landed in the islands of Asia known to Europeans as the Indies. Believing this, he called the Native Americans that he met *los indios* (lohs EEN-dee-ohs). That term later became the English word *Indian*, the name mistakenly used to describe the many peoples who inhabited the Americas (see map, page 6).

La Navidad. On Christmas day, the *Santa María* ran aground off a large island that the Spanish called La Española (lah es-pahn-YOH-lah), or Hispaniola (hihs-pahn-YOH-luh). With the help of the Taino, Columbus used some of the ship's timber to build a fortress on the island. He named the fort La Navidad (lah nah-vee-DAHD), or "The Nativity," for its link with Christmas. Columbus then picked 39 crew members to stay at the fort, while the rest returned to Spain.

In January 1493, the *Niña* and the *Pinta* headed out to sea, leaving La Navidad and its settlers behind them. After four storm-tossed months, the battered ships landed in Spain. They carried cargoes intended to dazzle the Spanish monarchs into backing another expedition—exotic parrots, golden trinkets, strange plants, and six Native American captives. Columbus sent a letter to the king and queen in Seville, promising proof "of a world beyond imagining."

Taking Another Look

1. How did the Spanish begin their conquests in the Americas?

2. What first impressions did Columbus have of the Native Americans?

3. **Critical Thinking** Imagine you are a member of the 1492 expedition. What would you cite as the expedition's two most important accomplishments? Why?

2 RESISTANCE AND CONQUEST
◆ How did the Spanish conquer Native
◆ Americans in the Caribbean?

In September 1493, Columbus led a second expedition across the Atlantic. This time, the Spanish sent some 17 fully equipped ships. On board were cannon and soldiers armed with swords and crossbows. There were also five priests, who had vowed to convert the Native Americans to **Christianity**, the religion based on the teachings of Jesus. Some 1,200 to 1,500 colonists also rode on the ships. Among them were several hundred *hidalgos* (ee-DAHL-gohs), or gentlemen. Their aim was to win new lands and fortunes.

Soldiers, priests, and colonists—these were the groups that would build an empire for Spain in the Americas. Their arrival started a clash of cultures that shook the Americas for the next 500 years.

Resistance. In November 1493, the large fleet anchored in what is now Salt River Bay in St. Croix, U.S. Virgin Islands. Here four Native American men and two women desperately attacked the ships threatening their home island. Their fierce response to the Spanish arrival stunned Columbus. The Spanish easily won the fight at Salt River Bay, but the struggle was the first armed resistance to Spanish settlement of the Americas.

Other incidents followed. When the Spanish tried to land on present-day Jamaica, Native Americans stoned them. The Spanish returned with guns, shields, and crossbows. In the battle that followed, 16 to 18 Native Americans lost their lives.

A fanciful view of La Navidad, the first European fort in the Americas. When the Spaniards demanded gold, Native Americans attacked and burned the fort.

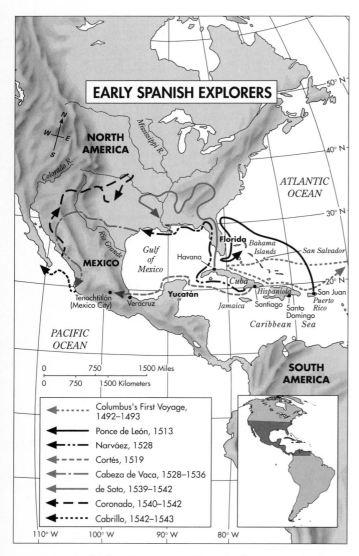

EARLY SPANISH EXPLORERS

NORTH AMERICA

Mississippi R.

Colorado R.

Rio Grande

MEXICO

Gulf of Mexico

Havana

Cuba

Yucatán

Tenochtitlán (Mexico City)

Veracruz

Jamaica   Santiago

PACIFIC OCEAN

ATLANTIC OCEAN

Florida

Bahama Islands

San Salvador

Hispaniola

Santo Domingo

San Juan

Puerto Rico

Caribbean Sea

SOUTH AMERICA

0	750	1500 Miles
0	750	1500 Kilometers

Columbus's First Voyage, 1492–1493

Ponce de León, 1513

Narváez, 1528

Cortés, 1519

Cabeza de Vaca, 1528–1536

de Soto, 1539–1542

Coronado, 1540–1542

Cabrillo, 1542–1543

110° W   100° W   90° W   80° W

To the Spanish it was a "New World." But not for long! Within 50 years of Columbus, explorers fanned out over much of the southern part of North America.

In December, the Spanish fleet dropped anchor at the little **presidio** (prih-SEED-ee-oh), or fort, at La Navidad. The fort lay in ruins, the bodies of its Spanish defenders scattered about. Columbus learned that the Spaniards at the fort had demanded gold, food, and labor from the Taino.

"Bad feelings arose," one Spaniard wrote. "To eliminate this outrage, . . . [the Taino] attacked the Christians in great force."

Conquest. Columbus now moved to build a second settlement on Hispaniola. He named it La Isabella in honor of Spain's Queen Isabella. This time, however, he used Spanish soldiers to strike fear into the Taino. The soldiers rode about on huge horses, animals unknown to Native Americans. Snarling attack dogs trotted beside them. To show their power, the soldiers fired off guns that spit out flames, smoke, and deadly musket balls.

Columbus forced the Taino to aid in the building of La Isabella. He ordered them to bring gold to him as taxes. He also rounded up some 550 Taino to be shipped in chains to Spain as slaves. One Spaniard reported that, to escape capture, some Taino women "left their infants anywhere on the ground and started to flee like desperate people."

In late 1494, the Taino rebelled against Columbus's policies. But the Spanish hunted down the rebels, unleashing attack dogs with the cry *Tómalos!* ("Get them!") A Spanish soldier named Bartolomé de Las Casas (lahs KAH-sahs) witnessed the terrible scene. Las Casas, who later became a priest, predicted,

This tactic begun here . . . [will soon] spread throughout these Indies and will end when there is no more land nor people to subjugate [conquer] and destroy in this part of the world.

Word of such violent incidents reached back to Spain. The Spanish rulers grew increasingly unhappy with Columbus's lack of ability as a ruler. Even so, the promise of wealth from the Caribbean islands led the Spanish rulers to back

Columbus on two more expeditions. By 1503, Columbus and his mostly Spanish crews had explored islands throughout the Caribbean, as well as parts of Central and South America. Although Columbus would die in 1506 insisting he had reached the Indies, the Spanish soon realized that they had stumbled across a "New World," a continent unknown to Europeans.

Conquistadors and *Adelantados*.

To take control of the land from Native Americans, Spanish rulers sent conquistadors, or explorer-soldiers, to the Americas. They included ambitious young Spanish nobles such as Juan Ponce de León (POHN-seh deh leh-OHN), who sailed with Columbus in 1493. Ponce de León took part in the conquest of Hispaniola and went on in 1508 to lead a force that took control of Puerto Rico. Joining him were other adventurers such as Juan Garrido (gah-RREE-doh), a free African.

◆ Known as *el conquistador negro*, or the Black Conquistador, **Juan Garrido** traveled from Africa to Spain. There he converted to Christianity and enlisted in the service of Spain. News of Columbus's voyages spurred Garrido to seek his fortune in the Americas. He fought beside Ponce de León in Puerto Rico and later took part in the conquest of present-day Mexico. Garrido served Spain for more than 30 years. In 1538, he received an estate in the Americas as his reward.

Native Americans tried to resist the conquistadors. A Taino leader named Hatuey (ah-too-AY) fled Hispaniola rather than become a slave. He later fought the Spanish as they tried to settle Cuba. Hatuey was killed, but he became a hero among Cubans who sought to end Spanish rule in the 1800s (see Chapter 14).

By the mid–1500s, the conquistadors had broken Native American resistance in much of the Caribbean. They were aided in their conquest by deadly European diseases, such as smallpox, that nearly wiped out the Taino and other Caribbean peoples. Spain now moved to set up a system to govern its lands in the Caribbean. On island after island, Spain appointed **adelantados** (ah-del-ahn-TAH-dohs), or governors, to rule the Spanish settlements. These settlements brought a new, Spanish way of life to the Caribbean. Most followed patterns first set on Hispaniola—the blueprint for empire.

Taking Another Look

1. What three groups of Spanish settlers helped build an empire in the Caribbean?
2. Why were the Spanish able to defeat the Native Americans?
3. **Critical Thinking** The Spanish called Puerto Rico the "Key to the Indies." Look at the map on page 14. Why do you think the island got this nickname?

3 EXPERIMENT IN EMPIRE BUILDING
◆ How did Hispaniola serve as a model for Spanish empire-building in the Americas?

Spanish settlement of Hispaniola got off to a shaky start. For two years, La Isabella hung on the edge of disaster. The hot, humid tropical weather drained the strength of settlers who were accustomed to the milder climate of Spain. Starvation threatened as supplies of salted meat, olive oil, and dried biscuits ran short. Settlers, however, would not eat unfamiliar Native

The Spanish forced the Native Americans to labor for them. Here Native Americans on Hispaniola bring in gold to be weighed by the Spaniard at the table.

American foods such as sweet potatoes, yucca, and cassava (kah-SAH-vuh). Surrounded by the island's natural supplies of food, many of them died of hunger awaiting shipments of food from Spain.

Columbus ordered settlers, including *hidalgos*, to work in the fields. However, many were too sick to work. Others refused to work with their hands. Instead, they demanded slaves to do the hard labor. By 1496, disease and starvation had ruined the settlement. Columbus ordered his brother, Bartholomew, to move survivors to what seemed to be a healthier area along the southern coast of Hispaniola. They named the new settlement Santo Domingo.

A Spanish City in the Americas. Santo Domingo offered many advantages. It lay along the mouth of a river that emptied into a fine natural harbor. Freshwater streams watered the fertile soil near the settlement. The site offered another attrac-

tion, as well. Small amounts of gold glittering in the sandy beds of the streams lured settlers into staying.

Columbus was an able sailor, but a poor governor. In 1500, complaints about his rule of Hispaniola led the Spanish rulers to take control of the island. They made Santo Domingo the center of Spain's holdings in the Caribbean. Here the Spanish built the first cathedral, the first hospital, and the first university in the Americas. They also set in place a system of rule that became the model for Spain's empire in the Americas.

Masters and Peasants. In 1501, Spain appointed Nicolás de Ovando (oh-VAHN-doh) *adelantado* of Hispaniola. Before he sailed to Santo Domingo, Queen Isabella instructed him to end conflicts among settlers over the labor of Native Americans. She ordered Ovando not to enslave the few remaining Taino. Rather, he was to resettle them throughout the colony so that the Spaniards could use their labor equally.

Ovando found it easier to distribute land than human beings. This led to the growth of the **encomienda** (en-koh-mee-EN-dah) system. Under the system, a settler received a grant of land known as an *encomienda*. The grant gave the owner, or **encomendero** (en-koh-men-DEH-roh), the right to use the labor of Native Americans living on the land. In exchange, the *encomendero* promised to convert those Native Americans to Christianity, pay them wages, and treat them fairly.

Under the *encomienda* system, Native Americans were tied to the land, much as peasants in Europe were. An entire Native American community might be put to work tilling land, digging for gold, or doing anything else the *encomendero* might want. The system fueled settlers' dreams of wealth and luxury. The system soon spread to Puerto Rico, Cuba, and Spain's other American holdings.

A Voice of Protest. Under the *encomienda* system, Native Americans suffered many abuses. In 1510, a group of Roman Catholic priests organized to protest the injustice. In December 1511, Fray Antonio de Montesinos (mohn-teh-SEE-nohs) delivered the first public protest against the system. From the church in Santo Domingo, he asked:

> Tell me, by what right or justice do you hold these Indians in such a cruel and horrible servitude? On what authority have you waged such detestable [awful] wars against these people who dwelt [lived] so quietly and peacefully in their own land? . . . Why do you keep them so oppressed and exhausted, without giving them enough to eat or curing them of the sicknesses they incur [get] from the excessive labor you give them? . . . Are you not bound to love them as you love yourselves? Don't you understand this? Don't you feel this?

The sermon stung the conscience of conquistador Bartolomé de Las Casas. Las Casas had come to Hispaniola with Ovando in 1502. He had helped Ovando set up the *encomienda* system that Montesinos now spoke out against. Las Casas tried to repent for his actions by becoming a Roman Catholic priest. In 1510 he was the first priest ordained in the Americas. Las Casas recorded Montesinos's speech in his diary. Still, he refused to give up his own *encomienda*, arguing that he treated his Native Americans fairly.

In 1512, Las Casas traveled to Cuba with Diego Velázquez (veh-LAHS-kes), the island's first governor. Here, he worked to convert Native Americans to Christianity. For his services, Velázquez awarded Las Casas yet another *encomienda*.

Las Casas stayed in Cuba as a parish priest in the newly founded village of Sancti Espíritu (SAHN-tee es-PEE-ree-too). While preparing a sermon, Las Casas read a passage in the Bible that convinced him "that everything done to the Indians thus far was unjust." He gave up his *encomiendas* and devoted his life to ending the system.

Las Casas wrote fiery protests to the pope in Rome and the king in Spain, calling for an end to *encomiendas*. In 1516, the king showed his concern by naming Las Casas "Protector of the Indians." But the Spanish crown did not officially end the *encomienda* system until 1549. By that time, other people had replaced Native Americans in the mines and fields of Spain's colonies in the Americas— enslaved Africans.

Taking Another Look

1. What were some of the firsts that took place at Santo Domingo?
2. What were the goals of the *encomienda* system?
3. **Critical Thinking** What proposals might Las Casas and Montesinos have suggested to reform Spain's colonial policies?

4 OUT OF AFRICA
◆ How did the large-scale arrival of
◆ enslaved Africans affect the history of the Caribbean?

They called themselves Yoruba, Bini, Igbo, Asante, and many other names that were well known along the West Coast of Africa. The Spanish and other Europeans called these peoples "black gold." These humans were a source of profit and wealth to the traders who sold them as slaves.

In the mid–1400s, the first shiploads of enslaved Africans were carried to the markets of Lisbon, Portugal. Soon Spain, too, opened its doors to the slave trade. By the early 1500s, Spain was ready to extend African slave trade to the Americas.

Turning Point in History. In 1505, a key event in the history of Africa and the Americas took place. In that year, the king of Spain sent 17 Africans to work in the copper mines of Hispaniola. A few months later, he promised to send 100 more. In 1510, he shipped another 50 Africans to the island. In the years to come, this trickle of enslaved Africans across the Atlantic swelled into a flood of millions. Their journey became the largest forced migration of human beings in world history.

The king had sent the Africans to replace Native Americans as workers. Those Native Americans were dying by the thousands as a result of mistreatment and diseases introduced by the Europeans. The king was also responding to demands by priests such as Las Casas to end the harsh treatment of Native Americans. Because of the high cost of enslaved Africans, Las Casas believed that slaveholders would treat them well. "The labor of one [African]," advised Las Casas, "[is] more valuable than that of four Indians; every effort should be made to bring many [Africans] to Hispaniola."

The king and Las Casas expected Africans from the tropics to adjust easily to the Caribbean. They did adjust to the Caribbean, but the Africans died just as quickly as Native Americans in the brutal conditions of slavery. "I cannot understand how so many [Africans] have died," wrote the king in 1511 to the governor of Hispaniola. "Take good care of them."

Unlike Native Americans, however, enslaved Africans could be replaced with other captives from West Africa. It was expensive to purchase and ship these captive Africans. But *encomenderos* on Hispaniola had found a way to help pay the costs. In 1515, they loaded several wooden boxes into ships anchored in the harbor at Santo Domingo. The boxes contained the island's first shipments of sugar, a product in much demand in Europe. Sugar became the "white gold" of the Caribbean.

Plantations and Sugar Mills. Columbus had brought the first sugar cane to Hispaniola from the Canary

Sugar cane being harvested. Why was the labor of enslaved people from West Africa so important to the economy of the Spanish Caribbean?

Islands, off the coast of Africa, in 1493. The crop thrived in the warm climate. But settlers lacked an effective way to process the cane into a form that could be sold.

In 1515, an enterprising Spaniard named Gonzalo de Vedosa (veh-DOH-sah) set up a horse-powered sugar mill in Santo Domingo that could grind large batches of the cane. A short time later, the Spanish introduced water-powered mills on the island, too. The syrup produced in the mills could later be made into molasses and sugar.

The growth of sugar mills went hand in hand with the growth of slavery. *Encomenderos* needed field hands to plant, tend, and cut the sugar cane. They needed workers to run the sugar mills. To meet this growing demand, the Spanish monarch in 1517 approved an *asiento* (ah-see-EN-toh), or contract. Under it, some 4,000 African captives were shipped to Hispaniola.

Other contracts for the shipment of enslaved Africans followed. The African slave trade soon spread beyond Hispaniola. Spanish *encomenderos* brought it with them as they carved out new plantations in Puerto Rico, Cuba, and Jamaica.

A Life of Bondage and Misery. The Atlantic slave trade left a trail of misery from Africa to the Caribbean. Untold numbers of Africans died on forced marches to slave-trading stations on the West African coast. Countless others died in the horrible journey across the Atlantic known as the **Middle Passage**. On the slave ships, chained Africans lay packed together in filthy cargo holds swarming with rats.

Once in the Caribbean, enslaved Africans faced more misery. They sweated in hot fields and toiled in often dangerous sugar mills. For their labor, they received only small portions of food, clothing that

was often little better than rags, and miserable huts for shelter.

By the mid–1500s, the number of enslaved Africans equaled or outnumbered the European population on some Caribbean islands, such as Hispaniola. "There are so many [Africans] in this island as a result of the sugar factories," noted one Spanish writer, "that the land seems to be . . . an image of Africa."

To control the enslaved Africans, the Spanish used brutal means of punishment—branding, whipping, even hanging. Yet Africans endured the cruel treatment and kept themselves and their traditions alive in the Caribbean. Over time, African and Spanish ways mixed with those of Native Americans to produce the vital cultures of Puerto Rico, Cuba, and the Dominican Republic.

Taking Another Look

1. How did the sugar industry increase demand for enslaved Africans?

2. How did the arrival of large numbers of enslaved Africans affect the development of the Caribbean?

3. **Critical Thinking** One historian wrote of the Caribbean in the late 1500s, "Europe reigned; but Africa governed." What might the historian have meant?

LOOKING AHEAD

When the Caribbean failed to yield rich supplies of gold, Spanish explorers set their sights on the mainland that lay to the west. The Spanish soon added what is now Mexico to their kingdom. But, as on the Caribbean islands, Spanish ways of life did not completely replace already existing cultures. Instead, Spanish, African, and Native American cultures blended there as a new way of life took shape.

RETHINKING COLUMBUS DAY

In 1892, the 400th anniversary of Columbus's landing in the Americas was a time of great celebrations in the United States. That year, for example, the city of Chicago hosted the World's Columbian Exposition in Chicago. There, no fewer than 70 portraits of the Italian explorer stared out at visitors to one of the first World's Fairs. The focus of many celebrations was the arrival of Europeans in the Americas.

One hundred years later, the focus of the celebrations had shifted. Many Latinos saw little reason to celebrate European "discovery" of the Americas. Even today, for example, Dominicans recall Spain's colonial policies in Hispaniola with a shudder. They believe it to be bad luck to mention Columbus's name.

Waves of protest greeted plans to celebrate Columbus's arrival. Some Native Americans called for a day of mourning, rather than of celebration. Some Caribbean nations chose to call October 12, not Columbus Day, but rather "The Encounter of Two Worlds." Other nations call it *el dia de la Raza* (the Day of the People).

In the end, the 500th anniversary of Columbus's voyage was a display of historical interdependence. No longer was the story of the Americas to be told simply from a European point of view. Europeans, Native Americans, and Africans had all had a part in that story and in the molding of Latino cultures in the Americas.

CLOSE UP: Chapter 1

The Who, What, Where of History

1. **Where** did the Spanish build their first settlements in the Americas?
2. **Who** was Juan Garrido?
3. **Who** was Hatuey?
4. **What** was the first permanent Spanish city in the Americas?
5. **What** was the *encomienda* system?
6. **Who** was Bartolomé de Las Casas?
7. **What** was the Middle Passage?

Making the Connection

1. What was the connection between European diseases and Spanish conquest of the Americas?
2. What was the connection between sugar plantations and the large-scale arrival of enslaved Africans in the Caribbean?
3. Which event happened *first:* the end of the *encomienda* system or the arrival of enslaved Africans in the Americas?

Time Check

1. In what year did the Spanish arrive in the Americas?
2. Why is the year 1505 a turning point in history?

What Would You Have Done?

1. If you had been living in Seville, Spain, in 1493, would you have joined Columbus's second expedition as a settler? Why or why not?
2. If you had been one of the priests who opposed the *encomienda* system in 1510, what arguments would you have used to persuade the Spanish king and queen to end the system?

Thinking and Writing About History

1. Write a journal entry explaining the impact of Columbus's voyages to the Americas from the point of view of a Spanish official, an enslaved African, a Catholic priest, or a Native American.

2. Imagine you are a Taino fleeing Hispaniola in 1502 to seek shelter among Native Americans in Cuba. Write a dialogue in which you explain what has taken place on your home island.

Building Skills: Interpreting Primary Sources

Writing history is like putting together the pieces of a puzzle. To build a picture of the past, historians must examine and fit together many pieces of information from the period under study. These pieces of information are called *primary sources*. Primary sources include paintings, photographs, maps, diaries, eyewitness accounts, and so on.

Historians complete the puzzle by writing a description or analysis of the past based upon the primary sources they have studied. This account is known as a *secondary source*. That is, it is a secondhand account of the times. This book is a secondary source. However, it also contains primary sources such as the quote on page 17.

Practice interpreting primary sources, by studying the drawing on this page of Native American women in 1572. Then follow the steps below.

1. Identify the drawing's most important visual details. They are the drawing's "facts."

2. Write down some of the things that the visual details tell you about Native American life.

3. Now organize this information into a paragraph about Native American life in 1572. Why is your paragraph a secondary source?

Express Yourself!

Reread Section 1 (pages 11–13). Then, with a partner, draw two pictures showing the first meeting of the Spanish and the Taino. One picture should show the meeting from a Spaniard's point of view. The other should show the meeting from a Taino's viewpoint. Write captions explaining the pictures. Display your pictures on a bulletin board or wall of your classroom.

A Native American method of baking bread

SECTIONS

1 Seeking Adventure and Gold

2 Marching to Tenochtitlán

3 Toppling an Empire

Motecuhzoma, emperor of all the Aztecs, one night climbed to the top of an observatory and saw a blazing comet. It was an omen of death, both for him and for his powerful image.

Struggle for an Empire

(1500–1525)

THINKING ABOUT THE CHAPTER

How did the Spanish conquer a Native American empire in what is now Mexico?

In 1485, Catalina Pizaro Altamirano de Cortés gave birth to a son in the windswept Spanish province of Estremadura (es-treh-mah-DOO-rah). Here mountains and dusty plains covered much of the land. The region was best suited for sheepherding. Catalina and her husband, Martín Cortés de Monroy (mohn-ROI), knew the land offered their son little opportunity for wealth. As *hidalgos,* or minor nobles, the couple could train their son for one of three professions: the law, the priesthood, or the army. The couple chose the law.

At age 14, Hernán Cortés set out for the University of Salamanca (sah-lah-MAHN-kah). Cortés studied law there for two years. But the teenager found himself increasingly drawn to events across the Atlantic. Dreams of conquest and glory filled his mind. In 1502, he returned home to tell his parents that he was giving up the law. Cortés believed that his fortune lay in the Americas.

Although saddened by the decision, Cortés's father agreed to help his son. He wrote a letter introducing Hernán to a cousin from Estremadura—Nicolás de Ovando, governor of Hispaniola. Ovando promised to help the teenager settle on that island as a farmer. Hernán, however, had other plans. He dreamed of picking up a sword, not a plow.

In time, Cortés's search for adventure led him to what is now Mexico. This chapter tells the story of that journey. From that journey, the culture of the present-day Mexican people would emerge.

1 SEEKING ADVENTURE AND GOLD
◆ Why did the Spanish set out to explore
◆ lands west of Cuba?

Si tuviera dineros
No fuera en verdad.

"If I had money, I'd surely not go." These are words from a popular Spanish song of the early 1500s. That song captured the feelings of many Spanish settlers bound for Hispaniola and other islands in the Caribbean. Like Cortés, those settlers sailed westward to seek opportunities denied to them in Spain.

Cortés first landed in Hispaniola in 1504. The teenager was blunt about why he had come to the Americas. Said Cortés, "I came to get gold, not to till [work] the soil like a peasant."

From Farmer to Conquistador. There was no longer much gold to be found on Hispaniola, however. If Cortés wanted gold, he would have to find it somewhere else. But Ovando reminded him that by law Spanish settlers shipped to Hispaniola had to live there for five years. He then assigned Cortés a medium-sized *encomienda* to oversee.

Cortés soon became friends with Diego Velázquez, the island's assistant governor. Like Cortés, Velázquez had dreams that life on Hispaniola did not satisfy. In 1511, Velázquez won permission to conquer the island of Cuba. Cortés marched with Velázquez during the conquest. For his service, Cortés received a large estate and several gold mines.

Rumors of Gold. Velázquez, now governor of Cuba, soon decided to explore rumors of a rich empire on the American mainland, some 120 miles (192 kilometers) west of Cuba. Columbus had sailed along the coast of the mainland in 1502. On that voyage, he met an ocean-going canoe "from a province called Maia [Maya]." The canoe was filled with trade goods—roots, grains, copper axes, and turquoise ornaments.

The people in the canoe were very different from the Taino that the Spanish had met. Unlike the Taino, they did not treat the Europeans as gods. Instead, wrote one crew member, "They indicated arrogantly [proudly] to our men that they should make way, and made threats when [we] offered resistance."

In 1517, Velázquez sent Francisco Hernández de Córdova (er-NAHN-des deh KOHR-doh-vah) to find out more about these people known as the Maya. Hernández landed on the shore of the Yucatán Peninsula, on the southeastern edge of present-day Mexico. The Maya, however, drove the Spanish soldiers back to their ships.

The next year, Velázquez sent out a

1504	Cortés lands in Hispaniola.
1511	Velázquez takes over Cuba.
1519	Cortés claims Yucatán Peninsula for Spain.
1519–1521	Cortés conquers Aztec Empire.

second expedition, commanded by Juan de Grijalva (gree-HAHL-vah). As the ships sailed along the Yucatán coast, the sailors saw towns "so large that the city of Seville [in Spain] could not be better or larger." Grijalva did not explore the mainland. Before he sailed back to Cuba, however, a group of Maya paddled out to meet Grijalva. One Spaniard reported,

> They brought gold cast in bars . . . a beautiful gold mask, a figurine [statue] of a man with a half mask of gold, and a crown of gold beads.

Voyage to the Yucatán. Bored with his life as a farmer, Cortés had closely followed the news of the two expeditions to the mainland. From the Hernández expedition, Cortés learned that he would need an army to march inland. From the Grijalva expedition, he learned that there was gold to be found.

Cortés asked Velázquez to give him command of the next expedition to the mainland. Velázquez knew that Cortés was ambitious. He feared letting Cortés out of his sight. Cortés, however, offered to pay the costs of the expedition himself. Velázquez then agreed, but not before planting spies among Cortés's crew.

Cortés convinced some 550 Spaniards to join the expedition. He then added 200 native Cubans and Africans. Cortés bought gunpowder, crossbows, and iron lances. He also made sure the expedition included horses and attack dogs dressed in armor.

The sight of Cortés's army led Velázquez to have second thoughts. He feared that he had given Cortés too much power. Rumors spread that Velázquez might cancel the expedition. In February 1519, before Velázquez could do so, Cortés's ships sailed.

Cortés had defied the government for the hope of winning wealth and fame. Unless he succeeded in finding a golden empire to the west, he faced the possibility of prison or death on his return.

This is the only portrait of Cortés drawn by someone who actually knew him. Cortés is shown towards the end of his life, holding his coat of arms.

Taking Another Look

1. Why did many Spaniards travel to Hispaniola in the early 1500s?
2. What did the Spanish learn in their early contacts with the Maya?
3. **Critical Thinking** How did the voyage of Cortés differ from the voyages undertaken by Columbus?

2 MARCHING TO TENOCHTITLÁN

◆ How did the Spanish gain entry into
◆ the heart of the Aztec empire?

The 11 Spanish ships soon reached Cozumel (koh-soo-MEL), an island along the eastern Yucatán coast. Cortés ordered several dozen soldiers to join him in the rowboats. Next to Cortés sat a Maya slave captured on the Hernández expedition. He spoke just enough Spanish to act as interpreter for Cortés.

Upon reaching shore, Cortés marched to a nearby Maya village. Speaking through the interpreter, Cortés ordered the Maya to give up their gods. The startled Maya watched while the Spaniards entered a temple and pushed statues of the Maya gods to the ground. Cortés then ordered the Maya to kneel and to accept the Roman Catholic religion.

The armed strangers and shattered statues shocked the Maya into surrender. As they knelt, Cortés announced that they were now subjects of the king of Spain. The conquest of Mexico had begun.

Pressing Inland. On the Yucatán coast, Cortés met Jerónimo de Aguilar (ah-gee-LAHR), one of two survivors of a 1511 shipwreck. Aguilar had learned to speak the Maya language well. He now joined the expedition.

After a violent storm, the ships landed near present-day Tabasco, Mexico. Stories of the Spanish had already reached the Tabascans (tah-BAHS-kahns). When the Spanish tried to land, thousands of armed Tabascans stood ready to resist.

His experiences with Velázquez in Cuba had prepared Cortés to fight. He knew how to use Spanish horses and cannon to awe the Native Americans. Horses and cannon allowed the outnumbered Spanish to overcome Tabascan resistance. As the price of surrender, Cortés demanded that the Tabascan *caciques* (kuh-SEEKS), or chiefs, convert to the Roman Catholic religion practiced by the Spanish.

After the battle, Cortés gained a new member for his expedition—a Native American woman named Malintzin (mah-LEEN-tseen). Malintzin spoke Mayan and Nahuatl (NAH-waht-l), the language of the powerful Aztec people, who lived inland, to the west. From Malintzin, he heard stories of the Aztec, who ruled his dreamed-of golden empire. She also told him of a god, whom the Aztec believed would return one day from the east. As Cortés prepared to march west, this knowledge gave him an advantage over the Aztec.

The Return of Quetzalcoatl. In the Aztec capital of Tenochtitlán, Emperor Motecuhzoma (moh-teh-koo-SOH-mah) paced about nervously. A messenger from the coast had brought disturbing news of strange sights of visitors there.

Unsure of what or whom his frightened subject might have seen, Motecuhzoma sent two trusted officials to the coast. The officials soon returned to the capital with their report.

Our lord and king, it is true that strange people have come to the shores of the great sea. . . . They have very light skin, much lighter than ours. They all have very long beards, and their hair comes only to their ears.

Motecuhzoma turned away in silence. According to legend, a light-skinned Aztec god called Quetzalcoatl (ket-sahl-koh-AHT-l), or the Feathered Serpent, had sailed across the sea in ancient times. The god, who opposed human sacrifice, had promised to return in the year One Reed and reclaim his land. The current year, the year these strangers had arrived, was One Reed.

Motecuhzoma now made a decision that would help end his empire. Because of the legend of Quetzalcoatl, he viewed the strangers as gods rather than as men invading Aztec lands. He sent messengers carrying rich gifts to the coast. "When you see the god," instructed Motecuhzoma, "say to him: 'Your deputy, Motecuhzoma, has sent us to you. Here are the presents with which he welcomes you home to Mexico.'"

The Lure of Gold. Malintzin, who was called Doña Marina (DOH-nyah mah-REE-nah) by the Spaniards, translated the message for Cortés. Cortés allowed the messengers to dress him in clothing they had brought as gifts. They spread other gifts at his feet.

Cortés stared coldly at the messengers and said, "And is this all? Is this your gift of welcome? Is this how you greet people?" He ordered the messengers put in chains.

Cortés then put on a display of Spanish power. Cannon spit out iron balls that shattered trees. Soldiers held snarling dogs within feet of the messengers. When Cortés finally freed the terrified Aztecs, he

On his way to the Aztec capital, Cortés met Aztecs carrying gifts for him. Cortés rejected the gifts, replying coldly, "I and my companions suffer from a disease of the heart which can be cured only by gold."

An Aztec drawing shows the Spanish march on Tenochtitlán. At the head of the column are the bearded Cortés and Malintizin, the Native American woman who helped Cortés communicate with the Aztecs.

said, "I and my companions suffer from a disease of the heart which can be cured only by gold."

The messengers hurried the 200 miles (320 kilometers) to Tenochtitlán. When the emperor heard their story, he seemed frozen, unsure what to do next. Cortés, meanwhile, prepared to march to Tenochtitlán.

Win or Die. First, though, Cortés ordered the building of a small settlement on the shores of the Caribbean. The Spanish named it *la Villa Rica de Vera Cruz* (lah VEE-yah REE-kah deh VEH-rah kroos), or "the Rich Town of the True Cross." Soldiers voted Cortés leader of the new settlement, later known as Veracruz.

Cortés now took a bold action. He sank all his ships, except one. He sent that vessel to Spain with news of the expedition, which he hoped would win the favor of the king. With the ships gone, his soldiers had no hope of retreat. Cortés had given his

soldiers but one choice in the battle to come—win or die.

Into Aztec Lands. On August 16, 1519, the Spanish began their westward march into the Mexican highlands. Along the way, they met **vassals**, or subjects, of the Aztecs. A picture of harsh Aztec rule began to emerge. Cortés heard stories of forced tribute, the goods and produce paid by a conquered people to a conqueror. He also learned of captives taken as slaves. Many of these captives were killed as sacrifices to Aztec gods.

Cortés planned to show these vassals that the Spanish were mightier rulers than the Aztec. The Spanish proved their strength in several battles against Aztec vassals. The Spanish also demonstrated their hatred of the practice of human sacrifice. The Spanish destroyed bloody altars and built Christian shrines in their place.

On his march, Cortés formed alliances with peoples who wanted to shake off Aztec

This Spanish map of Mexico City was drawn in 1528. By then, the great Aztec buildings of Tenochtitlán had been torn down and Mexico City, the new Spanish city, was being built.

rule. Many of these Native Americans joined the march. Cortés's army soon swelled into the thousands.

An Enchanted Vision. For weeks, the Spanish marched along a steep mountain trail that rose sharply from the tropical coast. They trudged through volcanic ash, salt lakes, and sand.

In early November 1519, the Spanish finally passed beneath the volcanoes that guarded the entrance to the Valley of Mexico, center of the Aztec empire. In the valley below, they saw Tenochtitlán—the largest city in the Americas—spread out at their feet. One soldier, Bernal Díaz (DEE-ahs), later recalled:

> Gazing on such wonderful sights, we did not know what to say or whether what appeared before us was real. . . . These great . . . buildings . . . all made of stone, seemed like an enchanted vision. . . . Indeed, some of our soldiers asked whether it was not all a dream.

Taking Another Look

1. What advantages did Cortés have over the Maya and Aztec?

2. Why did Cortés destroy all his ships but one at Veracruz?

3. **Critical Thinking** How might history have been different if Motecuhzoma had viewed the conquistadors as men rather than as gods?

3 TOPPLING AN EMPIRE

◆ How did the Aztec defeat pave the
◆ way for the rise of a new people in what is now Mexico?

Tenochtitlán sat on an island in the center of a sparkling lake. A series of broad causeways, or raised roads, connected the city with the mainland. Thousands of Aztec crowded the roads to stare as the Spanish army approached. The Spaniards gazed at the crowds nervously. How would these people react to their arrival?

Cortés rode his horse over one of the causeways into the city. As he approached, servants carried Motecuhzoma toward him in a golden chair. When the Aztec emperor stepped down, they spread embroidered cloth on the ground so he would not soil his feet.

Cortés dismounted and walked toward the emperor. The two leaders saluted each other. Then, Motecuhzoma greeted Cortés as Quetzalcoatl and welcomed him back. The Spaniards breathed more easily. For the moment, the Aztec looked on them as gods.

Gardens and Markets. Servants guided the Spanish to luxurious rooms in the heart of the city. For the next few weeks, the Spanish acted as sightseers. They visited zoos filled with exotic birds and animals. They ate rich meals of strange foods at the palace. The Spanish soldiers felt Tenochtitlán compared favorably with European cities such as London and Rome. They remarked on its great cleanliness. (The Aztec washed city streets and carried wastes from the city each day.)

The Aztec did their marketing in Tenochtitlán's twin city, Tlatelolco (tlah-tel-OHL-koh). There the Spanish found stalls packed with merchandise. Bernal Díaz listed dozens of items—gold, precious stones, feathers, cotton, tobacco, dyes, honey, and more. "I wish I could finish telling of all the things which are sold there," wrote Díaz, "but they are [too] numerous."

Toward War. As the weeks passed, many Aztec came to realize that their guests were not gods, but men. "They were swollen with greed," said one Aztec. "They hungered for gold like wild pigs." Meanwhile, Spain's hatred of the Aztec practice of human sacrifice deepened.

As tensions increased, Cortés made a daring move to protect his Spanish troops. He took Motecuhzoma hostage. Cortés reasoned that the Aztec would not attack his army so long as their emperor was in Spanish hands. But Cortés's move only increased Aztec anger.

Doña Marina heard rumors of a planned Aztec attack. She warned Cortés of the danger. Cortés, though, had other problems on his mind. A Spanish force sent by Velázquez to take Cortés prisoner had landed at Veracruz. Cortés gathered about 260 troops and marched to meet the new arrivals.

Cortés left Pedro de Alvarado (ahl-vah-RAH-doh) in charge of the Spanish at Tenochtitlán. Alvarado gave Aztec nobles permission to hold a religious festival in a

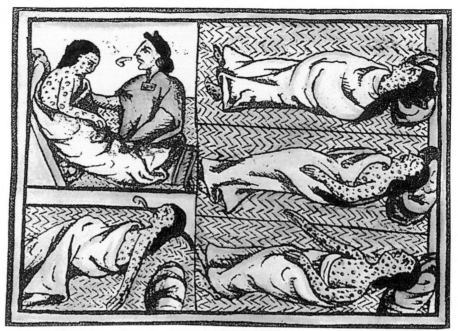

It was smallpox as much as Spanish arms that destroyed the Aztecs. Said one Aztec, "The illness was so dreadful that no one could walk or move. So they simply starved to death in their beds."

temple plaza. As they sang and danced, Alvarado ordered soldiers to murder the Aztec there.

News of the massacre sent shock waves through the city. Aztec soldiers now took up arms against the Spanish. The Spanish retreated into the royal palace, where they put Motecuhzoma in chains. Although vastly outnumbered, the Spanish used their guns to hold off attackers. Soon, the attacks stopped and a tense calm settled over the city. The Aztecs had decided to use the soldiers as bait to trap Cortés.

La noche triste. Cortés returned to Tenochtitlán in triumph. He had met Velázquez's troops and convinced them to join him by telling them of Aztec gold. But triumph soon turned into disaster. Cortés led 1,300 Spanish troops into Tenochtitlán to rescue Alvarado.

Cortés marched through empty streets to reach the palace. Once the Spaniards were inside, however, the Aztec attacked. Spanish cannon, muskets, and crossbows turned back the attackers, but just barely.

In desperation, the Spanish dragged Motecuhzoma to the palace roof. They thought the sight of him would make the Aztec stop fighting. Instead, it added to Aztec anger. Someone hurled a rock at the emperor. One story is that Motecuhzoma later died from that blow. Another is that the Spanish killed him.

As food and water ran out, Cortés planned a breakout from the city. On the misty night of June 30, 1520, the Spaniards moved, as quietly as possible, toward one of the causeways. Escape had seemed within sight when suddenly, thousands of Aztec fell on the Spanish. Cortés and several hundred troops slashed their way to freedom. But some 450 Spanish died, on what became known as *la noche triste* (lah NOH-cheh TREES-teh), or "the night of sorrow."

A Silent Ally. As Spanish soldiers recovered from their wounds outside Tenochtitlán, Cortés convinced his Native American allies to give him more help. Together, the Spaniards and Native Americans laid siege to Tenochtitlán.

As their forces ringed the city, another, silent ally joined them. The Spanish had carried deadly smallpox germs to Tenochtitlán. Soon, an epidemic swept the city. "The illness was so dreadful that no one could walk or move," wrote one Aztec. "So they simply starved to death in their beds."

An Aztec noble named Cuauhtémoc [kwow-TEH-mohk] had become the Aztec ruler. With thousands of people dying inside the city, he tried to break the siege.

◆ **Cuauhtémoc** was the nephew of Motecuhzoma. Unlike his uncle, he saw the Spanish not as gods, but as men who wanted to be conquerors. To save the empire, he led one last bold assault against the Spanish. But the smallpox epidemic had left the Aztec too weak to defeat the Spanish and their allies.

On August 13, 1521, Cuauhtémoc surrendered to Cortés. In the next months, he suffered insults and tortures. But Cortés failed to break his spirit. Finally, the Spanish hanged the last Aztec emperor.

Cuauhtémoc's courage has made him a hero among the Mexican people. Today, it is his statue, rather than one of Cortés, that greets visitors to Mexico City.

By late August, the Spanish had destroyed the Aztec empire. Tenochtitlán lay in ruins. Thousands of Native Americans in the Valley of Mexico, both Aztecs and allies of the Spanish, lay dying of disease. This was the situation as Cortés prepared to build a new empire for Spain.

Taking Another Look

1. Why did Tenochtitlán impress the Spanish?

2. What factors contributed to the Aztec defeat?

3. **Critical Thinking** What does the story of Cuauhtémoc reveal about the way present-day Mexicans view their Aztec heritage?

LOOKING AHEAD

Conquest of the Aztec sent a flood of gold and silver pouring into Spain. It also opened the doors of Mexico to a steady stream of Spanish settlers. In the next decades, Mexico would become the center of a vast Spanish empire in the Americas.

Cuauhtémoc was only 18 years old when he became the last ruler of the Aztec empire. This portrait was done by an Aztec artist after the Spanish conquest.

REDISCOVERING AZTLAN

Our forebears dwelt in that bliss-ful, happy place called Aztlan. . . . Our ancestors went about in canoes and made floating gar-dens upon which they sowed maize [corn], chili, tomatoes . . . beans and all kinds of seeds.

The Spanish had barely entered Tenochtitlán in 1519 when they heard wonderous tales of Aztlan (AHS-tlahn), the original Aztec homeland. These stories sent the Spanish in search of Aztlan into what is today the U.S. Southwest.

The Spanish saw that region as land to be conquered. The descen-dants of the Aztec saw the region as their ancestral homeland. When Mexicans shook off Spanish rule in 1821, they used Aztlan as a symbol of independence. Later, they deeply mourned the loss of the land to the United States in the 1840s. Aztlan had again fallen to a foreign "conqueror."

Today, many Mexican Americans have strong feelings about Aztlan. In the 1960s, when Mexican Americans began a struggle to win their full rights as U.S. citizens, they used Aztlan as a symbol of the movement. In Aztlan, Mexican Americans found a tie that bound them to a Mexican past stretching back to before Tenochtitlán.

CLOSE UP: Chapter 2

The Who, What, Where of History

1. **Where** was Hernan Cortés born?
2. **Who** was Malintzin (Doña Marina)?
3. **What** was Nahuatl?
4. **Who** was Motecuhzoma?
5. **What** is tribute?
6. **What** was the name of the Aztec capital?
7. **What** was *la noche triste*?
8. **Who** was Cuauhtémoc?

Making the Connection

1. What was the connection between the conquistadors and the spread of the Roman Catholic religion?
2. What was the connection between Malintzin (Doña Marina) and Cortés's conquest of the Mexico?

Time Check

1. Place the following in the correct order of Spanish settlement: Mexico, Hispaniola, Cuba.
2. What important event in Mexican his-tory took place on August 13, 1521?

What Would You Have Done?

1. Imagine that you are an adviser to the king of Spain. You have just received two requests: one from Velázquez demanding punishment of Cortés for treason and one from Cortés asking for recognition of Veracruz. What action would you advise the king to take?
2. Suppose you were a *cacique* of one of the peoples conquered by the Spanish. Would you side with Cortés or side with your Aztec rulers? Why?

Thinking and Writing About History

1. Draft a letter that Cortés might have written to his parents in late 1521. The letter should describe the highlights of Cortés's life since his departure from Spain.

2. Based on information in the text, write a travel guide for visitors to Tenochtitlán. Be sure to point out all the wonders of the city. Design at least one illustration for your travel guide.

3. Imagine that you are an Aztec priest who wishes to write an essay about the conquest of your empire by the Spanish. Write your essay about the fall of the Aztec empire from the point of view of an Aztec. You may wish to illustrate your essay.

Building Skills: Developing Empathy

History is more than just the study of facts. It is the story of people—their dreams and fears, their triumphs and defeats. To see the human side of history, historians use primary sources such as those given in the last chapter. These sources bring alive faces and voices from the past. For example, ask a friend to read aloud the eyewitness description of Tenochtitlán by Bernal Díaz on page 28. Close your eyes and imagine what it would have been like to be with the Spanish on that day. How might you have felt?

Your answer to this question will help you to develop empathy for the Spanish. Empathy is an understanding of the feelings of other people. To develop empathy for the Aztec at the time of their defeat, read the following poem by an unknown Aztec writer. Then answer the questions.

How can we save our homes, my
  people?
The Aztecs are deserting the city:
The city is in flames, and all
is darkness and destruction. . . .

Weep, my people:
know that with these disasters
we have lost the Mexican nation.
The water has turned bitter,
The food is bitter!
These are the acts of the Giver
  of Life.

1. What does the poet tell you about the fate of Tenochtitlán?

2. These lines are from a series of poems known as Aztec "songs of sorrow." What lines in the poem convey that sorrow?

3. Write two sentences to express the effect the fall of Tenochtitlán had upon the Aztec.

4. What does the last line of the poem tell you about the Aztec poet? If you could rewrite these two lines, how would you change them?

Express Yourself!

Choose one or two classmates as partners. On a piece of paper, write down all the vocabulary words in this chapter. The vocabulary words appear in heavy, bold type. In addition, write down any other words or terms that you are not familiar with. First, define these words. Then, draw pictures that help explain their meaning. When you are finished, share your "illustrated dictionary" with your classmates.

SECTIONS

1 Extending Spain's Reach

2 New Religious Voices

3 The Columbian Exchange

4 A Center of Spanish Culture

By the 1600s, when this picture was painted, Mexico had developed distinctive ways of life. High flying Native American dancers, *mestizo* musicians, and wealthy *peninsulares* symbolize the new ways.

CHAPTER 3

New Ways of Life

(1521–1650s)

THINKING ABOUT THE CHAPTER

What new ways of life developed in Spain's colonies in the Americas?

In late August 1521, flames still burned in the rubble of Tenochtitlán. The Spanish conquerors set up a camp outside the shattered city. There, the soldiers eagerly awaited their share of treasure from the fallen Aztec empire. Hopes ran high that each share would be very large.

When Cortés finally gave the soldiers their rewards, their mood of celebration turned sour. A soldier on horseback received only 100 pesos. That amount would pay barely a fifth the cost of a horse. Foot soldiers received even less.

The angry soldiers listened as Cortés tried to explain. First, he pointed out the losses. Huge amounts of treasure lay at the bottom of canals, either dropped there by soldiers on the Night of Sorrow or dumped there by the Aztec on the eve before surrender. Of the treasure that remained, one fifth was reserved for the Spanish crown and one fifth for the captain-general (Cortés). The remaining three fifths had to be divided among more than 400 officers and soldiers.

For weeks, soldiers complained. Some talked of finding new empires to conquer. A few scrawled protests on the walls of Cortés's home. One soldier scribbled, "Not content with the captain's share, he takes a royal share as well."

In the end, tempers cooled and most soldiers grudgingly agreed to help Cortés build a new mainland colony for Spain. Like the earlier conquerors in the Caribbean, they would get their pay in the form of Native American land and labor. This chapter traces the founding of New Spain, the name given to the former Aztec empire and lands bordering it, and the ways of life that developed there.

1 EXTENDING SPAIN'S REACH
◆ How did the Spanish take firmer hold
◆ of the Americas after 1521?

In early 1522, Native American workers filled the ruined city of Tenochtitlán. *Caciques* who once served Aztec nobles now supplied work crews of defeated Aztec and their former slaves for the Spanish. The sound of crashing stone filled the city as workers smashed statues of Aztec gods and goddesses and pulled down temples. From the toppled stones of Tenochtitlán came the building blocks for a new Spanish capital.

Place of the Mexicas. The Spaniards had trouble pronouncing Tenochtitlán. Therefore, they began calling the city Mexico, or "Place of the Mexicas" (meks-HEE-kahs). The Aztec believed their gods had given them the name Mexica when

Veracruz, the first European outpost in Mexico, was built in 1519 with Native American labor.

they first arrived in the region. As Aztec buildings fell, the name Mexico City took hold. The name firmly linked the new city with its Aztec past.

More than a name connected Mexico City and Tenochtitlán. A Spanish architect named Alonso García Brava (gahr-SEE-ah BRAH-vah) planned the new city along the same lines as Tenochtitlán. A central plaza, or public square, replaced the Aztec ceremonial center. The palaces of Aztec nobles

35

1524	Pedro de Alvarado explores the Yucatán Peninsula.
	Franciscans arrive at Veracruz.
1531	Vasco de Quiroga founds the Hospital de Santa Fé.
1533	Francisco Pizarro conquers the Inca empire.
1535	Antonio de Mendoza appointed first viceroy of New Spain.
1542	New Laws end the *encomienda* system.
1545	Silver discovered near Mexico City.
1551	University of Mexico is founded.

gave way to the homes of conquistadors. Churches or cathedrals grew up on or near the foundations of old Aztec temples. Workers filled in canals with rubble to create streets.

The Spanish designed the city, but Native American labor built it. One observer noted:

> [Native Americans] were responsible for finding the construction material, the masons and carpenters. . . . They carried everything on their backs. They dragged stones and beams with ropes, . . . singing and shouting, with voices that never ceased night or day.

The work claimed many Native American lives. Within three years, however, a new city was built. "Mexico City," boasted Cortés, "will soon be the most noble . . . in the known world!"

In the Footsteps of Cortés. As Mexico City took shape, Cortés handed out *encomiendas* throughout New Spain. Again, some conquistadors felt cheated. They grumbled that they were not getting enough tribute from Native Americans assigned to their land. They hungered for a chance to taste the glory won by Cortés.

In 1524, Cortés gave dissatisfied soldiers their chance. He sent Pedro de Alvarado into southern Yucatán to search for the fabled Maya empire. Unknown to the Spaniards, that empire had long since declined (see page 4). With some 400 soldiers, Alvarado plunged into the dense Central American rain forest searching for lost cities.

Alvarado waged a brutal campaign against the Maya he did find. He set fire to their villages and sent thousands of Maya to Caribbean sugar plantations as slaves. His conquests added what are now Guatemala and parts of Honduras and El Salvador to New Spain. Bitter memories of Alvarado lived on among the Maya long after his death in 1541. Many Maya continued to resist rule from Mexico City until well into the 1800s.

Into South America. As Alvarado slogged through the rain forest, Francisco Pizarro landed on the western coast of South America. In 1533, Pizarro and a band of about 200 soldiers trudged over the Andes Mountains to capture the fabulous Inca empire (see page 4). Pizarro's conquest gave Spain a South American colony named Peru.

Never again would the Spanish find glittering empires like those of the Aztec and Inca. Even so, the adventures of Cortés and Pizarro inspired conquerors to march into other parts of the Americas.

Conquistadors were not the only Spaniards whose efforts added to Spain's empire. After the first conquests, Roman Catholic priests came to the Americas in growing numbers. Their efforts helped shape the new culture that emerged in Spanish America.

Taking Another Look

1. What role did Native Americans play in the founding of Mexico City?

2. Why did Spanish conquerors explore what is now Central America?

3. **Critical Thinking** Why are the accomplishments of Cortés and the other conquistadors not as widely praised today as they once were?

2 NEW RELIGIOUS VOICES

How did efforts to spread Christianity affect the lives of Native Americans?

In 1524, a dozen **friars** got off a Spanish ship anchored at Veracruz. These men were priests, members of a Roman Catholic religious group, or order, called the Franciscans. They had come to the Americas to teach their religion to Native Americans. Dressed in simple brown robes, the friars walked barefoot over 200 miles (320 kilometers) of rugged trails to reach Mexico City.

As the friars neared the city, Cortés rode out to greet them. Behind him followed a huge procession of Native Americans. They stared in amazement as Cortés knelt before the friars and begged forgiveness for his sins against the native peoples. The Native Americans wondered, who were these brown-robed men to have such power over the mighty Cortés. The Native Americans would soon learn the answer, as the Catholic priests became a vital part of Spain's American empire.

Spreading Christianity. The humble friars quickly earned the respect of many Native Americans. Said one Aztec,

Like us they go about poorly clad and barefoot, partaking of the same food we eat, abide [live] in our midst, and deal meekly [kindly] with us.

There were similarities between the Roman Catholic faith preached by the friars and traditional Native American beliefs. Like the friars, the Native Americans believed in life after death. Both groups also believed in a Supreme Being. The Christian saints reminded Native Americans of their own lesser gods and goddesses.

Still, some Native Americans resisted the friars' efforts to convert them to Christianity. They urged the friars to respect ancient ways. One Aztec priest pleaded,

And now, must we destroy the ancient principles of life? Listen, [Franciscans], do not force something on your people that will bring them misfortune.

Aztec drawing shows Spanish priests destroying Aztec temples. What is the artist's point of view?

For many Native Americans, however, misfortune had already come. The old gods and goddesses had failed to rise up in anger as the Spanish smashed their temples. Strange illnesses—measles, mumps, and typhus—swept through them. Yet the Spanish seemed largely untouched by these diseases.

In despair, many Native Americans converted to the new religion taught by the friars. Fray (or Father) Toribio de Benavente (ben-ah-VEN-teh), known to Native Americans as Motolinía (moh-toh-lee-NEE-ah), "the Poor Man," claimed that the friars converted thousands in 1524 alone. In time, Catholicism became the chief religion in Spanish America.

Start of the Mission System. Other religious orders—Dominicans, Augustinians, and Jesuits—soon took up the work started by the Franciscans. Many priests were deeply touched by the suffering that Native Americans endured from disease and forced labor. A Dominican priest named Vasco de Quiroga (kee-ROH-gah) decided to take action. In 1531, he won permission to set up a **mission,** a settlement devoted to spreading Christianity.

Quiroga named his mission Hospital de Santa Fé. He described the settlement as "a home for children, a school, and a community lodging." At its height, the settlement numbered some 30,000 people.

The Native Americans who lived at Santa Fé learned European crafts and methods of farming. Quiroga demanded they attend church regularly. But he also limited their workday to six hours. He also made sure that products raised on the mission farm were distributed fairly. Other missions soon appeared in New Spain.

As disease reduced Native American populations, priests won permission to resettle the people of scattered villages into larger communities. These were called ***congregaciones*** (kohn-greh-gahs-YOHN-es). Pulled from their villages, Native Americans found themselves subject to strict rules aimed at teaching them Spanish ways.

The *congregaciones* put Native Americans to work for the benefit of the religious orders that ran them. They provided priests with the labor to build churches, raise food, and produce crops for sale in Spain. Over time, the *congregaciones* greatly enriched the Roman Catholic church and helped make it the largest landowner in New Spain.

Taking Another Look

1. Why did many Native Americans accept the Roman Catholic religion?

2. What was the main purpose of the missions?

3. **Critical Thinking** In what ways were the *congregaciones* similar to *encomiendas*? How were they different?

3 THE COLUMBIAN EXCHANGE

◆ How did the growth of Spanish
◆ colonies lead to the spread of new
ways of life?

In 1521, Gregorio Villalobos (vee-ya-LOH-bohs) unloaded a herd of cattle onto the beach at Veracruz, in New Spain. The four-legged invaders soon proved as troublesome to Native Americans as the two-legged ones.

Turned loose on fields outside Mexico City, the cattle trampled crops and grazed on tender shoots. The Spanish forbade Native Americans from slaughtering the cattle. So the herds increased dramatically. One Franciscan friar proudly announced in the mid–1500s, "They [the cattle] have so multiplied that it seems they are native to the country!"

The cattle, however, were not native to the Americas. The Spanish had brought them from Europe, first to the Caribbean islands and then to the mainland. Cattle were just one of the many new items introduced to the Americas by the Spanish. These items were part of the **Columbian Exchange**, as the exchanges among peoples of different cultures during the 1500s have become known.

Unwanted Immigrants.
By 1526, several thousand people from Europe and Africa had come to live in Mexico City. The ships that carried them across the Atlantic also carried many unwelcome passengers —rats, cockroaches, and weeds, whose seeds slipped into the cargo.

Outdoing those pests in their destructive power were the germs of diseases new to the Americas. Because Native Americans had never been exposed to these diseases, they had no resistance to them. The diseases spread like wildfire. Some scientists today estimate that from 50 to 90 percent of the native population of the Americas died of those diseases.

Old Foods in a New Land.
Not all the things Europeans carried to the Americas had such bad effects. As settlers from Europe set out for the Americas, they brought familiar foods with them. To satisfy their taste for meat, the Spanish brought herds of cattle, pigs, sheep, and goats to raise in their new home.

Europeans also brought crops that were new to the Americas. They packed sacks of wheat and rye for bread, and grape clippings for wine. Native American laborers soon found themselves growing those and other strange plants—peach, apple,

Three products that found their way around the world as part of the Columbian Exchange were the pumpkin, gourd, and taro root.

orange, and lemon trees; onions, radishes, and much more.

From the Americas.
Traffic did not flow in just one direction across the Atlantic. Ships sailed from the Americas to Europe, Africa, and Asia with new items for sale. American foods such as squash, chilies, pumpkins, tomatoes, and peanuts began to appear on tables and in cooking pots around the world.

Two of the most important foods from the Americas were potatoes and maize (corn). These crops proved more resistant to bad weather and easier to store than wheat or oats. They helped save generations of peasants in Europe, Africa, and Asia from famine or food shortages.

The Americas also introduced new medicines to the world. Native American healers eased fevers with teas brewed from moss. That moss turned out to be rich in penicillin. They lessened the effects of malaria with cinchona (sin-KOH-neh) bark, which contained quinine. They rubbed painful fever sores with juice squeezed from aloe leaves.

From Africa.
Natural remedies could not halt the march of disease through

Native American populations. So the use of enslaved Africans as laborers spread from the Caribbean to the American mainland. By the late 1500s, nearly 60,000 enslaved Africans lived in New Spain.

The slave trade opened the way to other cultural exchanges. African foods such as yams, blackeyed peas, and bananas traveled to the Americas on slave ships. Other foods returned with the ships to Africa. Such present-day staples as corn, peanuts, oranges, avocados, and papaya all came to Africa from the Americas.

New Ideas and New Peoples. The ships that sailed the Atlantic in the 1500s carried more than trade items. They carried people and their ideas.

Contacts among different peoples speeded **cultural diffusion**, or the spread of cultures across global regions. Nowhere was the mixing more obvious than in New Spain. There, the peoples of four continents—Africa, North and South America, and Europe—came together and developed new ways of living.

Taking Another Look

1. What foods did the Spanish bring from Europe to New Spain?

2. Why did the slave trade expand from the Caribbean to the mainland?

3. **Critical Thinking** How did the Columbian Exchange promote cultural diffusion?

4 A CENTER OF SPANISH CULTURE

◆ What was it like to live in New Spain in the 1500s?

In the summer of 1566, merchants in Mexico City loaded silver into wagons. Armed guards rode beside the wagons as they rumbled along dirt roads east toward Veracruz. In that Caribbean port, people eagerly awaited the first sight of the Spanish fleet from Seville. The arrival of the fleet would start the yearly silver fair. For 20 to 30 days, merchants of New Spain would trade their silver for such luxuries as furniture, glassware, and the latest fashions from Spain.

LATINO HERITAGE

Sor Juana

Sor Juana wrote many different types of poems: love poems, religious poems, poems about life in the court of the Viceroy of New Spain. Although most of her work was in Spanish, some poems had parts written in African or Native American tongues. In the selection below, Sor Juana explains that she values the beauty of art more highly than material goods.

Costliness and wealth bring me no
   pleasure;
the only happiness I care to find
derives from setting treasure in my mind,
and not from mind that's set on treasure.

Yo no estimo tesoros ni riquezas;
y así, siempre me causa más contento
poner riquezas en mi pensamiento
que no mi pensamiento en las riquezas.

Six months later, the sleepy Pacific port of Acapulco came alive. Here, lookouts scanned the seas for the Manila galleons, two huge ships from Spain's Asian colony in the Philippines. Again, merchants awaited the start of another silver fair. This time, their silver bought silks, pearls, spices, and other luxuries from Asia.

The two yearly fairs poured tons of silver into Spain's treasury. In less than 45 years, Mexico City had become the capital of Spain's most profitable colony.

A Jewel in the Spanish Crown.
King Carlos V considered New Spain the brightest jewel in the Spanish crown. To ensure efficient running of the colony, he changed the way it was governed. In 1535, Carlos took the responsibility of governing New Spain out of the hands of the conquistadors and gave it to a **viceroy,** or royal representative. (In 1544, Spain set up another viceroyalty among the Inca lands that Pizarro had conquered in Peru.)

The discovery of huge veins of silver northwest of Mexico City in 1545 brought new wealth to Spain. Silver became the most important part of New Spain's economy. Some people tried to develop manufacturing in New Spain, but people in Spain worried that colonial manufacturing would compete with their own businesses. Thus, the Spanish passed laws to discourage such enterprises.

That policy left New Spain with few industries to fall back on when the silver ran out. But that time lay far in the future. In the late 1500s and 1600s, Mexico City glittered with wealth.

La Capital.
At the height of the silver boom, the splendor of La Capital (lah kah-pee-TAHL), as Mexico City was known, awed many visitors. Carriages trimmed in gold and silver clattered down stone streets. Bells in the towering cathedral of Mexico called the people to morning and evening religious services. Students rushed to classes held at the University of Mexico, founded in 1551. Printing presses, first set up in 1537, published a wide range of books by local authors.

People on both sides of the Atlantic read the poetry of Sor (Sister) **Juana Inés de la Cruz** (sohr HWAH-nah ee-NES deh lah kroos). Legend holds that Juana began to study books at age 3. As a teenager, Juana begged her mother to allow her to dress as a man so that she could attend the university, which was closed to women. Horrified, her mother turned down the request. That left Juana with the two choices open to women at the time—marriage or joining a convent as a nun.

At 17, Juana chose the convent, where she might study freely. Because she was a nun, however, her poetry came to the attention of church officials. Many of them thought it was wrong for a woman to pursue such intellectual interests. When she wrote a scholarly criticism of a sermon, one church official demanded she stop her writing. The anger of church officials finally broke Sor Juana's spirit. She gave up writing poetry and sent officials a letter, using her blood as ink, in which she renewed her vows as a nun. In 1695, at age 43, Sor Juana died.

Social Divisions.
The treatment received by Sor Juana was one example of

inequalities common in New Spain. Such inequalities separated not only men and women, but also separated social classes.

In New Spain, most wealth and power belonged to the **peninsulares** (peh-neen-soo-LAH-res), or settlers born in Spain. The Spanish crown gave many privileges to the *peninsulares*. They held the highest offices in the church and the government, including the office of viceroy.

After the *peninsulares* came the **criollos** (kree-OH-yohs), people born of Spanish parents in the Americas. The *criollos* could not hold important positions in the government. But many enjoyed great wealth. Some owned silver mines or huge country estates called **haciendas** (ah-SYEN-dahs). The *criollos* took great pride in their contribution to the economy of New Spain. Many of them deeply resented the *peninsulares*. Tensions between the classes would lead to revolution in the Spanish colonies during the 1800s.

The **mestizos,** (mes-TEE-sohs) or people of mixed Spanish and Native American ancestry, took over many of the skilled jobs in Mexico City. In the 1550s, they represented less than 20 percent of the population. But their numbers grew over time. Eventually, Mexico would become a *mestizo* society.

At the bottom of colonial society stood the Native Americans and enslaved Africans. Many enslaved Africans became skilled artisans. Often, they served as overseers of Native American workers.

Another group in New Spain was the **mulattoes** (muh-LAHT-ohs), people who had one parent of European and one of African descent. Mulattoes sometimes found acceptance among *mestizos* or Africans.

Native Americans in New Spain.
The Native Americans who survived con-

quest and disease provided the backbone of New Spain's labor force. Native peoples built mansions and churches, tilled the soil, mined for silver, and performed most of the basic tasks of colonial life.

In 1542, the crown bowed to pressure from priests such as Bartolomé de Las Casas (see page 16) to end mistreatment of Native American laborers. The so-called New Laws passed by the crown did away with the *encomienda* system. The laws set off a wave of protest in Mexico City. "Provisioning [supplying] of this city . . . cannot be done unless it is with Indians," warned one official. "The mines cannot be worked without [the forced labor of] the Indians," added another.

The outcry forced the crown to change its laws. Although the *encomienda* system died, Spain allowed a system of **peonage** (PEE-uh-nihj) to grow up in its place. Under this system, Native Americans received a wage for their work on *haciendas*. But the wage was so low that workers, or **peons** (PEE-uhns), had to borrow heavily from *hacienda* owners. As a result, most peons spent their lives in debt to the owners.

In Mexico City, most Native Americans lived in poverty. They crowded into adobe huts at the edge of the city. Furniture seldom included more than a rough bench, table, and chair. Some Native Americans supported themselves by selling local produce such as prickly pears, chilies, or beans. A few worked in *obrajes* (oh-BRAH-hes), workshops that produced textiles, pottery, or handicrafts.

Among the hardships endured by Native Americans in the 1500s and 1600s were the efforts by Europeans to strip them of their own culture. In missions, priests taught Native Americans to speak Spanish and to follow the Roman Catholic faith. On *haciendas,* owners dressed

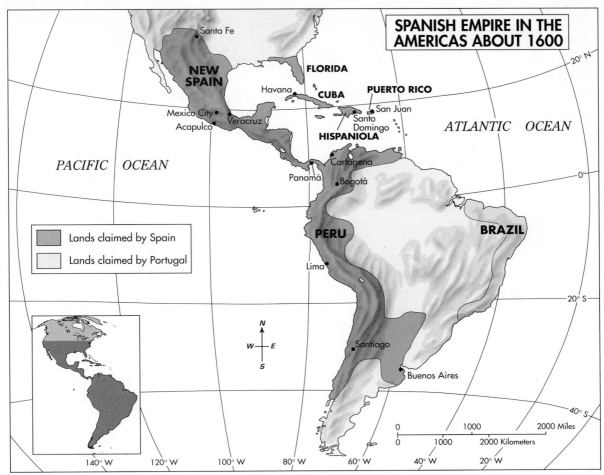

SPANISH EMPIRE IN THE AMERICAS ABOUT 1600

Santa Fe

NEW SPAIN

FLORIDA

Havana
CUBA

PUERTO RICO
San Juan

Mexico City
Acapulco · Veracruz

Santo
Domingo
HISPANIOLA

ATLANTIC   OCEAN

PACIFIC   OCEAN

20° N

Cartagena

Panamá
Bogotá

0°

PERU

BRAZIL

Lima

20° S

Lands claimed by Spain

Lands claimed by Portugal

N
W — E
S

Santiago

Buenos Aires

40° S

0   1000   2000 Miles
0   1000   2000 Kilometers

140° W   120° W   100° W   80° W   60° W   40° W   20° W

By 1600, Spain's holdings were vast. What was its easternmost settlement?

Native Americans in loose-fitting cotton trousers or dresses similar to those worn by European peasants.

In seeking to change Native Americans, however, the Spanish also changed. They added Native American foods to their tables. They picked up Nahuatl and Maya words. They threw Native American blankets across their beds. Through such simple acts, a slow blending of cultures took place. This blending produced the *mestizo* culture of modern Mexico.

Taking Another Look

1. How did the Spanish crown attempt to take control of New Spain?

2. What social classes existed in New Spain?

3. **Critical Thinking** Examine the picture on page 34. What additional details does this picture provide about life in New Spain?

LOOKING AHEAD

The flowering of New Spain prompted settlers to dream of founding other mainland colonies. Some Spaniards pushed south into Central and South America. Others turned north, toward what would one day become the United States.

THE GIFT OF MAIZE

Now, at that time, the people had no corn. . . . They and the animals lived on fruits, also roots that they found in the forest. However, there was corn in the world. It was hidden under a great rock. No one knew about it except the leaf-cutter ants.

Those words begin an ancient Maya story about the discovery of maize, or corn, by humans. Most Native American groups relied on maize as a main source of food. Stories about the importance of maize are found in many American cultures.

When the Spanish arrived in the Americas, Native Americans taught them how to bake and fry corn. The Spanish also learned how to grind corn to make flat pancakes called *tortillas.*

Spanish ships transported maize around the world. Soon, people in Europe, Africa, and Asia were enjoying the taste of corn. Today, corn is a basic food for millions of people. Dried corn stalks fill cribs in the villages of Nepal in Asia. Corn is also used in Ghana, Kenya, and Tanzania in Africa.

In the United States, many people eat corn in Native American and *mestizo* dishes. Tamales, tacos, and burritos are but a few of the corn dishes that have come to the United States from the kitchens of Mexico.

CLOSE UP: Chapter 3

The Who, What, Where of History

1. **Where** did Pedro de Alvarado search for the Maya empire?
2. **Who** was Francisco Pizarro?
3. **Where** was the Inca empire located?
4. **What** religion became the dominant faith in Spanish America?
5. **What** is cultural diffusion?
6. **Who** was Juana Inés de la Cruz?
7. **What** were the main social classes in New Spain?
8. **What** was the peonage system?

Making the Connection

1. What was the connection between Tenochtitlán and Mexico City?
2. What was the connection between colonization of the Americas and the Columbian Exchange?

Time Check

1. Place the following events in chronological order: (a) the end of the *encomienda* system, (b) the arrival of Roman Catholic friars in New Spain, (c) start of the mission system.
2. In which year was the University of Mexico founded?

What Would You Have Done?

1. Imagine you are a Native American living outside Mexico City in 1531. Vasco de Quiroga has just asked you to live at his mission at Santa Fé. Would you accept the offer? Why or why not?
2. If you had been a friend of Sor Juana, what advice would you have given her after her mother forbid her to attend

the university? How would you have advised her after the church demanded she stop writing?

Thinking and Writing About History

1. Design a brochure encouraging merchants in Mexico City to attend one of the annual silver fairs. Mention the two locations of the silver fairs and the items that can be purchased at each fair. Also, explain how the fair benefits both Spain and New Spain.

2. Write an essay about the Columbian Exchange entitled "Changing the Diets of the World." At the end of your essay, tell which of the foods you eat today were part of the Columbian Exchange of the 1500s.

Building Skills: Identifying a Point of View

Identifying points of view is an important skill to develop. A *point of view* is an opinion or attitude a person has about an event or issue. A person's point of view is influenced by his or her education, reading, experiences, family, and friends.

To identify someone's point of view, you must first determine the issue or event under consideration. Next, look for clues that signal a person's opinion or attitude toward that issue or event. Words or phrases such as *should, ought, I believe,* or *I think,* signal an opinion. Also, note how the speaker or writer uses facts. Is he or she using facts in a straightforward, or objective, way? Or is he or she using them to support an argument, or point or view?

To practice identifying points of view, read the selection below. It is an excerpt from a letter written in 1556 by the archbishop of Mexico, Fray Alonso de Montufar (mohn-too-FAHR), to his clergy. Then, answer the questions that follow.

The . . . sumptuous [luxurious] *and superfluous* [unnecessary] *works being erected by the religious* [priests] *in the Indian villages at the Indians' expense should be remedied* [stopped]. *With respect to monasteries, in some places they are so grandiose* [elaborate] *that . . . they would more than suffice for Valladolid* [the Spanish royal court]. . . . *It is nothing for a religious* [friar] *to begin a new work . . . and to bring Indians to work on it in gangs of five hundred, six hundred, or a thousand . . . without paying them any wages or even giving them a crust of bread.*

1. What issue is discussed in the letter?
2. What is Fray Montufar's point of view on this issue?
3. What words helped you to identify his point of view?
4. What facts does Fray Montufar use to support his point of view?

Express Yourself!

Reread Section 3. Then, form a small group and create a booklet that shows some of the foods, plants, animals, and ideas that were part of the Columbian Exchange. On each page of your booklet, draw a picture of one item from the exchange. Next, write the name of the culture the item originally came from. Then, explain how the item was introduced to another culture.

This picture of St. Augustine was drawn by a European artist who had never been there. What details do not seem accurate?

SECTIONS

1 La Florida

2 Outposts of Empire

CHAPTER 4

Reaching Out from the Caribbean

(1513–1695)

THINKING ABOUT THE CHAPTER

What importance did Florida and the Caribbean islands have in Spain's American Empire?

Lucas Vázquez de Ayllón (VAHS-kes deh eye-YOHN) set sail from Hispaniola in July 1526. He was leading an expedition north, to the mainland of America. Some 600 people were packed into six ships. They included soldiers, farmers, a doctor, a surgeon, a pharmacist, a few women and children, 100 enslaved Africans, and 3 Dominican friars. Among the friars was Antonio de Montesinos, a fierce critic of the *encomienda* system.

In late August, the fleet landed in what is now Winyah (WIHN-yoh) Bay, South Carolina. From there, the ships edged south along the sandy Atlantic coast looking for a good place to settle. Ayllón finally stopped at a site along Sapelo (SAHP-uh-loh) Sound in present-day Georgia.

There, the settlers built a small wooden town named San Miguel de Guadalupe (sahn mee-GEL deh gwah-dah-LOO-peh). The town lasted less than six months. Frigid winds and disease struck down nearly two thirds of the settlers, including Ayllón. Enslaved Africans, seeing a chance at freedom, fled to live among Native Americans. Faced with disaster, the remaining settlers risked the wintry seas to sail back to Hispaniola. Only 150, including Montesinos, survived.

Spain would make other efforts to start settlements in the southeastern part of what is today the United States. Most of those efforts would be launched from the Caribbean islands. This chapter explores significant events in the development of Spanish Florida and the Caribbean.

1 LA FLORIDA
◆ Why did Spain want to settle Florida?
◆

In 1513, soldier-explorer Juan Ponce de León set out to investigate rumors of a land north of Puerto Rico. On April 2, Ponce de León spied a tree-covered beach. The day was Easter Sunday—the *Pascua Florida* (PAHS-kwah floh-REE-dah), or "Feast of Flowers," as the Spanish called it. In honor of the day, Ponce de León called the land La Florida.

Exploring La Florida. The Spanish would spend many years trying to plant a colony in La Florida. The lands the Spanish called La Florida in Ponce de León's time stretched north from present-day Florida to Delaware Bay and west to northern Mexico. In 1521, Ponce de León landed with some 200 settlers and soldiers on the west coast of La Florida. Here, battles with Native Americans cost Ponce de León his life.

Others followed in Ponce de León's footsteps. Expeditions led by Pánfilo de Narváez (nahr-VAH-es) in 1528 and Hernando de Soto (deh SOH-toh) in 1539 probed the region. Spanish soldiers marched through parts of what are now Florida, Georgia, the Carolinas, Tennessee, Alabama, Mississippi, Arkansas, Louisiana, and Texas. The expeditions added to Spain's knowledge of the continent. But the explorers found no new golden empires.

Attempts to settle the area also ended in failure. For example, in 1559, Tristán de Luna y Arellano (LOO-nah ee ah-reh-YAH-noh) led some 1,500 well-supplied soldiers and settlers to Ochuse (oh-CHOO-seh), near present-day Pensacola. They had barely arrived when a huge storm swept down on the colony. After the storm, Ochuse fell victim to disease, starvation, and, finally, failure.

The French Threat. In September 1561, the Spanish crown, disgusted with the lack of success in Florida, banned all further efforts at colonization. Within months, however, Spain reversed its decision. Spanish sailors had spotted French settlers in Florida, along what is the St. Johns River, near present-day Jacksonville.

The news sent King Felipe II of Spain into a rage. The French had dared to "trespass" on Spanish territory. Felipe suspected that France wanted to use Fort Caroline, as the settlement was known, for a base for pirates. Both France and England had grown rich by attacking Spain's treasure ships as they sailed from New Spain to Europe.

Spain needed to destroy Fort Caroline and build a colony of its own. King Felipe found the person who could do the job. At the moment, that person was locked up in a prison in Seville.

Pedro Menéndez de Avilés (men-EN-des deh ah-vee-LES) had been born in Spain in 1519. As a teenager, Menéndez had sailed to the Caribbean. There, he earned a reputation as a fierce fighter of pirates. Menéndez prowled the seas looking for the French, English, and Dutch pirates who seized treasure from Spain's Caribbean ports and slow-moving Spanish galleons.

Menéndez's courage and daring in time earned him the position of captain-general of Spain's West Indies fleet. To protect Spanish treasure, he set up a **convoy system.** In this system, Spanish warships sailed alongside the treasure-filled galleons to protect them from raiders. Menéndez sometimes used the fleet to smuggle goods into the Caribbean at a hefty profit for himself. It was this activity that had landed him in prison.

In 1565, King Felipe released Menéndez and ordered him to drive the French from Florida. By August, Menéndez had arrived at his new post in Florida.

A New Settlement. On September 20, Menéndez and his soldiers wiped out Fort Caroline. He put all the settlers "to the knife," except for women, children, and several Roman Catholic men. Menéndez then set about building a Spanish fort at a site to the south he called St. Augustine. To guide the conduct of the soldiers, he issued the Ordinances of Governances. It was the first European code of laws enacted in what is now the United States.

In gratitude, King Felipe made Menéndez governor of Cuba and La Florida. Menéndez used Cuba as a base from which to send ships and supplies to the struggling settlement. He also ordered Jesuit friars into the area.

Slowly, a tiny Spanish outpost grew on the northern edge of the Spanish empire. Over the years, pirates looted it. English ships attacked it. But Spain hung on to St. Augustine. It became an important part of a system of defenses along the rim of the Caribbean. Today, St. Augustine is the oldest European city in the United States.

Taking Another Look

1. What area originally made up La Florida?

2. Why did the Spanish build a colony at St. Augustine?

3. **Critical Thinking** How did the Spanish experience in La Florida differ from colonization efforts in New Spain?

2 OUTPOSTS OF EMPIRE

Why did Spain seek to fortify its bases throughout the Caribbean?

The defense of La Florida was important to King Felipe of Spain. That outpost could slow the growth of French colonies in North America. Felipe ordered the governor of Puerto Rico to supply Pedro Menéndez with soldiers, horses, and cannon.

The king's order did not please the governor. He knew that Puerto Rico could barely defend itself, let alone some far-off outpost in La Florida. The governor was more concerned about a new enemy that had sailed into the waters around Puerto Rico. The English called them *sea dogs;* the Puerto Ricans called them *piratas* (pee-RAH-tahs), or pirates.

1513   Juan Ponce de León lands in Florida.

1526   Lucas Vázquez de Ayllón leads an expedition to America.

1565   Pedro Menéndez de Avilés establishes St. Augustine.

1588   England defeats the Spanish Armada.

1595   Sir Francis Drake attacks San Juan.

1607   England establishes a colony at Jamestown, Virginia.

Securing the Caribbean. The sea dogs were English sailors. They sailed without official support from England. Even so, these **privateers,** or owners of private ships that served as war ships, delighted the English with their bold acts. Spanish settlers in the Caribbean, however, saw the sea dogs as foreign pirates who set fire to their ports and seized their ships. Governors throughout the Caribbean begged Spain for protection.

Spain moved slowly at first. Spanish interest had shifted from the Caribbean to the mainland with the discovery of gold and silver in New Spain and Peru. Islands in the Caribbean had become little more than naval bases to service ships headed in or out of the Gulf of Mexico. Crops such as sugar cane, cattle, and tobacco became the islands' main source of income.

Because Spanish officials considered mainland silver and gold to be more important than crops, they came to value the Caribbean islands mainly for their location. Scattered through the sea routes that led to New Spain, the islands were of greater worth as presidios, or forts, than as income-producing settlements. Their

purpose was to turn back invaders headed into the Gulf.

The islands of Puerto Rico and Cuba protected entry to the Caribbean. They were often the first or last stops for ships crossing the Atlantic. As attacks on Spanish ships increased, Spain built strong defenses for harbors at San Juan, in Puerto Rico, and Havana, in Cuba.

Two huge stone forts protected the harbors of the two ports. As the English sea dogs raided the islands, Spain strengthened the two forts and built others as well. By 1590, Puerto Rico's governor could boast, "[The forts] are the strongest . . . in all of the Indies. Now the people of the country sleep in security."

The English Threat. The Puerto Rican governor had spoken too quickly, however. In 1588, the tides of world power had shifted. In a great sea battle off the coast of England, the English had defeated the powerful Spanish Armada. With Spain unable to defend its sea lanes, the English and other nations moved into the Caribbean.

In 1595, sea dog Sir Francis Drake, who the Spanish called *el Dragón* (el-drah-GOHN), or the Dragon, attacked San Juan. The islanders fought back, steadily shelling the English ships. One cannonball hit Drake's cabin and knocked a stool out from under him.

Although the English sailed away in defeat, they returned again in three years. This time, an epidemic had weakened Puerto Rico's defenders. In 1598, the English pushed into San Juan. For 65 days, the Puerto Ricans battled back against the English. When at last the English pulled out, they looted the city and set it ablaze.

As the 1600s opened, the English began to build colonies in North America. While the people of San Juan struggled to rebuild their city, another Spanish outpost, this one on the mainland of North America, came under attack. England moved to seize La Florida from Spain.

St. Augustine in the Balance.
Settlers at St. Augustine faced a difficult and often dangerous life. Farmers barely coaxed enough crops from the sandy soil to feed the people of the settlement. Ships out of Havana and other Caribbean ports were St. Augustine's lifeline. They carried in badly needed supplies to keep the settlement going.

Settlers at St. Augustine also found themselves exposed to constant attack from the sea. In 1586, *el Dragón* burned the town to the ground, while settlers hid in the surrounding forests. But, like the people of Puerto Rico, the people of St. Augustine rebuilt their town from the ashes.

As the 1600s began, English pressure on St. Augustine increased. In 1607, England established a colony at Jamestown, Virginia. There, English settlers experienced the same hardships endured 100 years earlier by the first Spanish settlers in the Americas. The Spanish watched with concern as England tried to build Jamestown and other colonies in North America. The settlement at St. Augustine took on added importance in the race for empire. If the English took

From Florida to the easternmost islands of the Caribbean, Spain felt the increasing pressure of France and England in the 1600s. What did the Spanish Crown do to protect against this pressure?

By the 1600s, the port of Havana had become the busiest port in the Americas. In this picture there are many details, including Morro Castle at left, that show Havana's importance. What other details show this?

St. Augustine, they would be able to use it as a port to launch raids against Spanish ships carrying gold and silver from the colonies. English control of St. Augustine would also put the ports of Havana and San Juan in danger of attack.

In 1672, Spain ordered new defenses built at St. Augustine. That year, work began on a fort called Castillo de San Marcos (kahs-TEE-yoh deh sahn MAHR-kohs). Craftworkers, many of whom were enslaved Africans, were sent to Florida from Havana, Cuba. For more than 20 years, stonemasons carved out huge blocks of coquina (koh-KEE-nah), a rock made of seashells, to build the fort's walls. By 1695, most of the workers had gone from St. Augustine. They left behind a structure that helped protect Spain's claim on Florida well into the 1700s. Today, that fort is one of the United States' major historical landmarks.

Taking Another Look

1. How did the Spanish view of its Caribbean colonies change in the mid-1500s?

2. Why did the Spanish seek to fortify St. Augustine?

3. **Critical Thinking** Imagine you are a Spanish official in 1600. How would you respond to a proposal to abandon St. Augustine?

LOOKING AHEAD

As Spain extended its reach into Florida, it also cast its eyes to lands along the northern frontier of New Spain. The next steps in Spanish exploration and settlement would take place there, in what would one day become the southwestern United States.

In 1743, Spanish officials in Havana, Cuba, decided to establish another settlement in La Florida. They sent two Jesuit priests, Fray Guiseppe Saverio Alagna (ah-LAHG-nah) and José María Mónaco (MOH-nah-coh) to start a settlement between the Miami River and Biscayne (bihs-KAYN) Bay. With the help of Spanish soldiers and Native Americans, the two priests built a wood fort at the mouth of the Miami.

When the fort was completed, Fray Alagna rushed back to Havana to report that a Cuban foothold had been established in southern Florida. Alagna asked that officials send Cuban families and additional troops to the settlement, called Santa María de Loreto (SAHN-tah mah-REE-a deh loh-REH-toh).

By now, officials in Cuba had decided that a colony in Florida would be too expensive to maintain. Fortifications would be needed to fend off attacks by enemies of Spain. Cuban officials ordered the priests to return home.

More than 200 years later, thousands of Cuban refugees poured into the city of Miami. They were fleeing a communist government led by Fidel Castro. City officials welcomed the refugees at a building known today as Freedom Tower. That building stands near the site once occupied by Santa Maria de Loreto. In coming to Miami, the refugees built on a heritage older than the United States itself.

CLOSE UP: Chapter 4

The Who, What, Where of History

1. **Where** was the first Spanish colony in the present-day United States?
2. **Who** was Juan Ponce de León?
3. **What** parts of the present-day United States did Hernando de Soto explore?
4. **Who** founded St. Augustine?
5. **What** were the Ordinances of Governances?
6. **What** port did Spain fortify on the island of Puerto Rico?
7. **Where** is Castillo de San Marcos?

Making the Connection

1. What was the connection between Fort Caroline and St. Augustine?
2. What was the connection between the English colony at Jamestown, Virginia, and construction of Castillo de San Marcos?

Time Check

1. Why was the year 1588 a turning point in the history of the Americas?
2. Which happened first: the defeat of the Spanish Armada or the looting of San Juan by the English?

What Would You Have Done

1. If you had lived in Santo Domingo in 1526, would you have volunteered to help Ayllón build his new settlement? Why or why not?
2. Imagine you are the king or queen of Spain in 1570. You need to select a new governor to replace Menéndez in La Florida. What qualities would you look for in a governor? Explain.

Thinking and Writing About History

1. Write a story for a newspaper in Seville on one of the following events: (a) Ayllón's failed attempt at settlement; (b) de Soto's expedition; (c) the founding of St. Augustine.

2. Write a speech a Spanish official in St. Augustine might have delivered in 1695 honoring the completion of Castillo de San Marcos.

Building Skills: Interpreting a Historical Map

Most people are familiar with topographic maps and political maps. A *topographic* map presents information about elevations on earth. A *political* map shows the boundaries of countries, states, or regions. A *special purpose* map presents information on a specific topic. Special purpose maps include rainfall maps, population maps, and time zone maps. What other kinds of special purpose maps can you identify?

The special purpose map on this page is called a historical map. A *historical map* shows events or developments at a particular time in the past. Like any other map, a historical map includes a number of tools to help you read it. The map title presents the subject of the map. Map labels provide more information. Look at the map below. Then, answer the questions.

1. What is the subject of this map?
2. What harbors did Spain fortify?
3. What do the arrows symbolize?
4. Based on this map, why do you think settlers at St. Augustine felt especially vulnerable to attack?

Express Yourself!

Choose a partner. Together review the information about Pedro Menéndez de Avilés on page 48 and Sir Francis Drake on page 49. Pretend Menéndez and Drake are meeting for the first time. Write a dialogue for these two people that tells how each feels about his country and his duty. When you are finished, read your dialogue for the class.

How Spain protected its valuable Caribbean ports.

Guarded by mounted soldiers, Native Americans were marched to work near the San Francisco presidio. Said one friar: "The Indians complain bitterly at having to work so that the soldiers may eat."

SECTIONS

1 The Kingdom of New Mexico

2 Across the Rio Grande

3 Along the Pacific Coast

CHAPTER 5

The Spanish Borderlands

(1536–1784)

THINKING ABOUT THE CHAPTER

How did Spain establish settlements in New Mexico, Texas, and California?

In 1687, a friar named Eusebio Kino (KEE-noh) left Mexico City on a rugged, dusty trail the Spanish called *el Camino del Diablo,* or the "Devil's Highway." Carved out of the desert by Native Americans, the trail snaked northward across the present-day border of Mexico and Arizona. Fray Kino used the route to head into the **Spanish Borderlands,** the name given to the northern lands of New Spain. Fray Kino was both a Jesuit priest and a geographer. Thus, he looked forward both to converting new peoples and to mapping new lands.

Kino stopped briefly among the Pima people who lived on the Río San Miguel in what is today the Mexican state of Sonora. There he built a mission named Nuestra Señora de los Dolores (NWEH-strah seh-NYOH-rah deh lohs doh-LOH-res). He used the mission as his home base for more than 24 years. But his restless spirit never let him remain there for long. Known as the "padre [priest] on horseback," Kino made more than 40 expeditions throughout the borderlands. He started some 25 missions there. One of these, San Xavier del Bac (sahn sah-vee-ER del bahk), still stands in Tucson, Arizona.

Kino dreamed of building a system of missions and trails that would span the borderlands all the way to the Pacific Ocean. Officials in Mexico City thought the plan too costly. Although Kino died in 1711, his dream did not die with him. This chapter traces events that led the Spanish to make part of Kino's dream a reality. The story begins in the early 1500s with the first Spanish *entradas* (en-TRAH-dahs), or expeditions, into what is now the U.S. Southwest.

1 THE KINGDOM OF
◆ NEW MEXICO
◆ Why did the Spanish push into the borderlands north of New Spain?

In 1536, a slave trader named Nuño de Guzmán (goos-MAHN) was riding through the northwestern portion of New Spain. He was searching for Native Americans to take captive. Although enslaving Native Americans had been outlawed by Spain, some settlers still bought Native Americans to labor as slaves in silver mines or fields. Instead of Native Americans, Guzmán stumbled upon a group of Spaniards in rags. They were the only survivors of Pánfilo de Narváez's Florida expedition (see page 47).

On July 24, the leader of the group, Alvar Núñez Cabeza de Vaca (kah-BEH-sah deh VAH-kah) walked into Mexico City with three other survivors—two *hidalgos* like himself and an enslaved African named Estevánico (es-teh-VAH-nee-koh). Their appearance sparked a wave of excitement. The wanderers had walked from the Gulf of Mexico almost to the Gulf of California. Their 6,000-mile (9,600 kilometer) journey gave the Spanish their first glimpse of the borderlands. The Spaniards of Mexico City eagerly waited to hear their stories.

In Search of Golden Cities. Cabeza de Vaca told a hair-raising tale of survival. But the part of the story that interested people most was a report he received from one group of Native Americans. It told of a city filled with turquoise and emeralds. Perhaps riches to match the empire of the Aztecs lay to the north.

This possibility fired the imagination of Don Antonio de Mendoza, the first viceroy of New Spain. He ordered Francisco Vásquez de Coronado (koh-roh-NAH-doh) to march into the borderlands in search of the golden cities. In February 1540, Coronado led his expedition out of Mexico City. Some 300 adventurers including three women, 1,000 Native Americans, 6 priests, and 1,500 horses and pack animals headed north.

Instead of golden cities, Coronado found the adobe villages of the Zuñi. The Spanish called these villages "pueblos," the Spanish word for towns. Coronado's soldiers killed many people of the pueblos, earning the lasting hatred of the Zuñi.

For the next two years, Coronado marched through much of present-day Arizona, New Mexico, Texas, Oklahoma, and Kansas searching in vain for golden cities. In the spring of 1542, his ragged, half-starved force returned to Mexico City. The only gold carried by Coronado was his gold-plated armor.

55

1540–1542 Francisco Coronado explores much of what is today the U.S Southwest.

1598 Juan de Oñate establishes first settlement in the Kingdom of New Mexico.

1680 Popé's revolt drives Spanish from New Mexico.

1692 Diego de Vargas retakes New Mexico for Spain.

1718 Spanish priests and soldiers establish mission at San Antonio in Texas.

1769 Gaspar de Portolá orders building of mission at San Diego, California.

1776 Spanish soldiers and priests found San Francisco settlement.

Rediscovery. Trips such as Coronado's helped end the hopes of finding cities like Tenochtitlán to the north. A boom in silver mining in New Spain focused attention on areas closer to Mexico City (see Chapter 3). Gradually, however, settlers began to move north from the mining towns.

Slave catchers entered into the borderlands to capture Native Americans to work in the mines. Priests moved north to win new converts in the borderlands. Some of the older mines began to run out of silver and miners pushed north to the borderlands, seeking new sources of ore.

The flurry of activity in the north led King Felipe II to take control of the borderlands. The king announced creation of a new state within New Spain to be known as the Kingdom of New Mexico. In the 1580s, he opened the position of "governor and captain general" of New Mexico to the highest bidder. The winner was Juan de Oñate (oh-NYAH-teh).

"Passed This Way." Oñate, the son of a wealthy silver-mine owner, dedicated himself to making the new colony a success. "I shall give your majesty a new world, greater than New Spain," he pledged. The king helped Oñate round up settlers by promising to make them *hidalgos* if they remained in New Mexico for five years.

In 1598, after many delays, Oñate set out on a grand expedition. It included some 500 people—soldiers, women, children, enslaved Africans, and Native American and *mestizo* servants. A cloud of dust swirled about them as 83 carts and 7,000 cattle pushed north.

In September, after nearly nine months on the trail, Oñate stopped in northern New Mexico near the present-day town of Española. He ordered workers to build a settlement. Friendly Native Americans fed and housed the group during the building.

Good relations with the Native Americans proved short-lived. In 1599, Oñate tried to convert the Native Americans to Christianity. When people at the Acoma pueblo resisted, Oñate turned Spanish cannons, guns, and swords against them. He savagely punished the survivors as an example to other pueblo peoples who resisted.

In 1600, he ordered settlers to build a new capital named San Gabriel (sahn gah-bree-EL) along the banks of the northern Rio Grande. Unaware of how large the continent was, Oñate also set out to find an easy route to the Pacific. On a trail near what is today El Morro National Monument, Oñate carved into a rock an inscription that reads in part: "There passed this way the *Adelantado* Don Juan de Oñate." That carving still exists today.

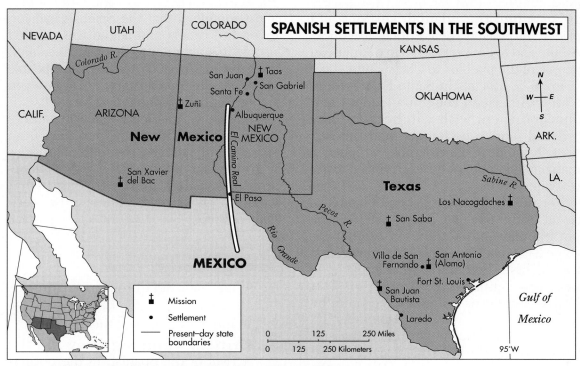

SPANISH SETTLEMENTS IN THE SOUTHWEST

NEVADA · UTAH · COLORADO · KANSAS · CALIF. · ARIZONA · OKLAHOMA · ARK. · LA. · Texas · MEXICO

Colorado R.
San Juan · Taos · San Gabriel · Santa Fe · Zuñi · Albuquerque · NEW MEXICO · New Mexico · El Camino Real · San Xavier del Bac · El Paso · Rio Grande · Pecos R. · Sabine R. · Los Nacogdoches · San Saba · Villa de San Fernando · San Antonio (Alamo) · Fort St. Louis · San Juan Bautista · Laredo · Gulf of Mexico · 95°W

N W E S

✝ Mission
● Settlement
— Present–day state boundaries

0 125 250 Miles
0 125 250 Kilometers

From the 1600s to the 1800s, Spanish friars and soldiers established a string of missions across what is today Arizona, New Mexico, and Texas. In which present-day state were the oldest missions?

The inscription was soon the only trace of Oñate in the region. His heavy-handed rule of settlers and harsh treatment of Native Americans led Spanish officials to recall him. In 1609, a new *adelantado,* Pedro de Peralta (peh-RAHL-tah), arrived in San Gabriel.

Building Santa Fe. In the winter of 1609–1610, Peralta moved settlers to a new site along the fertile banks of a tributary, or branch, of the upper Rio Grande. Here they built a new capital named Santa Fe, or "Holy Faith."

Santa Fe became the second oldest Spanish town, in the present-day United States. By the 1630s, some 250 Spaniards and as many *mestizos* lived or worked on *ranchos* (rahn-chohs), or small farms,

around the town. A string of 25 missions grew up along a network of Native American trails that connected pueblos in the area.

To obtain supplies, pack trains of mules headed into Mexico City along a 1,500-mile (2,400-kilometer) trail known as *el Camino Real*, or "the Royal Road." The trains carried items for trade such as hides, piñon nuts, and *mantas* (MAHN-tahs), or blankets woven by Native Americans. Aside from this slim trade, however, officials in Mexico City paid little attention to Santa Fe.

The Pueblo Revolt. The pueblo peoples never fully forgot earlier brutality by the Spanish. But, for many years, they lived in an uneasy peace with their neigh-

57

bors. Trouble, however, began again in the 1670s when the Spanish settlers and priests increased their efforts to collect tribute and to convert the Native American people of the pueblos to Christianity.

In 1675, officials in Sante Fe seized 47 Native American religious leaders and charged them with witchcraft. They ordered four to be hanged and the rest brutally whipped. One of those whipped, a man named Popé (poh-PEH), vowed to get revenge.

For nearly five years, Popé planned a revolt of the pueblos. In August 1680, he put his plan into action. On August 10, some 2,000 pueblo peoples rose up against the Spanish. Settlers in the countryside fled into Santa Fe for protection. But Native Americans outnumbered them by more than two to one. On September 15, the Native Americans permitted the survivors to leave the town and flee to Spanish settlements further down the Rio Grande. Popé then ordered Santa Fe to be looted and burned.

For the next 13 years, the borderlands belonged to Native Americans alone. The pueblo peoples—among them the Hopi, Zuñi, and Acoma—had driven out the Spanish. But the unity created by opposition to the Spanish did not last. Traditional divisions among the pueblo peoples grew again. Also, Popé made a serious mistake. He traded Spanish horses to the Apache. The Apache began to use these horses to attack the pueblos.

Rebuilding Santa Fe. After Popé's death in 1688, Spain began to reconquer the borderlands. Both England and France had planted colonies in North America. So Spain wanted to keep New Mexico in order to protect New Spain.

In 1692, Diego de Vargas (VAHR-gahs) marched into New Mexico with only about 200 soldiers. He calmly rode into pueblos and announced that the Spanish had forgiven the rebels and asked the startled people to surrender to Spanish rule. With the growing threat of Apache raids, people in pueblo after pueblo agreed. Vargas even retook Santa Fe without firing a shot.

In 1693, Vargas led some 800 settlers into Santa Fe. With the help of allies from surrounding pueblos, the settlement slowly grew again. It formed the first stepping-stone in Spain's march through what would in time become the southwestern United States.

Taking Another Look

1. What lands did Coronado explore?
2. Why did Spain seek to plant a colony in the borderlands in the late 1500s?
3. **Critical Thinking** How did the arrival of the Spanish in the borderlands affect the Native Americans who lived there?

2 ACROSS THE RIO GRANDE
◆ Why did the Spanish attempt to build settlements in Texas?

In July 1714, Captain Diego Ramón (rah-MOHN) sat stunned in his office at San Juan Bautista (bow-TEES-tah), a lonely Spanish outpost on what is now the Mexican side of the Rio Grande. Before him stood a group of traders from French Louisiana. The traders had crossed the huge stretch of Spanish land called Texas to reach San Juan Bautista.

Ramón immediately grasped the danger of the situation for New Spain. If French traders could make the trip, so could a French army. He warned in a letter, "If his Majesty does not intervene, the French will be masters of all this land."

Painted on a cowhide early in the 1700s, this scene shows mounted Native Americans allied with the Spanish attacking an Apache village. Why did some Native Americans ally themselves with the Spanish?

Into East Texas. Ramón and Louis St. Denis, the leader of the traders, were unable to speak each other's language. But St. Denis spoke Caddo and a Caddo woman named Angelina could translate St. Denis's words into Spanish for Ramón.

Angelina, the translator, considered the mission at San Juan Bautista one of two homes. As a chief among the Caddo, Angelina kept close ties with her people in eastern Texas. But she loved the mission, too. She had grown up among the priests, who taught her the ways of the Spanish and converted her to Catholicism.

Angelina used her knowledge of Spanish to serve her people as a translator. She also helped the Spanish to extend their influence into Texas by acting as a negotiator with the Caddo and other Native Americans of the region. Today, Angelina County is the only Texas county named in honor of a woman.

Speaking through Angelina, St. Denis offered Ramón a deal. If the Spanish would allow St. Denis to open a trade route to New Mexico, he would help them win converts among Native Americans.

St. Denis persuaded the Spanish to accept his offer. Working with Angelina, St. Denis helped set up a string of missions and presidios from San Juan Bautista to the present-day cities of Nacogdoches (nak-uh-DOH-chuhz) and San Augustine.

San Antonio. The actions of the French spurred the Spanish into taking control of Texas. In 1718, a group of priests and soldiers arrived at a river in central Texas. On its west bank they built the Misión San Antonio de Valero (vah-LEH-roh). The mission later became better known to history as the Alamo.

San Antonio barely survived. Disease and backbreaking farm labor discouraged many Native American people from living at the mission. Few settlers from New Spain to the south wanted to relocate to the lonely outpost. Finally, priests at the mission appealed to Spain for help.

In 1731, the Spanish king sent some 200 farm families from the Canary Islands to San Antonio. But these islanders showed little interest in the rigid routines of mission life. They built their own village nearby named Villa de San Fernando (VEE-yah deh sahn fer-NAHN-doh). It was the first civilian settlement in Texas. The mission and village later became the modern city of San Antonio.

Holding Onto Texas. By the 1740s, only a string of thinly settled missions and presidios connected Texas with New Spain. The Texas plains were really controlled by the Apache, who had entered the region in the 1720s. The Apache, like other peoples of the plains, had mastered the use of the horse. Deadly accurate Apache arrows, fired from the backs of their galloping horses, defeated many enemies, including the Spanish.

However, the Texas plains still attracted the Spanish. The region seemed perfect for grazing wild cattle and the wild horses called **mustangs.** To control the plains,

This drawing from the 1600s shows a Spanish officer armed to ride into battle against the Native Americans of Texas.

the Spanish handed out more than 20 *ranchos.* These later grew into towns such as Laredo, Texas. These towns faced constant threat of attack from the Apache and, later, the Comanche. But the *ranchos* had their own defenders in the form of the **vaqueros** (vah-KEH-rohs)—tough Spanish, *mestizo,* or Native American cattleherders.

In New Spain, *peninsulares* looked down on *vaqueros* as peons. But on the Texas plains, the *vaqueros* gained a new respect. They learned to live and fight on the backs of horses. Their courage and skill became famous. "To be a *vaquero,*" went one saying, "is to be a hero."

The *vaqueros* developed a way of life that became widespread in what later became the western United States. Their words and clothing became famous. Even today, people use the words of the *vaqueros. Corral, lazo* (lasso), *bronco, chaparreras* (chaps)—these and other words recall New Spain's *entrada* into Texas.

Taking Another Look

1. How did the French try to gain control of Texas?
2. How did the Apache limit Spanish settlement?
3. **Critical Thinking** How did *vaquero* culture influence the culture of the United States today?

3 ALONG THE PACIFIC COAST

◆ How did friars and *poblanos* affect the
◆ development of California?

In February 1768, Spanish soldiers evicted 15 Jesuit priests from the mission at Loreto in Baja, or lower, California. The soldiers watched as the black-robed Jesuits boarded a ship.

The king of Spain, like other European rulers at the time, had come to fear the power of the Jesuits. The religious order had built a worldwide network of missions and trading stations. So, in the 1760s, the rulers of Spain, France, and Portugal cracked down. Thousands of Jesuits were exiled and their property seized.

The mission now belonged to another religious order, the brown-robed Franciscans. Their leader, Fray Junípero Serra (SEHR-rah), welcomed the work that lay ahead. Soon he would help carry the cross and the sword into Alta, or upper, California.

Nueva California. The Spanish first heard about Alta California from Juan Rodríguez Cabrillo (kah-BREE-yoh), one of Cortés's soldiers. In 1542, Cabrillo had sailed from the Pacific coast of New Spain as far north as present-day Santa Monica Bay. Cabrillo hoped to find the golden cities of a legendary island called California. Instead, he found dozens of Native American villages.

Cabrillo's report dampened the interest of gold-hungry Spaniards in *Nueva California,* or "New California." In the 1760s, however, reports of British and Russian ships off the Pacific coast renewed Spanish interest in settling New California. A member of the royal court named José de Gálvez (GAHL-ves) convinced the king to let him build a series of missions and presidios along the Pacific coast. The missions and forts would help secure the land for Spain. Each mission would lie no more than one or two days' march from another.

By Land and Sea. Gálvez appointed Gaspar de Portolá governor of both Baja and Alta California. He placed the task of building missions in the hands of Fray Serra. He put the soldiers assigned to the expedition under the command of Captain Rivera.

On January 9, 1769, the expedition set out for Alta California. Two groups sailed by sea; another two marched by land. All four groups met with hardship and disaster. The sailors faced stormy seas and a lack of food and water. The soldiers, mule drivers, and Native Americans faced food shortages and disease.

On July 1, 1769, the land and sea parties met along a strip of sandy beach. "It was a day of great rejoicing and merriment for all," wrote Serra in his diary. But the loss of life had been great. Nearly one-quarter of those on the expedition had died. Even so, Portolá ordered work to begin on San Diego, the first mission and presidio in Alta California.

"Good Land for Planting." While soldiers worked, Portolá headed north. Together they mapped the lands and picked sites for farms, missions, and towns. A soldier named Juan Crespi

(KRES-pee) was struck with the richness of Alta California. In describing the future site of Los Angeles, Crespi wrote:

It has good land for planting all kinds of grain and seeds, and is the most suitable site . . . for a large settlement. . . . [It has] a large vineyard of wild grapes and an infinity [endless supply] of rosebushes in full bloom. All the soil is black.

Over the next four years, the expedition built only a few missions. From the start, Serra's friars found few Native Americans willing to stay on the missions unless forced to by soldiers. Farming made little sense to Native Americans who lived by hunting, fishing, and gathering abundant wild food. Also disease and harsh discipline made the missions places of death in the minds of many Native Americans.

Nevertheless, Fray Serra stuck to his goal—the conversion of "thousands of souls." In 1775, he returned to Mexico City to plead for supplies. His appeal revived the plan of Fray Kino (see page 55). Officials decided to open an overland route between the supply-rich missions of the northern borderlands and the struggling missions of the Pacific coast.

In 1774, Juan Bautista de Anza (AHN-sah), a Spanish soldier, scouted a route. With Kino's maps to guide him, Anza marked out a trail from what is now Arizona to San Gabriel (see map, page 63). From here, he made his way north. With Anza's help, Serra founded a mission at San Francisco. Serra named it after his personal hero, St. Francis of Assisi, the founder of the Franciscans.

The Missions. By the last years of the 1700s, however, missions and presidios formed stepping-stones up the California coast. Between 1769 and 1834, an estimated 30,000 Native Americans lived at the missions of Alta California.

The missions brought new ways of life to native Californians. Before the arrival of the friars, hundreds of different groups of Native American peoples had lived along the coast. Some of these people rebelled against the mission system and were killed. Countless more died of European diseases. The surviving Native Americans found themselves taught a new religion and a strange new language.

Days at the mission opened and ended with the sound of the chapel bell. A **mador** (MAH-dohr), usually an older male Native American, made sure the converts attended religious services. A **maestra** (mah-ES-trah), or female chaperone, watched out for the girls and young women.

In between church services, Native Americans labored in the mission workshops or in the mission's fields. As a result of their efforts, California blossomed with some 260,000 orange trees. Plants that were first grown at the missions still bloom throughout the area—mission grapes, mission olives, and mission figs.

The Poblanos. Despite the influence of the missions, the *mestizo* culture of California did not grow out of mission life. Instead, it developed in the pueblos, or towns, that grew up in towns near the missions. Here **poblanos** (poh-BLAH-nohs), or civilian settlers from New Spain, built thriving communities such as Los Angeles and San Jose.

The eldest males of the founding families of Los Angeles were part of a new mix of people that was developing in Spanish North America. They included two Spaniards, four Native Americans, one *mestizo,* two mulattoes of black and

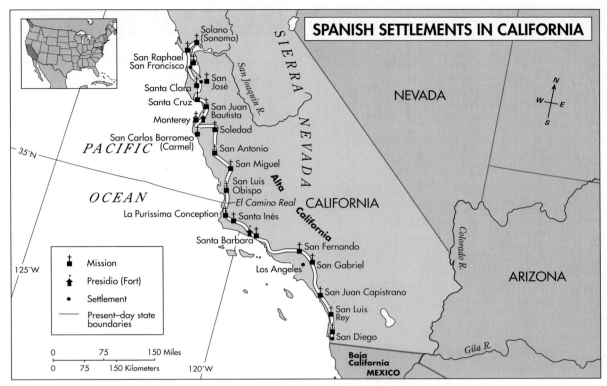

SPANISH SETTLEMENTS IN CALIFORNIA

Solano (Sonoma)
San Raphael
San Francisco
Santa Clara
San José
Santa Cruz
San Juan Bautista
Monterey
Soledad
San Carlos Borromeo (Carmel)
San Antonio
San Miguel
San Luis Obispo
El Camino Real
La Puríssima Conception
Santa Inés
Santa Barbara
San Fernando
Los Angeles
San Gabriel
San Juan Capistrano
San Luis Rey
San Diego

SIERRA NEVADA
Alta California
CALIFORNIA
San Joaquín R.
PACIFIC
OCEAN
35°N
125°W
120°W

NEVADA
ARIZONA
Colorado R.
Gila R.
Baja California
MEXICO

✝ Mission
⬛ Presidio (Fort)
• Settlement
— Present–day state boundaries

0   75   150 Miles
0   75   150 Kilometers

In less than half a century from 1769 to the early 1800s, the Spanish built a string of presidios and missions along the coast of what is today the state of California. Why did all this activity suddenly take place?

Spanish ancestry, and one person of Native American and mulatto ancestry. By the early 1800s, people of mixed ancestry made up the majority of the population of Los Angeles and other pueblos.

Taking Another Look

1. Why did Spain encourage the settlement of Alta California?

2. How did the mission system affect the lives of Native Americans in what is today California?

3. **Critical Thinking** Study the map on this page. (a) How did location influence where missions were built? (b) Why were ties with Mexico so loose?

LOOKING AHEAD

As Spanish missions stretched north along the Pacific coast, English colonists along the Atlantic coast struggled to gain independence from their home country. In 1776, these colonists announced the creation of a new nation, the United States of America.

Spain would come to the aid of those colonists in their struggle against England, then the most powerful nation in the world. Thanks in part to the help of Spain, the English colonies would win their independence. Not long after that, Spain's colonies in the Americas would be so inspired by the North American struggle that the colonists would seek to throw off Spanish rule.

On July 24, 1694, 20 armed Spanish soldiers and their Native American allies attacked the Jémez pueblo in New Mexico. In the fighting that followed, 84 members of the pueblo died. Rather than surrender to the Spanish, several people jumped off the high mesa where the pueblo was located. According to legend, a vision of the pueblo's patron saint, San Diego, appeared and guided the jumpers to safety.

Since that time, the Jémez pueblo has held a great feast honoring San Diego. For years, traders have come from near and far to take part in the great feast. Navajo spread their silver and turquoise jewelry on blankets. Farmers from surrounding pueblos hang up dried chilies and blue corn to sell. Weavers display *mantas,* or cloths, for sale.

The event celebrates a union of cultures. San Diego Feast Day honors a saint introduced to the Jémez by Christian friars. But, after people leave morning church services, they go to the central plaza to watch traditional Jémez dances and honor the earth, the sky, *and* San Diego. First, the Pumpkin clan dances, then the Turquoise clan. In the background, a church bell rings. The sights and sounds mark the blend of Spanish and Native American ways that characterize New Mexico today.

CLOSE UP: Chapter 5

The Who, What, Where of History

1. **What** were the Spanish Borderlands?
2. **Where** did Francisco Vásquez de Coronado explore?
3. **Who** was Popé?
4. **Who** was Angelina?
5. **What** deal did Louis St. Denis offer to the Spanish?
6. **Who** were the *vaqueros?*
7. **Where** was the first Spanish mission in Alta California?

Making the Connection

1. What was the connection between Apache raids on pueblos and Diego de Vargas's takeover of New Mexico in 1692?
2. What was the connection between French interest in North America and the founding of Texas?

Time Check

1. How many years passed between Fray Eusebio Kino's arrival in Alta California and the arrival of Fray Junípero Serra?
2. In what year did Juan de Oñate begin his expedition into New Mexico?

What Would You Have Done?

1. If you had been an adviser to Captain Diego Ramón in 1714, what advice would you have given him about Louis St. Denis's offer?
2. Imagine you are a *mestizo* in Mexico City. You have just heard about the new pueblos in California. What reasons might encourage you to move to the new frontier?

Thinking and Writing About History

1. Imagine that you had traveled with Fray Eusebio Kino during his travels through northern Mexico and Arizona in the late 1600s and early 1700s. Write two or three journal entries describing your travels and Kino's work. You may wish to research about Kino's life and about the geography of the Mexican borderlands.

2. Write a news article about the pueblo revolt of 1680 that might have appeared in a newspaper in Mexico City. Try to include answers to the following questions commonly asked by reporters: *Who? What? Where? When? Why? How?*

3. Write a brief skit describing the experiences of a young Native American who has been sent to one of Fray Junípero Serra's new missions.

4. Write a speech that might have been given upon the founding of Los Angeles in 1781. Use your school or local library to find additional information about this event.

Building Skills: Forming Inferences

What did the chapel at San Antonio look like in the late 1700s? To find out, read the following eyewitness account:

The Indian quarters form a square about the mission with attractive porticoes [porches], with the whole being watered by a beautiful irrigation ditch. . . . Besides this, a well was dug to forestall [prevent] the lack of water in case of being besieged by the enemy. To safeguard it, the door is fortified. At the entrance to the chapel a small watch-tower was built, with loopholes for three swivel guns which . . . are carefully guarded.

From this description, you may come up with the idea that friars at the mission feared being attacked. Notice that this idea is not stated anywhere in the selection. Instead, this idea comes from putting together clues from the selection. Can you identify some of these clues?

Whenever you look for unstated ideas, you are "reading between the lines." That is, you put together clues to come up with new insights about a topic or a subject. These insights are called *inferences*.

To practice your skill at forming inferences, study the map of Spanish settlements in New Mexico and Texas on page 57. Then answer these questions.

1. Why do you think the settlements and missions are generally located near each other?

2. What might you infer about the land around the El Camino Real between El Paso and Albuquerque? Explain.

Express Yourself!

Study the maps on pages 57 and 63. Many of the names of places are Spanish. That is because Spanish settlers lived there and named them. Find a map of the state you live in. Be sure your map shows the names of many cities and towns. Choose two or three students to work with. Make a list of all the place names that are Spanish. Then, try to identify place names that are French. When you are finished, find out if any areas of your state were once controlled by the Spanish or French.

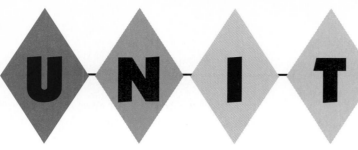

UNIT 2

TOWARD INDEPENDENCE
(1763–1840s)

Mission in New Mexico

Chapter

6 The Spanish and the American Revolution (1763–1783)

7 The Road to Latin American Independence (1783–1825)

8 Life in the Mexican Borderlands (1820s–1840s)

Simón Bolívar

Unit 2 traces the rise of independence movements in the British and Spanish colonies of the Americas. Spain was one of the European powers that gave important aid to the British colonists as they fought for freedom. Spanish colonists, too, soon began independence movements of their own. However, as you will read, differences between the British and Spanish colonies meant that their revolutions took different forms and had different results.

For more than a hundred years, Spain, Britain, and France fought a series of bloody wars for empire. In 1763, at the close of the French and Indian War, the British won Canada, Florida, and all the land between the Appalachian (ap-pah-LAY-chuhn) Mountains and the Mississippi River from the French. The Louisiana Territory, or all the land west of the Mississippi and east of the Rocky Mountains, went to Spain. Britain and Spain were now the largest landholders in the Americas.

◆ ◆ In The United States ◆ ◆

Among Britain's North American lands were 13 colonies on a narrow strip between the Atlantic Ocean and the Appalachian Mountains. Nearly 4 million people lived in this area, most of them on farms.

The British Colonies in 1763. Like the Spanish, the British had built their colonies at the expense of the Native Americans. Although a few colonists tried to deal fairly with the Native Americans, most simply wanted their lands. The British found no huge empires to conquer,

like that of the Aztec in Mexico. Instead, settlers killed the Native Americans or drove them deeper into the interior of the North American continent.

The British colonists, in such colonies as Georgia, Virginia, North Carolina, and South Carolina, followed the example of the Spanish in using enslaved Africans to meet a severe labor shortage. The first Africans arrived in the British colonies as **indentured servants** in the early 1600s. An indentured servant was a person who agreed to work for a certain length of time in return for passage to the colonies. A few years later Africans arrived in the colonies as slaves. A century later, the slave system had taken hold throughout the British colonies, especially in the South.

White Europeans in the British colonies, on the other hand, enjoyed a degree of freedom unknown in Spanish America or in most European nations. In the British colonies, a poor family could hope to rise to the middle or even the upper class.

There was greater political liberty for whites in the British colonies, as well as more economic opportunity. British settlers brought to North America a tradition of self-government. White males who owned a certain amount of property could vote for members of local and colonial governments.

By 1763 nearly every colony had a two-house **legislature**, or lawmaking body. Each colonial legislature had to answer to a governor, who was appointed by the monarch. The legislatures and governors had to answer to the British ruler and to **Parliament,** the British lawmaking body. For many years, Parliament left the colonies largely free to manage their own

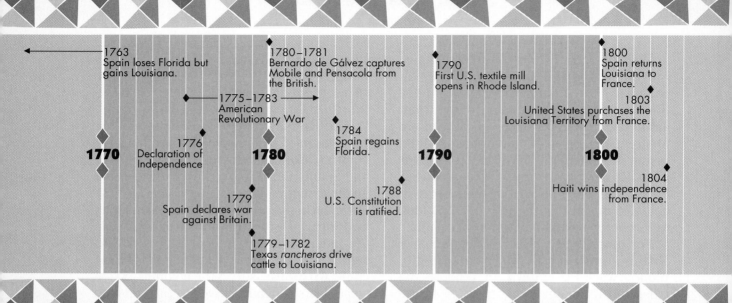

1763
Spain loses Florida but
gains Louisiana.

1780–1781
Bernardo de Gálvez captures
Mobile and Pensacola from
the British.

1790
First U.S. textile mill
opens in Rhode Island.

1800
Spain returns
Louisiana to
France.

1775–1783
American
Revolutionary War

1803
United States purchases the
Louisiana Territory from France.

1770

1776
Declaration of
Independence

1780

1784
Spain regains
Florida.

1790

1800

1779
Spain declares war
against Britain.

1788
U.S. Constitution
is ratified.

1804
Haiti wins independence
from France.

1779–1782
Texas *rancheros* drive
cattle to Louisiana.

affairs. The British colonists thus had much experience with self-government.

Roots of Conflict. After the French and Indian War, however, the colonists began to feel the heavy hand of British rule. First, the British government barred colonists from moving west of the Appalachian Mountains. It did that to prevent further trouble between Native Americans and colonists seeking new lands to settle. Then Parliament passed new taxes on the colonists to help pay for the war that had recently ended.

Many colonists believed that since they were not represented in Parliament, it had no right to tax them. The slogan "No taxation without representation!" began to echo throughout the colonies. Although Parliament dropped the hated taxes, it soon passed others to replace them.

This pattern of new taxes followed by angry protests was repeated several times.

Each time, the colonists' outcry grew angrier. Finally, the British government clamped down on the colonies. Parliament passed tough laws that limited the powers of colonial governments. The colonists begged the king to repeal these laws. Instead, he sent troops to enforce them.

A War for Independence. In April 1775, British soldiers, known as **Redcoats**, and colonial **Minutemen**, or citizen soldiers, fired on each other at the Massachusetts towns of Lexington and Concord. Little did either side realize that the shots were heard around the world.

Word of the uprising reached colonists in Mexico and South America who were unhappy with Spanish rule. Their excitement grew when they learned that the British colonists had boldly issued a **Declaration of Independence** on July 4, 1776. The document rang with phrases about liberty and equality. It also spoke of

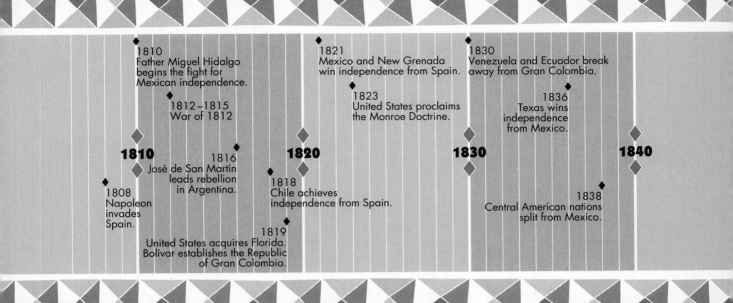

1810
Father Miguel Hidalgo begins the fight for Mexican independence.

1821
Mexico and New Grenada win independence from Spain.

1830
Venezuela and Ecuador break away from Gran Colombia.

1812–1815
War of 1812

1823
United States proclaims the Monroe Doctrine.

1836
Texas wins independence from Mexico.

1810

1816
José de San Martín leads rebellion in Argentina.

1820

1830

1840

1808
Napoleon invades Spain.

1818
Chile achieves independence from Spain.

1838
Central American nations split from Mexico.

1819
United States acquires Florida. Bolívar establishes the Republic of Gran Colombia.

governments "deriving [receiving] their just powers from the consent of the governed." Like British colonists, many Spanish colonists knew of these revolutionary ideas from reading the books of European thinkers. But before this, no people had dared act on such principles.

The Spanish colonists followed the course of the American Revolution with great interest. They were not surprised when the British colonists suffered a string of defeats against the most powerful nation in the world. What did surprise them was that after the colonists scored a stunning victory at Saratoga, New York, in 1778, first France, then Spain, joined the war on the side of the rebels.

In 1783, the former British colonists and the British signed the Treaty of Paris, ending the war. Under the terms of the treaty, Great Britain recognized the United States of America as an independent nation. It was bounded on the west by the Mississippi River, on the north by the Great Lakes and Canada, and on the south by Florida. Pablo Vizcardo (vees-KAHR-doh), a Spanish American priest, paid tribute to the colonists in these words:

The valour [bravery] with which the English colonies of America have fought for liberty, which they now gloriously enjoy, fills our own indolence [idleness] with shame.

A New Law of the Land. For a while, it looked as if the new American nation might break up into 13 separate, squabbling states. Then, in 1787, delegates gathered in Philadelphia to draw up a new plan of government. That plan became the basis of the **U.S. Constitution.** It created a **federal system** of government for the nation. Under the federal system, powers are divided and shared between the state governments and a central government that is supreme over them.

Like the Declaration of Independence, the Constitution served as an inspiration to freedom-loving people in Spanish America and throughout the world. Even so, the signers of the Constitution compromised on African slavery. They barred Congress from ending the importation of slaves before 1808. They allowed slavery itself to continue.

An Expanding Nation. Soon after 1787, the young nation began to stretch its boundaries. A treaty with Spain in 1795 helped U.S. settlers in the Northwest Territory. This was a huge area lying north of the Ohio River and east of the Mississippi. Under the treaty, settlers won the right to float their farm produce down the Mississippi to the Spanish port of New Orleans. From there they could ship it to the East Coast or overseas.

In 1800, however, France forced Spain to surrender New Orleans and Louisiana. U.S. farmers now grew alarmed that the French would close New Orleans to them. In 1803, in one of the most spectacular real estate deals in history, President Thomas Jefferson bought the entire Louisiana Territory from France for $15 million. This deal came to be known as the **Louisiana Purchase.**

The War of 1812. In 1812, the United States fought a "second war of independence" against Great Britain. The United States, still a young nation, found that Britain was taking advantage of it by violating U.S. rights at sea. The United States also wanted to stop Britain from arming Native Americans in the Northwest Territory. Some U.S. citizens even hoped that the United States could take

The U. S. Declaration of Independence inspired people around the world, including Latin America. A small Chinese porcelain shows the Declaration's signing.

Canada from Great Britain.

The war ended with neither nation being the winner. But the United States did receive some gains from the war. It showed that it could stand up to the world's most powerful nation. As a result, its own confidence and self respect grew. With renewed spirit, the United States continued to expand to the west.

The United States also turned its attention southward to Spanish Florida. Already, in 1810, some U.S. citizens had seized West Florida. Now the United States pressured Spain to give up East Florida. Spain agreed to sell Florida to the United States for $5 million.

The Monroe Doctrine. By 1823, Spain had lost more than Louisiana and Florida. As you will read in the next section, most of its American colonies had won independence as well. U.S. President James Monroe and his secretary of state, John Quincy Adams, worried that Spain or other European countries might try to regain control of the newly independent nations. They feared that such actions might, in time, threaten the United States.

With this possibility in mind, President Monroe issued a warning to European powers not to meddle in the affairs of the independent nations of the Americas. He also declared that Europeans must not try to establish more colonies in the Americas. In return, the United States promised to stay out of European affairs and not take part in any European war. These statements about U.S. policy in Latin America became known as the **Monroe Doctrine.**

A Thriving Economy. The U.S. economy grew during the period after the War of 1812. New Englanders built the first U.S. textile mills, and manufacturing began to take hold in the region. In other parts of the United States, farming was still the main occupation. Settlers in western states and territories mainly grew corn and wheat. In the southern states, cotton became the region's big cash crop. As cotton-growing spread, so did slavery.

This led to sharp conflict between the North and the South.

Taking Another Look

1. Why did the colonists resent British policy after 1763?

2. What new territory did the United States acquire after 1787?

3. **Critical Thinking** What do you think were the turning points in the colonists' struggle to become a strong independent nation?

◆◆ **In Latin America** ◆◆

The successful struggle for independence by Great Britain's colonists nation served as an inspiration to many people in the world, but none more so than those in the Spanish colonies of Latin America. If their neighbors to the north could free themselves of British control, they wondered, why could they not rid themselves of Spanish control?

The Spanish Colonies in 1763. Unlike Britain, Spain kept its colonies under tight control. The chain of command began with the king and the Council of the Indies in Spain. It continued in the Americas through the king's personal representatives, the viceroys. The viceroys selected local officials in the colonies. Often dishonest, these officials saw that every aspect of life was closely watched.

In the 1700s, a new line of Spanish kings introduced reforms. The changes aimed to promote better government and loosen restrictions. But many colonists felt the reforms did not go far enough.

Spain's American colonies occupied a larger area than all of Europe. Yet, relatively few Spaniards had moved to those colonies. In the early years of conquest, most of the Spaniards were single men. They took Native Americans and Africans for both workers and wives. As a result, there was much more mixing of ethnic groups than in the British colonies.

A social division that had begun soon after Spain founded its first American colonies became a serious problem by the 1800s. The *peninsulares*, Spanish colonists who were natives of Spain, continued to hold the highest positions in government, the military, and the Roman Catholic Church. The power of the *peninsulares* was increasingly resented by the *criollos*, Spaniards who had been born in the colonies. Although they were often wealthy landowners and business people, the *criollos* were not permitted to hold the highest positions in government.

The French Revolution.
Spanish *criollos* wanted changes in government, but they were not yet ready to rise up in rebellion. The people of France were the first people to act on the model of the American Revolution. In 1789, an angry mob stormed the Bastille (bas-TEEL), a prison in Paris. They were rebelling against years of corrupt rule by their monarchs and an unfair system of taxation, in which the poorest people paid the most.

Like the Americans, the French hoped to establish a government in which citizens had a direct voice. But soon, different groups began to struggle for control of the French Revolution. Violence spread. Thousands of people, including the French king, Louis XVI, were beheaded. In time, a strong leader, Napoleon Bonaparte (nuh-POH-lee-uhn BOH-nuh-pahrt) seized power. A man of vast ambition, Napoleon dreamed of ruling all of Europe. In 1808, he invaded Spain and put his brother Joseph on the Spanish throne.

Independence Movements.
Napoleon's takeover of Spain was the spark that set off rebellion against Spanish rule in Latin America. On September 16, 1810, in the tiny village of Dolores (doh-LOH-rehs) in Mexico, a *criollo* priest, Father Miguel Hidalgo (ee-DAHL-goh), sounded the cry of revolt against Spanish rule in Mexico. Hidalgo led an army of thousands of *mestizos* and Native Americans against Spanish rule.

Within a year, however, Spanish authorities captured and executed Hidalgo. But other leaders, like the *mestizo* priest and soldier José María Morelos (moh-REH-lohs), kept up the fight. Finally, in 1821 a *criollo* soldier, Agustín de Iturbide (ee-toor-BEE-deh), toppled Spanish rule in Mexico, as well as Central America, then a part of Mexico.

In South America, Simón Bolívar (boh-LEE-vahr), in the north, and José de San Martín (sahn mahr-TEEN), in the south, led the independence movements. In 1819, after years of fighting and many setbacks, Bolívar established the independent republic of Gran Colombia (grahn koh-LOHM-bee-ah). It was made up of the present-day countries of Venezuela, Ecuador, and Colombia.

Meanwhile, in Argentina, San Martín freed his native land. He then assembled his famous "Army of the Andes" to cross those towering mountains and liberate Chile. Next, he moved on the Spanish stronghold of Lima, in Peru. San Martín's and Bolívar's forces joined and, in 1824, finally drove the Spanish out. By 1826, all that remained of Spain's once huge empire in the Americas were the colonies of Cuba and Puerto Rico.

After Independence.
The overthrow of Spanish rule brought division rather than unity to Latin America. Bolívar and other leaders had dreamed of one big fed-

Voices of the Times

Those people, reared in freedom and accustomed to independence, are no longer inclined to suffer with resignation [patience].

— Bernardo de Gálvez, governor of Spanish Louisiana, 1785

eral republic like the United States, but that was not to be. Vast distances, towering mountains, burning deserts, and thick rain forests separated the regions of South America. Also, the various regions had had no practice in working together. In 1830, the year Bolívar died, worn-out and bitter at the age of 47, Gran Colombia split into three nations. A few years later, Central America left Mexico and divided into five republics. Eventually, 17 nations took shape from what had been Spain's American colonies.

The revolutions in Latin America did accomplish one thing that the American Revolution had failed to achieve. That was the **emancipation**, or freeing, of the enslaved Africans in several republics. Otherwise, the social structure stayed much the same. The *criollos* stepped into positions of power that were left empty by the *peninsulares*. *Mestizos* and Native Americans had also fought in the revolutionary armies, but they remained as oppressed as before.

The struggles for independence in Latin America lasted more than ten times as long as the American Revolution, from 1810 to 1898, when Cuba was freed. Those wars also caused much greater damage. Overseas trade stopped, and mines lay idle, as did many farms. Cities filled with hordes of poor people displaced by the fighting. *Criollo* leaders drew up constitutions modeled on the U.S. Constitution. But with no experience of self-government, they had trouble getting their plans to work. So, along with economic hard times, they faced a long period of political confusion.

Taking Another Look

1. List three differences between the Spanish and British colonies.

2. Why did Napoleon's takeover of Spain lead to wars for independence in Latin America?

3. **Critical Thinking** In what ways did the revolutions in Latin America succeed and in what ways did they fail?

The flags of many different countries decorate a diplomatic ball held at a Spanish California settlement. Wealthy californios lived a gracious life and owned huge estates in Spanish California.

Under the leadership of Bernardo de Gálvez, on horseback, Spanish troops blew up the ammunition storehouse and took the important British fortress at Pensacola in Florida.

SECTIONS

1 Supplying the Patriot Side

2 Joining the Fight

3 The First Cattle Drives

CHAPTER 6

The Spanish and the American Revolution

(1763–1783)

THINKING ABOUT THE CHAPTER

How did the Spanish help the United States gain independence from Britain?

In May 1775, 13 of Britain's North American colonies were about to declare their independence. Aware that they would have to fight for their freedom, colonial leaders asked George Washington of Virginia to organize an army. When his officers reviewed the colonies' military supplies, they discovered that they had only 10,000 pounds (4,500 kilograms) of gunpowder. That was enough for each soldier to shoot just nine times. One officer later recalled that Washington "was so struck [by the news] that he did not utter a word for half an hour." Not surprisingly, finding more weapons and ammunition became a major goal for the army.

In July 1776, a few days after the Declaration of Independence was signed, George Gibson of Virginia left Fort Pitt (now Pittsburgh), in Pennsylvania, on a secret mission. Disguised as traders, he and a crew of 16 traveled down the Ohio and Mississippi rivers to New Orleans. They carried a message for Luis de Unzaga (oon-SAH-gah), the governor of Spanish Louisiana. The **Patriots**, as those fighting for independence were called, appealed to the "known generosity of the Spaniards." The Patriots pleaded for guns, gunpowder, blankets, medicine, and other supplies.

Gibson and the others were still officially British subjects and trespassers in Spanish lands. Publicly, the governor had to order Gibson's arrest. But Unzaga—and Spain—wanted to help the Patriots in their fight against Spain's enemy, Britain. Secretly, Unzaga agreed to ship 9,000 pounds (4,050 kilograms) of gunpowder up the Mississippi River to Patriot forces at Fort Pitt and another 1,000 pounds (450 kilograms) by sea to Philadelphia. Those shipments marked the start of Spanish involvement in the American Revolution.

1 SUPPLYING THE PATRIOT SIDE

◆ How did the Spanish aid the Patriots early in the American Revolution?

Even as Unzaga was secretly shipping supplies to Washington's army, a new governor was on his way to Louisiana. The Patriots wondered whether that governor would continue to support them in their fight against the British. After all, Spain had not yet taken a stand in the conflict. Officially, it was **neutral**—that is, it supported neither side.

The Patriots' Western Lifeline. The new governor was a Spanish army officer named Bernardo de Gálvez (GAHL-ves). At the age of 29, he was a veteran of wars on three continents. Now he planned to use the knowledge and experience he had gained to protect Louisiana. Gálvez knew

SNAPSHOT OF THE TIMES		
1763	Spain gains control of Louisiana territory.
1776	British colonies in North America issue Declaration of Independence.
1777	Gálvez begins to aid the Patriot cause secretly.
1779	Spain declares war against Britain. Spanish organize first cattle drive from Texas to Louisiana.
1781	British army surrenders to Patriot army at Yorktown.
1783	Treaty of Paris signed.

that Britain was Spain's chief rival in North America. He also believed that aiding the Patriots would weaken British power.

Gálvez knew that no army can survive without a supply line. He knew that the Patriots lacked a dependable one. This was especially true for those who lived west of the Appalachian Mountains. Colonists there were cut off from the Atlantic coast for much of the year. In the spring, rain turned trails into mud, and in winter, they were blocked by ice and snow.

The only highways west of the Appalachians were rivers—particularly the Mississippi. After the French and Indian War (1754–1763), Spain had won control of the Mississippi when France had given Spain the Louisiana Territory in return for help in fighting the British. Although Britain had won all of France's other territories on the continent in the war, it recognized Spain's rights to Louisiana.

To those who worked out the peace treaty that ended the French and Indian War, the Mississippi River was a natural boundary between English and Spanish lands. In reality, the river did not divide the lands west of the Appalachians; it united them. The river linked widely scattered Spanish, French, British, and Native American settlements.

The people who lived along the Mississippi and its many branches depended on the river for trade and transportation. New Orleans was therefore the most important city in the region. It linked places as far east as Fort Pitt to the Gulf of Mexico and the Atlantic Ocean.

Gálvez and Louisiana. As a soldier, Gálvez understood the importance of New Orleans and the Mississippi. But Gálvez was more than a military officer.

Bernardo de Gálvez was born in 1746 into a family known for its service to Spain. His father was captain-general of Guatemala and later served as viceroy of New Spain. His uncle was one of the nation's most powerful officials. Some say that only King Carlos III had more power than that uncle, José de Gálvez.

At the age of 16, Bernardo was already making a name for himself as a lieutenant in the army. At 19, he accompanied his uncle on a tour of New Spain. In the years that followed, he would fight for Spain in Europe, on Mexico's northern frontier, and in North Africa.

Gálvez's background gave him a deeper understanding of Spanish goals in the Americas than most officials had. The young governor was also more willing than most to take risks to reach those goals. He was even willing to bend the law, if that would strengthen Louisiana and weaken Britain.

Gálvez feared that Louisiana would not remain a Spanish colony unless it attracted more settlers. However, Spain's offical policy discouraged immigration. But Gálvez tried to attract settlers from the British colonies by offering land and opportunities for trade. Although such settlers had to become Spanish citizens, Gálvez did not pressure them to convert to Roman Catholicism, Spain's official religion.

Gálvez and the Patriots. Gálvez quickly responded to the Patriots' pleas for aid. Soon after arriving in Louisiana, in January 1777, he met with Oliver Pollock, a business owner who lived in New Orleans and openly supported the Patriots. Pollock hoped to persuade Gálvez to support the Patriot cause.

Gálvez required little persuasion. By July, he had slipped 2,000 barrels of gunpowder, lead, and clothing past British forts on the Mississippi to the Patriots. He also encouraged King Carlos III of Spain to lend the Patriots large sums of money secretly.

Gálvez helped the Patriots in other ways as well. Under the treaty that ended the French and Indian War, he could not keep the British from using the Mississippi River. He could, however, limit their use of the port of New Orleans. He could also protect Patriot ships by pretending to seize them and then releasing them when the British ships had gone.

A New American Expedition. Throughout 1777 and 1778, Governor Patrick Henry of Virginia sent letters to Gálvez asking for more help. In those letters, he suggested that Spain use the war to regain East and West Florida. The

Bustling New Orleans, at the mouth of the Mississippi River, became the lifeline for U. S. Patriots living west of the Appalachians. How did Bernardo de Gálvez use North American geography to help the Patriots?

Spanish had lost both to Britain after the French and Indian War.

Gálvez did not need encouragement. He was eager for revenge. He saw his chance to win back lost lands for Spain. An open attack on British forts, however, would mean an end to Spanish neutrality. So Gálvez waited for the right time to act. A military expedition by the Patriots brought the chance for which Gálvez was looking.

In March 1778, a Patriot captain, James Willing, set out for New Orleans from Fort Pitt with 30 volunteers. His mission was to carry a packet of secret messages to New Orleans. Along the way, Willing and his men raided and burned British holdings in West Florida. They captured dozens of enslaved Africans and carted off as many valuables as they could carry.

Willing's raids angered many Anglo Americans, or people of British descent, in West Florida. They became supporters of the British. Willing's raids also led the British to strengthen their posts in West

Florida. Those posts threatened not only the Patriots but also Spanish Louisiana.

Gálvez soon learned how serious that threat really was. The British knew that the Spanish were aiding the Patriots. Now, Spanish spies brought him word that the British were planning to invade Louisiana.

Taking Another Look

1. How did the Mississippi River unite Spanish and British colonists?

2. Why was Gálvez's help so critical to the success of the Patriots?

3. **Critical Thinking** How did Gálvez help Spain by helping the Patriots?

2 JOINING THE FIGHT

What part did the Spanish play in fighting the British during the American Revolution?

In early summer of 1779, Spain formally declared war against Britain. Gálvez, however, had prepared for war long before the news reached him in late August.

The Fight for the Mississippi.

On August 27, 1779, Gálvez set out for British Fort Bute, at Manchac, on the Mississippi River. With him were 170 veterans, 330 recruits newly arrived from Mexico and the Canary Islands, 80 African American volunteers, and 7 Anglo Americans, including Oliver Pollock. The tiny army trudged through the thick forests of southern Louisiana. Their supplies were hauled upriver on barges.

All along the 90 miles (144 kilometers) to Manchac, Gálvez stopped at settlements to sign on more volunteers. He also visited Native Americans who were allies of Spain. They, too, supplied soldiers for the mission. By the time Gálvez reached Fort Bute in early September, his army had more than doubled.

The Spanish easily captured Fort Bute. They then marched to the larger and better-armed British fort at Baton Rouge (bat-'n RYOOZH). This time, Gálvez sent a few soldiers ahead to cut communications between Baton Rouge and the next fort on Gálvez's list, the one at Natchez (NACH-ihz). In the meantime, the remaining troops set up camp near Baton Rouge.

Gálvez knew that conquering the fort at Baton Rouge would not be as easy as capturing Fort Bute. The British had more troops at Baton Rouge. Their fort also had thick walls and was surrounded by a ditch 18 feet (5.4 meters) wide and 9 feet (2.7 meters) deep.

As Gálvez studied the area, he noticed a small grove of trees near the fort. It looked like a place from which the British might

The Spanish colonies of the Americas helped the United States win independence from Britain. What was the northernmost battle the Spanish fought?

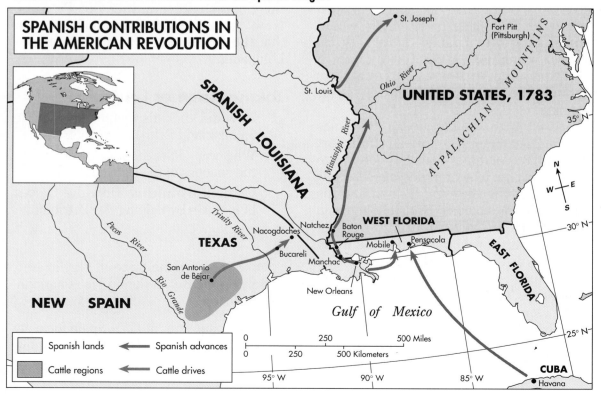

SPANISH CONTRIBUTIONS IN THE AMERICAN REVOLUTION

UNITED STATES, 1783

St. Joseph
Fort Pitt (Pittsburgh)
St. Louis
Ohio River
Mississippi River
APPALACHIAN MOUNTAINS
35° N

SPANISH LOUISIANA

Pecos River
Trinity River
Nacogdoches
Natchez
Baton Rouge
WEST FLORIDA
Mobile
Pensacola
EAST FLORIDA
30° N

TEXAS
Bucareli
Manchac

San Antonio de Béjar

Rio Grande

New Orleans

Gulf of Mexico

NEW SPAIN

25° N

CUBA
Havana

| | Spanish lands | ← Spanish advances |
| | Cattle regions | ← Cattle drives |

0   250   500 Miles
0   250   500 Kilometers

95° W   90° W   85° W

expect an attack to come. So on the night of September 20, he sent a small group of soldiers there to distract the British. They noisily chopped down trees, built barricades, and fired on the fort from time to time. While they worked, the rest of Gálvez's army quietly set up cannon on the other side of the fort.

The British were convinced that the Spanish planned to charge from the grove. They bombarded it all night long. The next morning, they discovered their mistake, but by then, it was too late. The Spanish soldiers and cannon were dug in. They could now fire on the fort whenever they wished.

That afternoon, the British surrendered the fort at Baton Rouge. That same day, they also surrendered their fort at Natchez to a small band of Gálvez's soldiers. In less than a month, Gálvez had removed all threat of a British invasion of Louisiana from West Florida.

Two more battles gave the Spanish total control of the Mississippi Valley. In 1780, they turned back a British attack at St. Louis. Then, in 1781, the Spanish and their Native American allies captured the British settlement of St. Joseph, far to the north, on the shore of Lake Michigan.

Moving on Mobile. After his victory at Baton Rouge, Gálvez prepared to move against Mobile (moh-BEEL) and Pensacola (pen-sah-KOH-luh), the two key British forts on the Gulf of Mexico. In January 1780, Gálvez sailed from New Orleans with a fleet of 12 ships. On board the ships was an army of 754 soldiers. It was made up of regular Spanish troops, Native American allies, African Americans, Anglo Americans, and volunteers from Spain's colonies in the Caribbean.

The Spanish ships entered Mobile Bay on February 10. To control the entrance to the bay, Gálvez left some troops and cannon on Mobile Point. The rest of the army sailed into the bay, where they were later joined by more troops from Cuba.

While Spanish sailors diverted the British by opening fire, Gálvez's troops landed and set up camp just outside the fort. On March 9, they began a full-scale attack. Five days later, they had taken the fort. As a reward for the capture of Mobile, the king promoted Gálvez to field marshal and put him in charge of all Spanish operations against the British in North America.

Conquering Pensacola. Gálvez had hoped to follow up his success at Mobile by quickly attacking Pensacola, the capital of West Florida. Spanish officials in Cuba, however, failed to send Gálvez more soldiers. Gálvez knew that the British in Pensacola had as many soldiers and Native American allies as he did. They also had the advantage of a strong position to defend. In fact, the British were so sure of themselves that they were preparing to retake Mobile.

Gálvez was furious. He went to Cuba to cut through the red tape that threatened his plans. Using his family connections, he persuaded Spanish officials to help him. Gálvez returned to the Gulf of Mexico with 64 warships and 4,000 troops.

Gálvez immediately sent 500 soldiers to Mobile to keep the city safe from British attack. The rest of his troops sailed into Pensacola Bay on March 8, 1781. A few weeks later, they were joined by still more troops from Cuba.

By late March, Gálvez was ready to attack Pensacola. Week after week, his men bombarded the British positions. Then on May 8, the Spanish hit the building where the British stored their ammunition. The explosion killed 85 men and knocked a huge hole through the wall that surrounded the fort. Two days later, the Spanish took Pensacola.

A Lingering War. In the fall of 1781, the British surrendered to George Washington's Patriot army at Yorktown, Virginia. The Spanish, however, continued their fight against the British. By the spring of 1782, Gálvez had captured the British naval base at New Providence, in the Bahamas. Then, as he prepared for an even larger campaign against the Caribbean island of Jamaica, the diplomats in Paris reached a peace agreement.

By 1783, the war was over. Gálvez's actions had aided both Spain and the Patriots. He had helped Washington's army by removing the threat of a British attack from the Gulf Coast. He had also kept a supply line open to Patriot troops west of the Appalachians. At the same time, Gálvez had not only protected Spanish Louisiana but also regained control of both East and West Florida.

Taking Another Look

1. How did Gálvez and his troops secure the Mississippi Valley?

2. Why were Mobile and Pensacola major objectives for the Spanish?

3. **Critical Thinking** How might the outcome of the American Revolution been different if the Spanish had backed the British instead of the Patriots?

3 THE FIRST CATTLE DRIVES

◆ How did cattle from Texas help win the
◆ American Revolution?

Every military leader knows that an army "travels on its stomach." That means

After more than 200 years, Mission Espíritu Santo is still a noble sight. The mission supplied most of the Texas longhorn cattle for the dangerous cattle drive to Louisiana to feed Gálvez's army.

that soldiers must have supplies of food to be able to fight. Bernardo de Gálvez certainly knew this. In the 1700s, however, Louisiana did not produce enough food to meet the needs of a large army. Gálvez, though, had a good idea of where he could find enough food for his troops.

As a young captain in the Spanish army, Gálvez had helped guard Mexico's northern borderlands. He had traveled as far north as the Pecos River. There he first learned of the great herds of cattle that roamed near the Spanish missions at San Antonio de Béjar (sahn ahn-TOH-nee-o deh BEH-hahr) in the province of Texas. Now Gálvez wanted to use those herds to feed his army. Texas missionaries and *rancheros* (rahn-CHEH-rohs), or owners of ranches, were more than willing to sell their cattle to Gálvez. There was, after all, little market for their herds in sparsely settled Texas.

A Dangerous Journey. It took a while for things to get done in Spain's American empire. However, eventually, permission was granted by the governor. Then the *rancheros* were able to start their drives. They rounded up cattle and prepared to set out on the cattle trail. But how were they to get this cattle to Louisiana? The Texans were in a constant state of war with some Native Americans of Texas. The Comanche, in particular, were determined to force the Spanish from the area.

The *rancheros* planned to drive their animals from the missions to Nacogdoches (see map, page 78), then push on to Louisiana. The job of finding a safe route to Nacogdoches fell to Joseph Félix Menchaca (men-CHAH-kah). As a lieutenant in the Spanish army, he had the task of protecting the *vaqueros* (vah-KEH-rohs), or cowhands, and their herds. Menchaca was also a *ranchero*. He stood to profit if he could find a way to get the cattle to Louisiana.

The Comanche controlled the most direct path to Nacogdoches. So Menchaca and his group took a less direct route southeast from San Antonio de Bexar, then across the Trinity River near Bucareli. Only then did they dare use the road to Nacogdoches.

Menchaca and his vaqueros made a safe first trip, leaving a large herd with Gálvez. However, others were not so lucky. Despite the many precuations they took, many of the cattle drives ended in tragedy. There were too few Spanish troops to provide enough protection from the Comanche.

Still, between 1779 and 1782, Texans delivered more than 9,000 head of cattle to Gálvez's army in Louisiana. Thanks to them, the Spanish forces never lacked for food as they attacked the British.

Taking Another Look

1. Why did Bernardo de Gálvez take an interest in northern Texas?

2. Why were cattle drives dangerous?

3. **Critical Thinking** How important was the role of Texas in helping the colonists defeat the British in the American Revolution?

LOOKING AHEAD

The Treaty of Paris in 1783 formally ended the American Revolution and Spain's war with Britain. Spain's empire in the Americas seemed secure for the moment. In just a few years, however, the United States, Spain's former ally, would move against Spanish lands in North America. In addition, the ideas of liberty that sparked the American Revolution would help to set off rebellions throughout Spain's empire in the Americas.

The city of New Orleans usually brings to mind French styles and flavors. Although the French founded New Orleans and controlled it for over 40 years, the city has a strong Spanish feeling as well.

New Orleans was the center of Spanish government in Louisiana from 1762 to 1800. When fire destroyed the city in the late 1700s, the Spanish colonists rebuilt using Spanish styles of architecture. Today, the lacy iron grillwork that decorates many balconies is a trademark of the city. In addition, Spanish arcades, fountains, and shaded patios grace the streets of New Orleans' French Quarter.

To protect the city against future fires, the Spanish established building codes. All roofs had to be made of slate or tile. Walls were to be of brick covered with stucco.

One of New Orleans most famous landmarks is Jackson Square. Although named for U.S. President Andrew Jackson, the square is laid out in the Spanish style. Facing the square is the St. Louis Cathedral. Nearby stands the Cabildo, or government house, from which Spain ruled the territory of Louisiana. When the United States purchased Louisiana from the French in 1803, the official transfer of territory took place in the Cabildo. Today, the Cabildo serves as a museum and monument to the history of this great city.

CLOSE UP: Chapter 6

The Who, What, Where of History

1. **What** river was the Patriots' lifeline in the West?
2. **Who** was Bernardo de Gálvez?
3. **What** did Gálvez do to aid the Patriot cause in the West?
4. **Who** were the *rancheros*?
5. **Where** did the cattle drives begin?

Making the Connection

1. What was the connection between the Mississippi River and settlements west of the Appalachian Mountains?
2. What was the connection between Spain and Great Britain's conflict and the outcome of the American Revolution?

Time Check

1. When did the government of Spanish Louisiana begin its involvement in the American Revolution?
2. How many years passed from Spain's declaration of war against Britain to Gálvez's capture of Pensacola?
3. When did the Spanish begin cattle drives from Texas to Louisiana?

What Would You Have Done?

1. Imagine that you are Bernardo de Gálvez demanding help from Spanish officials for your attack on Pensacola. What arguments would you use to persuade the officials to give you soldiers and weapons?
2. If you had been a Spanish citizen of Louisiana, would you have chosen to help the Patriots or to remain neutral? Explain your decision.

Thinking and Writing About History

1. Write a paragraph explaining the importance of the Mississippi River and the city of New Orleans to the success of the Patriot cause.

2. Imagine you are Bernardo de Gálvez. Write a report to Spanish officials explaining why helping the Patriot cause would also help the Spanish.

Building Skills: Recognizing Relevant Information

Yesterday, a blizzard covered your city. You want to know how many inches of snow fell in yesterday's storm. An article in the newspaper tells you the following:

[1] The blizzard yesterday was one of the worst to hit our community. [2] More than 18 inches of snow fell in some areas. [3] Others received up to a foot of snow. [4] High winds caused drifts of 6 and 7 feet. [5] Many residents were trapped in their homes.

Which of the sentences in the article are *not* necessary to give you the information you want?

The sentences you chose are examples of *irrelevant* information. They do not give you the *relevant,* or significant, information you want—the amount of snow that fell in yesterday's storm.

Recognizing relevant information will help you focus your reading and think more clearly about a topic.

Each of the questions below is followed by three facts. On a separate sheet of paper, write an *R* next to the letter of a fact relevant to the topic. Write an *I* if the fact is irrelevant.

1. Why was the Mississippi River important to Patriot success in the West?
   a. Louisiana became a Spanish colony after the French and Indian War.
   b. Bernardo de Gálvez aided the Patriots with money and supplies.
   c. The Mississippi linked western settlements and was crucial as a supply line.

2. How did Gálvez secure Louisiana from British invasion?
   a. Spain was neutral when the British colonies declared independence.
   b. Gálvez captured British forts along the Mississippi River.
   c. Gálvez recaptured East and West Florida from the British.

3. Why were Texas *rancheros* willing to sell their cattle to Gálvez's army?
   a. There was no large market for cattle in sparsely settled Texas.
   b. The governor refused to allow cattle drives.
   c. Cattle drives involved long and dangerous journeys.

Express Yourself!

Reread the biography of Bernardo de Gálvez on page 76. Use a dictionary to define any words you do not know. Then, pretend that you will be interviewing Governor Gálvez. Choose a partner and together write four or five questions you would like to ask Gálvez about his life and career.

This painting celebrates Mexico's independence from Spain. In it, Father Miguel Hidalgo, who started the rebellion, places a crown of freedom on a woman representing Mexico.

CHAPTER 7

SECTIONS

1 Challenges in the North

2 Independence for Mexico

3 Changes in Spanish America

The Road to Latin American Independence

(1783–1830)

THINKING ABOUT THE CHAPTER

How did revolutions in the late 1700s and early 1800s affect Spanish colonies in the Americas?

In 1792, on the 300th anniversary of Columbus's first voyage to the Americas, a *criollo* priest issued a call for revolution. In his *Letter to Spanish Americans*, Juan Bautista Vizcardo y Guzmán (vees-CAHR-doh ee goos-MAN) of Peru argued that "the preservation of natural rights, above all the preservation of personal freedom and property," is "the bedrock [foundation] of any human community." He urged those living in Spanish-controlled colonies to "reclaim our God-given rights."

The letter caused a sensation. Revolutionaries like Francisco de Miranda (mee-RAHN-dah) of Venezuela, who was living in Philadelphia at the time, made copies. Miranda and others then smuggled those copies into Spanish colonies, from Argentina to Louisiana. Not everyone admired the letter. Spanish officials tried to track down and destroy every copy. But they could not stop the spread of the letter or of the ideas that inspired it.

By 1792, ideas much like those set down in the letter had already led to three revolutions. In 1783, the new United States had won its freedom from Britain. Six years later, a revolution had begun in France. In 1791, the French Revolution had inspired enslaved Africans in the French colony of Haiti to begin their own struggle for freedom. In the early 1800s, those three revolutions and the ideas that sparked them would change Spanish America in ways that no one could have guessed.

1 CHALLENGES IN THE NORTH
◆ How did the Spanish lose control of
◆ Louisiana and Florida?

On July 14, 1784, the king of Spain held a grand ball to celebrate the return of East and West Florida to Spain after the American Revolution (see page 79). But even as he rejoiced, his officials in North America were uneasy. In their view, Louisiana and other Spanish provinces in North America were in danger of being overrun by what they saw as the "active, industrious, aggressive" citizens of the new United States.

Guarding Spanish Claims. Those officials had good reason to worry. In 1784, Spain was already quarreling with the United States over Florida's northern border. The Americans insisted it lay along the 31st parallel (see map, page 50). Spain thought it should be over 100 miles (160 kilometers) to the north.

The king responded to the threat by promoting men like Bernardo de Gálvez (see Chapter 6) to key positions along the border with the United States. They were professional soldiers who believed that new policies were needed to protect Spanish provinces and help them grow rich.

Gálvez might well have shaped such policies. But just three years after the American Revolution ended, he died of a fever. Although the men who took his place tried to carry out his ideas, they lacked his energy and power.

Reclaiming Florida. Vicente Manuel de Zéspedes (SES-peh-des) became governor of East Florida in 1784. He shared Gálvez's belief that Spain's policies had to change if the nation was to hold on to its colonies. Zéspedes was convinced that the best way to protect Florida was by building "a living wall of industrious [active] citizens."

When he arrived in Florida's largest settlement, St. Augustine, in June 1784, the colony was home to only about 1,500 Europeans. Many of those people were soldiers. Very few Spanish settlers still lived in the province. Most had left when the British had taken Florida in 1763.

Zéspedes urged those settlers to return. He recruited newcomers from Spain. He also encouraged settlers to come to Florida from other parts of Europe.

In time, dozens of different languages, including English, were spoken on the streets of St. Augustine. Some English-speakers were British planters and traders who had decided to remain in the province after it was returned to Spain. Others were from the new United States. Many of them had supported Britain during the American Revolution. Others were African Americans who had escaped from slavery in the United States.

Building the Economy. Policies made in Spain sometimes got in the way of Zéspedes's "wall of industrious citizens."

Those policies crippled efforts to build Florida's economy. For example, in the 1700s and early 1800s, tar, pitch (waterproofing material), and turpentine were used to keep wooden ships watertight. Known as **naval stores**, the three forest products were very valuable.

The Spanish navy spent huge sums of money each year buying naval stores from other countries. A Florida planter named Francis Philip Fatio tried to get permission to build a naval stores business. First, though, in addition to the governor's support, he had to win the backing of dozens of royal officials.

In time, Fatio won permission, but only after the king had sent agents to inspect his property and study his plans. Fatio and other business people were annoyed by such long delays. They were also bothered by trade regulations. Spanish law, for example, required products made in the colonies to be sold only in Spain. Colonial business owners wanted to be free to sell their products to the highest bidder—even if that bidder was not Spanish.

In order to help Florida prosper, the governor did not enforce Spanish trade laws strictly. In 1806, for example, of the 42 ships that docked in St. Augustine only 5 flew the flag of Spain. The rest were from ports in the United States.

A Weakening Spanish Hold in Florida. In spite of Zéspedes's efforts, Spain's control of Florida grew weaker. Events in Europe were to blame.

As you have read, a revolution broke out in France. Within a few years, wars growing out of that revolution had spread across Europe. Spain found itself dragged into those wars. At times, its own independence was threatened. As a result, Spain could spare little attention to events along the border with the United States. In 1795, Spain decided to stop trying. It signed a treaty with the United States that made the 31st parallel Florida's northern border.

Changes in Louisiana. Esteban Miró (mee-ROH), the governor of Louisiana, faced problems much like those of Zéspedes in Florida. Settlers from

The governor's house at St. Augustine, as it looked about the time of the American Revolution. Despite the efforts of Spanish governors, Spain's control of Florida grew weaker as the United States grew stronger.

the United States were moving west toward Louisiana. In 1783, there were only 12,000 Anglo Americans in all of Kentucky. Seven years later, the territory had 73,000 people. Other U.S. territories bordering Louisiana grew almost as quickly.

In 1784, Spain responded to the flood of newcomers by closing the lower part of the Mississippi River, and the port of New Orleans to all but Spanish traders. U.S. farmers in Kentucky and Tennessee were outraged. The only way they could get their flour, bacon, and other goods to market was by floating them downriver to the Gulf of Mexico.

The farmers quickly discovered that the governor of Louisiana was no more eager to enforce the new laws made in Spain than they were to obey them. His colony needed food grown by U.S. farmers. However, Miró's willingness to overlook the law did not satisfy U.S. farmers. They regarded the use of the river as a right, not as a favor that could be withdrawn. They continued to press for free use of the river.

New Immigration Policies. Miró had an idea for dealing with pressure from Anglo American settlers. At his urging, in 1788, Spain began to offer Anglo Americans free land in the Mississippi Valley. The governor hoped that the Anglos who came as settlers would become good Spanish citizens. He felt if there were enough such settlers, neither the United States nor Britain would ever try to seize Louisiana.

The new policy helped boost Louisiana's population from 20,000 in 1782 to 45,000 in 1792. It also helped West Florida grow. Indeed, West Florida's Natchez district now had so many Anglos that when the king named a new governor in 1789, he was careful to choose someone who spoke English well.

Spain's Retreat. In the end, the future of Louisiana and the two Floridas was not decided by officials in North America but by events in Europe. War there drained Spain's resources. The treaty Spain signed with the United States in 1795 marked the start of a retreat from North America. It set the 31st parallel as Florida's northern border. It also allowed U.S. citizens free use of the Mississippi.

Five years later, Spain secretly returned all of Louisiana to France. In 1803, French leaders sold the territory to the United States. This Louisiana Purchase did not satisfy the desire of U.S. citizens for more land. They claimed more and more Spanish territory. By 1810, they were insisting that the Louisiana Purchase included a large chunk of West Florida as well. U.S. troops and settlers soon moved into West Florida.

As the pressure from the United States increased, the Spanish decided to give up East and West Florida rather than try to defend them. In 1819, Spain and the United States signed the Adams-Onís (AD-uhmz oh-NEES) Treaty. Under it, the United States got all Spanish lands east of the Mississippi. In return, the United States gave up its claim that Texas was included in the Louisiana Purchase.

Taking Another Look

1. How did Spanish officials try to strengthen Spain's control over Louisiana and the two Floridas?

2. How did events in Europe affect Spanish control of the three provinces?

3. **Critical Thinking** Do you think Spain would have been able to keep Florida and Louisiana if Spanish governors had strictly enforced Spanish law? Why or why not?

2 INDEPENDENCE FOR MEXICO

◆ How did Mexico's struggle for independence affect its northernmost provinces?

Before dawn on September 16, 1810, church bells rang out in the small Mexican town of Dolores. The startled villagers rushed to the church. The local priest, Father Miguel Hidalgo y Castilla, greeted them with a call to revolution. They must, he shouted, "recover from the hated Spaniards lands stolen 300 years ago." Hidalgo's cry touched off a struggle for freedom that did not end until 1821.

Revolution in Mexico. Hidalgo belonged to a group of *criollos* who had been plotting a revolution for many months. Members of the group saw themselves not as *criollos* but as Spanish Americans, who wanted to govern their own country. They were tired of being ruled by *peninsulares*—people born in Spain.

Although Hidalgo was captured and executed by a firing squad in less than a year, the independence movement continued. Among those who kept it alive was a 19-year-old *criolla* named Leona Vicario (vee-KAH-ree-oh).

◆ **Leona Vicario** kept widely scattered groups of Mexican rebels in touch with one another, by writing coded letters to women in the groups. She also ran a secret printing press that published articles supporting the idea of rebellion.

In time, Spanish officials arrested Vicario and put her in prison. After her release, she rejoined the fight for Mexico's freedom. She built a secret cannon factory in Tlalpujahua (tlahl-poo-HAH-wah). There, workers made the weapons that would help win the revolution.

The Fight for Texas. After the death of Father Hidalgo, a number of his supporters fled from Mexico. Among them was a wealthy *criollo* named Bernardo Gutiérrez de Lara (goo-tee-ER-res deh LAH-rah) who settled in New Orleans. There, he joined forces with Augustus Magee, a former officer in the U.S. Army. The two men decided to work together to free Texas from Spanish rule. Neither bothered to ask Texans whether they wanted to be free.

By 1812, the two men had signed up 200 volunteers for their army. Among the recruits were Native Americans, Texas *vaqueros*, French traders, Anglo American adventurers, and even a few outlaws. Many were attracted by promises of 40 dollars a month and free land.

The army invaded Texas in 1812 and quickly captured Nacogdoches, La Bahía (lah bah-EE-ah), and San Antonio. But their success rapidly came undone. The rebels began to quarrel over plans for the future of Texas. Rebels from the United States wanted Texas to become part of that nation. Gutiérrez and his Texas supporters wanted the province to be part of an independent Mexico. The feuding rebels could not push back Spanish troops when they arrived to recapture San Antonio. The Spanish drove the rebels back to Louisiana.

Mexico finally won its independence from Spain on February 24, 1821. New Spain's northern provinces, including Texas, became part of Mexico. Now, it was up to the government of the young republic to deal with the pressure of settlers from the United States.

Reaction in the West. The new Republic of Mexico also included the provinces of California and New Mexico. Although people in both provinces had followed news of Mexico's revolution, few had taken part in it. Most had no reason to drive out the Spanish. Spanish soldiers protected their settlements from attack by foreigners and Native Americans.

An incident in 1818 had reminded *californios* how open to such attack their settlements were. In that year, Hipólito Bouchard (boo-CHARD), a privateer, or commander of a privately owned warship, arrived in California. Bouchard sailed into Monterey Bay and called on the townspeople to join the revolution against Spain. When the townspeople showed no interest in driving out the Spaniards, Bouchard and his crew set the town on fire. Then they sailed south to Santa Barbara and San Juan Capistrano (kah-pees-TRAH-noh), where Spanish soldiers and *californios* turned back the invaders and forced them to return to South America.

Nuevomexicanos were equally concerned about their security. Until the late 1700s, the Apache had often raided Spanish settlements in New Mexico. Slowly, the Spanish army had reduced that threat. As a result, by the early 1800s, New Mexico was beginning to grow and expand. *Nuevomexicanos* had no interest in risking that growth by attacking Spanish soldiers.

Once the Mexican revolution was over, however, both California and New Mexico organized huge celebrations, much like those held when a new king was crowned. Now, however, cries of *"¡Viva la independencia!"*—"Long live independence!"—replaced shouts of *"¡Viva el rey!"*—"Long live the king!"

Taking Another Look

1. What led Mexicans to launch a fight for independence in 1810?

1783	United States wins independence from Britain.
1784	Spain regains control of East and West Florida.
1789	French Revolution begins.
1800	Spain secretly returns Louisiana to France.
1803	France sells Louisiana to the United States.
1810–1821	Mexican Revolution
1819	Republic of Gran Colombia established.

2. Why did the fight to free Texas from Spanish control fail?

3. **Critical Thinking** Why did most *californios* and *nuevomexicanos* support the Spanish soldiers before the Mexican revolution? Why do you think they supported the new Mexican government after the revolution?

3 CHANGES IN SPANISH AMERICA

◆ How did revolutions affect Spain's
◆ colonies in South America and the Caribbean?

Revolutions in Europe and the Americas brought changes not only to Mexico but to all of Spanish America. Change came slowly, however. The struggle for independence in South America was a long and bloody one.

Across the Andes. In June 1819, an army of more than 2,000 soldiers struggled to cross the mighty Andes Mountains of South America. They had set out from

bly from the bitter mountain cold. One soldier later wrote:

> Nobody could get any warmth, for there was not as much as a hut [for shelter].... The icy wind cost many a life; men fell marching, and many died within a few minutes.

Despite the hardships, the rebel army made it across. On August 7, 1819, the little army faced 3,000 veteran Spanish troops at Boyacá (boh-yah-KAH), near Bogotá. In the fierce battle that followed, the Spanish lost over 1,000 soldiers. The ragged army had won another important battle in the long struggle for independence in South America.

Independence for South America. Simón Bolívar of Venezuela had planned the march over the Andes and led the troops to victory at Boyacá. Bolívar was a wealthy *criollo*. Inspired by the ideals of the French Revolution, he had vowed to free South America from Spanish rule.

As had been the case in Mexico, revolts had broken out all across South America in 1810. Bolívar had joined the one in Venezuela. For years, the struggle seesawed back and forth. The rebels made some gains, only to be defeated by the Spanish. In time, though, bold moves such as Bolívar's march over the Andes helped the rebels gain the upper hand.

Soon after the victory at Boyacá, Bolívar established the Republic of Gran Colombia. This included present-day Venezuela and Colombia. He then joined forces with another revolutionary leader, José de San Martín, whose armies had freed Argentina and Chile. The combined forces now freed Ecuador and Peru. By

INDEPENDENCE FOR LATIN AMERICA

UNITED STATES

ATLANTIC OCEAN

CUBA 1898
HAITI (French) 1804
DOMINICAN REPUBLIC (Santo Domingo) (1821 from Spain, 1844 from Haiti)
Gulf of Mexico
MEXICO 1821
Puerto Rico (Spanish to 1898, then U.S.)
BELIZE 1981 (British Honduras)
Caribbean Sea
GUYANA (British) 1966
SURINAME (Dutch) 1975
GUATEMALA 1821
HONDURAS 1821
EL SALVADOR 1821
NICARAGUA 1821
COSTA RICA 1821
PANAMA (from Colombia 1903)
ECUADOR 1822
VENEZUELA 1821
French Guiana
COLOMBIA 1819 (New Granada)
BRAZIL (Portuguese) 1822
PERU 1824
BOLIVIA 1825
PACIFIC OCEAN
N
W E
S
PARAGUAY 1811
0   750   1500 Miles
0   750   1500 Kilometers
CHILE 1818
ARGENTINA 1816 (Rio de la Plata)
URUGUAY (1825 from Spain, 1828 from Brazil)

Former Spanish colonies
1821 Date of independence
Gran Colombia (1819–1830)
United Provinces of Central America (1823–1838)

In the 15 years between 1810 and 1825, Spain and Portugal lost their huge empire in the Americas. By 1825 only Cuba and Puerto Rico remained colonies.

the hot, flat plains of Venezuela. They were marching toward the city of Bogotá (boh-goh-TAH), the capital of the Spanish territory of New Granada. There they hoped to surprise the Spanish army, defeat it, and win independence for New Granada.

Higher and higher into the snowcapped mountains the army marched. Wearing thin summer uniforms, they suffered terri-

1825, the revolutionaries had won. South America was free of Spanish rule.

The Faithful Islands. The men and women who won independence for the nations of Spanish South America were inspired by the ideals of the French Revolution. Other Latin Americans, especially wealthy *criollos*, were horrified by the killing and destruction during that revolution. On the islands of Puerto Rico and Cuba, the *criollos* were even more frightened by a slave revolt that had taken place closer to home. This one had taken place in Haiti and was led by former slave Toussaint L'Ouverture. The French colony of Haiti shared the island of Hispaniola with Spanish Santo Domingo. The *criollos* feared that revolutions in Spanish America would encourage their own slaves to rebel.

Until Haitians began their fight for freedom in 1791, Haiti was the world's largest producer of sugar. As the revolt of enslaved Africans spread over the island many planters were killed. Others fled the country.

Cubans and Puerto Ricans saw a business opportunity in the sudden collapse of Haiti's sugar industry. In Cuba, wealthy planters persuaded the Spanish government to end restrictions on their sale of sugar to other nations. New laws also opened the island to more slaves. In 1790, Cuba had produced only 14,000 tons (12,701 metric tons) of sugar. By 1805, the island was turning out 34,000 tons (30,845 metric tons) a year.

As production grew, so did the demand for slave labor. In 1791, Cuba had only 40,000 enslaved Africans, about 10 percent of the number in Haiti. Over the next few decades, planters would bring over 600,000 enslaved Africans to Cuba to work in the sugar cane fields. The story was much the same in Puerto Rico. It, too, became a major sugar producer and importer of enslaved Africans.

As slavery grew on the islands, so did planters' fears of a slave rebellion like the one in Haiti. Indeed, the planters had good reason to be afraid. Haitians took over neighboring Santo Domingo from 1801 to 1805 and again from 1822 to 1844. (Santo Domingo freed itself from Haitian rule in 1844 and became an independent nation called the Dominican Republic.) Cuba experienced major slave rebellions in 1810 and again in 1812.

Wealthy planters in Cuba and Puerto Rico relied on Spain to put down such rebellions. Thus, they had no wish for independence from that nation. Even though they were not always happy with the Spanish government's policies, most planters remained loyal to Spain. Cuba and Puerto Rico were Spain's last colonies in the Americas.

Taking Another Look

1. How did the French Revolution affect South Americans?

2. How did the slave revolt in Haiti affect Cuba and Puerto Rico?

3. **Critical Thinking** How do you account for differences in the way various Spanish provinces responded to events in other countries?

LOOKING AHEAD

The northern provinces of California, New Mexico, and Texas saw relatively little fighting or destruction during the struggle for Mexican independence. The people of those provinces now tried to accept their new Mexican government. But that government was far away. It did not always respond swiftly to the special needs of the people there.

THE END OF SLAVERY IN SOUTH AMERICA

During his struggle to free Venezuela from Spanish rule, Simón Bolívar turned to Haiti for help. In return for supplies and weapons, the leaders of Haiti asked Bolívar to emancipate, or free, African slaves in Venezuela. Bolívar readily agreed to this condition. He had come to detest slavery and had already freed the slaves that belonged to his family.

Slavery in South America was already in decline by the time the Spanish colonies were fighting for independence. Many African slaves had won their freedom by serving in the military. New laws had been passed that freed others. Still, the abolition, or end, of slavery did not come quickly or easily.

Within a few years after independence, nearly all the former colonies in South America had ended the slave trade. Complete emancipation, took longer. In Colombia, emancipation came in 1821. In Peru, fighting among various factions after independence delayed emancipation until 1854.

In Mexico, slavery was not abolished until 1829. Yet, most of the former Spanish colonies freed African slaves before other nations did. Great Britain did not abolish slavery until 1833. The abolition of slavery in the French colonies occurred in 1848. The end of slavery in the United States did not come until after the Civil War, in 1865.

CLOSE UP: Chapter 7

The Who, What, Where of History

1. **What** three revolutions inspired rebellion in Spain's colonies?
2. **Who** was Vicente Manuel de Zéspedes?
3. **What** are naval stores?
4. **What** was the 31st parallel?
5. **Where** in Spain's colonies did the first independence movement begin?
6. **Who** was Father Hidalgo?
7. **Who** was Simón Bolívar?
8. **Where** did Bolívar gain his first victory?
9. **What** were the faithful islands?
10. **Who** led the slave revolt on Haiti in 1791?

Making the Connection

1. What was the connection between revolutions in Europe and the Americas and Spain's loss of control over its colonies?
2. What was the connection between the Mexican revolution and independence from Spain for Texas, California, and New Mexico?
3. What was the connection between independence in Haiti and the loyalty of Cuba and Puerto Rico to Spain?

Time Check

1. What event in 1783 inspired revolutions in Spanish America?
2. In what year did Spain give up its province of Florida to the United States?
3. How many years passed between the beginning of Mexico's revolution and its independence from Spain?

What Would You Have Done?

1. If you had been a Spanish citizen of Florida or Louisiana, would you have agreed with Spain's policies to control the economy of your province? Explain.

2. Imagine you had been a citizen of Spanish California when Mexico finally gained its independence in 1821. Would you have remained in California or moved to Spain? Explain your decision.

Thinking and Writing About History

1. Imagine you are a businessperson in Spanish Florida. Write a letter to the king in Spain explaining how you think policies can be changed to build the province's economy.

2. Write a paragraph explaining the causes and effects of the following sequence of events in Spain's Caribbean colonies: Haiti's sugar market collapses; sugar production in Cuba and Puerto Rico increases dramatically; more labor is needed to work in the sugarcane fields; major slave rebellions occur in Cuba in 1810 and 1812; planters need the protection of Spain.

Building Skills: Skimming and Scanning

Suppose you want to get a general idea of the kind of information in a chapter before you read it carefully. Or maybe you want to find a piece of information quickly. Skimming and scanning will help you do both of these.

In skimming, you skip words in order to read rapidly and get an overview of the text. Scanning involves reading quickly to find a particular piece of information. Skim and scan Chapter 7 in order to answer the questions below.

1. What is the title of the chapter?

2. What are the titles of the three main sections of the chapter?

3. Skim and scan to find the chapter section that contains the following information:

   a. An account of Simón Bolívar's movement to free South America from Spanish rule.

   b. A discussion of the changes in Louisiana that affected the relation ship between Spain and the United States.

   c. The reactions of people in New Mexico and California to revolution in Mexico.

   d. The details about how the Mexican Revolution began.

   e. Information concerning Spain's control of Florida.

4. Skim each major section and write a statement that answers the question at the beginning of the section.

Express Yourself!

With two or three classmates, study the Snapshot of the Times box on page 89. Use the events listed in the box to make a timeline with pictures or illustrations. First, draw a line across a large piece of paper. Then, make marks on the timeline for the dates you decide to show. Choose at least three events from the timebox. Draw pictures to illustrate these events or use pictures from magazines and newspapers. Display your illustrated timeline in the classroom.

The remote frontier towns of Spanish New Mexico, such as Mesilla, were both fortresses and religious centers for the residents.

Life in the Mexican Borderlands

(1820s—1840s)

SECTIONS

1 Life in New Mexico

2 Life in Mexican California

3 Changing Ways in Texas

THINKING ABOUT THE CHAPTER

How did life in Mexico's northern provinces change after Mexico became independent?

Like most women in the early 1800s, Juana Briones de Miranda (bree-OH-nes deh mee-RAHN-dah) married young and devoted herself to caring for her family and helping friends and neighbors. Briones lived in California, which had fewer than 4,000 people of Spanish descent. Briones's marriage did not last, however. After leaving her husband, she secured a grant of land in what is now San Francisco. There she built a prosperous *rancho*.

Briones had the kind of independent spirit found in women and men throughout Mexico's northern provinces of Texas, New Mexico, and California. Much of that independence and courage was due to the harshness of living conditions at the farthest edges of Spanish settlement. Life there differed greatly from life in the great cities of Mexico and Spain. Those differences often sparked disagreements that strained relations between Mexico and its three northern provinces.

1 LIFE IN NEW MEXICO
◆ What was life like in New Mexico in
✦ the early 1800s?

To many Mexicans and Anglos in the early 1800s, New Mexico seemed as far away as the North Pole and almost as uninviting. Yet to *nuevomexicanos* (NWEH-voh-meh-hee-KAH-nohs), or Spanish-speaking settlers in New Mexico, those distances were part of the attraction of the province. As one governor noted, "They [the *nuevomexicanos*] love distance which makes them independent."

Frontier Towns. Some settlers were drawn to New Mexico by grants of land made to groups of families willing to start new settlements in the borderland. These grants were given at first by the Spanish, and later by the Mexican, government. Under a grant, each family received a small plot of farmland, as well as the right to graze livestock and cut timber from lands held by the community as a whole.

Spain and, later, Mexico also gave land to people who were willing to recruit settlers to come to New Mexico. Once a community was built, these people were expected to be *patrones* (pah-TROHN-es) to their villagers. A *patrón* not only governed a community but also cared for its people. In addition, a *patrón* provided for the town's defense.

Every town in New Mexico was a fortress. Villagers and *patrones* learned how to defend their communities in battle. They also learned the value of allies. Over

SNAPSHOT OF THE TIMES

1821	Mexico wins independence.
1825	Stephen Austin leads 300 families from the United States to Texas.
1829	Mexico abolishes slavery.
1835	New Mexican villagers protest new taxes.
1848	California missions secularized.

the years, most towns built alliances with Native Americans of the pueblos, who also suffered from raids by the Apache and Comanche.

Making a Living. Townspeople depended on one another for more than defense. Families tried to grow or make most of what they needed. They also traded for items they did not produce. In town squares, they exchanged vegetables for leather goods or pottery for mutton.

A few towns were large enough to support a full-time craftsworker. Often, it was a blacksmith who melted down scrap iron to make hardware. Sometimes, it was a weaver or a *santero* (sahn-TEH-roh), a carver of wooden statues of saints.

Every fall, a few villagers traveled to Taos (TAH-ohs), New Mexico, for the big trading fair. There they sold food to Anglo and French trappers who needed to stock up for the winter. Many people from the pueblos attended the fair, as did groups of Plains Native Americans. Merchants from Chihuahua (chee-WAH-wah), Mexico, also came to Taos, with mule trains loaded with chocolate and other luxuries.

The Social Order. The people in New Mexico were interdependent. They relied on one another for goods, security, and

95

their livelihoods. Yet they did not view all of their fellow townspeople as equals. Each person had a particular position in the social order, similar to that in Mexico or Spain.

At the top of New Mexican society were *españoles* (es-pahn-YOH-les), or Spaniards. All *patrones* were *españoles,* as were all government officials. At the bottom of the social scale were **genízaros** (hen-EE-sah-rohs), Native Americans who no longer lived among their own people or who had been captured and then freed. In between were *mestizos,* individuals of mixed European or Native American descent.

However, ethnic background alone did not determine a person's place in society. It was possible for a person to move from one class to another. A wealthy landowner, no matter what his or her heritage, could be considered a Spaniard if he or she accepted the Catholic religion and Spanish culture. One poor *nuevomexicano* even rose to the highest office in the province.

Manuel Armijo (ahr-MEE-hoh) was born near Albuquerque to a very poor family. As a young man, he worked as a *vaquero,* or cowboy, and later as a shepherd. When he saw a chance to make money by raising sheep, he was quick to take advantage of the opportunity. By the early 1800s, he was one of the richest men in the province. He went on to serve as governor and was the last person to hold that office while the province was still part of Mexico.

A career in the military was another way by which poor young men could advance in society. So was marriage to a woman of a well-to-do family.

Peace, Trade, and Wealth. Until the late 1700s, there were few opportunities for anyone in New Mexico to get rich. Villagers and *patrones* produced food mainly for their own use. The province was too isolated for trade to grow.

The constant danger of raids by Native Americans also discouraged trade. Then Spain made a series of treaties with two of the Native American groups, the Comanche and the Ute (yoot), who had been attacking New Mexican towns and farms. For the first time, New Mexico was at peace.

With peace, trade began to grow. As it did, some *nuevomexicanos,* like Armijo, suddenly had a chance to make their fortune by raising sheep in large numbers for sale. By the early 1800s, *nuevomexicanos* were driving as many as 400,000 sheep each year down the Rio Grande Valley to El Paso and then on to Chihuahua 600 miles (960 kilometers) away.

Partidos and Peonage. After Mexico won its independence in 1821, the new government encouraged settlement in New Mexico. It did so by offering generous land grants to **ricos** (REE-kohs), wealthy individuals, interested in raising sheep. Some of the new grants were enormous. The *ricos* recruited some workers from Mexico. Others were New Mexican villagers now trapped in what was known as the **partido** (pahr-TEE-doh) system.

Under the *partido* system, a villager agreed to take care of a *rico's* flock of sheep. In return, the villager received a share, or *partido,* of the newborn animals. In addition, the *rico* usually paid the

Ignacio Rodríguez Galván

After Mexico won independence from Spain, its writers began to stress the country's special identity. Ignacio Rodríguez Galván was a leading Mexican poet of the early 1800s. These lines from his masterpiece, *Profecia de Guatimoc* ("Prophecy of Cuauhtémoc," the last Aztec emperor), show the anti-Spanish, pro-Native American feeling that marked his writing.

Nada perdona el bárbaro europeo.
Todo lo rompe, y tala, y aniquila
Con brazo furibundo.
   Es su placer en fúnebres desiertos
La ciudades trocar (¡ Hazaña
   honrosa!).
Ve el sueño con desdén, si no reposa
Sobre insepultos muertos.

The cruel European forgives nothing.
He breaks and he destroys and he
   wipes out
With a wild purpose.
   He takes pleasure in turning cities
Into desert wastes (Honorable, indeed!)
He views sleep with scorn if he cannot
   rest
On unburied bodies.

---

herder a cash advance for services. The herder could then use the money to build up his own herd.

In bad times, however, the herder could not repay the money and was in debt to the *rico*. The herder then had to work for the *rico* to pay off the debt. Although the *partido* system seemed to offer poor people a chance to build herds of their own, it often led to a lifetime of working off debt.

A New Opportunity for Wealth.

Until 1821, *nuevomexicanos,* like other Spanish colonists, could trade only within the Spanish empire. Government officials banned foreigners from trading in New Mexico. But after independence, those rules no longer applied.

A number of Anglo traders arrived in Santa Fe with pack trains loaded with goods. Their profits were enormous. However, the risks were equally enormous. Some traders never reached their destinations. Some died in blizzards, windstorms, or accidents along the trail. Still others were killed in battles with Native Americans.

Conflicts Among *Nuevomexicanos.*

The growth of trade widened the distance between the rich and poor *nuevomexicanos.* Even villagers who were still independent feared that they, too, might become peons. That fear touched off a revolt when a new governor from Mexico imposed new taxes. In 1837, angry villagers banded together with some Native Americans of the pueblos and marched on the capital at Santa Fe. Within weeks, they had killed the governor and installed one of their own people in his place.

At first, the *ricos* supported the rebellion. After all, they, too, resented new taxes. The rebels, however, tried to limit the power of the *ricos.* Then a group of *ricos* led by Manuel Armijo helped the

Mexican army end the rebellion. Although they restored order for a time, that did not bring peace to New Mexico.

Taking Another Look

1. How did isolation from the main centers of Mexico shape life in New Mexico?

2. What was the *partido* system?

3. **Critical Thinking** If you were a young, poor *nuevomexicano*, what could you do to become rich?

2 LIFE IN MEXICAN CALIFORNIA

How did life in Mexican California change from 1820 to 1840?

The years from the 1820s to the 1840s were years of change in California. As in New Mexico, some of the changes were sparked by the desire to expand the economy. In 1823, California was the home of 21 Roman Catholic missions that stretched from San Diego, in the south, to Sonoma, in the north. Seventeen years later, all 21 missions had been abandoned and their lands were privately owned.

The Breakup of the Missions. To the Spanish and, then, the Mexican government, the missions hindered economic growth in California. The missions held much of the best farming and ranching land in California. Further, the missions had almost total control of the labor force, which in the 1820s consisted mostly of Native Americans.

The Mexican government **secularized** the California missions, or removed them from religious ownership or use, in 1833.

Native Americans who had once been forced to stay at missions now no longer had to live and work there. Even though

they had been promised land, tools, and seed, few Native Americans chose to stay at the missions. Many Native Americans resented the way they had been treated at the missions. Some moved to the wilderness. Others went to work on *ranchos* or in towns.

By 1848, all 21 missions had been secularized. Most of the mission lands ended up in the hands of government officials and their friends. For example, a young army officer named Mariano Guadalupe Vallejo (vah-YEH-hoh) acquired most of the fertile land of the San Francisco Solano (soh-LAH-noh) mission in the Sonoma Valley as well as another huge tract. These holdings—248,642 acres (100,625 hectares)—made him one of California's largest landowners at the time.

Most of the mission lands were turned into *ranchos,* or ranches. In 1808, the year Vallejo was born, there were only about 20 *ranchos* in California. Between 1834 and 1846, the number grew to about 700. Almost all of that land was devoted to raising cattle. *Californios,* or Spanish-speaking settlers in California, were eager to take advantage of a new trade that was developing.

Hides and Tallow. Until the 1820s, most *californios* raised cattle mainly for their own use. Then, in 1822, companies from Great Britain and Massachusetts negotiated contracts with California missions and *ranchos* for hides and tallow.

At that time, the shoe industry was growing in New England and Great Britain. As a result, cowhide to be made into shoe leather was in great demand. So was **tallow,** a substance made from the fat of slaughtered animals. In the early 1800s, tallow was used to make candles, the main source of light in homes and businesses, and soap.

Mariano Vallejo, wealthy *californio*, shown with daughters Maria and Luisa and three grandchildren, played a leading role in bringing California into the U.S.

As the hide and tallow trade flourished, California's ties to Britain and the United States grew stronger. Indeed, some traders from the United States began to settle in California and became Mexican citizens. Many married into local Mexican families.

Rancho Life. The growing trade in hides and tallow changed the way *californios* lived. As in New Mexico, the gap widened between rich and poor. Mariano Vallejo's *rancho* suggests how large that gap had become.

Vallejo and his family lived in a huge adobe house on the plaza in Sonoma. There, they entertained in style. Celebrations of weddings, holidays, and other special events often lasted for a week or more. Guests enjoyed dances, horse races, bull fights, banquets, and picnics. Dozens of servants cared for the house and the family.

Most of the servants and workers on the *ranchos* were Native Americans who were trapped by debt in the peonage system. Their anger and resentment contributed to the unrest that grew in California during the 1830s and 1840s.

A Shaky Future. Some former mission residents joined other Native Americans in raids on *ranchos* and other settlements. Many wealthy *californios* expected help from the Mexican government, but it never arrived.

At the time, Vallejo was California's military commander. He voiced his concerns to the Mexican government:

> Daily throughout the whole extent of [California], with the exception of this frontier, where I maintain a military force of 40 men at my own expense, there are Indian raids which ravish [ruin] the fields . . . and destroy the only effective wealth of the country, cattle and horses.

Mexico did little about Vallejo's concerns and those of other Californians. As a result, California's ties to Mexico weakened, even as its ties to the United States became firmer. By 1846, Vallejo was openly supporting efforts to make California part of the United States.

Taking Another Look

1. How did the growth of trade shape life in California?
2. What caused the political unrest in California in the 1830s and 1840s?
3. **Critical Thinking a.** How was life in Mexican California similar to life in New Mexico? **b.** How was it different?

3 CHANGING WAYS IN TEXAS

◆ Why did the Mexican government
◆ encourage U.S. citizens to settle in
Texas?

To the small number of Mexicans who lived in Texas in 1821, the year of Mexican independence, the mere mention of the word Comanche sent them reaching for their rifles. Year after year, the Comanche had swept down from the north and reduced homes and ranches to ashes. Small wonder that few Mexicans were willing to become *tejanos* (teh-HAHN-nohs), as Mexican settlers in this least developed northern province were called.

Mexicans also hesitated to move to Texas because the province was so far from the more populated Mexican areas to the south. Why should they abandon familiar homes to scratch out a living in a strange and dangerous land? Both Spain and the Mexican government that ruled after 1821 reluctantly decided that to populate Texas, people from other nations, including the United States, would have to be encouraged to settle there.

Life in Texas. By the 1820s, there were about 2,500 *tejanos* living in Texas. They were scattered in tiny settlements and on huge *ranchos* near the Rio Grande. Some farmed near a presidio, mission, or town. But most were involved in raising cattle.

Only a few thousand *tejanos* and Anglos lived in Texas in the early 1800s. Though they lived in fear of Comanche raiders, Anglos and *tejanos* were able to celebrate at festivals, such as this one in San Antonio.

Some *rancheros* sold their herds in Mexico by driving them south across the Rio Grande to the neighboring province of Tamaulipas. Other *tejanos* found a market for their cattle in Cuba and on other islands in the Caribbean. Still others preferred to sell their livestock in Louisiana, a market that had been opened up through the daring of *vaqueros* during the American Revolution (see Chapter 6).

At first the government sought settlers from within Mexico. But Mexico's population was not large. Hundreds of thousands of people had died in the wars of independence, including many young men. Mexico then turned to Europe, encouraging Europeans to emigrate to Texas. But young people from the countries of western Europe preferred to emigrate to the more settled areas of the United States. Many had relatives or friends in the busy cities of the eastern United States. Reluctantly, Mexico opened its Texas frontier to waiting settlers from the United States.

A Plan for Settlement. To encourage immigration into Texas, Spain decided to offer land grants to **empresarios** (em-preh-SAHR-yohs), or agents willing to recruit settlers. In 1821, Spanish officials made an agreement with Moses Austin, a former U.S. miner living in Louisiana. Austin would be given a huge tract of land on the Brazos River if he brought 300 families from Louisiana to Texas.

Before the agreement could be carried out, however, Mexico became independent, and Spain lost control of Texas. At about the same time, Austin died. His son, Stephen F. Austin, persuaded the Mexican government to approve the grant that had been promised to his father.

By 1825, Stephen Austin had brought 300 families to Texas. In time, he persuaded another 900 families to settle in Texas.

All of them made their homes on Austin's grant along the Brazos River.

This grant was the first of many awarded to U.S. citizens. In the next 12 years, nearly 28,000 Americans came to Texas. By 1830, in fact, there were five times as many U.S. settlers in Texas as there were *tejanos*.

Many of those settlers brought enslaved African Americans. Much of the land the U.S. settlers occupied was ideal for cotton, a crop in great demand in the United States and Britain. With the labor of those they had enslaved, the newcomers hoped to raise cotton.

By 1830, Anglos, U.S. settlers in Texas, numbered about 7,000. Meanwhile, the *tejano* population had grown slowly to about 3,000. As the Anglo population mushroomed, Mexican officials worried once more. Would Anglos take over Texas from Mexico?

Taking Another Look

1. Why were so few Mexicans willing to settle in Texas?
2. Why did the Mexican government encourage people from the United States to settle in Texas?
3. **Critical Thinking** Why do you think Texas had fewer settlers in 1820 than New Mexico or California?

LOOKING AHEAD

Under the government of Mexico, the provinces of New Mexico, California, and Texas underwent many changes. They grew in population and in economic strength. They came to rely less and less on the central government of Mexico. For all three provinces, even greater changes were in store when they would become part of the United States.

A MASTER CARVER

The year was 1802. In an isolated Spanish settlement along the frontier of New Mexico, a wood carver began to create a figure from a piece of cottonwood. After carving, the statue was brightly painted. The carver, called a *santero,* was a craftsworker who fashioned images of saints. The saint, or *santo,* might have stood in the village church. Or perhaps it had a place in the home of a wealthy *patrón.*

The art of carving *santos* has been passed from one generation to the next for more than 200 years. At the beginning of the 1900s, however, the art appeared to be dying out. People began buying machine-produced religious objects instead of the hand-carved images. A *santero* named José Lopez was determined to preserve the heritage of his ancestors. But rather than color the images, Lopez carved *santos* that he left unpainted.

Lopez's son, George, continues his father's work. Now in his 90s, George Lopez is a master carver. "It's in the blood. It's part of my name," he says. Lopez creates his figures with a penknife, sandpaper, and a few simple tools. To ensure that his art will not die, Lopez is teaching his skills to the younger members of his family. Lopez was honored by the Folk Arts Program of the National Endowment for the Arts as an artist who has kept alive the tradition of the *santeros.*

CLOSE UP: Chapter 8

The Who, What, Where of History

1. **What** was a *patrón?*
2. **Where** in New Mexico did the annual trading fair take place?
3. **Who** was Manuel Armijo?
4. **What** two products enriched California ranchers in the 1800s?
5. **What** were *tejanos?*
6. **Where** was Moses Austin's land grant?

Making the Connection

1. What was the connection between the status of Native Americans on California *ranchos* and growing unrest there in the 1830s and 1840s?
2. What was the connection between granting land to *empresarios* and the number of U.S. settlers moving to Texas?

Time Check

1. When were restrictions against trade with foreigners lifted in New Mexico?
2. In what year did Mexico secularize the California missions?

What Would You Have Done?

1. Imagine you had been born a poor person in New Mexico but had acquired wealth and status through ambition and hard work. Would you have supported the system of *partido?* Explain your answer.
2. As a California ranch owner would you have agreed with Governor Vallejo's efforts to make California part of the United States? Why or why not?

Thinking and Writing About History

1. Choose a classmate to work with. Imagine that the two of you have decided to become *patrones*. Based on what you have read about life in New Mexico in this chapter, create a list of rules for the community you are about to build. Also, make a list of the type of craftsworkers you would want to recruit for the town.

2. Imagine you are a reporter visiting a *rancho* in California, and you ask to interview the workers. Write an article describing their reactions to their working conditions.

3. Imagine you are Stephen Austin. Create an advertisement urging Anglo settlers to emigrate to Texas.

Building Skills: Main Ideas and Details

Just as chapters and chapter sections contain main ideas, paragraphs also have main ideas. Usually there is a single sentence in a paragraph that tells what the paragraph is about. The rest of the sentences in the paragraph give details that support the main idea. Keeping track of the main ideas as you read will help you to understand and remember the main points the writer is making.

In the following paragraph, the first sentence gives the main idea:

Yet ethnic background alone did not determine a person's place in society. It was possible for a person to move from one class to another. A wealthy landowner, no matter what his or her heritage, could be considered a Spaniard if he or she accepted the Catholic religion and Spanish culture. *One poor nuevomexicano even rose to the highest office in the province.*

1. Read the paragraph below and then write the sentence that states the main idea.

Vallejo had specific ideas for protecting the province. He suggested that the governor have both civil and military authority. He also wanted Mexico to send at least 200 more soldiers to help defend the province. And he urged that the government recruit more farmers and artisans.

2. The main idea is not always in the first sentence of a paragraph. Read the paragraph below and write the sentence that states the main idea.

The new trade did not bring much money to California. It was based on a system of barter. Californios traded their hides and tallow for everything from pins and needles to pianos and billard tables. Trading ships increasingly resembled floating shopping malls.

Express Yourself!

On a piece of paper, write down all the terms that appear in this chapter in bold, or heavy type. Write down any other words or terms you are not familiar with. Next to each word, write its definition. In addition, draw pictures or symbols that show the meaning of two or three of these words. Then, write a sentence for each word you have defined.

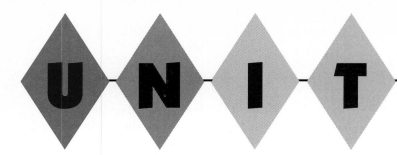

UNIT ——— 3

A TIME OF UPHEAVAL
(1830–1870)

Lorenzo de Zavala

Chapter | 9   Revolt in Texas
(1820s–1836)

10   War Between the
United States and Mexico
(1838–1848)

11   Foreigners in Their Own Land
(1848–1870s)

Battle of San Pascual

THE BIG PICTURE

Voices of the Times

The North Americans have conquered whatever territory adjoins them. In less than half a century, they have become masters of extensive colonies which formerly belonged to Spain and France, and of . . . territories from which have disappeared the former owners, the Indian tribes.

— Mexican general Manuel Mier y Terán, 1829

Unit 3 describes a time of great unrest and change in both the United States and Latin America. The United States continued to expand until its borders stretched from the Atlantic Ocean to the Pacific. But expansion focused attention on the problem of slavery. This issue increasingly divided the North and South.

Latin Americans, meanwhile, grappled with the question of what form their new governments should take. In Mexico, political struggles so drained the nation's strength that its northern provinces became easy targets for an expanding United States.

◆◆ In The United States ◆◆

From 1830 to 1860, the United States was undergoing great changes. The country was in the process of changing from a mostly agricultural nation to one in which industry played a larger and larger role. The reactions of one visitor, Domingo Faustino Sarmiento (sahr-mee-EN-toh), give a picture of the United States at that time through the eyes of a Latin American.

Progress Aplenty. On a visit to the United States in 1847, Sarmiento, a writer, educator, and future president of Argentina, found much to admire. Having fled harsh rule in his own land, he appreciated the liberty that U.S. citizens enjoyed. He also envied their material progress. The United States had been blessed with a fine system of rivers. The Yankees, as he called the Americans, had improved that system. They built canals, "thereby creating an internal navigation system covering a distance greater than that between America and Europe." They had also built "a great national highway"—the National Road—from Cumberland, Maryland, to Vandalia, Illinois.

Sarmiento further marveled at the nation's many telegraph lines, railroads, and steamboats, and at how much they were used. "If God were suddenly to call the world to judgment," Sarmiento wrote, "He would surprise two thirds of the population of the United States on the road like ants."

Sarmiento also admired the factories of the North, as well as the Yankee willingness "to try anything." If, for example, an advertisement for a new kind of plow appeared in one paper, the next day every paper in the country carried it. "Soon the new machines are put on sale, and a year later they are in use all over the Union."

The Problem of Slavery. But for all its progress, the United States still permitted slavery. Sarmiento called slavery "the deep ulcer [sore] . . . which threatens to corrupt the robust [strong] body of the Union!" Sarmiento felt that George Washington and the other framers of the

105

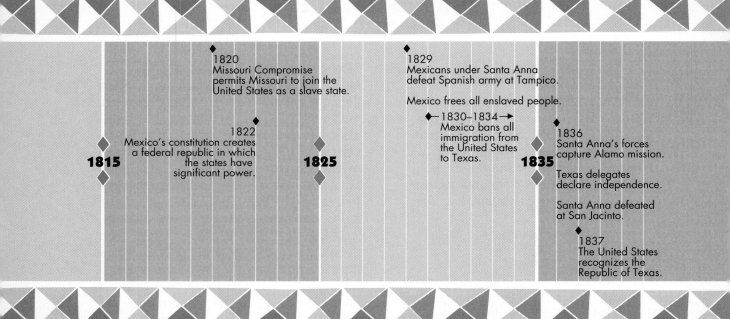

1815

◆ 1820
Missouri Compromise permits Missouri to join the United States as a slave state.

◆ 1822
Mexico's constitution creates a federal republic in which the states have significant power.

1825

◆ 1829
Mexicans under Santa Anna defeat Spanish army at Tampico.

Mexico frees all enslaved people.

◆ 1830–1834 →
Mexico bans all immigration from the United States to Texas.

1835

◆ 1836
Santa Anna's forces capture Alamo mission.

Texas delegates declare independence.

Santa Anna defeated at San Jacinto.

◆ 1837
The United States recognizes the Republic of Texas.

Constitution had made a "fatal error" in not abolishing this system. Instead, U.S. leaders had continued to make compromises over slavery.

The **Missouri Compromise** of 1820, for example, permitted Missouri to join the Union as a slave state, while Maine came in as a free state. This was done to keep the number of slave and free states equal. In addition, the Missouri Compromise barred slavery from the area north of latitude 36°30' in the Louisiana Territory, but allowed it in the area south of that line.

Nevertheless, by the 1830s, Northern **abolitionists** were demanding an immediate end to slavery throughout the nation. Stung by the abolitionists' attacks, Southerners answered with arguments in which they tried to justify slavery. Noted Sarmiento, "Slavery . . . has been made the soul of the society which exploits [takes advantage of] it."

Pushing West. Sarmiento was awed by the advance of the United States toward the Pacific Ocean. The line of U.S. settlement was pushing west at the rate of 700 miles (1,100 kilometers) per year. In the 1820s, rugged fur trappers and traders called **Mountain Men** led this westward march. They blazed trails and discovered passes through the mountains. By the late 1840s, U.S. settlers poured through those passes into the Oregon Country, a rich farming area beyond the Rockies.

The settling of Oregon led to a dispute, and even the possibility of war, with Great Britain, which also claimed the area. As Sarmiento noted:

Everything would have remained peaceful . . . but the Yankee spirit, like the condor [a large South American vulture] when there is blood, smelled good lands, rivers, forests, and ports.

106

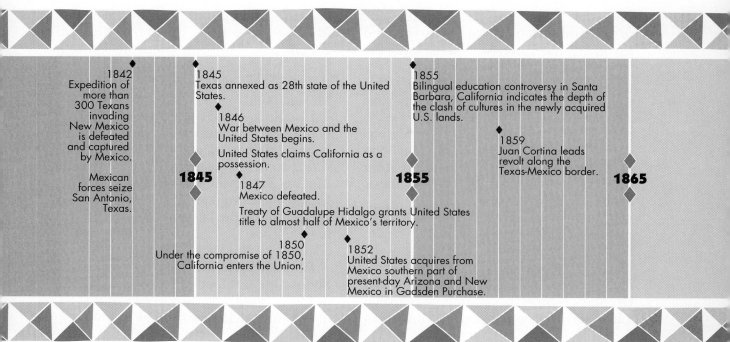

1842
Expedition of more than 300 Texans invading New Mexico is defeated and captured by Mexico.

Mexican forces seize San Antonio, Texas.

1845

1845
Texas annexed as 28th state of the United States.

1846
War between Mexico and the United States begins.

United States claims California as a possession.

1847
Mexico defeated.

Treaty of Guadalupe Hidalgo grants United States title to almost half of Mexico's territory.

1850
Under the compromise of 1850, California enters the Union.

1852
United States acquires from Mexico southern part of present-day Arizona and New Mexico in Gadsden Purchase.

1855

1855
Bilingual education controversy in Santa Barbara, California indicates the depth of the clash of cultures in the newly acquired U.S. lands.

1859
Juan Cortina leads revolt along the Texas-Mexico border.

1865

The Oregon question was settled in 1846, with the United States gaining valuable territory. As in other lands claimed by the United States, most U.S. settlers disregarded Native American rights to the land.

Pushing South. By the late 1820s, huge stretches of land where cotton could be grown had drawn thousands of U.S. citizens into Texas. That region was then part of newly independent Mexico. Under Mexican law, these immigrants had to become Mexican citizens, follow Mexican laws, practice Roman Catholicism, and pay taxes to the Mexican government.

Few did so. Instead, they expected to go on enjoying the rights of U.S. citizens. They complained bitterly when they felt that those rights were violated by the Mexican government.

Alarmed at the number of U.S. settlers, the Mexican government tried to discourage their immigration by ending slavery.

But Southerners disregarded the law. Then Mexico banned further immigration from the United States. U.S. settlers ignored the ban and kept coming.

A new government came to power in Mexico in 1835 and tried to tighten control over Texas. The U.S. immigrants protested, claiming that they no longer had any say in how they were governed. Soon a revolt was underway. Some *tejanos*—Mexicans living in Texas—were also unhappy with the new Mexican government. They joined the immigrants in fighting for and winning independence from Mexico. In 1836, the Lone Star Republic of Texas was proclaimed.

War With Mexico. For the next nine years, Texas remained an independent republic. The United States did not **annex** Texas (add Texas to its territory) because Mexico threatened war if it did so. Also, many Northerners did not want another

107

slave state joining the Union. In the end, the argument of those who favored expanding the nation won out. In 1845, the United States annexed Texas.

The next year, the United States sent troops into a disputed area between Texas and Mexico. When the Mexicans tried to defend this area, which they regarded as theirs, the U.S. government accused them of invading the United States. Fighting soon broke out, and the United States declared war on Mexico.

Although the Mexicans fought hard in defense of their homeland, victory went to the United States. Under the terms of the Treaty of Guadalupe Hidalgo (gwah-dah-LOO-peh ee-DAHL-goh) of 1848, the Rio Grande became the boundary between Texas and Mexico. Mexico gave up almost half of its lands, an area that was called the **Mexican Cession**. In return, Mexico received $15 million from the United States, which also agreed to respect the rights of former Mexican citizens in the Mexican Cession.

In 1853, in a deal known as the **Gadsden Purchase,** the United States bought another big chunk of Mexican territory, consisting of parts of southern New Mexico and Arizona, for $10 million. The United States wanted this land because it seemed to be the best route for a railroad to California.

Another State, Another Compromise. Soon after California had become U.S. property, gold was discovered there. So many gold seekers swarmed to the area

When Mexico finally gained independence from Spain in 1821, it covered a vast area. However, it soon lost much of its land to the growing United States. What area did it lose in the Mexican Cession? In the Gadsden Purchase?

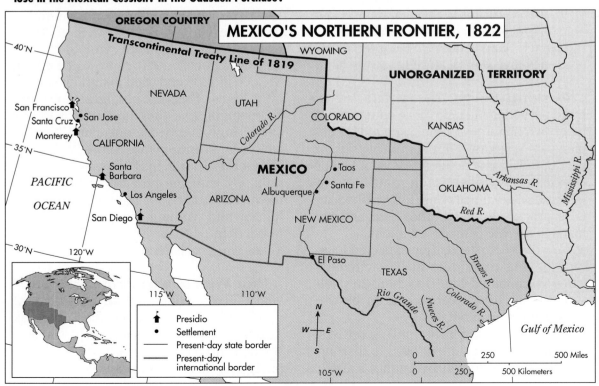

MEXICO'S NORTHERN FRONTIER, 1822

that California sought to be admitted to the Union as a free state.

The result was the **Compromise of 1850**. Under the compromise, California entered the union as a free state. In other parts of the Mexican Cession, the principle of **popular sovereignty** would be followed. This meant that the people in a territory would decide whether or not they wanted slavery there. Congress also passed a tougher law requiring the return of **fugitive,** or runaway, slaves.

U.S. citizens desperately hoped the dispute over slavery was now over. But with the push of settlers into new territory in the 1850s, it flared up again and again. By 1860, the United States stood on the brink of civil war.

Taking Another Look

1. What kinds of progress did the United States make between 1830 and 1850?
2. Why did expansion bring compromises over slavery?
3. **Critical Thinking** How was the discovery of gold in California a mixed blessing for the United States?

◆◆ In Latin America ◆◆

By 1830, most Latin American lands had thrown off Spanish rule. Now that they were independent, they had to find ways to rebuild their nations and create new governments for their people after years of brutal warfare. In many nations, *caudillos* (kow-DEE-yohs), or military strongmen, took charge of the governments. This proved to be the case in Mexico.

A New Republic. While U.S. citizens were pushing west and south and arguing over slavery, Mexicans struggled to come up with an effective form of government. Three hundred years of Spanish rule, followed by 11 destructive years of war with Spain, made this task very difficult. As a result, Mexico went through a series of short-lived governments.

In 1822, Agustín de Iturbide, the *criollo* general who had helped topple Spanish rule in Mexico, declared himself emperor. He became Mexico's first *caudillo*, shutting down newspapers that criticized him and then dismissing the country's legislature. In 1823, his government collapsed. Soon after, the Central American states separated from Mexico and formed their own short-lived nation.

In Mexico City, delegates gathered to draw up a new plan of government. Some wanted a federal republic like that of the United States. There, states shared power with a central goverment. Other delegates argued for a central government with very strong powers. They believed that Mexico was not ready for the looser federal form. Said one delegate, "We are . . . slaves who have just unshackled their chains." But pointing to the success of the United States, the federalists won.

Mexico's constitution of 1824 created a federal republic in which the states had more power than in the United States. State legislatures rather than the people chose the president. The president was also given special powers in emergencies, and both the clergy and the military had special rights.

Mexico's first two presidents were unable to cope with the huge economic problems facing the nation. Its third president, Anastasio Bustamante (boos-tah-MAHN-teh), made himself a military dictator. His overthrow in 1832 set the stage for the rise to power of General Antonio López de Santa Anna (SAHN-tah AHN-ah). Santa Anna was to become

Mexican and U.S. armies fought in the Battle of Buena Vista in 1847.

Mexico's most important political leader for the next 20 years.

A Centralized State. In 1833, Santa Anna seemed a champion of Mexican liberty. This *criollo* native of Veracruz had fought in the war for independence from Spain and had stopped a Spanish attempt to invade Mexico in 1829. He had also helped bring down two dictators, Iturbide and Bustamante.

Little wonder that Santa Anna was elected president in 1833 by a huge majority of the state legislatures. In 1836, he replaced the federal constitution of 1824 with a new one.

The constitution of 1836 created a centralized state. The states became military departments controlled by political bosses chosen by the president. The president's term of office was also extended from four to eight years. But no president would rule for that long. During the next several years, governments came and went rapidly. Santa Anna himself was in and out of office nine times!

Trouble From the North. Many of Mexico's states were angered by their loss of power to the central government. Revolts broke out in many parts of Mexico. The most serious of these was in Texas. Mexico refused to recognize the independence of Texas because it hoped to reconquer its former province.

Mexico also had to deal with invasions by foreign powers. In 1838, it turned back an invasion by France. This occurred after it could not pay claims by French citizens in Mexico for damage done to their property during the war for independence. Then in 1847, Mexico lost its war with the United States.

That war was a disaster for Mexico. It cost the nation almost half its territory. The war also left a legacy of bitterness and hatred toward the United States.

The war did, however, strengthen the stirrings of Mexican **nationalism,** or pride in one's country. It took several years for this nationalism to develop. Right after the war, Mexico was as divided as ever. But when, in 1853, Santa Anna sold even more of Mexico to the United States in the Gadsden Purchase, Mexican patriots had had enough. A revolt against Santa Anna broke out that changed the course of Mexican history.

Reform. In 1855, a group of reformers led by Benito Juárez (HWAH-res), a Zapotec Native American, succeeded in overthrowing Santa Anna. The reformers passed laws aimed at curbing the power of the military and the church. Then, in 1857, they put a new constitution into effect. It restored the federal system of government and, for the first time, gave Mexicans a bill of rights. Now, freedom of speech and of the press, and equality before the law were guaranteed.

Some of the reforms angered officials of the Roman Catholic Church. The church had become an extremely powerful force in Mexico. New laws ordered that church and state be separated and that the government take over all church property. The church struck back by threatening to **excommunicate,** or deny religious rites to, anyone who swore loyalty to the new constitution.

Feelings ran so high that civil war broke out. The victory of Juárez and the reformers in that struggle marked the beginning of a more stable period in Mexico. Nevertheless, as you will see in Unit 4, the nation first had to suffer yet another invasion from abroad.

Elsewhere in Latin America. Other Latin American countries besides Mexico underwent periods of trouble after they became independent. In Argentina, for example, a struggle raged between the *porteños* (pohr-TEH-nyohs), or people who lived in the port city of Buenos Aires, and the *gauchos* (GOW-chohs), or cowboys of the pampas (PAHM-pahs), or grasslands. While the *porteños* wanted a strong central government based in Buenos Aires, the *gauchos* preferred local control. In 1835, a *caudillo* from the pampas, Juan Manuel de Rosas (ROH-sahs), took advantage of the strife to come to power. He ruled from Buenos Aires as a military dictator until 1852.

As in Mexico, dictatorship finally gave way to reform in Argentina. Domingo Faustino Sarmiento, whose views on the United States you read earlier, was elected president in 1868. Sarmiento gave his country a system of public education modeled on that of the United States. He also called for improvements in farming and saw to it that railroads and settlers reached across the pampas. In Argentina and other Latin American countries, stable governments brought economic development, often with the help of Great Britain, which supplied trained people, money, and equipment.

Taking Another Look

1. How did Mexicans respond to the U.S. victory in the war?

2. How did Santa Anna's switch to a centralized government bring disaster to Mexico?

3. **Critical Thinking** Why do you think Mexico had so much trouble ridding itself of oppressive governments?

111

The village of San Antonio was a center of *tejano* life in the early 1800s, when this picture was painted. The Alamo mission is shown in this painting. Can you find it?

SECTIONS

1 A Time of Unrest

2 Alarms in Texas

3 Texas Gains Independence

Revolt in Texas

(1820s–1836)

THINKING ABOUT THE CHAPTER

Why did Texas break away from Mexico in 1836?

"How strange are these people from the North," observed José Sánchez after a visit to Texas in 1828. "The Americans . . . eat only salted meat, bread made by themselves out of corn meal, coffee, and home-made cheeses. To these the greater part . . . add strong liquor."

Sánchez was part of a Mexican government team surveying conditions in Texas. At the head of the mission was General Manuel de Mier y Terán (mee-ER ee teh-RAHN), a scholarly soldier. He shared his government's concern about the flood of Anglo settlers in Texas. In the green valleys of the Colorado and Brazos rivers, Mier y Terán noted how Anglo settlers ran affairs their way and ignored Mexican laws. He saw, too, that Mexico had few soldiers or officials to enforce the government's laws in the distant province.

On his return to Mexico City, Mier y Terán issued a stern warning of the danger Anglo settlement presented. "Either the government occupies Texas *now,* or it is lost forever." Mexico did take steps to control the province. However, new laws led to unrest—and rebellion.

1 A TIME OF UNREST

◆ What political divisions contributed to
◆ unrest in Mexico?

The Anglo *empresario* Stephen F. Austin (see Chapter 8) considered himself a loyal Mexican citizen. He spoke the Spanish language fluently. He signed official papers *Esteban* Austin, using the Spanish form of his first name.

Despite Stephen Austin's commitment to Mexico, most other Anglo settlers had little loyalty to their new country. As one Mexican official warned, the North American colonists in Texas were Mexicans in name only.

Two Cultures. In the 1820s, Texas was home to two cultures—one *tejano* and the other Anglo. In general, the two groups lived apart. *Tejanos* lived in San Antonio and Goliad and in towns around them.

Tejano social life centered around the Catholic Church. Some *tejanos* were small-scale farmers. Many others worked on cattle ranches. Few of the *tejanos* got rich from cattle raising. It was a demanding business. Cattle drives were dangerous. Floods and other natural disasters as well as raids by the Comanche or Apache could bring ruin.

In general, *tejanos* welcomed Anglo settlers who settled in rural communities in East Texas. They hoped the newcomers would make life more secure and help Texas grow. Anglos, however, remained isolated in their own communities. They set up their own schools. Few Anglos learned Spanish and most were Protestant. They also did not wish to become Mexicans as the government had hoped.

Many Anglos had little use for *tejanos.* They felt a sense of superiority to the Mexicans. Still, some well-to-do *tejanos* established friendly relations with the newcomers.

Federalism or Centralism? Although Texas was far from Mexico City, events in the south affected Mexico's northern frontier. The 1820s were a time of turmoil in Mexico. The wars for independence from Spain had left the country's leaders deeply divided.

On one side were the liberals. They supported **federalism,** the system of government under which the individual states would share power with the central government in Mexico City. They also wanted to reduce the power of the Catholic Church, end special privileges, and protect freedom of the press.

On the other side were the conservatives. They favored **centralism,** with power concentrated in the national government. Conservatives wanted to keep society as it was, with power in the hands of the wealthy. They wanted to protect the power that the Catholic Church had in Mexico. They also believed some censorship of the press was necessary to help maintain order.

After Mexico won its independence in 1821, rival leaders maneuvered for power. Often *caudillos*, military leaders, seized control of the Mexican government. The most successful *caudillo* was a man who would have great influence on Mexican life for more than 30 years.

At the age of 17, **Antonio López de Santa Anna** won a medal for bravery—as a soldier fighting for Spain in Mexico. On the banks of the Medina River, he helped crush Mexican rebels. During the wars of independence, Santa Anna rose through the ranks. Then, with a shrewd sense of timing, he switched sides just as Mexico won independence from Spain.

In the turmoil that followed, Santa Anna pushed his way to the top. At first, he favored the liberals. Santa Anna was a clever politician. He managed to keep a loyal following even when he changed sides to favor the conservatives.

Santa Anna won fame as a talented military leader. In 1829, he turned back a Spanish army that had landed at the port of Tampico. The Spanish invasion was part of an effort to reconquer Mexico. Mexicans hailed him as the "Victor of Tampico."

Santa Anna saw himself as the "Napoleon of the West." He believed he had been chosen by God to save Mexico. Time and again, Mexicans turned to him to lead the country. He held the office of president 9 different times in his career.

At first, *tejanos* and Texas Anglos supported Santa Anna. They were federalists who wanted to protect states' rights. They did not want the government in Mexico City dictating to them. When Santa Anna changed sides, however, they no longer saw him as a hero.

Taking Another Look

1. Why did *tejanos* and Anglos have little to do with each other?
2. What were the major political divisions in Mexico in the 1820s?
3. **Critical Thinking** Why do you think a leader like Santa Anna was able to gain and hold power in Mexico?

2 ALARMS IN TEXAS

Why did Mexico want to stop Anglo immigration into Texas?

Despite political unrest, Mexico kept a watchful eye on Texas and its growing Anglo population. The government put General Mier y Terán in charge of colonization. The general complained he had too little help and issued more warnings:

There is no physical force that can stop the entrance of *norteamericanos* [North Americans], who are exclusive owners of the coast and the border of Texas.

In 1830, the government tried to stop the flood of settlers from the United States. By then, Anglos greatly outnumbered *tejanos* and more were arriving daily.

Mexican Fears. Mexican leaders understood Mier y Terán when he pointed out that "the North Americans have conquered whatever territory adjoins them." They knew the United States was eager to acquire Texas. In 1826, it offered $1 million for Texas. A few years later, President Andrew Jackson raised the offer to $5 million. Another Mexican, Lucas Alamán (ah-lah-MAHN), echoed the alarm: "Texas will be lost for this Republic if adequate measures to save it are not taken."

In 1829, Mexico passed a law freeing all

1829   Mexico abolishes slavery.

1830 – 1834   Mexican government bans immigration of Anglos to Texas.

1833   Stephen Austin petitions the Mexican government for Texas statehood.

Austin is jailed in Mexico City.

1834   Santa Anna imposes strong central government on Mexico.

1835   Texan army defeats Mexican army at the Alamo.

1836   Mexican army kills Texan defenders of the Alamo.

Texas declares independence.

Battle of San Jacinto ends war in Texas.

enslaved people. Mexicans had few slaves, so the law was mostly aimed at Anglo slave owners in Texas. It was meant to discourage other slave owners from settling in Texas. The next year, the Mexican Congress banned further Anglo immigration. It also planned to enforce trade regulations, such as taxes on goods imported from the United States.

Rumblings in Texas. These measures brought furious protests from Anglos in Texas. But as in the past, Anglos refused to obey the new laws, and Mexico was unable to enforce them. Between 1830 and 1834, when the ban on immigration was lifted, as many as 12,000 Anglos with enslaved African Americans moved into Texas. In response to protests, Mexico allowed Texas slaveowners to "free" enslaved African Americans and then sign them to lifelong work contracts.

Discontent increased in the early 1830s. Anglos talked about defending their rights. More radical Anglos took action. They attacked Mexican soldiers and talked openly about Texas independence.

Desire for Statehood. Moderate Anglos, like Stephen Austin, and their *tejano* friends were more cautious. They wanted Texas to become a separate state within Mexico. At the time, Texas was part of the neighboring state of Coahuila (koh-ah-WEE-lah). Its capital, Saltillo (sahl-TEE-yoh), was more than 300 miles (480 kilometers) southwest of San Antonio. Texans resented having to travel so far to do business with the government.

In 1833, Stephen Austin went to Mexico City with a petition asking the government to grant Texas statehood within Mexico. The petition also asked for reforms such as the right to trial by jury. In response, Santa Anna pointed out that Texas had fewer than half the 80,000 people needed to become a state. However, Mexico agreed to permit trial by jury in Texas. It also ended the ban on Anglo immigration.

While in Mexico City, Austin was arrested. In a letter that fell into government hands, he had urged Texans to set up their own state even without the government's consent. After seven months in prison, he was released.

Santa Anna's Turnabout. In 1834, Santa Anna moved away from his earlier liberal reforms and began backing conservative goals. He set out to build a strong central government and impose his will on all of Mexico.

The Federalists felt betrayed. Unrest erupted across Mexico's borderlands. There was unrest in California, New Mexico, and Texas in the north. Santa Anna was soon busy crushing the rebellions.

There were two battles of the Alamo. In the first one in 1835, Mexican soldiers held out for 41 days before being overwhelmed by Texas volunteers. About half the Texas force was made up of *tejanos*.

A Time of Decision. In Texas, weary riders brought news of revolts to *tejanos* and Anglos. The moment of decision had come.

Among the *empresarios* who had brought settlers to Texas was Lorenzo de Zavala (sah-VAH-lah). Born in Yucatán, Zavala had served in Mexico's liberal government. When Santa Anna turned on the liberals, Zavala fled to Texas. Zavala had close business ties with Anglo leaders. He urged them to join with *tejanos* in fighting against Santa Anna and centralized government control.

Tejanos faced an especially difficult choice. Should they remain loyal to Mexico, which was dominated by a centralist government they disliked? Or should they join with the Anglos, who in turn would dominate them? By 1835, Anglos outnumbered *tejanos* 10 to 1.

Anglos, too, were divided. Stephen Austin headed the "peace" party. Along with Zavala and others, he hoped that by resisting central control they could restore federalists to power and remain a state within Mexico. William B. Travis headed the "war" party. Texas, he felt, should declare independence at once.

Headed for War. By mid-1835, armed clashes had occurred between Travis and Mexican forces. In October and November, fighting spread. More and more Texans now talked about separating from Mexico.

A few *tejanos* were delegates to a convention that discussed what action to take. Many were suspicious of the Anglos. In turn, Anglos distrusted *tejanos*. An Anglo leader called it "bad policy to . . . trust Mexicans in any matter connected with our government." Among prominent Mexicans, only Lorenzo de Zavala allied himself with the Anglos.

In response to attacks on Mexican forces, Santa Anna sent General Martín Perfecto de Cós (per-FEK-toh deh KOHS) to Texas with an army of 600. Rumors spread that Cós planned to haul 800 Texans to Mexico City in chains.

Those stories helped unite Texans. Austin stopped using the name Esteban and organized an army. With 200 volunteers, about half of them *tejanos*, Austin surrounded Cós and his army. For 41 days, the Mexicans held out in the Alamo, an abandoned mission in San Antonio. As cannons punched holes in the old mission's walls, Cós finally surrendered and withdrew from Texas. The victors began to rebuild the shattered walls in case they, too, might have to defend the Alamo.

Santa Anna had just crushed an uprising in the Mexican state of Zacatecas (sah-kah-TEH-kas), but he was determined to bring Texas back into line. Claiming he "preferred the hazards of war to the . . . life of the [presidential] palace," he raced north with an army of 6,000.

The army had to cross rain-swollen rivers. Hungry and tired, soldiers and horses collapsed. Many soldiers were untrained recruits. Some were Maya from southern Mexico who did not speak Spanish.

With about 1,500 soldiers, Santa Anna pressed ahead of the rest. In late February 1836, his group reached San Antonio. Most residents of the city had fled. But 182 rebels led by William Travis had prepared to hold the Alamo.

Taking Another Look

1. Why did Mexico pass new laws affecting settlers in Texas?

2. How did Anglos respond to the new laws?

3. **Critical Thinking** Juan Almonte (ahl-MOHN-teh), a Mexican official, claimed that Anglos "seek nothing more than pretexts [excuses] for a revolution whose first object will be separation from Coahuila and afterwards from the Republic." Agree or disagree with this statement, giving reasons for your answer.

3 TEXAS GAINS INDEPENDENCE
◆ How did Texas gain independence from Mexico?

By day, Gregorio Esparaza (es-pah-RAH-zah) loaded and fired the cannon. At night, he rested inside the battered chapel of the Alamo. Would the next day bring the final attack? He knew only too well what the outcome would be. Santa Anna, whose forces surrounded the Alamo, had placed a bright red banner on the highest steeple in San Antonio. Its message: No mercy for the defenders of the Alamo.

Esparaza was one of seven *tejanos* who had volunteered to defend the Alamo. Like the other defenders, he must have wondered why no relief forces had arrived. Early on, *tejanos* Colonel Juan Seguín (seh-GWEEN) and Antonio Cruz had slipped away, hoping to cross enemy lines to get help. Had they been captured?

Esparaza looked at his wife and children huddled nearby. Did he also think about his brother, Francisco, who had chosen to fight on the other side in this war?

Second Siege of the Alamo. Santa Anna's siege of the Alamo began on February 23, 1836. For the defenders, hope of rescue faded slowly. Although

Seguín had spread word of their desperate plight, he was unable to bring help.

On March 6, Santa Anna's forces stormed the battered mission. Wave upon wave of Mexicans fell in the assault. Urged forward by officers, more swarmed over the bodies of the fallen and fought their way into the mission. In the end, all the defenders were killed. Esparaza's family and a few others survived.

Declaring Independence. While Santa Anna surrounded the Alamo, Texans were meeting in Washington-on-the-Brazos. On March 2, 1836, delegates at this convention declared Texas independent. Two *tejanos*, José Antonio Navarro (nah-VAHR-roh) and Francisco Ruiz (RWEES), signed the document. So, too, did Lorenzo de Zavala. Delegates then chose David Burnet as president and Zavala as vice-president of Texas.

Independence still had to be won on the battlefield, however. Sam Houston, a former governor of Tennessee, was put in command of the army. Then came the news of the fall of the Alamo.

More bad news soon followed when Mexican forces captured 365 rebels at Goliad, south of San Antonio. Santa Anna sent orders to kill all the prisoners. They were pirates and traitors to Mexico, he claimed, and deserved no mercy.

Santa Anna pursued Houston and his forces as they retreated eastward. Settlers, too, fled before the Mexican army.

Battle of San Jacinto. When the revolt began, Texans called for help from the United States. Volunteers poured into Texas, including men like Davy Crockett who died at the Alamo. News of the Alamo and Goliad brought new waves of fighters.

As Houston's forces increased, he felt strong enough to attack.

On April 21, at the San Jacinto River, Santa Anna's soldiers rested after eating their midday meal. The general expected Houston to attack the next day. For some reason, the Mexicans did not post lookouts. Suddenly, the camp awoke as Texans stormed in shouting "Remember the Alamo" and "Remember Goliad."

Houston had caught the Mexicans by surprise. Within minutes, the attackers killed 600 Mexicans in revenge for Santa Anna's massacres. They also took 400 prisoners. Among the prisoners they discovered Santa Anna, disguised in peasant clothes.

Santa Anna was forced to sign two treaties. In them, he agreed to recognize the independence of Texas and accept its southern border at the Rio Grande. The Mexican Congress at once rejected the treaties, saying they had been signed under pressure.

The Republic of Texas. With the war over, the Republic of Texas wanted to join the United States. U.S. President Andrew Jackson welcomed Texan independence but opposed the admission of Texas as a new state. He did not want to risk a war with Mexico. Also, because Texas permitted slavery, admission would raise conflicts in Northern states where opposition to slavery was strong.

Tejanos had mixed reactions to independence. A few had fought for the cause. But most had had little reason to join the battle. They did not expect the change of government to affect their lives. After independence, however, Anglo dislike for *tejanos* remained widespread.

Colonel Seguín was the most prominent *tejano* in the battle for independence. He

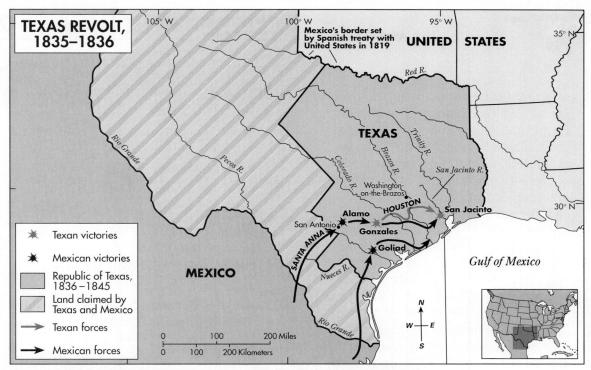

TEXAS REVOLT, 1835-1836

Mexico's border set by Spanish treaty with United States in 1819

UNITED STATES

TEXAS

Red R.

Rio Grande

Pecos R.

Colorado R.

Brazos R.

Trinity R.

San Jacinto R.

Washington-on-the-Brazos

Alamo   HOUSTON   San Jacinto

San Antonio   Gonzales

SANTA ANNA   Goliad

MEXICO

Nueces R.

Gulf of Mexico

Rio Grande

* Texan victories
* Mexican victories
Republic of Texas, 1836–1845
Land claimed by Texas and Mexico
→ Texan forces
→ Mexican forces

0   100   200 Miles
0   100   200 Kilometers

N W E S

The Texas fight for independence was brief, but bloody. Who won the battle at Goliad? In what direction did Mexican forces move after the battle at the Alamo? Where was the final major battle of the war?

had done heroic duty scouting for Houston in the days before the battle of San Jacinto. After the war, however, Anglos treated him with suspicion. In 1841, hounded by anti-Mexican prejudice, he had to flee with his family to Mexico. Sadly, he concluded he had become a "foreigner in my native land."

A few *tejanos* had better luck. *Ricos,* or wealthy landowners, like Lorenzo de Zavala benefited from independence. They profited from the trade that grew up between Texas and the United States.

LOOKING AHEAD

For Mexicans, the loss of Texas was a great blow. The Mexican government refused to recognize the independence of Texas. It continued to send military expeditions in attempts to retake the province.

Yet, for Mexicans the worst was yet to come. The United States was looking hungrily at lands to its west. The desire of the United States to expand would soon bring that nation into conflict with Mexico. The cost, for Mexico, would be enormous.

Taking Another Look

1. Describe three key events in the Texas struggle for independence.

2. What role did *tejanos* play in the Texas revolt?

3. **Critical Thinking** If you had been a *tejano* in 1836, what stand would you have taken on Texas independence? Give reasons for your position.

119

TEJANO PLACE NAMES

Have you ever wondered how places get their names? The cities of Corsicana and Seguin in Texas owe their names to *tejanos* who took part in the 1836 fight for independence.

The city of Corsicana is the seat of government of Navarro County in east central Texas. The city's name is related to the Mediterranean island of Corsica. An immigrant from that island settled in Texas when the region was under Spanish control. The immigrant's son, José Antonio Navarro, assisted Stephen Austin when Austin first started his colony on the Brazos River. Navarro was also one of three *tejano* signers of Texas's declaration of independence. Both Navarro County and Corsicana were named in honor of the Navarro family.

Seguin, a city east of San Antonio, gets its name from another prominent *tejano* family. Erasmo Seguín owned a ranch near San Antonio. During the first siege of the Alamo, he contributed horses, mules, and food to the Texan Army.

His son, Juan Seguín organized a company of *tejano* volunteers that fought alongside the Texas forces in many battles, including San Jacinto. Juan Seguín did not speak English. He used an interpreter to communicate with Sam Houston and other Anglo commanders. The city of Seguin adopted the family's name—without the accent.

CLOSE UP: Chapter 9

The Who, What, Where Of History

1. **Who** was Manuel de Mier y Terán?
2. **Where** did most *tejanos* live?
3. **Who** was Antonio López de Santa Anna?
4. **Who** was Steven Austin?
5. **Who** was Lorenzo de Zavala?
6. **Who** was Martín Perfecto de Cós?
7. **What** happened at the Alamo during the Texas struggle for independence?
8. **Where** did the final battle of the Texas war take place?
9. **What** happened to Juan Seguín after Texas gained independence?

Making The Connection

1. What was the connection between Santa Anna's return to Mexican centralism and the war in Texas?
2. What was the connection between the Republic of Texas and the United States?

Time Check

1. Which event happened *first*: Santa Anna begins to build a strong central government in Texas, Steven Austin is arrested in Mexico City, General Cós surrenders at the Alamo?
2. In what year did Texas win independence?
3. How much time passed between the Texas declaration of independence and the battle of San Jacinto?

What Would You Have Done?

1. Imagine that you are a *tejano* delegate to the Texas convention in 1835.

Would you vote to support the 1824 constitution of Mexico or to declare Texas independent? Why?

2. If you had been a U.S. citizen in 1836 would you have wanted Texas to join the United States? Why or why not?

Thinking And Writing About History

1. Imagine that you are a soldier in Santa Anna's army at the Alamo in 1836. The siege is just beginning. Write a diary entry describing your experiences and thoughts.

2. Suppose you are a *tejano* who just fought with Sam Houston at San Jacinto. Write a letter to a cousin in Mexico City describing the battle.

3. Imagine that you are a Texas legislator after the Battle of San Jacinto. Some people want to put Santa Anna on trial for war crimes. Others want to send him back to Mexico. Write a speech recommending a course of action.

Building Skills: Distinguishing Fact from Opinion

As you study history, teachers will often ask you to give the facts about people and events. At other times, they will ask for your opinion about a person or event. Facts and opinions are different, but they are connected.

A *fact* is a statement that you can check or test to see whether it is true. The statement "General Santa Anna led the Mexican army against the Texans" is a fact. You can look it up in reference books to see whether it is true or not.

An *opinion* is a person's attitude or thoughts about something. An opinion is neither true nor false. Consider the statement "Santa Anna could have defeated the Texas rebels if he hadn't stopped for a rest." That is an opinion. You cannot prove it true or untrue. The fact is that Santa Anna did not defeat the Texas rebels.

Facts and opinions are related because we form opinions based on facts. A person might hold the opinion that Santa Anna could have defeated the Texans because of the following facts: Santa Anna's army was bigger than Houston's, the Mexican general had a long record of successes in battle, and many of Houston's soldiers were raw recruits.

Read the statements below. Then, on a separate sheet of paper, write the numbers of the sentences that state opinions.

1. Santa Anna called himself "the Napoleon of the West."

2. The Texans should have shot Santa Anna after the war.

3. Stephen Austin was the wisest leader the Texans had.

4. The Roman Catholic Church and the *ricos* favored centralism.

5. Federalism is a better form of government than centralism.

6. Sam Houston was a better military leader than Santa Anna.

Express Yourself!

Study the map of the Texas Revolt on page 119. On a sheet of paper, draw your own outline map of Texas. Mark the places where major battles of the Texas revolution took place. For each place, write a brief description of what happened and why it was important.

SECTIONS

1 Background to War

2 Mexico and the United States at War

3 Aftermath of War

In 1854, Mexican and U.S. troops met at Mesilla, New Mexico, to transfer power over territory in the Gadsden Purchase from Mexico to the United States.

CHAPTER 10

War Between the United States and Mexico

(1838–1848)

THINKING ABOUT THE CHAPTER

How did the Mexican lands of Texas, New Mexico, and California become part of the United States?

People in the northern Mexican town of Matamoros (mah-tah-MOH-rohs) came out of their homes to watch as several dozen Mexicans, Cherokee, and Caddo rode north, toward Texas. The aim of the riders was to stir up armed opposition by *tejanos* within the Republic of Texas.

The year was 1838—two years after the Battle of San Jacinto (see page 118). The defeat of the Mexican army in that battle had brought independence to Texas. The Mexican government, however, did not recognize the Republic of Texas. It was determined to take Texas back.

The group from Matamoros rode across Texas, to regions

in the north and east. Along the way, the Mexicans spoke with Kickapoo, Choctaw, and other Native Americans. The Mexicans offered to return the hunting lands that Anglo settlers had been taking from Native Americans if they joined Mexico in the fight against the Anglos. The Native Americans, angry at the rough treatment they had received from the Anglos, found the offer attractive.

Small groups of Mexicans, *tejanos*, and Native Americans then attacked Anglo colonies across northern Texas. Mexican military commanders, meanwhile, made plans for a full-scale invasion of Texas. Those plans collapsed, however, when a civil war broke out in northern Mexico in 1838. As a result, the drive to reconquer Texas had to be postponed.

1 BACKGROUND TO WAR
◆ Why did war break out between
◆ Mexico and the United States in 1846?

The creation of the Republic of Texas had confirmed fears that many Mexicans held about their northern neighbor, the United States. Many Mexicans were sure that the Texas revolt against Mexico in 1836 was part of a U.S. plot to steal Texas. They believed the United States wanted to take New Mexico and California as well.

Recognition by the United States. The United States officially recognized the Republic of Texas as an independent nation in 1837. Mexicans were far from happy with this action. But at least the United States had not moved to annex Texas, that is, make it a part of the United States. Many U.S. citizens and most Anglos in Texas favored just such a move. But people in the Northern United States did not wish to see another slave state enter the Union.

Mexicans were not reassured that the United States did not annex Texas immediately. The United States had given up its claim to Texas "forever" in a 1819 treaty with Spain (see page 87) but Mexicans feared that such promises could easily be broken.

Arguing Over a Border. Mexicans had long held that the southern border of Texas lay along the Nueces (noo-AY-suhs) River (see map, page 125). That river had been the border since Spanish times. But Texans insisted that the border lay farther to the west and south, at the Río Bravo del Norte—or the Rio Grande, as the Texans called it.

The Rio Grande begins in the mountains of Colorado. It flows south through New Mexico, then past El Paso, Laredo, and Matamoros to the Gulf of Mexico. If the Rio Grande were the border, Texas would be a huge republic indeed. A large area of Mexico's province of New Mexico would be part of Texas under this claim. Texas would be so big that the United States might decide to annex Texas after all.

To support its claim to the disputed land, the Texas government sent a force of more than 300 armed men toward New Mexico's capital, Santa Fe, in 1841. But Native Americans captured most of the expedition's horses. Then the Texans got lost before reaching Santa Fe.

Manuel Armijo, the governor of New Mexico, learned of the Texans' approach. He and the Mexican army were waiting for them. Suffering from thirst and exhaustion, the ragged Texans surrendered without a fight. Mexican soldiers then chained the Texans together and marched them across 2,000 miles (3,200 kilometers) of deserts and mountains to prison in Mexico. For the Mexican people, this was a revenge of sorts for the humiliating way Texans had treated

General Santa Anna after the Battle of San Jacinto (see page 118).

"El Desierto Muerto." The area claimed by Texas that lay south and west of the Nueces River was called *"el desierto muerto,"* or the dead desert. The Comanche claimed it as a hunting ground, and almost no one else lived there.

At times, the governments of both Mexico and Texas sent war parties across the "dead desert" to attack more settled areas. Twice in 1842, Mexican soldiers seized San Antonio, some 75 miles (120 kilometers) north of the Nueces. Retreating after the second attack, the Mexican soldiers captured all 67 male Texans of San Antonio.

In response, a troop of Texas volunteers raided Laredo on the Rio Grande. Having done so, the main force withdrew. But a group of the volunteers marched farther on into Mexico. A Mexican force captured them and, when the Texans attempted to flee, shot every tenth man. These incidents made clear that Texas and Mexico were headed for a showdown.

The Annexation Crisis. Not long after the Laredo incident, a new crisis arose. The Texas government passed a resolution claiming lands as far west as California. The resolution drew U.S. attention to Texas. U.S. leaders knew that Texas had already signed trade treaties with Great Britain. They feared that Texas might make an alliance with Great Britain. If it did, then one day a vast Texas empire, closely tied to Europe's mightiest power, might reach all the way to the Pacific Ocean. Such an empire would challenge the power of the United States in North America.

U.S. leaders would not risk such a possibility. They decided to ignore the 1819 treaty in which the United States had promised not to annex Texas. Members of Congress who favored U.S. expansion then overcame the opposition of the anti-slavery forces. In February 1845, the U.S. Congress voted to annex Texas as the 28th state.

An "Insulting" Offer. Mexico was furious at the U.S. move. It recalled its ambassador from Washington and the Mexican army prepared for war. But the U.S. President, James K. Polk, thought Mexico might still be willing to negotiate over its claim to Texas.

Polk sent a U.S. agent, John Slidell, to Mexico to work out an agreement. Actually, Polk had his eyes on more than Texas. He told Slidell, in addition to trying to settle the Texas question, to offer $5 million for New Mexico and up to $25 million for California.

Upon hearing of the U.S. offer, the Mexican public exploded in outrage. Mexicans were insulted that the United States thought Mexico would be willing to accept money in exchange for land. Military officers forced Mexican President José Joaquín Herrera (eh-RREH-rah) to resign. They accused him of "seeking to avoid a necessary and glorious war."

Guns Along the Rio Grande. Faced with Mexico's refusal to sell its land, President Polk took steps that brought the nations to the brink of war. Polk had already sent U.S. troops to the Nueces River at Corpus Christi (see map, page 125). When Mexico refused Slidell's offers, Polk ordered General Zachary Taylor and his 3,500 soldiers south to the Rio Grande. A small unit of U.S. soldiers began building what they called Fort Texas just across the river from Matamoros.

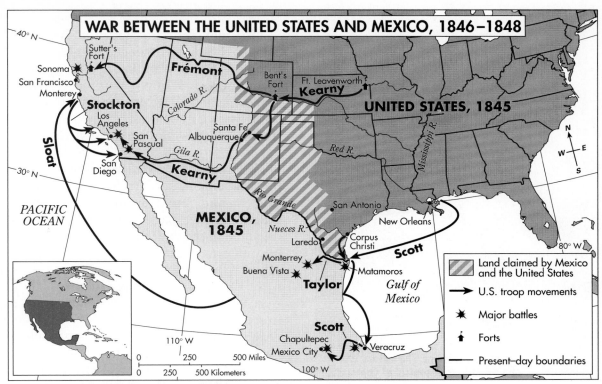

WAR BETWEEN THE UNITED STATES AND MEXICO, 1846–1848

A dispute over the territory in cross-hatching led to a brief but bloody war. The United States had three aims: to occupy Mexico, to take California and New Mexico, and to march on Mexico City.

The Mexican commander at Matamoros, General Mariano Arista (ah-REES-tah), was furious that U.S. soldiers would build a fort on Mexican soil. He warned U.S. forces to move back north of the Nueces. Then on April 23, 1846, Arista sent 1,600 men across the Rio Grande. The Mexicans fired on a unit of U.S. soldiers. Sixteen of the soldiers fell dead or wounded.

The skirmish was just what President Polk had been waiting for. When news of it reached Washington on May 9, Polk asked Congress to declare war. He announced, "Mexico has . . . shed American blood on American soil." Most members of Congress accepted Polk's claim that land south of the Nueces was "American soil." They granted Polk's request. The United States and Mexico were at war. Many U.S. citizens opposed the war, feeling that it was unjust and also that it might add more slave-holding territory to the Union.

Many Mexicans, on the other hand, favored the war. They saw it as the chance to reclaim stolen lands and halt U.S. expansion. General Arista spoke for many when he said, "Forced into war, we enter a struggle that cannot be avoided without failing in what is most sacred to man."

Taking Another Look

1. What lands did both Texas and Mexico claim?

2. Why did the United States fear Texas expansion to California?

3. **Critical Thinking** In your opinion, which side "started" the war? Explain.

At the battle of San Pascual, a band of *californios* defeated a force of U.S. soldiers. The victory was temporary. Soon the U.S. took control of California.

2 MEXICO AND THE UNITED STATES ◆ AT WAR

◆ What factors contributed to the U.S. victory over Mexico?

With music playing and flags flying, Mexican soldiers crossed the Rio Grande to repel the invading U.S. army. For three days, boats shuttled across the wide river near Matamoros, carrying Mexican troops to the northern shore.

General Arista's plan was to wipe out General Taylor's army as it carried supplies to Fort Texas. Arista was confident of victory, for he had almost three men to every one of Taylor's.

Taylor, however, was the better general. His army killed or wounded an estimated 1,200 Mexicans in two battles on May 8 and 9, 1846. Three days after their confident crossing of the Rio Grande, the Mexican soldiers retreated to the south side of the river.

The war had not started well for Mexico. It soon worsened. The Mexicans faced a U.S. war plan that had three aims: to occupy northern Mexico, to take California and New Mexico, and to march on Mexico City and force Mexico to surrender. The first aim had been achieved.

The Loss of California. Long before the war began, settlers from the United States had been coming to Upper California (see page 99). Many of them dreamed of the day when California would become part of the United States. Mexican officials had allowed in the immigrants from the United States. However, they were keeping a watchful eye for any moves to separate California from Mexico.

At Sonoma, California, Manuel Vallejo (see page 98), a well-known *californio* rancher and military commander, answered a knock on his door on the morning of June 14, 1846. Facing him were 40 armed Anglos. They took Vallejo prisoner, along with 17 others. The Anglos declared California independent and hoisted a flag bearing the image of a grizzly bear. They announced the creation of the Bear Flag Republic.

No word of the war between the United States and Mexico had yet reached California. Still, creation of the Bear Flag Republic touched off U.S. naval attacks on Monterey and Los Angeles. Both surrendered, and the United States claimed possession of California.

The Charge at San Pascual. The *californios*, however, were not yet beaten. In September, they took back Los Angeles. Then came word that General Stephen W. Kearny and 100 U.S. soldiers were approaching. Kearny had seized New Mexico in August and was planning to help in the takeover of California.

General Andrés Pico (PEE-koh) and a small force of *californios* rode east to meet the U.S. troops at the Native American village of San Pascual (sahn pahs-KWAHL). Pico and his soldiers were waiting on horseback in the early morning darkness of December 6, 1846. They heard the creak of leather and whispered words in English. U.S. guns barked, and 160 of the Mexican horsemen rode off in retreat. But this was a trick. As planned, it drew the U.S. soldiers deep into a trap.

Suddenly, the fleeing Mexican riders reined in their horses. Turning around, they charged into the ranks of the surprised U.S. soldiers. One third of the Americans fell dead or wounded.

The victory of the *californios* at the Battle of San Pascual did not end U.S. advances. With reinforcements from San Diego, Kearny went on to recapture Los Angeles in January 1847. Nearby, General Pico surrendered to Frémont. The war in California was over.

The Invasions of Mexico. Meanwhile, Mexicans struggled to push back U.S. armies advancing to Mexico from the north. General Santa Anna took command of the Mexican army. The general was older now, limping about on a wooden leg. (His left limb had been smashed by a French shell at Veracruz in 1838.)

Santa Anna led 15,000 men against General Zachary Taylor's army in the Battle of Buena Vista (BWEH-nah VEES-tah) in February 1847. In the hard-fought battle, the Mexicans at one point almost surrounded the U.S. forces. However, greater numbers of U.S. cannon brought defeat to Santa Anna's army.

With his remaining forces, Santa Anna then turned to face a bigger threat. In early March, General Winfield Scott and some 10,000 U.S. troops landed at Veracruz on

◆ **SNAPSHOT OF THE TIMES**

1845	United States annexes Texas.
1846	U.S. Congress declares war against Mexico.
	Anglos in California announce the creation of the Bear Flag Republic.
1846–1847	Battle of San Pascual
1847	Battle of Buena Vista
	Mexican cadets defend Chapultepec.
	U.S. General Scott takes Mexico City.
1848	Mexico and the United States sign the Treaty of Guadalupe Hidalgo.

the Gulf Coast. After capturing the fortress there, they set off on the long route over the mountains to Mexico City.

The Boy Heroes at Chapultepec. By September 1847, the U.S. Army had fought its way to the gates of Mexico City. There, Santa Anna made a last-ditch effort to stop Scott's advance. All day on September 12, 1847, U.S. artillery shells came down on Mexican troops. The hour for the final assault had come.

The U.S. troops aimed their main attack at Chapultepec (chuh-POOL-tuh-pek) Castle, built on a high rocky hill just outside the city. Once the Spanish viceroy's castle, Chapultepec was now Mexico's National Military Academy. Cadets at the academy, some as young as 13, were among the 1,000 Mexican soldiers who resisted a much larger U.S. force.

Heavy U.S. artillery fire fell on Chapultepec, shattering walls and ceilings.

127

U.S. troops climbed the castle walls, setting off brutal hand-to-hand fighting in the castle. Finally, when all hope was lost, the Mexican commander surrendered.

Some of the cadets, however, refused to give up. Francisco Márquez (MAHR-kes), Agustín Melgar (mel-GAHR), Juan Escutia (es-KOO-tyah), Fernando Montes de Oca (OH-kah), Vicente Suárez (SWAH-res), and Juan de la Barrera (bah-RREH-rah) fought to the bitter end. Escutia, fearing that U.S. soldiers would seize the Mexican flag, hauled it down and ran for a stairway. Struck by a bullet, he fell to his death on the rocks below. The six youths went down in history as *los niños héroes*—"the boy heroes." Today, a monument at the foot of Chapultepec Castle honors their memory.

After taking Chapultepec, the U.S. soldiers stormed into Mexico City. General Scott entered the city as a conqueror on September 14, 1847. To the dismay of Mexicans, U.S. marines raised a U.S. flag above the "Halls of Montezuma," the National Palace. The war had ended.

Taking Another Look

1. What was the Bear Flag Republic?
2. Why are *los niños héroes* remembered?
3. **Critical Thinking** Why was it hard for Mexico to defend California?

3 AFTERMATH OF WAR

◆ What promises did the United States make in the Treaty of Guadalupe Hidalgo?

Early in February 1848, diplomats of Mexico and the United States met at the village of Guadalupe Hidalgo (gwah-dah-LOO-peh ee-DAHL-goh), just outside Mexico City, to sign the peace treaty ending the war. It was a sad day for Mexico. The Treaty of Guadalupe Hidalgo granted the United States title to almost half of Mexico's territory. The pain of the loss was made greater when news spread that nine days after the signing of the treaty, gold had been discovered in California.

Terms of the Treaty. The treaty set the Rio Grande as the southern border of Texas. It recognized Texas as a part of the United States. In addition, it turned over to the United States all of what is presently California and New Mexico, Arizona, Nevada, Utah, as well as part of today's Colorado, and Wyoming. (Five years later, the United States bought the southern parts of present-day Arizona and New Mexico from Mexico in the so-called Gadsden Purchase.)

In return, the United States agreed to pay Mexico $15 million. It also agreed to pay off $3.25 million of Mexico's debt to U.S. citizens.

Protection for the People. Many Mexicans worried about how *californios, tejanos,* and *nuevomexicanos* would be treated by the U.S. government and U.S. citizens. One Mexican diplomat said:

Our race, our unfortunate people, will have to wander in search of hospitality in a strange land, only to be ejected [thrown out] later. Descendants of the Indians that we are, the North Americans hate us . . . and they consider us unworthy to form with them one nation and one society.

Because of such fears, Mexico's negotiators insisted that the treaty include protection for Mexicans who lived in the lost territories. The treaty gave those people a choice. They could move south into what

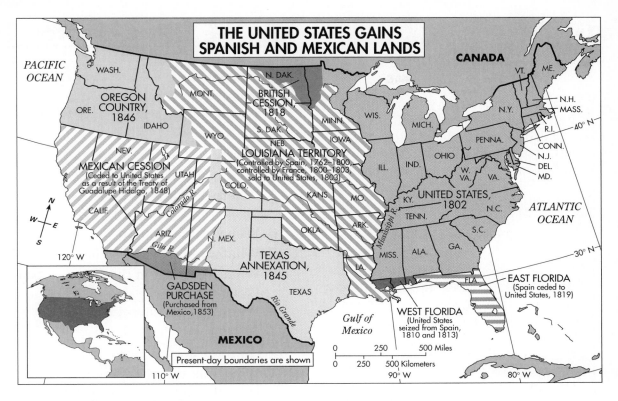

THE UNITED STATES GAINS SPANISH AND MEXICAN LANDS

PACIFIC OCEAN

CANADA

WASH.

OREGON COUNTRY, 1846

ORE.

IDAHO

MEXICAN CESSION
(Ceded to United States as a result of the Treaty of Guadalupe Hidalgo, 1848)

NEV.

UTAH

CALIF.

ARIZ.

Gila R.

120° W

GADSDEN PURCHASE
(Purchased from Mexico, 1853)

MEXICO

110° W

MONT.

WYO.

COLO.

N. MEX.

TEXAS ANNEXATION, 1845

TEXAS

Rio Grande

Colorado R.

N. DAK.

BRITISH CESSION, 1818

S. DAK.

NEB.

LOUISIANA TERRITORY
(Controlled by Spain, 1762–1800, controlled by France, 1800–1803, sold to United States, 1803)

KANS.

OKLA.

MINN.

IOWA

MO.

ARK.

LA.

WIS.

ILL.

MISS.

MICH.

IND.

OHIO

KY.

TENN.

ALA.

W. VA.

VA.

N.C.

S.C.

GA.

Mississippi R.

UNITED STATES, 1802

VT.

ME.

N.H.

MASS.

N.Y.

R.I.

CONN.

N.J.

DEL.

MD.

PENNA.

40° N

ATLANTIC OCEAN

30° N

FLA.

EAST FLORIDA
(Spain ceded to United States, 1819)

WEST FLORIDA
(United States seized from Spain, 1810 and 1813)

Gulf of Mexico

0   250   500 Miles
0   250   500 Kilometers
90° W

80° W

Present-day boundaries are shown

What territories were lost by Mexico as a result of the war between Mexico and the United States? What lands on this map were not directly won or purchased from Mexico?

remained of Mexico and continue to be Mexican citizens. Or they could stay on and enjoy "all the rights of citizens of the United States according to the principles of the Constitution."

It was a difficult choice. Some 2,000 *californios* and *nuevomexicanos* decided to accept Mexico's offer of small farms and move south. A far larger number remained in what was now the United States.

Taking Another Look

1. What lands did Mexico give up under the Treaty of Guadalupe Hidalgo?

2. How did the treaty seek to protect *californios, nuevomexicanos,* and *tejanos?*

3. **Critical Thinking** Why do you think more *californios* and *nuevomexicanos* chose to stay in lands controlled by the United States after the war than chose to move to Mexico?

LOOKING AHEAD

The Treaty of Guadalupe Hidalgo brought an end to open war between Mexico and the United States. But it did not end the distrust and suspicion that many people in each nation felt toward those in the other. The former Mexicans in the areas that now were part of the United States faced especially difficult times in the years after the war.

129

For hundreds of years, church bells have chimed through the Spanish Plaza in what is today downtown Los Angeles. Today, the church bells remind listeners of the history of the Plaza, which has been a part of Los Angeles since the founding of the city in 1781.

The first plaza was laid out when a group of settlers founded the Pueblo de Los Angeles—the town of Los Angeles. After floods destroyed that site, a new plaza was rebuilt nearby between 1800 and 1812. The homes of wealthy Los Angeles *californios* ringed the plaza. However, most of these homes disappeared long ago. One exception is Lugo House, the oldest two-story building in Los Angeles. It was built in 1840 by Don Vincente Lugo (LOO-goh).

Nearby is Olvera Street, named for Don Agustín Olvera (ohl-VEH-rah), who fought against U.S. forces in 1846. Olvera Street is one of the oldest streets in Los Angeles. Today, shops and restaurants line the street, some housed in adobe buildings dating back to the 1800s. Every December, Mexican Americans stage the pageant of *Las Posadas* (lahs poh-SAH-dahs), the lodgings. It depicts Mary's search for a place to give birth to her baby, Jesus. Los Angeles residents treasure the Spanish Plaza and Olvera Street as reminders of the small town Los Angeles once was.

CLOSE UP: Chapter 10

The Who, What, Where of History

1. **Where** is the Nueces River?
2. **What** did Texans call the Río Bravo del Norte?
3. **Where** was *el desierto muerto*?
4. **Who** was José Joaquín Herrera?
5. **Where** did Zachary Taylor build Fort Texas?
6. **Who** was Mariano Arista?
7. **What** was the Bear Flag Republic?
8. **What** happened in the Battle of San Pascual?
9. **Where** is Chapultepec Castle?

Making the Connection

1. What was the connection between U.S. annexation of Texas and the war between the United States and Mexico?
2. What was the connection between the U.S.-Mexican War and the creation of the Bear Flag Republic?

Time Check

1. In which year did Texas send an expedition to Santa Fe?
2. How long after the United States annexed Texas did the United States declare war on Mexico?
3. In what year was the Treaty of Guadalupe Hidalgo signed?

What Would You Have Done?

1. Imagine that you are an adviser to the Mexican government in 1838. What strategy would you propose for recovering Texas?

2. If you had been a Mexican negotiator for the Treaty of Guadalupe Hidalgo in 1848, what rights would you have requested for *californios, tejanos,* and *nuevomexicanos?*

3. Imagine that you are a *californio* rancher in 1848. Will you move to Mexico or stay in California?

Thinking and Writing About History

1. Imagine that you are a resident of Matamoros in the spring of 1846. Write a letter to a friend telling about the invasion of the U.S. soldiers.

2. Write the story of the Battle of San Pascual as one of the *californio* participants might have told it to a grandchild many years after the event.

3. Reread the section about the boy heroes at Chapultepec. Write a poem or short story that describes their defense of the castle.

Building Skills: Stating the Main Idea in Your Own Words

You are at your desk and the student behind you whispers a question. "Did you read the chapter last night?" "Sure I read it," you reply. From behind, the student says, "Well, what's it about?" You try to explain but are unable to find the words. "Oh, it's about Mexico and the United States and things like that. You know." Your classmate probably does not know. And it sounds as though you need to think about the *main ideas* of the chapter.

One way to be sure that you understand and remember the main ideas of what you read is to put them into your own words. Read the following paragraph:

The equipment of the two armies was far from equal. Mexican cannons fired solid balls that hit the ground and bounced, so that U.S. soldiers often could jump aside. U.S. cannons, on the other hand, fired shells that hit the ground and burst, splattering metal balls that tore soldiers' arms and limbs. The U.S. artillery had a longer range besides.

1. On a separate sheet of paper, write the sentence that states the main idea of the paragraph. Next, try to rewrite the sentence in your own words.

2. Find the main idea of the following paragraph and write a sentence that states it in your own words.

The Treaty of Guadalupe Hidalgo included protection for Mexicans who lived in California, New Mexico, and Texas. Articles Eight and Nine of the treaty gave those people a choice. They could remain Mexican citizens and move south. Or else they could stay on and enjoy "all the rights of citizens of the United States according to the principles of the Constitution."

Express Yourself!

Create a calendar of the events of the war between Mexico and the United States from 1846 to 1848. Work with a group of classmates to list the month and year of six or seven events of the war. When you finish, write each event at the top of a separate piece of paper. Write the month and year of the event as well. Then, create an illustration for each event. Display your calendar in your classroom.

Many Mexicans suffered by becoming Mexican Americans. The Lugo family of Los Angeles had their 30,000 acre ranch reduced to 400 acres by 1870 because land was taken by Anglo squatters.

SECTIONS

1 Living Under a New Flag

2 Land Claims and Courts

3 Looking for Justice

CHAPTER 11

Foreigners in Their Own Land

(1848–1870s)

THINKING ABOUT THE CHAPTER

What were some results of the United States' takeover of Mexican lands?

"Gold in California! A bonanza!"

Word of the 1848 discovery of gold at Sutter's Fort in northern California spread like wildfire. The discovery came just days before the Treaty of Guadalupe Hidalgo turned California over to the United States.

Many *californios* headed for the mines, hoping to strike it rich. Don Antonio Coronel (koh-roh-NEL), from Los Angeles, organized one party of *californio* gold-seekers. Luck was with them. A woman in the group, Dolores Sepúlveda (seh-POOL-veh-dah), found a gold nugget that weighed 12 ounces (.336 kilograms).

But their good fortune lasted only briefly. Soon, a flood of new people poured into California to join the search.

California's population jumped from 10,000 in 1848 to 110,000 by the end of 1849, and more than 250,000 in 1852. Most of the newcomers were Anglos from the eastern United States. They considered Spanish-speaking people to be "foreign" intruders in California. Mob violence and lynchings took the lives of many miners of Mexican descent. The violence and the hostility of newcomers forced *californios* such as Coronel to give up the search. Sadly, Coronel declared, "For me, gold mining is finished."

Californios had glimpsed the future. They, and the Spanish-speaking natives of all the conquered borderlands, would be treated as second-class citizens. Often, they would be sneered at and deprived of their rights. *Californios*, *nuevomexicanos*, and *tejanos* would soon feel like foreigners in their own land.

1 LIVING UNDER A NEW FLAG
◆ How did life change for Mexicans
◆ who now found themselves U.S. citizens?

About 75,000 Mexicans and 180,000 Native Americans lived in the lands that the United States took from Mexico. Anglos tended to look down on both these groups. Most Anglos would have agreed with the words of a U.S. soldier who said, "The Mexican, like the poor Indian, is doomed to retire [retreat] before the more enterprising [ambitious] Anglo-Americans."

Opportunity Calls. Mexican Americans, however, were practical people. They did not intend to retreat. Indeed, many were eager to take advantage of new opportunities. For the owners of large southern California *ranchos*, for example, the gold-mining boom offered the chance of a lifetime. Gold miners needed to eat, and the *ranchos* could provide plenty of beef. Because of the increased demand, the price of longhorn cattle rose from $1 or $2 a head before the gold rush to $70 in 1849.

People from the Mexican state of Sonora, just south of present-day Arizona, were also enterprising. Merchants piled their goods onto mules and headed for California's mines. Thousands of other Sonorans came to prospect for gold or take jobs as mule drivers, cooks, and laborers.

As gold seekers poured into California, mining towns sprang up. Many of these boomtowns had a Mexican flavor. One of them was Hornitos (ohr-NEE-tohs), which grew up around a Mexican miner's gold strike. Anglo, Chinese, and other miners came, but Hornitos kept its Mexican character. Many of its businesses were owned and operated by people of Mexican descent.

A Change in Government. U.S. rule brought great changes to the government of the former Mexican borderlands. California's booming population quickly qualified it for statehood. With its large Anglo majority, California gained admission to the Union in 1850.

New Mexico's 60,000 residents, however, were almost wholly of Mexican or Native American descent. With no gold rush to attract Anglo settlers, Mexican Americans remained in the majority for many decades. New Mexico and Arizona (which became a separate territory in 1863) did not become states until 1912. Moreover, most of the top government jobs in the two territories were held by Anglos appointed by officials in Washington.

When the borderlands were part of Mexico, the *ricos* had controlled government. Now that their lands were under U.S. control, they made every effort to hold on to their influence. To do so, they joined with Anglos in local governments. This tactic worked best in New Mexico, where the Anglo population grew slowly. New Mexico's landowners, for example, became political bosses. They had influence because they could control the votes of workers on their estates. Some *ricos* of New Mexico served in the territorial legislatures and as delegates to the U.S. Congress.

In northern California, the *ricos* had less influence because Anglos quickly outnumbered Latinos there and in the state as a whole. In southern California, however, Mexican Americans were more numerous than Anglos for a few decades after 1850. There, old *californio* families kept some of their political power.

Writing California's Constitution.

There were 48 delegates to the 1849 convention that wrote California's first state constitution. Of those delegates, eight were Spanish-speaking *californios*. They were eager to protect their own rights as landowners and as members of the Spanish-speaking minority.

They had some success. For example, they blocked a move to limit the right to vote to Anglos. They insisted that all state laws be printed in Spanish as well as in English. They also insisted that tax assessors be elected locally. This would help *californios* protect themselves from being taxed more than Anglos.

Some new California laws were based on Spanish and Mexican laws rather than U.S. laws. Since Anglos had little experience dealing with rights to water in a dry land, California followed Spanish and Mexican practices. Laws dealing with mineral rights and mining also followed

"The whole country resounds with the cry of 'gold! GOLD! GOLD!'" said a California newspaper describing the gold rush. People rushed to California to get rich quick. The *californios* were now seen as "foreigners."

Spanish customs. California also adopted a property law based on Spanish traditions. It gave married women greater rights over property than they would have had under Anglo law.

Discrimination. As the Anglo population of California grew larger, the legislature paid less attention to the concerns of *californios*. It began to pass laws that harmed Latinos. One example was the Foreign Miners' Tax of 1850.

Anglo gold-seekers argued that "foreigners" should not be allowed to "steal" a precious national resource like gold. They pressed the legislature to pass a tax of $16 a month on all foreign miners. Included among the "foreigners" were *californios*. These people were natives of California. They had lived their whole lives there. By the terms of the Treaty of Guadalupe Hidalgo of 1848, they were U.S. citizens. Yet the act lumped the *californios* with miners from Mexico and from other Spanish-speaking countries, such as Chile and Peru. Passage of the tax was followed by outbreaks of mob violence against *californios* and against foreigners. As a result, thousands of Latinos left the goldfields.

Another California law, passed in 1855, showed the feelings of many Anglos toward Mexican Americans. The act allowed police to arrest people who had no visible means of support. It was applied almost solely against people of Spanish descent.

Taking Another Look

1. Why did California become a U.S. state long before New Mexico and Arizona did?

2. **a.** Where did Mexican American *ricos* have the most influence? **b.** Why?

3. **Critical Thinking** In what ways did *californios* come to feel like foreigners in their native land?

2 LAND CLAIMS AND COURTS
◆ How did many Mexicans lose their
◆ lands after the United States took possession of the Southwest?

Vicente Peralta watched in horror as Anglo settlers moved onto his 19,000-acre (7,600-hectare) Rancho San Antonio, along the eastern shore of San Francisco Bay. The settlers put up fences that kept Peralta's cattle from reaching the best grazing land. They threatened to shoot anyone who tried to stop them.

Other *californio* landowners faced similar problems. Yet the Treaty of Guadalupe Hidalgo had promised *californios* and other former Mexicans the "free enjoyment of their liberty and property." What had happened?

Examining the Land Grants. *Ricos* like Peralta held their large estates under land grants issued either by Spain or by Mexican authorities after Mexico became independent in 1821. When the United States took over, some 800 land grants had been issued in California. Another 300 had been given in New Mexico. The grants gave **title,** or ownership, to millions of acres of land. Some of the grants were held by Anglos who had married into pioneer Spanish families. Most, however, were held by people of Spanish descent.

Many Anglo newcomers were unhappy with the land grants. They claimed that the holders of the grants were not putting the vast acreages to productive use. In reality, the Anglos wanted more land for themselves.

1848	Discovery of gold in California brings a flood of Anglo settlers to the region.
1850	California becomes a U.S. state.
	California passes Foreign Miners' Tax.
1851	Land Act of 1851 allows for the examination of land titles in California.
1854	U.S. government begins survey of land in New Mexico.
1855	California law allows police to arrest people with no visible means of support.
	El Clamor Público founded.
1873	Juan Nepomuceno Cortina arrested in Mexico.

Because of such feelings, the U.S. Congress called for reviews of land grants in California and New Mexico. The reviews forced landowners to spend a great deal of money on lawyers to defend their title claims. While most titles were upheld, the costs of defending them were very high. Many people had to sell off part of their land in order to pay the costs.

Some Anglos took advantage of the review of land titles. They moved onto the *ranchos* as **squatters,** or illegal settlers. They built cabins and put up fences. If the landowner lost his or her title to the land, the squatters would be there to claim a piece of it.

The Land Act of 1851. Under the Land Act of 1851, the federal government set up a commission to examine land titles in California. The commission's work was not easy. The boundaries of the land grants were often uncertain. One corner of the property might be described in a land grant as located at "a bullock's [young bull's] skull." Another corner might be by "a sycamore tree." Deeds and other documents were often missing.

The commission's work took four years. Court appeals dragged on for a dozen years more. Meanwhile, squatters continued to grab more *rancho* lands. At the Peralta ranch, squatters rounded up Peralta cattle and took them to market. They cut down orchards for lumber. They even blocked off the doorways of the homes of the aging Peralta and his sons. Finally, the Peraltas could bear it no longer. They gave up their land and moved out.

In all, the land commission examined 813 titles. It rejected only 32. But legal expenses, squatters, and fraud cost many landowners like the Peraltas vast stretches of land. By the 1880s, the land grants of *californios* had shrunk to one fourth their former size.

Land Ownership in New Mexico and Texas. In New Mexico, a federally appointed land surveyor began work in 1854. That work dragged on year after year. By the time the title checking ended, more than 60 years had passed. During this time, many families lost their lands to squatters or were forced to sell them to pay lawyers' and court fees.

Land ownership in Texas presented fewer problems. Most of the original land grants had been made to *empresarios* (see page 101). The *empresarios,* in turn, had sold off land to settlers. Good records had been kept, and local land boards had settled most land claims during the time that Texas was a republic.

Taking Another Look

1. What legal grounds did *ricos* have for their land claims?
2. On what grounds did Anglos challenge the land claims of Mexican Americans?
3. **Critical Thinking** In your opinion, did the United States fulfill its treaty obligation to protect the property rights of Mexican Americans? Explain.

3 LOOKING FOR JUSTICE

◆ How did Mexican Americans respond
◆ to the prejudice and discrimination they faced in their new nation?

Manuel Domínguez (doh-MEEN-ghes) was a man of influence among *californios*. He had served as a delegate to California's constitutional convention of 1849. He had signed the state's first constitution. He was a county supervisor and a respected landowner.

In 1857, Domínguez appeared in a San Francisco court to testify for a defendant. But he was not permitted to be a witness. The opposing lawyer quickly pointed out that Domínguez was a *mestizo,* someone who was part Native American. Under the law, Native Americans could not testify in court.

If a well-known and respected man like Domínguez faced such treatment, what was life like for most ordinary men and women of Spanish descent? Mexican Americans and Mexican citizens faced harsh and constant discrimination in the years after the U.S. takeover of the borderlands.

The U.S. flag flies over the San Fernando Cathedral in San Antonio, Texas. While everyday life seemed to go on as usual after the U.S. takeover, Mexican Americans often faced harsh discrimination.

Seeking to Adjust. Most Mexican Americans attempted to adjust peacefully to their new situation. They accepted U.S. rule and did their best to live by the new laws. A Los Angeles newspaper of the 1850s *El Clamor Público* (el klah-MOHR POO-blee-koh) (see page 140), advised its readers to give up "all bygone traditions, and become Americanized all over—in language, in manners, in customs and habits."

For most people, adjustment meant keeping old ways but trying to adapt them to new realities. Some Mexican Americans set out to learn English, but most of them continued to speak mainly Spanish. They also continued to practice the Roman Catholic religion in a state that was now largely Protestant. But they tried to follow the advice of *El Clamor Público* in other parts of their lives. No matter what Mexicans did, however, most of them had an uneasy sense of being powerless in their own land.

Social Bandits. Some Mexican Americans were unwilling to play by rules that were stacked against them. Some of them became outlaws. They robbed banks and stagecoaches and rustled cattle. Their acts caused terror among Anglos, who saw them as bandits.

But some Mexican Americans saw these people as heroes, just as Anglos saw Robin Hood as a hero. To them, the bandits were avenging the wrongs done to the Mexican people. Historians use the term **social bandit** to describe an outlaw who claims to be acting on behalf of an oppressed group.

LATINO HERITAGE

El Carroferril

Many Mexican Americans worked building the first railroads in the U.S. Southwest in the 1800s. In the evenings, the workers would sing songs or tell stories. *El Carroferril* (The Iron Horse) was one of the songs they sang.

Ahí viene el carroferril,
Con dirección de Durango;
El que se embarca en el,
Díos no mas sabe hasta cuando.

Allí viene el carroferril,
Vamos a ver donde está;
Ah, qué gusto nos dará,
Cuando ló veamos venir.

Ahí viene el carroferril,
Viene cargado de indianas;
Viene quebrando los precios
A las tiendas mejicanas.

Here comes the railroad
Heading toward Durango;
Whoever gets on it,
It'll be till only God knows when.

There comes the railroad,
Let's go and see where it is;
How happy we'll be
When we see it coming.

Here comes the railroad,
It comes loaded with calicos;
Forcing down the prices
In the Mexican stores.

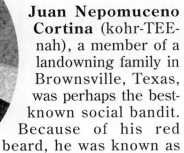

Juan Nepomuceno Cortina (kohr-TEE-nah), a member of a landowning family in Brownsville, Texas, was perhaps the best-known social bandit. Because of his red beard, he was known as "the red robber of the Rio Grande."

Cortina's outlaw career began in 1859. As he was having coffee in a Brownsville cafe, he saw a sheriff beating up a *vaquero* who had worked for the Cortina family. "Take it easy," Cortina shouted. The sheriff cursed Cortina, who then pulled a gun and shot the sheriff in the shoulder.

Cortina escaped. Two months later, though, he returned to Brownsville with a small army. They took the city and raised the Mexican flag.

For 14 years, Cortina and his band raided ranches and towns along the border, issuing calls to rebellion. In one such call, Cortina said, "Mexicans! . . . The voice of revelation [divine truth] whispers to me that to me is entrusted the work of breaking the chains of your slavery."

Texas Rangers chased Cortina through southern Texas and northern Mexico, but they never caught him. Finally, in 1873, Mexico's president had Cortina arrested. However, because of his popularity, he was soon released. Cortina later served as acting governor of a state in northern Mexico.

Legends and Reality. Many legends grew up about the daring exploits of social bandits. Among the well-known were Joaquín Murieta (moor-YEH-tah) and Antonio Moreno (moh-REH-noh) of California, and Sostenes L'Archeveque (lahr-cheh-VEH-kay) of New Mexico. These men and others became the subjects of many popular songs and stories.

The social bandits became heroes because they were seen as fighting back against Anglo oppression. Many Mexican Americans applauded the words that bandit Tiburcio Vásquez spoke at his trial:

> A spirit of hatred and revenge took possession of me. I had numerous fights in defense of what I believed to be my rights and those of my countrymen. I believed that we were being deprived of the social rights that belonged to us.

Taking Another Look

1. What does the fact that Manuel Domínguez could not testify in court show about the way Mexican Americans were treated?

2. What is the difference between a social bandit and an ordinary outlaw?

3. **Critical Thinking** If Latinos of Mexican descent were treated so badly, why do you think many of them followed the advice of the Los Angeles newspaper to adjust to the new conditions?

LOOKING AHEAD

The takeover of Mexican lands by the United States resulted in oppression of the people who were now Mexican Americans. Some people adjusted to the new conditions. Others resisted. Relations between Mexican Americans and their Anglo neighbors remained tense and often violent through the mid–1800s. As you will read in the next unit, events on the national scene shifted the focus away from the U.S. Southwest and West to growing conflict over slavery.

EL CLAMOR PÚBLICO

Californios of the 1850s read their weekly copy of *El Clamor Público*, (The Public Outcry) with great interest. The Spanish-language newspaper carried news of issues and events that directly concerned them. It also suggested ways that Mexican Americans could fight for their rights.

Published in Los Angeles, *El Clamor Público* was a forerunner of such present-day newspapers as *El Diario/La Prensa* in New York City and *La Opinión* in Los Angeles. A 20-year-old journalist named Francisco P. Ramírez (rah-MEE-res) started *El Clamor Público* in 1855. The paper lasted four years and carried stories that encouraged Latinos to work hard and get an education. The paper urged schooling for girls as well as boys and wrote about acts of discrimination against Mexicans. To help its readers learn English, *El Clamor Público* printed a page that carried articles in English and Spanish.

Ramírez believed that Mexican Americans should be proud of their history. Like the Spanish-language newspapers of today, *El Clamor Público* carried messages of pride and hope to the Spanish-speaking community in the United States.

CLOSE UP: Chapter 11

The Who, What, Where of History

1. **Where** is the state of Sonora?
2. **What** was a *rico*?
3. **What** laws of Mexican and Spanish tradition became part of California's state constitution?
4. **What** was the Foreign Miners' Tax of 1850?
5. **Who** was Vicente Peralta?
6. **What** is a squatter?
7. **What** was the Land Act of 1851?
8. **Who** was Manuel Domínguez?
9. **What** are social bandits?
10. **Who** was Juan Nepomuceno Cortina?
11. **Who** was Joaquín Murieta?

Making the Connection

1. What was the connection between the gold rush and California's becoming a U.S. state?
2. What was the connection between squatters and the Land Act of 1851?

Time Check

1. How long did it take for California's population to rise from 10,000 to 250,000?
2. Tell the year in which the following events occurred: California becomes a U.S. state; New Mexico and Arizona become U.S. states.
3. Where was the process of examining land grants completed first—in California, New Mexico, or Texas? Why was this so?

What Would You Have Done?

1. Imagine that you are the defense

lawyer in the trial at which Manuel Domínguez was to testify. The judge has just disqualified Domínguez as a witness. What arguments would you present to try to change the judge's mind on this issue?

2. Suppose you were a *tejano* rancher in 1859 and Juan Nepomuceno Cortina wanted to hide on your ranch. Would you let him? Why or why not?

Thinking and Writing About History

1. You are a resident of northern Mexico in 1848 and have just decided to go to the California gold fields. Write a letter to a friend explaining why.

2. Imagine that you are a reporter who is sent to a Sonoran mining camp in California that was destroyed by an Anglo mob. Write a news story describing the scene and telling what happened.

3. You are a young journalist who wants to start a Spanish-language newspaper in Santa Fe in the 1850s. Write a memo describing your plans to people whom you wish to persuade to loan you money for the project.

4. Imagine that you are a member of the California senate in the 1850s. Draft a bill, or a proposal for a law, to protect the civil rights of Mexican Americans and Mexicans in the United States.

Building Skills: Main Ideas in a Chapter Section

In previous chapters, you practiced finding the main idea of a paragraph and stating a main idea in your own words. You also used the titles and section headings of your textbook to keep track of main ideas.

Now you will combine those skills to restate the main idea of a chapter section.

Section 1 of Chapter 11 begins on page 133. On a separate sheet of paper, write the title of the section. Next write the question that follows the title. Then write one sentence that states the section's main idea. If you are not sure what to write, turn the section-opening question into a sentence.

Now look at the sentence you have written. It is probably too general. Try to improve it. Skim the section and its bold-face headings. Then rewrite your sentence, making it more specific.

For instance, suppose for the main idea of Section 1 you wrote, "Mexicans who found themselves U.S. citizens after 1848 experienced many changes in their lives." How could you make that sentence more specific? Perhaps a sentence like this would do: "A flood of Anglo gold seekers to California after 1848 undermined the power and status of Mexicans there."

Follow the same steps for Sections 2 and 3 of this chapter. Look at the section title and the question that follows it. Write a sentence that gives the main idea of the section. Then skim the section and rewrite your main idea, making it more specific.

Express Yourself!

In this chapter, you read how many Mexican Americans kept some of their traditional customs while learning about new "American" customs. Interview a family member or friend that emigrated to the United States from another country. Find out what customs he or she still practices from their country of origin. Discover what new "American" customs have been adopted. Report your findings to the rest of the class.

UNIT 4

A TIME OF GROWTH

(1860–1920s)

Puerto Rican Patriots in 1898

Antonio Maceo

Chapter

12 Latinos in the U.S. Civil War
(1861–1865)

13 A Changing World
(1860 s–1912)

14 The Cuban-Spanish-American War
(1868–1898)

15 Puerto Rico and Cuba Under
United States Control
(1898–1920s)

THE BIG PICTURE

Voices of the Times

It is my duty . . . to prevent, through the independence of Cuba, the U.S.A. from spreading over the West Indies and falling with added weight upon other lands of Our America.

— José Martí, Cuban writer and patriot, 1895

Unit 4 describes the role people of Latin American descent played in the U.S. Civil War and in the changing United States during the late 1800s. It also describes how Cuba and Puerto Rico, Spain's last two colonies in the Americas, struggled for independence during this period. They gained that independence, only to come under the control of a more powerful nation—the United States. U.S. involvement with these islands brought new elements to the story of the Latino experience in the United States.

◆◆ In The United States ◆◆

The latter half of the 1800s was a critical time for the United States. A civil war erupted in 1861 that almost broke the United States into two separate nations, one slave, one free. The war ended in 1865 with the North as victor. The Union was preserved and slavery was abolished. The United States then entered a time of remarkable economic and territorial growth.

A Bloody Civil War. In the 1850s, the United States went through a series of crises over African American slavery. The issue was whether slavery should be allowed in the western territories. That issue split the northern and southern states into two increasingly hostile camps.

A new political party, the Republicans, sprang up to oppose the spread of slavery. In 1860, that party's candidate, Abraham Lincoln, won election as President of the United States. The Southern states then **seceded,** or separated, from the Union. They set up their own government, known as the Confederate States of America, or the **Confederacy.**

Fighting between the Union and the Confederacy broke out in 1861. The Civil War lasted four destructive years. During that time, about 620,000 people were killed. Latinos fought on both sides in the war (see Chapter 12).

Reconstruction. The Union victory in 1865 was followed by a difficult period known as **Reconstruction**. While punishing white Southerners, Congress tried to ensure equality for African Americans. The **13th, 14th,** and **15th Amendments** freed enslaved African Americans, made them citizens with equal rights under the law, and gave African American males the right to vote. No women were allowed to vote at this time.

White Southerners resisted granting the freed African Americans their new rights. By the time Reconstruction ended in 1877, most Southern states had passed so-called **Jim Crow laws**. These laws aimed to **segregate,** or separate the two races, and to keep African Americans in an inferior position.

A Network of Railroads. While the nation went through political changes

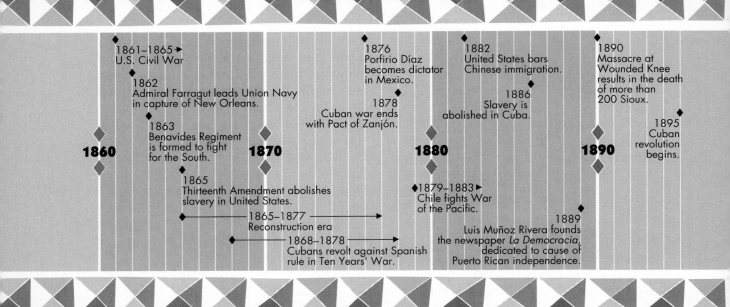

1861–1865 →
U.S. Civil War

1862
Admiral Farragut leads Union Navy in capture of New Orleans.

1863
Benavides Regiment is formed to fight for the South.

1860

1865
Thirteenth Amendment abolishes slavery in United States.

1865–1877
Reconstruction era

1868–1878
Cubans revolt against Spanish rule in Ten Years' War.

1870

1876
Porfirio Díaz becomes dictator in Mexico.

1878
Cuban war ends with Pact of Zanjón.

1879–1883 →
Chile fights War of the Pacific.

1882
United States bars Chinese immigration.

1886
Slavery is abolished in Cuba.

1880

1889
Luis Muñoz Rivera founds the newspaper *La Democracia*, dedicated to cause of Puerto Rican independence.

1890
Massacre at Wounded Knee results in the death of more than 200 Sioux.

1895
Cuban revolution begins.

1890

after the Civil War, the growth of industry in the United States boomed. This was especially true in the North and Midwest. Aiding this growth was a new railroad system that tied the nation together.

During the war, the federal government called for the building of a transcontinental railroad to link the East Coast with California. The first transcontinental railroad was completed in 1869 by Chinese and Irish immigrant workers. By 1890, more than 166,700 miles (268,000 kilometers) of railroad track crisscrossed the nation. Over this rail system, products—and people—could travel more quickly and inexpensively than ever before.

New Industries. By the late 1800s, there were more products to ship over that rail system. More and more industries used methods of **mass production**—ways of making huge quantities of goods cheaply and quickly. New sources of ener-

gy and new technology aided mass production. Oil was refined into kerosene for lamps or used to lubricate machinery. Electricity powered everything from light bulbs to street cars. Telegraphs and telephones speeded communication and helped make industry more efficient.

As the output of factories increased, businesses themselves grew larger. Businesspeople like oilman John D. Rockefeller and steel king Andrew Carnegie tried to take control of their industries. They created giant corporations, such as Standard Oil and U.S. Steel, that came to have great influence in all aspects of U.S. life.

A Flood of Immigrants. The nation's huge new industries needed workers. Many U.S. citizens, including large numbers of African Americans, left farms for new jobs in city factories. In addition, huge numbers of immigrants poured into the

144

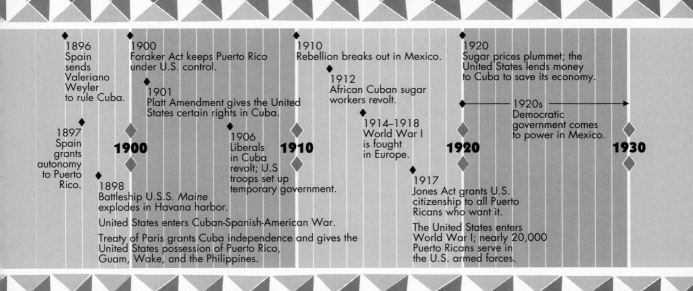

1896 Spain sends Valeriano Weyler to rule Cuba.

1897 Spain grants autonomy to Puerto Rico.

1898 Battleship U.S.S. *Maine* explodes in Havana harbor.

United States enters Cuban-Spanish-American War.

Treaty of Paris grants Cuba independence and gives the United States possession of Puerto Rico, Guam, Wake, and the Philippines.

1900 Foraker Act keeps Puerto Rico under U.S. control.

1901 Platt Amendment gives the United States certain rights in Cuba.

1906 Liberals in Cuba revolt; U.S troops set up temporary government.

1910 Rebellion breaks out in Mexico.

1912 African Cuban sugar workers revolt.

1914–1918 World War I is fought in Europe.

1917 Jones Act grants U.S. citizenship to all Puerto Ricans who want it.

The United States enters World War I; nearly 20,000 Puerto Ricans serve in the U.S. armed forces.

1920 Sugar prices plummet; the United States lends money to Cuba to save its economy.

1920s Democratic government comes to power in Mexico.

1900   **1910**   **1920**   **1930**

United States. Between 1877 and 1890, more than 6 million immigrants entered the country.

Previous immigrants to the United States had mostly come from western and northern Europe. Most of the new immigrants were from eastern and southern Europe. Others came from China and Japan. Some newcomers from Spain's Caribbean colonies of Puerto Rico and Cuba built new communities in Florida and New York.

Despite their contributions to their new land, immigrants—whether from Europe, Asia, or Latin America—often met with prejudice and discrimination from native-born U.S. citizens. In 1882, for example, the U.S. Congress passed a law barring Chinese immigration. Suspicion and hatred of the "different" newcomers would continue for many years.

Settlement of the West. The new railroads brought a rush of people to the West. Some were miners who hoped to strike it rich in the newly discovered gold, silver, and copper mines of the West. Others looked to build vast cattle ranches that rivaled those of Latin America. Still others took advantage of cheap land and improved farm machinery to put thousands of acres under the plow.

Much of the land in the U.S. West had once been Mexican. The Mexican Americans who lived there, in southern California, Arizona, and New Mexico, had made up the majority of the population. The flood of newcomers changed this. As Mexican Americans became a minority in their own land, they suffered from increasing prejudice and discrimination.

A similar fate awaited the very first settlers of the West. More and more Native Americans were killed or forced from their homelands onto **reservations.** These reservations usually consisted of land no one else wanted. There the Native

Americans were expected to give up hunting and become farmers. The Native Americans fought back in a series of tragic wars that climaxed with the massacre of about 200 Sioux at Wounded Knee in South Dakota in 1890.

A New Expansionist Spirit. As the United States became more settled, Americans looked beyond their borders for new lands in which to extend their power and influence. Growing U.S. industries needed new markets for the goods that they produced as well as cheap sources of raw materials.

People who believed that the United States should expand pointed to a book called *The Influence of Sea Power Upon History* by Alfred Thayer Mahan, a U.S. navy officer. In it, Mahan argued that, to become great, the United States had to have access to world markets. To do so, the United States needed ships to carry its goods, a navy to protect the ships, and naval bases and refueling stations throughout the world.

Expanding in the Pacific and Latin America. In the spirit of Mahan's message, the United States began spreading its influence in the Pacific and Latin America. It joined other Western powers in China. To ensure that U.S. companies would have the same opportunities as other foreign companies in China, the United States supported the **Open Door policy**. Under this policy, no nation that wanted to invest in China could be kept from doing so.

The United States had long claimed that the Monroe Doctrine (see page 71) gave it a special role and special rights in Latin America. Citing the Monroe Doctrine, the United States stepped in to help settle disputes between Venezuela and European nations in 1895 and 1902.

The United States also became involved in a struggle between Spain and its colony Cuba, which was seeking self-government. Cuban rebels had been fighting for freedom for years. The United States finally went to war with Spain in 1898. As a result of the Cuban-Spanish-American War that followed, the United States gained control of Cuba and Puerto Rico.

Thereafter, U.S. interest and power in Latin America grew. In 1902, President Theodore Roosevelt declared the United States to be "the policeman of the West." Two years later, he announced that the United States had the right to exercise "international police power" over any Latin American nation that could not control internal disorders.

Roosevelt acted to back up these statements. When the Dominican Republic could not pay its debts to European countries, he had the United States take charge of the country's financial affairs. Roosevelt also showed how far the United States would go into the affairs of Latin American nations by his actions in Panama (see page 196).

Taking Another Look

1. **(a)** What gains did African Americans make as a result of the Civil War? **(b)** How were these gains limited by the Jim Crow laws passed in Southern states after the Civil War?

2. Why were some U.S. citizens interested in expanding the nation's borders in the late 1800s?

3. **Critical Thinking** Do you think the United States was justified in getting involved in the affairs of other American nations? Explain your answer.

Benito Juárez, perhaps Mexico's most beloved leader, introduced many reforms in government that helped improve the condition of Mexico's poor.

In Latin America

The second half of the 1800s saw important changes taking place in Latin America as well as in the United States. Larger countries such as Mexico, Argentina, and Chile began to make progress on the rocky road to economic and political stability for their citizens.

Juárez in Mexico. In the years that followed Mexico's loss in its war with the United States (see page 126), a Mexican Indian named Benito Juárez rose to power. Juárez became one of his country's most beloved political figures. He introduced many reforms in government. He reduced the power of the military and tried to keep the affairs of the government and church completely separate. A devout Roman Catholic, he introduced a policy of tolerance for all religions in Mexico. In 1861, he became Mexico's first president of Native American descent.

A Foreign Emperor. Six months after Juárez became president, an empty treasury forced him to suspend payments on Mexico's debt to foreign countries. The French ruler, Napoleon III, used this move as an excuse to send troops to Mexico.

By 1863, the French had defeated the Mexican army and marched into Mexico City. There, an Austrian noble named Ferdinand Maximilian, who was an ally of France, was proclaimed Mexico's new emperor.

Juárez and his followers, however, continued to resist foreign rule. Once its Civil War was over, the United States began supplying the Mexicans with arms. Sensing that the Mexicans could not be defeated, Napoleon III ordered the French troops home. Left with little military support, Maximilian was captured by Juárez's army in May 1867 and executed.

The Díaz Dictatorship. One of the Mexicans who led the fight against Maximilian was the *mestizo* Porfirio Díaz (DEE-ahs). After Juárez died in 1872, Díaz rose to power and ruled the country as a dictator from 1876 to 1911. Díaz used his power to push for economic progress. In doing so, he welcomed investment from companies in Britain and the United States. Under Díaz, new railroads were built and copper mines and oil fields developed. Manufacturing expanded. The economy improved. As it did, businesspeople, landowners, and foreign investors reaped the benefits.

147

Most Mexicans did not share in the economic growth of their country. Widespread poverty and Díaz's harsh rule aroused resentment among the people and led to the outbreak of rebellion in 1910. Díaz was forced out of office in 1911. A period of civil war followed that ended with a new democratic government coming to power in Mexico in the 1920s.

Economic Growth.

Elsewhere in Latin America, newly stable governments promoted economic development, also with foreign help. Like the United States, these countries had enormous natural resources. But unlike the United States, they lacked the money and means to develop them.

Industrialized nations like Great Britain needed raw materials for their industries and cheap food for their workers. They had money to invest. They also needed new markets for their goods. Increasingly, these industrialized nations looked to Latin America.

Changes in Argentina.

Starting in the late 1850s, the British forged strong economic ties with Argentina. They built thousands of miles of railroad track stretching across the grassland, or pampas. They brought in British cattle to be bred and raised on huge ranches there. The cattle were shipped from British-built docks at the port of Buenos Aires to Britain in specially designed refrigerated steamships.

In addition to money for investment, Argentina needed workers. Like the United States, Argentina met this need by encouraging immigration from abroad. By 1914, foreigners made up about 30 percent of Argentina's population, compared to only about 13 percent in the United States. Most of these immigrants came from Spain and Italy.

Growth in Chile.

Aid from abroad also helped spark an economic boom in Chile. Chile's main resources were nitrates, which were used in fertilizer and copper production. From 1879 to 1883, Chile fought the War of the Pacific to gain control of nitrate-rich lands from Bolivia and Peru. Foreign investors, mostly British, soon bought up about two thirds of the nitrate fields. British-built railways transported the fertilizer to ports along the Pacific coast. From those ports, it was carried to farmlands in Europe and in the United States.

The economies of these Latin American nations depended on the prosperity of the industrial nations. Hard times abroad could easily mean economic disaster for them. Furthermore, the wealth that came from this foreign investment did not benefit the majority of the people. There was a huge gap between the wealthy few at the top of the society and just about everybody else at the bottom.

The End of Spanish Rule.

While Europeans invested in various Latin American countries, Cuba and Puerto Rico, Spain's last colonies in the Americas, struggled to free themselves from that nation's control. As you will read in Chapter 14, the United States entered the fight in 1898. After a brief war, Spain lost its colonies. But Cuba and Puerto Rico did not gain full independence. The United States took over Puerto Rico and played a major role in the affairs of Cuba. This action angered and humiliated people on both islands.

Other Latin Americans watched these developments with anger and alarm. They worried about how far the people of the United States would go in their quest for power over the peoples of Latin America.

After a brief but bloody war, Spain was expelled from Cuba and Puerto Rico. Here the Spanish general, Toral, is shown surrendering the city of Santiago, Cuba, to U.S. forces.

Central America. As you have read (page 73), shortly after Mexico became independent, five countries of Central America—Guatemala, El Salvador, Honduras, Nicaragua, and Costa Rica—withdrew from Mexico. They set up their own federation, called the United Provinces of Central America. These countries, plus Belize and Panama, make up what we now think of as Central America.

The federation broke up in 1838, and the original five nations went their separate ways. Largely agricultural, these countries concentrated on the growth and export of coffee and bananas. Foreign investors, especially from Germany and the United States, were attracted by the profits to be made from these crops. One U.S. company, the United Fruit Company, came to dominate the banana trade and other parts of the economy of Central America. In addition, it controlled the politics of several countries of the region.

Coffee and banana prices were subject to the ups and downs of the world market. When world prices were high, the compa-nies and wealthy Central Americans prospered. When world prices were low, Central American economies suffered. But the poverty-stricken workers who labored on the coffee and banana plantations rarely benefited from good times. They also suffered most during bad times.

Workers grew to resent the power of the foreign-owned companies. They also felt anger toward the United States. That nation was showing its growing willingness to intervene in the affairs of their countries to protect U.S.-owned businesses.

Taking Another Look

1. **(a)** Why were the French able to set up an empire in Mexico? **(b)** Why did the empire collapse?

2. How were the economies of Latin American countries dependent on Europe and the United States?

3. **Critical Thinking** Compare and contrast the economies of Argentina and Chile with those of the Central American countries.

SECTIONS

1 The Civil War in the U.S. Southwest

2 Fighters for Two Flags

Former Mexican lands of the U. S. Southwest became a battleground for Confederate and Union forces during the Civil War. Latinos fought on both sides.

CHAPTER 12

Latinos in the U.S. Civil War

(1861–1865)

THINKING ABOUT THE CHAPTER

What part did Latinos play in the U.S. Civil War?

Loreta Janeta Velázquez nervously approached the train that would take her from New York to Canada. She prayed that she would not be found out. She knew that Northern authorities were on the lookout for her. As a spy for the Confederacy, she was carrying important documents and a great deal of money for the Southern cause. If she were caught, she might have to pay with her life.

Velázquez's heart skipped a beat when she saw that a Northern detective, who had been pointed out to her by a friend, was about to board the same train as she. Years later, Velázquez recalled, "At Rochester [New York] . . . to my infinite horror, he [the detective] entered the car where I was and took a seat near me."

Fortunately for her, the detective did not recognize her.

Loreta Velázquez as shown in her normal clothes and in her disguise as a Confederate officer. After the Civil War, Velázquez wrote a book describing her wartime deeds.

Then, as she she left the train he took an interest, she reported.

> The detective seemed determined to be as polite to me as he could; and on leaving the cars he carried my satchel [suitcase], containing eighty-two thousand dollars belonging to the Confederate government. . . . I took the satchel from him, and thanking him for his attention, proceeded to get out of his sight as expeditiously [quickly] as I could.

Before Cuban-born Velázquez became a spy, she had served the South as a soldier. Disguised as a man, she became a Confederate army lieutenant and fought at the battle of Bull Run in 1861. But she was found out to be a woman and discharged from the army. Still determined to fight, she disguised herself again, rejoined the Confederate army, and was wounded in the Battle of Shiloh in 1862. Only after being discovered a second time did Velázquez give up the army for good. She then became a spy in Washington, D.C., where she worked for a top-secret government office.

1 THE CIVIL WAR IN THE U.S. SOUTHWEST

◆ Why was control of the New Mexico Territory important to both the Union and the Confederacy?

Loreta Velázquez was only one of nearly 10,000 Latinos who fought for either the North or the South in the U.S. Civil War. Those Latinos faced the same hard decisions about which side to support that other U.S. citizens did.

Choosing Sides. Today, we may wonder why Latinos would want to fight on the side that defended slavery. But not all who did so felt they were defending slavery. Some supported the Confederacy for reasons that had nothing to do with slavery. Similarly, many Latinos who fought for the Union were not concerned about putting an end to slavery.

Many Latinos chose sides based on personal reasons. Velázquez's husband had been killed while fighting for the Confederacy. She was determined to avenge his death. Some Latinos fought for the Confederacy simply to defend a beloved homeland from invasion. Also, some Latinos were drafted into service and had no choice of sides.

New Mexico. Latinos made up the majority of the 200,000 people who lived in

After Confederate forces had taken Santa Fe and Albuquerque, they were defeated at Glorieta Pass with the help of a daring raid led by Manuel Chaves.

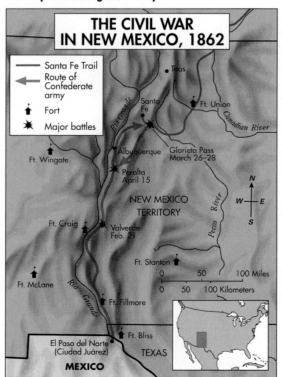

THE CIVIL WAR
IN NEW MEXICO, 1862

— Santa Fe Trail
← Route of Confederate army
↑ Fort
✷ Major battles

Taos
Santa Fe
Ft. Union
Rio Grande
Canadian River
Albuquerque
Glorieta Pass
March 26–28
Ft. Wingate
Peralta
April 15
NEW MEXICO
TERRITORY
Pecos River
Ft. Craig
Valverde
Feb. 21
Ft. Stanton
0   50   100 Miles
0   50   100 Kilometers
Ft. McLane
Rio Grande
Ft. Fillmore
El Paso del Norte
(Ciudad Juárez)
Ft. Bliss
TEXAS
MEXICO

the huge New Mexico Territory in 1861 at the outbreak of the Civil War. This territory included what are now the states of New Mexico and Arizona. This region was extremely valuable both to the Union, which held it, and to the Confederacy, which wanted it.

If the South could take over New Mexico, it would be able to advance directly to the gold mines of California, to the west, and the silver mines of Colorado, to the north. At the same time, it could expand slavery to the southwestern territories. It could also build a railroad across the region to link California with the rest of the Confederacy. These moves would do much to strengthen the South.

Texans in Action. Texas had been one of the first slave states to **secede**, or withdraw, from the Union in 1861. Many Texans needed little prodding to attack neighboring New Mexico. Texans and New Mexicans had been bitter enemies as far back as the 1830s, when Texas laid claim to New Mexican land. Many Anglo Texans were prejudiced against Latinos, who made up the majority of the population of New Mexico.

When the Civil War broke out in 1861, a force of Texans attacked Mexicans and Mexican Americans who were living in the Rio Grande region of Texas. Many Latinos then fled to Mexico. Others fought back and raided Anglo ranches and farms, making off with cattle, sheep, and cotton.

Attack on New Mexico. To the west, in New Mexico, however, most Latinos felt far removed from the events of the Civil War. In their eyes, it was an Anglo war, and they felt no great loyalty to either side. A few wealthy Latino landowners, however, sympathized with the Confederacy. They had much in common with the slave owners of the South. They ran their ranches with laborers called peons, who were bound to work on the ranches to pay off debts. Further, the landowners blamed the government in Washington for not having made New Mexico a state. In late 1861, some landowners even plotted to turn part of New Mexico into a Confederate territory.

However, an attack on New Mexico by Confederates from Texas led many New Mexicans to become involved in the war on the Union side. Near the end of February 1862, a Confederate force under the command of Brigadier General Henry Hopkins Sibley moved up along the Rio Grande and took New Mexico's two largest cities, Albuquerque and Santa Fe. Sibley's plan was to take over New Mexico and then invade Colorado, Utah, and California.

This brought the war literally to the New Mexicans' doorsteps, threatening their homes. New Mexicans could no longer say they did not care which side won the war. Many quickly enlisted as volunteers in the militia and in the regular Union army.

The Battle at Glorieta Pass. A Union force of New Mexico volunteers was dispatched from Fort Union, east of Santa Fe, to stop the Confederates. Commanded by Major John M. Chivington, the troop was guided by Lieutenant Colonel Manuel Chaves (CHAH-ves).

◆ **Manuel Chaves (1818–1889)** was nicknamed El Leoncito (leh-ohn-SEE-toh), the Little Lion, and for good reason. He had been a fighter all his life. As a teenager, Chaves had sided with the rebels during Mexico's war for independence. Because of this, his uncle, territorial Governor Manuel Armijo (ahr-MEE-hoh), threatened his life. Chaves was forced to flee from Santa Fe to St. Louis, Missouri.

Chaves returned to Santa Fe a few years after Mexico had won its independence and became a rancher. He later served as chief scout for U.S. soldiers in their fight against the Apache. He was in charge of Fort Fauntleroy in north-western New Mexico when the Civil War began.

To meet the invading Confederates, on March 26, 1862, Chivington's regiment filed into a high, narrow mountain pass of the Santa Fe Trail known as Glorieta Pass. There they met the Confederates head-on. The fighting was fierce as soldiers on both sides shot from behind boulders and thick cedar trees. One Confederate described the scene in a letter to his wife:

On they [the Union soldiers] came to what I supposed was certain destruction, but nothing like lead or iron seemed to stop them. . . . In a moment these devils had run the gauntlet [survived the ordeal] for a half mile, and were fighting hand to hand with our men in the road.

The Confederates retreated, but the fighting was not over. Reinforcements came to join the Confederates, and they prepared for a bigger battle.

At dawn on March 28, Chaves led 490 New Mexico volunteers on a daring raid. They cut westward across the mountains to a point south of the pass. As the main

1861	Civil War between the North and South begins.
1862	Farragut leads Union Navy in the capture of New Orleans.
	Confederate forces take Albuquerque and Santa Fe.
	Union Army led by Chaves defeats Confederates at Glorieta Pass.
1863	Cavada captured at Battle of Gettysburg.
	Benavides Regiment joins Confederate Army.
1864	Farragut captures Mobile, Alabama.
1865	Civil War ends.

Union group fought the Confederates, Chaves's men lowered themselves down a 200-foot (61-meter) mountain using ropes and leather straps. They took a small Texan guard completely by surprise and captured the Confederates' supply train. They then destroyed the wagons and burned all the supplies.

Without enough food and water to keep them going, the Texans called for a truce that night. Then they limped back home along the Rio Grande. The Confederacy never tried to take New Mexico again.

Thanks to Chaves and his men, the Battle of Glorieta Pass was a clear victory for the Union. Today, it is proudly referred to by New Mexicans as the "Gettysburg of the West." At the great Battle of Gettysburg, fought in Pennsylvania in 1863, Union forces prevented a Confederate invasion of the North. If Chaves's men had not been able to destroy the Confederates' supplies, the Confederate army might have continued on to

California and Colorado. The Civil War might have dragged on much longer than it did.

Taking Another Look

1. What caused many New Mexicans to come to the Union's support?

2. How did Manuel Chaves help win the battle at Glorieta Pass?

3. **Critical Thinking** How do you think the Civil War in New Mexico might have affected the attitude of Latinos there toward the United States?

2 FIGHTERS FOR TWO FLAGS

◆ Who were some of the other outstand-
◆ ing Latinos who fought in the Civil War?

The southwestern territories were not the only place in which Latinos took part in the Civil War. Wherever there were Latinos in any numbers, they engaged in the war, either by fighting or by being active in other ways.

A Confederate Colonel. Colonel Santos Benavides (beh-nah-VEE-des) was the highest-ranking Latino officer in the Confederacy. He was born in Laredo, Texas, and was elected mayor of his hometown at age 30.

Benavides formed a cavalry regiment of Mexican Americans to fight for the South in November 1863. The "Benavides Regiment" scored an important victory when its soldiers drove a force of invading Union soldiers out of Laredo. This victory helped to put an end to Union threats to Texas for the rest of the war.

A Spy for the South. Cuban-born Lola Sánchez, like Loreta Janeta Velázquez, was one of a number of women

"Damn the torpedoes! Full speed ahead!" Shouting these words, the Latino David Farragut urged his Union fleet to sail past floating mines into Mobile Bay in Alabama and capture the Confederate stronghold.

who provided important help for the Confederacy. Sánchez lived near Palatka, Florida, with her family. Union soldiers had arrested her father as a Confederate spy and imprisoned him at St. Augustine. The Sánchez house was occupied by Union soldiers to prevent any more trouble from the family.

Sánchez was furious and made up her mind to do everything she could to help the Confederate cause. One day, while serving Union officers who had occupied the Sánchez house, she overheard them talking about their plans for the next day. They spoke about raiding Confederate troops stationed nearby.

Sánchez sneaked out of the house past the guards and hurried through a thick forest to warn the Confederates. She returned from her mission an hour and a half later, arousing no suspicions among the officers. The next day, thanks to Sánchez's warning, the Confederate sol-diers were lying in wait for the surprised Union troops and captured them.

The "Old Salamander." No person of Spanish descent who fought in the Civil War is better known than David Farragut (FAR-uh-guht). Farragut was the hero of the battles of New Orleans and Mobile Bay and the first admiral of the U.S. Navy.

Farragut's father, Jorge (HOHR-heh) Ferragut, came to the American colonies from the Spanish island of Minorca during the American Revolution. He became a lieutenant in the South Carolina Navy and fought the British at Savannah and Charleston.

David Farragut, named James at birth, was born near Knoxville, Tennessee, in 1801. After his mother's death from yellow fever, young Farragut, with the consent of his father, was adopted by Captain David Porter. The boy took the name David in Porter's honor.

At age 9, Farragut served as a midshipman on board Porter's ship. He fought against the British in the War of 1812. He later fought pirates in the West Indies, served in the war with Mexico, and was made a captain, in 1855.

When the Civil War broke out, Farragut left his home in Norfolk, Virginia, and moved north to serve the Union. But the government was suspicious of him because he had lived most of his life in the South. Finally, however, Farragut was approved for active duty.

In January 1862, Farragut was put in command of the squadron that had the important job of **blockading**, or closing off, some of the Confederate ports on the Gulf of Mexico. In April, he led 17 ships in an attack against the South's largest port, New Orleans. After six days of fighting, Farragut captured New Orleans. His ability to dodge enemy fire in hostile waters earned him the nickname Old Salamander. A salamander is a small land and water animal that can slide easily around obstacles.

Farragut next sailed up the Mississippi River and bombarded Vicksburg, Mississippi. While he did not take the Confederate city, he weakened it. This allowed Union General Ulysses S. Grant to capture Vicksburg by land a year later. President Abraham Lincoln praised Farragut for his victories and promoted him to rear admiral.

The Battle of Mobile Bay. In August 1864, Farragut led an attack on the Confederacy's second largest port on the Gulf of Mexico—Mobile, Alabama. It was a dangerous mission. The Confederates had loaded hundreds of barrels with gunpowder and placed them across the entrance to Mobile Bay. These floating "torpedoes," as they were called, were rigged to explode if a ship bumped against them.

Lieutenant Robert Ely, aboard one of the four ships in Farragut's small fleet, wrote about the journey up the bay in his journal.

> We knew that the channel was full of them [torpedoes], but the Admiral acted upon the belief that they had been submerged [sunken] so long that a great part of them would not explode, and fortunately his surmise [opinion] proved correct. The ships, in cruising in, heard the continued snapping and pinging of those infernal [evil] machines, but the powder proved to be inferior, and although the percussion [fuses] exploded, the torpedoes remained harmless.

Not all the torpedoes were harmless. The ironclad U.S.S. *Tecumseh* hit a torpedo and exploded on contact. "She [the ship] sank in seven minutes, and only one ensign, the pilot, and four men were saved from her," wrote Ely.

Farragut was not, however, about to turn back. He took the lead with his wooden ship and shouted these famous words: "Damn the torpedoes! Full speed ahead!"

The other ships followed their brave leader and soon captured the Confederate ironclad *Tennessee*. The fort defending Mobile quickly surrendered. An important Southern port was sealed off for the remainder of the war. For his victory, Farragut was named full admiral, the highest rank in the U.S. Navy.

Farragut spoke Spanish and remained proud of his heritage throughout his life. He traveled throughout Latin America during his naval career and visited Spain on a goodwill voyage to Europe in 1867. He met Queen Elizabeth II of Spain, who told him, "I am proud to know that your ancestors came from my kingdom."

A Union balloon is about to be sent aloft to observe Confederate forces. From such balloons, Federico Cavada made sketches of the movement of the Confederates.

Balloons in War. Another Latino hero of the North used balloons, not ships, to help defeat the enemy. Cuban-born Federico Fernández Cavada (fer-NAHN-des kah-VAH-dah) served as a captain and engineer in the Union army. Cavada was an expert artist. The army put his talent to good use by sending him aloft in hot air balloons near the battle lines.

From the air, Cavada sketched what he observed of the enemy's troop movements. His sketches helped the Union forces in their battles.

Cavada was captured at the Battle of Gettysburg and sent to Libby Prison in Richmond, Virginia. He scribbled notes about his experiences there on old newspapers and scraps of paper and hid them from his Confederate guards in his shoes and socks. After his release in 1864, Cavada used these notes to write *Libby Life,* a book about his cruel treatment in the Confederate prison.

After the war, Cavada served as U.S. consul in the Spanish colony of Cuba for five years. In 1868, when the Cubans rose in revolt against Spanish rule, Cavada became commander-in-chief of the Cuban Revolutionary Army. He was captured trying to help a sick friend get out of Cuba and was executed by a Spanish firing squad on July 1, 1871. Moments before his death, Cavada threw his hat in the air and cried, "Goodbye, Cuba, forever!"

Taking Another Look

1. What famous words did David Farragut shout at the Battle of Mobile Bay? Explain their meaning.
2. How was Federico Cavada's talent as an artist used by the Union army?
3. **Critical Thinking** Which of the Latinos discussed in this section do you think contributed most to his or her cause in the Civil War? Explain.

LOOKING AHEAD

The Civil War ended in April 1865. Although the Union won, both the North and the South were exhausted. The toll in human lives was enormous. Much of the South was in ruins, and it was years before its economy recovered.

Nevertheless, the reunited nation underwent important changes. Its industries grew. The U.S. West and Southwest, where most Latinos then lived, became more closely connected with life in the rest of the United States. New immigrant Latino communities sprang up in other parts of the country. The United States took a growing interest in Latin American lands to the south.

157

A LATINO ASTRONAUT

As you have read, engineer Federico Fernández Cavada played an important role during the Civil War. He floated high over the Confederate army in hot air balloons and reported their positions. Cavada's reports contributed to Union victory and were a great service to his country.

Over 100 years later, another Latino was sent aloft in the service of the United States. But this Latino flew much higher than Cavada.

Franklin Chang-Diaz, a Costa Rican-born engineer and physicist, had dreamed of becoming an astronaut. He moved one step closer to his dream in 1980, when he was selected to be part of NASA's space program. In 1983, Diaz worked as part of the ground crew for the first space lab mission. Three years later, he was assigned duty aboard the shuttle *Columbia*. Diaz videotaped life in the shuttle with his fellow astronauts. But his most thrilling moment came when he spoke to the people of North and South America in Spanish. Diaz feels that his experience will help bring the people of these two continents closer together in their search for scientific knowledge.

Since his flight, Diaz has been working on a rocket that will increase the speed of a spacecraft to as much as three million miles an hour. As the first Latino in space, Diaz has won a place in history and science.

CLOSE UP: Chapter 12

The Who, What, Where of History

1. **Who** was Manuel Chaves?
2. **Where** did Chivington's regiment defeat Confederate forces from Texas?
3. **What** was the Benavides Regiment?
4. **Who** was Lola Sánchez?
5. **Where** did David Farragut earn the nickname "Old Salamander"?
6. **What** was Federico Fernández Cavada's contribution to the Union victory?
7. **Who** is Franklin Chang-Diaz and how did he earn fame?

Making the Connection

1. What was the connection between General Sibley's invasion of New Mexico and New Mexicans enlisting in the Union army?
2. What was the connection between Farragut's attack on Vicksburg and General Grant's victory there?

Time Check

1. Which of these events occurred first: the Battle of Mobile Bay, the battle at Glorieta Pass, Sibley's invasion of New Mexico?
2. When did Santos Benavides form a regiment of Mexican Americans to fight for the Confederacy?

What Would You Have Done?

1. Imagine you had been a friend of Loreta Velázquez. Would you have supported her decision to fight for the Confederate army after her husband's death? Why or why not?

2. If you had been a New Mexican, how would you have responded when Texans tried to take your land?

Thinking and Writing About History

1. Choose one of the following headlines. Write a brief newspaper article to go with the headline.

   Spy Loreta Velázquez Avoids Capture by Union Authorities

   "El Leoncito" Leads Daring Raid On Confederate Forces

   Farragut Ignores Torpedoes, Orders "Full Speed Ahead!"

2. Write a dialogue between two Latinos. One wants to join the Confederacy while the other wants to fight for the Union. Have each present his or her reasons.

3. Imagine that you are one of the commanders of the Union force at New Mexico. You have just participated in the battle at Glorieta Pass and must now make a report of the event for your superiors. In a brief report, describe the fighting from its beginning on March 26, 1862, to its end two days later.

Building Skills: Stating an Implied Topic Sentence

Chief Inspector Díaz is investigating the scene of a burglary. "Well," he says to his assistant, "there is no sign of a break-in, the thief knew just where to look for the money, and the butler has disappeared." "I see," replied his assistant. "Are you implying that the butler did it?"

To *imply* something is to state it indirectly. Without actually saying so, Inspector Díaz was implying that the butler was the thief. When you read for main ideas, you will find that writers often do not state them in a sentence. They may imply the main idea.

Read the following paragraph from Chapter 12.

When the Civil War broke out in 1861, a force of Texans attacked Mexicans and Mexican Americans who were living in the Rio Grande region of Texas. Many Latinos then fled to Mexico. Others fought back and raided Anglo ranches and farms, making off with cattle, sheep, and cotton.

Although not directly stated, the main idea of this paragraph is implied. In the state of Texas, the Anglo Texans and the Latino Texans were long-standing enemies.

Now read the following paragraph. Write what you think is the implied main idea on a separate sheet of paper.

At age 9, Farragut served as a midshipman on board Porter's ship. He fought against the British in the War of 1812. He later fought pirates in the West Indies, served in the war with Mexico, and was made a captain, in 1855.

Express Yourself!

Choose a classmate to work with. Pretend that you are cousins and that it is the Civil War. One of you lives in the South. The other lives in the North. Write brief letters to one another. Tell how the war is affecting you. Write whether you plan to join the army.

Ybor City, Florida, was built by Vicente Martínez Ybor for Cubans who worked in his cigar factory. Cubans came to Florida in great numbers after the start of Cuba's Ten Year War in 1868.

SECTIONS

1 New Spanish Immigration

2 Newcomers from Puerto Rico and Cuba

3 New Mexico

CHAPTER

13

A Changing World
(1860s–1912)

THINKING ABOUT THE CHAPTER

How did changing conditions in the United States affect Latinos in the late 1800s and early 1900s?

The Cubans who arrived in the swampland outside the city of Tampa, Florida, in the 1880s were not impressed. This place where they had been hired to work was filled with dangers and discomforts. These ranged from wild animals and fevers to swarms of biting insects. The flies were so thick that the new settlers had to wear goggles to keep them out of their eyes. Elígio Carbonell Malta (kahr-boh-NEL MAHL-tah), son of one of the first Cuban settlers, remembered:

In order to walk from one end of the village to the other a person had to resign himself to suffer as though he were contemplating [thinking of] a difficult journey across a desert. For the person who ventured out at night . . . it was indispensable [necessary] to carry a lantern or lamp which might permit him to avoid dangerous spots. It was also advisable to carry a rifle or revolver for protection in the event of meeting any dangerous animals or similar unexpected threats.

When one worker brought his new bride to the place, he wrote, "she burst out crying at what she saw. Wilderness, swamps, mosquitoes. . . ." She later asked her husband, "Why have you brought me to such a place?"

Tampa was just one of the places in the United States that received Spanish-speaking immigrants in the 1880s. Cuba was not the only land from which they came. Spain, Puerto Rico, and Mexico sent their share of newcomers. The new arrivals settled in the Northeast, the Midwest, and the Southwest.

In the period covered by this chapter, factories, mines, and railroads were turning the United States into a giant industrial power. The economic opportunities in this changing nation attracted many immigrants. The new Spanish-speaking immigrants joined with others from many nations to make the mix of people in the United States even more varied than it had been.

1 NEW SPANISH IMMIGRATION
◆ Why did immigrants from Spain come
◆ to the United States in the late 1800s?

When the Spanish conquistadors set foot on the lands of the Americas after 1492, they were drawn by visions of golden cities. These conquistadors, many of them soldiers or nobles, wanted to gain glory for themselves and an empire for Spain. In the late 1800s, Spaniards again began heading for the Americas. These newcomers were not nobles or soldiers. They were ordinary men and women who simply sought to better their lives.

At Home in the Americas. The large majority of Spanish immigrants who came to the Americas in the late 1800s settled in Cuba and Argentina. Smaller numbers settled in Brazil, Mexico, and Uruguay. The Spaniards who came directly from Spain to the United States in the late 1800s and early 1900s numbered only about 50,000. Most of them arrived after 1900.

Until 1890, most Spaniards in the United States lived in New York City, California, and Louisiana. New York was where most ships from Europe landed. Thus, many Spaniards, like other immigrants, settled there. California and Louisiana had once been parts of Spain's colonial empire. They attracted Spanish newcomers because elements of Spanish culture still existed there. California became the nation's main "Spanish state" between 1900 and 1910 because of immigrants from Mexico and Spain. After 1890, Spaniards also began settling in Florida, which already had Spanish-speaking exiles from Cuba.

Around 1900, large numbers of sugar workers left the region of Andalusía in Spain. They sailed to Hawaii, which was then a U.S. territory. There, they played a major part in building up Hawaii's sugar industry.

Beginning in 1900, shepherds and cattle herders from the Basque region of Spain began to leave their homeland. Many settled in parts of the U.S. West, especially Idaho (see page 234). The Basque sheepherders brought to the pastures of the Rocky Mountains a way of life that their ancestors had practiced in Europe since ancient times.

Why They Came. Spaniards came to the United States for many reasons. Some were drawn to the United States because they saw it as the land of the future. They thought it offered the best chance to improve their lives.

Some left home because there were too many people and too little good land for farming or ranching. Some left to escape military service. Like other European nations, Spain drafted young men into its army for long periods of time. Some of the Spaniards who came to the United States never intended to stay. They "commuted" back and forth across the Atlantic, keeping homes in both countries.

Taking Another Look

1. Where did Spanish immigrants settle in the United States and its possessions?

2. What kind of work did some Spaniards find in the U.S. West that was similar to what they did back home?

3. **Critical Thinking** Why do you think many more Spaniards settled in Latin America than in the United States?

2 NEWCOMERS FROM PUERTO RICO ◆ AND CUBA

◆ What brought Puerto Rican and Cuban immigrants to the United States in the 1800s?

In the late 1800s, Cuba and Puerto Rico were Spain's last colonies in the Americas. In September 1868, Puerto Ricans in the town of Lares rebelled against Spanish rule. Their uprising, called *el Grito de Lares*, "the Cry of Lares," aimed at winning independence. Spanish troops quickly crushed the rebellion. Some Puerto Ricans who fought the Spanish or support-

SNAPSHOT OF THE TIMES

1868	Puerto Ricans in the town of Lares rebel against the Spanish.
1876	Key West elects the first Cuban American mayor in the United States.
1880s	*Las Gorras Blancas* make raids on Anglo property in New Mexico.
1893	Puerto Rican cigar makers declare Christmas Eve "the Day of the Homeland," raising $12,000 for the independence movement.
1898	Cuban-Spanish-American War
1900	Immigrants from the Andalusia and the Basque regions of Spain begin arriving in the United States.
1912	New Mexico and Arizona become U.S. states.

ed the cause of independence emigrated. Many came to New York City.

After the Cuban-Spanish-American War of 1898 (see Chapter 14), large sugar plantations replaced small farms in Puerto Rico. Often, those plantations were built with North American investments. Many poor farmworkers labored on those plantations for such low wages that they could barely feed their families. A number of those workers emigrated to the United States in search of better opportunities.

Puerto Ricans in New York. New York City was the magnet that drew large numbers of Puerto Ricans in the years after the Puerto Rican rebellion. Many found work as *tabaqueros* (tah-bah-KEH-rohs), or cigar makers, in the city's cigar factories. In 1894, there were 3,000 cigar factories in New York City. Five hundred of them were owned by Latinos.

For members of the Puerto Rican community in New York City, the cause of freedom for Puerto Rico and Cuba was a major issue. Almost every social event was related to the liberation cause. Political clubs argued over what the status of Puerto Rico should be when free of Spanish rule. Should it be independent or be connected with the United States?

In every cigar factory, there was a committee in charge of raising money for the cause. In 1893, Christmas Eve was designated as *el Día de la Patria,* "the Day of the Homeland." Every worker in the cigar factories donated a day's pay to be given to the independence movement. In all, $12,000, a huge sum in those days, was collected.

Immigrant Dreams. Many Puerto Rican immigrants dreamed of a new life in the United States. Immigrant Bernardo Vega (VEH-gah) recalled his voyage to New York City in the early 1900s:

Towards the dawn of the first day, the passengers began to act as if they were all family members. We did not hesitate to discover one another's histories. The overriding theme of our conversations, however, was what we expected to find in New York City. With our first earnings we would send for our nearest relative. Later on at the end of several years we would return to the homeland with our savings. We all, more or less, set our sights on the farm we would buy or the business we would establish in our respective hometowns.

Many new immigrants joined clubs with others from the same countries. The girls in this photo were members of the Cuban Club in Ybor City. Why do you think new immigrants joined clubs? What purposes do you think clubs served?

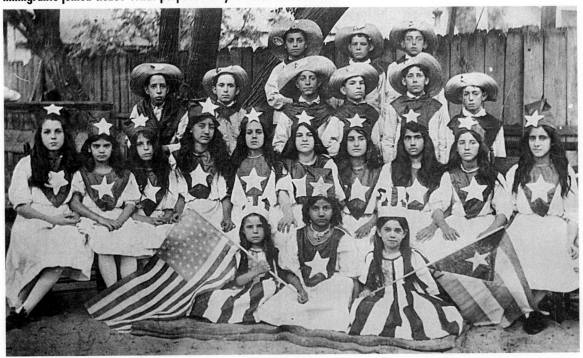

Not all the dreams of the Puerto Rican immigrants came true. However, many found steady work for decent wages in New York City. Wherever they went to live in the great city, the Puerto Ricans brought their culture and customs with them. The streets of their neighborhoods were lined with colorful grocery stores called *bodegas* (boh-DEH-gahs), Puerto Rican restaurants, and boardinghouses.

The Cubans in Key West. In the late 1800s, Puerto Ricans also moved to Florida. There they joined Cubans who had started living in the state in the 1870s. Cubans, too, had risen in revolt against Spanish rule in 1868. Unlike Puerto Rico's *Grito de Lares,* the Cuban revolt lasted ten long years (see page 173).

During those years of fighting and hardship, 100,000 Cubans fled the country. Many came to the United States. Those Cubans who were well educated and from the middle class settled in the big cities of the U.S. Northeast, like New York, Philadelphia, and Boston. There they could pursue their professions.

A much larger group of Cubans moved to Key West, Florida. This island off the coast of Florida is only about 90 miles (144 kilometers) from Cuba. In Key West, many Cubans worked in the cigar industry. By 1885, about 3,000 Cubans were working in the 100 cigar factories of the island.

Key West was a center of Cuban nationalism. Freedom from Spain was a constant topic of discussion among Cubans. A fiery Key West newspaper, *El Yara,* published a stream of editorials demanding independence from Spain. One such editorial said:

> To believe that [Spain] can give Cuba what it needs to make her prosper is a fantasy. There is only one road to salvation, the establishment of a Cuban republic where Cubans and Spaniards can find peace, work, and progress.

Cuban patriots visited Key West. They pleaded the cause of Cuban independence and raised money from workers in the cigar factories.

However, enthusiasm for Cuban independence did not make up for the low

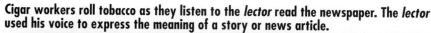

Cigar workers roll tobacco as they listen to the *lector* read the newspaper. The *lector* used his voice to express the meaning of a story or news article.

wages paid to cigar makers. Hardship struck when the demand for cigars fell in the United States. Many cigar makers lost their jobs. Not surprisingly, cigar workers organized labor unions. Several times they went on strike. Then, in 1886, a huge fire swept through Key West, destroying 16 cigar factories. The fire left hundreds of Cubans homeless and unemployed.

The Cigar Makers Move. With conditions in Key West so bad, one of the island's leading cigar manufacturers, Vicente Martínez Ybor (mahr-TEE-nes ee-BOHR), decided to move to the Florida mainland. Cheap land was available near the small city of Tampa. Ybor also thought he would have fewer labor problems to deal with. Ybor bought 40 acres (16 hectares) of swampy land a few miles from the Tampa business center.

Vicente Martínez Ybor was as much a dreamer as a businessperson. He looked at the swampland he had bought and pictured a company town where his employees could work, live, and raise their families. This community became a reality. It was called Ybor City, and Ybor controlled every aspect of life in it. He supervised the building of new homes for his workers. These homes were sold to the workers at low prices. If workers needed money for emergencies, Ybor would give them an advance on their pay. He threw picnics for workers and their families, stood in as godfather for their children, and gave them presents and food at Christmas.

Nevertheless, cigar workers did not want to rely on Ybor's generosity. The union activity that had started in Key West continued in Tampa. In January 1887, Ybor's workers struck for higher wages. Ybor then brought in new workers to replace the strikers. Violence broke out, resulting in the death of one worker and the wounding of three others. Although this strike was settled, conflict between workers and the owners of the cigar factories in Tampa continued for many years.

Readers in the Workplace. As time went on, cigar manufacturing spread to other Florida cities, such as Jacksonville and Ocala. Thousands more Cubans came to Florida where their skills of shaping Havana tobacco into high-grade cigars won them jobs.

All the factories followed a custom unique to the cigar-manufacturing industry. This was the use of a **lector** (lek-TOHR), a reader who read to the workers as they made the cigars. *Lectores* were given a try out and hired by the cigar workers and paid by them as well. The work, as *lector* Abelardo Gutierres Díaz (goo-tee-EH-rres DEE-ahs) explained, was not easy.

The *lector* had to be something of an actor. He had to breathe life into the protagonists [characters] in a story. The old lady—the old man: when they argued, when they yelled. All that. You know, it was not all that easy.

The *lector* . . . did not have the benefit of a loud-speaker system. It was all through the strength of one's voice. In one factory . . . which contained some 300 cigar workers, one had to read loud enough to be heard by everyone. It was an enormous effort. One enterprising *lector,* seeking to improve the system and there-

165

by make his life easier, introduced into the factory a [megaphone]. But the *lector's* voice through the [megaphone] annoyed the majority of workers; it was too metallic, they complained. In deference to [in response to] the workers' protest, the *lector* abandoned the [megaphone].

Many *lectores* read political articles, as well as popular novels, to the workers. As the struggle for independence grew in Cuba, the *lectores* became a powerful voice in its support. *Lectores* sometimes called on workers to join the fight. Often, they urged workers to support the cause with their time and money. After Cuba became independent, many *lectores* turned to reading political news articles and stories. Sometimes they read material that encouraged workers to strike or to demonstrate for better wages and working conditions. In time, this practice led managers to ban *lectores* from the factories.

Cigar manufacturing gave Cuban immigrants strong ties to their new communities in the United States. That was demonstrated when Cuba finally won independence in 1898. Some Cubans returned to their homeland. Many more, however, stayed in Florida, which they now considered their home.

Taking Another Look

1. What reasons brought Puerto Ricans to the United States in the 1800s? What reasons brought Cubans to the United States?

2. What roles did the *lector* fulfill in the cigar factories?

3. **Critical Thinking** If you were a cigar maker in Ybor City, what reading material would you want to have read to you as you worked? Explain your answer.

3 NEW MEXICO

◆ How did the movement of new people into the U.S. Southwest affect Latinos in New Mexico?

During the late 1800s, as you have read, many new immigrants moved to the United States. At the same time, however, groups of people moved within the United States as well. In the U.S. Southwest, these movements sometimes led to conflict as new Anglo settlers came in contact with long-time *nuevomexicano* residents.

Misunderstandings. For many years after the war with Mexico ended, in 1848, Latinos made up the largest part of the population in New Mexico and Arizona. Because of this, they had been spared some of the difficulties that other former Mexican citizens had faced soon after the war's end (see Chapter 11). By 1879, however, changes were taking place.

For example, the Atchison, Topeka and Santa Fe Railway had come to New Mexico. The railroad linked the isolated lands of the U.S. Southwest with the rest of the nation. The railroad also brought large numbers of Anglo settlers and businesspeople to the region for the first time. The newcomers saw in the vast land tremendous opportunity for progress.

The *nuevomexicanos* believed in progress, too. But for them, progress meant having enough land to farm and enough food to eat. For the newly arrived Anglos, progress meant new industries, like mining, more railroads, and large commercial farms. They viewed the *nuevomexicanos* and their culture as foreign, strange, and inferior.

Just as the Anglos did not understand the customs and traditions of the *nuevomexicanos,* the *nuevomexicanos* found the practices of the Anglos and their ideas on land use confusing. Many of them withdrew from the new society growing up around them and isolated themselves on their farms and in their villages. However, a few of them, particularly the *ricos,* welcomed the Anglos. They formed a partnership with the newcomers in order to hold on to their power and influence.

The *Gorras Blancas.* By the 1880s, New Mexico was experiencing a cattle boom. Anglo ranchers bought up or stole more *nuevomexicano* lands on which to graze their cattle (see page 136). They put up barbed wire fences, which *nuevomexicanos* called "the devil's hat-band," to confine their cattle and keep trespassers off.

Some *nuevomexicanos* decided to fight back to protect their way of life. At night, groups of these *nuevomexicanos* rode the countryside cutting fences, wrecking rail lines, and destroying Anglo property. The most famous of these groups called themselves *las Gorras Blancas* (GOH-rrahs BLAHN-kahs), or "the White Caps," after the masks they wore to hide their identity.

In 1890, they ruined 9 miles (14.4 kilometers) of barbed wire in just one night.

Anglo authorities saw *las Gorras Blancas* as a "lawless mob of several hundred Mexicans." But many *nuevomexicanos* saw them as heroes who were fighting for their land and homes. At least one Anglo judge agreed with them. After dismissing charges against a group of fence cutters, Judge James O'Brien told the New Mexico governor that "the so-called outrages are the protests of a simple, pastoral [animal-raising] people against the establishment of large landed estates . . . in their native territory."

The governor was not convinced. He threatened to call out federal troops to halt the raids. Thus warned, *las Gorras Blancas* soon gave up their raids. Instead, they turned to politics to preserve their culture. They formed a political party called *el Partido del Pueblo,* "the People's Party." After winning an election in 1894, however, the party split up because of disagreements among its leaders.

Latinos kept their traditions long after the U.S. takeover of New Mexico. Here, *nuevomexicanos* watch a religious procession in Santa Fe in 1895.

Nuevomexicano cowboys posed for this photograph in the 1890s. How would Anglo settlers change these Latino cowboys' way of life?

The Struggle for Statehood. As New Mexico's population grew, pressure to make it a state increased. The politicians in the U.S. Congress, however, resisted that pressure for years. They argued that New Mexico had too few people and was still too undeveloped for statehood.

New Mexicans thought those arguments made no sense. After all, territories like Wyoming and Idaho, with far fewer people than New Mexico, were admitted as states in the 1890s. The ugly truth was that Congress did not want to admit New Mexico to the Union while most of its people were Spanish-speaking, Roman Catholics of Mexican descent. One Congress member who opposed statehood called the *nuevomexicanos* "a race speaking an alien language."

The Constitutional Convention. In 1910, Congress finally agreed to admit New Mexico and Arizona as separate states. First, however, the territories had to draw up state constitutions. A constitutional convention met at Santa Fe on October 3, 1910.

One third of the 100 delegates were Latinos. Led by outspoken men like future governor Octaviano Larrazolo (see page 218), these delegates were determined that *nuevomexicano* rights would be protected under the new constitution.

The Latino delegates succeeded. One article of the constitution stated, "The rights, privileges and immunities, civil, political, and religious, guaranteed to the people of New Mexico by the Treaty of Guadalupe Hidalgo [see page 128] shall be preserved inviolate [unchanged]."

The constitution protected the right of a male citizen to vote regardless of his "religion, race, language or color." One article declared that "children of Spanish descent" would never be denied admission to the public schools. Nor would they ever be "classed in separate schools, but shall forever enjoy perfect equality with other children in all public schools."

Nuevomexicanos also agreed to a provision allowing women to vote in school elections. (Women were not permitted to vote at all in most states at the time.) They tried, unsuccessfully, to ban a provision for separate schools for African American students. A Southern newspaper warned the delegates that the U.S. Congress would reject the constitution if such a provision were included.

On January 6, 1912, New Mexico became the 47th state of the union. (Arizona was admitted as the 48th state on February 14, 1912). However, the struggle for equality for *nuevomexicanos,* as well as for other Latinos living in the United States, was far from over.

Taking Another Look

1. Over what issues did Anglo settlers and *nuevomexicanos* disagree?
2. Why did New Mexico have to wait until 1912 to become a state?
3. **Critical Thinking** What arguments would you have used to prevent the governor of New Mexico from calling out federal troops against *las Gorras Blancas*?

LOOKING AHEAD

In the later years of the 1880s and in the early 1900s, Spanish-speaking immigrants from Spain, Puerto Rico, Cuba, and Mexico joined the Latino population that had already made its mark on the culture of the United States. As the newcomers were making progress in their new country, Cuba and Puerto Rico entered the final stages of their struggles to free themselves from Spanish rule. In the next chapter, you will read how the two islands gained their freedom from Spain.

Latino delegates to New Mexico's state constitutional convention succeeded in securing a number of rights, including equality in education for Latino children.

LA PLACITA

Scattered across New Mexico are towns and villages whose Spanish names reflect their *nuevomexicano* origin. Names such as Jicarilla, Pinos Altos, and Tierra Blanca are reminders of the region's Latino heritage. When Anglos began to arrive in New Mexico, they sometimes changed the names of these towns. One such town was the Mexican village called *La Placita del Río Bonito,* "Little Plaza by the Pretty River."

Established by Mexican pioneers around 1849, La Placita was a farming center. Its adobe homes surrounded a central plaza, and a stone tower offered protection during frequent Apache raids. By the late 1860s, some 400 *nuevomexicanos* lived there.

Change came in 1869 when a group of Anglo businesspeople wanted to expand into the region. Urged on by the Anglos, Captain Saturnino Baca, military leader of La Placita, petitioned the territory's legislature to establish a new county called Lincoln. La Placita was then renamed as well.

Lincoln soon became a center of violence when Anglo ranchers fought Mexican farmers in what became known as the Lincoln County War during the 1870s. Today, Lincoln is not remembered as the peaceful La Placita but rather as a symbol of the lawlessness of the southwestern frontier.

CLOSE UP: Chapter 13

The Who, What, Where of History

1. **What** attracted Spanish newcomers to California and Louisiana?
2. **Where** in the United States did Basque immigrants settle?
3. **What** is *el Día de la Patria*?
4. **Who** was Vicente Martínez Ybor?
5. **What** is a *lector*?
6. **Who** were *las Gorras Blancas*?

Making the Connection

1. What was the connection between the increase in immigration to the United States from Puerto Rico and Cuba and the struggle for independence in those countries?
2. What was the connection between the construction of a railroad across the Southwest and the conflict between Anglos and *nuevomexicanos?*

Time Check

1. During which period was California considered the United States' main "Spanish state"?
2. In what year did New Mexico and Arizona become states?

What Would You Have Done?

1. Imagine that you are a Spanish farmer who is enduring hard times in Spain in the late 1800s and you decide to emigrate to the United States. Where in the United States would you choose to live? Explain.
2. As a *nuevomexicano* farmer in the Southwest, what would you have done to protect your property in the face of Anglo expansion? Explain.

Thinking and Writing About History

1. Imagine that you were among the Cubans who arrived to settle the area around Tampa during the 1880s. Write a letter to a friend describing the conditions of the region.

2. Imagine that you are a Puerto Rican *tabaquero* in New York City in the late 1800s who has been asked to raise money for the liberation cause. Write a speech you would give to other workers explaining the importance of the cause and urging them to support it.

3. Create a dialogue between an Anglo rancher and a *nuevomexicano* farmer on the issue of how to use land in the Southwest. Express the point of view of each person and the reason why he or she feels that way. At the end of the dialogue, write a paragraph explaining how you think the conflict could be resolved.

Building Skills: Recognizing a Generalization

Historians teach us about the past. Using primary and secondary sources, they interpret events in a way that helps us understand and appreciate history. The interpretations that historians make are based on generalizations about events or trends. A *generalization* is a broad conclusion based on many facts related to one another.

Here is an example of a generalization you might make after reading this chapter's introduction: "In the 1880s, the area around Tampa, Florida, was a dangerous place." The sentences below are examples of some of the facts that support this generalization.

For the person who ventured out at night . . . it was indispensable [necessary] to carry a lantern or lamp which might permit him to avoid dangerous spots. It was also advisable to carry a rifle or revolver for protection in the event of meeting any dangerous animals or similar unexpected threats.

To help you recognize generalizations, look for broad (not specific) statements and summarizing sentences, not examples.

Read the sentences below. Decide which sentences are generalizations. Then, on a separate sheet of paper, write the numbers of the sentences below that are generalizations.

1. Spanish immigrants settled in many regions of the United States.

2. About 50,000 Spaniards immigrated directly to the United States in the late 1800s and early 1900s.

3. New Mexico became a state in 1912.

4. The newspaper *El Yara* demanded independence for Cuba.

5. The *lector* played several roles in the cigar factories.

6. Anglo settlers and *nuevomexicanos* were in conflict with one another in several ways.

Express Yourself!

Choose two or three classmates to work with. Together, design a poster that supports one of the following causes: (1) independence for Cuba, (2) independence for Puerto Rico, or (3) statehood for New Mexico or Arizona. Be sure that your poster uses pictures and words that will influence others to support the cause.

In the fight for Cuban independence, patriots used tactics such as burning sugar cane fields owned by the Spanish.

The Cuban-Spanish-American War

(1868–1898)

SECTIONS

1 Background to Revolution

2 The War of 1895

3 Uncertain Victory

THINKING ABOUT THE CHAPTER

How did the United States become involved in fighting between Spain and its Caribbean colony Cuba?

To many people, what the 16-year-old boy had done was not serious. He had simply written a letter to a friend, accusing him of supporting Spain in a war against their home island of Cuba. The letter had come into the hands of the Spanish authorities who controlled Cuba. They were not pleased by the letter. They remembered that it was not the first time the writer of the letter had expressed feelings they saw as treasonous. After all, he had published patriotic poems and even put out his own newspaper called *Patria Libre* (PAH-tree-ah LEE-breh), "Our Free Country."

The writer had to be punished severely, the authorities decided. They therefore sentenced the young Cuban to six years of hard labor in a stone quarry. After serving a few months of his sentence, he was released and sent into exile in Spain. He was warned never to return to Cuba.

But José Martí (mahr-TEE) would not heed the warning. He would return to his beloved Cuba twice more in the remaining 26 years of his life. In the many years between the two visits, Martí would plead to the world the cause of his country's independence. That independence, won at great cost, was brief, followed by a period of U.S. control over Cuba.

1 BACKGROUND TO REVOLUTION
◆ What led Cubans to revolt against
◆ Spanish rule in the late 1800s?

By the mid-1800s, Spain's vast colonial empire in the Americas had shrunk to two islands in the Caribbean—Cuba and Puerto Rico. Mexico and the countries of Central and South America had fought for and won their freedom from Spain earlier in the century (see Chapter 7). Although no longer the strong world power it once was, Spain clung stubbornly to its last possessions. It was particularly determined not to give up Cuba, which the Spanish called the "ever faithful isle."

Cuba was still a source of wealth for Spain. The island's climate and rich soil were ideal for the production of sugar, tobacco, and coffee. Cuba's contribution to Spain's economy was not rewarded by the Spanish government. Spain took much and gave little in return. The Cubans were forced to pay high taxes, buy Spanish goods at very high prices, and suffer poor living and working conditions.

Stirrings of Independence. In 1821, Cuban anger exploded into a brief revolt, but the independence movement was crushed. Later, Simón Bolívar, the brilliant general, and liberator of several South American countries (see page 90), planned an invasion of Cuba and Puerto Rico with Mexican leaders. The invasion, however, never took place. One reason was that the United States at that time backed Spain's continued control of Cuba.

The United States had a strong interest in Cuba. It had traded with the island for many years and did not want revolution to end that profitable trade. However, many people in the United States sympathized with the Cubans' desire for freedom. The situation in Cuba reminded many U.S. citizens of their own nation's struggle for independence.

The Ten Years' War. In 1868, the Cubans tried once more to gain their independence. Under the leadership of wealthy Cuban planter Carlos Manuel de Céspedes (SES-peh-des), they demanded that Spain abolish slavery on the island and grant Cuba full independence. Spain refused, and the Cubans rebelled in what became known as the Ten Years' War.

In this conflict, the Cubans were led by two skillful commanders. Máximo Gómez (GOH-mes) was a tough professional soldier and a strong leader. His friend, Antonio Maceo (mah-SEH-oh), was an experienced fighter.

The war was a bitter one. The *insurrectos* (een-soo-RREK-tohs), as the rebels were called, were committed to winning independence. The Spanish, on the other hand, were determined to keep their colony. A statement by a Spanish officer in 1869 shows just how far the Spaniards would go to put down the rebellion:

Not a single Cuban will remain in this island, because we will shoot all those we find in the fields, on the farms, and in every hovel [crude dwelling]. We do not leave a creature alive where we pass, be it man or animal. . . . The island will remain a desert.

Sympathy for the Cubans ran high in the United States. Although the U.S. government did not get involved in the war, many private citizens and professional soldiers enlisted to fight in Cuba. Others brought arms and supplies to the rebels. Many U.S. citizens were captured on their arrival by the Spanish and hanged or shot. That further angered the U.S. public.

While the long war in Cuba dragged on, an uprising in Puerto Rico was quickly put down. The Puerto Ricans decided to abandon violence. They tried to negotiate with Spain for self-government, but they were unsuccessful. Many Puerto Ricans later went to Cuba and fought alongside Cubans in their war for independence.

In 1878, the Cuban war finally ended with an agreement called the Pact of Zanjón (sahn-HOHN). The Spanish government agreed to start political reforms. They also promised to pass laws abolishing slavery. In 1886, slavery was finally abolished, freeing thousands of African Cubans from bondage. But most of the reforms the Spanish government agreed to were never carried out.

After the war, many Cubans who had supported it fled to the United States, where they settled mainly in New York City and Tampa, Florida. As you read in Chapter 13, the Cuban cigar makers helped to create a new industry in the United States. The Cuban immigrants in the United States also played a major role in the ongoing struggle for Cuban independence from Spain. They formed committees that helped keep the independence movement alive. They also raised large sums of money to buy arms and other supplies for the struggle.

Taking Another Look

1. What reasons did Spain have for holding on to Cuba?

2. Why were the people of the United States sympathetic to the Cubans in their fight against Spain?

3. **Critical Thinking** Why do you think the Cubans' attempts to gain their freedom from Spain were not successful?

2 THE WAR OF 1895
◆ What part did Cubans in the United States play in the Cuban revolution?

In the years after the Ten Years' War, conditions in Cuba grew worse and worse. In 1894, the United States put a high **tariff**, or tax, on Cuban sugar coming into the country. As a result, the price of Cuban sugar rose sharply and sales fell drastically in the United States. The Cuban economy was nearly destroyed. The winter of 1894–1895 was a hard one for the Cuban people, and discontent led once more to war. This time, though, the war was launched not from within Cuba but from outside the island by Cuban immigrants living in the United States.

Martí as Leader. No Cuban contributed more to the coming struggle than José Martí. After he had been exiled to Spain, the young Martí earned a law degree there, then moved to Mexico. In Mexico, he wrote political essays and poems that expressed his desire for Cuban independence. Martí's democratic ideas led him to leave Mexico and later Guatemala, since both countries were run by dictators at the time. In 1878, Martí returned to Cuba under an **amnesty,** or general pardon. But he continued to be

"Let us rise up . . . for the true republic." With these words Jose Martí roused a crowd of Cuban Americans in Tampa in 1891. Martí, with jacket open at top of steps, is shown just after his famous speech.

active in the independence movement. His political activities soon forced him to leave the island again.

By 1881, Martí was living in New York City, where he would spend the next 14 years. He wrote and gave lectures all across the country demanding Cuban independence. He also formed the Cuban Revolutionary party to plan another war against Spanish rule. Martí urged Cuban immigrants in the United States to support the struggle in their homeland. He also taught Latin Americans about life in the United States through articles published in many Latin American newspapers.

Although Martí admired the democratic system of government in the United States, he was not blind to problems in the nation. Martí criticized the racial prejudice and **materialism,** or love of money and wealth, of his adopted country. He was especially concerned about the United States' growing influence in Latin America. He saw that influence as harmful to the countries of the region.

To Martí, the fight for Cuban independence meant more than just freedom from Spanish rule. It also meant freedom from all prejudice and injustice. Martí dreamed of a new Cuba, where all people would be brothers and sisters, regardless of their skin color or social position. In a historic speech to Cuban Americans in Tampa in November 1891, Martí electrified the audience with these words:

Let us rise up so that freedom will not be endangered by confusion or apathy [lack of interest] or impatience in preparing it. Let us rise up, too, for the true republic, those of us who, with our passion for right and our habit of hard work, will know how to preserve it. . . . And let us place around the star of our new flag this formula [motto] of love triumphant: "With all, and for the good of all."

Cuban Americans responded to Martí's call by donating a tenth of their weekly wages to buy guns and ammunition for the coming struggle.

◆ Among Martí's strongest supporters in Tampa were the African Cuban **Paulina Pedroso** (peh-DROH-soh) and her husband Ruperto. On his visits to Tampa, Martí stayed with the Pedrosos. Paulina nursed him back to health when he fell ill after an exhausting series of lectures. She helped set up groups to meet the needs of new immigrants. She raised money tirelessly for the cause of Cuban inde-

LATINO HERITAGE

José Martí

José Martí's skills as an organizer and political thinker helped bring lasting change to Cuba. His skills as a writer helped change Latin American literature as well. Martí wrote highly original essays and simple, moving poetry. The selections below are from his book *Versos Sencillos (Simple Verses)*. After Martí's death, some of those verses were set to music in the famous song *Guantanamera*.

Yo soy un hombre sincero
De donde crece la palma,
Y antes de morirme quiero
Echar mis versos del alma.

Oculto en mi pecho bravo
La pena que me lo hiere:
El hijo de un pueblo esclavo
Vive por él, calla y muere.

I am an honest man
From where the palms grow;
Before I die I want my soul
To shed its poetry.

My manly heart conceals
The pain it suffers; sons of
A land enslaved live for it
Silently, and die.

pendence. She and Ruperto even sold their modest home so that they could contribute to the cause. Years later, the Pedrosos returned to an independent Cuba. They were given a house rent-free by the government in return for the one they had given up. After their deaths, Tampa honored the Pedrosos with a plaque near where their house once stood. It describes Paulina as "one of the great women patriots of Cuba."

A Bitter War. By February 1895, all was in place for another uprising. Cubans returning from the United States had aroused the people and helped organize rebel soldiers. In April, José Martí himself returned to Cuba. He came not to write or speak out for Cuban independence, but to fight for it.

Martí's decision alarmed some Cuban rebels. They feared for the life of the man whose words inspired them. Their fears proved justified. On May 19, 1895, in a minor fight with Spanish troops, Martí was killed. He was one of the first to fall in the war, but his spirit remained very much alive.

General Máximo Gómez and Antonio Maceo returned from exile to lead Cubans in the War of 1895. Gómez knew that rebel forces were outnumbered nearly five to one by the Spanish and that the rebels had few guns and meager supplies. He therefore decided that the only way to win was to fight a **guerrilla war**. *Guerrilla* in Spanish means "little war." In fighting such a war, Gómez organized his men into small units and avoided facing the Spanish in major battles. Instead, rebel forces attacked the Spanish from concealed positions and then disappeared into the mountains or jungles.

Through two long and bitter wars of independence, Antonio Maceo fought to oust the the Spanish from his beloved Cuba.

"The Butcher" Arrives. In 1896, with the rebels gaining ground, the Spanish government sent General Valeriano Weyler (way-LEHR) to lead the fight against the Cubans. Weyler launched a brutal campaign that earned him the nickname in the United States of "the Butcher." A children's poem of the time summed up the hatred the Cuban people felt for Weyler when it said he had:

The instinct of a jackal, the soul of a
  dog.
Hypocrite! Coward! Vile and
  obscene!

Weyler declared **martial law**, which meant that the whole country, including

1868–1878 Cuba and Spain engage in the Ten Years' War.

1886 Slavery abolished in Cuba.

1895 War of 1895 begins.

José Martí is killed in a battle with Spanish troops.

1898 U.S.S. *Maine* explodes in Havana.

Cuban-Spanish-American War fought.

U.S. troops occupy Cuba.

United States gains Puerto Rico, the Philippines, Guam, and Wake from Spain.

civilians, was under the control of the army. Weyler also issued a *reconcentrado* (reh-kahn-sen-TRAH-doh), or reconcentration, order. Under this order, Cubans in the countryside were forcibly moved to towns and cities, where they were herded together behind barbed wire. There, they lived with little food and shelter and without proper sanitation facilities. Many became ill and died.

Now, with the people who had supplied the rebels out of the way, Weyler set their fields on fire to starve out the enemy. U.S. official William J. Calhoun described the destruction he saw while on a train trip through the Cuban interior.

The country outside of the military posts was practically depopulated [without people]. Every house had been burned, banana trees cut down, [sugar] cane fields swept with fire, and everything in the shape of food destroyed. . . . I did not see a sign of life, except an occasional vulture or buzzard circling through the air. The country was wrapped in the stillness of death and the silence of desolation [emptiness].

Fighting Back. Rebel General Gómez fought fire with fire. He set out to burn every remaining sugar cane field. He hoped that doing so would destroy the main source of Spanish wealth in Cuba and thus drive the Spanish out.

After two years of war, trade and business had come to a standstill. Cuba was on the brink of disaster. U.S. President William McKinley called for an end to the conflict. He asked Spain to grant Cuba some form of self-government. If the war continued, McKinley warned, the United States would step in.

In 1898, a new, more liberal government came to power in Spain. The Cubans' fight for independence had severely weakened Spain. The new government wanted peace badly. It removed Weyler from command. The new Spanish government also promised new reforms for Cuba.

Cubans, however, were no longer willing to accept reforms. What they wanted was complete independence. On January 12, 1898, a riot broke out in Havana. President McKinley feared that U.S. citizens and property would be endangered. He sent the battleship U.S.S. *Maine* to Cuba on a "courtesy visit" as a further warning to Spain. The visit had an unexpected outcome.

Taking Another Look

1. How did José Martí gain support for Cuba's struggle from Cuban Americans?

2. What war tactics did the Cubans and the Spanish use against each other during the War of 1895?

3. **Critical Thinking** José Martí considered himself a citizen not only of Cuba but of all the Americas. From what you know of his life, explain whether he was justified in thinking of himself in that way.

3 UNCERTAIN VICTORY
◆ How did Cuba come under the control
◆ of the United States?

On February 9, 1898, the *New York Journal* printed a letter about President McKinley on its front page. The letter included this description of McKinley:

[He is] weak and a bidder for the admiration of the crowd, and, besides being a common politician who tries to leave a door open behind himself while keeping on good terms with the jingos [people who demanded war with Spain] of his party.

The letter raised a storm because it had been written by the Spanish ambassador to the United States, Enrique Dupey de Lôme (doo-PAY deh LOHM), to a friend. De Lôme was immediately forced to resign. But the letter damaged the already strained relations between the United States and Spain. Worse was yet to come.

The *Maine*. Six days after the de Lôme letter appeared, the battleship U.S.S. *Maine* exploded in Havana harbor. Some 260 of the 350 sailors aboard the *Maine* lost their lives in the explosion.

The sinking of the *Maine* caused an uproar in the United States. A number of U.S. citizens, including future President Theodore Roosevelt, accused the Spanish of blowing up the battleship. Although an investigation many years later stated that the explosion was probably the result of an accident, most Americans at the time agreed with Roosevelt.

"Destruction of the War Ship *Maine* Was the Work of an Enemy," screamed a front page headline in the *New York Journal*. The newspaper's publisher, William Randolph Hearst, thought that a strong campaign for war with Spain would increase the circulation of his newspaper. So his newspaper played up every anti-Spanish story. His sensational brand of reporting was called **yellow journalism**. It was also practiced by Hearst's rival, Joseph Pulitzer, in the *New York World*.

Hearst and Pulitzer competed for readers by seeing who could be the more startling. One Hearst headline became a war cry for U.S. soldiers in the coming war: "Remember the *Maine*! To hell with Spain!"

On April 18, the U.S. Congress recognized the independence of Cuba and ordered Spain to withdraw from the island. Spain refused. On April 24, Congress declared war.

The Ten-Week War. On June 14, 1898, a U.S. military force of 17,000 men set sail for Cuba from Tampa. Six days later, the two U.S. commanders, General William R. Shafter and Admiral William T. Sampson, met with General Calixto García, the local Cuban rebel commander. García suggested that U.S. troops come ashore at Daiquirí (deye-kee-REE) and Siboney (see-boh-NAY) (see map, page 180). Once ashore, the U.S. troops joined García's soldiers and attacked the Spanish outside the city of Santiago.

One half of the U.S.-Cuban force attacked a Spanish-held stone fort at El Caney (el kah-NAY). The rest led an assault on the main Spanish defenses on Kettle Hill and San Juan Hill. The Rough Rider Regiment, with their second-in-command, Lieutenant Colonel Theodore Roosevelt, charged up Kettle Hill. Among the Rough Riders were African Americans and Latinos, including Captain Maximiliano Luna. The battle was a bitter victory. While 215 Spanish died, so did 205 U.S. soldiers, with many more wounded.

With U.S. troops surrounding Santiago on the land, Spanish Admiral Pascual Cervera y Topete (ser-VEH-rah ee toh-PEH-teh) tried to get away from the city by sea. U.S. ships followed the Spanish fleet, however, and captured or sank every vessel. On July 17, Santiago surrendered.

Soon after, Major General Nelson A. Miles invaded Puerto Rico and met with little resistance from the Spanish there. Meanwhile, Commodore George Dewey

had completely destroyed the Spanish fleet in Manila Bay in the Philippine Islands, Spain's Asian colony. U.S. land troops then landed in Manila, the Philippine capital. By August, the Cuban-Spanish-American War was over. It had lasted a brief ten weeks.

After the Fighting. On December 10, 1898, Spain and the United States signed a peace treaty. Under the agreement, Spain granted full independence to Cuba. It also turned over to the United States Puerto Rico, the Philippines, and the Pacific islands of Guam and Wake. In exchange, the United States paid Spain $20 million.

After 400 years of Spanish rule, Cuba seemed to be free. But was it actually free? The United States set up a military gov-

In 10 weeks of 1898, combined U.S. and Cuban forces drove the Spanish from their final American colonies. Cuba and Puerto Rico were free of Spanish rule. But the United States now played a major role in both countries.

In triumph, U.S. troops raise their flag over a government building in Havana. Spain was ousted from Cuba. When would the Americans leave?

ernment to run the island, in order to restore normal conditions. That government would also prepare the way for free elections in Cuba.

Yet many people in Cuba, in the United States, and throughout Latin America were concerned by the U.S. victory. They wondered if the United States would really pull out of Cuba. U.S. companies had large investments on the island. Would they pressure the U.S. government to take over the island? Nicaraguan poet Rubén Darío (roo-BEN dah-REE-oh) wondered what José Martí would have thought about the outcome of the war. Darío asked "what that Cuban [Martí] would say today in seeing that under the cover of aid to [Cuba], the 'monster' [a term Martí sometimes used for the United States] gobbles it up."

Taking Another Look

1. What two events helped lead up to the Cuban-Spanish-American War in 1898?

2. What did the United States gain from taking part in the war with Spain?

3. **Critical Thinking** Do you think the United States was right to occupy Cuba after the war? Why or why not?

LOOKING AHEAD

The war of 1898 was a turning point in the history of Latin America. Cuba and Puerto Rico were now free of Spanish rule. Spain had lost the last pieces of an empire that had once stretched from the southern tip of South America well into what is today the United States. In place of Spain, the United States had become a dominant Caribbean power. Yet freedom from Spain did not bring true independence to Cuba and Puerto Rico. The United States would play a strong role in both countries for many years to come. You will read about this influence in the next chapter.

GUANTÁNAMO BAY

Located in Guantánamo (gwahn-TAH-nuh-moh) Bay on the eastern coast of communist Cuba is a small U.S. naval base. It has been there since 1903—five years after the end of the Cuban-Spanish-American War.

As you have read, the United States set up a military government in Cuba after the war. In 1901, the U.S. Congress announced the conditions under which the United States would end its occupation of Cuba. One of the conditions was the establishment of a U.S. naval base on Guantánamo Bay.

Surrounded by a 10-foot (3-meter) high fence with a 24-hour guard, some 7,000 U.S. servicepeople and their families live and work at this outpost. Homes, supermarkets, and a golf course supply these Americans with what one writer called "all the comforts of a small midwestern town."

The United States pays an annual rent of $4,085 for Guantánamo. After the communist revolution in 1959, U.S. relations with Cuba turned sour. Cuba now refuses to cash the checks, insisting that the United States is in Guantánamo illegally. Except for about 30 Cubans who work on the base, Guantánamo is forbidden to Cubans.

Cuban leader Fidel Castro has called the base "a dagger plunged into Cuban soil." In addition, many U.S. military experts think the base no longer holds any real strategic value. For now, however, it remains a U.S. military outpost in the Caribbean.

CLOSE UP: Chapter 14

The Who, What, Where of History

1. **What** did Cuba contribute to the economy of Spain?
2. **Who** were Carlos de Céspedes, Máximo Gómez, and Antonio Maceo?
3. **What** is a tariff?
4. **Who** was José Martí?
5. **What** did Paulina and Ruperto Pedroso contribute to the struggle for Cuban independence?
6. **Where** did the incident with the U.S.S. *Maine* take place?
7. **Who** was Calixto García?

Making the Connection

1. What was the connection between uprisings in Puerto Rico and rebellion in Cuba?
2. What was the connection between Cubans in the United States and the War of 1895?

Time Check

1. When did the first major uprising against Spanish rule occur in Cuba?
2. How many years passed between the first uprising and the end of the Ten Years' War?
3. In what year did the United States declare war on Spain?

What Would You Have Done?

1. Would you have agreed with José Martí's decision to return to Cuba or would you have urged him to continue his fight for independence from outside the island? Explain.
2. If you had been a Cuban American who supported Cuban independence,

how would you have reacted to the final outcome of the Cuban-Spanish-American War?

Thinking and Writing About History

1. Reread the excerpt from José Martí's speech (page 176). Then, in your own words summarize Martí's ideas about the meaning of freedom.

2. Write an article entitled "The Role of Yellow Journalism in U.S. Intervention in Cuba." Describe what yellow journalism is and give examples. Tell whether you think this kind of journalism is practiced today.

3. If you had been a U.S. citizen who read about the explosion of the U.S.S. *Maine,* how would you have reacted? What course of action would you have suggested to the U.S. government? Write an editorial for the *New York Journal* that expresses your opinion and your plan of action.

Building Skills: Recognizing a Generalization

In the last chapter you learned about *generalizations,* broad statements based on many related facts. Read the account below of Spain's relations with Cuba and answer the question that follows.

Cuba was still a source of wealth for Spain. The island's climate and rich soil were ideal for the production of sugar, tobacco, and coffee. Cuba's contribution to Spain's economy was not rewarded by the Spanish government. Spain took much and gave little in return. Cubans were forced to pay high taxes, buy Spanish goods at incredibly high prices, and suffer poor living and working conditions.

1. In your notebook, number the sentences in the quotation from 1 to 5. Which of the sentences contain generalizations?

Read the following excerpt by a historian regarding the explosion of the battleship *Maine.* Then, answer the questions that follow.

To this day no one knows how the Maine was blown up, yet her destruction, quite illogically, was by far the most important single precipitant [cause] of war with Spain. Nothing could have brought home to the American republic more forcibly the disordered conditions in Cuba and the proposed solution that the island be freed. The American people no longer reasoned—they felt.

2. According to this selection, what was the key reason the United States declared war on Spain?

3. Based on this selection, what generalization can you make about the effect of the *Maine's* destruction on the United States' decision to intervene in Cuba?

Express Yourself!

Choose a classmate to work with. Together, pick one of the following people: José Martí, Carlos de Céspedes, Máximo Gómez, Antonio Maceo, or Paulina Pedroso. Review the information about that person in the text. Write down at least five questions you would want to ask that person. Then, write answers to your questions from the point of view of the person you chose. With your partner, read your interview for the class.

Not all Puerto Ricans greeted the arrival of U.S. troops with open arms. The members of the Aguila Blanca (White Eagle) party shown here were among those who opposed the U.S. presence.

SECTIONS

1 The United States and Puerto Rico

2 The Republic of Cuba

CHAPTER 15

Puerto Rico and Cuba Under United States Control

(1898–1920s)

THINKING ABOUT THE CHAPTER

What did control by the United States mean for Puerto Rico and Cuba?

General Nelson A. Miles was a veteran of the U.S. Civil War and wars against Native Americans. Yet the invasion of Puerto Rico during the U.S. war with Spain was unlike anything else in Miles's long military career. His troops landed on the southern coast of Puerto Rico on July 25, 1898. Realizing that the war was already lost in Cuba, the Spanish put up little resistance.

The Puerto Ricans, on the other hand, welcomed the U.S. arrival. When journalist Richard Harding Davis arrived in the town of Como ahead of the U.S. troops, the mayor surrendered to him and proclaimed a fiesta, or celebration. In

17 days, it was all over. Puerto Rico was entirely in U.S. hands. Only 4 U.S. soldiers had been killed and 40 wounded.

One U.S. newspaper called the campaign "General Miles' Gran' Picnic and Moonlight Excursion in Puerto Rico." Correspondent Davis wrote more soberly in *Scribner's Magazine,* "It is a beautiful island, smiling with plenty and content . . . and it came to us willingly, with open arms. But had it been otherwise, it would have come to us."

Yet, the enthusiasm that Puerto Ricans felt for the first U.S. troops did not last much longer than the invasion itself. Likewise in Cuba, the U.S. takeover did not turn out as Cubans had expected. The United States soon found itself thought of as an invader rather than a liberator. For many years to come, Puerto Ricans and Cubans would view their neighbor to the north with suspicion.

1 THE UNITED STATES AND PUERTO RICO

◆ What kind of government did the United States provide for its new possession?

At the time of the U.S. invasion, Puerto Rico was a small island of nearly one million people. It was a country of small farms that produced a variety of crops. Many people lived in poverty. Few children went to school. Only 13 percent of all Puerto Ricans could read and write.

Self-Rule. Even with these problems, the Puerto Ricans were better off politically than their Cuban neighbors. In 1897, after years of negotiation, Puerto Rico was granted **autonomy** by Spain. This meant that, although still a Spanish possession, Puerto Rico had a great degree of self-rule. It could send representatives to Spain's legislature. Puerto Rico's own parliament—part elected and part appointed by Spanish officials—for the most part controlled its own affairs.

In March 1898, Puerto Rican voters chose their first parliament under the new arrangement. The elected officials took office on July 17, 1898. Eight days later, U.S. troops landed in Puerto Rico and the parliament was sent home. Yet many Puerto Ricans were pleased with the U.S. arrival. Most Puerto Ricans believed their lives would improve even more with U.S. help. Surely, many people reasoned, the United States, as a democracy, would help Puerto Rico gain full independence more rapidly than Spain would have done.

A Military Government. In his first public speech, General Miles, the new military governor, seemed to promise as much:

> We have not come to make war upon the people of a country that for centuries has been oppressed but on the contrary to bring you protection . . . to promote your prosperity and to bestow upon [give] you the . . . blessings of the liberal institutions of our government.

But the United States had no intention of bestowing independence on Puerto Rico. There were two reasons for this. First, it felt that the people had no experience in self-rule. Thus, U.S. government officials believed Puerto Ricans were not ready for total political freedom. Second, the location of the island, at the entrance to the Caribbean, was important to the defense of the United States and its interests in the region. To ensure the safety of those interests, the United States felt that it must control Puerto Rico.

However, the U.S. government was ready to make improvements in the lives of the Puerto Rican people. Accordingly, it built roads, bridges, hospitals, and schools. But under U.S. rule Puerto Rico came to have a "one-crop economy." U.S. companies made sugar the island's most important product. Before long, Puerto Rico's economy was largely dependent on selling sugar to the United States.

The Foraker Act. The first U.S. government in Puerto Rico was a military one and it was temporary. It lasted only two years. A civil government was put in place in 1900 under the **Foraker Act.** The Foraker Act was named for U.S. Congressman Joseph B. Foraker. He was one of the most outspoken backers of a policy of U.S. expansion.

According to the Foraker Act, Puerto Rico would remain politically under the control of the U.S. government. The upper body of the two-house legislature and the governor of Puerto Rico would be appointed by the U.S. President. The lower house would be elected by the Puerto Ricans. All legislation would be subject to review by the U.S. Congress. Although a Puerto Rican representative could sit in the U.S. House of Representatives, that representative could not vote. Soon after the Foraker Act took effect, U.S. politicians were saying proudly, "We have organized the government of Puerto Rico and its people now enjoy peace, freedom, order, and prosperity."

Many Puerto Ricans reacted angrily to the Foraker Act. The act brought them no closer to the **home rule,** or self-government, that most of them had expected. The most outspoken critic of the act was Luis Muñoz Rivera (moo-NYOS ree-VEH-rah). He called it "unworthy of the United States which imposed it and of the Puerto Ricans who have to endure it."

Luis Muñoz Rivera (1859–1916) dedicated his life to the cause of Puerto Rican independence. In 1889, he founded the newspaper *La Democracia,* devoted to freedom for his country. Unlike some nationalists, Muñoz Rivera was willing to work with Spain to gain self-government. That willingness was harshly criticized by some other Puerto Ricans.

However, Muñoz Rivera's tactics worked. He was elected head of a new liberal government in Puerto Rico only months before the U.S. invasion. Muñoz Rivera tried to work with the U.S. government as he had with the Spanish to gain full rights for his people. In 1910, Muñoz Rivera moved to Washington, D.C., as the island's representative in Congress. For six years he worked tirelessly to change the Foraker Act. He died before the passage of the Jones Act (see below), which provided for greater Puerto Rican self-government.

The Jones Act. Puerto Ricans continued to demand a greater share in the governing of their island. In 1917, the U.S. Congress moved in this direction by passing the **Jones Act.** The new law granted U.S. citizenship to all Puerto Ricans who wanted it. Most Puerto Ricans accepted this offer, although a small number refused. They believed, as Muñoz Rivera did, that for Puerto Ricans to do so "would interfere with their ambitions for independence."

Under the Jones Act, Puerto Rican voters could elect the upper house of the Puerto Rican legislature. However, the governor and other key officials continued to be appointed by the U.S. President.

The new law was passed just before the United States entered World War I. Although the Jones Act did not please those Puerto Ricans who wanted greater self-government, the majority of Puerto Ricans supported the United States in the war. Nearly 20,000 Puerto Ricans served in the U.S. armed forces, while islanders raised $10 million in war bonds.

Statehood and Economic Rights.

Some Puerto Ricans, such as labor leader Santiago Iglesias (ee-GLES-ee-ahs), were more interested in winning economic rights than political ones. After the war, Iglesias, head of the Puerto Rican Socialist party, led a movement for statehood. He argued that, if Puerto Rico were a U.S. state, it would have more control over its economy and be able to improve workers' lives.

Iglesias had much to complain about. The *jíbaros* (HEE-bah-rohs), the workers on the sugar plantations and the tobacco farms, made up a large part of the island's population. They lived in extreme poverty.

After a visit to the island, one U.S. governor reported seeing "farm after farm where lean underfed women and sickly men repeated again and again the same story—little food and no opportunity to get more." In fact, the island's welfare remained under the control of the U.S.-appointed governors. Some of these governors named many native Puerto Ricans to government positions.

Other governors, however, had little understanding of the island or its people. One such governor declared, "There is no room on this island for any flag other than

1898	Cuban-Spanish-American War
	U.S. troops land in Puerto Rico.
1900	Foraker Act goes into effect.
1901	Cuba adopts Platt Amendment.
	U.S. troops pull out of Cuba.
1902	U.S. base established at Guantánamo Bay.
1906	Cuban Liberal party revolts.
1912	African Cuban sugar workers' revolt supressed.
1917	U.S. Congress passes the Jones Act.
	United States enters World War I.

the Stars and Stripes." That governor's attitude was shared by other U.S. officials. In the 1920s, Puerto Rican leaders requested greater home rule from U.S. President Calvin Coolidge. Coolidge responded that they should be grateful for what freedom they did have.

Cultural Imperialism.

Many Puerto Ricans wanted independence from the United States not only for political and economic reasons but for cultural reasons as well. They accused the United States of **cultural imperialism,** the desire to wipe out the culture of the island.

The longer the United States ruled the island, they feared, the more Puerto Rico would become like the United States. In the process, Puerto Ricans' folklore, literature, language, and even their customs would vanish.

Many of these fears were not realized, however. Few Puerto Ricans abandoned Spanish for English. By and large, the culture of Puerto Rico kept its distinctive qualities. Nevertheless, the fear that it would be wiped out remained a key point in the patriots' campaigns against the United States. Every time a U.S official or visitor called the island "Porto Rico," the fears of the patriots were reinforced.

Taking Another Look

1. How did the Foraker Act limit Puerto Rican independence?

2. What did Luis Muñoz Rivera do to help Puerto Rico become more free of Spanish and U.S. domination?

3. **Critical Thinking** If you were a Puerto Rican patriot in 1898, how do you think you would have reacted to the U.S. occupation of your island?

2 THE REPUBLIC OF CUBA

◆ What part did the United States play in the affairs of Cuba after that nation became independent of Spain?

After the Cuban-Spanish-American War, the United States treated Cuba very differently from the way it treated Puerto Rico. The Cubans were seen as better able to handle self-government. Also, the United States had no desire to go to war against Cuban rebels who had already fought for many years against the Spanish. On the other hand, the United States had no intention of giving up its investments in the Cuban sugar industry. If the rebels took over the country, that profitable trade might be in danger.

The U.S. Army in Charge. By 1900, Cuba was exhausted from years of warfare. There were 1.5 million Cubans, down by 200,000 from 1895. The United States set up a military government to improve living conditions and pave the way toward self-government.

General Leonard Wood, commander of the Rough Riders, was the most prominent military governor. Under his leadership, employment rose, education was improved, and new roads, bridges, and sewer systems were built.

Perhaps the greatest problem in Cuba was the deadly disease yellow fever, known as "yellow jack." The cause of the disease was unknown. Thousands of people in Cuba and other Latin American nations lost their lives to the disease each year. Many more U.S. soldiers died of yellow fever than were killed in the fighting during the Spanish-Cuban-American War.

A Cuban doctor, **Carlos Juan Finlay** (1833–1915), was the man who found the key to the mysterious disease. In 1881, Finlay had proposed that yellow fever was spread by the bite of a particular kind of mosquito called *Aëdes aegypti*. His theory had been rejected by scientists in Cuba and the United States.

But in 1900, an American Yellow Fever Commission, led by Major Walter Reed, was desperate to find a cure for yellow fever. Reed and his team used mosquitoes from eggs given them by Finlay to bite volunteer soldiers. All those bitten by the mosquitoes came down with the disease. Now the commission had proof of the cause of yellow fever. A sanitary campaign, originally suggested by Finlay, was begun on the island and wiped out the dangerous mosquito. Thanks to Finlay's pioneering work, the terror of yellow fever was ended.

A wave of Cuban flags held by Cuban students celebrates Cuban independence in 1902. The Stars and Stripes no longer flew over Cuba, but the United States continued to have great power.

The Platt Amendment. Cubans continued to press for full independence and the end of U.S. occupation. In 1901, U.S. troops finally pulled out. But the United States was not willing to cut all its ties to Cuba.

As an important step to self-government, the Cubans drew up a constitution. The United States, however, insisted that the new constitution include an amendment that gave the United States certain rights in Cuba. This was the so-called **Platt Amendment.** Under it, the United States had the right to intervene in Cuba to preserve order and to establish naval bases on the island. In 1902, the United States leased land for a base on Guantánamo Bay (see page 182).

The Platt Amendment in effect made Cuba a **protectorate** of the United States. A protectorate is a country that is technically independent but is really controlled by a stronger power. Many Cubans were unhappy with the Platt Amendment, but accepted it as the price of independence. On May 20, 1902, the U.S. flag was lowered in Cuba and the new republic's first president Tomás Estrada Palma (es-TRAH-dah PAHL-mah) took office.

Two Revolts. An honest, well-intentioned man, Estrada Palma realized self-government would not be easy for a people who had lived 400 years under colonialism. Cuba had become a republic, he said, but it lacked citizens.

189

Estrada Palma was a member of the Moderate party. His presidency was hampered by the opposition of the Cuban Liberal party. In August 1906, the Liberals revolted. The United States, invoking the Platt Amendment, sent in troops and set up a temporary government.

A second Cuban republic was established in 1909, with José Miguel Gómez, head of the Liberal party, as president. Gómez watched U.S. forces leave Cuba on the new battleship *Maine*. As he did he announced, "Once again we are completely free."

Freedom for Gómez and his followers, however, meant a license to steal. Gómez was a popular president, but he was also a corrupt politician. In addition, he was insensitive to the needs of the Cuban people, especially Cubans of African descent.

In 1912, 4,000 African Cuban sugar workers rose in revolt. Panic swept the country. The United States sent a force of marines to protect U.S.-owned sugar mills. Soon, Cuban troops put down the revolt. However, from that time until 1959, African Cubans had little say in the political life of the country.

Political Corruption. In 1913, General Mario García Menocal (meh-noh-KAHL) of the Conservative party became president. He quickly proved to be even more corrupt than Gómez. Menocal had a fortune of $1 million when he became president; he is said to have left office with $40 million.

By the mid–1920s, Cubans were fed up with the corruption and greed that had marked the government for a decade and a half. They elected Gerardo Machado y Morales (mah-CHAH-doh ee moh-RAHL-es) as president. Machado promised to reject the Platt Amendment and create a new relationship with the United States.

He also promised reform. The Liberal party called Machado "the man the young Republic had been waiting for."

Unfortunately, Machado turned out to be no different from his predecessors. He was corrupt. He also ruled as a dictator, often ordering political opponents to be killed.

U.S. Businesses in Cuba. With Cuba experiencing the growing pains of a new republic, some U.S. politicians became impatient and spoke of the need to take greater control of the island. In reality, the United States already had a great deal of power there. U.S. businesses had bought up much of the country and its profitable sugar mills. Such companies often gave large sums of money to politicians and government officials in return for special favors and privileges.

One U.S. citizen living in Cuba described the situation there:

> This republic is not a creature of Cubans . . . but on the contrary it is of all-American manufacture. Americans built it. Americans set it up again when it fell flat. American influence is all that sustains it to this moment.

King Sugar. Under U.S. control, sugar went from being an important export to the backbone of the Cuban economy. By 1910, as much sugar was being produced on the island in one year as had been in the entire decade of the 1830s.

During World War I, sugar production in warring countries was shut down. Cuba became the major producer of sugar in the world. Sugar cane was planted everywhere on the island to cash in on the boom. The daughter of a Cuban tobacco farmer recalled:

Sugar was "king" in Cuba, as under U.S. control, sugar became the backbone of the Cuban economy. Some became fabulously rich, but most Cuban workers worked long hours in the fields for next to nothing.

Whole jungles . . . were fired and razed [demolished] to the ground to make way for the sugar cane. My parents were in despair for that most beautiful and fragrant tropical wood . . . blazing in sacrifice to the frenzy [craze] to cover the countryside with sugar cane.

Sugar prices climbed dramatically. In just five months the price of sugar jumped from $6\frac{1}{2}$ cents per pound (.45 kilograms) to $22\frac{1}{2}$ cents per pound. Cuban landowners and sugar mill owners grew fabulously rich. They called the time the "dance of the millions."

But the dance ended as quickly as it had begun. After the war, there was an oversupply of sugar on the world market. Prices plummeted to $3\frac{3}{4}$ cents by Christmas 1920. Banks failed and sugar mills closed. At the beginning of the 1920s, there were 209 sugar mills in Cuba. By 1930, the number was down to 157.

Taking Another Look

1. How did the Platt Amendment prevent Cuba from being totally independent of the United States?

2. Why was Cuba's one-crop economy both a blessing and a curse?

3. **Critical Thinking** Why were some Cuban presidents corrupt?

LOOKING AHEAD

As a result of the Cuban-Spanish-American War, the United States had a strong presence in the Caribbean. Puerto Rico was its possession and Cuba, its protectorate. The people of neither island were satisfied with U.S. control.

In time, Cuba would become free, while Puerto Rico would become more tightly joined to the U.S. political system. Meanwhile, many Latinos of both islands would come to make their homes in the mainland United States.

The Cuban-Spanish-American War was in progress as U.S. warships approached San Juan Bay, Puerto Rico. As the ships drew closer, the great fortress, El Castillo de San Felipe del Morro, came into view. Rising 140 feet (43 meters) above the ocean, "El Morro," as the fortress is called, stood strong against U.S. gunfire. Only the lighthouse, the fortress's highest point, was destroyed during the attack.

This was not the first time that El Morro had been attacked by Spain's enemies. During the late 1500s and early 1600s, the English and the Dutch had tried to take the fort. But both were driven back. For nearly 400 years, until the United States took over Puerto Rico, Spain's flag flew over El Morro.

Construction on El Morro began in 1539. Over the years, the fortress expanded into a six-level structure with tunnels, dungeons, and gun turrets. A mystery surrounds the construction of El Morro, however. Scientists are not sure where the stones to build the fortress came from. Some scientists think that Taino Native Americans led the Spanish to stone quarries on the island. Then, the Spanish may have forced the Taino to dig and carry the stone to the construction site.

Today, El Morro is one of Puerto Rico's most popular tourist attractions. It is a National Historic site and a World Heritage site.

CLOSE UP: Chapter 15

The Who, What, Where of History

1. **What** did the Foraker Act do?
2. **Who** was Luis Muñoz Rivera?
3. **What** was the Jones Act?
4. **Who** was Santiago Iglesias?
5. **What** was the Platt Amendment?
6. **Where** did the United States establish a naval base in Cuba?
7. **Who** was Gerardo Machado y Morales?

Making the Connection

1. What was the connection between Puerto Rico's location and U.S. interest in the island?
2. Explain the relationship between the Jones Act and U.S. citizenship for Puerto Ricans.
3. Explain the relationship between Puerto Rico's one-crop sugar economy and Santiago Iglesias's movement for statehood.
4. What was the connection between U.S. business interests in Cuba and the growth of the sugar economy?

Time Check

1. How many years passed between the passage of the Foraker Act and the Jones Act?
2. Place the following events in the correct chronological order: José Miguel Gómez becomes president of Cuba; revolt of the Cuban Liberal party; passage of the Platt Amendment; U.S. base established at Guantánamo Bay.
3. In what year did African Cuban sugar workers revolt?

What Would You Have Done?

1. If you had been a Puerto Rican leader who had a chance to represent your country in the U.S. Congress in the early 1900s, would you have accepted the position? Explain your answer.

2. Imagine you are a Cuban rebel who fought for independence from Spain and welcomed the U.S. victory. How would you react to the Platt Amendment? Explain.

Thinking and Writing About History

1. Reread the excerpt from General Miles's speech on page 185. Imagine that you are a Puerto Rican who heard the general's speech. Write a letter to a friend expressing your hopes about the future of Puerto Rico based on this speech.

2. Write a letter to U.S. President Calvin Coolidge addressing his response to Puerto Ricans' demand for greater home rule. You may write your letter from the point of view of a Puerto Rican or of someone living in the United States.

3. Imagine that you are a speech writer for Cuban presidential candidate Gerardo Machado y Morales. Write a speech that Machado could deliver to the people asking for their support.

Building Skills: Making a Generalization

We make generalizations all the time. Suppose you are in a video store looking for a particular adventure film. Eventually you find it among the comedy films. A few days later, you look for a favorite mystery and find it also included in the comedy sec-

tion. From these experiences, you might make the generalization that the store is careless about its filing.

Read each of the following groups of related facts. Use the facts to make a *generalization,* a broad conclusion based on each group of facts.

1. a. The United States considered Puerto Rico important to its interests in the Caribbean.

   b. The governor of Puerto Rico was appointed by the U.S. President.

   c. Laws passed by Puerto Rico's legislature had to be reviewed by the U.S. Congress.

   d. A representative of Puerto Rico could sit in the U.S. Congress but could not vote.

2. a. Cuba drew up a constitution and became an independent republic.

   b. The United States insisted that Cuba include in its constitution the Platt Amendment.

   c. The United States established a permanent naval base at Guantánamo Bay in Cuba.

   d. After a revolt in Cuba in 1906, the United States set up a provisional government there.

Express Yourself!

Choose two or three classmates to work with. Discuss the actions of the United States in Puerto Rico and Cuba after the Cuban-Spanish-American War. Then, design a poster that tells how your group feels about U.S. actions in either Puerto Rico or Cuba. Use pictures and symbols to show how you feel. When you are done, display your poster in class.

UNIT 5

CHANGES IN A NEW CENTURY

(1900–1945)

Pecan Shellers' Strike in 1938

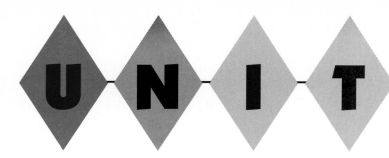

Chapter

16 The Mexican Revolution and New Patterns of Immigration (1900–1920)

17 Latinos and World War I (1914–1920)

18 From Boom to Depression (1920–1940)

19 Latinos and World War II (1941–1945)

Latino Soldier in World War I

THE BIG PICTURE

Voices of the Times

They paid very poor salaries. But I thought it was good because where I came from I used to work ten hours for $1.25, 12 cents an hour. . . .Then I came here and they paid $1.25 for eight hours—it was good.

— Frederico López, immigrant
from Mexico, 1916

Unit 5 follows the story of Latinos in the United States through the first half of the 1900s. In 1910, a revolution in Mexico brought a dramatic increase in Mexican immigration to the United States. The new Mexican immigrants, along with other Latinos in the United States, felt the great social changes during this period. Those changes included two world wars and the worst period of economic hard times the nation had ever known.

◆◆ In The United States ◆◆

By 1900, the United States was one of the leading industrial countries of the world. It was stretching its power beyond its own borders. As you will read, industrial growth and foreign expansion brought both advantages and problems.

Prosperity and Progressivism. When the 20th century began, the United States was wealthier than it had ever been. Its expanding railroads, industries, and agriculture provided jobs for a steady stream of immigrants from Latin America as well as from Europe.

Along with prosperity came problems. Many city people lived in housing that was crowded and unhealthful. Corruption in government was widespread. Big businesses had become very powerful. Often they showed little concern for the people who labored for them. Workers earned very little for long hours of work, and conditions in many factories were unsafe.

A group of reformers, known as **Progressives,** set out to solve these and other problems. Under pressure from Progressives, laws were passed to protect consumers. One law provided for the inspection of meat and banned the use of harmful chemicals in food. New election laws gave voters more power. Laws limiting child labor and workers' hours were passed. In 1912, Massachusetts became the first state to pass a minimum-wage law for women.

The Progressives were mostly concerned with conditions in Northern and Midwestern cities. They did little to aid Latinos, most of whom still lived in the Southwest and California. Also, some well-known Progressives held prejudices against immigrants.

Such prejudices and feelings of superiority toward immigrants made life difficult for newcomers from Latin America. When those attitudes combined with the desire to advance U.S. economic interests in the Americas, the result was repeated U.S. interference in Latin American affairs.

A Canal Across Panama. As the United States and the European powers developed worldwide trade, their merchant ships and naval vessels had to travel between the Atlantic and Pacific oceans.

195

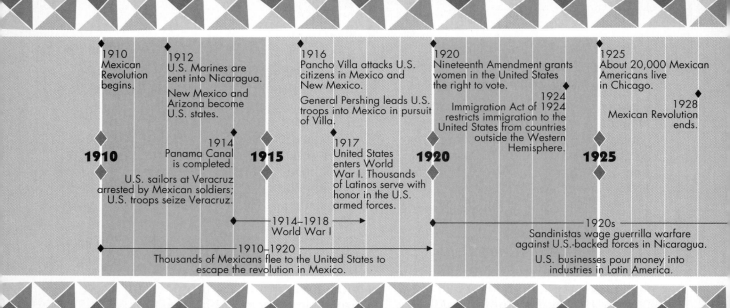

1910
Mexican Revolution begins.

1912
U.S. Marines are sent into Nicaragua.

New Mexico and Arizona become U.S. states.

1914
Panama Canal is completed.

U.S. sailors at Veracruz arrested by Mexican soldiers; U.S. troops seize Veracruz.

1916
Pancho Villa attacks U.S. citizens in Mexico and New Mexico.

General Pershing leads U.S. troops into Mexico in pursuit of Villa.

1917
United States enters World War I. Thousands of Latinos serve with honor in the U.S. armed forces.

1920
Nineteenth Amendment grants women in the United States the right to vote.

1924
Immigration Act of 1924 restricts immigration to the United States from countries outside the Western Hemisphere.

1925
About 20,000 Mexican Americans live in Chicago.

1928
Mexican Revolution ends.

1910   **1915**   **1920**   **1925**

1914–1918
World War I

1910–1920
Thousands of Mexicans flee to the United States to escape the revolution in Mexico.

1920s
Sandinistas wage guerrilla warfare against U.S.-backed forces in Nicaragua.

U.S. businesses pour money into industries in Latin America.

To do so, they had to make the long trip around the southern tip of South America. A canal across narrow Central America would cut the Atlantic-to-Pacific voyage in half.

In 1882, a French company began digging a canal across Panama, but it gave up years later when it ran out of money. The United States then moved into the picture. At that time, Panama was part of Colombia. President Theodore Roosevelt offered Colombia $10 million for the right to build a canal through its territory. When Colombia turned the offer down, Roosevelt was even more determined to get the canal built.

Roosevelt encouraged a group of Panamanians who wanted independence in Panama to stage a revolution. When the revolution broke out in Panama in 1903, a U.S. warship *just* happened to be on the spot to keep Colombia from ending the revolt. A few weeks later, the newly independent Republic of Panama signed a treaty with the United States. The treaty gave the United States control of the 10-mile-wide (16-kilometer-wide) Canal Zone for the same sum Colombia had refused.

Construction of the canal began in 1904. The labor of 30,000 African West Indian workers was vital to the success of the project. The canal was completed in 1914.

The so-called **gunboat diplomacy** that Roosevelt had used to get the right to build the Panama Canal drew strong protests from Colombia and other Latin American countries. Not until the 1920s did the United States apologize and pay Colombia $25 million. By then, with 5,000 ships passing through the canal each year, protecting it had become a cornerstone of U.S. policy in Latin America.

Policing Latin America. Ten years before the Panama Canal was finished, the United States' growing interest in Latin America had led President Theodore

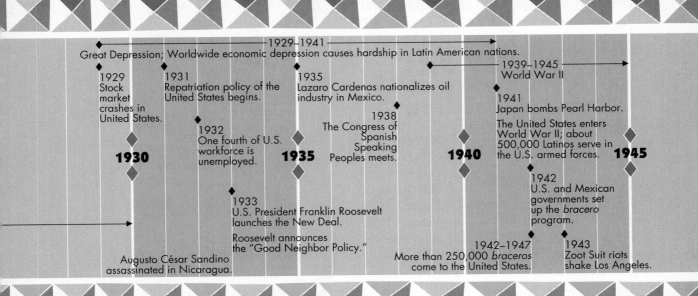

1929–1941
Great Depression; Worldwide economic depression causes hardship in Latin American nations.

1929
Stock market crashes in United States.

1931
Repatriation policy of the United States begins.

1935
Lazaro Cardenas nationalizes oil industry in Mexico.

1939–1945
World War II

1941
Japan bombs Pearl Harbor.
The United States enters World War II; about 500,000 Latinos serve in the U.S. armed forces.

1930

1932
One fourth of U.S. workforce is unemployed.

1935

1938
The Congress of Spanish Speaking Peoples meets.

1940

1945

1942
U.S. and Mexican governments set up the *bracero* program.

1933
U.S. President Franklin Roosevelt launches the New Deal.

Roosevelt announces the "Good Neighbor Policy."

Augusto César Sandino assassinated in Nicaragua.

1942–1947
More than 250,000 *braceros* come to the United States.

1943
Zoot Suit riots shake Los Angeles.

Roosevelt to make a major statement of policy. That statement became known as the **Roosevelt Corollary** to the Monroe Doctrine (see page 146). Roosevelt announced that the United States would exercise an "international police power" in the Americas. It would step in if Latin American countries could not pay their debts to other nations, or when they were guilty of "wrong-doing."

The United States first used this power in 1905 when the Dominican Republic did not pay its foreign debts. Later, the United States also stepped into Cuba, Haiti, and Nicaragua. In each of those countries, the United States trained special armies, whose commanders later seized power as military dictators.

It was little wonder, then, that in 1913 the Argentine author Manuel Ugarte (oo-GAHR-teh) wrote to newly elected U.S. President Woodrow Wilson. Ugarte demanded that "the stars and stripes cease

to be a symbol of oppression [unjust use of power] in the New World." Nevertheless, Wilson not only sent U.S. marines to Haiti and the Dominican Republic but also invaded Mexico twice.

World War I. The outbreak of war in Europe in 1914 directed the attention of the United States away from Latin America for a time. The war pitted Germany and Austria-Hungary against Great Britain, France, and Russia. With fighting taking place in many parts of the globe, the conflict became known as World War I.

At first, the United States tried to remain neutral and not support either side. But after Germany made submarine attacks against U.S. ships, the United States declared war against it in 1917.

Many Latinos were among the U.S. troops who fought in Europe. On the home front, Mexican immigrant farmworkers helped supply food to the soldiers. Many

Mexican Americans also left California and the Southwest to fill factory jobs in cities of the Midwest and Northeast.

Isolationism and Intolerance. After the end of World War I in 1918, the United States decided it did not wish to get deeply involved in the affairs of European nations. This policy, known as **isolationism**, did not apply to Latin America, however. During the 1920s, U.S. businesspeople continued to pour money into Cuban sugar, Central American bananas, Chilean copper, and Venezuelan and Mexican oil. By 1929, U.S. investment in Latin America totaled over $5 billion. With such a huge financial stake, it was not surprising that the United States continued to meddle in Latin American affairs.

Meanwhile, at home, many U.S. citizens looked upon immigrants, including Latinos, with growing dislike and suspicion. Many immigrants were suspected of holding radical beliefs. Large numbers of immigrants were arrested and sent back to their home countries at this time. Congress also passed laws sharply cutting back on immigration from Europe and Asia. Some people also wanted to limit immigration from Mexico. But huge U.S. agriculture companies successfully argued that they needed the cheap labor of Mexican immigrants.

The Roaring Twenties. Tired of war and of Progressives' efforts at reform, many people in the United States concentrated on having a good time during the 1920s. New forms of mass entertainment like the radio, the phonograph, and the movies helped make that possible. U.S. movies became popular throughout the world. Even in remote villages of Latin America, people thrilled to the images of Hollywood film stars. They also danced to

In the depths of the Great Depression. With no hope of a job, this man was left to survive by selling apples in the streets of a U.S. city.

a new kind of music, called jazz, developed by African Americans.

Important changes were taking place for women in the United States at this time. More and more women entered the work force. The 19th Amendment to the Constitution, enacted in 1920, gave women the vote. In the home, vacuum cleaners and electric irons and refrigerators made housework easier and gave women more time to explore other interests.

The Great Depression. The good times ended suddenly in 1929 when prices on the stock market plunged. Thousands of businesses closed. In this **Great Depression,** millions were thrown out of work. By 1932, one fourth of the U.S. work force was unemployed.

Always among the last to be hired and first to be fired, Latinos, like African Americans, were especially hard hit by the Great Depression. Claiming that illegal Latino immigrants were stealing jobs from U.S. citizens, the government sent about 400,000 Mexicans back to Mexico.

The New Deal. President Franklin D. Roosevelt, elected in 1932, launched what he called a **New Deal** to rescue the United States from the Great Depression. In his inaugural address in March 1933, the President declared, "The only thing we have to fear is fear itself." The President believed that it was the federal government's responsibility to make those "needed efforts" to lead the nation to economic recovery.

In the first 100 days Roosevelt was in office, Congress, at his urging, passed more than a dozen New Deal laws. These laws affected many parts of U.S. life. For example, large numbers of banks had closed during the depression. Therefore, one of the first New Deal laws set up rules for banks that would protect the money the banks held for depositors.

To put people back to work, Roosevelt launched a **public works program.** Under it, roads, post offices, and schools were built. For unemployed young men, Roosevelt called for the Civilian Conservation Corps (CCC). Millions of young men, including many Latinos, became CCC workers. They planted trees, built bridges, dug reservoirs, and developed parks.

New Deal programs also gave money for food and housing to those who could not find work. Later, the New Deal created the Social Security system to provide pensions for retired people. It also provided unemployment benefits for people who had lost their jobs.

The reforms of the New Deal improved the lives of many people in the United States. But the programs did not end the Great Depression. However, the New Deal did change the ideas of many people about government. Under Roosevelt, the federal government assumed the responsibility of helping to solve the nation's economic and social problems.

World War II. In 1939, World War II broke out in Europe. On one side were the Allies, notably Great Britain, France, and, later, the Soviet Union. They feared the Axis powers, Germany and its allies, Italy and Japan. Germany's leader, Nazi dictator Adolf Hitler, had declared that he was out to conquer the world.

The United States was drawn into the war in December 1941, after the Japanese bombed the U.S. naval base at Pearl Harbor, Hawaii. Along with millions of other U.S. citizens, Latinos performed often heroic duty in the armed forces. On the home front, Latino women and men moved into better-paying jobs in wartime industries. Thousands of **braceros** (brah-SEH-rohs), or contract laborers, from Mexico helped meet the need for farmworkers. But tensions between Anglos and Latinos continued. During the war years, such tensions sometimes led to the outbreak of riots.

Taking Another Look

1. How did the United States get the right to build the Panama Canal?

2. Why did the United States send Mexicans back to their homeland in the 1930s?

3. **Critical Thinking** Why do you think the U.S. isolationist policies of the 1920s applied to Europe but not to Latin America?

In Latin America

At the beginning of a new century, Latin Americans faced growing threats to their economic and political freedom from the United States. At the same time, a number of Latin American nations made increasing efforts to cope with enormous social problems at home.

Revolution and Reform. The early 1900s brought both revolution and reform to Latin America. In Mexico, a revolution that began in 1910 started a period of political and social change that continued for many years. Some 14 years later, a Mexican president, Lázaro Cárdenas (CAHR-deh-nahs), was still trying to keep the unfulfilled promises of that revolution. Cárdenas distributed millions of acres of land to peasants, built many rural schools, and worked to strengthen the labor movement. His most dramatic move, however, was the government takeover, or **nationalization,** of the oil industry. That industry had been dominated by powerful British and U.S. companies.

In many Latin American nations, however, economies continued to rely on exports of raw materials and agricultural products to industrialized nations. Foreign businesses and investors continued to play key roles in the economies of these nations. As these export businesses grew, however, workers in them began to organize in labor unions. They fought for better wages and working conditions. The workers also pushed for a greater voice in the governments of their nations.

Democracy moved ahead slowly in the region. The Argentine government, for example, granted the right to vote to all males in 1912. Chile moved toward a more representative system of government as well. Meanwhile, the republic of Uruguay tried to make the welfare of its people secure through a system of public education, an eight-hour workday, old-age pensions, and other measures. Despite these changes in other nations, rule by *caudillos* did not disappear in Latin America.

World War I. Eight Latin American republics, most of them in Central America and the Caribbean, declared war on Germany and its allies in World War I. But the other Latin American nations decided to sit out the conflict.

Mexico remained neutral despite a tempting offer from Germany. In exchange for Mexican support, the German foreign secretary, Arthur Zimmermann, offered to return to Mexico all the lands it had lost to the United States during the "War of the North American Invasion" (1846–1848). The Mexican government turned down the proposal.

From Enemies to "Good Neighbors." The nations of the Americas had formed the Pan-American Union in 1889. This organization was set up to deal with problems common to those nations. Almost from its founding, the Latin American members strongly protested U.S. interference in the affairs of member countries. Such interference continued after World War I.

For example, U.S. Marines had been sent to Nicaragua in 1912. An armed resistance movement grew up to oppose the U.S. occupation led by a reform-minded army officer, Augusto César Sandino (sahn-DEE-noh). Sandino's followers waged a fierce guerrilla war against the U.S. presence in their country during the 1920s. Sandino was gunned down by the U.S.-trained Nicaraguan National Guard in 1934.

That same year, President Franklin D. Roosevelt announced a new U.S. policy

A U.S. Marine plane bombs Sandinista positions in this 1930 picture. The Sandinistas waged a guerrilla war against U.S. influence in Nicaragua.

toward Latin America. It became known as the "Good Neighbor Policy." Under the policy, the United States promised to respect the rights of Latin Americans.

In times before the Good Neighbor Policy, the United States would probably have taken swift action when Mexico nationalized its oil properties in 1938. Under the Good Neighbor Policy, however, it did not send in troops. Instead, it let a commission decide how much Mexico had to pay the U.S. companies for their lost investments.

Hard Times. By 1933, Latin America, too, was caught in the grip of the Great Depression. Many foreign businesses and individuals could no longer invest in the region. Latin American countries faced an ever-shrinking demand for their exports. Thus, they did not have the money with which to buy needed manufactured goods from the United States and Europe.

Economic problems gave rise to political problems. Governments rose and fell quickly in many Latin American nations. Some countries, therefore, took action to gain more control over their economies. Nations such as Argentina, Mexico, and Brazil increased their attempts to industrialize. By doing so, they hoped to decrease their dependence on investment from the United States and Europe.

World War II and Latin America. When war first broke out in Europe in 1939, various Latin American nations joined with the United States in declaring neutrality. Before the war was over, though, every Latin American country had joined the conflict on the Allied side. Although the Latin American nations supported the Allies, Mexico and Brazil were the only countries to actually send troops.

By the end of the war, the United States had become the most powerful nation in the world. Latin Americans hoped that in return for their wartime support the United States would finally use its power and wealth to help them in solving their problems. Within the United States, Latinos harbored similar hopes of greater economic opportunities and a better life. In the next unit, you will see to what extent these hopes were realized.

Taking Another Look

1. What steps were taken by Latin American countries to deal with their problems in the 1930s?

2. Why was Latin America especially hard hit by the Great Depression?

3. **Critical Thinking** If you were a Mexican citizen, how might you have reacted to the news of the nationalization of your country's oil industry?

Sick of the injustice under the dictator Díaz, Mexican peasants formed armed bands to topple the government. Their hope: to get a government that would improve their lives.

SECTIONS

1 Background to Revolution

2 A Long Struggle

3 North from Mexico

The Mexican Revolution and New Patterns of Immigration

(1900–1920)

THINKING ABOUT THE CHAPTER

What impact did revolution in Mexico have on Latinos in the United States?

One day in January 1910, a short, quiet man approached the longtime president of Mexico, Porfirio Díaz. He identified himself as Francisco I. Madero (mah-DEH-roh), a landowner. He told Díaz that the man chosen for vice-president was cruel and would be a very poor leader if anything should happen to the aged Díaz.

Then the man astonished the dictator by offering himself as Díaz's next vice-president. Díaz might well have had a good laugh over the man's bold suggestion. But less than a year and a half later, Díaz was on his way into exile. Madero, on the other hand, would become Mexico's new president.

Madero helped begin a revolution in Mexico that brought about great changes and led to the migration of many thousands of Mexicans to the United States.

1 BACKGROUND TO REVOLUTION
◆ Why did a revolution break out in
◆ Mexico in 1910?

General Porfirio Díaz, a *mestizo* hero, became president of Mexico after overthrowing the successor of Benito Juárez (page 147) in 1876. Díaz's motto was "little politics, much administration." It was another way of saying that he intended to run the country his way, with no political opposition.

Growth and Dictatorship. In his 30 years in power, Díaz tried to modernize Mexico. He built factories, oil wells, mines, and railroads. When Díaz became president, Mexico had 287 miles (460 kilometers) of railroad track. When he left, there were 15,000 miles (24,000 kilometers) of track. He built wide boulevards and stately buildings in the capital, making Mexico City one of the most beautiful cities in the world. He encouraged trade by opening the door to investment from the United States and European countries.

But there was a dark side to Díaz's regime. The profits that poured into the country enriched the few and left the vast majority of Mexicans as poor as ever. Poor Mexican farmers were deprived of their property. Díaz sold most of it to large landowners. These poor farmers were then forced to work on large estates as peons.

Three thousand families owned over half the land in Mexico. Foreigners owned over half the oil wells and mines. As one bitter political opponent put it, Mexico under Díaz had become "the mother of foreigners and the stepmother of Mexicans."

Díaz would accept no dissent from his rule. Enemies and opponents were jailed, executed, or driven into exile.

Opposition from the North. Mexican exiles in the United States worked to overthrow Díaz. They collected money, clothes, medicine, and guns to support a rebellion. Ricardo and Enrique Flores Magón (FLOH-res mah-GOHN) were among the leaders of this movement. They published a newspaper in San Antonio and later in St. Louis, Missouri, calling for the overthrow of Díaz. The brothers also tried to organize Mexican workers into labor unions. They believed that the unions would help change Mexican society.

Madero at first chose to oppose Díaz with words and ideas rather than guns. Gradually, Madero won the support of the Mexican people and became a threat to Díaz's power. Although Díaz had rejected him as a possible candidate for vice-president, Madero was nominated for president by an opposition party in 1910. Díaz had him thrown into jail until after the election, which Díaz won easily.

Madero fled to Texas after his release. He reluctantly took sides with the Flores Magóns and issued a call for revolution. Madero realized that violence was the only way to remove Díaz from power. Madero gained support from all over Mexico. In early 1911, the stage was set for a final showdown between the Mexican people and their dictator.

Taking Another Look

1. How did Porfirio Díaz's economic policies affect the majority of Mexicans?

2. Why did Díaz win the election of 1910?

3. **Critical Thinking** Why do you think Francisco Madero changed his strategy for fighting Díaz after the election in 1910?

2 A LONG STRUGGLE

◆ What did the Mexican revolutionaries seek to accomplish?

Francisco Madero's call for revolution was a call to arms for Mexicans sick of the injustice of Díaz. Small revolutionary bands across the country attacked soldiers and destroyed railroads and private factories. The country was thrown into turmoil. Díaz's own ministers saw how serious the situation was and called on the president to resign. Díaz fled Mexico in 1911 and settled in France, where he died four years later.

A New President. In 1911, Madero was elected Mexico's new president. He believed that with the overthrow of Díaz, the revolution was complete. However, many Mexicans wanted more than a political change. They wanted far-reaching social and economic changes in their country. Most of all, they wanted the redistribution of land among the Mexican people. This meant breaking up the *haciendas* and returning the lands to villages or to individual farmers.

Madero was too weak to lead the country into such bold reforms. He found himself caught between those who wanted change and those who wanted to keep the system as it was. As one writer put it, Madero was "a dove fluttering in a sky filled with hawks."

General Victoriano Huerta (WER-tah), who had helped Madero to power, now decided to seize it for himself. In 1913, he had Madero killed and proclaimed himself president. Huerta introduced some reforms, but the way he had seized power angered many revolutionaries. They turned to another supporter of change, Venustiano Carranza (kah-RRAHN-sah). The Mexican Revolution, which some thought was over, was only beginning.

The United States in Veracruz. The U.S. government had a strong interest in the outcome of the Mexican Revolution. It was concerned that the fighting would affect U.S. property and business interests in Mexico. Believing that Carranza would bring stability to Mexico, U.S. President Woodrow Wilson supported him against Huerta.

Francisco "Pancho" Villa, the Mexican revolutionary, was a hero to some people and a villain to others. What is your opinion of Villa?

On April 12, 1914, a group of U.S. sailors in Veracruz were arrested by Huerta's soldiers. They were soon released with an apology to the U.S. government. But the U.S. naval commander was not satisfied. He demanded that the Mexicans give a 21-gun salute to the U.S. flag. When President Huerta refused, President Wilson supported the naval commander and ordered U.S. troops to seize Veracruz. The real reason for this act was to prevent the shipment of weapons from Veracruz to Huerta's forces in Mexico City.

The United States held Veracruz for most of 1914. In that time, Huerta was overthrown, and Carranza became president. However, some of the revolutionary leaders who had supported Carranza became disappointed with him. They felt he would not make the radical changes in the country's economy they thought were necessary. Chief among these radicals were the peasant leaders Francisco "Pancho" Villa (PAH-choh VEE-yah) and Emiliano Zapata (sah-PAH-tah).

Villa Strikes Back. Villa had hoped that the United States would support him in his efforts to become president of Mexico. When President Wilson instead backed Carranza, Villa decided to retaliate. Early in 1916, he killed 16 U.S. mine employees in northern Mexico. He then crossed the border and attacked the town of Columbus, New Mexico, killing another 18 people.

The U.S. government was outraged. President Wilson sent General John J. Pershing into Mexico to capture Villa. People in northern Mexico, for whom Villa was a hero, helped him hide from the U.S. soldiers. After 11 months, Pershing gave up the search. Meanwhile, many Mexicans were outraged that the United States had invaded their country for the second time in two years.

A Hero of the Revolution. The key to Mexico's future, some revolutionaries believed, lay in economic and social reform. The most outspoken of these leaders was Emiliano Zapata.

Emiliano Zapata earned his living raising livestock in a small village in the state of Morelos. He knew how important land was to his people, who farmed small plots. Zapata saw the revolution as a way to give land to people who lived their lives out in deepest poverty and in debt to wealthy landowners. His slogan was *Tierra y libertad*, "Land and Liberty". Since neither Madero nor Carranza had done much about land distribution, Zapata refused to lay down his weapons.

After Carranza came to power, Zapata returned home to Morelos, where he worked to carry out his plan of redistributing the land. In 1919, Zapata was lured into a trap by one of Carranza's supporters. As he rode through the gates of a *hacienda* for a scheduled meeting, Zapata was gunned down in a hail of bullets. His death was mourned by the poor people of Mexico, for whom he was the hero of the revolution.

A New Constitution. Two years earlier, in 1917, Carranza had approved a new constitution. Some parts of Zapata's plan for giving land to the poor were written into the constitution. The constitution also gave the government vast new powers. It set up schools in poverty-stricken areas of the country. It also recognized labor

Torn from their homes by the fierce fighting between armed bands, Mexican villagers flee to the United States taking with them only what they can carry.

unions and limited the influence of the Roman Catholic Church.

The important changes were set in place. But there would be more upheavals before the revolution was over. Carranza was killed in 1920 and a new general, Alvaro Obregón (oh-breh-GOHN), took control of Mexico. He ruled until 1928, when he too was assassinated.

The long, bloody Mexican Revolution was at an end. Yet it would be many years before the promise of the revolution would be realized.

Taking Another Look

1. What kinds of social and economic changes did Mexicans want President Madero to carry out?

2. What events led to the U.S. seizure of Veracruz?

3. **Critical Thinking** Compare Francisco Madero and Venustiano Carranza. How were they similar? How were they different?

3 NORTH FROM MEXICO
◆ How did the many Mexicans who
◆ moved to the United States during the years of the Mexican Revolution live?

Although the Mexican Revolution eventually improved the lives of Mexicans, it did so at a fearful price. In the long struggle, about a million Mexicans, one out of every fifteen people, died. Many of these victims were innocent peons caught in the crossfire between warring sides. Other thousands of Mexicans fled north to the United States to escape the chaos, violence, and famine. As one immigrant explained, "I had to come to the United States because it was impossible to live down there with so many revolutions."

The New Immigrants. Between 1910 and 1920, the newcomers streamed across the U.S. border on foot, on horseback, in wagons, and on railroad trains. What they wanted most was food, jobs, and safety. If they also found liberty, that was a bonus.

Safety and the promise of a better life were not the only reasons Mexicans immigrated to the United States at this time. Some saw their neighbor to the north as a place filled with excitement and adventure. "It was my dream to come here," said Jesús Garza (GAHR-sah), a 24-year-old *mestizo*, who crossed the border into San Antonio against the wishes of his parents.

1910	Porfirio Díaz elected president of Mexico.
	Mexican Revolution begins.
1910–1920	Thousands of Mexicans immigrate to the United States.
1911	Francisco I. Madero becomes president of Mexico.
1914	U.S. troops seize the city of Veracruz.
1916	Pancho Villa kills U.S. citizens in Mexico and in Columbus, New Mexico.
	U.S. General Pershing pursues Villa in Mexico.
1917	Venustiano Carranza approves new Mexican constitution.
1919	Emiliano Zapata is killed.
1920	Alvaro Obregón becomes president after Carranza is killed.

Most of the newcomers were poor farmers who had been forced off their land by fighting in the revolution. But also among them were many other Mexicans. There were soldiers who had fought for the different revolutionary leaders and were now on the wrong side. There were also supporters of the various governments who were now seeking refuge from political persecution. There were also Mexicans with enough money to start businesses in the United States. In fact, this flood of immigrants included people of more varied backgrounds than any other group of Mexican newcomers that have entered the United States before or since.

One of those that came was Pablo Mares (MAH-res). He found work in an Arizona mine. Here is what he had to say about his adopted country:

The work is very heavy, but what is good is that one lives in peace. There is no trouble with revolutions nor difficulties of any kind. Here one is treated according to the way in which one behaves himself and one earns more than in Mexico. I have gone back to Mexico twice . . . but I have come back, for in addition to the fact that work is very scarce there, the wages are too low . . . . I think that as long as we have so many wars, killing each other, we will not progress and we shall always be poor.

Not all Mexican immigrants were happy in the United States. Some found the United States unfriendly and prejudiced. One newcomer observed,

It is not as happy . . . a life as it is in Mexico. They have no *fiestas* [festivals] or *serenatas* [concerts] and no places for *paseos* [walks] in the evening. If you walk in the streets in the evening, you suffer insults from uncouth [rude] persons. . . . The life here is very cheerless in contrast to Mexico. The neighbors are other nationalities and they are very hostile instead of friendly.

The Barrio. Most of the Mexicans who settled in cities of the Southwest lived in **barrios** (BAHRR-ee-ohs). A *barrio* is a section of a city where there are large numbers of Latinos. *Barrios* offered newcomers a sense of security. Here they lived among relatives and friends from the same Mexican communities. They formed social clubs and visited Mexican American grocery stores, bakeries, restaurants, and barbershops. Spanish was the language of the *barrios*. Employers found workers for the expanding economy of the Southwest in the *barrios*.

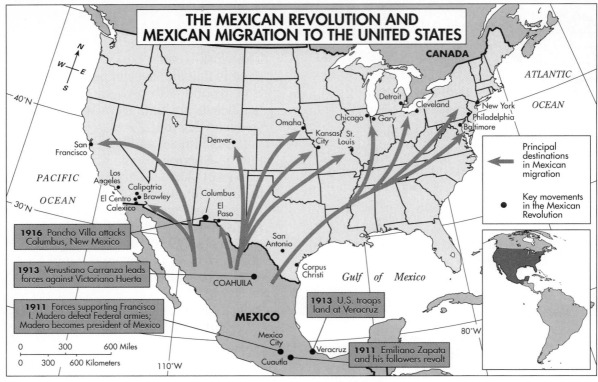

THE MEXICAN REVOLUTION AND MEXICAN MIGRATION TO THE UNITED STATES

1916 Pancho Villa attacks Columbus, New Mexico

1913 Venustiano Carranza leads forces against Victoriano Huerta

1911 Forces supporting Francisco I. Madero defeat Federal armies; Madero becomes president of Mexico

1913 U.S. troops land at Veracruz

1911 Emiliano Zapata and his followers revolt

Principal destinations in Mexican migration

Key movements in the Mexican Revolution

During the years of the Mexican Revolution, many Mexicans came to the United States. What Southwest U.S. cities received the most immigrants?

The largest *barrio* was in Los Angeles. It had a population of 30,000 Mexican-born Americans in 1920, almost three times more people than had been there in 1910. By 1925, Los Angeles had a larger Mexican population than any other city except Mexico City. Other cities with large *barrios* were El Paso and San Antonio.

Conditions in many of the *barrios* were frightful. People lived in old, overcrowded buildings. There was poor sanitation, few public services, and high rates of sickness and disease.

The Work Picture. In the early 1900s, the Southwest was booming economically. U.S. businesspeople saw Mexicans and Mexican Americans as a source of cheap labor for new mines and factories. In addition, tracks had to be laid for the Southern Pacific and Santa Fe railroads. These railroads were recruiting more than a thousand Mexican workers a month.

Gradually, Mexican Americans made their way to the U.S. Midwest. They worked for railroads, steel mills, and meatpacking plants there. Sometimes, northern steel companies recruited Mexicans as strikebreakers. The Mexicans desperately needed the work, but by taking these jobs, they often found themselves in conflict with workers who were out on strike. Chicago became the largest Mexican center outside the Southwest, with 4,000 Mexican Americans there by 1920.

Most Mexicans were unskilled workers and could not read or write English. For this reason, they worked at the lowest paying jobs. A farmworker earned between $1.00 and $1.50 a day. The highest pay was in mine work, where a worker could earn as much as $5.00 a day. Still, these rates were many times higher than what Mexican Americans would have earned as farm workers in Mexico. There the rate was about 16 cents a day.

Migrant Workers. As agriculture developed in the U.S. Southwest, farms there grew larger. These new farms required armies of workers to harvest the crops. Since different crops became ready for harvesting at different times of the year in different regions, workers moved from region to region with the seasons. They became **migrant workers** in California, Arizona, New Mexico, Colorado, and Texas. The workers traveled from state to state to bring in harvests of sugar beets, cotton, fruits, and vegetables.

Groups of migrant worker families moved together from place to place. Women and children often joined the men in the fields. The workday lasted from dawn to dark. A family might live and work in more than five widely spaced places a year. Wages were low, and living conditions primitive.

Since such work was seasonal, migrant workers had to scrounge for odd jobs during the off seasons. Men were lucky to find work on irrigation projects, dam building, and road construction. Young boys helped out by delivering newspapers.

Many women also worked. They took jobs as servants, laundry workers, and cooks in the homes of Anglos in the off seasons. As more and more Mexican Americans opened their own businesses in *barrios*, sales and clerical jobs also opened up for women.

Discrimination and Hostility. In Santa Barbara, California, an Anglo who drove a wagon earned $4.50 a day. A Mexican American who did the same work was paid $2.50 a day. In many places, the easiest jobs were given to Anglos. The hardest, dirtiest tasks were given to Mexican Americans. When labor unions were organized in some industries, Mexican Americans were usually not allowed to join.

Such job discrimination was only one part of the hostility that Mexican Americans faced from Anglos. Anglo workers were hostile because they feared Mexican Americans would take jobs away from other U.S. citizens. Mexican American children were forced to attend segregated schools.

Mexican Americans were accused of clinging to their own ways and not being willing to enter the mainstream of U.S. society. This was strange since, at the same time, many Anglos thought of Mexican Americans as only temporary immigrants, who would go back to Mexico when there was no longer any need for their labor.

Many Mexican immigrants also hoped to return to their homeland. Large numbers did, crossing and recrossing the border. For others, however, the United States became their new homeland.

Taking Another Look

1. Why did Mexicans come to the United States from 1910 to 1920?

2. What work opportunities were there for new immigrants?

3. **Critical Thinking** If you had been an immigrant from Mexico in 1915, what would have persuaded you to remain in the United States?

LOOKING AHEAD

The Mexican Revolution that began in 1910 brought changes to Mexico and to the United States as well. The Mexicans who came to the United States altered the face of the U.S. Southwest and the other regions in which they settled. The Mexican American community would grow in size and influence throughout the entire United States.

ARTISTS OF THE REVOLUTION

Trains back from the battlefield unloaded their cargoes . . . the wounded, the tired, exhausted, mutilated soldiers, sweating. . . . In the world of politics it was the same, war without quarter, struggle for power and wealth . . .

This quote, from Mexican artist José Orozco (oh-ROHS-koh), helps explain how images from the Mexican Revolution influenced his art. Orozco, along with Diego Rivera and David Siqueiros (see-keh-EE-rohs), was an artist during the revolution. Eventually, they became Mexico's most famous artists of the period.

The three artists used the mural, an art form that dates back to Aztec times, to develop a truly Mexican style of art. Their murals were gigantic in size and used powerful images to portray not only the people and events of the revolution, but also the history of Mexico. The murals champion the causes of the poor and landless, and often depict native Mexicans as the symbol of Mexico's spirit.

After the revolution, Orozco, Rivera, and Siquerios painted murals in a number of public buildings. Often called the "shouting walls," these murals can be seen in Mexico today. Through the murals the ideas of these artists still reach the people of Mexico.

CLOSE UP: Chapter 16

The Who, What, Where of History

1. **What** were the results of Porfirio Díaz's regime in Mexico?
2. **Who** was Francisco Madero?
3. **Who** was Emiliano Zapata?
4. **What** was the U.S. response to Pancho Villa's raid on Columbus, New Mexico?
5. **What** are three reasons Mexicans gave for immigrating to the United States?
6. **What** is a *barrio*?

Making the Connection

1. Explain the relationship between distribution of land and wealth in Mexico and the Mexican Revolution.
2. What was the connection between the Mexican Revolution and the migration of thousands of Mexicans to the United States?

Time Check

1. When did the Mexican Revolution begin?
2. In what year did the United States invade Veracruz?

What Would You Have Done?

1. Imagine that you support Francisco Madero as president of Mexico. How would you advise him to carry out the goals of the revolution?
2. Imagine you are a Mexican immigrant to the United States in 1915. Write a letter to a friend in Mexico explaining why you immigrated. Would you urge your friend to follow you north? Why or why not?

Thinking and Writing About History

Below are the words to two songs about U.S. General Pershing's search for Pancho Villa. The first song was written by some of Villa's followers. The second came from Pershing's soldiers.

A. *Maybe they have guns and canons,*
Maybe they are a lot stronger.
We have only rocks and mountains,
But we know how to last longer.

B. *Our horses, they were hungry,*
And we ate parched corn.
It was [awful] hard living
In the state of Chihuahua,
Where Pancho Villa was born.

Compare the songs and answer the questions below.

1. What information do the songs give about the revolutionaries in Mexico?
2. What information do they give about the U.S. troops?
3. Write an essay about Pershing's search for Villa based on these songs.

Building Skills: Primary and Secondary Sources

When historians want to find out what happened at a certain time in the past, they look for clues. Some of their clues come from *primary sources,* original documents written at the time of an actual event. Autobiographies, journals, letters, legal records, and firsthand accounts of an event are all primary sources. *Secondary sources* are accounts written at a later date that explain or interpret an event from the past. Secondary sources include history books or biographies.

Study the list of sources below. On a separate sheet of paper, write the letters of the primary sources and explain why each is a primary source.

a. a book called *Heroes of Mexico,* by Morris Rosenblum, published in 1969
b. President Wilson's message to Congress on U.S. relations with Mexico, August 27, 1913
c. an article titled "Black Jack's Mexican Goose Chase," from *American Heritage* magazine, June 1962
d. eyewitness accounts of Pancho Villa's exploits by journalist John Reed, written for the *New York World*, 1913 to 1914
e. "Zapata Remembered," an article by P. Hamill in the October 1990 issue of *Travel Holiday*
f. a declaration called "Plan of Ayala," issued by Emiliano Zapata on November 27, 1911
g. a photograph of Pershing's soldiers on the march in Mexico, taken in 1916

Express Yourself!

In this chapter, you have read about Mexican immigration to the United States in the early 1900s. Have you ever moved to a new country or a new neighborhood? What was that experience like for you and your family? Interview a member of your family, a friend, or a classmate who has moved to a new place. Ask how the new home is different from the old home. What does he or she miss most about the old home? What does he or she like best about the new home? Write the answers to these questions on a piece of paper. Then, report your findings to the class.

In 1920, Governor Octaviano Larrazolo attended the American Day Parade in Santa Fe. It honored the soldiers from New Mexico who served in World War I, many of whom were Latinos.

SECTIONS

1 Going to War

2 Growing Immigration

3 Moving North

CHAPTER 17

Latinos and World War I

(1914–1920)

THINKING ABOUT THE CHAPTER

How were Latinos affected by the United States' entry into World War I?

It was September 12, 1918. World War I was nearly over, but not for U.S. Army private Marcelino Serna (SER-nah). From his trench, the young Mexican American could see across the bomb-pitted field to the German lines. From time to time, a helmeted head would pop up, followed by shots fired in Serna's direction.

Serna waited for the right moment to return fire. Just as he squeezed his trigger, he felt the sting of an enemy bullet on his cheek. Realizing, however, that this was only a flesh wound, he pumped more bullets toward the enemy trench. Then he launched a hand grenade at the German line.

When the smoke from the grenade cleared, Serna received a surprise. Out of the trench climbed 24 dusty German soldiers, their arms raised in surrender. Serna then marched his captives to his unit's headquarters.

For his brave action, Serna received the Distinguished Service Cross, one of the army's highest awards. Later acts of heroism earned him other honors—two Purple Hearts, the Victory Medal, and the French *Croix de Guerre*. Serna did not receive the U.S. top award, the Congressional Medal of Honor. According to one of his officers, this was only because Serna could not read or write English well enough to fill out the necessary reports.

Private Serna was just one of the thousands of Latinos who served with honor in the armed forces in World War I. In addition, thousands of Latinos filled jobs at home that were needed to keep the wartime economy running at top speed.

1 GOING TO WAR

◆ What roles did Latinos play in the U.S.
◆ armed forces during
  World War I?

World War I broke out in Europe in 1914 (see page 197). U.S. President Woodrow Wilson pledged to keep the nation out of the conflict. By 1917, however, a German policy under which their submarines sank U.S. merchant ships caused him to change his mind. In April, the United States went to war against Germany and its allies.

When the United States entered the war, the army had only about 200,000 men. Congress quickly passed a draft law that called about 3.8 million men into the armed forces. Thousands of those who served were Latinos. But they had to overcome a variety of difficulties to fight for the United States.

Puerto Ricans and World War I. At the beginning of 1917, Puerto Ricans were not citizens of the United States. The island was still governed by the Foraker Act (see page 186). As the chance of war

grew, President Wilson pushed Congress to pass a bill granting Puerto Ricans citizenship. Just two months before war was declared, Congress passed the act. A month later, President Wilson signed the Jones Act. That granted Puerto Rico a new government and Puerto Ricans some of the rights of U.S. citizens (see page 186).

Puerto Ricans could now join the U.S. Army. A regiment of soldiers from Puerto Rico became part of the regular army in May 1917. Puerto Ricans were also eligible for the draft. Some 235,000 registered, and about 18,000 of these were called up for service.

Mexican Americans Go to War. Mexican Americans faced other difficulties in trying to serve the United States during World War I. First, many U.S. citizens were suspicious of the loyalty of Mexican Americans. This was caused in part by the discovery that Germany had tried to persuade Mexico to fight on its side in the war (see page 200). When 200 Mexican American laborers went on strike for better wages, many Anglos called the action German inspired.

In addition, anti-Mexican feeling had been deepened by Pancho Villa's raid on New Mexico in 1916 (see page 205). So strong was the reaction to Villa's attack that Los Angeles officials asked the federal government to deport Mexican immigrants. Violence against Mexican Americans was widespread in Texas. Even the Texas Rangers were accused of being involved in the murder of *tejanos*.

Serving Their Country. Like Marcelino Serna, thousands of young Mexican American men decided to serve their country despite the harsh way many of them were treated. The exact number of Mexican Americans who served in the war is not certain. However, the percentage of

Mexican Americans who volunteered was greater than that of any other ethnic group in the nation.

The armed services did not quite know what to do with these Latino volunteers. Many of them could not speak or write English fluently. Therefore, they were not allowed to finish their military training and were kept at the training centers. Other volunteers, however, were sent to the front in Europe.

Félix Sánchez of New Mexico fought and was wounded in the fierce Meuse-Argonne offensive. This was an important Allied victory in France during World War I.

Those who did see action served with courage and distinction. Another outstanding soldier in addition to Marcelino Serna was 19-year-old Nicolás Lucero (loo-SEH-roh) from Albuquerque, New Mexico. Lucero received the French Croix de Guerre for destroying two German machine gun positions.

While many Latinos were volunteering and going off to war, most Mexican Americans were finding ways to serve their country on the home front. The southwestern United States was the center of operations for the largest number of these Mexican Americans.

Taking Another Look

1. What was the attitude of many Americans about the loyalty of Mexican Americans during World War I?

2. How did Marcelino Serna and Nicolás Lucero earn their medals?

3. **Critical Thinking** If you were a Mexican American living in the United States in 1917, would you have volunteered to fight? Give reasons for your answer.

2 GROWING IMMIGRATION

◆ How did World War I lead to an
◆ increase in immigration from Mexico?

Large-scale [agricultural] production would be impossible without the Mexican field labor. Without the Mexicans, costs would be increased fifty percent.

With these words, an official of a California agricultural company explained why Mexicans were encouraged to cross the border to work in the United States during World War I. In the five years from the start of the war to 1919, the year after the war ended, hundreds of thousands of Mexicans immigrated to the United States.

Many of these Mexicans were escaping from the violence and disorder of the Mexican Revolution (see page 206). Not only were they fleeing the actual fighting, but they also feared starvation when farms and businesses were destroyed. Others of those who fled had supported one or another of the revolutionary groups trying to gain control in Mexico and had fled when their group was defeated. Whatever the reasons for leaving their country, Mexicans knew that there were job opportunities in the United States. Many of these were created by the demand of wartime agriculture and industry.

New Jobs. The demand for the labor of Mexican immigrants was especially high in the U.S. Southwest. Agriculture and industry were expanding there. But many U.S. citizens who worked in those areas had been drafted into the armed forces.

The jobs of those workers had to be filled. Thus, Mexican immigrants were hired to work in the cotton fields of Arizona and on the sugar beet farms of California and Colorado. They also labored in the copper mines of New Mexico and built railroad lines throughout the U.S. West.

The high demand for labor helped improve conditions for some Mexican Americans who had been in the United States for a generation or more. For the first time, they were able to move into higher-paying, skilled industrial jobs. Mexican American women, who often had

---

World War I Honor Roll

David Barkley—First Latino to receive the Medal of Honor. Barkley volunteered to spy on the position of the German army. He died in action, but his maps of the area were carried to his unit by his partner. The unit was then able to launch a successful attack against the Germans.

Nicholás Lucero—Received the French Croix de Guerre for destroying two German machine gun positions and for keeping constant fire on enemy positions for more than three hours.

Marcelino Serna—Awarded the Distinguished Service Cross for single-handedly capturing 24 German prisoners. For later actions, Serna received the French Croix de Guerre, the Victory Medal with three bars, and two Purple Hearts.

---

to add to the family income, took jobs in garment factories, fish canneries, and food-processing plants.

The Rush to California. California attracted large numbers of Mexican immigrants and Mexican Americans from other states. Agriculture was booming in California. By 1918, Mexicans and Mexican Americans made up the largest group of workers in the fertile Imperial Valley. Those who worked on the railroads also found seasonal work bringing in the fruit and vegetable harvests.

Industry, too, was growing in California. Shipyards, rubber factories, and other industries were working overtime to meet the wartime needs of the country. Industry and agriculture leaders wanted to be sure that they had a steady supply of workers for their businesses. They pressured the federal government to ignore the immigration laws requiring immigrants to be able to read and write in English. They also persuaded the government to drop the eight-dollar tax that each Mexican entering the United States had to pay. They argued that if the flow of Mexican immigrants was cut back, businesses would have to pay higher wages to attract other workers. This would mean that the prices of their products would have to rise, harming the economy.

Colonias and Barrios. The new Mexican immigrants who worked in agriculture settled together in communities they called *colonias* (koh-LOH-nee-ahs). They organized *colonias* in villages near where they worked. As more people moved north, the *colonias* grew so large that new ones had to be started.

Mexican immigrants who flowed into the U.S. Southwest during WWI often lived together in *colonias* and *barrios*. *El Brillante* market shown below was owned by a Latino. It served the residents of a *colonia* of Mexicans in Santa Barbara, California.

One Mexican American, Ernesto Galarza (gah-LAHR-sah), recalled how his *colonia* grew in the years leading up to World War I:

> The *colonia* was like a sponge that was beginning to leak along the edges, squeezed between the levee [earthen dam], the railroad tracks, and the river front. But it wasn't squeezed dry because it kept filling with newcomers who found families who took in boarders. . . . Crowded as it was, the *colonia* found a place for these *chicanos*, the name by which we called unskilled workers born in Mexico and just arrived in the United States.

The Mexicans who settled in cities lived in all-Latino neighborhoods they called *barrios*. Most *barrios* were in poorer sections of cities with run-down housing. Services such as garbage collection and sanitation facilities were poor. As late as 1920, 92 percent of the homes in the Los Angeles *barrio* had no gas and 72 percent lacked electricity. However, they did have bustling shops and restaurants with Mexican products and foods. The movie houses played Spanish and Mexican films and the theaters performed plays in Spanish. In short, the *barrios* were places where Mexican Americans could feel at home.

Mexican Americans who lived in the *colonias* and *barrios* helped newcomers adjust to life in their new country in many ways. For example, they set up mutual aid societies called **mutualistas** (moo-twah-LEES-tahs).

Mutualistas provided help in civil-rights matters. They also collected money for the sick and for the families of the dead. Sometimes, they served as labor organiza-tions. *Mutualistas* also sponsored social and cultural events and activities, such as fiestas. These events helped keep alive the immigrants' Mexican heritage. The consti-tution of one *mutualista* gave its purpose as follows:

> To bring closer together . . . the rela-tions of the Mexicanos . . . in order that they extend to each other the hand of brotherly love for their pro-tection, mutual benefits, and to pro-cure [secure] through all legal means the moral and material betterment of its members.

Voices of Dissent. Not every immi-grant was happy with life in the United States. Some, like Carlos Almanzán (ahl-mahn-SAHN), who led a back-to-Mexico campaign, were quickly disappointed with the United States. Almanzán worked in a brick factory in Los Angeles where he was paid four dollars for an eight-hour day. The pay was good for that time, but it was not enough to keep him from returning to Mexico. He wrote:

> I don't believe that I will ever return to this country for I have spent the hardest days of my life; it is here where I have worked the hardest and earned the least. . . . Besides, the peo-ple here don't like us.

But a growing number of Mexican Americans fought back against poor work-ing conditions and prejudice. Here is how Elías Sepúlveda of Nogales, Arizona, react-ed to racism at work:

> I was working in the bakery of an American and an American baker came and in front of me asked him why he had a "Mexican" working when the Americans had greater

need of that work. I answered that I was a "Mexican" but that I had more right than he to the work. First because I was an American citizen born in the United States and secondly because I was from Arizona, and I told him that I could even teach him the Constitution of the United States. When he heard me speak English he left, but in order to show the owner that I wasn't in love with working for him I asked for my time [quit] in three days. . . . When I am among Mexicans I feel better than when I am among the Americans.

Labor Organizations. Quitting a job was one way of protesting. But few Mexican Americans could afford to do that. Instead, they formed unions or joined existing ones to improve their lives as workers. In 1917, in one California town, Mexican workers formed a union called *Trabajadores Unidos* (United Workers) and struck for higher wages. After two weeks, they won a five-cent-an-hour increase.

In many other cases, strikers faced violence at the hands of local authorities. In 1917, Mexican mine workers in Arizona went on strike. Local authorities charged them with undermining the war effort. They forced the strikers into freight cars and dumped them in the desert near the Mexican border without food or water. In other cases, strikers were beaten and strikebreakers were hired to put down the strikes.

Political Gains. New Mexico achieved statehood in 1912 (see page 169). The new state was a center of Mexican culture and growing political power. Here, Mexican Americans who had lived in the region for generations took pride in their past. They called themselves *Hispano* (ees-PAH-no) to distinguish themselves from the more recent immigrants.

In 1918, Mexican American **Octaviano A. Larrazolo** (lah-rrah - SOH - loh) became New Mexico's third governor. Larrazolo was born in Chihuahua, Mexico, in 1859. On a trip to Tucson, Arizona, when he was still a youth, Larrazolo was shocked to see Mexican Americans living under the worst conditions. He made a vow to spend his life improving conditions for his people. He studied law and later entered politics. Settling in New Mexico, Larrazolo fought to have the new state constitution spell out the right of Mexican Americans to vote, hold office, and sit on juries. In 1918, he was elected governor. In office, he was a strong supporter of Latino rights. He favored the teaching of public school students in both English and Spanish. He later served the people of New Mexico as a U.S. Senator.

Old Immigrants and New. Mexican immigrants continued to enter the United States through the World War I years. Some more-established Latinos began to resent the newcomers. They felt that the newcomers were increasing the competition for jobs. This kept wages low, because employers could decrease wages and still find workers. This was particularly true for unskilled agricultural work.

Dissatisfaction with existing conditions led many Mexican Americans—war veterans and war workers alike—to look beyond the Southwest for new opportunities. The most promising possibilities seemed to lie in the states of the Middle West and the Northeast.

Agricultural workers, many of whom were Mexican immigrants, found seasonal work packing peaches in an orchard in New Mexico. Low wages, long hours, and dreadful conditions forced some workers to form unions and strike.

Taking Another Look

1. What reasons did Mexicans have for coming to the United States during the war years?

2. Explain the terms *colonias* and *barrios*.

3. **Critical Thinking** Describe the ways in which Mexican Americans helped one another and improved their lives during World War I.

3 MOVING NORTH

◆ How did Mexican American
◆ communities develop in the Middle West and Northeast?

When 20-year-old Ricardo López (LOH-pes) came home to Salinas, California, from army duty in February 1919, he was wearing a clean, pressed uniform, polished shoes, and a proud smile. After warm family greetings, Ricardo gave out souvenirs he had brought home from France, where he had served.

In the weeks that followed, his family noticed that Ricardo was a changed man. He had more self-confidence. He was more serious. The war had brought about great changes in the way Latinos like Ricardo viewed themselves. Latino soldiers returning from Europe had seen a world they had hardly known existed.

Their war experiences made them want a better life for themselves and their families. They came home ready to find better-paying jobs than picking cotton, sugar beets, and fruits and vegetables. These Mexican Americans, and many others, were drawn from their homes by the promise of better work in the booming factories of the U.S. Middle West and Northeast.

City Life in the Middle West. Many of the Mexican Americans who sought new challenges settled in large cities of the Middle West such as Detroit, Chicago, St. Louis, Kansas City, Omaha, Cleveland, and Gary, Indiana. Here they worked at unskilled jobs in steel mills, stockyards, and factories. But the jobs provided a step up the economic ladder for Mexican Americans because pay scales were higher than in the Southwest.

SNAPSHOT OF THE TIMES

1914	World War I begins.
1917	U.S. enters World War I; thousands of Latinos serve in the U.S. Army with honor.
	The Jones Act makes Puerto Ricans eligible for the U.S draft.
	Trabajadores Unidos is formed.
1918	Mexicans and Mexican Americans make up the largest group of agricultural workers in the Imperial Valley.
	Mexican American Octaviano A. Larrazolo elected governor of New Mexico.
	World War I ends.

A steel strike in Chicago in 1919 allowed thousands of Mexican Americans to find work replacing the strikers. At the start of the 1920s, a wave of Mexican Americans from the Southwest arrived in Chicago. Many went to work at the city's restaurants and hotels. By 1925, Chicago had 20,000 Mexican Americans, the largest population of Spanish-speaking people outside the Southwest.

Yet these cities were strange and cold to the Mexican Americans. To survive in this new environment, they settled together in large *barrios*. There they could keep their customs and traditions alive and help one another.

The Northeast. From the Middle West, some Mexican Americans moved farther east. About 3,000 Mexican Americans found jobs with the Pennsylvania Railroad. They worked to maintain railroad lines as far east as Altoona, Pennsylvania.

Many of these workers and their families then left the railroad and found other jobs in the Northeast. Some worked in the coal mines and steel mills of Pennsylvania. About one thousand Mexicans were brought in from Texas to work at Bethlehem Steel during a strike at the plant. Others resettled in New York City and Baltimore, Maryland.

Prejudice and Racism. The newcomers to the cities were victims of the same kinds of prejudice that they had encountered in the Southwest. In some respects, their experiences were even worse.

In the cities of the Middle West and Northeast, they came in contact with immigrants from Poland, Hungary, Italy, and other Central and Eastern European countries. These people viewed the Mexican Americans, who were willing to work for less money than they, as rivals for jobs. In addition, they viewed the newcomers from the Southwest as inferiors. In Chicago, Mexican Americans were not permitted to attend services at Roman Catholic churches in some Eastern European parishes.

In some cases, Mexican Americans suffered the same kind of discrimination as African Americans. For example, in East Chicago, two movie theaters required Mexican Americans to sit in the segregated balcony reserved for African Americans.

The police in the cities treated Mexican Americans harshly. They were quick to arrest them for the smallest offenses. Chicago police sometimes forced false confessions to crimes by beating innocent Mexican American prisoners. Few arrested Mexican Americans could afford qualified lawyers to defend them.

By the end of World War I, there were more than 65,000 Mexican Americans living in the Middle West and Northeast. Ten times that number lived in the U.S. Southwest. These Mexican Americans worked to secure their place in U.S. society as the years known as the Roaring Twenties began.

Taking Another Look

1. What factors led Mexican Americans to move from the Southwest to the unfamiliar Middle West and Northeast?

2. What kinds of jobs did Mexican Americans find when they moved north?

3. **Critical Thinking** What were the advantages and disadvantages for Mexican Americans in the Middle West and Northeast?

LOOKING AHEAD

The war years had a great impact on the Mexican American community. For those who fought in the war, it was an opportunity to show their patriotism to the United States. For those who remained on the home front, jobs were plentiful, although they did not raise most Mexicans above the poverty level. Job opportunities brought many Mexican Americans from the Southwest to the cities of the Middle West and the Northeast.

However, storm clouds soon gathered on the economic horizon. They would usher in one of the most difficult periods in U.S. history. Before long, Mexican Americans and other Latinos would suffer with the rest of the country the consequences of the Great Depression.

LATINO HERITAGE

Registro de 1918

Important current events often inspired Mexican *corridos,* or ballads. The lines below are from *Registro de 1918* (Registration 1918), a *corrido* sung by Mexican Americans in the U.S. Army going to France to fight in World War I.

Adiós Laredo lucido
con sus torres y campanas,
pero nunca olvidaremos
a tus lindas mexicanas.

Good bye Laredo highlighted
by your towers and bells
but we shall never forget
your beautiful Mexican women.

Ya nos llevan a pelear
a unas tierras muy lejanas
y nos llevan a pelear
con los tropos alemanas.

They are taking us to fight
to some distant land
and taking us to fight
the German troops.

Ya nos llevan a pelear
a distintas direcciones,
y nos llevan a pelear
con differentes naciones.

They are taking us to fight
in separate directions
and taking us to fight
with different nations.

MUTUAL AID IN SANTA BARBARA

To bring closer together . . . the relations of the Mexicans, especially the members that form this Club in order that they extend to each other the hand of brotherly love for their protection, mutual benefits, and to procure through all the legal means the moral and material betterment of its members.

These words are from the constitution of the *Club Mexicano Independencia,* a *mutualista* founded in the *barrio* of Santa Barbara, California, in 1917. The CMI, as it was known, was not the only *mutualista* in Santa Barbara, but it was unique in that only people born in Mexico could be members. The founders of CMI wanted it to be a nationalistic Mexican group whose members would keep alive Mexican heritage. As the last president of the club put it, "I am Mexicano, my sons who were born here could not belong to the Club because they are American citizens."

The club was not a political group, but it did speak out to defend all Mexicans against racism and prejudice. Most of CMI's responsibilities centered around helping needy or sick members and sponsoring social activities. Through its work, CMI gave hundreds of Mexicans a sense of community and togetherness.

CLOSE UP: Chapter 17

The Who, What, Where of History

1. **Who** was Marcelino Serna?
2. **What** effect did the high demand for labor in the Southwest have on Mexican Americans living in that region?
3. **Where** is the Imperial Valley?
4. **What** were *colonias*?
5. **What** was the role of the *mutualistas* in Mexican American life?
6. **What** was the *Trabajadores Unidos*?
7. **What** opportunities existed for Mexican Americans in the North?

Making the Connection

1. What was the connection between the Jones Act and Puerto Rican soldiers in the U.S. Army?
2. What was the connection between the expansion of U.S. agriculture and industry and the increase in immigration from Mexico?
3. What was the connection between the "Hispanos" and newly arrived Mexican immigrants?

Time Check

1. When did Puerto Ricans become eligible for the U.S. draft?
2. In what year did Octaviano A. Larrazolo become governor of New Mexico?

What Would You Have Done?

1. Imagine that you are a Mexican American during the 1910s. Whose reaction to discrimination would you have supported, Carlos Almanzán's or Elías Sepúlveda's? Explain.

2. Imagine that you are a young Mexican in the 1920s and you have decided to emigrate to the United States. Would you choose to move to the Southwest or to the cities of the Middle West or Northeast? Explain.

Thinking and Writing About History

1. Write an editorial for a newspaper expressing your opinion about the heroism of Marcelino Serna. Discuss the failure of the United States to award him the Congressional Medal of Honor.

2. Imagine that you are a Mexican American who supports the formation of unions for Mexican American agricultural workers. Write a speech in which you explain the benefits of forming a union. In addition, describe the risks that may be involved in trying to form a union.

3. Imagine that you witnessed the scene described by Elías Sepúlveda on page 217. Write a letter to a friend describing your feelings about what you witnessed.

Building Skills: Interpreting a Primary Source

Have you ever read a mystery novel in which all the clues seem to point to one suspect, but you find out in the end that someone else committed the crime? To be a good detective, you have to interpret clues carefully. A good historian also has to interpret carefully the sources he or she uses.

Since *primary sources* often express opinions, historians must decide what value to place on opinions found in a particular source. Sometimes, opinions are not based on facts and may be biased by a person's prejudices.

Imagine you are a historian writing a book about the Mexican Americans in the *barrios.* You find an article written in 1912 about how Mexican Americans lived.

It says in part:

They are unsettled . . . move readily from place to place, and do not lease or acquire land. But their most unfavorable characteristic is their inclination to form colonies and live in a clannish [close-knit] manner.

You need to interpret the article and decide how much value to place on it. Answer the questions below to help you make your decision.

1. Explain the difference between facts and opinions.

2. List the facts and opinions.

3. Are any of the opinions based on facts?

4. How could you find out?

5. If you knew that this article was written by an Anglo reporter, how much value would you place on the opinion stated? Explain.

Express Yourself!

Pretend that you are the owner of a large factory in a city located in the Northeast or Middle West. Choose two or three classmates to work with. Together, create a pamphlet to attract Latinos to the city in which your factory is located. Be sure to describe the advantages of living in the Northeast or Middle West. Use any Spanish words that you may know in your pamphlet. You may wish to illustrate your pamphlet with pictures.

Council 4 was the local branch of *La Orden de Hijos de América,* The Order of the Sons of America, in Corpus Christi, Texas. Its members were dedicated to fighting for civil rights for Mexican Americans.

SECTIONS

1 Boom Times of the 1920s

2 Hard Times and the New Deal

3 Organizing for Strength

CHAPTER

18

From Boom to Depression

(1920–1940)

THINKING ABOUT THE CHAPTER

How did life change for Latinos in the United States during the 1920s and 1930s?

Shortly after World War I, teenager Ernesto Galarza took a summer job in the fields near Folsom, California. He lived in a camp near the fields with other Mexican American workers and their families. That summer, illness swept through the camp. Workers suspected that the water they used for cooking, drinking, and washing was contaminated.

Galarza wanted to have the water inspected. He went to see a lawyer whom his civics teacher had recommended. The lawyer promised Galarza that he would arrange this.

However, Galarza's visit with the lawyer turned out to be important for another reason as well. Galarza would always remember the advice the lawyer offered: "Tell the people in the camp to organize. Only by organizing will they ever have decent places to live."

In the years that followed, Galarza took the lawyer's advice to heart. He helped organize Mexican American field workers into labor unions. These labor unions could bargain with employers for better wages and working conditions.

The 1920s and 1930s saw the first serious efforts to improve conditions for Mexican American farmworkers. In those years, Latinos in towns and cities also formed organizations to help them gain the rights to which they were entitled.

1 BOOM TIMES OF THE 1920s
◆ How did Mexicans and Mexican
◆ Americans share in the good times of the 1920s?

After a brief business slump in the early 1920s, the U.S. economy boomed. People across the nation flocked to stores to buy goods that had been in short supply during World War I. Factories turned out products in record numbers. Jobs were plentiful.

In Mexico, however, jobs were scarce. When there was work, it paid very little. As in the past, the land to the north seemed to promise a better life. More than half a million Mexicans crossed the border into the United States during the 1920s. By 1930, the United States had more than 1.2 million residents of Mexican heritage.

Narrowing the Open Doors. After World War I, immigrants once again flocked to the United States. Many U.S. citizens felt uneasy about that immigration. This was due, in part, to a mood of isolationism that gripped the nation at that time (see page 198). U.S. citizens wanted to cut themselves off from the problems of the rest of the world after the bloody world war. The uneasy feelings also arose from the longheld distrust of foreigners that many U.S. citizens shared.

In the early 1920s, Congress passed two laws sharply cutting back on immigration. The **Emergency Quota Act of 1921** set temporary quotas, or limits, on immigration from outside the Western Hemisphere. The **Immigration Act of 1924** lowered those limits and made them permanent. The laws also put an end to the immigration of Asians. However, neither law limited immigration from Canada or Latin America.

Debating Mexican Immigration. In the U.S. Southwest, anti-immigration feelings were particularly strong against Mexicans. Some U.S. citizens wanted to slash immigration from Mexico. They also wanted to set limits on the number of immigrants from the rest of Latin America.

Labor leaders were among the most active opponents of immigration from Latin America. They argued that it was unfair for U.S. workers to have to compete against Mexican immigrants, who worked for very low wages. Many employers, meanwhile, strongly opposed limiting immigration from Latin America. Railroad operators and owners of large farms wanted a steady supply of Mexican workers to whom they could pay low wages.

Congress decided not to restrict Mexican immigration. However, U.S. immigration officials set up the Border Patrol in 1924 to stop Mexicans from slipping into the country illegally. But the Border Patrol had little success. Almost as many Mexicans entered the country illegally during the 1920s as entered legally.

Organizing. Most Mexican immigrants did not apply for U.S. citizenship. Their goal was to earn some money and

Men and women learn English in a language class in San Antonio, Texas, in 1921. One of the important goals of Latino civil rights groups was to teach Latinos to speak, read, and write English as a means of gaining full rights.

go back home. But the return to Mexico might be many years away. So the immigrants formed organizations to help them with their day-to-day problems. Mexican American citizens, who also shared many of the same problems, did likewise.

Some organizations worked to build pride in Mexican heritage. They held *fiestas* and parades to celebrate Mexican national holidays like the *Cinco de Mayo,* honoring a victory against the French in 1862.

Women often took the lead in organizing dances and celebrations. In some communities, they started theater groups. They also organized chapters of the *Cruz Azul Mexicana,* the Mexican version of the Red Cross.

In the 1920s, the mutual-aid societies, known as *mutualistas* (see page 217), played an important part in the lives of Mexicans and Mexican Americans. Each *mutualista* had from 20 to 120 families as members. The societies provided member families with insurance against fire and illness. As Mexican Americans became secure in their new country, many started small businesses. *Mutualistas* often provided loans for such ventures.

Fighting for Their Rights. Some organizations were formed to fight for Latino civil rights. In the early 1920s, there was a brief business slump. Rumors spread that all Mexicans would be deported. Concerned Latinos met in Kansas City and formed *La Liga Protectiva Mexicana,* or The Mexican Protective League. The league dissolved once the economy improved and the threat of deportation ended.

In San Antonio, Texas, Mexican Americans created *La Orden de Hijos de América,* The Order of the Sons of America, in 1921. The group fought to win for Latinos "all the rights and privileges . . . extended by the American Constitution."

Similar goals inspired the formation of the League of United Latin American Citizens, or LULAC. Created by Mexican Americans at Harlingen, Texas, in 1928, the league later spread to 21 states. Besides opposing discrimination, LULAC organized "400 Clubs" to teach English to Latino preschoolers. The object was to ensure that each child starting first grade had a basic vocabulary of at least 400 English words.

LULAC was different from most other Mexican American organizations. Members of LULAC stressed that they considered themselves citizens of the United States first and Mexican Americans second. They did not hold this view because they were ashamed of their Mexican background. Rather, Mexican Americans felt that this was the best way to win the equal rights that were due them as citizens.

Taking Another Look

1. Why did railroad operators and owners of large farms oppose limits on Mexican immigrants?

2. How did *mutualistas* help Mexican Americans?

3. **Critical Thinking** Do you think the founders of LULAC were wise in setting up their goals? Explain your answer.

2 HARD TIMES AND THE NEW DEAL

◆ How did the Great Depression affect
◆ Latinos?

Mexicans and Mexican Americans working in the fields of California paused in their work. They watched as the stream of battered cars and old pickup trucks clattered by. The vehicles were piled high with bedding, boxes, and other household goods. They were carrying Anglo farm families from the drought-stricken states of Arkansas, Oklahoma, and Texas to California. There, the families hoped to rebuild their lives.

For most Californians, the new arrivals offered more proof of how hard the Great Depression had hit the United States. For Mexicans and Mexican Americans in California, the new arrivals also posed a threat. Farm owners would begin to hire these and other unemployed Anglos to replace Mexicans and Mexican Americans in the fields.

Deeper into Poverty. The Great Depression that began in 1929 spread rapidly across the United States and the rest of the world (see page 198). Consumers sharply reduced their purchases of food and other goods. Factories closed and wages fell. People desperately looked for work. In the early 1930s, from one quarter to one third of U.S. workers were without jobs.

In the U.S. Southwest, farm output was cut back. That made it even harder for migrant workers to earn a decent living. Many migrants worked fewer days and for lower wages than in previous years. Increasing numbers of women, who normally worked at home, joined men in the fields when work was available. Mexicans and Mexican Americans who had jobs in meat-packing plants, steel factories, and on railroads found themselves working only a few days a week. Often, they could get no work at all. Many families could barely afford one meal a day.

Only a relatively small number of Mexican Americans owned land. But many of these lost their property because they were unable to pay taxes. In New Mexico alone, up to 8,000 Mexican Americans lost their land.

The Depression dragged on into the 1930s. Resentment against Mexican immigrants grew. Many were turned away from jobs by employers who preferred hiring Anglos. People demanded that Mexican immigrants return to Mexico. Newspapers ran angry letters in which writers argued, "Let's take care of our own first. Foreigners should go back where they came from."

Even the President, Herbert Hoover, joined in the attack on Mexican immigrants. He claimed that they were taking jobs away from U.S. citizens. He thus blamed them for causing unemployment.

Repatriation. The feelings of anger grew into a drive to **repatriate** Mexicans—that is, to return them to their homeland. In 1931, the Hoover administration announced a plan to deport Mexicans and others living in the country illegally. Hoover hoped that any jobs they held would go to U.S. citizens.

The government first tried to convince Mexicans that it was in their interest to leave the country voluntarily. Many Mexicans did leave rather than face unemployment, poverty, and continuing prejudice.

Other immigrants did not wish to leave. The U.S. Immigration Service began roundups of Mexicans and Mexican Americans. Both Mexicans and Mexican Americans had to prove that they were in the United States legally. If they could

not, they would face deportation. Unfortunately, even many Mexicans who had entered the country legally had lost their immigration documents. They were among those who were deported.

Meanwhile, some states joined with the federal government in applying pressure on Mexicans and Mexican Americans. Relief agencies in California, Texas, and Colorado threatened to cut off aid to Mexicans if they did not leave the country. In New Mexico, even Mexican Americans whose ancestors had lived in the territory when it was ceded to the United States were forced out.

Luisa Moreno (see page 232), a fighter for the civil rights of Mexicans, blasted the repatriation policy with these words:

These people . . . have contributed their endurance, sacrifices, youth, and labor to the Southwest. Indirectly, they have paid more taxes than all the stockholders of California's industrialized agriculture, the sugar beet companies and the large cotton interests that operate or have operated with the labor of Mexican workers.

Going Home. Despite such protests, the repatriation program continued. One writer described the deportations at a Los Angeles railroad station in 1931:

The loading process began at six o'clock in the morning. Repatriados [those being deported] arrived by the truckload,—men, women, and children,—with dogs, cats, and goats; half-open suitcases, rolls of bedding, and lunchbaskets. It cost the County of Los Angeles $77,249.29 to repatriate one trainload, but the savings in relief amounted to $347,468.41 for this one shipment.

Workers reconstruct the San José y San Miguel de Aguayo Mission in San Antonio, Texas, during the 1930s. These workers, many of whom were Latinos, were part of a federally funded work program created under the New Deal.

At border crossings, such as the bridge between El Paso, Texas, and Juárez, Mexico, cars full of *repatriados* (reh-pah-tree-AH-dohs) formed long lines. Some *repatriados* crossed the border on foot. One group waited in Juárez for a month before the Mexican government provided trains to carry them south.

As a result of the campaign of fear, about half a million Mexicans were repatriated during the 1930s. Some 65,000 Mexicans were forced to leave. The others returned to Mexico on their own.

Latinos and the New Deal. In March 1933, President Franklin D. Roosevelt took office. He launched his New Deal to rescue the United States from the Depression (see page 199). The New Deal was made up of a variety of programs. Many of them were helpful to Mexican Americans. Puerto Ricans who were settling in New York City and the Cubans who worked in Florida were also helped.

Like many other U.S. residents, jobless Latinos swallowed their pride and accepted relief (or "welfare") payments.

Other Latinos found jobs on New Deal public works projects. They built bridges, roads, public buildings, and parks. Some New Deal programs hired writers and artists. Among them were Mexican Americans who, using traditional Mexican themes, painted murals and created other works of art for public buildings.

A change in policy in 1937 barred noncitizens from jobs in the main public works program. That meant Mexican immigrants could no longer hold such jobs—not even if their husbands, wives, or children were U.S. citizens. Many states and local governments also barred noncitizens from public jobs.

Some New Deal programs provided outright cash payments to those who had no other income. Some Mexican Americans received more in relief payments than they earned from low-paying jobs. When

1921	The Emergency Quota Act is passed.
	The Order of the Sons of America is formed.
1924	The Immigration Act sets quotas on immigration from outside the Western Hemisphere.
	The Border Patrol is established.
1927	The Confederation of Mexican Workers is founded.
1928	Mexican Americans organize LULAC.
	La Unión de Trabajadores del Valle Imperial stages a strike.
1929	The Great Depression begins.
1931	President Herbert Hoover approves repatriation of Mexicans.
1933	New Deal is launched.
	Mexican strawberry pickers strike for higher wages.
	Confederación de Uniones de Campesinos y Obreros Mexicanos is formed.
1938	Luisa Moreno organizes *El Congreso de Pueblos de Habla Español.*

this was revealed, a huge outcry developed. A new system was started. Under it, Mexicans received less than Anglos.

Taking Another Look

1. Why was it difficult for Latinos to earn a living during the 1930s?

2. Who were the *repatriados?*

3. **Critical Thinking** How effective was the New Deal at helping Latinos survive the Depression?

3 ORGANIZING FOR STRENGTH
◆ How did Latinos fight for better work-
◆ ing conditions during the Great Depression?

A Mexican American field worker described how he was hired in the 1930s:

> I was . . . hired by a . . . contractor or a straw boss [supervisor] who picked up crews in town and handled the payroll. The important questions that were in my mind—the wages per hour . . . whether the beds would have mattresses and blankets, the price of meals, how often we would be paid—were never discussed, much less answered, beforehand. Once we were in camp, owing the employer for the ride to the job, having no means to get back to town except by walking and no money for the next meal, arguments over working conditions were settled in favor of the boss.

An important New Deal law was the Wagner Act. It protected the right of workers to organize labor unions. However, the law did not apply to migrant workers. Thus, when migrant workers began to organize unions, they often faced brutal opposition from farm owners.

Taking Up the Struggle. Organizing unions among workers in any occupation was a hard job. But among farmworkers, it was even more difficult. In the first place, the supply of workers was usually larger than the number of jobs. Thus, if one set of workers walked off the job, a grower had no trouble hiring replacements. Moreover, most workers had no savings to fall back on in case of a strike. It was hard for them to give up wages for the days, weeks, or months that a strike might last.

In the 1930s, some national labor unions thought agricultural workers were too hard to organize. However, these Mexican cotton pickers in San Joaquin Valley, California, organized their own union against brutal opposition from growers.

National unions like the American Federation of Labor (AFL) made little effort to organize agricultural workers. One labor leader remarked: "Only fanatics [unreasonably eager people] are willing to live in shacks or tents and get their heads broken in the interest of migratory laborers."

As Mexican workers grew in number during the 1920s, they made efforts to organize. The first lasting union of Mexican workers was the *Confederación de Uniones Obreras Mexicanas,* the Confederation of Mexican Workers (CUOM). Formed in Southern California in 1927, the union grew to about 3,000 members.

Another new union was *La Unión de Trabajadores del Valle Imperial,* The Union of Workers of the Imperial Valley. It orga-

nized a strike of cantaloupe pickers in 1928. As often happened in labor disputes, law officers sided openly with the growers. Officials labeled strike leaders Communists. They shut down the union's offices and staged mass arrests. Still, the union achieved some of its goals in the strike.

The Strawberry Strike. In May 1933, some 1,500 Mexican strawberry pickers at El Monte, California, demanded 25 cents an hour or 65 cents a crate. The growers who employed them were mostly Japanese immigrants who rented land at high prices from Anglos. The growers argued that if they paid higher wages they could not make a profit. So *la huelga* (WEL-gah), or the strike, began.

As strawberries ripened and then rotted in the fields, strikers with signs bearing slogans picketed the fields. Police arrested marchers for "disturbing the peace." Finally, the owners offered the union a contract with a wage of 20 cents an hour. That was not what the strikers had demanded, but they claimed a victory. At least, they now had a contract.

Out of the strike came a new union called the *Confederación de Uniones de Campesinos y Obreros Mexicanos,* the Confederation of Unions of Mexican Farm Workers and Laborers (CUCOM). Within a year, CUCOM claimed to have about 10,000 members.

A Hard Struggle.

For the next few years, shouts of *¡Viva la huelga!* (*On with the strike!*) rang through the fields of California. Cherry pickers, peach pickers, and cotton pickers all used strikes to try to get higher wages. In Texas, sheep shearers and pecan shellers were among those who went on strike.

However, employers organized as well. A California growers' group successfully pressured the legislature to pass laws to restrict union activity. Employers also used harsh methods to fight the unions. Some hired armed guards to help crush strikes. Others paid thugs to break up union meetings.

Meanwhile, new kinds of farm machinery reduced the need for seasonal labor. After a 1938 strike by Mexican pecan shellers in San Antonio, Texas, the Southern Pecan Shelling Company introduced mechanical shellers. By 1941, the company needed only 600 workers instead of the 10,000 it had formerly used. Field work, too, was increasingly handled by machines. From mechanical beetpickers to mobile packing sheds, machines reduced the need for hired labor.

Seeking Civil Rights.

During the Texas pecan shellers' strike, growers used violence to try to defeat the strikers. Such methods deeply disturbed a woman who had come to San Antonio, Texas to help the workers.

Born in Guatemala, **Luisa Moreno** had been a newspaper reporter in Mexico City before moving to New York City with her husband and infant daughter. With her husband out of work, Moreno took a job as a seamstress in a sweatshop to support the family.

The miserable working conditions made her angry. Moreno yearned to do something to improve the situations of those around her. She decided to become a professional union organizer. She organized cigar makers in Florida, New York, and Pennsylvania. Then she went to Texas to help the pecan shellers, most of whom were Mexican and Mexican American women. She was outraged at the way people in power bullied the pecan shellers. Moreno concluded that she "could not organize workers in the face of violence and terror." So she turned her attention to the protection of Latino civil rights.

Moreno traveled around the country speaking to Latino farmworkers, steel workers, and miners. She met with the members of *mutualistas* in many *colonias* and *barrios.* Moreno also talked about Latino civil rights with elected officials like Dennis Chávez (CHAH-ves), speaker of New Mexico's House of Representatives and later a U.S. senator.

Mexican women shell pecans by hand in San Antonio, Texas. Workers employed by the Southern Pecan Shelling Company struck for higher wages in 1938. The company resorted to violence to try to break the strike.

In 1938, she brought all those groups together in Los Angeles for the first nationwide conference of Spanish-speaking people. Those present included Mexican Americans, Puerto Ricans, Cuban Americans, and others. They created a new nationwide confederation. It was called *El Congreso de Pueblos de Habla Español,* (kohn-GREH-soh deh PWEH-blohs deh AH-blah es-PAH-nyol) The Congress of Spanish-speaking Peoples.

The congress held regional conferences for Latino young people. It helped to organize Mexican, Puerto Rican, and Cuban communities around the country to action. The organization's membership rose to more than 6,000. But it came under attack as "Communist" and "un-American." Then it ran out of money. In the 1940s, the *Congreso* faded away. Still, it had taken important steps in building ties among Latinos.

Taking Another Look

1. Why was it difficult to organize Mexican field workers into labor unions?

2. What new union grew out of the strawberry pickers' strike of 1933?

3. **Critical Thinking** Why did Luisa Moreno change from working for labor unions to working for Latino civil rights?

LOOKING AHEAD

By 1940, the Great Depression was coming to a close. The labor turmoil in the fields began to die down. The approach of World War II put an end to a period of organization and struggle. During the war, Latinos would fight for their nation abroad. They would also discover new opportunities on the home front.

233

Despite the Great Depression, the Basque people of Mountain Home, Idaho, kept up their tradition of an annual "sheepherders overall dance" during the 1930s. Men in overalls and women in colorful gingham dresses snapped their fingers and tapped their feet as they danced the *jota* (HOH-tah), a popular folk dance.

The Basque homeland is divided between Spain and France. Many Basques speak Spanish as well as Euskara, the Basque language. Euskara, however, is very different from Spanish.

Some 20,000 to 30,000 Basques were living in the United States during the Depression. One of the largest Basque communities was located in Boise, Idaho. Basques also lived in other western states as well as in Florida and New York.

Basques who came to the United States often worked first as shepherds (see page 161). Sheepherding is a common occupation in the Basque's homeland in the rugged Pyrenees (PIHR-uh-nees) Mountains. Before long, however, many Basques started dairy farms or became gardeners or miners. Others opened restaurants or boardinghouses. One Basque American, Ramon Navarro, became a star of silent movies.

Today, Basque Americans can be found in a range of occupations. Each year Basques relive their traditions in a festival held at Elko, Nevada.

CLOSE UP: Chapter 18

The Who, What, Where of History

1. **What** were the Emergency Quota Act of 1921 and the Immigration Act of 1924?
2. **What** were the 400 Clubs?
3. **What** was CUOM?
4. **What** is repatriation?
5. **Where** did the 1933 strawberry pickers' strike take place?
6. **Who** was Luisa Moreno?
7. **What** was *El Congreso de Pueblos de Habla Español*?

Making the Connection

1. What was the connection between the end of World War I and the migration of Mexicans to the United States?
2. What was the connection between the Great Depression and the repatriation of Mexican immigrants?

Time Check

1. How many years passed between the start of the Great Depression and President Hoover's repatriation plan?
2. In which year was the first nationwide conference of Spanish-speaking peoples held?

What Would You Have Done?

1. Imagine that you are a Mexican American parent in the 1920s. Would you register your children in a 400 Club? Why or why not?
2. Imagine that you are a Mexican crop picker in the 1920s and 1930s. Do you think that you would join a union? Why or why not?

Thinking and Writing About History

1. Imagine that it is the 1930s. You have returned from Chicago to your Mexican village. Write to a friend from the village who remained in Chicago. Explain your feelings about being back in the village.

2. Imagine that you are a delegate to The Congress of Spanish-speaking Peoples in 1938. Write a speech that outlines what you hope the congress will accomplish.

Building Skills: Classifying Information

Imagine trying to shop in a clothing store that did not *classify* clothing by style and size. It might take you all day to find something that fit you.

Classifying means grouping or arranging items into classes, or categories, based on similarities. We classify pieces of information for the same reason we classify sweaters and shoes—to keep them organized and to find what we want easily.

In this chapter, you have read how the prosperity of the 1920s and the Great Depression of the 1930s brought changes to the lives of Latinos. Classifying those changes will help you remember what you have learned. Three categories you might use to classify the changes are *population patterns, work,* and *relations with non-Latinos.*

Review the chapter, looking for changes. On a separate sheet of paper, organize changes into a chart like the one below. Note that a sample entry has been made in each category. Be sure to include at least three other entries in each category in your chart.

After you complete the chart, review it. In which category do you think the changes were most important? Write a paragraph explaining your choice.

Express Yourself!

With two or three classmates, study the Snapshot of the Times box on page 228. Use the events listed in the box to make a timeline with pictures or illustrations. First, draw a line across a large piece of paper. Then, mark the dates you wish to show. Choose at least three events and draw pictures to illustrate them. You may also use pictures from magazines or newspapers.

CHANGES IN THE LIVES OF LATINOS DURING THE 1920s AND 1930s

Population Patterns	Work	Relations With Non-Latinos
Large numbers of Mexicans came to the U.S. in the 1920s	More Latinos worked in industry.	U.S. isolationist mood makes many Anglos uneasy about immigration

U.S. troops storm ashore against heavy fire at Salerno, Italy, in 1943. Among the troops was the 141st Infantry Regiment from Texas, which contained a large number of Latinos.

SECTIONS

1 Latinos in the Armed Forces

2 The Home Front

3 Facing Prejudice

236

CHAPTER 19

Latinos and World War II

(1941–1945)

THINKING ABOUT THE CHAPTER

How did World War II affect the lives of Latinos in the United States?

Félix Longoria (lohn-GOH-ree-ah) was among the many Latinos who served—and died—fighting for the United States in World War II. After the war, Longoria's body was brought back to his hometown of Three Rivers, Texas. But the town's only funeral home refused to hold services for him because he was a Mexican American. The case drew national attention. In time, Longoria was buried with full military honors in Arlington National Cemetery, across the Potomac River from the nation's capital.

Over the four years after the Japanese attack on Pearl Harbor, roughly 500,000 Latinos served in the U.S. armed forces. Latinos volunteered for, or were drafted into the army, the navy, and the marines. Latinas enlisted in the Women's Army Corps. In fact, Latinos volunteered for the armed forces in World War II at a higher rate than any other group of citizens. Yet the Longoria case was a sad reminder that discrimination still blocked Latinos from full participation in U.S. society.

1 LATINOS IN THE ARMED FORCES

◆ What was military service like for
◆ Latinos during World War II?

Adolfo Garduno (gahr-DOO-noh) of Las Vegas, New Mexico, was mostly skin and bones when he reached a Japanese prison camp in the Philippines in 1942. Garduno was one of the lucky ones. He, at least, had survived the "Bataan Death March." Thousands of other U.S. and Filipino soldiers were not so fortunate.

The Bataan Death March. The death march was one of the early horrors of the war. Japan had attacked the Philippines, then a U.S. possession, at the same time it bombed Pearl Harbor. Large numbers of Mexican Americans were serving in the Philippines. Because they spoke Spanish, they could work easily with Spanish-speaking Filipino soldiers.

The Japanese pushed U.S. and Filipino troops back onto a 30-mile (48-kilometer)-long neck of land called the Bataan Peninsula. Garduno was among some 78,000 soldiers and 26,000 civilians trapped on Bataan. Food supplies rapidly shrank. The soldiers became weak with hunger. They fought fiercely, but had to fall back. In April 1942, four months after the Japanese attack began, the soldiers surrendered.

Then came the death march. The Japanese marched their half-starved captives through the forests of Bataan to prisoner-of-war camps 70 miles (112 kilometers) away. Several thousand prisoners,

including many Mexican Americans, fell by the wayside and died.

Who Served? The thousands of Latinos who served in the armed forces during World War II made up a cross-section of the Latino population in the United States. Some 400,000 were Mexican Americans, while 65,000 were Puerto Ricans. Others traced their ancestry to Cuba, to Central or South America, to Spain or Portugal. After Mexico entered the war on the side of the Allies in 1942, many Mexican citizens also fought in the U.S. armed forces.

Latinos served on all major fronts of the war. They fought in North Africa, in Sicily, in Italy, in the D-day invasion of France. Latinos were among the U.S. troops who slogged through the jungles of Burma. They flew on bombing missions over Germany and Japan.

Mexican Americans made up a large part of units recruited from states like New Mexico and Texas. A New Mexico unit known as the Santa Fe Battalion laid railroad tracks across the North African desert. Trains brought supplies over those tracks to the combat soldiers who drove German and Italian troops out of North Africa in 1942 and 1943.

Medals for Valor. Many Latino soldiers won medals for bravery. In the summer of 1943, Allied forces invaded Sicily. Sergeant Manuel S. Gonzales (gohn-SAH-les) of Texas earned a Distinguished Service Cross for heroism during that invasion. He charged a German machine-gun unit and wiped it out with hand grenades.

On the islands of the Pacific, Marine Private First Class Guy "Gabby" Gabaldón (gah-bahl-DOHN) used "the gift of gab" to persuade hundreds of Japanese soldiers to surrender. Gabaldón had been raised by a

Japanese American family in East Los Angeles and spoke excellent Japanese. On the island of Saipan, Gabaldón would make his way into the jungle where Japanese soldiers were hiding in caves. Speaking in Japanese, he would promise them food and water and good treatment if they surrendered. He received a Silver Star for talking over 1,000 of the enemy into giving up.

The highest U.S. military decoration is the Congressional Medal of Honor, awarded for exceptional bravery. Seventeen Mexican Americans earned this award in World War II. One Medal of Honor went to Private José P. Martínez, a former sugar beet worker from Colorado. Refusing to be pinned down by Japanese fire while under attack in the Aleutian Islands, Martínez charged forward, leaping into trenches occupied by enemy troops. He suffered fatal injuries in his daring assault.

Sergeant Cleto Rodríguez of San Antonio, Texas, won the Medal of Honor. He attacked a Japanese position in the Philippines and killed 82 of its defenders.

Expanded Horizons. Service in the war opened up new opportunities for many Latinos. For some, it was the first time away from their hometown. They met

Latinos from other parts of the United States and made friends among other ethnic groups.

After the war ended, in September 1945, many Latinos took advantage of the **GI Bill of Rights.** Congress had passed that law to provide benefits to veterans to help them in their return to civilian life. Some used the money for training in job skills. Others used it to attend high school or college or to start new businesses. Many moved out of the *barrios* of the cities and bought homes in the spreading suburbs.

Latino veterans found new roles in their local communities. Some joined organizations like the American G.I. Forum. This group was started in Texas in reaction to the Félix Longoria incident (see page 236). The Forum fought for equal treatment for Latino veterans in postwar life. Many of those veterans had been rejected for membership in the older veterans' organizations like the American Legion.

Taking Another Look

1. Most Latinos who served in the U.S. armed forces in World War II came from which two national groups?

2. How did the GI Bill of Rights help Latino war veterans?

3. **Critical Thinking** Why might a young Latino or Latina have volunteered for the armed services in World War II?

2 THE HOME FRONT
◆ How did World War II offer new
◆ opportunities for Latino workers in the United States?

As young male factory and farm workers marched off to war, employers desperately looked for replacements. Women,

older men, teenage girls, and boys too young to be drafted suddenly found themselves choosing among many possible jobs. Almost overnight, the Great Depression (see page 198) faded away.

Rush to the War Factories. Like other U.S. citizens, Latinos joined the rush to the war factories. Mexican Americans left farms and ranches and small towns. Piling their belongings into cars or trucks, they moved to Denver or Tucson or Los Angeles or Seattle. For the many Mexican American women who found work, taking home weekly wages was a thrilling experience. They gained a new sense of self-worth.

Puerto Ricans too were eager to take war jobs. Some 70,000 Puerto Ricans lived on the mainland at the start of the war. During the war, army transport ships carried still more workers from Puerto Rico to the mainland to help fill war-related jobs.

Lowering Barriers. Before the war, Latinos who sought jobs in industry had faced an invisible barrier. No matter how able they were, Latinos and Latinas were rarely allowed to work at skilled or even semiskilled jobs.

The federal government for the first time tried to end such discrimination. In 1941, under pressure from African Americans, President Franklin D. Roosevelt set up the **Fair Employment Practices Committee** (FEPC). It aimed at ending discrimination in war industries. Any company that held a federal contract was required to treat people equally, whatever their race or background.

Through his work with the FEPC, Dr. Carlos E. Castañeda (kahs-tah-NYEH-dah), of the University of Texas, helped open up new opportunities for Mexican Americans.

Carlos E. Castañeda was born in a small town on the Mexican side of the Rio Grande. He moved to Texas with his family at the age of 10. Dr. Castañeda became a leading historian and taught at the University of Texas for more than 30 years.

As a special assistant to the FEPC, Dr. Castañeda sought to improve opportunities and working conditions for Mexican Americans in Texas. In 1945, he was behind an FEPC order directing an oil company to change its policy toward Mexican American workers and promote those it had kept at lower work levels.

The FEPC helped Latinos, African Americans, and other ethnic minorities move up to better jobs. In 1930, only 15 percent of Latino workers were in skilled or semiskilled jobs. By 1950, the proportion had gone up to 35 percent.

The *Bracero* Program. The flood of new workers into industry was not enough to fill all available jobs. Farmers needed helpers to tend and harvest crops. Railroads were short of hands. Both agriculture and railroads were vital war industries. The farmers and the railroads looked to the south—to Mexico—to get the workers they needed.

To meet the labor shortage, in July 1942 the U.S. and Mexican governments set up what was called the ***bracero*** program. *Braceros* (from the word *brazo* or arm) were hired hands or laborers. Under the program, U.S. farmers hired *braceros* to harvest sugar beets, cotton, corn, onions, and other crops. Each year, after the crops were in, the *braceros* returned to Mexico. A related, but separate, program supplied *braceros* to the railroads.

The Mexican government insisted that the programs include safeguards such as a minimum wage of 30 cents an hour and protection against discrimination. The *bracero* program stirred controversy from the start. U.S. labor unions argued that it would result in lower wages for U.S. citizens. They also claimed it would prevent farmworkers from organizing unions. Farm owners objected that the wages they would have to pay the *braceros* were too high. Many Mexican Americans opposed the program, too. They argued that Mexican citizens should be admitted as regular immigrants, free to seek any job they could get.

But *braceros* were eager to work. At that time, 30 cents an hour was far more than they could earn in Mexico. Mexican workers rushed to join the program. From 1942 to 1947, more than 250,000 *braceros* came to the United States. U.S. business owners profited from the cheap labor. After the war, they urged that the *bracero* program be extended. Congress agreed with the business owners. Before the plan ended in 1964, another 4.5 million *braceros* had worked in the United States.

ptMojados* in Texas. In Laredo, Texas, a cafe had a sign on its door that read, "Negroes, Mexicans, and dogs not allowed." Such cruel evidence of open discrimination angered officials of the Mexican government. They considered Texas the most hostile of all states for people of Mexican ancestry. Mexico announced that no *bracero* could go to work in Texas.

However, Texas farmers and ranchers found other ways of hiring Mexican citizens. They hired Mexicans who had crossed the border illegally, sometimes by swimming across the Rio Grande. Such "unofficial" Mexican workers were often called *mojados* (moh-HAH-dohs), or "wetbacks."

Unlike *braceros*, the *mojados* had no formal protection from the government. Employers did not have to pay them a minimum wage or offer any of the other benefits *braceros* received. If a *mojado* objected about his wages or working conditions to an employer, the employer could threaten to have him deported.

A truckload of Mexican *braceros* heads for the cotton fields of New Mexico's Pecos Valley. Why do you think that one observer of the labor scene in the U.S. Southwest called the *bracero* program a grower's "dream of heaven"?

Life of a *Bracero*. For a typical *bracero*, life in the United States was hard. The *bracero* was away from his family, doing backbreaking work, and living in poor housing. But the lure of more money than they could make in Mexico made the experience bearable for most *braceros* in spite of the hardships.

One *bracero*, Juan Garza began his wartime travels in a small village in central Mexico. One day in early spring of 1943, he joined some of his neighbors to walk to a nearby town. There, recruiters were taking applications for the *bracero* program. Some of Garza's neighbors paid bribes to recruiters to ensure that they would be accepted into the program. But Garza had no money to offer for bribes. He decided to take his chances and apply anyway. Garza was lucky. He was accepted.

With 40 other men, Garza boarded a bus. They rode all night and all the next day. At the border, they switched to another bus. Finally, they reached their destination, a farm in California.

For the next six months, Garza moved from farm to farm, tending and harvesting crops. At the end of the day, Garza's back ached from all the lifting and stooping. He had to pay high prices for food that was often badly prepared and not to Mexican tastes. The bunkhouses where he slept were often run-down shacks. Sometimes the roofs leaked when it rained. On weekends, the men piled into a truck to go to town. If town was too far away, they stayed at the bunkhouse and played cards or sang songs.

When Garza returned to Mexico after six months, he had saved about $500 to help his family get through the winter. The following spring, like many other Mexicans, Juan Garza set off for another season as a *bracero*.

Taking Another Look

1. How did World War II open up new opportunities for Latinos in U.S. farms and factories?

2. What was the *bracero* program and why was it started?

3. **Critical Thinking** From the point of view of a Mexican peasant, what were the advantages and disadvantages of the *bracero* program?

3 FACING PREJUDICE
◆ What forms of prejudice and
◆ discrimination did Latinos face during World War II?

Sergeant Macario García came home from the war with the prized Congressional Medal of Honor. In Germany, he had attacked two enemy machine-gun nests single-handedly. But at the Oasis Cafe in Sugarland, Texas, García was not a war hero. He was simply "a Mexican." The management refused to serve him and ordered him to leave. When García refused, a fight broke out. Finally, the Sugarland sheriff came and broke up the fight.

The wartime deeds of Latinos won them new respect from some Anglo Americans. However, much prejudice and discrimination against Latinos still remained. In fact, attacks on Latinos reached new heights during the war years.

Zoot Suits and *Pachucos*. In the early years of the war, Los Angeles was a battleground between gangs of Anglo and Mexican American youths. As a badge of honor, Mexican American teenagers adopted a flashy style of clothing that sent a clear message: "I'm me and I'm proud. Don't mess with me."

For Mexican American teenage boys, the "in" thing to wear on a night out was the **zoot suit**. The zoot suit featured an oversized jacket with wide lapels and padded shoulders. High-waisted, baggy pants narrowed to a snug fit at the cuffs. A broad-brimmed hat completed the look. Girls who hung out with zoot-suiters had their own distinctive style. They wore sweaters, short black skirts, black stockings, and sandals.

The Mexican American young men who adopted such styles were known as *pachucos* (pah-CHOO-kohs). The young women were known as *pachucas* (pah-CHOO-kahs). They represented only a fraction of Mexican American young people, but they stood out. When *pachuco* gangs got in trouble, many Anglos blamed Mexican Americans as a group. The police, meanwhile, were ready to crack down on the gangs at the slightest excuse.

Los Angeles police arrested 22 members of a Mexican gang and charged them with taking part in a murder in August 1942. Although 17 were convicted, a higher court ruled that their trial had been unfair and freed the youths.

1939	World War II begins in Europe.
1941	Japanese army attacks Pearl Harbor.
	U.S. enters World War II.
	Fair Employment Practices Committee aims to end discrimination in war industries.
1942	Mexico joins the Allied powers.
	Bataan Death March kills thousands of U.S. soldiers.
	Bracero program allows Mexican laborers to work in the United States.
1943	Zoot-suit riots shake Los Angeles.
1945	World War II ends.
	Congress passes GI Bill of Rights.

Targets of Violence. In the late spring of 1943, two weeks of violence known as the "zoot-suit riots" shook Los Angeles. The term is misleading, for the zoot-suit-wearing *pachucos* were mainly the victims rather than the rioters. Anglo sailors and soldiers were the ones who committed most of the violence.

Los Angeles newspapers had whipped up feelings against Mexican Americans in the months before the riots. The newspapers ran sensational stories about *pachuco* gangs. The police assumed that all zoot-suiters were criminals and arrested masses of them. A Mexican American complained, "We're Americans for the draft but Mexicans for jobs and for the police."

On the night of June 3, 1943, a group of soldiers and sailors reported to police that *pachucos* had attacked them in a Mexican American neighborhood of Los Angeles. On the nights that followed, hundreds of soldiers and sailors roamed Los Angeles in taxis. When they spotted someone in a zoot suit, they piled out and beat him up. Sometimes, gangs of Anglos invaded movie theaters and dance halls and ripped the zoot suits off the *pachucos* they found there.

Newspapers egged the rioters on, implying that zoot-suiters were being taught a necessary lesson. The police did little to stop the attackers. In one incident, an eyewitness reported:

> Four boys came out of a pool hall. They were wearing the zoot-suits that have become the symbol of a fighting flag. Police ordered them into arrest cars. One refused. He asked: "Why am I being arrested?" The police officer answered with three swift blows of the night-stick across the boy's head and he went down. As he sprawled, he was kicked in the face. Police had difficulty loading his body into the vehicle because he was one-legged and wore a wooden limb.

The Los Angeles riots finally ended when military police stepped in and began arresting the soldiers and sailors. But zoot-suit riots spread to Chicago, Detroit, and other cities.

The rioting soon led the Mexican ambassador in Washington to protest to the U.S. government over the way Mexican Americans were being treated. The U.S. State Department's Office of Inter-American Affairs took action. It set up the Spanish-Speaking People's Division

THE ARTIST'S VIEW

Carlos Vierra, Zia Mission, *Museum of Fine Arts, Santa Fe, New Mexico*
In the 1920's, painter Carlos Vierra became alarmed at the decay of
centuries-old Spanish missions. Vierra created a series of 16 paintings of
New Mexico missions as they had appeared when they were first built.

Bronze head; Nigeria, Metropolitan Museum of Art, New York. Photo by Schector Lee The proud face of a Benin king looks out from this dark bronze figure dating from the 1500s. Today, Benin kings still wear caps and chokers similar to those worn by this figure. The different cultures of enslaved Africans who were brought to the Americas became one of the three main roots of today's Latino culture.

Silver Chalice, Los Angeles County Museum of Art, Gift of William Randolph Hearst This chalice, or communion cup, was crafted in Mexico City about 1575. Made of silver, wood, and feathers, it has fine carvings of religious scenes, including the Twelve Apostles. This is a beautiful example of the art of Spanish culture, the second of the three main groups that combined to create today's Latino culture.

Taino wood chair. The Granger Collection Carved from a single piece of wood, these chairs were used by chiefs, priests, and important warriors. This chair is shaped like a hammock, which the Taino used in place of beds. Native American culture is the third great root of today's Latino culture.

*L*egendary Origin of Tenochtitlán, *From Codex Mendoza, Aztec; ca.1540; M.N.A.H., Biblioteca. Laurie Platt Winfrey.* A codex is a handwritten book combining writing and pictures. This one tells the history of the Aztec people. It shows the settlement of the valley of Mexico. Tradition says that an eagle landing on a cactus guided the Aztecs to the spot where they built their capital. The drawings at the bottom show Aztec conquests of neighboring people. Around the outside are emblems with days of the week and Aztec gods.

Painted pine cupboard, California, International Museum of Folk Art, Museum of New Mexico Spanish designs join with Native American materials and bright colors in this 19th-century *trastero,* a huge pine cupboard. In creating everything from furniture to blankets to buildings, the Spanish drew heavily on Native American styles. Spanish artists also used the bright paints that Native Americans developed from local minerals.

Pottery mug, Museum of New Mexico, Photo by John Lei, Omni-Photo Communications, Inc. Pottery making was a respected art of the Native Americans of the Southwestern United States. This bowl and mug, dating from the 1600s, show the mixture of ancient native American traditions and new Spanish styles. The distinctive shapes are very much in the Pueblo tradition. The glazed finish reflects the influence of the Spanish settlers.

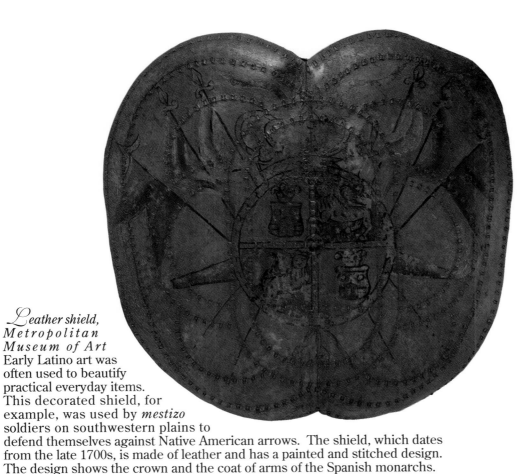

Leather shield, Metropolitan Museum of Art Early Latino art was often used to beautify practical everyday items. This decorated shield, for example, was used by *mestizo* soldiers on southwestern plains to defend themselves against Native American arrows. The shield, which dates from the late 1700s, is made of leather and has a painted and stitched design. The design shows the crown and the coat of arms of the Spanish monarchs.

Frederico Cavada, The Battle of Fredericksburg
Historical Society of Pennsylvania, Philadelphia
From a balloon high above the battle, Federico
Cavada made sketches during the U.S. Civil War
that were used by Union forces to study the movement of Confederate armies. Later, he turned a
sketch of the Battle of Fredericksburg into
this panorama of color and movement. After the
U.S. Civil War, Cavada returned to his native
Cuba to fight for freedom from Spain. Captured by
the Spanish, he was executed by firing squad.

José Salazar, Don Luis de Penalver y Cardenas, *Louisiana State Museum*
José Salazar, who was born in Mérida, Mexico, was the first professional artist in the city of New Orleans. His works, including this portrait of the bishop of Louisiana, are the only paintings still existing
from the period of the Spanish occupation (1764—1803). The scroll-
like ornament at the lower left is called a *cartouche.* It is typical of traditional Spanish paintings.

Santo, *J. B. Ortega, International Folk Museum, Museum of New Mexico*
This *santo* of St. Ninode Atocha was carved in wood by a modern day santero, J.B. Oretga. Santos figures are an art form that developed in the Spanish borderlands soon after Spanish settlement. The art of creating santos has been passed from generation to generation by the *santeros*. The subjects that the *santos* depict may be male or female groupings but they are always religious figures.

The Holy Trinity, Santo, International Folk Museum, Museum of New Mexico
Santos, or religious images, were a way for artisans in the Spanish borderlands to express their faith. Often, as with this *santo*, the three figures of the Trinity are shown joined together. *Santeros* still pursue their art today in the U.S. Southwest. The painted or carved figures decorate homes, private chapels, and churches. Often, *santos* are carried in religious processions.

Xavier Martínez, Afternoon in Piedmont, *Collection of the Oakland Museum, gift of Dr. William S. Porter.*
The word *poetic* has been used to describe the work of Xavier Martínez. His *Afternoon in Piedmont* used as its source James Whistler's famous painting of his mother. Martínez moved that scene to a window of his house and used his wife as the central figure. Martínez was born in Guadalajara, Mexico, in 1869. He moved to San Francisco when his stepfather, a diplomat, was transferred there. Later, he taught at the California School of Fine Arts.

Miguel Pou, Ciqua, *Museo de Arte de Ponce, Puerto Rico, Fundación Luis A. Ferré*
Miguel Pou drew upon his Caribbean heritage in this oil-on-canvas portrait of a
Puerto Rican man. He studied education at Normal School in Hyannis, Massachusetts,
later taught public school in Puerto Rico, and founded the Miguel Pou Academy of
Puerto Rico in 1910. His work has been exhibited in Puerto Rico and the United States.

Julio Alpuy, The Couple from the Valley, *Courtesy of the artist. Photo by Tony Valez.*
This huge painting on wood was created by Uruguayan artist Julio Alpuy, who
now lives in the United States. The piece is more than five feet long, almost four
feet tall, and more than three inches deep.

Fernando Botero, La
Familia Pinzon, *Museum
of Art, Rhode Island
School of Design*
Poking gentle fun at his
subjects, the Colombian-
born painter, Fernando
Botero, has an unusual
style that makes it possible to recognize his paintings immediately. Botero
uses an exaggerated style
to portray people as stuffy
and pompous. He also
uses the bright colors
often used in the traditional folk art of Colombian
peasants. Botero was
born in Medellin,
Colombia. He studied in
Colombia, Italy, France,
and Spain. He now lives
in New York City.

Rosa Ibarra, Women Reading, *Museo del Barrio,*
In her paintings, Rosa Ibarra celebrates the strengths and achievements of Latino women. The daughter of a Puerto Rican artist,
Ibarra, paints figures that suggest meditation, stillness, and friend-
ship. While her Puerto Rican heritage is important to her, she
gives her figures characteristics of *all* national and ethnic groups.
She paints women as powerful, colorful subjects. Her paintings
communicate the strength, warmth, and vitality of women.

Carmen Lomas Garza, Empanadas (Turnovers), *Courtesy of the artist.* The paintings of Carmen Lomas Garza explore memories of her childhood in Kingsville, Texas. An active member of *El Movimiento* of the 1960s, Garza uses painting to preserve the traditions of Chicano families. In *Empanadas,* she shows an activity from her family's past, the making of turnovers. By celebrating the activities of her childhood, she encourages fellow Latinos to celebrate their tradition of strong family ties.

Julio Larraz, Hurricane,
Courtesy of the artist. Nora Haime Gallery
In this painting, the artist takes a vantage point from space, seeming to look down on the earth. The Cuban American artist says, "Air travel has caused me to look differently at the world. While traveling by plane, instead of reading or eating, I would look out the window and do water colors." Larraz's paintings are *abstract*. They show forms and colors not as a photograph would capture them, but how they appear in the artist's mind.

𝒜dolfo Piantini, Niña, *Courtesy of the Artist.*
Adolfo Piantini is a Dominican artist, who now lives in New York City. His pictures reflect the life of poor people of the Dominican Republic and the United States. On a visit to Santo Domingo, he was outraged by the poverty and decided to use his talent to publicize the plight of the poor. "I felt that my work was far from over. There were the ghetto children left aside by so-called progress, living in the silence of their cardboard homes."

Luis Jimenez, Sodbusters, *Courtesy of Luis Jimenez. Photo by Eduardo Fuss.*
At the age of six, Luis Jimenez was helping his father make neon signs in his native El Paso, Texas. Today, Jimenez's huge, colorful figures grace many U.S. cities. The muscular farmer in *Sodbuster* dominates the main street of Fargo, North Dakota. Jimenez molds his massive creations out of fiberglass and then paints them in brilliant colors.

to fight prejudice and discrimination. The office had only limited success, however. Thus, although the war years brought economic gains to Mexican Americans and other Latinos, everyday life still held much bitterness and pain.

Taking Another Look

1. What were the zoot-suit riots?
2. What role did the newspapers play in the zoot-suit riots?
3. **Critical Thinking a.** What did zoot suits mean to the young people who wore them? **b.** What did they mean to the soldiers and sailors who rioted?

LOOKING AHEAD

In the years after World War II, conditions for Latinos in U.S. society would continue to change at a rapid pace. Some Latinos would find better jobs and live in better homes. Larger numbers of immigrants from Latin America would arrive in those years. The postwar period would also see a drive to guarantee equality for Latinos in all aspects of U.S. life.

In June 1943, U.S. soldiers, sailors, and marines roamed the streets of Los Angeles beating up Mexican wearers of zoot-suits. Here, the servicemen have stopped a streetcar to see if it carried any zoot-suiters.

THE *PACHUCO* IMAGE

The defiant image of the *pachuco* did not end in the 1940s. Recent generations have looked upon the *pachuco* era as a time when Mexican Americans began to show pride in their heritage in the face of oppression.

The actor Edward James Olmos (OHL-mohs) brought the strut and swagger of the *pachuco* to the stage in the 1978 musical drama *Zoot Suit* by Luis Valdéz. The play was based on a sensational 1942 murder trial in Los Angeles. A judge and jury sent more than a dozen *pachuco* gang members to San Quentin prison for allegedly murdering a boy who belonged to a rival gang.

Later, an appeals court dismissed the convictions because the judge and prosecution had shown open bias against Latinos. Bias also distorted newspaper coverage of the trial. Such coverage aroused anti-Latino feelings that were unleashed in the "zoot-suit riots" a year later.

Olmos, himself a Mexican American, grew up in the *barrio* of East Los Angeles. Several of his movie roles have shown his pride in being Latino. In *The Ballad of Gregorio Cortéz*, he played a Mexican hunted down by Texas Rangers. In *Stand and Deliver*, he portrayed Jaime Escalante, the Bolivian-born math teacher who inspired a class of Latino high-school students to high achievement.

CLOSE UP: Chapter 19

The Who, What, Where of History

1. **Who** was Félix Longoria?
2. **Where** is Bataan?
3. **What** was the Santa Fe Battalion?
4. **Who** was Guy "Gabby" Gabaldón?
5. **What** was the GI Bill of Rights?
6. **What** was the American G.I. Forum?
7. **What** was the Fair Employment Practices Committee?
8. **Who** was Dr. Carlos E. Castañeda?
9. **What** are *braceros*?
10. **Who** were *pachucos* and *pachucas*?

Making the Connection

1. What was the connection between Félix Longoria and the American G.I. Forum?
2. What was the connection between the Fair Employment Practices Committee and the need for factory workers during World War II?

Time Check

1. How many years passed between the Japanese attack on Pearl Harbor and the end of World War II?
2. In what year did the zoot suit riots occur?

What Would You Have Done?

1. If you had been a World War II veteran, how would you have used your benefits under the GI Bill of Rights? Explain.
2. If you had lived in a Mexican village in the 1940s, would you have applied to go to the United States as a *bracero*? Explain.

3. Imagine that you returned from military service in World War II and were refused service in a restaurant because of your cultural background. What would you do?

Thinking And Writing About History

1. It is 1942. Write a memo to the President of the United States telling him whether or not you support the *bracero* program.

2. Write an editorial for a Mexican newspaper commenting on the zoot-suit riots of 1943.

Building Skills: Drawing Conclusions

A *conclusion* is a statement that is supported by facts. Every conclusion must have facts to support it. For example, the following sentence is a conclusion: "The lives of *braceros* were hard, but *braceros* were better off than *mojados*." What facts support this conclusion? Here is one supporting fact: "The government guaranteed *braceros* a minimum wage of 30 cents an hour." Here is another: "*Mojados* had no formal protection from either the Mexican or U.S. government."

Each conclusion below has a set of facts that follows it. Some facts support the conclusion; others do not. For each conclusion, write the letters of the facts that support it.

1. Latinos served on all major fronts in the war.

   a. Large numbers of Mexican Americans served in the Philippines.

   b. Sergeant Manuel S. Gonzales earned a medal for bravery in Sicily.

   c. Private First Class Guy Gabaldón grew up in East Los Angeles.

2. Service in the armed forces created new opportunities for many Latinos.

   a. The GI Bill of Rights helped many Latinos get an education.

   b. Many Latinas went to work in war factories.

   c. Latino veterans were eligible for job training after the war.

3. Not everyone supported the *bracero* program.

   a. Mexico refused to let *braceros* work in Texas.

   b. Labor unions argued that *braceros* were taking jobs away from U.S. workers.

   c. Mexican American leaders said that Mexican citizens should be admitted as regular immigrants rather than as *braceros*.

Express Yourself!

Choose one of the Latino war heroes whom you read about in this chapter. Write an epitaph, a brief message or poem that appears on a gravestone, in memory of that person. The epitaph should mention the person's name and describe his or her actions during World War II. The following is an example of an epitaph: "Here lies Félix Longoria, a brave soldier who fought for his country during World War II. Although denied burial in his hometown, he was honored with a burial at Arlington National Cemetery."

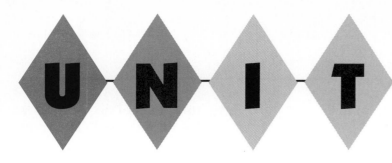

UNIT 6

A CHANGING POSTWAR WORLD

(1945–1980)

Cuban refugees in 1965.

César Chávez

Chapter

20 The Great Migration from
Puerto Rico
(1945–1980)

21 New Arrivals from the
Caribbean
(1945–1970s)

22 The Struggle for Equal Rights
(1950s–1970s)

23 New Immigrants from Central
and South America
(1950s–1970s)

24 A Growing Voice
(1950s–1980)

THE BIG PICTURE

Voices of the Times

All we need is the recognition of our right to full and equal coverage under every law which protects every other working man and woman in this country.

— César Chávez, Mexican American labor organizer, 1969

Unit 6 describes how Latinos fared in the years from the end of World War II to 1980. Those years were marked by a bitter rivalry between the United States and what was then the Soviet Union. They were also marked by a revolution in Cuba and political troubles elsewhere in Latin America. In those unsettled conditions, new waves of Latinos arrived on U.S. shores. During the same period, African Americans launched a movement to gain their civil rights. That movement helped inspire Latinos to fight for full political and economic equality.

◆◆ In The United States ◆◆

A bitter rivalry developed between the United States and the Soviet Union after World War II. That rivalry had a major influence on life in the United States between 1945 and 1980. The rivalry also had a huge influence on the political and economic life of the United States in those years.

The Cold War Begins. Although the United States was the most powerful nation in the world at the end of World War II, the Communist government of the Soviet Union quickly challenged that position. The Soviet Union took over much of Eastern Europe. It also developed its own atomic weapons. Almost as soon as the two **superpowers,** as the United States and Soviet Union were called, began to enjoy the benefits of peace, they were caught up in what became known as the **Cold War.** It was a "cold" war because the conflict between the two nations stopped just short of military combat.

The United States became committed to stopping the spread of communism in Europe, Asia, and Latin America. Through what was called the Marshall Plan, it sent billions of dollars in aid to the war-torn nations of Western Europe. In addition, it formed a military alliance with ten European nations and Canada known as the North Atlantic Treaty Organization (NATO).

The United States also convinced the 20 Latin American nations to line up on its side in the Organization of American States (OAS) in 1948. The OAS was founded to promote goodwill, trade, and peace among the nations of the Americas. The member nations also pledged to help defend one another from military threats.

The Cold War became a hot war in 1950, when Soviet-supported North Korea invaded U.S.-backed South Korea. A United Nations (UN) fighting force, mostly U.S. troops, was sent to South Korea to drive the North Koreans back. But when UN forces advanced into North Korea, Communist China joined the war on North Korea's side. The Korean War ended three years later with neither side able to claim a victory.

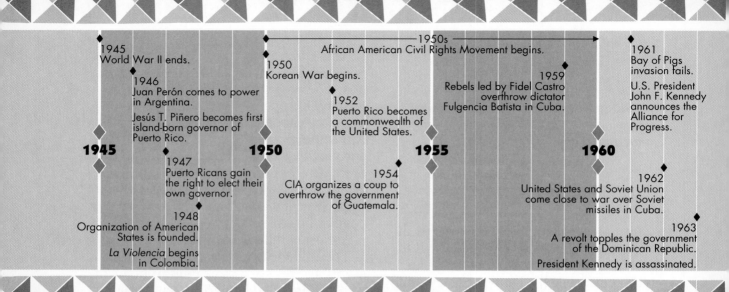

1945
World War II ends.

1946
Juan Perón comes to power in Argentina.

Jesús T. Piñero becomes first island-born governor of Puerto Rico.

1945

1947
Puerto Ricans gain the right to elect their own governor.

1948
Organization of American States is founded.

La Violencia begins in Colombia.

1950s
African American Civil Rights Movement begins.

1950
Korean War begins.

1952
Puerto Rico becomes a commonwealth of the United States.

1950

1954
CIA organizes a coup to overthrow the government of Guatemala.

1959
Rebels led by Fidel Castro overthrow dictator Fulgencia Batista in Cuba.

1955

1961
Bay of Pigs invasion fails.

U.S. President John F. Kennedy announces the Alliance for Progress.

1960

1962
United States and Soviet Union come close to war over Soviet missiles in Cuba.

1963
A revolt topples the government of the Dominican Republic.

President Kennedy is assassinated.

A New "Red Scare." The effects of the Cold War were not limited to foreign policy. As happened after World War I, a **"Red scare,"** or fear of communism, swept the nation. Some Congressional leaders, government officials, and newspaper columnists spread the word that U.S. Communists and Soviet agents were everywhere. The Communists, they claimed, were undermining the U.S. government and way of life.

The anti-Communist drive heated up during the 1950s. In 1953, a New York couple, Julius and Ethel Rosenberg, were put to death for having passed along to the Soviet Union details of the atomic bomb. In a second case, a British scientist who had worked on the U.S. atomic bomb project admitted he had also given the Soviet Union secret information about the construction of the atomic bomb.

The anti-Communist feeling reached its peak in the early 1950s when Senator Joseph McCarthy of Wisconsin charged that the State Department and the U.S. Army were riddled with Communists. McCarthy offered no proof of his charges. But his anti-Communist campaign filled the nation's television screens for months.

Eventually, McCarthy's bullying tactics proved his undoing. By the time he died in 1957, the Red scare had run its course. But the term **McCarthyism** has remained in the English language. It means to charge people with political disloyalty on the basis of little or no evidence.

The Fabulous Fifties. U.S. citizens of the 1950s had more to do than worry about communism. In those years, they were busy taking advantage of the post-World War II prosperity. Wartime restrictions on the production of consumer goods had ended. The economy was in high gear. People rushed to buy television sets, refrigerators, dishwashers, and other comforts.

Many people moved out of the cities and

250

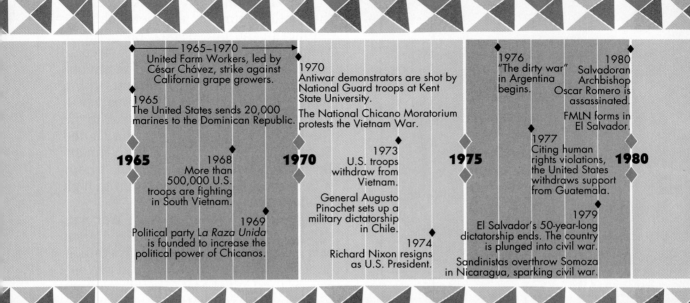

1965–1970
United Farm Workers, led by César Chávez, strike against California grape growers.

1965
The United States sends 20,000 marines to the Dominican Republic.

1965

1968
More than 500,000 U.S. troops are fighting in South Vietnam.

1969
Political party *La Raza Unida* is founded to increase the political power of Chicanos.

1970
Antiwar demonstrators are shot by National Guard troops at Kent State University.

The National Chicano Moratorium protests the Vietnam War.

1970

1973
U.S. troops withdraw from Vietnam.

General Augusto Pinochet sets up a military dictatorship in Chile.

1974
Richard Nixon resigns as U.S. President.

1976
"The dirty war" in Argentina begins.

1977
Citing human rights violations, the United States withdraws support from Guatemala.

1975

1980
Salvadoran Archbishop Oscar Romero is assassinated.

FMLN forms in El Salvador.

1979
El Salvador's 50-year-long dictatorship ends. The country is plunged into civil war.

Sandinistas overthrow Somoza in Nicaragua, sparking civil war.

1980

bought homes in the suburbs. Meanwhile, with well-to-do city dwellers moving out, the cities began to suffer from a loss of income from taxes. Many cities could no longer provide as many public services or as much aid to needy people as they once had. Many older neighborhoods in cities became the homes of new immigrants from Latin America. Latinos began making their mark on U.S. culture, especially in the entertainment field. The Cuban-born bandleader Desi Arnaz (ahr-NAHS) and the Chilean-born pianist Claudio Arrau (AHR-row), for example, became household names to the millions who owned television sets.

Lured by the promise of mainland life, record numbers of Puerto Ricans took advantage of cheap air fares to leave their island home. They moved to New York and other northeastern cities. Large numbers of African Americans also moved from the South to cities in the North and Midwest.

The Civil Rights Movement. Many Latinos and African Americans lived in poverty. Most Latinos and African Americans were treated as second-class citizens. In the 1950s, African Americans began a drive to gain the civil rights they had long been denied. Their first big victory came in 1954 when the U.S. Supreme Court ruled in *Brown* v. *Board of Education* that **segregation,** or separation of race, in public schools was illegal.

Led by a dynamic young minister, the Reverend Dr. Martin Luther King, Jr., African Americans pressed for equal rights in other areas as well. In struggling for their rights, African Americans used nonviolent methods such as mass marches and sit-ins. Responding to their protests, in 1964 and 1965, Congress passed new civil rights laws. These laws prohibited segregation in public places and protected African Americans' right to vote.

The civil rights laws were part of what President Lyndon B. Johnson called his

251

At an August 1971 rally, this *chicana* was part of a group that marched in Sacramento, California to protest discrimination against Mexican Americans.

The Vietnam War. East Asia became the battleground for another Cold War conflict in the mid–1960s. Like Korea, Vietnam had been divided into two countries: North Vietnam, with a Communist government, and South Vietnam, with a supposedly democratic one. When North Vietnamese guerrillas tried to reunite the country under communism, the United States sent soldiers to help South Vietnam. By 1968, more than 460,000 U.S. troops were fighting in South Vietnam, with high casualties.

Opposition to the Vietnam War was widespread. Protesters organized giant peace marches. Young men burned their draft cards. The strong opposition was one reason the United States withdrew from Vietnam. In March 1973, the last U.S. troops pulled out of Vietnam. Within a year, the South Vietnamese army was defeated and the country fell into the hands of the Vietnamese Communists.

1968—a Violent Year. In 1968, at the height of antiwar protests, violence rocked the nation. An assassin's bullets killed Martin Luther King, Jr. A few months later, Presidential candidate Robert Kennedy, who had been campaigning against the Vietnam War and for greater civil rights, was gunned down. His death came less than five years after a gunman had killed his brother, President John F. Kennedy.

Riots broke out after King's death. They left areas of many U.S. cities like Los Angeles looking like war zones. Then later that summer, police and National Guard troops attacked antiwar protestors at the Democratic National Convention in Chicago. The Republican candidate, Richard M. Nixon, won the presidency with an appeal to the "Silent Majority"—all those who feared the unrest that seemed to be sweeping the nation.

Great Society program. Other Great Society measures aimed at providing better schools, medical care, and housing. Latinos benefited from these programs.

Latinos also followed the example of the African American Civil Rights Movement in pushing for social justice. César Chávez organized Mexican American migrant farmworkers into a new union, the United Farm Workers. It won higher wages and better working conditions after a five-year-long strike, from 1965 to 1970, against California grape growers.

Meanwhile, in the urban *barrios* of California and the Southwest, a **Chicano** (chee-KAH-noh), or Mexican American, movement sprang up. Chicanos (the men) and chicanas (the women) expressed their pride in their Mexican heritage. Movement members worked through a variety of organizations for better housing, for educational opportunities, and for jobs. Puerto Rican groups pursued similar goals.

A Decade of Disappointment. In the 1970s, the United States finally pulled out of Vietnam, but not before more violence had erupted on the home front. In May 1970, National Guard troops shot and killed four antiwar protesters at Kent State University in Ohio. That summer, police attacked a large Chicano antiwar demonstration in Los Angeles, killing a number of people, including Rubén Salazar (sah-lah-SAHR), a popular Mexican American journalist. Four years later, Richard Nixon became the first President to resign, because of the Watergate scandal. The affair involved illegal campaign activities by his aides and an attempted coverup by the President himself.

U.S. citizens were angered in 1979 when revolutionaries in Iran, angry at U.S. support of their former ruler, the shah, stormed the U.S. embassy. They took more than 50 Americans hostage. The Americans were held for over a year before being released. In the words of President Jimmy Carter, the country seemed to be suffering from a "malaise," a sense of social and moral uneasiness.

Taking Another Look

1. Where did the Cold War become a fighting war?
2. What is McCarthyism?
3. **Critical Thinking a.** How did the African American Civil Rights Movement affect Latinos' fight for civil rights? **b.** What methods do you think were most effective in gaining civil rights for both groups

◆▪◆ **In Latin America** ◆ ◆

During the postwar years, Latin Americans continued their efforts to achieve social reform and a greater degree of economic independence for their nations. Those efforts often involved force. Sometimes the efforts led to clashes with the United States over its fear that communism might spread in Latin America.

Changes in Argentina and Guatemala. In 1946, Juan Perón (peh-ROHN) came to power in Argentina as a new type of reform-minded *caudillo*. Together with his actress-wife, Evita, he championed the cause of the urban *descamisados* (des-kah-mee-SAH-dohs), or shirtless ones, as workers were called. Perón also sought to reduce foreign control over the economy by having the government take over the railroads and utilities.

The United States saw no threat of communism in Perón's government. But in 1951, when Guatemalan president Colonel Jacobo Arbenz Guzman started on a program of land reform, the United States reacted differently. A powerful U.S. company, the United Fruit Company (see page 149), was the largest single landowner in Guatemala. It controlled a large part of Guatemala's economy. The Arbenz plan to redistribute land among the peasants would have wiped out the United Fruit Company's holdings.

The United States quickly moved to protect the company and to stop what it said was a Communist government. The U.S. Central Intelligence Agency (CIA) organized an invasion of Guatemalan exiles in 1954. The Arbenz government was overthrown, and a government that backed U.S. interests more strongly replaced it. Latin Americans deeply resented the U.S. action in Guatemala. So strong was this anti-U.S. feeling that when Vice-President Richard M. Nixon visited Latin America in 1958, angry mobs attacked his motorcade and almost overturned his car.

The Cuban Revolution. Since the 1930s, Cuba had suffered under the brutal dictatorship of Fulgencio Batista (bah-TEES-tah). Then, in 1959 Batista was overthrown by a rebel army led by Fidel Castro, a former law student who became a revolutionary guerrilla. Once in power, Castro denounced the United States and embraced communism. He seized Cuba's farms and industry, thereby removing them from the control of U.S. companies or private Cuban owners. The United States fought back by cutting off all trade with Cuba. Cuba then turned to the Soviet Union for aid. At the beginning of 1960, the U.S. broke off relations with Cuba.

As Castro moved toward communism, thousands of Cubans fled the island. By the spring of 1961, the Cuban exile population in the United States numbered nearly 100,000. Many of those exiles dreamed of overthrowing Castro and returning to Cuba. That April, President John F. Kennedy agreed to support an invasion of Cuba by an exile army. The army of about 1,400 landed at the Bay of Pigs. They were quickly surrounded and captured. The invasion then collapsed.

In October 1962, the Soviet Union installed nuclear missiles on Cuba. A dangerous face-off followed, in which the United States and the Soviet Union stood on the brink of nuclear war. The Soviets finally agreed to withdraw the missiles.

Cuba's revolution continued. Cut off from the United States and most of the Latin American nations, Cuba had to depend on enormous amounts of aid from the Soviet Union to keep its economy going. But the revolution did succeed in wiping out illiteracy and greatly improving education, health care, and housing. Castro and his associate Ernesto "Che" Guevara (ghe-VAH-rah) became heroes to many young people in both the United States and Latin America.

The Alliance for Progress. To improve relations with Latin America, in 1961, President John F. Kennedy announced a new policy, known as the Alliance for Progress. The United States promised to give money for social reform and economic development to democratic governments in Latin America.

However, democratic reformers like Fernando Belaúnde Terry (beh-lah-OON-deh TEH-ree) in Peru and Eduardo Frei (FRAY) in Chile were unable to accomplish much. Belaúnde was thrown out of office by a military coup. Given the choice between reform governments with Communist leanings and dictatorships that supported U.S. interests, the U.S. government continued to prefer the latter.

Trouble in the Dominican Republic. In the Dominican Republic, for example, the rule of dictator Rafael Trujillo (troo-HEE-yoh) finally gave way to a democratic government with plans for reform in 1961. But a military takeover soon ended that government. In the turmoil that followed, thousands of Dominicans fled to the United States. In 1965, fearing that a new revolt might produce another Cuba, U.S. President Lyndon Johnson sent in 20,000 troops. They remained until new elections were held in 1966. This new U.S. intervention aroused the anger of many Latin Americans.

A Socialist Government in Chile. In 1970, Chile became the first Latin American country to elect a Socialist president, Salvador Allende (ah-YEN-deh). He pursued an active program of land reform. He also nationalized copper mines and many banks and industries. Allende also reopened relations with Cuba.

In 1973, the Chilean military moved against Allende. The Chilean president was killed, and the government became a

Sandinistas celebrate the fall of the Somoza government in Nicaragua.

dictatorship under General Augusto Pinochet (pee-noh-SHEH). It soon became clear that the United States had assisted in Allende's overthrow. When the role of the United States became known, many Latin Americans protested. To them, it was yet another example of U.S. interference in their affairs.

Gathering Storm in Central America. As the 1970s began, Guatemala, El Salvador, and Nicaragua all suffered under the harsh rule of dictators. Those rulers freely used the army to crush any opposition. After Guatemalan "death squads" had slaughtered over 30,000 people, the U.S. government withdrew its support in 1977. This was part of President Jimmy Carter's new policy of cutting off aid to countries that violated human rights.

In 1979, El Salvador's almost 50-year-long dictatorship ended. A joint military and civilian **junta** (HOON-tuh), or ruling council, then came to power. But the civilians were forced out of the junta, and the country plunged into civil war.

That same year in Nicaragua, a revolutionary guerrilla movement overthrew the corrupt government of the Somoza (soh-MOH-sah) family. The U.S. government had backed the Somozas since the 1930s because of their anti-Communist stand. The revolutionaries called themselves **Sandinistas** after Augusto César Sandino, who had opposed the U.S. occupation of Nicaragua in the 1930s (see page 200). At first, the United States supported the new Sandinista government. That policy changed as the Sandinistas made changes that many in the United States thought were too radical.

The strife in Central America continued into the 1980s. Conditions there would help send a flood of refugees from the region to the United States in the coming years.

Taking Another Look

1. Give three examples of U.S. involvement in Latin America in the 1960s and 1970s.

2. How was the Allende government of Chile different from other governments of Latin American nations?

3. **Critical Thinking** Do you think the United States would have intervened in Latin America as often as it did in the 1960s and 1970s if there had been no Cold War? Explain your answer.

255

More than a half century of U.S. colonial rule was ended in 1952 when Puerto Rico's commonwealth status became official and the flag of Puerto Rico proudly flew over the island.

CHAPTER 20

The Great Migration from Puerto Rico
(1945–1980)

THINKING ABOUT THE CHAPTER

What changes helped increase Puerto Rican migration to the United States after World War II?

In the autumn of 1949, Verania González (gohn-SAH-lehs) boarded a plane bound for New York. As the plane cut through the clouds, the 17-year-old from San Juan, Puerto Rico, wondered what her new life would be like. She spoke only Spanish. But her sister Nilda lived in a Puerto Rican neighborhood in the South Bronx section of New York City. Nilda had promised to introduce Verania to many new Puerto Rican friends.

Within hours of landing, Verania caught her first glimpse of the South Bronx. Here she spotted Spanish signs in the windows of Puerto Rican *bodegas*, or small grocery stores. She heard the sounds of Spanish in the streets. She found a Spanish Protestant church like the one she had worshiped in at home. She also met Luis Cancel (kahn-SEL), a 17-year-

SECTIONS

1 A New Form of Government

2 Meeting New Challenges

3 Lending a Helping Hand

old Puerto Rican born in the United States. Remarked Luis to a friend, "I'm going to marry that girl."

In 1952, Luis kept that promise. The couple took up a new life in the South Bronx amid a growing Puerto Rican population. Today, the Cancels take great pride in their two homelands. Luis explains, "I am a United States citizen, *and* I am a Puerto Rican." As both Puerto Ricans and New Yorkers, Luis and Verania lived through a time of many changes in their native land and in the growing Puerto Rican community in the United States.

1 A NEW FORM OF GOVERNMENT

◆ How did the political status of Puerto Rico change after World War II?

In 1952, the same year that Verania and Luis married, there was a turning point in Puerto Rican history. That summer, on July 25, Governor Luis Muñoz Marín (mah-REEN) raised the Puerto Rican flag next to the U.S. flag at El Morro (see page 192), the fortress guarding San Juan harbor. His act was the official birth of the *Estado Libre Asociado de Puerto Rico* (es-TAH-doh LEE-breh a-soh-SYAH-doh deh PWER-toh REE-koh), or Free Associated State of Puerto Rico. Puerto Rico was now a **commonwealth** of the United States. As a commonwealth, it was no longer a U.S. colony. It was now a self-governing nation with political and economic ties to the United States.

Shaking Off Colonial Bonds.

Although Puerto Rico had been a colony, Puerto Ricans were U.S. citizens. But they could not elect their own governor (see page 187). Patriotic Puerto Ricans searched for a way to end the island's colonial status. Followers of Luis Muñoz Marín embraced the idea of *autonomismo* (ow-toh-noh-MEES-moh), or self-government, in free association with the United States.

Luis Muñoz Marín, the son of Luis Muñoz Rivera (see page 186), had studied in the United States. There he established himself as a gifted writer. But Muñoz Marín burned with a desire to finish the struggle for independence and home rule started by his father. In the 1930s, Muñoz Marín returned to Puerto Rico from the United States to take up his father's cause.

On July 22, 1938, Muñoz Marín visited the tiny inland town where his father had been born. Here, he announced the start of a new political party called the *Partido Popular Democrático* (Popular Democratic party), or PPD. He chose as an emblem the profile of a *jíbaro,* or peasant, wearing a straw hat called a *pava* (PAH-vah). Under the emblem, Muñoz Marín wrote the words: *Pan, Tierra y Libertad* (Bread, Land, Liberty). These words became the slogan of the PPD.

An Island Commonwealth. World War II was a turning point in the struggle to end colonial rule in Puerto Rico. About 65,000 Puerto Ricans fought for the United States in that conflict. Their service won support for the idea of Puerto Rican self-government. Colonial empires around the world had been shattered during the war. The United States also moved to break up its own colonial empire.

In 1946, U.S. President Harry S. Truman named Jesús T. Piñero (pee-NYE-roh) as Puerto Rico's first island-born gov-

1938 Luis Muñoz Marín establishes the Popular Democratic party in Puerto Rico.

1940s–1970s The great migration brings a million Puerto Ricans to the mainland.

1946 Jesús T. Piñero becomes the first island-born governor of Puerto Rico.

1950 Public Law 600 makes Puerto Rico a commonwealth of the United States.

1952 Puerto Rican constitution goes into effect.

1961 Antonia Pantoja helps found ASPIRA.

1967–1979 South Bronx Project creates bilingual programs in nine public libraries.

ernor. A year later, Congress gave Puerto Ricans the right to elect their own governor. In a landslide election, voters swept Muñoz Marín into office.

In 1950, the United States adopted Muñoz Marín's plan for *autonomismo*. On July 4, President Truman signed Public Law 600. Known as the Constitution Act, the law declared,

> Fully recognizing the principle of government by consent, this act is now adopted . . . so that the people of Puerto Rico may organize a government pursuant [according] to a constitution of their own adoption.

Under the law, Puerto Rico became a commonwealth. As a self-governing country, Puerto Rico could elect its own officials, fly its own flag, and adopt its own

national anthem. Puerto Ricans retained U.S. citizenship and remained subject to the military draft. But as members of the commonwealth, they paid no federal income taxes.

Puerto Ricans adopted a new constitution, modeled after the U. S. Constitution. Muñoz Marín put the constitution into effect on the anniversary of the date U.S. troops first took control of the island from Spain. On July 25, 1952, Puerto Rico ended 54 years of colonial rule.

Voices of Dissent. On March 1, 1954, shots rang out from the gallery of the U.S. House of Representatives. A woman named Lolita Lebrón (leh-BROHN) cried out, "Free Puerto Rico now!" Bullets struck five representatives before police seized Lebrón and her three male companions.

At their trial, the four attackers spoke out in favor of complete independence for Puerto Rico. Few Puerto Ricans supported such violent tactics. However, the incident revealed the split among Puerto Ricans over the island's commonwealth status.

Three quarters of Puerto Rican voters had approved the nation's new constitution in 1952. Yet, debate continued over the future of the island. The debate led to the creation of two new political parties: the Puerto Rican Independence Party (PIP) and the New Progressive Party (PNP). The views of these parties, along with those of the PPD, continue to influence Puerto Rican politics today.

The *independentistas* (een-deh-pen-den-TEES-tahs) who formed the PIP call for an end to all political ties with the United States. They believe that independence is the only way to free Puerto Rico from what they call crippling dependence on the United States. That dependence, they

Under "Operation Bootstrap," Muñoz Marín's program to modernize Puerto Rico, mainland companies were encouraged to build factories on the island. Here is a 1970s electric plant in Hato Rey.

believe, holds back Puerto Rico's cultural and economic growth.

The *estadistas unidos* (es-tah-DEES-tahs oo-NEE-dohs) of the PNP want Puerto Rico to become a state of the United States. They believe that only through statehood can Puerto Rico truly become a part of the economic and political system of the United States. In particular, they want the right to be represented in Congress and to vote for the President of the United States.

Under the guidance of Muñoz Marín, the PPD defeated its rivals for more than 20 years. During this time, Puerto Rico experienced an era of extraordinary growth. It also saw the movement of tens of thousands of Puerto Ricans to the mainland United States.

Taking Another Look

1. How did World War II help end Puerto Rico's status as a colony?

2. How did Public Law 600 change Puerto Rico's political status?

3. **Critical Thinking** Imagine you are living in Puerto Rico in 1955. Which political party would you support? Why?

2 MEETING NEW CHALLENGES
◆ What challenges faced Puerto Ricans
◆ on the island and on the mainland?

Governor Muñoz Marín hoped to instill a sense of pride among *puertorriqueños* (pwer-toh-rree-KEH-nyos), as the people of Puerto Rico called themselves, after centuries of colonial rule. To accomplish this, he created a program known as *¡Jalda Arriba!* (HAHL-dah ah-RREE-bah), or **Operation Bootstrap.** It was designed to improve the economy and living conditions of Puerto Ricans.

A Drive to Modernize. Under Operation Bootstrap, Muñoz Marín challenged Puerto Ricans to pull themselves "up by their bootstraps." To provide the jobs they needed to do that, Muñoz Marín invited U.S. companies to build factories and plants in Puerto Rico. Through foreign investment, Muñoz Marín hoped to transform Puerto Rico from an agricultural society into a modern industrial society.

Not everyone supported efforts to lure mainland industry to the island. Critics called the policy "perfumed colonialism." Nevertheless, Muñoz Marín's popularity won the votes to push the program.

Operation Bootstrap brought great changes to the island. In 1952, there were only 82 factories in Puerto Rico. Once Operation Bootstrap got under way, new factories seemed to open almost every day. By 1970, the island boasted more than 1,000 factories. Those factories created thousands of new jobs.

Workers crowded into public housing projects built by the government. New paved roads crisscrossed the country. *Jíbaros* no longer lived on isolated farms cut off from the cities. Large farms were broken up and parceled out to farm workers. New schools were built, and the number of Puerto Ricans who could read and write soared.

Moving to the Mainland. During the 1950s and 1960s, wages rose and unemployment dropped in Puerto Rico. Even so, higher wages and more plentiful jobs could be found in the United States. So, many Puerto Ricans decided to move to the mainland.

Before World War II, few people from Puerto Rico traveled to the United States. A boat trip might cost a worker a year's wages. After World War II, widespread use of the airplane changed this situation. By the late 1940s, air fares dropped to less than $50.

In 1930, only about 53,000 Puerto Ricans lived in the mainland United States. Of this number, 45,000 lived in New York City. Between 1940 and 1950, more than 200,000 Puerto Ricans arrived in the United States. In that single decade, the size of the Puerto Rican community in New York City jumped to some 187,000. Throughout the 1950s and 1960s, more than 50,000 Puerto Ricans arrived each year at airports in New York, Chicago, Newark, Philadelphia, and other cities.

The 1970 U.S. Census provided a glimpse of what has become known as "the great migration." By that time, nearly 1.4 million people of Puerto Rican descent lived in the United States. The Puerto Rican population of New York City totaled 817,712. This figure was nearly double that of San Juan! Some people called New York "the Puerto Rican capital of the world."

Shown on their wedding day in 1952, Verania and Luis Cancel take great pride in their two homelands, one in the South Bronx, the other on Puerto Rico.

A Cold Greeting. Many Puerto Ricans who arrived in New York in the 1950s exclaimed: *"¡Hace mucho frío!"* ("It's very cold!") The cool climates of northern cities, where most Puerto Ricans settled, contrasted sharply with the warm climate of their sunny home island. So too did the constant chatter in English.

The new arrivals adjusted to climate differences. But language differences proved more difficult to handle. Prejudice against those who could not speak English was widespread. When one recent arrival went to an unemployment office to find work, a clerk snapped, "Go learn English before you come to this office."

In the 1950s and early 1960s, few programs existed to help Puerto Ricans and other Spanish-speaking people make their way in the English-speaking world. Adults faced forms and applications written in English. Spanish-speaking children struggled to pass courses taught in English.

Discouraged by the language barrier, some newcomers returned home. Others, like Verania Cancel, learned English on the job. But even those Puerto Ricans who spoke English often felt unwelcome. In giving their reactions to life on the mainland, Puerto Ricans commonly complained, *"La gente son fría."* ("The people are cold.")

The Stain of Racism. One of the reasons Puerto Ricans felt Americans were cold to them was the racism practiced by many U.S. citizens. In Puerto Rico, the fact that an individual's African or Native American heritage was reflected in their physical appearance had little effect on how they were treated. Some of the outstanding heroes of the Puerto Rican people were of African descent. They included Rafael Cordero (kohr-DEH-roh), who dedicated himself to teaching the poor, and José Celso Barbosa (bahr-BOH-sah), a doctor who founded the Republican party of Puerto Rico.

In the United States, Puerto Ricans were shocked to find that African Americans suffered from severe prejudice and discrimination. Now the same attitudes were directed at those Puerto Ricans who did not look "white." Puerto Ricans could not help wondering how much the people of the United States really valued democracy.

Land of Opportunity? Most Puerto Ricans who came to the mainland United States started at the bottom of the economic ladder. In the 1950s, nearly 92 percent of all Puerto Ricans working in the United States held semiskilled or unskilled jobs. Many worked as bellhops, messengers, cooks, and dishwashers. Others took jobs in factories, especially in New York's garment district.

PUERTO RICANS IN NEW YORK CITY AND ON THE MAINLAND, 1950–1970

1st Generation (Born in Puerto Rico)

Year	New York City	Rest of Mainland	Total	Percentage In NYC
1950	187,420	38,690	226,110	82.9
1960	429,710	185,674	615,384	69.8
1970	473,300	336,787	810,087	58.4

2nd Generation (Born on the Mainland)

Year	New York City	Rest of Mainland	Total	Percentage In NYC
1950	58,460	16,805	75,265	77.7
1960	182,964	89,314	272,278	67.2
1970	344,412	236,964	581,376	59.2

From 1950 to 1970, did the percentage of Puerto Ricans living on the mainland who lived in New York City rise or fall?

"My father did piece work as a laundry presser," recalled Luis Cancel. "He worked 70 hours a week for $15 a week." As a teenager, Luis worked as a laundry presser. After he married, Luis took a job in the millinery, or hatmaking, trade. Verania found work in a pocketbook factory.

Still other Puerto Ricans came to the United States as seasonal farmworkers. After harvesting Puerto Rico's sugar crop in June, they headed to New Jersey farms. Here they picked cranberries and other crops by hand, working long hours for minimum wages.

Some Puerto Ricans in time found more skilled work. Luis Cancel, for example, became a purchasing agent for a large manufacturer of business machines. Others, however, remained trapped in low-paying jobs or found no work at all. In the 1960s, the unemployment rate among Puerto Ricans was twice that of non-Latino white workers. At the same time, Puerto Rican families earned only half the average income of non-Latino white families. Some 30 percent of all Puerto Rican families on the mainland lived below the **poverty line,** or the income required to meet minimum family needs.

Education statistics were also discouraging. In the 1960s, crime and drugs crept into city schools. The percentage of Puerto Rican students leaving high school before graduating soared. In warning of the seriousness of the situation, Puerto Rican educator Richard Rivera observed, "The Puerto Rican student who drops out of school has nothing to 'drop into' except low wages, unemployment, or underemployment."

Faced with the grave problems of their people, Puerto Rican community leaders took action. Some joined the protest movements of the late 1960s and 1970s (see Chapter 22). You will read about what others did to help Puerto Ricans in the next section.

Taking Another Look

1. What was the goal of Operation Bootstrap?
2. What problems faced Puerto Ricans on the mainland in the 1950s and 1960s?
3. **Critical Thinking** Congressman Herman Badillo (bah-DEE-yoh) described Puerto Ricans as "strangers in their own land." What do you think he meant by that?

3 LENDING A HELPING HAND

◆ What programs helped Puerto Ricans to build new lives on the mainland?

"How can a poor community help itself?" As Puerto Ricans struggled with this question, the Puerto Rican government came up with a solution. In 1947, the

Luis Palés Matos

Luis Palés Matos (1898–1959) was one of the leading Puerto Rican poets of the mid-1900s. In these lines from his poem "Ten con ten" he notes how a blending of peoples created a new culture in the Caribbean. Puerto Rico is one of the Antilles islands.

Y así estás, mi verde antilla,	And thus you are, my green Antille isle,
en un sí es que no es de raza,	In a yes and a no over race,
en ten con ten de abolengo	In neither one nor the other of ancestry
que te hace tan antillana . . .	that makes you so Antillean . . .
Al ritmo de los tambores	To the rhythm of the drums
tu lindo ten con ten bailas,	You dance a pretty neither this nor that,
una mitad española	one half Spanish,
y otra mitad africana.	the other African.

Office of the Commonwealth of Puerto Rico was set up. Governor Muñoz Marín viewed the office as a "bridge" between the island and the mainland. It would offer Puerto Ricans on the mainland the help that many federal, state, and city agencies failed to provide.

Helping Newcomers. In 1948, the Office of the Commonwealth opened in New York City. The office acted as an employment service, translator, and guide to city services. It also worked for and won the passage of laws to help seasonal workers who came to the mainland from Puerto Rico. The laws forced farm owners to provide contracts to the seasonal workers. Those contracts clearly stated the terms of employment, including hours, wages, health insurance, and more.

The Office of the Commonwealth grew along with migration. By the mid–1950s, regional offices had opened in Chicago and in Camden, New Jersey. But even the expansion failed to keep up with the pressing problems created by the arrival of hundreds of thousands of Puerto Rican migrants.

Organizing the Community. In the 1950s and 1960s, a number of different groups took shape. Some, such as the Puerto Rican Merchants Association, encouraged the growth of small businesses. Others, such as the Puerto Rican Family Institute, provided assistance to troubled families. The Puerto Rican Forum was one of several groups that sought to instill pride among Puerto Rican youth.

As the 1960s unfolded, many organizations took aim at two of the most pressing problems facing Puerto Ricans—the language barrier and the high dropout rates among Puerto Rican students. Antonia Pantoja (pahn-TOH-hah), one of the

263

founders of the Puerto Rican Forum, became a leader in this movement. In 1961, Pantoja helped set up ASPIRA (ahs-PEE-rah), named after the Spanish for "strive" or "achieve." ASPIRA dedicated itself to promoting educational achievement. "Strive to learn" was its challenging motto.

To promote higher education, Pantoja started ASPIRA clubs in New York, Puerto Rico, and Washington, D.C. She also established the Universidad Boricua (oo-nee-ver-see-DAHD boh-REE-kwah), with centers in New York and Washington. Here students from Puerto Rico and the mainland took advanced courses in many areas.

While Pantoja championed higher learning, another project took shape in the libraries of New York City. The project aimed at "Puerto Ricans ages 1–99." One of the people behind this project was a librarian named Pura Belpré (bel-PREH).

Stories From Puerto Rico. The reading room at the Bronx library exploded in applause as Pura Belpré started her puppet show. A beloved character called Juan Bobo (HWAHN BOH-boh) had taken the stage in Belpré's puppet theater. Belpré's voice and hands brought Bobo to life as she retold a traditional Puerto Rican folktale called "Juan Bobo and the Queen's Necklace."

"Strive to Learn" was the challenging motto of ASPIRA. Here, in an ASPIRA classroom in New York City, students young, middle aged, and old took courses in many different subjects.

When the show ended, the 67-year-old storyteller packed up the puppets and headed to another library in the South Bronx. As she walked toward her car, a child's voice begged her to wait. The child quickly introduced her grandmother. "Please tell her a story," pleaded the child. Standing between two parked cars, Belpré told yet another tale. Tears spilled down the grandmother's cheeks as she relived her Puerto Rican childhood.

A Sense of Pride. Belpré's puppet shows formed part of what became known as the South Bronx Project. From 1967 to 1979, the New York Public Library set up nine branch libraries aimed at reaching the Spanish-speaking population of the South Bronx. For Belpré, the program offered one more chance to "develop a sense of pride . . . in Puerto Rican children."

Belpré had come to New York City in 1920 at age 17. While visiting a library, she watched as a librarian helped a group of teenagers. Silently Belpré made a wish. "If only I could do what this lady is doing for the rest of my life, I'd be the happiest person in the world."

In 1921, Belpré's wish came true when the New York Public Library hired her as a special Spanish-speaking assistant. Belpré was the first Puerto Rican librarian hired by the city. She worked to bring Puerto Rican culture to readers. As part of that effort, she wrote the first collections of Puerto Rican folktales published in the United States. In 1982, New York City honored Belpré with the Mayor's Award of Honor for Arts and Culture.

Belpré worked on the South Bronx Project with Lillian López, the program's director. López and Belpré helped make the libraries **bilingual,** or capable of offering services in two languages. They hired bilingual staff and bought bilingual materi-als—films, books, newspapers, and more. Under their direction, libraries in the South Bronx became cultural centers.

A Growing Presence. Economic hard times in the 1970s forced deep cutbacks in many federal programs. These cutbacks ended the South Bronx Project. As the project drew to a close, a new generation of Puerto Ricans came of age. Born of Puerto Rican parents in the United States, these young men and women numbered in the hundreds of thousands.

By 1980, Puerto Ricans formed the second largest Spanish-speaking community in the United States. More than 2 million Puerto Ricans now lived on the mainland, while an estimated 3.3 million lived on the island. Although Puerto Ricans still faced staggering problems, they were gaining the power to make their voices heard. As the 1980s began, Puerto Ricans on the mainland reexamined their role in U.S. society (see Chapter 26).

Taking Another Look

1. How did the Puerto Rican government help mainland Puerto Ricans?
2. What was the purpose of Aspira and the South Bronx Project?
3. **Critical Thinking** Why do you think Pura Belpré used traditional folktales working with Puerto Rican children?

LOOKING AHEAD

Between 1945 and 1980, Puerto Ricans witnessed remarkable changes. During the same time, immigrants from other Latin American lands also began arriving in the United States. Unlike Puerto Ricans, they fled political upheaval and revolution at home. Their arrival added new cultural richness to the nation's growing Latino population.

RELIGIOUS DIVERSITY

When James Cancel visited his grandparents' home in Puerto Rico during the 1970s, he awoke each morning to the sounds of mass in the Catholic church next door. At that time, nearly 80 percent of all Puerto Ricans practiced Roman Catholicism. But James belonged to the Pentecostal (pehn-tuh-KAWS-tuhl) church in which his parents worshiped.

The Pentecostal church has an approach to religion that appeals to many Puerto Ricans unsettled by changes on the island or the mainland. Explained James's father Luis, "The Church filled a spiritual need."

Today, the Pentecostal church is but one of many Protestant sects making inroads in Latin America.

In 1992, about 40 million Latin Americans had converted to Protestantism. This trend prompted some observers to ask, "Is Latin America turning Protestant?"

The answer is no. The majority of Latin Americans still practice the Roman Catholic faith. But changes in Latin American societies have opened the door to new religions, including traditional African or Native American faiths. The result has been an increase in religious diversity. Latin Americans who travel to the United States bring those beliefs with them, adding to religious diversity in the United States as well.

CLOSE UP: Chapter 20

The Who, What, Where of History

1. **Where** in the United States did Verania and Luis Cancel live?
2. **What** are *bodegas?*
3. **Who** was Luis Muñoz Marín?
4. **What** political party adopted the slogan *Pan, Tierra, Libertad?*
5. **What** is a commonwealth?
6. **Who** are the *independentistas* and the *estadistas unidos?*
7. **Who** are the *jíbaros?*
8. **What** was "the great migration"?
9. **Where** did many seasonal Puerto Rican farmworkers take jobs in the United States?
10. **What** was the original purpose of the Office of the Commonwealth?
11. **What** challenges faced Puerto Rican migrants in the 1950s and 1960s?
12. **Who** was Antonia Pantoja?
13. **What** was the South Bronx Project?
14. **Who** was Lillian López?

Making the Connection

1. What was the connection between Public Law 600 and the creation of the Puerto Rican commonwealth?
2. What was the connection between Operation Bootstrap and the modernization of Puerto Rico?
3. What was the connection between the rise of airline travel and "the great migration"?

Time Check

1. What is the importance of July 25, 1952, to Puerto Ricans?

2. Which political party developed first, PNP, PPD, or PIP?

3. Which two decades saw the greatest migration of Puerto Ricans to the mainland?

What Would You Have Done?

1. Imagine that you are a *puertorriqueño* or a *puertorriqueña* in the 1950s. Would you support an Operation Bootstrap project to build a factory in your town? Why or why not?

2. Suppose you are a member of a Puerto Rican group in the 1950s or 1960s. What *one* problem would you suggest that the group focus on? Why?

3. Imagine that you were a student in the South Bronx in 1976. What arguments would you have given the city government to continue the South Bronx Project?

Thinking and Writing About History

1. Write a news story describing the importance of the ceremony at El Morro on July 25, 1952. Try to include answers to the questions *Who? What? When? Where? Why?* and *How?*

2. Create a short skit in which Luis Muñoz Marín explains his program to an inland village of *jíbaros*.

Building Skills: Interpreting Historical Statistics

The U.S. Constitution requires that a census of the population be conducted to determine the number of representatives each state is entitled to in Congress. The first national census took place in 1790.

Since that time, the government has conducted a national census every ten years, with smaller surveys taken in between.

The statistics compiled by the U.S. Census Bureau provide an important source of historical data on population patterns in the United States. The table on page 262 provides statistics on changes within the Puerto Rican community during the years 1950 to 1970. The titles and labels help you interpret these statistics. For example, the main title tells you that these figures will give you information about Puerto Ricans in New York City *and* in the United States. To practice interpreting historical statistics, answer the questions below.

1. Where in the United States did most Puerto Ricans live in 1950?

2. How many second-generation Puerto Ricans were born in New York City in 1960?

3. Based on the table, would you expect the number of second-generation Puerto Ricans to increase or decrease in the 1980s? Explain.

4. How do the figures help explain why Puerto Rico established the Office of the Commonwealth in New York City? How do the figures support the decision to open offices elsewhere in the 1950s?

Express Yourself!

Imagine that a family from Puerto Rico was going to settle in your neighborhood. Choose a partner to work with. Together, list five or six important ideas that you think would help this family to live in your community.

Having built a new life in the United States, Marta Gutiérrez is shown with her son Fernando in their Miami home. Marta and Enrique Gutiérrez first supported Castro, but came to oppose him.

CHAPTER 21

New Arrivals from the Caribbean

(1945–1970s)

THINKING ABOUT THE CHAPTER

What events in Cuba and the Dominican Republic led new Spanish-speaking groups to the United States?

Marta and Enrique Gutiérrez began their married life in the storms of revolution. Years of dictatorship under Cuba's Fulgencio Batista had driven Enrique into the **underground,** the name given to secret antigovernment movements. The underground aimed at the overthrow of Batista and his government. As a revolutionary, Enrique faced death by firing squad if captured by Batista's troops.

In 1958, a young lawyer named Fidel Castro inspired Enrique, Marta, and thousands of other Cubans with dreams of reform. "We hoped to replace corruption with honesty, tyranny with democracy," recalled Marta. People from all parts of Cuban society—peasants, laborers, merchants, doctors, lawyers, and other professionals—shared in this vision.

SECTIONS

1 **Upheaval in Cuba**

2 **A Growing Cuban Presence**

3 **Turmoil in the Dominican Republic**

As you will read, Batista's government crumbled before the wave of popular support for Castro. On New Year's Eve 1958, Batista boarded a plane carrying him to exile in the Dominican Republic. There, another dictator, Rafael Trujillo, offered Batista shelter. In little more than two years, Trujillo would also fall, not to a revolution but to an assassin's bullet.

This chapter tells the story of the revolutions that swept Cuba and the Dominican Republic in the late 1950s and early 1960s. These political upheavals brought hundreds of thousands of Cubans and Dominicans to the United States. Among them were Marta and Enrique Gutiérrez.

1 UPHEAVAL IN CUBA
◆ Why did many people flee Cuba after
◆ the 1959 revolution?

On January 1, 1959, Havana exploded in celebration. Thousands of people poured into the streets singing and chanting. Some held signs that read *Gracias Fidel* (Thank you, Fidel). Everywhere people dressed in black and red—the colors of the revolution. Years later, Marta Gutiérrez recalled the scene:

> The day was very emotional. It was like looking at a whole country caught up in a new beginning. At that time, nearly everyone had faith in Castro. We hoped to set up a new democratic government respected by the people and respected by the world. It was a magic moment. But the dream soon went sour.

The Downfall of Corrupt Rule. The Cuban people had often seen their dreams of good government go sour. As you read in Chapter 15, many Cuban presidents had promised reform. Most, however, had been corrupted by huge sums of money offered to them by businesses in Cuba. Many of these businesses were owned by U.S. corporations. The reform presidents often became corrupt dictators. By 1933, the people had had enough of the iron rule of President Machado (see page 190). First, an army revolt ousted Machado. Then, two months later, a young army sergeant named Fulgencio Batista, supported by university students, brought a new president into power. From 1933 until 1959, Batista was the real power in Cuba. At first, he exercised power mostly through presidents who owed their position to him. But in 1952, Batista himself seized power and ruled as a dictator.

Batista had the support of the United States throughout his rule. He even managed to persuade the United States to cancel that part of the Platt Amendment that permitted U.S. intervention in Cuba (see page 189).

Batista also gained the support of U.S.-owned businesses in Cuba. These businesses viewed Batista as a leader who protected their interests. He did not disappoint them. U.S. business in Cuba and the Cuban economy in general prospered during Batista's rule. Batista helped himself to a share of the prosperity and built up a huge fortune. However, most of the Cuban people still lived in poverty.

Batista's reign began to crumble in 1956. In that year, Fidel Castro and his revolutionaries began attacking army posts and government offices. At that time, Castro had the support of many businesspeople, church officials, and landowners. These groups were worried that the differences between the few rich and the many poor would doom Cuba to years of revolutionary struggle. They persuaded the U.S.

Early in 1958, these members of Fidel Castro's underground assembled in the mountains at the eastern end of Cuba. Within hours of this photograph, they would launch an attack against a nearby government army post.

government to halt the sale of arms to the Batista government.

Castro's forces then stepped up their fighting. By the end of 1958, Batista had lost most of his support and decided to flee. When he flew out of the country to the Dominican Republic, he carried with him a large share of the national treasury.

Into Havana. With Batista gone, Castro left his base in the Sierra Maestra mountains on the southeastern edge of Cuba. He led some 800 guerrillas on a 500-mile (800-kilometer) march to Havana. At Castro's side walked his brother Raúl and

Argentine revolutionary Ernesto "Che" Guevara. Millions of Cubans turned out to cheer the rebels.

On January 8, Castro and his army entered Havana. The rebellion was over. But the revolution had just begun. In February 1959, Cubans overwhelmingly elected Castro prime minister of a new government. Armed with political power, he set out "to revolutionize Cuba from the bottom up." In an interview with reporters, he remarked, "Revolutionaries are not born, they are made by poverty, inequality, and dictatorship." He promised to eliminate all these conditions in Cuba.

Winds of Change. The Cuba that Castro seized held great promise. In 1959, it ranked among the most highly developed nations in Latin America. It had the third-highest life expectancy in the region. It also had the fifth-highest **per capita income,** or the average annual income per person. Cuba rivaled many industrialized nations in the number of automobiles, television sets, radios, and doctors. But Cuba's wealth was not evenly distributed. "It is a rich country with too many poor people," said Castro.

In April 1959, Castro traveled to the United States to appeal for economic aid. But he met a chilly reception. U.S. officials distrusted Castro's brother Raúl and Che Guevara. Both of them supported communism. The meeting left Castro angry and bitter.

That spring, Castro began his reform of Cuban society. He increasingly looked to communism as a model for that reform. He favored state ownership of land and businesses instead of private ownership. He also looked to the Soviet Union to support his government with money and arms.

In May 1959, Castro set up the Agrarian Reform Law. This law took aim at the *latifundia* (lah-tee-FOON-dee-ah), or large commercial farms owned by wealthy people or agricultural companies. Castro used the law to break up the *latifundia* into **communes**. These were farms jointly owned and worked by formerly landless peasants.

Castro also raised taxes on foreign investors. U.S. sugar companies alone controlled almost 75 percent of the farmland in Cuba. These companies were angered when Castro raised their taxes. The United States struck back by cutting its sugar imports from Cuba. Sugar trade with the United States made up a major part of Cuba's exports.

A New Political State. Meanwhile, Castro went ahead with his plans to reshape Cuba. He began a massive road-building project. He tried to reduce the economy's dependence upon sugar by ordering farmers to plant other crops. He also launched a massive education project to fight illiteracy in Cuba.

In 1961, Castro organized some 300,000 people, including 100,000 high-school students, into teaching brigades. Armed with a basic textbook titled *Venceremos* (We Shall Overcome), these teachers headed into the countryside to teach peasants to read and write.

To enact his programs, Castro tightened his control over the nation. He seized plantations and businesses from hundreds of Batista supporters. He also moved to nationalize the economy, or put it under state control. The Cuban government took over hundreds of millions of dollars' worth of property owned by U.S. businesses. But Castro went far beyond punishing the United States and Batista supporters. Cubans who had no ties to Batista or the United States also lost their businesses.

Rumblings of Dissent. By mid–1959, some Cubans were having second thoughts about Castro. They felt he now was totally following the Communist line of his brother Raúl and Che Guevara. People assumed it was they who urged Castro to build a Communist state.

Enrique Gutiérrez, about whom you read at the beginning of this chapter, served as the director of the Ministry of Architecture for Castro. But he objected to the nation's move toward communism. So once again he joined the underground, but this time to work against Castro.

Enrique's wife Marta printed anti-Castro literature in her shop in Havana. In late 1959, she learned that authorities had

1956	Fidel Castro begins a revolt in Cuba.
1959	Castro is elected prime minister of Cuba.
1961	Dominican dictator Rafael Trujillo is assassinated.
	The Bay of Pigs invasion
1962	The Cuban Missile Crisis
1963	A revolt topples the government of the Dominican Republic.
1965	U.S. marines invade the Dominican Republic.
	The Camarioca boatlift from Cuba
1978	Antonio Guzmán is elected president of the Dominican Republic.

discovered her husband's activities. At the time, Enrique was on business in Central America. When he called home, Marta warned him not to return to Cuba.

Enrique flew to Puerto Rico. Marta hurriedly joined him there with their 1-year-old daughter. Everything they owned was left behind.

The Cuban Exodus. In 1959 and 1960, thousands of Cubans like the Gutiérrez family left the island. As **political exiles,** or people who leave a country for political reasons, they hoped one day to reclaim Cuba from Castro. Some Cubans traveled to other Spanish-speaking nations such as Mexico and Spain. Others went to Puerto Rico. But most went to Miami, Florida.

The Miami of 1959 was a sleepy vacation town. People traveled there to visit its beautiful Atlantic beaches. But it was not the beaches that attracted Cuban political exiles to Miami. It was the fact that only a 200-mile (360-kilometer) span of water separated Miami and Cuba. From Miami, the exiles could imagine seeing their homeland just over the horizon. They also saw Miami as a base from which they could regain control of Cuba.

Brigade 2506. In the summer of 1960, hundreds of Cuban exiles, some only in their teens, headed to boot camps hidden in the mountainous jungles of southern Guatemala. Here, agents from the U.S. Central Intelligence Agency (CIA) trained the exiles for an armed invasion of Cuba. That summer the Cuban recruits named their unit Brigade 2506, after the serial number of a comrade who had died in an accident.

By the time John F. Kennedy became President in January 1961, some 1,400 Cubans stood ready to invade Cuba. They believed that the invasion would set off a major uprising in Cuba. Kennedy reluctantly backed the plan. But too many people were involved in the operation for it to remain a secret. Castro knew the attack would come, he just did not know when or where. So he readied his own army of some 20,000 soldiers.

In the early morning hours of April 17, 1961, Brigade 2506 landed on the beaches surrounding the Bay of Pigs on the southern coast of Cuba. In the hours that followed, Castro threw his full force at the invaders.

In Miami, Cuban exiles sat glued to their radio and television sets waiting for news of the invasion. The final outcome sent many into despair. The Bay of Pigs invasion was a failure. Of the invaders, 129 were killed, and 1,180 were sentenced to Cuban prisons. Although only a young child at the time, Cuban American lawyer

Ana María Escagedo (es-kah-HEH-doh) recalled the impact upon her family:

The family firmly believed the United States government would intervene in Cuba. They thought we would go home soon. Right after the Bay of Pigs invasion, they knew that would never happen. I remember the great sadness of the day. My family now knew they would not be able to go home. So they started to build new lives in the United States.

Taking Another Look

1. What changes did Castro bring to Cuba?
2. Why did many Cubans flee the island in 1959 and 1960?

3. **Critical Thinking** Why was the failed Bay of Pigs invasion a turning point in the history of Cuban Americans?

2 A GROWING CUBAN PRESENCE

◆ How did large numbers of Cubans come to the United States in the 1960s and 1970s?

The time was October 1962. Cubans called the affair the October Crisis. People in the United States called it the Cuban Missile Crisis. It involved a showdown between the United States and what was then the Soviet Union. The dispute began when the United States discovered that bases for Soviet nuclear missiles were being built on Cuban soil.

The United States played an active part in events in the Caribbean region during the 1960s and 1970s, as this map shows. In what countries did anti-Castro forces train in preparation for the Bay of Pigs invasion?

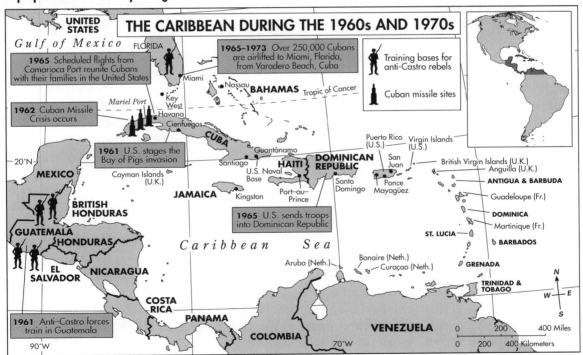

THE CARIBBEAN DURING THE 1960s AND 1970s

1965 Scheduled flights from Camarioca Port reunite Cubans with their families in the United States

1965–1973 Over 250,000 Cubans are airlifted to Miami, Florida, from Varadero Beach, Cuba

Training bases for anti-Castro rebels

Cuban missile sites

1962 Cuban Missile Crisis occurs

1961 U.S. stages the Bay of Pigs invasion

1965 U.S. sends troops into Dominican Republic

1961 Anti-Castro forces train in Guatemala

273

Sealing Off Cuba. The presence of Soviet missile bases in Cuba brought the Cold War to the doorstep of the United States. It also brought the world to the brink of nuclear war. President Kennedy ordered a naval **blockade** of Cuba. Until the Soviet Union agreed to remove the missiles, U.S. warships would prevent other military supplies from being sent to the island.

After the crisis ended in November, 1962, Cuba banned all flights to and from Miami. Until this time, an average of 1,500 Cubans had been arriving in Miami each week. Between 1959 and October 1962, more than 150,000 Cubans had moved to the United States. In the next three years, only about 30,000 slipped out. Some braved choppy seas to sail for Florida in small boats. Others traveled to the United States through so-called "bridge countries" such as Spain or Mexico.

The Second Wave. In 1965, Cuba opened its doors again when the United States and Cuba made a formal agreement. This agreement allowed Cubans to join family members already in the United States. The response startled both nations. Cuban exiles sailed from Florida in hundreds of boats to the Cuban port of Camarioca (kah-mah-ree-OH-kah). Here they took friends and relatives aboard the boats and headed for the United States.

The so-called Camarioca boatlift led Cuba and the United States to set up a system to control migration. In September 1965, the two nations established regularly scheduled flights between Miami and Cuba. Empty planes left Miami almost every day. They returned filled with relatives of Cubans already in the United States. On average, a Cuban **refugee,** or person displaced by war or persecution, arrived in Miami every ten minutes.

Over the next eight years, some 2,800 flights carried almost 260,000 Cubans from their homeland into the United States. Soon after their arrival, thousands of these refugees met U.S. Army Major Mercedes Cubria (KOO-bree-ah).

Born in Guantánamo, Cuba, in 1903, **Mercedes Cubria** became a United States citizen in 1924. In 1943, she enlisted in the Women's Army Corps (WAC) to serve her nation in World War II. As part of U.S. Counter Intelligence, Cubria gathered information against the enemy in both World War II and the Korean War. Her bravery earned Cubria the rank of major, making her the WAC's first Cuban American officer.

Major Cubria retired in 1953. But, in 1962, the U.S. Army recalled her to service. For the next 11 years, she helped process the Cuban refugees into the United States. In 1972, the Army promoted her to lieutenant colonel. In 1973, at age 70, Cubria finally retired. She chose to spend her remaining years among the many Cubans who had come to call Miami their home.

Between 1959 and 1973, nearly 10 percent of Cuba's six million people left the island to make their homes throughout the Americas and parts of Europe. In 1973, faced with a tremendous drain on the island's human resources, Castro sharply cut down on the number of exit permits granted to Cuban citizens. By this time, however, the Cuban population of Miami had grown to almost 300,000.

Castro's growing ties with the Soviet Union led the United States to oppose his government. These Cuban refugees gathered at a rally in Miami in 1961 to express their support for the position the United States had taken.

The Lure of Freedom. In 1974, Miguel Seco (SEH-koh) feared he would never get out of Cuba. At age 14, he had only one year before the government would draft him for military service. Years before, his parents had applied for exit permits to join their families in Spain. "We were really leaving for political reasons," explained Miguel. "But we dared not to say it."

As a ninth-grade student, Miguel had spent his entire life under Castro. Miguel recalled,

> My generation had no frame of reference other than Castro's government. Our only other history or view of the world came to us through our parents. They always began stories about the past with the word *antes* (AHN-tees), or "before." Whenever we heard the word *antes,* we knew they meant "before the revolution."

No matter what his teachers told him, Miguel knew he lacked freedom. In Cuba, officials discouraged the practice of religion. Because Miguel clung to his Roman Catholic faith, he could not hold any student office. Also, he knew that Cuba might deny his father an exit permit. Said Miguel, "He was a doctor, and the state needed professionals like him."

Bridge to the United States. In late 1974, Miguel's mother received word that she could take her two sons to Spain. As the family had feared, Miguel's father was refused permission to leave.

With little more than the clothes on his back, Miguel boarded a Soviet plane bound for Madrid. As the plane took off, a flood of emotion filled him. He thought, I'm free! I'm free! Nobody will ever tell me what to do again!

Once in Spain, Miguel's mother applied for visas to the United States. A year later, the family flew to Miami. Here Miguel began a new life. Miguel later remembered his first day at Booker T. Washington Junior High School. "All I could say was 'My name is. . . . I live at. . . .' That was the extent of my English." Upon graduation, Miguel not only spoke

275

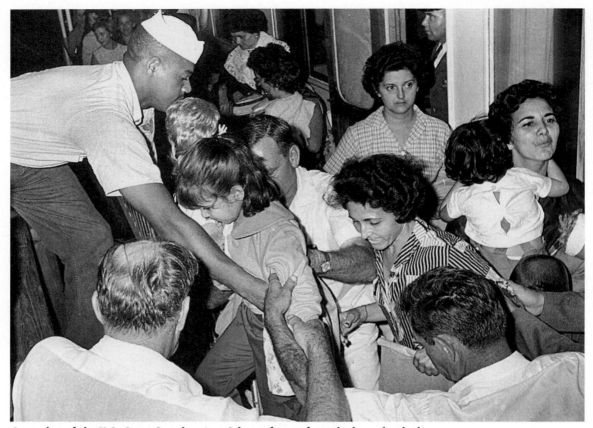

A member of the U.S. Coast Guard assists Cuban refugees from the boat that had carried 108 of them to Key West. They were part of the Camarioca boatlift, the second major wave of refugees to flee Castro's Cuba.

English; he also won one of three Human Relations Awards from his school.

Miguel went on to Miami High School in the section of the city known as Little Havana. Filled with Spanish-speaking people, Little Havana was the center of the Cuban community in the United States. Although Miguel left to study art history at colleges and universities outside Florida, his heart remained in Miami. In the 1980s, he returned to work in the city's growing artistic community.

Putting Down Roots. By the time Miguel graduated from Miami High School, more than one million Cubans lived in the United States. Nearly 99 percent chose to settle in urban areas. Of all

the cities in the United States, Miami remained the first choice. Cubans settled in smaller numbers in cities such as New York City, Newark and Jersey City, New Jersey, Los Angeles, and Chicago.

By 1980, nearly half the nation's Cuban population lived in Dade County, Florida, where Miami is located. They helped make Miami one of the key centers of Latino culture in the United States. As Ana María Escagedo explained, "The migration of the 1960s made Miami a big city. In the 1970s, the hard work of the Cuban people turned it into a great city."

The Cuban Americans had lived through a dizzying series of events that led them from revolution in Cuba to life in the United States. During these years, political troubles on the neighboring island of Hispaniola sent thousands of other immigrants to the United States.

Taking Another Look

1. What obstacles did Cuban immigrants face in getting to the United States?

2. Why did Cuba seek to curb immigration after 1973?

3. **Critical Thinking** In what ways are the stories of Mercedes Cubria and Miguel Seco similar and in what ways are they different?

3 TURMOIL IN THE DOMINICAN ◆ REPUBLIC
◆ Why did Dominican immigration to the United States increase in the 1960s?

On May 30, 1961, 13-year-old Daysi Parris (pah-RREES) was studying in her school in Santo Domingo, the capital of the Dominican Republic. Suddenly, sirens sounded all over the city. Sensing that something terrible had happened, Daysi's teacher and the school principal quickly rushed the children of the school into minivans. They loaded relatives of Dominican dictator Rafael Trujillo aboard one van. Children of parents who worked for the government were ordered into another van. Because Daysi's father worked as a chef for Trujillo, she found herself on the government van.

When Daysi arrived home, her mother grabbed her. She quickly told Daysi the news. "Trujillo has been killed."

End of an Era. The news spread like wildfire through the Dominican Republic, the nation that shares the island of Hispaniola with Haiti. Some Dominicans refused to believe that Trujillo had been killed. But slowly it became known that a blaze of gunfire had cut down the dictator on a lonely road just outside the city. The assassination marked the end of an era for the Dominican Republic.

An Uncertain Future. Trujillo had taken control of the Dominican Republic in 1930. Trujillo and the state had been one. Although the nation's constitution guaranteed free elections, there were no free elections. Never was there any doubt about who would win. During one election, a state-controlled newspaper announced Trujillo's victory even before the votes had been counted.

Trujillo used the island's economy to make himself wealthy. By 1960, observers estimated Trujillo to be the richest person in the world. He richly rewarded his supporters and mercilessly punished suspected enemies. Everyone knew that a concrete building called *La Cuarenta* (kwah-REN-tah) housed political prisoners. They nicknamed it "Trujillo's torture chambers."

When Trujillo died, angry Dominicans lashed out at his supporters. Even his chef was harassed. Daysi Parris recalled,

It was a nightmare. Everybody who worked for Trujillo fled their houses and left everything behind. They took only what they could carry. It was like the end of the world. What did I feel? Fear!

Daysi's family decided to apply for visas to leave the country. Her mother had two daughters and a sister in the United States. She had thought about joining them for some time. But now she made the decision to go.

The immigration office looked like a madhouse. Lines and lines of people

277

pushed and shoved one another. Daysi's mother gave up and turned to a lawyer for help. A few weeks later, visas in hand, Daysi's family joined a flood of immigrants to the United States.

Changing Patterns. Under Trujillo, few people left the Dominican Republic. In 1960, only some 750 people legally immigrated to the United States. After his death, that number swelled to 20,000 a year. Because many left illegally, the numbers may have been much higher.

In 1962, Juan Bosch (BOHSH) was elected president in the nation's first free election. However, Bosch's plans for reform angered some former supporters of Trujillo. Bosch's government was overthrown and unrest shook the island. The political and economic confusion drove large numbers of middle-class and professional people from the Dominican Republic.

In 1965, a popular democratic revolution broke out in the Dominican Republic. U.S. President Lyndon B. Johnson feared that the Dominican Republic might become the next Communist base in the Caribbean. He ordered the U.S. Marines into the Dominican Republic to put down the revolution.

In 1966, Dominicans elected former Trujillo supporter Joaquín Balaguer (bah-lah-GHER) president. Shortly after that, the U.S. Marines left the island. However, many nations condemned the United States for another intervention in Latin American affairs.

With backing from the United States and the Dominican military, Balaguer restored political order to the island. Balaguer introduced some social reforms to the Dominican Republic as well. But unrest and uncertainty continued to drive Dominicans from the island. Even the peaceful elections of 1978, when Balaguer turned the office of president over to the popular Antonio Guzmán Fernández, did not stop the flow of emigrants. By then, a large Dominican community already existed in the United States.

The Early Arrivals. Most of the Dominicans who came to the United States in the 1960s headed for New York City. Daysi Parris's sister Margarita, a medical student at Columbia University, found her family a six-room apartment in the Bronx. They were the first Dominican family in what would soon become a mainly Dominican neighborhood.

Daysi was amazed by all the changes. Like other new arrivals from the Caribbean, she was uncomfortable with the cold weather. "I still shiver thinking of it," remembered Daysi. After leaving her open country home outside Santo Domingo, the tall apartment buildings stunned her. As she walked up the stairs to her new apartment, she cried, *"Muchas puertas! Muchas puertas!"* (Many doors! Many doors!)

The next shock came at school. Daysi spoke only Spanish. The teacher conducted her lessons in English. "It was very hard," explained Daysi, "but I had to learn English fast." She also ran into a new idea of race. Many of her classmates considered Daysi, a dark-skinned Dominican, an African American. But Daysi saw herself as a *mestizo,* "a person with mixed-up beautiful colors." Like many Dominicans, she saw herself as a blend of peoples and cultures since her family background included Spanish, Dutch, English, African, and Native American ancestors.

As the 1970s passed into the 1980s, events pushed a second, much larger wave of Dominicans into the United States. By the 1990s, Dominicans would become the

In 1960, Dominicans who had been exiled from their homeland gathered in New York City to demonstrate against dictator Rafael Trujillo. Less than a year after this rally, Trujillo was dead, killed by an assassin.

nation's fastest-growing immigrant group. (For more on Dominican Americans, see Chapter 28.)

Taking Another Look

1. Why did many Dominicans flee their island after Trujillo's death?

2. Why did the United States intervene in the Dominican Republic in 1965?

3. **Critical Thinking** What do you think was the biggest challenge faced by teenage Dominican immigrants such as Daysi Parris in the early 1960s? Explain.

LOOKING AHEAD

Dominicans left their homeland for many of the same reasons that brought other newcomers to the United States. Like most immigrants, Dominicans had problems adjusting to the ways of their new homeland. As the number of Latinos increased in the United States, they began to organize to win full rights as U.S. citizens. Inspired by the Civil Rights Movement of the 1950s and 1960s, Mexican Americans, Puerto Ricans, and others joined in a rights campaign of their own.

LATINO JEWS

In the cemetery near Miami's Temple Emanu-El, inscriptions in Hebrew, English, and Spanish mark the stone slabs above the graves. The presence of Spanish inscriptions pays tribute to Miami's community of Latino Jews.

The first Latino Jews arrived in the Americas soon after Columbus. Seeking to escape religious persecution in Spain and elsewhere, they built new lives on islands in the Caribbean and the rest of Latin America. Over time, many of these settlers developed a language known as **Ladino**—a language that combines elements of Spanish, Portuguese, and Hebrew.

In the 1930s, the rise of fascism in Europe forced a new wave of Jewish immigrants into the Americas. Because of immigration restrictions in the United States, many settled in Cuba, the Dominican Republic, and on other islands in the Caribbean.

During the Cuban Revolution, Jews who did not support Castro fled the island. Those who were successful business owners found their property seized and their lives threatened. Most Cuban Jews joined the huge wave of exiles to Miami. Between 1959 and 1980, more than 14,250 of Cuba's estimated 15,000 Jews left the island. Today these exiles and their descendants consider themselves part of Miami's Cuban American population.

CLOSE UP: Chapter 21

The Who, What, Where of History

1. **Who** is Fidel Castro?
2. **What** did Fidel Castro do to Cuba's *latifundia?*
3. **What** is a political exile?
4. **Where** did most Cuban political exiles settle in the United States?
5. **What** was Brigade 2506?
6. **Where** did the CIA train Cuban troops who volunteered to invade Cuba?
7. **Who** was Mercedes Cubria?
8. **Who** was Rafael Trujillo?
9. **What** was the U.S. response to the assassination of Trujillo?
10. **Where** did most Dominican immigrants settle in the 1960s?

Making the Connection

1. What was the connection between Fulgencio Batista and Rafael Trujillo?
2. What was the connection between communism and the Cuban exodus to the United States?
3. What was the connection between events in Cuba and the U.S. decision to intervene in the Dominican Republic?

Time Check

1. Explain the importance of the following years to the history of Cuban Americans: 1959, 1961, 1962, 1965.
2. Which of the following events occurred last: the Bay of Pigs invasion; the Cuban Missile Crisis; the election of Castro as prime minister of Cuba?

3. In which year was Rafael Trujillo assassinated?

What Would You Have Done?

1. Suppose you lived in Cuba in late 1959. Would you apply for an exit permit? Why or why not?

2. Imagine that you are a Cuban teenager in Miami in 1960. Would you volunteer for Brigade 2506? Explain.

Thinking and Writing About History

1. Write a skit in which a Cuban American family discusses its reactions to the Bay of Pigs invasion.

2. Write a speech that Miguel Seco might have delivered on the day he received the Human Relations Award from Booker T. Washington Junior High School.

3. Imagine that you are a Dominican teenager who has just arrived in New York City. Write a letter to your friend back home describing your first impressions of New York City.

Building Skills: Drawing Conclusions

Whenever you *draw conclusions*, you are making informed judgments based upon available information. You do more than summarize data in a broad-based statement, as you do when you make a generalization. Instead, you are interpreting the data to determine what the facts tell you about a topic, an idea, or an event.

To practice drawing conclusions, read the selection below written by Pedro Reboredo, mayor of West Miami, Florida. Reboredo describes changes in Miami since the arrival of Cuban refugees.

The face of Miami and South Florida has changed during the past twenty years. Especially after 1965, when Cuban refugees, who had begun arriving in 1959, realized that we wouldn't be going back to Cuba. We began to really buy into the American dream. Most are decent middle-class people who came from Havana. Like myself, almost all arrived penniless.

The Southwest Eighth Street area [Calle Ocho] is known as Little Havana. Cubans have renovated that section of Miami very nicely. And much of the high-rise buildings that have made Miami's skyline famous have been designed by Cuban architects. Miami has become the trade center for Latin America.

1. What conclusion can you draw about Reboredo's opinion of the Cuban contribution to Miami?

2. What statements in the selection support your conclusion?

3. What conclusion can you draw about how Cuban Americans such as Reboredo view their relationship with Latin America?

4. How did you conclude this?

Express Yourself!

Create a comic strip about the experiences of a member of your family or a friend who has immigrated to the United States. First, choose one event to write about, such as the first day of school or the first trip to a store. Next, make a list of the characters that will be in your comic strip. Then, summarize the story you will tell. Finally, write the dialogue and draw pictures to show the action.

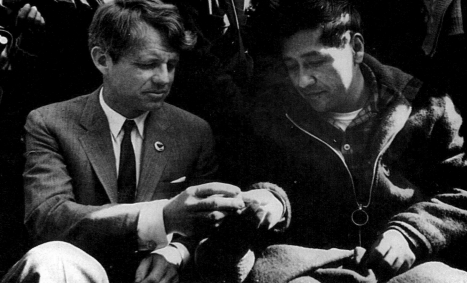

César Chávez (right) helped focus the nation's attention on the problems of Latino farmworkers. In 1968, Presidential candidate Robert F. Kennedy offered his support to Chávez's cause.

SECTIONS

1 *La Causa*

2 A Time for Action

CHAPTER 22

The Struggle for Equal Rights

(1950s–1970s)

THINKING ABOUT THE CHAPTER

What were some of the Latino rights movements that took shape in the 1960s and 1970s?

Twenty-four-year-old César Chávez wanted to have nothing to do with Fred Ross, the Anglo who had asked to see him. "Probably just another university student studying the *barrio*," thought Chávez. It seemed that every time anyone at Stanford, Berkeley, or San Jose State wanted to investigate *barrio* life, they came to the tough San Jose neighborhood where Chávez lived. The neighborhood was known as *Sal Si Puedes* (SAHL see PWEH-des), or "Get Out If You Can." Chávez explained:

That's what that *barrio* was called, because . . . not too many could get out of it. . . . Anyway, we were sick and tired of people coming around asking us stupid questions.

When Ross finally tracked down Chávez, he startled the young Mexican American with a request. He asked Chávez and his wife Helen to work with the Community Service Organization (CSO) in registering migrant workers to vote. Chávez remarked, "He did such a good job of explaining how poor people could build power that I could even taste it."

In the summer of 1952, young Chávez joined the CSO as a volunteer. As a migrant worker himself, Chávez spent the day picking apricots. At night, he knocked on doors for the CSO. Within two months, Chávez had registered more than 4,000 voters.

Then Chávez's boss fired him for urging the workers to form a union. However, the CSO quickly hired him as a full-time employee. Although Chávez did not know it at the time, he had taken the first steps to becoming one of the leaders in a great Latino struggle for equality.

1 LA CAUSA

◆ How did migrant farmworkers win
◆ greater rights in the 1960s?

In 1962, a debate raged among delegates to a CSO convention held in Calexico, Mexico. César Chávez was by that time the general director of the CSO. He had asked the delegates at the convention to support a union of farmworkers. He felt a union was the only way migrant workers could ever win fair treatment from landowners. Usually, whenever migrants asked for better working conditions, their employers replaced them with *braceros,* the contract workers from Mexico (see page 240).

The delegates voted down Chávez's request because they thought a union had no chance of success. Chávez then made a decision. "I resign," he announced. As he walked out, people pleaded, "You can't quit." One rich member offered him $50,000 if he would keep his CSO job. But money was not the issue. In fact, Chávez had even offered to give up a year's salary if the CSO backed a farmworkers' union. So, with little more than $1,200 in savings, Chávez started the organizing on his own.

The Black Aztec Eagle. With the support of his wife Helen, Chávez headed to the town of Delano. It was a farming community in the fertile heart of California's Great Central Valley. There the couple worked on one of the area's more than 70 grape farms.

Chávez drew up a map that showed every town and farming camp in the valley. In the next six months, he visited each spot on the map. Along with Helen and their eight children, Chávez handed out more than 80,000 postcards to migrant workers in the valley. The cards asked them about their wages. It also asked them if they were willing to form a union. Some workers scribbled notes in pencil on the cards. "Do you think we can win?" asked one. "I hope to God we win!" wrote another.

Built on the People. Chávez refused all outside support. That included turning down money from the American Federation of Labor and Congress of Industrial Organizations (AFL-CIO), the largest labor organization in the United States. In later years, Chávez explained why he did so:

I have always believed that, in order for a movement to be lasting, it must be built on the people. . . . Money by itself will not get the job done. . . . If workers are going to do anything, they need their own power. They need to involve themselves in meaningful ways.

Chávez hoped to organize farmworkers into a union run by the workers themselves. He called the union the National Farm Workers Association (NFWA). Soon, even people who could not read or write recognized the NFWA emblem—a black Aztec eagle set against a bold red flag. "When this eagle flies," said the flag's designer, Manuel Chávez, "the problems of the farmworkers will be solved!" This was the start of *La Causa* (lah KOW-sah), "The Cause," the name the farmworkers gave to their movement.

Reasons for Organizing.
Few Mexican Americans doubted the need for an organization like the one Chávez was building. Mexican Americans suffered heavily from the effects of discrimination. In 1960, Mexican American families earned just two thirds of the average annual income of Anglo families. Also, the average Mexican American had finished fewer than nine years of school.

In the early 1960s, Mexican American migrant farmworkers sweated in the fields for 14 to 16 hours a day. They might return home with as little as five dollars in their pocket. Out of this tiny sum, they had to buy food and pay rent on the run-down shacks or cheap motel rooms in which they lived. Because migrant worker families moved as the seasons changed, few of their children went to the same school for any length of time. As a result, not many finished school. César Chávez, for example, left school at the end of the eighth grade. By that time, he had attended more than 30 schools throughout California.

Migrants—Legal and Illegal.
In 1951, the U.S. government extended the *bracero* program it had begun during World War II. Landowners continued to truck *braceros* in and out of Mexico as the seasons changed. They paid the *braceros* the lowest wages possible. They often used them as strikebreakers. With *braceros* working in the United States only part of the year, it was hard to get them to join the farmworkers' union.

Even more difficult to sign up were the large numbers of Mexicans who entered the United States illegally (see page 240). These illegal immigrants had to work for very low wages. However, they dared not complain. To do so meant **deportation,** being expelled, from the United States.

Winds of Change.
Mexican American farmworkers saw the NFWA as the only way to make landowners pay a living wage. They knew the owners might fire them. But they hoped to hold onto their jobs long enough to launch a *huelga*, or "strike." This might force landowners to meet their demands.

Strikes against unfair treatment were nothing new to Mexican Americans. As early as 1903, Mexican and Japanese sugar-beet workers went on strike in Ventura, California. Mexicans and Mexican Americans took part in a series of strikes during the Great Depression (see page 231).

Farm owners would do almost anything to crush such strikes. In 1947, for example, more than 1,000 migrant workers waged a bitter two-year strike against the powerful Di Giorgio Fruit Corporation near Bakersfield, California. The farm owners filed expensive lawsuits against strike leaders. They also brought in hundreds of strikebreakers. Guards armed with guns and attack dogs patrolled fields

César Chávez's concern for migrant farmworkers lasted throughout his life. In 1988, he went on a hunger strike to protest the use of harmful pesticides on crops. Chávez died in 1993, still working for *La Causa*.

to keep out the strikers. The workers held out for two years, but in the end their strike was broken.

In the 1960s, events began to turn in favor of the farmworkers. In 1964, protests by the CSO and other groups forced the government to end the *bracero* program. This removed an important tool for breaking strikes from the hands of farm owners. Farmworkers also benefited from the African American Civil Rights Movement being waged at that time. (See page 251.) Many civil rights workers stood ready to offer support to the striking farmworkers.

But, just as African Americans played the major part in the Civil Rights Movement, Latinos took the lead in *La Causa*. The movement was about more than wages. *La Causa* expressed the dignity and pride of the nation's Latino population.

"¡Viva la Huelga!" Chávez wanted to move slowly. "You can't strike and organize at the same time," he remarked. But events moved beyond his control.

On September 8, 1965, Filipino farmworkers went on strike at a vineyard near Delano. The leader of the Filipinos, Larry Itliong (IHT-lee-awng), asked Chávez to back them. Chávez didn't know what to do. "That morning of September 8, a strike was the furthest thing from my mind," recalled Chávez. "All I could think of was 'Oh, God, we're not ready for a strike.'"

On September 16, Mexican Independence Day, Chávez put the question of whether to join in the strike to the members of the NFWA. Nearly 2,000 voices answered Chávez with cries of *"¡Huelga! ¡Huelga!"* With less than $100 in its strike fund, the NFWA joined the picket lines. In this crisis, Chávez relied on Dolores

285

Huerta (WER-tah), vice-president of the NFWA, for advice and guidance.

Dolores Huerta traced her roots back to the first Spanish settlers of New Mexico. Like Chávez, Huerta grew up as a migrant worker until her mother saved enough money to buy a hotel in Stockton, California. Her mother rented rooms to farmworkers and *braceros*. Sometimes she let families stay without paying so that they would have enough money for food. Huerta silently promised herself that one day she, too, would help Mexican American migrants.

In 1952, Dolores got her chance. That year, Fred Ross asked her to join the CSO. Huerta soon met Chávez, and the two formed a team. When Chávez left the CSO in 1962, Huerta gave up her teaching job to join César and Helen Chávez in Delano. Together, they founded the NFWA. All three remained active in it for over 30 years.

New Tactics. The first major strike Chávez and Huerta took part in put them on picket lines at a vineyard owned by the Di Giorgio Corporation. There, striking farmworkers walked the picket lines chanting, *"¡Viva la huelga!"* ("On with the strike!"). But Huerta and Chávez knew it would take more than pickets and cheers to defeat Di Giorgio. So they asked for help from civil rights workers and from the clergy. They also appealed to newspapers and TV, making the strike headline news.

As the strike spread, resistance among vineyard owners stiffened. Chávez and Huerta called on people across the nation to join in a **boycott** of, or refusal to buy, grapes picked by nonunion workers. In March 1966, Chávez led farmworkers on a 300-mile (480-kilometer) march from Delano to Sacramento, the capital of California. There 10,000 farmworkers and their supporters held a huge rally. They demanded that vineyard owners be forced to negotiate with the union. Yet even this show of strength failed to push vineyard owners into talks.

A Political Force. By early 1968, Chávez had come to fear that the continuing strike might lead to violence. Like Dr. Martin Luther King, Jr., in the African American Civil Rights Movement, Chávez favored the use of nonviolent tactics. On February 14, Chávez began a fast against violence. Day after day, Chávez went without food. National attention focused on the leader who risked his health in the name of nonviolent change.

On March 11, Chávez finally bowed to doctors' demands to end the fast. In an emotion-filled scene, U.S. Senator and candidate for President Robert F. Kennedy knelt beside Chávez in prayer. The Senator's wife, Ethel Kennedy, handed Chávez a small piece of Mexican *semita* (seh-MEE-tah) bread. Another 300 loaves were shared by the crowd. A spokesperson then read a speech for the badly weakened Chávez:

> We are poor, but we have something the rich do not own—our bodies and our spirits and the justice of our cause.

Next, Kennedy took the microphone. "I come here as an American citizen to honor César Chávez," declared Kennedy. He

1962 César Chávez resigns from the CSO and begins to form the NFWA.

1963 Reies López Tijerina founds the Federal Land Grant Alliance.

1965 Corky Gonzales founds *La Cruzada Para la Justicia*.

1966 *Aliancistas* occupy a portion of Kit Carson National Forest.

1969 José Angel Gutiérrez organizes *La Raza Unida*.

1970 National Chicano Moratorium meets to protest Vietnam War.

Vineyard owners sign the first contracts with the NFWA.

The Young Lords stage a takeover of a rundown hospital in New York City.

1972 The NFWA joins the AFL-CIO under the name United Farm Workers.

then pledged to fight for the rights long denied to migrant workers—health insurance, fair wages, recognition of their union, and more. Kennedy never got a chance to keep that promise. On June 5, 1968, an assassin's bullet took his life.

New Battles. The spirit of the March 11 gathering lived on after Kennedy's death. *La Causa* had become a political force in its own right. In 1970, vineyard owners finally recognized the union. In 1972, the AFL-CIO granted a charter to the union, which now took the name United Farm Workers (UFW).

After the Delano strike, Chávez and Huerta took the UFW into new battles. They tried to get other large farm owners, such as lettuce growers, to sign contracts with the UFW. They won some battles and lost others. Not all farmworkers joined the UFW. Even so, labels saying the produce had been picked by union workers began appearing in many supermarkets. Some consumers even refused to buy vegetables or fruits without the label.

As the UFW moved in new directions, the influence of *La Causa* reached from the farms into the *barrios*. There, a new generation of Mexican Americans led a movement to gain full civil rights for the nation's Latinos. Not everyone agreed with that movement's bold, outspoken leaders. But, as you will read in the next section, few could ignore them.

Taking Another Look

1. Why did Chávez and Huerta found the NFWA?

2. What tactics did the NFWA use to force vineyard owners to negotiate with the union?

3. **Critical Thinking a.** If you were a Mexican American migrant worker, would you join the NFWA? **b.** Why or why not?

2 A TIME FOR ACTION

◆ What were some of the goals of
◆ Latino activists in the late 1960s and 1970s?

In late 1965, strikers at the DiGiorgio vineyard roared with laughter as they watched a handful of farm workers perform an *acto* (AHK-toh), a fast-moving play. The play poked fun at the vineyard owners and promised victory for the union. Under the skillful direction of Mexican American playwright Luis Valdez (vahl-DES), such *actos* became the basis of an active theater group called *El Teatro Campesino*.

Soon Valdez's theater group moved from the vineyards of Delano to theaters around the United States. Said Valdez, they "became a vibrant [lively] element for the whole Chicano community."

Chicanos and Chicanas. Valdez used the terms *Chicano* and *Chicana* to express pride. They were shortened forms of *Mexicano* and *Mexicana*, the names commonly used by Mexicans to identify themselves. Before the mid–1960s, *Chicano* and *Chicana* generally referred to recent arrivals from Mexico.

As the Latino rights movement took shape, however, some young activists proudly claimed the names for themselves. Young men called themselves *Chicanos*. Young women called themselves *Chicanas*. However, not all Mexican Americans liked the term. Some felt that it did not reflect the fact that they were U.S. citizens.

In an effort to pin down the meaning of the term, Mexican American journalist Rubén Salazar offered his own definition. "A Chicano," he wrote in 1970, "is a Mexican American with a non-Anglo image of himself." The definition became

The successes of *La Causa* helped fuel the drive for Latino rights. Here, an angry activist protests discrimination against Mexican Americans at a rally in front of the California State Capitol in 1971.

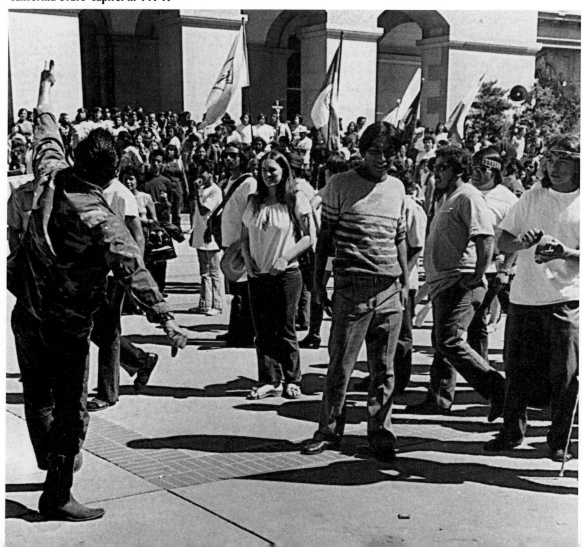

widely accepted by Chicanos and Chicanas who took part in the push for Latino rights that was known as *El Movimiento* (el moh-vee-mee-EN-toh), or The Movement.

Radical Actions.

El Movimiento was a new, more radical phase of the Mexican American drive for full rights. At first, most members of *El Movimiento* followed the lead of César Chávez and tried to keep their protests nonviolent.

However, when changes proved slow in coming, some leaders resorted to more extreme courses of action. One of these leaders was the son of a Texas sharecropper named Reies López Tijerina (tee-heh-REE-nah). He was known by the nickname *El Tigre* (el TEE-greh), the "Tiger."

Like Chávez, Tijerina grew up working in the fields. He educated himself when he was not working. Then he went on to become a preacher who traveled among poor farmworkers throughout the Southwest. During his travels, Tijerina came to believe that the problems of Mexican Americans were caused by the loss of land once held by their ancestors. To solve these problems, according to Tijerina, the land should be returned to them.

To regain lost lands in New Mexico, Tijerina founded the *Alianza Federal de Pueblos Libres* (ah-lee-AHN-sah fe-DEH-rahl deh PWEY-blohs LEE-bres), the Federal Land Grant Alliance, in 1962. Members of the *Alianza* were called **aliancistas** (ah-lee-ahn-SEES-tahs). They asked the United States and Mexico to study old land grants. *Aliancistas* hoped that the land would be returned to Mexican Americans who had held the grants when the territory belonged to Mexico. When both governments turned down the request, Tijerina began to practice **civil disobedience,** or the refusal to obey laws considered to be unjust.

Defying the Government.

In 1966, the *aliancistas* occupied a part of an old land grant in New Mexico's Kit Carson National Forest. They then declared themselves the "Republic of San Joaquín." They also arrested several U.S. forest rangers for "trespassing." Federal officials pressed charges against Tijerina and his group.

In June 1967, Tijerina announced that his group planned to hold a meeting in Coyote, a small town in northern New Mexico. Officials blocked the meeting and arrested several organizers. Feeling that their right to free assembly had been violated, some 20 armed *aliancistas* attacked the courthouse at Tierra Amarilla and freed *aliancistas* in the jail there. Tijerina and his men then left town with two hostages.

In response, some 400 National Guard, 200 state police, 2 tanks, and several helicopters moved into the area. They rounded up dozens of Spanish-speaking people and held them in a camp before capturing Tijerina and the *aliancistas*.

Tijerina was tried, convicted, and sentenced to a two-year prison term. After his release, he worked to improve the lives of poverty-stricken Mexican Americans through nonviolent change. By this time, the Chicano movement had spread throughout the Southwest.

Fighting for Justice.

Another Mexican American activist was Rodolfo "Corky" Gonzales. Gonzales was a man with a fascinating background. Born in a *barrio* in Denver, Colorado, he grew up working in the fields with his parents, who were migrant workers. Despite constant moves, the gifted Gonzales managed to graduate from high school at age 16. He went on to become a professional boxer. But his heart lay with Mexican Americans in the Denver *barrio* of his youth. So, at age 27, Gonzales quit boxing and returned to Denver.

Gonzales became active in politics. He served as the first Mexican American district captain for the Democratic Party in Denver. He headed the city's "Viva Kennedy" campaign for John F. Kennedy during the 1960 presidential election. Later, Gonzales worked in antipoverty programs started by President Lyndon Johnson.

Yet, like Tijerina, Gonzales grew impatient with the slow pace of change. In 1965, Gonzales founded *La Cruzada Para la Justicia* (lah kroo-SAH-dah PAH-rah lah hoos-TEE-see-ah), The Crusade for Justice. As the group's slogan, he chose *Venceremos* (ven-seh-REH-mohs). The slogan expressed in Spanish the words made famous by Dr. Martin Luther King, Jr.: "We shall overcome."

The Crusade for Justice focused on two main goals—pride in Latino culture and self-help. The Crusade established a ballet company, a legal defense fund, a day-care center, a weekly newspaper (*El Gallo*), and a bilingual school. To honor the school, Gonzales dedicated his poem *"Yo Soy Joaquín"* ("I Am Joaquín") to the school's students. The poem became one of many great pieces of art and literature that flowed out of the Chicano movement. (See Chapter 24.)

To reach bilingual students all over the country, Gonzales organized the Chicano Youth Liberation Conference. On Palm Sunday 1969, more than 1,500 students attended the opening session of the conference. There they discussed what it meant to be a Chicano or a Chicana.

A New Political Party. On the day that Gonzales opened his conference, another Chicano leader, José Angel Gutiérrez, led about 2,000 people on a protest march in Del Rio, Texas. At the Del Rio courthouse, Gutiérrez taped a written statement to the courthouse window. The statement called for loyalty to the United States and cultural independence for Mexican Americans.

After this protest, Gutiérrez organized a new political party called *La Raza Unida* (lah RAH-sah oo-NEE-dah), which means The United People. The party aimed at gaining political control for Chicanos in about 20 counties in south Texas where they made up a majority of the residents.

The party's first step toward that goal came in Gutiérrez's hometown of Crystal City, Texas. In 1970, Mexican Americans gained control of the school board and the city council. The new officials hired bilingual teachers and started special programs in Mexican American culture.

Rodolfo "Corky" Gonzales argued that Chicanos could gain full rights and greater influence in society by building political power from the local level up.

José Angel Gutiérrez was only 22 when he came to national attention. He began to organize *La Raza Unida* political party to fight discrimination against Mexican American students in Texas public schools.

La Raza Unida ran other candidates for county and state government in Texas. Soon, branches of *La Raza Unida* opened in other states with large Mexican American populations. These included Colorado, New Mexico, Arizona, and California. Although the party never gained the power its founders hoped for, its successes showed that Mexican American voters could show their strength through the ballot box.

Protesting the Vietnam War. The Chicano movement was gaining power in the summer of 1970. That August, leaders of a group called the "Brown Berets," organized the National Chicano Moratorium, a protest against the war in Vietnam. About 20,000 people gathered in Laguna Park in Los Angeles to hear speakers such as Corky Gonzales and César Chávez.

Before the speakers could take the stage, police moved in to break up what

had been a peaceful gathering. Fighting broke out between protesters and police. It spilled out of the park and into the surrounding streets. In the confusion that followed, riot police fired tear gas. One canister struck and killed Rubén Salazar, the nation's leading Chicano journalist.

The events of the day showed the depth of Chicano anger at the war and the effect it had on their lives. Latinos fighting in Vietnam had a 19-percent casualty rate compared to a 12-percent rate for U.S. soldiers as a whole. While Latinos bore this burden, federal programs that might have helped them at home were being cut because the costs of the war were so high.

Lasting Achievements. Not all Mexican Americans agreed with the tactics of the Chicano movement. Many opposed the angry meetings and the civil disobedience. Senator Joseph Montoya (mohn-TOH-yah) of New Mexico, for example, criticized Chicano occupation of federal lands. But most supported the movement's broad goals. These included respect for the Latino heritage, an increased Latino voice in politics, and equal opportunities for Latinos in business and education.

Efforts to reach these goals resulted in several lasting achievements. In 1968, President Lyndon Johnson signed the Bilingual Education Act. This law directed school districts to set up bilingual classes for students not fluent in English. That same year, Mexican Americans founded the Mexican American Legal Defense and Education Fund (MALDEF). MALDEF gave money for legal efforts to advance the civil rights of Mexican Americans.

The rights movements of the 1960s and 1970s also encouraged Mexican American voters to use their political muscle. In the 1960s, they sent four Mexican Americans to Congress, including New Mexico's Joseph Montoya. In 1974, voters in two states elected Mexican American governors—Jerry Apodaca (ah-poh-DAH-kah) in New Mexico and Raúl Castro in Arizona. This trend continued into the 1980s and 1990s (see Chapter 30).

The Expanding Struggle. The civil rights struggles waged by African Americans and Mexican Americans encouraged other young Latinos into action. Some young Puerto Ricans, for example, set up the Young Lords organization to fight for their rights.

The Young Lords were ready to take direct action to bring about change. In 1970, a group of Young Lords in New York

One way of helping Mexican Americans win full rights was to improve education programs. The class shown here is part of the "English on Wheels" school in California, set up to teach English to migrant farmworkers.

Some Puerto Ricans, angered by continuing discrimination, joined the Young Lords. This group called on Puerto Ricans to "Wake up . . . defend what's yours" and called for radical action to achieve equality.

City staged a takeover of a run-down hospital in a Puerto Rican neighborhood. They used the takeover to push for improved health care in the South Bronx, a part of New York City.

The Young Lords also backed an "open admissions" policy in education. This policy promised a place in one of New York City's many public colleges to any student who graduated in the top half of his or her class.

A Growing Presence. The protests of the 1960s and 1970s made all Americans aware of the power of Latinos in U.S. affairs. By the start of the 1980s, Mexican Americans numbered nearly 9 million. Puerto Ricans numbered more than 2 million. In all, Latinos made up the nation's second-largest ethnic group. Only African Americans outnumbered them. As you will read in Unit 7, a strong Latino presence helped shape the United States in the closing years of this century.

Taking Another Look

1. What were some of the goals of the Chicano movement?
2. Why did some Mexican Americans object to use of the term *Chicano*?
3. **Critical Thinking** What do you think are the two most important gains of the Latino rights movements of the 1960s and 1970s? Explain.

LOOKING AHEAD

The rights won by Mexican Americans and other Latinos came at a time of growing immigration from Central and South America. Political and economic troubles in these regions brought larger numbers of Spanish-speaking people to the United States. Their arrival gave yet more variety to the nation's booming Latino community. That community closely linked the United States with the rest of the Americas.

Women can no longer be taken for granted. . . .It's way past the time when our husbands can say, "You have to stay home!"

So said unionorganizer Jesse López de la Cruz in 1967. De la Cruz had spent many years picking grapes, apricots, beets, and cotton. Chávez asked her to join the NFWA in 1962. By 1967, de la Cruz was one of its key leaders, bringing hundreds of women into the union.

The 1960s and 1970s produced a new generation of Latina activists. Dolores Huerta was a driving froce behind the NFWA. In the 1970s, Vilma Martínez emerged as the president of MALDEF.

Many Latina women joined the feminist movement of the 1970s. Others focused on advancing the rights of Spanish-speaking women. Francisca Flores set up the Chicana Service Action Center to offer vocational training toLatinas. The Los Angeles based *Comisión Femenil Mexicana Nacional* prepared Latinas for leadership roles.

These efforts seemed to have paid off. By the 1980s, women were appointed to high posts in the federal government. In the 1990s, three Latinas were elected to Congress. One of these, Lucille Roybal-Allard of California promised to "emphasize the importance of women, making sure they are a part of the political process."

CLOSE UP: Chapter 22

The Who, What, Where of History

1. **What** was the NFWA?
2. **What** is the meaning of *huelga?*
3. **Where** did the first major NFWA strike take place?
4. **Who** is Dolores Huerta?
5. **What** was *La Causa?*
6. **Who** was Rodolfo "Corky" Gonzales?
7. **What** was *La Raza Unida?*
8. **Who** were the Young Lords?

Making the Connection

1. What was the connection between the *bracero* program and *La Causa?*
2. What was the connection between the Civil Rights Movement and the organization of Mexican American migrant farmworkers?
3. What was the connection between the Vietnam War and the Chicano movement?

Time Check

1. In what year did the first NFWA boycott begin?
2. Which of the following was organized first—*El Movimiento, La Causa,* or *La Raza Unida?*

What Would You Have Done?

1. Imagine that it is 1965 and you have just received a post card from César Chávez. The card asks whether you would join a new union—even though the decision may cost your job. How would you respond? Why?
2. Suppose you are a college student of Mexican ancestry in 1969. Would you

prefer to be called a Mexican American or a *Chicano/Chicana?* Explain.

3. Imagine that you have just read a statement by Senator Joseph Montoya criticizing the occupation of parts of Kit Carson National Forest. Would you support Montoya's statement? Why or why not?

Thinking and Writing About History

1. Write an on-the-spot television report describing the end of César Chávez's antiviolence fast.

2. Write an *acto* that might have been performed by *El Teatro Campesino* during the Delano grape strike.

3. Design a time line showing some of the key events in the Latino rights struggle of the 1960s and 1970s. Write a brief description of each event on the time line and illustrate at least three events with drawings or pictures from magazines and newspapers.

Building Skills: Identifying Point of View in Poetry

The poetry of a time period can tell you a great deal about the ideas, feelings, and life styles of a people. Reading poetry as a source of historical data requires searching for hidden clues that help unravel the poem's deeper meaning. In looking for the poem's message, keep in mind that most poems have a *point of view,* or an attitude, toward the subject under discussion. This point of view will tell you a lot about the poet's message.

The poem on this page was written by an anonymous poet in Mexico. It is very popular among Mexican and Mexican American farmworkers today. In the 1960s, César Chávez hung a copy of this poem in the main office of the UFW. Read this poem, and answer the questions that follow.

My father . . .
could never write a poem,
But when he lined up his plow
with a pine tree on a distant hill,
he made a furrow
straight as an arrow,
across the length of his
labor.

My father . . .
could not write very many words,
But when he brought in
his crop
in the heat of a summer afternoon,
he created
a poem . . . from the earth.

1. What is the subject of the poem?
2. What attitude does the poet take toward farmworkers?
3. What details in the poem support your answer?
4. Why do you think Chávez chose to hang this poem in the UFW office?

Express Yourself!

Choose two or three classmates to work with. Together, create a poster that encourages people to join the National Farm Workers Association. You may wish to use the symbol of the black Aztec eagle. Think of other symbols, or signs, you could use on your poster. When you have finished the poster, put it up for display in your classroom.

Sylvia Jordan moved from Guatemala to the United States in 1959, when she was in junior high school. Today, Jordan runs a daycare center and school for African American children.

SECTIONS

1 Struggle for Democracy in Central America

2 New Voices from South America

CHAPTER 23

New Immigrants from Central and South America

(1950s–1970s)

THINKING ABOUT THE CHAPTER

What conditions in Central and South America helped set the stage for increased immigration to the United States?

¿Qué pata puso ese huevo? ("What duck laid that egg?") As a child growing up in Guatemala, Sylvia Jordan heard that expression many times. It meant, who are his or her parents? Explained Sylvia, "In Guatemala, [an important part of] a person's [social standing] was the ability to trace their family." Sylvia's family on her mother's side went back to the first Spanish founders of Guatemala. The family name, Jordan, reflected her grandfather's origin in Ireland.

Sylvia felt totally Guatemalan despite her mixed ancestry. In 1959, however, her mother decided to move to Miami.

Sylvia said, "Suddenly I didn't fit." In junior high school, Sylvia noticed the absence of Latino students. Only three other Spanish-speaking students were in her class, two Colombians and one Puerto Rican.

Within a year, though, the situation changed. Sylvia recalled, "Cuban students started arriving. They talked about revolution. They talked about Fidel Castro."

In 1960, Sylvia could not possibly know that soon tens of thousands of other Spanish-speaking people would leave Latin America for the United States. This chapter tells the story of the conditions in Central and South America that brought those new immigrants to the United States.

1 STRUGGLE FOR DEMOCRACY IN CENTRAL AMERICA

♦ How did political conflict spread through Central America after World War II?

In 1954, Sylvia Jordan got her first glimpse of the political warfare that would soon rip Guatemala apart. That year, a **coup** (koo), a sudden overthrow of the government, shook the nation of Guatemala. "I remember the gunshots. I remember the government cutting all the lights in Guatemala City," said Sylvia. "But I did not know about U.S. intervention then. What I remember is all the talk about communism."

A Decade of Reform. The roots of the 1954 coup in Guatemala reached back to 1944. In October of that year, a revolution brought Juan José Arévalo (ah-REH-vah-loh) to power. Arévalo called for economic reforms aimed at helping landless peasants. Large landowners felt uneasy as Arévalo handed out lands from German-owned plantations seized during World War II. Their discomfort increased when Arévalo allowed unions of workers to challenge the power of plantation owners.

Arévalo called his programs "spiritual socialism." During the Cold War of the late 1940s and 1950s (see page 249), however, *socialism* meant communism in the minds of many U.S. leaders. The fears of U.S. leaders increased when a small, vocal Guatemalan Communist party was formed in 1949.

In 1951, Jacobo Arbenz Guzmán won election as president. He had the backing of Guatemalan students and peasants. Arbenz saw the holdings of the *latifundias,* or large farms owned by businesses, as the key to improving conditions in Guatemala. In 1952, Arbenz seized unplanted *latifundia* lands. He wanted to turn these over to the peasants, many of whom lived on the edge of starvation.

In that move, the U.S.-owned United Fruit Company lost 85 percent of its lands. Arbenz paid the company and other landowners. But the owners complained bitterly because he paid for the land at the same low values that the owners used when figuring their taxes.

From Reform to Repression. Arbenz's reforms, if they continued, would sharply reduce U.S. influence in Guatemala. U.S. leaders moved to make sure they did not. In 1954, U.S. President Dwight D. Eisenhower approved a plan by the Central Intelligence Agency (CIA) to topple Arbenz. Using Honduras and El Salvador as bases, the CIA trained an army led by a Guatemalan military officer named Carlos Castillo Armas (kahs-TEE-yoh AHR-mahs).

In 1954, the army invaded Guatemala. "The bombing and fighting went on only a short period of time," explained Sylvia

Colombian soldiers stop protesters during a demonstration. Political unrest rocked many South and Central American countries during the 1970s and 1980s.

Jordan. "But the outcome of the coup totally changed the history of Guatemala."

Power now passed to the military. The new government jailed student and peasant leaders who opposed the coup. As opposition increased, so did oppression. In the 1960s, thousands of people fell victim to **death squads.** These were bands of military thugs who murdered those suspected of opposing the government.

With the rise of Fidel Castro in Cuba (see page 271), the United States grew increasingly concerned over the spread of communism to Central America. U.S. leaders failed to take action against the anti-Communist government of Guatemala. However, in the 1970s, violations of **human rights**—the basic rights of people as human beings—grew widespread in the country. The United States cut off aid to Guatemala until the violations ended.

The violations, however, did not end. In the 1980s, they increased. The result was a huge wave of Guatemalan refugees into the United States.

Challenging the Dictatorships. In the late 1970s, political unrest spread to other parts of Central America. In nation after nation, people challenged long-standing dictatorships. Several factors helped account for the unrest.

The Cuban revolution and aid from Castro's government encouraged some rebel leaders in other Latin American countries to take up arms. Other people drew hope from new policies of the Roman Catholic church. In 1968, church leaders publicly called for "social justice" for the poor. Coverage of human rights abuses in the media created more opposition.

The first explosions came in El Salvador. A string of brutal military governments there had kept the people terrorized since 1932. In the late 1970s, Salvadorans took action. Students, industrial workers, peasants, and clergy spoke out against the terror.

In 1977, world attention focused on El Salvador when government troops killed a rural priest named Rutilio Grande

(GRAHN-deh) who was working for reform. The archbishop of San Salvador, Oscar Romero (ROH-meh-roh), blasted the government. Romero then threw the weight of the Roman Catholic church behind the movement to bring reform to El Salvador. His efforts cost Romero his life. In March 1980, an assassin's bullet killed him.

In October 1980, rebel groups formed the Farabundo Martí National Liberation Front (FMLN). The group took its name from Agustín Farabundo Martí, the leader of a 1932 uprising. As the 1980s opened, civil war swept over El Salvador. In the next ten years, nearly one quarter of the nation's population fled. Many came to the United States.

End of a Dynasty. As turmoil rocked El Salvador, rebels tried to wrestle Nicaragua from the grip of the Somoza family. With U.S. backing, the Somozas had ruled Nicaragua since 1936 (see page 255). To many Nicaraguans, the Somozas represented U.S. domination. Nationalists looked back in pride to Augusto Sandino, who led a peasant army against the U.S. Marines in 1926 (see page 200). In 1961, guerrillas organized the Sandinista Front for National Liberation (FSLN). Named after Sandino, the Sandinistas vowed to finish the fight he had started in 1926.

In 1979, the Sandinistas triumphed and overthrew Somoza. The victory over Somoza cost 50,000 Nicaraguan lives. But as soon as one war ended, another began. As Cuban and Soviet aid flowed into Nicaragua, U.S. aid flowed into the hands of groups known as the **Contras** (KOHN-trahs). *Contra* is the Spanish word for "against." These groups were against the Sandinista government. Thus, the stage was set for another civil war and another wave of exiles from Central America (see Chapter 28).

Taking Another Look

1. Why did President Arbenz take land belonging to the United Fruit Company?
2. What factors led people to challenge dictatorships in Central America?
3. **Critical Thinking** Do you think the U.S. response to communism in Central America was just? Explain.

2 NEW VOICES FROM SOUTH AMERICA

♦ What events helped trigger increased immigration from South America after World War II?

In 1968, a chance meeting at a New York City party brought Mónica Hernando (er-NAHN-doh) and Rodolfo Singer together. Two years later, the Argentine couple married. Although they took up life in New York City, they hoped some day to return to Argentina. They even bought an apartment in Buenos Aires to prepare for their eventual return.

Memories of Argentina. Both Mónica and Rodolfo treasured their memories of Argentina. Mónica fondly recalled her years in an old Buenos Aires neighborhood known as San Telmo. Mónica remembers, "Artists lived there, and tourists visited all the tango cafes."

Rodolfo grew up in the city of Córdoba. He attended festivals in the mountains that surround the city. There he listened to the romantic stories and tales that are part of the folklore of the country.

With such warm memories, why didn't the couple return home? "Things started getting bad in the 1970s," explained Singer. "Did you ever hear of 'the dirty war'? Well, 'the dirty war' made up our minds. It convinced us to stay in the United States."

Search for Stability. The troubles Singer referred to arose in 1976, when military leaders seized power in Argentina. What followed was six years of fear known as "the dirty war." Singer recalled, "The military just went crazy. If you opposed the government, you became one of the *desaparecidos,* 'the disappeared ones.'" The terror of "the dirty war" sent 75,000 Argentines to the United States.

New Immigration Patterns. The large-scale arrival of South Americans was part of a change in immigration patterns that had begun shortly after World War II. Between 1820 and 1930, only 113,000 immigrants from the entire continent of South America arrived in the United States. By 1970, the number of first- and second-generation South Americans in the United States had grown to some 350,000. In 1980, it reached more than 500,000.

Immigration to the United States was made easier by the relatively low cost of airline travel. In the 1960s and 1970s, $300 or $400 could buy a one-way ticket. While that sum was too much for peasants and most industrial workers, it was well within reach of middle-class and professional people who wanted to flee political or economic troubles.

The first large group of South Americans to arrive came from Colombia. From 1948 to 1962, Colombia reeled from *la Violencia* (vee-oh-LEN-see-ah), "the Violence." This time of government repression, banditry, and guerrilla warfare sent some 32,000 Colombians to the United States. Continued turmoil pushed that number up to over 100,000 by 1976. In 1973, political coups in Uruguay and Chile sent citizens of those nations to the United States. Then, after 1976, came the Argentines.

Political crisis flared into violence in a number of Central American countries. In what year did the Sandinistas overthrow Somoza in Nicaragua?

CONFLICT IN CENTRAL AMERICA

Gulf of Mexico

CUBA

20°N

• Mexico City

MEXICO

BELIZE (BRITISH HONDURAS)
• Belmopan

1961 Anti–Castro Cubans train for Bay of Pigs in Guatemala

GUATEMALA

1954 U.S. helps overthrow leftist government in Guatemala

Guatemala City •

HONDURAS

• Tegucigalpa

15°N

San Salvador •

EL SALVADOR

Caribbean Sea

1970s Unrest between right and left in El Salvador flares into violent outbreaks

NICARAGUA

1979 Sandinistas overthrow Somoza in Nicaragua

Managua •

PACIFIC OCEAN

San José •

Panama Canal

10°N

COSTA RICA

Panama City •

0   150   300 Miles

PANAMA

0   150   300 Kilometers

COLOMBIA

90°W   85°W   80°W

New Cultural Voices. The new South American immigrants added to the nation's mix of Latinos. Their cultural presence could be felt in many ways. One example was Chilean author and teacher Fernando Alegría (ah-lee-GREE-ah).

Born in 1918, **Fernando Alegría** grew up in a crowded neighborhood in Santiago. He studied in both Chile and the United States. In 1947, Alegría earned a doctoral degree from the University of California at Berkeley. That same year, he was appointed a professor of Spanish American literature at Berkeley. But, even though he lived in the United States, Alegría kept close ties to Chile. In 1977, he founded a magazine called *Literatura chilena en el exilio.* (*Chilean Literature in Exile*). Alegría used the magazine to promote Chilean writers and, at the same time, to protest human rights abuses in Chile.

As the 1980s opened, large South American communities existed in New York, Los Angeles, Miami, and in many other cities in the nation. While those communities took root, new immigrants from South America continued to arrive in the United States.

Taking Another Look

1. Why did people flee Argentina in 1976?
2. In what way were conditions in other countries similar to those in Argentina, and what were the results?

SNAPSHOT OF THE TIMES

1948–1962 *La Violencia* creates turmoil in Colombia.

1951 Jacobo Arbenz Guzmán becomes president of Guatemala.

1954 CIA stages a coup in Guatemala.

1961 The Sandinista Front for National Liberation is founded in Nicaragua.

1968 The Roman Catholic church calls for social justice for the poor.

1976 "The dirty war" begins in Argentina.

1977 Salvadoran priest Rutilio Grande is killed by government troops.

1979 Sandinistas overthrow Somoza.

1980 Archbishop Oscar Romero of El Salvador is assassinated.

The FMLN is formed in El Salvador.

3. **Critical Thinking** Compare the immigrants from Central America to those of South America. Based on what you have read, in what ways are they similar? In what ways are they different?

LOOKING AHEAD

As more and more Spanish-speaking immigrants arrived in the United States, Latino influence was being felt across all areas of U.S. life. Latino artists, writers, and entertainers brought new variety to the nation's culture.

Years ago, in the early 1900s, the tango was considered the dance of the lower class. But then other classes in Argentina discovered it. Today, the whole world knows about the tango.

That was how Rodolfo Singer described the tango. Like most Argentines, Singer is well informed about the tango. Historians still debate whether its roots lie with the first Spanish settlers of Argentina or with the enslaved Africans they transported there. But like Argentina itself, the tango is a blend of influences. The instruments that accompany the tango show the cultures that have formed it—Spanish guitar, Italian violin, and a German accordion.

The tango first hit the United States in the 1920s. Here the sultry music of the tango blended with the sounds of jazz. When movie idol Rudolph Valentino took up the tango, so did millions of others.

Unlike most dance crazes, the tango did not die in the 1920s. In fact, it experienced a surge of popularity in the 1970s when waves of Argentines came to the United States. In New York City, one of these arrivals, Abel Malvestiti, founded *Amigos del Tango* (Friends of the Tango). In 1985, New York showed its love for the music and the dance in the smash Broadway hit *Tango Argentino*. When asked the reason for the tango's success, Malvestiti replied, "It is the music of the people."

CLOSE UP: Chapter 23

The Who, What, Where of History

1. **What** is a coup?
2. **What** did Jacobo Arbenz Guzmán hope to achieve by redistributing land?
3. **Who** was Archbishop Oscar Romero?
4. **Who** were the Sandinistas?
5. **What** was "the dirty war"?
6. **Where** did *la Violencia* occur?
7. **Who** is Fernando Alegría?

Making the Connection

1. What was the connection between the Cold War and U.S. intervention in Central America?
2. What was the connection between "the dirty war" and the *desaparecidos?*
3. Explain the connection between political coups and increased immigration from Central and South America after 1950.

Time Check

1. Which happened *first*—the Cuban revolution, CIA intervention in Guatemala, or the fall of the Somoza regime?
2. Why might some people call 1977 a turning point in the struggle in El Salvador?

What Would You Have Done?

1. By the late 1970s, death squads roamed both Guatemala and El Salvador. Would you have risked speaking out against the government? Why or why not?
2. Suppose you were living in Guatemala, El Salvador, or Nicaragua

in 1979. Would you have left your home? Explain.

3. Imagine you lived in Argentina during "the dirty war" or in Colombia during *la Violencia*. What, if any, action could you have taken to protest the violence?

Thinking and Writing About History

1. Imagine you are a Guatemalan living in the United States in 1976. Write an editorial urging the United States to end the human rights violations in Central America.

2. Write a brief eulogy, or funeral speech, that a Salvadoran peasant might have given for Archbishop Oscar Romero or Father Rutilio Grande.

3. Prepare a press release on the collapse of the Somoza regime from the points of view of each of the following: the U.S. government, the Cuban government, the Sandinistas.

4. Design a skit in which Rodolfo and Mónica Singer tell their children about Argentina.

5. Imagine that you are a Latino activist who wants to end violence in one of the nations mentioned in this chapter. Draw up a petition for presentation to the United Nations.

Building Skills: Recognizing Propaganda

When people hear the word *propaganda,* they often think of something underhanded or evil. But propaganda is neither good nor bad. It is simply a method for using ideas or information to sway people's opinions. The following are some widely used propaganda techniques:

1. *Glittering generalities:* broad, sweeping statements that sound good but in fact mean little.

2. *Name calling:* trying to devalue something by attaching a bad label to it.

3. *Bandwagon:* trying to win support for something by conveying the idea that "everybody is doing it."

4. *Testimonal:* having a well-known person endorse an idea or a product.

5. *Plain folks:* showing that something comes from ordinary, down-to-earth people and therefore is good.

6. *Card stacking:* distorting facts and evidence to present only one side of an issue favorably.

7. *Transfer:* trying to shift the positive associations from a person or thing to something not directly related.

Propaganda played an important role in the 1954 coup in Guatemala. Working with one or two of your classmates, write a piece of propaganda that the CIA might have distributed to influence Guatemalans to back the coup. Then, challenge the rest of the class to identify the techniques you used to write your propaganda.

Express Yourself!

On a piece of paper, write down all the terms that appear in this chapter in bold, or heavy, type. Write down any other words or terms that are not familiar to you. Work with a partner and write the definition of each term. Next, draw pictures or symbols that show the meaning of two or three of the words. Then, write a sentence for each word you have defined.

The Puerto Rican Traveling Theatre was one of the organizations formed during the Puerto Rican cultural revival. The theater performed works by Puerto Rican playwrights in the streets of New York City.

SECTIONS

1 New Cultural Perspectives

2 Reshaping Popular Culture

CHAPTER 24

A Growing Voice

(1950s–1980)

THINKING ABOUT THE CHAPTER

How have Latinos enriched the cultural life of the United States?

"I felt the need to see the rest of the world," explained Antonio Martorell (mahr-toh-REL), recalling his first visit to the United States. In 1954, at age 15, he had left Puerto Rico for California. There, Martorell stayed with an aunt. "My Aunt Irma was a pioneer," said Martorell. "She came to the U.S. quite early for Puerto Ricans."

Martorell was a pioneer, too. Together with other Puerto Rican artists, he helped chart new directions in the arts. Martorell earned a degree in international relations from Georgetown University. But his first loves were art and literature. So upon graduation in 1961, he headed to Spain to study painting.

Martorell then returned to Puerto Rico. There, he became involved in the *Instituto de Cultura Puertorriqueña,* the Institute of Puerto Rican Culture. Martorell found himself caught up in a great cultural movement. He explained:

The Institute was involved in a kind of cultural renaissance [rebirth] at the time. Most of the artists were inclined toward Puerto Rican independence. This feeling gave us a sense of community. We were using our art to help build a national identity. It was really quite exciting.

In the 1960s, Martorell became known as one of the island's leading painters. Since that time, he has helped promote Puerto Rican culture on the mainland through shows at *El Museo del Barrio,* the Museum of the Barrio, and workshops at Hostos Community College, both in New York City. This chapter describes how the activities of Latinos such as Martorell have enriched the culture of the United States.

1 NEW CULTURAL PERSPECTIVES
◆ How have Latino artists and writers
◆ added new dimensions to U.S. culture?

One of the key figures in the movement for the cultural independence of Puerto Rico was Celia Vice (VEE-seh). Like other Puerto Ricans, Vice took great pride in the political freedoms won by Puerto Rico as a commonwealth (see Chapter 20). But she wanted to increase Puerto Rico's cultural independence as well. For centuries, the island had lived in the shadow of Spain. Then it had come under the control of the United States. "Many think that Puerto Ricans have no history, no heritage, no great talents," explained Vice.

To help change that situation, the New York businesswoman founded Puerto Rican Heritage Publications. In the 1950s, she flew back and forth between island and mainland searching for authors and "hidden treasures" to publish. She then worked to get these literary works by Puerto Ricans into schools and libraries around the United States. In 1960, the Puerto Rican community of New York honored Vice for her efforts in bringing Puerto Rican culture to a wider audience.

A Sense of Identity. Vice was but one figure in the Puerto Rican cultural revival of the 1950s and 1960s. Those years saw a burst of activity among artists and writers on both the island and the mainland. In 1955, Puerto Rico set up the *Instituto de Cultura Puertorriqueña.* The Institute soon became a center for creative artists. As Antonio Martorell explained: "The Institute and its artists were very close-knit with other cultural ventures. We worked with music, film, theater, and much more."

While at the Institute, Martorell helped design sets for plays by René Marqués. Marqués wrote of the unsettled lives of many Puerto Ricans. He wrote about *jíbaros,* or peasants, who moved from their homes in the mountains to new homes in the cities. Marqués also wrote about Puerto Ricans moving from the island to the mainland. In plays such as *La Carreta (The Oxcart),* Marqués appealed to Puerto Ricans to return to their homeland. He urged them to preserve their culture.

Other writers treated similar themes in novels and poems. For example, José Luis González, Pedro Juan Soto, and Luis Rafael Sánchez revealed the dark side of life on the mainland. They also poked fun at "Americanized" Puerto Ricans. Like Marqués, they celebrated the rural roots of Puerto Rican culture. The *jíbaro* was a symbol of those roots.

Nuyoricans. Most Puerto Ricans on the mainland put down roots in New York City. Inspired by the Civil Rights Movement of the 1950s and 1960s, a new generation of writers and artists took pride in their identity as **nuyoricans** (noo-yoo-REE-kahns). Nuyoricans are second-generation Puerto Ricans born and raised in the continental United States. Nuyorican writers and artists found a spiritual home in the Nuyorican Poets Cafe, founded by poet Miguel Algarín (ahl-gah-REEN).

Opened in the 1960s, the Poets Cafe gave nuyorican writers a place where they could read their works to a sympathetic audience. Some of today's most talented nuyorican poets first read there, including Victor Hernandez Cruz, Tato Laviera (lah-vee-EH-rah), Miguel Piñero, and Sandra María Esteves (es-TEH-ves).

By the 1970s, a large amount of nuyorican literature had emerged. Many nuyorican authors were bilingual. They wrote in both Spanish and English. Most also thought of themselves as bicultural, with roots in both the United States and Puerto Rico. Some, such as Tato Laviera and Sandra María Esteves, took special pride in their African-Caribbean heritage.

In 1976, Laviera wrote his first novel, *La Carreta Made a U-Turn.* The book picks up on the story told in Marqués's *Oxcart.* But instead of taking readers back to Puerto Rico, the story leads them to New York City. His point is that Puerto Rico can be found in New York, too.

Puerto Rican works are now part of the mainstream of U.S. literature. There are dozens of nuyorican writers. Among them are Piri Thomas, Nicholasa Mohr, Ed Vega, and Judith Ortíz Cofer (ohr-TEES koh-fer). Piri Thomas, for example, stunned the literary world in 1967 when he published *Down These Mean Streets,* his picture of Puerto Rican life in New York.

Cultural ties between the island and the mainland remain strong. For example, Antonio Martorell lived and worked in Puerto Rico. However, he stayed in touch with the cultural activities of the Puerto Rican community in New York. He explained that to portray the Puerto Rican experience a writer or artist must deal with both the mainland and the island.

Puerto Rican artist Antonio Martorell explores new forms in his works. His "Rilkehaus," shown here at *El Museo del Barrio,* consists of variations of a portrait of poet Rainer Maria Rilke assembled into the form of a large room.

1955	The *Instituto de Cultura Puertorriqueña* is founded.
1960s	Nuyorican Poets Cafe opens.
	El Movimiento and the publication of *I Am Joaquín* spark the Chicano Renaissance.
	Salsa gains popularity in the United States.
1960	Celia Vice, founder of Puerto Rican Heritage Publications, is honored by the Puerto Rican community in New York.
1967	Piri Thomas publishes *Down These Mean Streets*.
1979	Tato Laviera writes *La Carreta Made a U-Turn*.
1990	Oscar Hijuelos becomes the first Latino to win the Pulitzer Prize for fiction.

The Cuban American Experience.

Unlike Puerto Ricans, the Cubans in the United States found their ties with the home island cut by revolution. In the 1960s, many Cuban artists and writers struggled with the idea that they were exiles.

For more than ten years after the Cuban community established itself in the United States, many of the best-known Cuban writers wrote of the heartbreaking move to the mainland. Some, such as Heberto Padilla (pah-DEE-yah), had supported the revolution, only to find their ideals betrayed. They moved to the United States holding onto dreams of one day returning to Cuba.

Lourdes Casal (kah-SAHL) was one of the writers who tried to adjust to life in the United States. But, like other new Spanish-speaking arrivals, Casal often felt caught between two cultures. Wrote Casal in one poem:

> Too Havanian to be a New Yorker,
> too much of a New Yorker to be
> —even to go back to being—
> anything else

Coming of Age in the United States.

In developing their art and literature, Cubans in the United States had a rich heritage to draw upon. The island had produced many literary and artistic masters. Their works blended Spanish and African-Caribbean influences. Cuban artists in the United States built on this tradition. "We've brought an intense Afro-Latin Americanism . . . to the world," explained Cuban painter José Bedia (BEH-dee-ah).

The generation of artists and writers who came of age in the United States added new elements to Cuban art and literature. They focused less on the experience of being exiles and more on Cuban culture in the United States. They described themselves as Cuban Americans. Celedonio Gonzales (gohn-SAH-les) wrote about Cubans who realize that Cuba is no longer theirs. Roberto Fernández tried to capture the unique culture of Little Havana.

Gonzales and Fernández wrote their first works in Spanish. Other Cuban American writers chose English. In *Latin Jazz,* Virgil Suárez captured the hopes and dreams of a Cuban family at the time of the Mariel boatlift (see page 349). In *The Mambo Kings Play Songs of Love,* Oscar Hijuelos (ee-HWEH-lohs) reached back to the 1940s and 1950s to describe the mambo craze in the United States. His powerful book won the Pulitzer Prize for fiction in 1990. Hijuelos was the first Latino ever to receive this important award.

GALLERY OF LATINO WRITERS

Julia Alvarez (AHL-vah-res) (1951–   ) Alvarez lived in the Dominican Republic until 1965. Amid the upheavals that followed the Trujillo assassination (see page 277), her family moved to the United States. There, Alvarez earned a master's degree in literature from Syracuse University. Both a poet and novelist, she won widespread fame with her first novel, *How the García Girls Lost Their Accents.*

Sandra Cisneros (1954–   ) Cisneros first became known with her collection of poetry called *My Wicked Wicked Ways.* Her first attempt at fiction, *The House on Mango Street,* won the Before Columbus Foundation American Book Award. Today this Mexican American poet, novelist, and short-story writer is working to "give Latina voices" a place in literature.

Roberto Fernández (1951–   ) In 1961, two years after Castro came to power, Fernández's family left Cuba. Today, Fernández belongs to a new generation of Cuban American writers who came of age in the United States. Fernández writes in Spanish about the Cuban community in exile. In works such as *La vida es un especial (Life Is a Bargain),* Fernández captures the essence of the exile culture, a culture he feels will soon vanish.

Isaac Goldemberg (1945–   ) Since moving to New York City from Peru in 1965, Goldemberg has been a leading force in encouraging Latino authors to write in Spanish. In his own poems and novels, Goldemberg writes about the varied cultural forces that have shaped Latin America. He writes of his own Peruvian heritage, which includes a Russian Jewish father and a mother with Spanish, Basque, Italian, and Quechua Native American ancestry.

Nicholasa Mohr (1935–) Born of Puerto Rican parents, Mohr grew up in *El Barrio* in New York City. As a child, she showed two talents—storytelling and sketching. In 1973, these talents came together to create an award-winning children's book called *Nilda.* Today, Mohr writes and illustrates books for people of all ages. In novels such as *El Bronx Remembered,* Mohr tells the story of Puerto Ricans on the mainland.

Heberto Padilla (1932–) Padilla backed the Cuban Revolution. But this writer/poet also valued literary freedom. In 1971, Cuban officials forced Padilla to publicly denounce his own poetry. Writers around the world pressured Cuba to grant exit permits to Padilla and his poet wife, Belkis Cuza Male (MAH-leh). Today Padilla teaches and writes in Princeton, New Jersey.

Luis Valdez (1940–) A founder of the Chicano theater movement, Valdez won national fame with his play *Zoot Suit.* In the 1980s, he moved from stage to film with his screenplay for *La Bamba,* the biography of Chicano rock-and-roll star Richie Valens. Today, Valdez has three words of advice for Latino young people: "Go for it!"

Rima de Vallbona (vahl-BOH-nah) (1931–) A longtime resident of Houston, Texas, Vallbona has kept strong ties with her native Costa Rica. As a scholar, Vallbona has done pioneering studies of Costa Rican women writers. As a writer, she has published a number of novels and collections of short stories in Spanish, including *Noche en vela (Sleepless Night)* and *La salamandra rosada (The Pink Salamander).*

GALLERY OF LATINO ARTISTS

Judith Baca (1946–) Baca helped pioneer the Mexican American mural movement in Los Angeles. Her best-known work is *The Great Wall of Los Angeles.* This huge mural, a half mile (.8 kilometer) long, took many years to complete. Nearly 200 scholars, artists, and staff assisted Baca. So did more than 450 young people from Los Angeles's many ethnic neighborhoods (see page 315).

Barbara Carrasco (kah-RRAH-skoh) (1955–) Carrasco first used her brush to give support to the causes of *El Movimiento.* Like other Chicana artists such as Yolanda M. Lopez, Carrasco paints strong images that challenge traditional views of Mexican American women. In 1990, Carrasco's works formed part of a three-year national tour titled Chicano Art: Resistance and Affirmation, 1965–1985 (CARA).

George Febres (1944–) Born in Guayaquil, Ecuador, Febres comes from a family that includes many famous Ecuadorans, including one of Ecuador's presidents. Febres, however, is the family's first artist. Today, Febres takes pride in his U.S. citizenship and his service in the Vietnam War. His works are in the collections of the New Orleans Museum of Art and the Smithsonian Institution.

Alberto Insua (EEN-swah) (1960–) A native of Lima, Peru, Insua uses his paintings to speak for him. "There are more than words to explain your feelings," says Insua. Stories from pre-Columbian myths spring from the bright colors and bold lines of many of his canvases. A resident of Washington, D.C., Insua is represented in many collections.

Antonio Martorell (1939–) Puerto Rico takes special pride in a generation of graphic artists like Martorell who came of age in the 1950s and 1960s. Martorell's prints have won international praise for their new techniques. Twenty-two of Martorell's posters form part of the permanent collection of *El Museo de Barrio* in New York City. (For more on Martorell, see pages 304–306.)

Octavio Medellín (meh-deh-YEEN) (1907–) Born in Matehuala, Mexico, Medellín moved to San Antonio, Texas, at the age of 13. After studying at the Art Institute of Chicago, Medellín traveled to Yucátan to study pre-Columbian art. His sculptures and paintings show the influence of his Native American ancestry. In 1969, Medellín opened his own art school in Dallas, Texas. Medellín's work appears in galleries around the world.

César Pelli (PEH-yee) (1922–) Argentine-born Pelli is one of the leading U.S. architects. Coming to the U.S. in 1922, Pelli began a career that eventually led to his appointment as dean of the School of Architecture at Yale University. Some of his most imaginative designs include the UN building in Vienna, Austria, and the U.S. Embassy in Tokyo, Japan.

Pedro Pérez (1951–) Pérez belongs to what is known to Cuban Americans as the "first-generation." In this group are artists who spent at least part of their lives in Castro's Cuba. Pérez works in an African-influenced style that is so much a part of the art of Cuba. Pérez has a Master in Fine Arts degree from the Maryland Institute of Art. His works have been exhibited in many galleries and museums including the Metropolitan Museum in New York and the Houston Fine Arts Museum.

GALLERY OF LATINO PERFORMING ARTISTS

Martina Arroyo (ah-RROH-yoh) (1936?–) College graduate, former high school teacher, and social worker, Arroyo was prepared to sing her first role as an operatic soprano in 1958, when the tent in which the performance was to take place blew down in a storm. From then on, however, her career took off. The New-York-born daughter of Puerto Rican professionals went on to sing leading roles at the Metropolitan Opera in New York City and in opera houses worldwide.

Julio Bacco (1966–) At only 19 years of age, Venezuelan-born Bacco captured the 1985 Gold Medal in Moscow's International Ballet Competition. A short time later, the American Ballet Theatre asked him to become a principal dancer. The offer brought Bacco to the United States. His first solo performance led critics to hail him as one of the brightest stars of the world of ballet.

Joan Baez (1941–) The daughter of a Mexican-born physicist, Baez became one of the leading folk singers of the 1960s. At that time, Baez used her voice to oppose the Vietnam War. In the 1980s, she joined other musicians to raise money to help end starvation in Africa. Baez celebrates her Latino heritage by including traditional Mexican ballads such as *"Gracias a la Vida"* ("Here's to Life") in her performances.

Pablo Casals (1876–1973) In 1939, Pablo Casals, one of the world's greatest cellists, made a decision. No longer would he live in his native Spain while fascist dictator Francisco Franco ruled. Casals settled first in France. Then, in 1956, he left for his mother's homeland, Puerto Rico. Casals helped make Puerto Rico a center of classical music. In the years since his death, Puerto Rico has continued to host the annual Casals Festival, a celebration of the world's great music.

Celia Cruz (1929–) When Celia Cruz left Castro's Cuba, the island lost the undisputed "Queen of Salsa." Says Cruz, "Castro never forgave me." Today, after more than 40 years as a musician, Cruz is still winning acclaim for the hot, spicy music she helped make famous. Together with Tito Puente, with whom she has appeared over 500 times, Cruz has taught the United States to dance to an Afro-Caribbean beat.

Horacio Gutiérrez (1948–) At age 11, Gutiérrez made his debut as a concert pianist with the Havana Symphony Orchestra. Two years later, his family joined the Cuban exile community in Miami. In 1970, Gutiérrez honored his adopted homeland by winning the silver medal at the Tchaikovsky Competition in Moscow. Today, Gutiérrez gives some 70 concerts a year, many with the world's most famous symphonies.

Tito Puente (1923–) In the 1950s, Puente carried the beat of Latin music from Puerto Rico to the mainland. His mastery of the saxaphone, clarinet, and many types of drums earned him the nickname *El Rey* (The King) of big-band mambo. In 1992, Puente commented on his broad appeal. "You see," he said, "instrumental music has no language problem."

Carlos Santana (1947–) Santana received his first music lessons in Jalisco, Mexico, from his violinist father. After moving to California, Santana took up rock-and-roll. When he added an Afro-Caribbean beat to his music, Santana created what has become known as Latin Rock. Since his 1969 appearance at the landmark Woodstock concert, Santana continues to influence young rock musicians today.

Chicano Voices. In the mid–1960s, a pamphlet in Spanish and English passed from hand to hand in Mexican American communities of the Southwest. It showed up on the picket lines of the United Farm Workers. Actors performed scenes from it in *barrio* street theaters. Entitled *I Am Joaquín/Yo Soy Joaquín,* it began:

I am Joaquín,
lost in a world of confusion,
caught up in the whirl of a
    gringo society.
confused by the rules. . . .

You read about this poem and its author, Rodolfo "Corky" Gonzales, in Chapter 22. Gonzales used Joaquín as a symbol for the Mexican American people. In the poem, he told of the historic struggles faced by Mexican Americans in the United States. The poem called upon Mexican Americans to cling to their culture and not to surrender it to the Anglo way of life. Written in 1967, the poem helped trigger the "Chicano Renaissance."

Writers of *El Movimiento*. The years following 1964 saw a whirl of artistic activity among Chicano writers and artists. They based their works on many sources. They looked to the Mexican past, a past that stretched back to the Aztec and Maya. They also drew upon the work of Mexican and Mexican American writers and artists. Most of all, Chicano writers and artists drew their inspiration from *El Movimiento,* the movement to increase pride in the Mexican heritage (see Chapter 22).

The effort to promote the causes and beliefs of *El Movimiento* led to a great out-pouring of literature. Most Chicano authors wrote in both Spanish and English. In poems, plays, novels, and short stories, they captured the textures of Mexican American life. Their works described the experiences of migrant farmworkers, *barrio* dwellers, and Latino youths.

From this generation of writers came such outstanding figures as the poet and writer Gary Soto, playwright Denise Chávez, and novelist Rolando Hinojosa (ee-noh-HOH-sah). New Latino publishing houses distributed the works of many of the writers. One of the most famous, Arte Público, is the leading publisher of Latino literature today (see page 318).

Chicano Art. Hundreds of artists were inspired by *El Movimiento*. They produced paintings, sculptures, prints, and posters. But among the most stunning achievements of Chicano artists were their community **murals,** or wall paintings.

The mural-making tradition grew from the Mexican past. Murals had covered the walls of ancient Maya and Aztec temples. Some of the best-known Mexican artists of the early 1900s, such as Diego Rivera and José Clemente Orozco, created famous murals.

In the 1960s and 1970s, Chicano artists built upon that tradition. They became known by such names as Los Four, the Royal Chicano Airforce, and *Las Mujeres Muralistas* (The Women Muralists). Chicano muralists helped organize the *barrios* into huge painting projects. They decorated neighborhoods, such as East Los Angeles, with sweeping pictures that celebrated the Mexican heritage.

Increasing Diversity. Added to the achievements of Puerto Ricans, Cubans, and Mexican Americans were the works of people from other parts of Latin America. In the decades following the 1960s, Dominicans, Central Americans, and South Americans were the fastest-growing

Latino groups in the nation. Their arrival added further richness and diversity to U.S. culture. For just a taste of the many and varied accomplishments of the nation's Latino artists, writers, and performers, see the Galleries on pages 308–313.

Taking Another Look

1. How did the *Instituto de Cultura Puertorriqueña* and the Nuyorican Poets Cafe serve the needs of Puerto Rican writers and artists?

2. How did the Cuban revolution affect Cuban American writing and art?

3. **Critical Thinking** Why do you think *I Am Joaquín* helped trigger the Chicano Renaissance?

2 RESHAPING POPULAR CULTURE

◆ How did Latinos influence popular culture in the United States?

For many non-Latino U.S. citizens of the 1940s and 1950s, music provided their first contact with Latino culture. In those years, the mambo, an exciting rhythmic dance, arrived in the United States from Cuba. The mambo developed into a craze that turned some Cuban performers into stars.

A Cuban musician named Desi Arnaz helped bring the sounds of Cuba into millions of living rooms. As the costar of one of the most popular television shows of the 1950s, "I Love Lucy," Arnaz gave the nation a weekly taste of Latino culture. Those years marked the beginning of a growing Latino influence on the culture of the United States.

The Great Wall of Los Angeles is the longest mural in the world. It tells the history of Los Angeles. Directed by Chicana artist Judith Baca, the mural was a community effort involving artists, storytellers, and neighborhood youth.

A New Latino Beat. The mambo craze brought an Afro-Caribbean beat to the United States. By the 1950s, Anglo audiences were ready to try another dance out of Cuba—the cha-cha. The enthusiastic response opened the door for other Latino rhythms and dances. Dominican artists introduced the United States to the merengue (meh-REN-geh). Puerto Rican groups popularized bombas (BOHM-bahs) and plenas (PLEH-nahs). In the 1960s, one of the most exciting sounds of all—salsa (SAHL-sah)—hit the scene. A mixture of styles born in the Caribbean, salsa blended the African and Spanish heritages shared by Latinos of the Caribbean.

Latino beats slowly crept into musical forms born in the United States. Jazz artists such as Chick Corea studied with Afro-Caribbean masters such as Mongo Santamaría (sahn-tah-mah-REE-ah) and Willie Bobo. Carlos Santana added Afro-Caribbean drums and rhythms to rock-and-roll. Singers from Latino backgrounds, such as Linda Ronstadt, added Spanish lyrics or ballads to their albums. By the 1980s, mainstream popular music in the United States reflected the influence of Latin Americans on U.S. culture.

A New Presence. As the number of Latinos in the United States grew, more and more Latinos could be seen on television screens and in movies. Audiences across the nation recognized such Latino actors and actresses as Rita Moreno, Raul Julia, and Edward James Olmos. Hollywood also began to recognize the talent of Latino directors. Luis Valdez, the founder of *El Teatro Campesino* (see page 287), was one

Los Lobos, a contemporary rock band from Southern California, has incorporated Mexican American themes and musical styles into their popular music. They perform in both English and Spanish on many of their albums.

of the Latino directors who made movies for the broad U.S. audience.

In the 1970s and 1980s, Latino names regularly showed up in the entertainment and sports sections of major newspapers. Latino artists performed in concert halls and dance halls. Latino sports stars triumphed in tennis, golf, baseball, football, boxing, and more. Each Latino group had its heroes and stars. Many of those individual heroes became national heroes as well. One outstanding example was Roberto Clemente (kleh-MEN-teh).

Roberto Clemente (1934–1972) grew up in Carolina, Puerto Rico. He knew the hard life and poverty of sugar-cane workers like his father. But the younger Clemente had a dream. He wanted to be a baseball player.

Through hard work and determination, Clemente fulfilled that dream. He became the star outfielder for the Pittsburgh Pirates and one of the best players in baseball history. Clemente broke record after record. He won 11 Gold Glove awards for fielding. He rapped out 3,000 hits, only the 11th man in the history of the game to rack up that many. He had a .317 lifetime batting average and played in 12 All-Star games.

But Clemente was also a hero away from the baseball diamond. He returned to Puerto Rico every winter to work with youths on the island. He planned a sports center for children. In 1972, when an earthquake hit Nicaragua, Clemente offered to help fly in supplies. En route to the disaster, his plane crashed. His death was mourned in Puerto Rico and throughout the United States. In 1984, the U.S. Congress approved a commemorative postage stamp to honor Clemente's achievements.

A Strong Latino Voice. By the 1990s, Latinos had become a strong cultural force within the nation. They helped enrich the United States through their talents and their diversity. Gone were the days when a Latino star such as Desi Arnaz stood out in a world of Anglo artists. Latino voices could now be heard throughout most of the country. The United States, as the fourth-largest Spanish-speaking nation in the world, has been enriched by Latino culture.

Taking Another Look

1. What was one of the first kinds of Latino music to become popular in the United States?

2. Why did more Latinos appear in movies and television shows during the 1970s and 1980s?

3. **Critical Thinking** Why do you think Latino directors such as Luis Valdez believed that it was important to make movies for the broad U.S. market, rather than for mainly Latino audiences?

LOOKING AHEAD

Latino writers, artists, and musicians have made a permanent mark on the culture of the United States. Their influence continued to grow through the 1990s, as the Latino population of the United States increased. The challenges and triumphs of the Latino people will become one of the most important influences as the United States moves into the 21st century.

The goal . . . [is] to get our hands on every piece of Hispanic literature that we can find.

That is how Nicolás Kanellos (kah-NEH-yohs) described a project called Recovering the Hispanic Literary Heritage of the United States. The project fulfills a 20-year-old dream held by Kanellos. With a 1992 grant from the Rockefeller Foundation and other foundations, Kanellos has launched a massive search for Latino literature from colonial times to 1960.

As a Professor of Spanish at Indiana University during the 1970s, Kanellos searched for a way to give a "voice to multiethnic Hispanic authors." First, he founded what is today *The Americas Review,* a highly respected literary journal. Then, in 1979, he founded Arte Público—the oldest and largest U.S. publisher of Latino literature.

Now based at the University of Houston, Arte Público has published some of the best-known contemporary Latino writers. With the grants he has received, Kanellos hopes to publish the talented Latino writers of the past. Program director Tomás Ybarra-Frausto predicts:

The fruits of this literary recovery project will broaden . . . what is studied . . . from kindergarten to graduate school.

CLOSE UP: Chapter 24

The Who, What, Where of History

1. **Who** is Antonio Martorell?
2. **Who** is Celia Vice?
3. **What** is the *Instituto de Cultura Puertorriqueña?*
4. **Where** is the Nuyorican Poets Cafe?
5. **What** role did *I Am Joaquín* play in the Chicano Renaissance?
6. **Who** were some of the leading chicano muralists?
7. **What** were some of the musical styles introduced to the United States by Latinos?
8. **Who** is Carlos Santana?
9. **Who** was Roberto Clemente?

Making the Connection

1. What was the connection between the *Instituto de Cultura Puertorriqueña* and Puerto Rican culture?
2. What was the connection between the Cuban Revolution and some of the earliest works of Cuban American writers?
3. What was the connection between *El Movimiento* and the Chicano Renaissance?

Time Check

1. Which decade saw a burst of cultural activities among nuyoricans, Cuban Americans, and Chicanos: 1940s, 1950s, or 1960s?
2. Which started *first*: *El Movimiento* or the Chicano Renaissance?
3. In what year did Congress honor the achievements of Roberto Clemente?

What Would You Have Done?

1. Imagine that you are a historian. Your assignment is to assess the Latino cultural movements of the 1960s. What common goal, if any, would you say these movements shared?

2. Imagine that you are Luis Valdez and it is 1969—the year he made his first film. What subject would you have chosen for your film? Explain.

Thinking and Writing About History

1. Write a review announcing the opening of the Nuyorican Poets Cafe that might have run in a Latino newspaper.

2. Write a poem entitled "Exile" from the perspective of a Cuban in the 1960s.

3. Review information on *La Causa* and *El Movimiento* in Chapter 22. Then design a poster that a Chicano artist might have drawn to promote one of the goals of these movements.

4. Write a two-minute radio commentary about the influence Latino music has had in the United States. Entitle your commentary: "The Musical Conquest of the United States."

Building Skills: Understanding Points of View

Every author has a *point of view,* or a particular way of looking at things. A person's point of view is influenced by his or her experiences, family, education, reading, and friends. An individual's point of view is also shaped, in part, by the times in which he or she lives. When you read a piece of fiction, a history book, a poem, or a biography, you need to be aware of the author's point of view.

Chicano writers in the 1960s took a bold view of their role in U.S. culture. Their works announced a cultural independence shaped by *El Movimiento*. Read the following lines from a poem written by Sergio Elizondo (eh-lee-SOHN-doh), and think about his point of view.

I, sir, am a Chicano,
because that is the name
        I gave myself.
No one gave me that name
I heard it and I have it.

        . . . .

American of Spanish
        descent,
What is that, my brother?
How long and empty it
                sounds.

1. Why does the poet favor the use of the term Chicano?

2. What is the poet's opinion of the phrase "American of Spanish descent"?

3. In what ways does the poem appeal to Mexican American pride?

4. Some Mexican Americans reject the word *Chicano.* What reasons can you suggest for their reactions?

Express Yourself!

Reread the information about Chicano art on page 314. Work with three or four classmates to create a community mural. On a large sheet of paper, use pictures and words to describe your community. You may draw your own pictures or cut out pictures from magazines or newspapers. Display your finished mural in the class.

UNIT 7

LATINOS TODAY

(1980–Present)

Mural by Dominican artist

Secretary of Housing and Urban Development, Henry Cisneros

Chapter

25 Mexican Americans Today
    (1980–Present)

26 Puerto Ricans Today
    (1980–Present)

27 Cuban Americans Today
    (1980–Present)

28 Central Americans and
    Dominicans Today
    (1980–Present)

29 South Americans in the
    United States Today
    (1980–Present)

30 Toward a New Century
    (1990–2000)

THE BIG PICTURE

Voices of the Times

Immigration. . . . It's a historical movement. People are coming up. They're diligent [hardworking] people. They need to, they want to be paid for their services. This [the United States] is a place where there's food and work and possibilities for a future.

— Ricardo Aguilar Melantzón, professor,
University of Texas at El Paso, 1990

Unit 7 brings the story of Latinos in the United States up to the present. It describes the great political, cultural, and social changes that are taking place as the nation moves toward a new century.

In The United States

When the results of the 1990 census were released, U.S. citizens realized how much the nation had changed in the ten years since the last census. Of its 249 million people, the percentage listed as white had dropped to 71.3. African Americans were now 12.1 percent of the population, up from 11.7 percent. The percentage of people of Latino origin had grown by about a third, to 9 percent. The percentage of people of Asian descent had almost doubled, to 2.9 percent.

These figures helped demonstrate the changing nature of U.S. society. The United States had once been thought of as a melting pot. In that melting pot, the cultures of the nation's many different ethnic groups were supposed to mix to make one "American" culture.

By the 1990s, however, a new image was replacing the melting pot. Now, it seemed, the United States was more like a multicultural rainbow. All groups still contributed to making one, united nation. But those groups were seen as individual, each keeping much of its special culture. This new image of the United States began to have an effect on the politics and economy of the nation.

A Conservative Mood. In the 1980s, many U.S. citizens became less interested in the drive for social justice that had marked the 1960s and early 1970s. They resented having to pay high taxes to support social programs such as welfare, public housing, and unemployment benefits. Ronald Reagan, a former governor of California who had once been a movie actor, became President in 1981. Reagan's policies reflected a new conservative mood in the nation, one that demanded fewer government programs and less government spending.

Reagan cut both taxes and government spending for social programs. The tax cuts greatly reduced the government's income. However, the nation's military spending rose steeply at the same time. Thus, the government had to borrow billions to pay its bills. This added to the huge **budget deficit,** in which the government was spending much more than it was taking in. The cuts in social programs hurt the poor, including many Latinos and African Americans.

President Reagan also took a conservative stand on civil rights. He was against **affirmative action** programs. Under these programs the federal government had required the hiring of women and

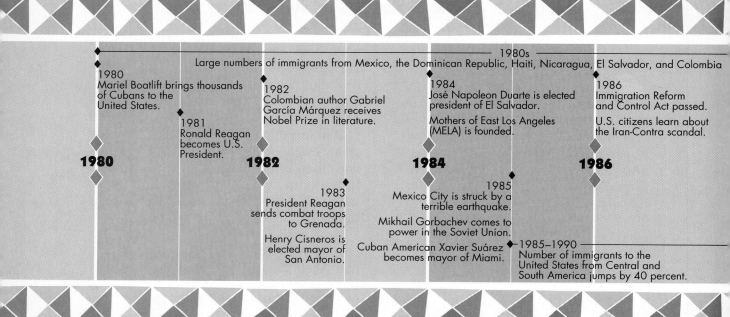

1980s
Large numbers of immigrants from Mexico, the Dominican Republic, Haiti, Nicaragua, El Salvador, and Colombia

1980
Mariel Boatlift brings thousands of Cubans to the United States.

1981
Ronald Reagan becomes U.S. President.

1982
Colombian author Gabriel García Márquez receives Nobel Prize in literature.

1984
José Napoleon Duarte is elected president of El Salvador.

Mothers of East Los Angeles (MELA) is founded.

1986
Immigration Reform and Control Act passed.

U.S. citizens learn about the Iran-Contra scandal.

1980

1982

1984

1986

1983
President Reagan sends combat troops to Grenada.

Henry Cisneros is elected mayor of San Antonio.

1985
Mexico City is struck by a terrible earthquake.

Mikhail Gorbachev comes to power in the Soviet Union.

Cuban American Xavier Suárez becomes mayor of Miami.

1985–1990
Number of immigrants to the United States from Central and South America jumps by 40 percent.

members of ethnic minorities to correct the effects of years of discrimination. He opposed busing to integrate the schools. The President did, however, appoint Lauro Cavazos (kah-VAH-sohs), Jr., as secretary of education, making him the first Latino member of a U.S. Cabinet.

The Prosperous 1980s. During Reagan's time in office, the country experienced the longest economic boom in U.S. history. The boom was especially visible in the Sunbelt, the states of the South and the West. Many computer and other high-tech companies brought prosperity to the region.

At the same time, however, the older cities of the Northeast and the Middle West went into a long decline. Their outdated factories often could not compete with newer, more efficient plants in other places. They contained growing numbers of unemployed workers, many of whom finally moved west or south to find work.

Most Latinos and African Americans did not share in the general prosperity of the times. Many were jobless. Many found themselves locked in the *barrios* and crumbling neighborhoods of the cities. Others were victims of the high crime rates there.

Controlling Immigration. During the 1980s, large numbers of immigrants from Mexico, the Dominican Republic, Haiti, Nicaragua, El Salvador, Colombia, and Asia entered the United States. This alarmed some U.S. citizens. They worried that the immigrants were taking jobs away from native-born citizens. They also feared that social-service programs were being strained to their limit. Experts pointed out, however, that the productivity and labor of new immigrants generally contributed more to the nation than the immigrants took from it.

Many people were also concerned about the large number of immigrants who entered the country illegally. The

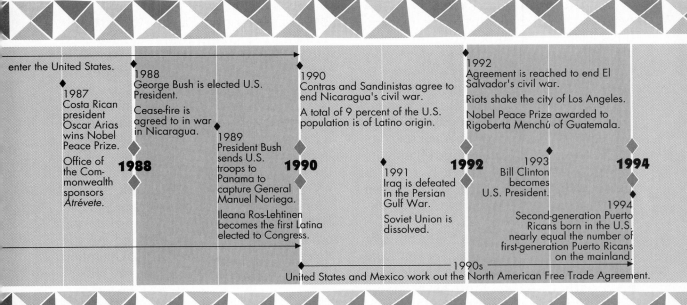

enter the United States.

1987
Costa Rican president Oscar Arias wins Nobel Peace Prize.

Office of the Commonwealth sponsors *Atrévete.*

1988

1988
George Bush is elected U.S. President.

Cease-fire is agreed to in war in Nicaragua.

1989
President Bush sends U.S. troops to Panama to capture General Manuel Noriega.

Ileana Ros-Lehtinen becomes the first Latina elected to Congress.

1990

1990
Contras and Sandinistas agree to end Nicaragua's civil war.

A total of 9 percent of the U.S. population is of Latino origin.

1991
Iraq is defeated in the Persian Gulf War.

Soviet Union is dissolved.

1992
Agreement is reached to end El Salvador's civil war.

Riots shake the city of Los Angeles.

Nobel Peace Prize awarded to Rigoberta Menchú of Guatemala.

1992

1993
Bill Clinton becomes U.S. President.

1994

1994
Second-generation Puerto Ricans born in the U.S. nearly equal the number of first-generation Puerto Ricans on the mainland.

1990s
United States and Mexico work out the North American Free Trade Agreement.

Immigration Reform and Control Act of 1986 granted amnesty, or a pardon, to undocumented immigrants who had come to the United States before January 1, 1982. The act also gave them a chance to apply for citizenship. At the same time, it set stiff penalties for employers who knowingly hired illegal immigrants.

Fighting Communism. In the early years of the Reagan administration, Cold War tensions rose again. President Reagan feared the spread of communism. He called the Soviet Union an "evil empire" and sped a U.S. military buildup.

Reagan cut off U.S. aid to the Sandinista government of Nicaragua. He took that action because the Sandinistas were backed by Cuba and the Soviet Union and because their programs had taken over businesses and private property in Nicaragua. Reagan supported the Nicaraguan Contras. They were rebels fighting to topple the Sandinistas.

Some people feared U.S. involvement in Nicaragua would lead to another war like that in Vietnam. Others believed that some Sandinista policies were necessary to improve conditions in Nicaragua.

In 1986, Americans were shocked to learn about what became known as the **Iran-Contra scandal.** The U.S. government had secretly sold arms to Iran, despite its own ban on such sales. It had then used the profits from the Iran deal to secretly arm the Contras. That was illegal because Congress had forbidden giving military aid to the Contras.

The Reagan administration also sent arms and military advisers to El Salvador. Its government was under attack by rebels who received aid from Nicaragua, Cuba, and the Soviet Union. In 1983, Reagan sent combat troops to the Caribbean island of Grenada when a radical group with Cuban ties took control of the government. The troops remained until a pro-U.S. government was elected.

323

The End of the Cold War. In 1985, a new leader, Mikhail Gorbachev (GOHR-buh-chawf), came to power in the Soviet Union. Economic conditions were very bad by this point. Gorbachev was forced to make sweeping reforms that resulted in much greater freedom for the people. By 1989, the weakness of the Soviet Union was so great that the Cold War was coming to an end. Communist governments toppled throughout Eastern Europe. In 1991, the Soviet Union itself was dissolved and replaced by a commonwealth of independent states.

The breakup of the Soviet Union brought an economic crisis to Cuba. As you have read, the United States refused to do business with Cuba so long as Castro's Communist government remained in power. Thus, the island nation had come to depend on the Soviet Union for trade and investment. With the Soviet Union's breakup, Cuba searched desperately for ways to increase its foreign trade.

The End of Good Times. The prosperity of the Reagan years had ended by 1990. The boom turned into a severe **recession,** or downturn in business. More and more Americans joined the ranks of the jobless and homeless.

The nation also woke up to the fact that it was saddled with a record-breaking budget deficit of $3.2 trillion. Adding to the nation's economic woes was the failure of hundreds of savings and loan associations. The government had to spend billions of dollars to protect the deposits of the associations' customers.

Action in Foreign Affairs. Reagan's Vice-President, George Bush, was elected President in 1988. During the campaign, Bush had said he hoped to take action on the nation's domestic problems. Instead, foreign affairs took up much of his time.

Late in 1989, President Bush sent 12,000 U.S. troops to Panama to overthrow and capture General Manuel Noriega (noh-ree-Eh-gah). Noriega was wanted in the United States on drug-trafficking charges. Although Noriega was convicted in U.S. court, many Panamanians and other Latin Americans resented the strong-arm tactics used to capture him.

In 1990, Saddam Hussein (hoo-SAYN), the ruler of Iraq, invaded the oil-rich country of Kuwait, on the Persian Gulf. After an economic boycott failed to move Saddam Hussein, the United States and several other UN members attacked and quickly defeated Iraq in an action called Operation Desert Storm.

Hard Times and Violence. The glow of victory in the Persian Gulf War soon faded. The nation's economic woes grew worse. The government reported that the number of people living in poverty was the highest since the early 1960s.

Critics warned that a lack of government programs to aid the poor and ethnic minorities was adding to the anger and despair among those groups. That anger and despair exploded into violence in Los Angeles in April 1992. Four white police officers had been charged with brutally beating an African American man. A widely shown videotape of the beating had convinced many people that the officers were guilty. The not-guilty verdicts in the case sparked days of looting, burning, and gunfire in mostly African American and Latino sections of the city. The violence brought new calls for programs to aid the cities.

A New Direction. In 1993, Democrat Bill Clinton took office as President. He had campaigned to reverse the policies of the Reagan-Bush years and make the federal government more active in social programs. He set about creating programs to

LATINO POPULATION IN THE UNITED STATES TODAY

Population (1990 Census)
- Under 100,000
- 100,000–399,999
- 400,000–999,999
- 1,000,000 or more

This map illustrates the current distribution of Latinos in the United States. Which states have over a million Latinos in their populations?

improve the economy, and provide affordable health care. He also appointed more women, Latinos, and African Americans to important government posts.

Taking Another Look

1. What conservative policies did President Reagan put into effect?

2. What military actions did the United States undertake while President Bush was in office?

3. **Critical Thinking** In what ways do you think that immigrants contribute to the United States?

◆◆ In Latin America ◆◆

Many of the same forces that acted on the United States during the 1980s and 1990s affected the nations of Latin America as well. Changing economic conditions and the end of the Cold War had major impacts on the region. Relations between the United States and Latin American nations were difficult at times, but there were signs of improvement.

Growing Democracy. As in other parts of the world during the 1980s, democracy was on the rise in Latin America. Elected governments replaced military dictatorships in Argentina, Ecuador, Bolivia, Peru, Uruguay, Chile, and Guatemala. Democratic government in Venezuela and Colombia dated back to the 1960s.

Democracy also took a step forward in Mexico. Since 1929, Mexico's elected government had been controlled by one party, the *Partido Revolucionario Institucional* (PRI). In the 1980s, however, several opposition parties began to challenge the PRI's dominance.

325

Bringing Peace to Central America.

In February 1987, Oscar Arias (AH-ree-ahs), the president of Costa Rica, took a bold step. He put forward a peace plan aimed at ending the fighting between the Sandinistas and the Contras in neighboring Nicaragua.

Costa Rica itself was a successful democracy with a strong tradition of providing social services for its people. Arias's plan reflected a widespread Latin American belief that peace should come from within the region rather than being imposed from the outside by the United States. For his efforts, he was awarded the Nobel Peace Prize of 1987.

Early in 1988, the left-wing president of Nicaragua, Daniel Ortega (ohr-TEH-gah), agreed to a cease-fire and peace talks with the Contras. In February 1990, the Sandinista government held a national election in hopes of ending the war. When Violeta Chamorro (chah-MOH-rroh), the opposition candidate, defeated Ortega, both sides agreed to stop fighting, and work to rebuild the shattered nation.

In El Salvador, the 1984 election of a moderate president, José Napoleon Duarte (DWAHR-teh), fueled hopes for an end to the civil war there. But Duarte failed to bring about much-needed land reform. Nor could he control the "death squads" that included many members of the Salvadoran military. These squads killed thousands of people in what they claimed was a struggle against communism.

Peace efforts continued, however, led by the Peruvian diplomat and secretary-general of the United Nations, Javier Pérez de Cuéllar (KWEH-yahr). Finally, in January 1992, the Salvadoran government and the rebels signed a peace agreement. The rebels promised to lay down their arms. The government, meanwhile, agreed to cut back its armed forces and give land to the peasants.

Economic Progress and Problems.

In the 1980s, governments of the various Latin American countries continued to promote industrial growth. They invested in factories turning out products like automobiles and home appliances. To widen the market for these goods, the governments lowered trade barriers with neighboring countries, while raising tariffs on goods imported from outside the region. Thanks to vigorous efforts by their governments, Brazil, Mexico, Argentina, and Venezuela became the region's leading industrial nations.

This development came at a high cost, however. All four countries borrowed heavily from banks in the United States and Western Europe. By the early 1980s, they had become four of the world's biggest debtor nations. They were also having difficulty repaying their debts.

Mexico, for example, had counted on the sale of oil to pay its debts. Mexico was the world's fourth largest oil producer. But a slump in world oil prices sent Mexico into an economic crisis. To make matters worse, terrible earthquakes struck Mexico in 1985. They caused thousands of deaths and billions of dollars in damage.

Economic hardships and political conflicts in Latin America led many people to leave the region in the 1980s. Many *indocumentados* (een-doh-koo-men-TAH-dohs)—undocumented workers—crossed the border into the United States. They kept coming despite the Immigration Reform and Control Act of 1986 (see page 323).

Changing Times.

By the mid–1990s, however, many of the Latin American countries were on the road to economic recovery. They had brought their rates of inflation down and were paying off their huge debts. In Mexico, in particular, industry was booming.

Many U.S. companies had set up factories in Mexico, where labor costs were cheaper than in the United States. In addition, Mexicans looked forward to a new agreement with the United States and Canada. Under this North American Free Trade Agreement, taxes and other laws limiting trade would be reduced and goods could move freely between the three countries. Mexicans hoped the agreement would open up new markets in the United States and Canada for their products.

After 500 Years. Despite the challenges and problems that remain, Latin Americans can point with pride to all they have accomplished in the 500 years since Columbus's first voyage. The rest of the world is paying increasing attention to those accomplishments.

In 1992, the Nobel Peace Prize went to Rigoberta Menchú (men-CHOOH), a Quiché Indian from Guatemala. Five years earlier, as you have read, that prize had gone to Oscar Arias, the president of Costa Rica. In 1990, the Nobel Prize in literature was awarded to the Mexican writer Octavio Paz (PAHS). In 1982, Gabriel García Márquez, the Colombian author, received the literature award.

Such awards are recognition of what is perhaps the greatest accomplishment of the past 500 years. That is the creation of rich new cultures in Latin America. In those cultures, the distinctive contributions of the Native American, European, and African peoples who shaped them remain clear.

Taking Another Look

1. What role did Oscar Arias play in bringing peace to Central America?

2. What factors contributed to hard economic times in Latin America in the 1980s?

3. **Critical Thinking** What signs were there that Latin America was in better shape economically in the 1990s than it was in the 1980s?

Past experiences with the United States left many people in Latin America suspicious of U.S. actions. Thousands of demonstrators gathered in Brazil to protest U.S. environmental policy during the Earth Summit there in 1992.

"We're not going to take it anymore!" said the Mothers of East Los Angeles when they heard of plans to build another prison in the neighborhood. How did they manage to stop the building?

Mexican Americans Today

(1980–Present)

THINKING ABOUT THE CHAPTER

What challenges face Mexican Americans as the nation heads into a new century?

The congregation boiled with anger when the pastor at the Roman Catholic Church of the Resurrection, told them alarming news in 1984. The state planned to crowd an eighth prison into their neighborhood of East Los Angeles.

This news moved women in the parish, such as Juana Gutiérrez to take action. They formed an organization called the Mothers of East Los Angeles (MELA). As MELA moved to block the prison, the state released more alarming news. In 1985, it announced plans to build the state's first giant hazardous-waste incinerator in the middle of East Los Angeles. "So there it was, plain and clear," said Aurora Castillo (kahs-TEE-yoh), who had joined with Gutiérrez in MELA. "Dump it all in our backyard!"

SECTIONS

1 A Tale of Three Cities

2 The Lure of *El Norte*

For the next six years, Castillo, Gutiérrez, and other members of MELA battled the state legislature. They organized protest marches and held midnight candle vigils. In the end, MELA kept both the prison and the incinerator out of their neighborhood. This chapter tells the story of other struggles and triumphs of Mexican Americans like the women of MELA.

1 A TALE OF THREE CITIES

◆ What is life like for the Mexican
◆ American populations of San Antonio, Los Angeles, and New York?

Imagine it is 1910. You are talking to an older Mexican man who has just arrived in the United States from south of the border. What if you told him that within his grandchildren's lifetime, millions of his fellow citizens would be living in the big cities of the United States.

"Impossible," he would insist. He probably thinks you are out of your mind, but is too polite to tell you so. After all, he would remind you, people whose ancestors were from Mexico would be country people. They would not be comfortable in the narrow streets and tall buildings of urban United States.

Times have changed faster than that man from 1910 could have imagined. The living proof is that today San Antonio, Los Angeles, and New York City have more residents with Mexican backgrounds than many cities in the land of their ancestors.

San Antonio. "The most Mexican of any U.S. city that does not sit directly on the border." That is how a reporter for *Newsweek* magazine described San Antonio, Texas. The 1990 Census seemed to uphold the description. About 48 per-

1983	Henry Cisneros elected Mayor of San Antonio.
1984	Founding of Mothers of East Los Angeles (MELA).
1986	U.S. Congress passes Immigration Reform Act.
1990	Census finds Mexican Americans making up 47.6 percent of people in San Antonio and 4.4 million Spanish-speaking people in Los Angeles.
	United States builds a steel fence to the west of El Paso attempting to stop migration from Mexico.
1991	Gloria Molina wins seat on Los Angeles County Board of Supervisors.
1993	Maquiladoras in Mexico border region number more than 1,000 and employ more than 600,000 people.

cent of the city's population, or more than 520,000 people, trace their roots to Mexico. San Antonio ranks as the nation's fourth-largest Latino city. Only Los Angeles, New York, and Miami have larger Latino populations.

The Flavor of Mexico. Evidence of close ties with Mexico are found everywhere in San Antonio. One of the city's two largest papers, the *San Antonio Light*, prints a daily weather map of Mexico. The city's top radio station, KXTN Tejano 107 FM, has made *tejano* music one of the hottest sounds in Texas. *Tejano* musicians such as Selena Quintanilla (keen-tah-NEE-yah) trace their musical roots directly to the *música de cantina* (MOO-see-kah deh kahn-TEE-nah) played in Mexican cafes. Also popular is Radio XEG, which broadcasts Mexican music straight from Monterrey, Mexico.

San Antonio's Mexican American population is young. Nearly 41 percent are under age 18. Another 28 percent are between 18 and 34. But these young people come from a well-established Mexican American community. Most families have lived in San Antonio for 30 years or more. They speak easily in both Spanish and English and expect their elected officials to do the same.

Mexican American voters in San Antonio first made their political power felt in the 1960s. At that time, they backed José Angel Gutiérrez and his new party, *La Raza Unida* (see page 290). In 1983, they elected Henry Cisneros (sees-NEH-rohs) as mayor, a position that put him in the national spotlight. (For more on Cisneros, see Chapter 30.) In 1992, voters in the San Antonio *barrio* sent Frank Tejeda (teh-HEH-dah) to Congress.

Today, Mexican American leaders in San Antonio are among the strongest backers of a plan to increase trade with Mexico (see page 335). "We are in the

Henry Cisneros is part of a generation of Latino leaders who came to power in the 1980s. Then mayor of San Antonio, Cisneros now holds a high position in the Clinton administration. What position does he now hold?

right place at the right time," says one leader. "We've got the Mexican American talent to make free trade a reality."

Los Angeles. No other city in the United States has a larger Latino population than Los Angeles, the "City of the Angels." Some 4.4 million Spanish-speaking people call Los Angeles home. Most of them have Mexican roots. Like San Antonio, the Latinos of Los Angeles are young. More than 37 percent are under age 18. Nearly 75 percent of Latinos in the city trace their origins to Mexico.

Mexican author Carlos Fuentes (FWEN-tes) points to the many gifts Mexican immigrants have brought to the city—foods, music, artistic styles, and a belief in *respeto* (res-PEH-toh), or respect. He also mentions language. "Los Angeles is now the second-largest Spanish city in the world," declares Fuentes. "We should rejoice in the culture we [Anglos and Mexicans] are creating together."

Changing East Los Angeles. This blend of cultures is clearest in thriving Mexican American East Los Angeles communities. Lynwood and Santa Fe Springs are two such communities. Through the efforts of groups like the Mothers of East Los Angeles (MELA), Mexican Americans have cleaned up entire blocks of East Los Angeles. Today well-kept houses and parks dot the area. Mexican stores and restaurants line the streets. So do dozens of Mexican speciality shops and local branches of Mexican banks.

Observers have said that such change has come about through hard work and the Mexican belief in *la familia,* or the family. Of all the ethnic groups in Los Angeles, Mexican Americans are the least likely to rely on public assistance. In 94 percent of all households, at least one family member holds a full-time job. Mexican American families are also twice as likely as other groups to live in two-parent households. Often, everyone over age 18 works to support the whole family.

A Political Voice. Because of the civil rights movements of the 1960s, Mexican Americans found a new political voice. When the Mothers of East Los Angeles needed help fighting the California legislature, Gloria Molina was there to join the fight.

The oldest of 10 children, **Gloria Molina** (moh - LEE - nah) grew up in the city of Pico Rivera, near Los Angeles. Her college years exposed Molina to the ideals of *La Causa.*

In 1991, voters in East Los Angeles chose Molina to speak for them. In a historic election, Molina won a seat on the powerful Los Angeles County Board of Supervisors. She was the first Latina to hold that position in 116 years—and the first woman ever.

Heading to New York. The sound of Spanish is nothing new in New York City. Puerto Ricans have long spoken the language there. But in the 1980s and 1990s, a new Spanish accent was heard on the streets as some 200,000 Mexicans migrated to New York.

Mexican Americans, such as radio correspondent María Hinojosa (ee-noh-HOH-sah), now feel at home in the city. But, explains this native of Mexico City, it was not that way when she first came to New York.

> When I arrived in New York in 1979, ... what a culture shock! ... Nowhere to get real tortillas; no chilis. And none of the Latinos had my accent!

These things are no longer true. Today fast-food vendors sell Mexican foods on the streets. Mexican music can be heard at the popular Roseland Ballroom. Each weekend Mexican bands such as *Los Tigres del Norte* play popular songs from "south of the border." A city-wide soccer league called *La Liga Mexicana de Fútbol* boasts some 42 teams.

Most new arrivals work at low-paying jobs. Many are *indocumentados* (een-doh-koo-men-TAH-dohs), who are forced to take whatever work they can find. Like other Mexican migrants, they usually send at least part of their wages home. Sometimes this money helps support entire villages. As time passes, many of the new arrivals become permanent residents of the community.

Taking Another Look

1. Why do some observers call San Antonio one of the nation's "most Mexican cities"?

2. What changes have Mexican Americans brought to Los Angeles and New York?

3. **Critical Thinking** One Mexican American predicted that heavy Mexican immigration to the United States would continue for years to come. Do you think this is true? Why or why not?

2 THE LURE OF *EL NORTE*

◆ Why have large numbers of Mexicans risked danger to come to the United States?

A thin man known only as Juan whispers: *"¡La línea divisoria!"* ("The dividing line!") Rosa and her children stare nervously at the waters of the Rio Grande. Juan earns his living as a *pollero* (poh-YEH-roh), or **coyote.** These are people who guide migrants without the necessary immigration papers across the border from Mexico to the United States. Juan gets $150 from each of the people he leads across the river. Rosa hands over the money sent by her husband, who is already in the United States.

Juan keeps watch for *la migra* (MEE-grah), the border guards of the Immigration and Naturalization Service (INS). He quickly blows up an old rubber raft. Then he signals Rosa and her children to make a dash for the river. Here everybody piles onto the raft. Juan paddles hard against the current. Once on the other side, he points to a hole in a chain-link fence that lines the muddy bank. Rosa and her children scramble through the hole and take their first steps onto U.S. soil.

Border Traffic. Such stories are repeated time and again as thousands of Mexicans attempt each year to slip across the 2,000-mile [3,200-kilometer] border between the United States and Mexico. Some like Rosa and her children, make the crossing with the help of coyotes such as Juan.

Other migrants make the journey on their own, wading across shallow parts of the Rio Grande. Still others, on the Mexican shore opposite El Paso, Texas,

A procession at the festival of the Virgin of Guadaloupe, held, not in the Southwestern United States but in Brooklyn, New York. There are more than 200,000 people of Mexican origin living in New York City.

wait for a chance to sprint across the Santa Fe Railroad bridge. Hundreds of miles to the west, many migrants race across the six-lane Interstate Highway 5 south of San Diego in a bid to reach the United States.

Once in the United States, *indocumentados* live in constant fear of *la migra*. Most undocumented migrants hold jobs and send their children to public schools. But for the most part, they do not stray far from the *barrios* where they live. Explains one undocumented worker, "If we can't show proof that we are legal, we've had it."

La Frontera. The area through which the undocumented immigrants pass is known as *La Frontera* (frohn-TEH-rah), or "the Frontier." Along this border region, U.S. and Mexican ways intermingle (See Focus On, page 336). But so do problems. When unemployment or inflation goes up in Mexico, so does the number of undocumented workers in U.S. border towns.

The United States tried to solve the problem of undocumented migration through the Immigration Reform Act of 1986 (see page 323). This law provides amnesty, or a general pardon, for **aliens,** citizens of another country, who could prove they had lived in the United States since January 1, 1982. At the same time, the act fined employers who hired undocumented workers.

The law has had mixed effects. Some 3.1 million aliens won amnesty. More than 2 million Mexicans were among them. However, many undocumented migrants did not have the necessary proof that they had lived in the United States since 1982. As a result, millions of migrants fall outside the law.

There are many critics of the 1986 immigration act. One such group is the Mexican American Legal Defense and Education Fund (MALDEF). It charges that the law's heavy fines have kept employers from hiring *any* Latinos, even legal immigrants or U.S. citizens. In addition, the law gave employers a weapon. It was possible for them to threaten undocumented workers with exposure if they demanded higher pay or better working conditions.

While debate raged over the act, in 1990 the United States built a 13-mile (21-kilometer) steel fence to the west of El Paso, the most heavily crossed portion of the border. But the fence did little to stop migration. In 1992, as dozens of children played near a hole in the fence, one border guard shrugged and said, "It stops no one."

A Changing Border Zone. What *has* slowed migration is the rise of ***maquiladoras*** (mah-kee-lah-DOH-rahs), or assembly plants, on the Mexican side of the border. In the mid–1960s, in an effort to bring jobs and U.S. dollars to its economy, Mexico invited U.S. companies to build assembly plants on the Mexican side of the border. U.S. companies saw the plants as a way to cut costs through the use of inexpensive labor.

Since 1965, the number of *maquiladoras* in the border region has grown from 12 to more than 1,000. By 1993, they employed about 600,000 workers. The factories turn out assembled parts for everything from children's games to electronic equipment.

The rise of the *maquiladoras* has helped business on both sides of the border. One Mexican American from the border area explained the effect that the *maquiladoras* have had on El Paso:

> A lot of our neighbors . . . have come from the North to manage the *maquiladora* industries that are being set up across the border in Juárez.
> . . . For every twelve *maquila* jobs created in Juárez, one job is created in El Paso. . . . The popular feeling is that the *maquiladora* program is here to stay.

However, the *maquiladoras* have their critics, too. The factories provide work. Yet wages are low and working conditions are poor. Most *maquiladora* workers receive

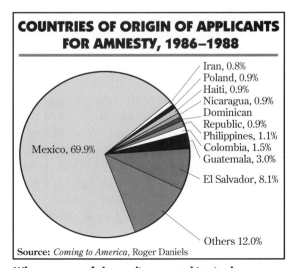

COUNTRIES OF ORIGIN OF APPLICANTS FOR AMNESTY, 1986–1988

Iran, 0.8%
Poland, 0.9%
Haiti, 0.9%
Nicaragua, 0.9%
Dominican Republic, 0.9%
Philippines, 1.1%
Colombia, 1.5%
Guatemala, 3.0%
El Salvador, 8.1%
Mexico, 69.9%
Others 12.0%

Source: *Coming to America,* Roger Daniels

What percent of the applicants on this pie chart have Latin American countries of origin?

Inside a Mexican *maquiladora*. What arguments are given by supporters and opponents of *maquiladoras*? With which side do you agree?

only about one dollar per hour. Many people also criticize the *maquiladoras* for polluting the air and water of the border region.

A Free-Trade Zone. To solve such problems and to promote economic growth, the United States and Mexico opened the 1990s by working out the North American Free Trade Agreement (NAFTA). When it goes into effect, the United States, Mexico, and Canada will join together in the world's largest free-trade region. In a free trade region, goods pass from one country to another without any tariffs, or taxes. These tariffs raise the price to the consumer.

The talk of closer ties between Mexico and the United States came at a time when the Mexican American population topped 13.3 million people. This was a gain of 10 million since 1960. Continued migration and agreements such as NAFTA promise to increase the influence of Mexican Americans in the decades ahead.

Taking Another Look

1. How did the 1986 Immigration Reform Act attempt to solve the problem of undocumented immigration?

2. Have U.S. attempts to slow illegal immigration from Mexico been effective? Explain your answer.

3. **Critical Thinking** Why do undocumented aliens risk the danger of coming to the United States, with the fear of being caught and expelled?

LOOKING AHEAD

One of the groups that Mexican Americans in New York City come in contact with is what has traditionally been the city's largest Latino group—the Puerto Ricans. In the 1990s, many Puerto Ricans are spreading out across the United States. Others are returning to Puerto Rico. This migration is extending the reach of Puerto Rican culture.

Eight times a day, dozens of people in El Paso pile aboard red-and-green trolley cars nicknamed Border Jumpers. In 1992 alone, more than 40,000 people made the 12-mile day trip into El Paso's twin city—Juárez, Mexico. Many of the riders are El Paso students interested in learning more about Spanish, Mexican, and Native American influences on the region.

Tour guides aboard the trolleys highlight dozens of cultural landmarks that link El Paso and Juárez. Along El Paso's famous Mission Trail, they point out white-washed missions built by the Spanish. The chain of missions continues into Juárez. Here, guides stop beside Our Lady of Guadalupe Mission Church. Built in the 1600s, the mission shows the blend of Spanish and Native American styles. This blend is based on the *mestizo* heritage of Mexico.

In Juárez, people jump off the trolleys to tour the old section of the city. Some of the people are tourists. Others are Mexican Americans from El Paso interested in picking up goods or visiting friends in Juárez.

Investors on both sides of the border hope to offer a similar service to the people of Juárez. When it is approved, the El Paso-Juárez Trolley Company will have blazed a new trail in goodwill throughout *La Frontera* (The Border).

CLOSE UP: Chapter 25

The Who, What, Where of History

1. **What** is the MELA?
2. **What** is *tejano* music?
3. **Who** is Henry Cisneros?
4. **Where** is the largest Latino population in the United States located?
5. **Who** is Gloria Molina?
6. **Who** are *la migra?*
7. **Where** is *La Frontera* located?
8. **What** are some parts of the Immigration Reform Act of 1986?
9. **What** is amnesty?
10. **What** are *maquiladoras*?
11. **What** is the North American Free Trade Agreement?

Making the Connection

1. What is the connection between the belief in *la familia* and the success of the Mexican American community in East Los Angeles?
2. What are some of the connections linking U.S. and Mexican border towns?
3. What is the connection between the Immigration Reform Act and increases in the Mexican American population?
4. What is the connection between *maquiladoras* and the North American Free Trade Agreement?
5. What is the connection between the North American Free Trade Agreement and increased business opportunities for Mexican Americans?

Time Check

1. Which came *first*—the Immigration Reform Act or the North American Free Trade Agreement?

2. When did the *maquiladora* program begin?

3. In what year did Latinos elect the first Latina member of the Los Angeles County Board of Supervisors?

4. What years saw the large-scale arrival of Mexican migrants in New York City?

What Would You Have Done?

1. Suppose you were a member of Congress in 1986. Would you have voted for or against the Immigration Reform Act? Explain reasons for your decision. Support your arguments by using the U.S. Constitution or Bill of Rights.

2. Imagine you are a Mexican American small-business owner in El Paso. How would you respond to President Clinton's 1993 decision to support the North American Trade Agreement? Why?

3. Suppose you are a Mexican migrant. In which of the following cities would you choose to settle: San Antonio, Los Angeles, or New York? Explain.

Thinking and Writing About History

1. Draft a petition that the Mothers of East Los Angeles might send to the California legislature. Keep in mind that a petition is meant to gather the signatures of voters.

2. In recent years, Mexican migrants have captured their experiences in the form of ballads, or poems sung to music. Write a ballad about a border crossing.

Building Skills: Identifying Valid Generalizations

Not all generalizations are *valid,* or true. Sometimes people misinterpret facts and form *invalid,* or faulty, generalizations. Other times, new facts turn up. When tested against those facts, a generalization may no longer be true.

Historians frequently weigh generalizations about the past. They study historical statistics to determine the accuracy of a statement.

Below are a number of generalizations about the people who applied for amnesty under the Immigration Reform Act of 1986. Using the statistics in the circle graph on page 334, decide whether each of these generalizations is valid. Cite statistics from the graph that prove your answer.

1. Most applicants for amnesty came from outside the Americas.

2. Few Spanish-speaking people applied for amnesty.

3. Almost half the applicants for amnesty were of Mexican descent.

4. More people from Central America applied for amnesty than from the Caribbean.

Express Yourself!

Choose two or three classmates to work with. Together design a poster for the Mothers of East Los Angeles. The poster should tell people in the community how the group wants to improve conditions in East Los Angeles. The poster should also invite people to join the group. When you are finished, display your poster in the classroom.

It rained on their parade, but that did not dim the pride of these spectators in New York City's annual Puerto Rican day parade. Since 1961, the parade has celebrated the contributions of New York's Puerto Rican community.

SECTIONS

1 On the Mainland

2 Ties to the Home Island

CHAPTER 26

Puerto Ricans Today

(1980–Present)

THINKING ABOUT THE CHAPTER

What new patterns of life have emerged among Puerto Ricans in the closing years of the century?

In September 1992, the sound of ringing phones filled the office of the Council of Spanish-Speaking People in Philadelphia. Speaking in both Spanish and English, the staff rattled off dates and locations for the annual Puerto Rican festival. Puerto Ricans from the island and the mainland poured into the city to join in a week-long celebration of their heritage.

The highlight of the festival was the Puerto Rican Day Parade. Some spectators waved Puerto Rican flags. Others sat atop cars with the names of Puerto Rican hometowns painted on the hoods.

When the parade ended, the neighborhood block parties began. Platters of special foods appeared—*arroz con gandules* (rice and pigeon peas), *carne de cerdo asada o frita* (roasted or fried pork), *pinchos* (shish kebob), *arroz con leche* (sweet rice pudding), and more. Disk jockeys filled the air with the sounds of *salsa* (SAHL-sah) and *bomba* (BOHM-bah), a jazzy, African-based music. With sparkling eyes, Lida Viruet (vee-RWET), visiting from upstate New York, recalled what it was like to be at the parade that day:

> People set aside their differences to celebrate the island. Everybody danced with everybody. Most danced *salsa*. But some danced *merengue* (meh-REN-geh), too. After that day, many of us went home and dreamed of Puerto Rico.

Like Lida, mainland Puerto Ricans value their island heritage. Some leave the mainland to return to the island. For those who remain, the island is always part of their vision of life.

1 ON THE MAINLAND
◆ What is life like for Puerto Ricans living in the United States today?

Lida Viruet first came to the mainland as a child with her family in the 1960s. Until the age of 4, she lived in New Jersey, where her father worked as a security guard. But her family longed for Puerto Rico. So they returned home to the coastal city of Mayagüez (mah-YAH-gwes).

On September 23, 1989, at age 23, Lida came back to New Jersey. This time, she traveled with her own children, Stephanie and Adrian, to seek a new life on the U.S. mainland.

A Hard Road. Lida arrived on the mainland armed with a degree in computer programming from the junior college at Mayagüez. Lida could read English, but she could not speak it well. So she worried about finding work. At first, she held several part-time jobs in the Puerto Rican community in Paterson, New Jersey. Then she moved to Bridgeton, New Jersey. Here Lida decided to put her education to work:

> I went to work as an interpreter helping teachers work with Mexican kids. Soon I became a full-time teacher's aide working with handicapped children.

In 1991, Lida moved to Wappingers Falls, New York. Here she took another job, working with people with disabilities. She also enrolled in college, taking classes in English and Community Mental Health. "Many times I feel like going back to Puerto Rico," Lida says. "But I want to show my kids that it's important to finish something. I'm going to finish college in the United States."

Changing Patterns. Lida's story shows some of the changes that have taken place in Puerto Rico and the United States since the great migration of the 1950s. (See Chapter 20.) A sharp decline in unskilled jobs in the United States has slowed the movement of unskilled workers from the island. Like Lida, many Puerto Rican migrants today possess some higher education or skills.

Migrants now do not automatically head for New York City. New York City still boasts the largest Puerto Rican population on the mainland. However, the percentage of Puerto Ricans living there has dropped from 80 percent in 1950 to less than 50 percent in the 1990s. Migrants in search of jobs have settled in other urban areas such as Chicago, Los Angeles, Philadelphia, Newark, Boston, Cleveland, and Hartford, Connecticut. Today Puerto Ricans live in every state of the Union, including more than 6,000 in Hawaii.

In addition to fanning out across the United States, many Puerto Ricans are migrating back to the island. About 90,000 Puerto Ricans travel to the mainland each year. Another 50,000 return to their Puerto Rican homeland.

A Second Generation. Louis and Verania Cancel, whom you read about in Chapter 20, came to the mainland in the 1950s. They plan to live in Puerto Rico after they retire. But their son James says he will stay in the United States. His sister Nilda, however, has chosen to move back.

James and Nilda belong to a large number of second-generation Puerto Ricans born and raised in the United States. By 1994, they nearly equalled the number of first-generation Puerto Ricans on the mainland. Some observers have said that the second-generation Puerto Rican lives with one foot on the island and one foot on the mainland.

Puerto Ricans on the island call second-generation Puerto Ricans **nuyoricans** (noo-yoh-REE-kahns). The term comes from the time when most Puerto Ricans lived in New York City. But the meaning has changed. Lida Viruet explains:

Today anybody who comes from the United States is a nuyorican. A nuyorican is somebody born on the mainland, but whose parents are Puerto Rican. It's a person who knows English.

Breaking the Cycle of Poverty. Some Puerto Ricans spend their lives in a hopeless cycle of poverty, from which they see no escape. Some youths do not attend school at all. Unable to find jobs, they pass the time on sidewalks in poverty-ridden areas of the cities. Drugs and crime are a fact of life. Puerto Ricans, African

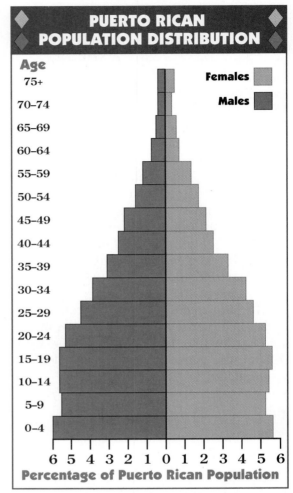

PUERTO RICAN POPULATION DISTRIBUTION

Age: 75+, 70–74, 65–69, 60–64, 55–59, 50–54, 45–49, 40–44, 35–39, 30–34, 25–29, 20–24, 15–19, 10–14, 5–9, 0–4

Females / Males

6 5 4 3 2 1 0 1 2 3 4 5 6
Percentage of Puerto Rican Population

Are there more Puerto Ricans in the 10–14 age group or the 20–24 age group?

Americans, and newly arrived immigrants from Caribbean islands such as Haiti and the Dominican Republic struggle to survive on the mainland.

According to the 1990 census, Puerto Ricans make up more than 11 percent of the total Latino population in the United States. Of all the Latino groups, the Puerto Ricans are the poorest. An estimated 37 percent of all Puerto Rican families have incomes below the U.S. government's poverty line.

Young Puerto Ricans caught in pockets of poverty have a tough time escaping. Yet many do make it out. By 1988, 54 percent of all Puerto Ricans between ages 25 and 34 had graduated from high school. The number of college graduates and Puerto Ricans in skilled jobs had gone up, too. Today nearly 15 percent of the Puerto Rican community holds skilled or professional jobs. This is especially true for second- and third-generation Puerto Ricans.

Atrévete. To help Puerto Ricans fight the cycle of poverty, agencies such as the Office of the Commonwealth launched a massive voter-registration drive in 1987. *"Atrévete"* (ah-TREH-veh-teh)—"I dare you to [register]"—challenged the agency. In 1993, the project claimed that more than 150,000 new voters had registered.

In 1992, Puerto Rican voters exercised their political muscle. That year, the largely Puerto Rican 4th Congressional district in Chicago swept Luis Gutiérrez into the House of Representatives. Voters in the 12th district of New York elected Nydia Velazquez, the first Puerto Rican woman ever elected to Congress.

Nydia Velázquez, the daughter of a sugar cane worker and his wife, overcame the poverty in her district that she now pledges to end. Born in 1953 in the rural town of Yabucoa (yah-boo-KOH-ah), Puerto Rico, Velázquez earned a master's degree in political science from the University of Puerto Rico.

After moving to New York City in the 1970s, Velázquez held a position in the Black and Puerto Rican Studies Department at Hunter College. She also served as secretary for the Office of the Commonwealth and took a commanding role in the start of *Atrévete.* In addition, she takes great pride in the creation of *Unidos Contra EL SIDA* (United Against AIDS). With the acquired immune deficiency syndrome (AIDS) claiming thousands of lives, Velazquez has vowed to work to curb its spread through research and education.

Islands of Hope. Rent an empty lot. Clean up the trash. Put up a small wooden house and plant gardens around it. That's the formula for building a *casita* (kah-SEE-tah). Today *casitas* represent hope and pride in the Puerto Rican heritage in New York City. As José Rivera explained:

People got tired of . . . the garbage and abandoned cars. . . . So they got together and planted community gardens and built these *casitas* . . . . People would come to the *casita* to play music or to celebrate holidays together.

The *casitas* have become cultural centers. Often, their builders ignore local laws when putting them up. City officials sometimes tear down the *casitas*, but the community builds new ones. During any summer in the 1990s, more than 50 *casitas* might be found throughout New York City's South Bronx.

For community organizers, the *casitas* are part of their efforts to combat drugs and crime. There, musicians write and perform *plenas* (PLEH-nahs), a kind of musical newspaper. The words of *plenas* tell people what is happening in the area. The lyrics from one *plena* warn young people to stay away from crack, a highly addictive drug. "Be careful of crack, you shouldn't smoke it. This sorry atrophy [waste], if you do not look out, will crack *you*!"

Other local musicians join with the *plena* artists. They sing *salsa* and write raps. Many of the raps are bilingual, throwing out lines that rhyme in both Spanish and English. Although written to a different beat than the *plenas*, many *salsa* and rap songs have the same purpose, to emphasize respect for the Puerto Rican culture.

Hanging On to a Heritage. A visit to *el barrio*, or the neighborhood, reveals the strength of Puerto Rican culture in

New York City today. One Puerto Rican community is East Harlem. In the *barrio*, which has been the center of Puerto Rican culture since the 1920s, *bodegas* (grocery stores) and *barberías* (bahr-beh-REE-ahs) (barber shops) still dot the neighborhood. During the summer, the Puerto Rican Traveling Theater sets up productions on the streets of East Harlem. Here Puerto Ricans turn out to listen to works by Miriam Colón (koh-LOHN), who founded the theater, and other Puerto Rican playwrights.

Nearby is el Museo del Barrio (el moo-SEH-oh del bah-RREE-oh), the Museum of the Barrio. Started in 1969 by a group of parents, educators, and artists, el Museo began as a one-room classroom in an East Harlem school. El Museo displays the art of talented Puerto Rican and other Latino artists.

From *casitas* to el Museo, Puerto Ricans have changed the look of New York City. In the century ahead, the Puerto Rican presence in the United States promises to increase. This raises a question in the minds of many Puerto Ricans. What will be the relationship between this large mainland community and people on the home island?

Rigoberto Torres, right, and John Ahearn enrich their South Bronx community in New York with brightly painted plaster casts of people in the neighborhood.

Taking Another Look

1. How have Puerto Rican patterns of migration to the mainland changed since the 1950s?

2. **a.** What progress have Puerto Ricans on the mainland made in recent years? **b.** What problems remain for Puerto Ricans who live on the mainland?

3. **Critical Thinking** Suppose you were a member of the *Atrévete* project. What arguments would you use to convince Puerto Ricans to vote?

The culture of traditional life in Puerto Rico is kept alive on the mainland by groups such as these playing *jíbaro* music. Playing on traditional instruments, their music tells of the island's rich folklore and history.

2 TIES TO THE HOME ISLAND

◆ What ties bind mainland Puerto Ricans
◆ to the home island today?

In Puerto Rico, they call the island community Levittown. "Levittown is New York," says James Cancel. "In Levittown, you can speak English. All the stores are the same as in the United States." Lida Viruet agrees. "Levittown looks just like the United States. You would hardly know you're in Puerto Rico."

Nuyorican Capital. Levittown lies on the northern coast of Puerto Rico, just across the harbor from San Juan. The community got its name from its builder, William J. Levitt.

The mainland Puerto Ricans who resettle in Levittown, Puerto Rico, soon find out how much life in the United States has touched them. The mainland Puerto Ricans who speak Spanish, often speak it differently from Puerto Ricans on the island. Sometimes the nuyoricans use entirely new words coined in the United States. An islander, for example, will point to a roof and call it *el techo* (TEH-choh). A New York Puerto Rican may point to the same roof and call it *el roofo*.

Some nuyoricans who make their homes on the island find that they do not know enough Spanish to communicate with the islanders. For such people, schools have set up classes in Spanish.

Political Views. One young nuyorican who traveled to the island was startled when someone in Levittown called him an *independentista* for hanging a Puerto Rican flag out his window. In the South Bronx, the action symbolized pride in Puerto Rico. In Levittown, it meant a vote for independence from the United States.

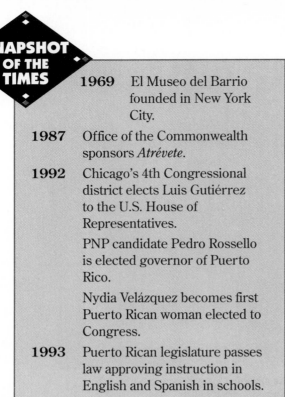

1969 El Museo del Barrio founded in New York City.

1987 Office of the Commonwealth sponsors *Atrévete*.

1992 Chicago's 4th Congressional district elects Luis Gutiérrez to the U.S. House of Representatives.

PNP candidate Pedro Rossello is elected governor of Puerto Rico.

Nydia Velázquez becomes first Puerto Rican woman elected to Congress.

1993 Puerto Rican legislature passes law approving instruction in English and Spanish in schools.

Puerto Ricans take politics seriously. The island has one of the highest rates of voter participation in the world. On election day, people turn out in great numbers to vote. Nearly everyone displays the symbol of one of the two main parties—the Popular Democratic Party (PPD) and the New Progressive Party (PNP). Members of the PPD proudly display a bright red peasant hat. Supporters of the New Progressive Party display a bright blue palm tree.

Issue of the 1990s. For Puerto Ricans, the single most important issue of the 1990s revolves around the island's political status. Most Puerto Ricans have strong political views. Few of them support the *independentistas* (see page 000). Instead, most tend to favor continued ties with the United States. But heated debate surrounds the issue of statehood. The PPD favors the present commonwealth status. The PNP supports statehood.

In November 1992, the two parties squared off against each other. The PPD attempted to knock out the PNP by running Victoria Muñoz, daughter of Muñoz Marín (see page 257), as its candidate for governor. The PNP chose Pedro Rossello (roh-SEH-yoh). In a close election, Rossello scored a victory with 49 percent of the vote. Muñoz won 45 percent, with the rest of the votes going to the *independentistas*.

The PPD has not surrendered. One official says, "If we become a state, we will lose our identity as Puerto Ricans." The PPD has centered its fight against a law enacted by the PNP-dominated legislature in January 1993. The law approved instruction in English and Spanish in the schools throughout the island. The PPD hopes to reverse this law through a **referendum,** or popular vote of the people. The referendum would eliminate the teaching of English in the schools. Many Puerto Ricans see Spanish as a key part of the Puerto Rican identity. Others see knowledge of English as a way to help Puerto Ricans advance in the U.S. economy.

Protecting the Environment. In July 1992, Lida Viruet visited her family in Mayagüez. She gasped at the development that had taken place during her years on the mainland. Lida said to her mother, "They tore down all my trees. What do they want—another New York City?"

James Cancel expressed a similar reaction on a recent trip to the island. "They built a major highway past my grandparents' house. It's all cement."

Despite differences over statehood and language, many Puerto Ricans today share a concern about the development of their island. Since the late 1970s, a strong environmental movement has taken shape. Puerto Ricans want to end the dumping of wastes by foreign-owned factories. They also want to stop unplanned development. With every highway and every housing project built, more trees are cut down.

The island still suffers from poverty and a high rate of unemployment. But many Puerto Ricans believe that simply building more factories is not the answer. They believe that carefully planned development is needed to protect the environment of the island.

Puerto Rico is moving to protect its two most precious natural resources—its land and water. Concern for the environment of the island even extends to Puerto Ricans in the United States. Says Lida Viruet, "I wrote a letter to the mayor of Mayagüez. I want the mayor to think more of the environment. I want the environment there for my children."

Taking Another Look

1. What differences do mainland Puerto Ricans experience when they move to the island?

2. What issues most concern Puerto Ricans today?

3. **Critical Thinking** What do you think might be some of the benefits and drawbacks of statehood for Puerto Rico?

LOOKING AHEAD

Life for many mainland Puerto Ricans has improved. But many still face the struggle of life in an alien culture. Many return to the island, where they see great changes taking place. Meanwhile, other groups of people from the Caribbean, the Cubans and Dominicans in the United States, also think—and worry—about the future of their islands.

Bridging two cultures, San Juan is both an "All-American" city, as this sign indicates, and a city rich in its traditional Puerto Rican heritage.

PUERTO RICAN DANCE

In 1987, Puerto Rican dancer Arthur Áviles auditioned for the famed Bill T. Jones dance company. Áviles calls himself a "nuyorican from Jamaica [New York]." Some thought the muscular young man would never make it into the modern dance company. But his raw power and grace won him a place among the company's dancers.

As Áviles introduces new styles to modern dance, other Puerto Rican dancers are bringing new flair to classical ballet. In 1980, Lolita San Miguel formed the Ballet Concierto de Puerto Rico. When the troop made its 1990 debut at New York City's Lincoln Center, critics gave it rave reviews. The *New York Times* called the company "one of Puerto Rico's best-kept secrets."

Like Áviles, San Miguel has brought new and different styles to dance. The dancers are not chosen on the basis of physical appearance, but for the spirit and flair they bring to the stage. She also has added Caribbean rhythms and beats to such dance classics as the *Nutcracker Suite*. In addition, she has brought new compositions from Latin America and introduced them to the world. In summing up the purpose of her troupe, San Miguel says, "We show the public that there's a lot of talent in the Caribbean. Another flavor, another rhythm."

CLOSE UP: Chapter 26

The Who, What, Where of History

1. **Where** do Puerto Ricans live on the mainland?
2. **Who** is a *Nuyorican*?
3. **What** is the purpose of the *Atrévete* project?
4. **Who** is Nydia Velazquez?
5. **What** activities take place at a *casita?*
6. **What** is a *plena?*
7. **What** is the Puerto Rican Traveling Theater?
8. **Where** was el Museo del Barrio founded?
9. **What** are some of the distinctive traits of Levittown, Puerto Rico?
10. **What** are the symbols of the Popular Democratic Party? Of the New Progressive Party?
11. **What** is the key issue facing Puerto Rican voters on the home island?
12. **Who** is Pedro Rossello?
13. **What** is a referendum?

Making the Connection

1. What is the connection between the decline in unskilled jobs in the United States and changing migration patterns from Puerto Rico?
2. What is the connection between *Atrévete* and the election of Puerto Rican representatives to Congress?
3. What is the connection between the issue of statehood and bilingual instruction in Puerto Rico?
4. What is the connection between rapid industrialization and the start of an environmental movement in Puerto Rico?

Time Check

1. In which year did *Atrévete* begin?
2. When was Luis Gutiérrez elected to the House of Representatives?

What Would You Have Done?

1. Imagine that you are a community organizer in the South Bronx. What arguments would you use to convince city officials to allow you to put up a *casita?*
2. Suppose you lived in Puerto Rico during the 1992 election. Would you have voted for the PPD or the PNP? Explain.

Thinking and Writing About History

1. Imagine that you are planning a Puerto Rican festival for your community. Create a list of the events that you would include. Explain the significance of each item on your list.
2. Write an essay in which you define what it means to be a second-generation Puerto Rican in the United States today.
3. Imagine that you are Lida Viruet. Write a letter to the mayor of Mayagüez in which you express your concerns about overdevelopment of the island.

Building Skills: Forming Generalizations Based Upon a Population Pyramid

In Chapter 15, you learned how to form a *generalization*, or true statement, based on the facts. A generalization, as you may recall, is a broad statement that summarizes information. A generalization uses qualifying words such as *most, few, usually,* and *generally.* These words signal that the generalization may no longer be valid, or true, if new information is discovered.

The population pyramid on page 340 provides factual data about the makeup of the Puerto Rican population in the 1980s. To form generalizations based upon this pyramid, you need to first identify the pyramid's key facts. What two classes of information are shown on the pyramid? Your answer to this question will give you the topic of your generalization. In this case, you will be generalizing about the age and gender of the Puerto Rican community. To help you form valid generalizations on this topic, answer the questions below.

1. Which age group is the largest in number?
2. How does the number of people over age 34 compare with the number of people under age 34?
3. What generalization can you make that accurately describes the balance of males and females in the Puerto Rican community?
4. How would you complete the following generalization? Most Puerto Ricans in the United States fall between the ages of_____ and _____.

Express Yourself!

Make a two-part bulletin board display for your classroom. One part will show pictures of Puerto Rico. The other part will show pictures of Puerto Rican neighborhoods in the United States. Work with a group to collect pictures from newspapers, magazines, and other places. You may also draw your own pictures.

The young people of Centro Mater are part of the story of accomplishments of the Cuban American community. Centro Mater became a home away from home for hundreds of young Cuban Americans.

CHAPTER
27

SECTIONS

1 New Waves of Refugees

2 A Strong Cuban American Presence

Cuban Americans Today

(1980–Present)

THINKING ABOUT THE CHAPTER

What patterns of life have emerged among Cuban Americans?

Sister Margarita Miranda wanted to help Cuban American children who were left alone after school while their parents worked. She knew the families had no choice. Often, both parents had to work just to get by. In other cases, only one parent had managed to escape from Cuba to Miami. Also, the move to the United States had upset the traditional Cuban family pattern. No longer was a grandmother, an aunt, or another relative on hand to help with the children.

In 1968, Sister Miranda asked the mothers at the school where she taught to help start an after-school play group. Mothers such as Lucía Suárez Escagedo eagerly agreed. After school, Lucía's 8-year-old daughter Ana María and her schoolmates were taken to the park in East Little Havana where the play group had been set up. There the children would play for hours until their parents could pick them up.

The play group at the park soon grew into Centro Mater (Mother's Center). One of the first day-care centers in Miami, Centro Mater became a home away from home for hundreds of Cuban American children. When thousands of needy families arrived from Cuba in 1980, Centro Mater jumped into the relief effort. That year, the city of Miami honored the center with a special award for its work with Cuban refugees. Centro Mater is only one of the many chapters in the story of the growth and accomplishments of the nation's Cuban and Cuban American community.

1 NEW WAVES OF REFUGEES
◆ What were some of the causes and
◆ effects of the Mariel Boatlift?

In the spring of 1980, a dispute broke out between Cuban leader Fidel Castro and the government of Peru. The quarrel began when a group of Cubans who were unhappy with the government, took shelter in the Peruvian embassy in Havana. Castro insisted that the embassy expel the group. Peru refused. It demanded that the people be allowed to fly to Lima, the capital of Peru.

On April 4, 11,000 Cubans stormed the Peruvian embassy asking that they too be flown to Lima. In response, Castro ordered the gates of the Peruvian embassy bulldozed open. He then startled the United States by announcing that the port of Mariel would be open to any U.S. resident interested in picking up Cubans who wanted to leave the island.

The Mariel Boatlift. The news electrified the Cuban community in Miami. Cuban Americans jumped at the chance to take family or friends off the island. Pedro Reboredo (reh-bor-REH-doh), the future mayor of West Miami, set out in a small motorboat to pick up relatives of his wife Norma.

Reboredo later recalled, "I was not familiar with how to operate the boat. We were bouncing around on the waves. Cuba is only 90 miles from Florida, but the trip took 14 hours." By the time he reached Mariel harbor, there were already 2,000 other boats from the United States there.

However, a surprise awaited the rescuers. Castro announced that they could not pick up friends and relatives unless they also agreed to take along other Cubans. These included people from the island's prisons and mental hospitals. The rescuers had no choice but to agree to Castro's strange requirement. Eduardo Suárez, a TV cameraman from Havana, remembered being crowded in with several convicted criminals on the way to Florida. They were among the 80 people on a boat meant to hold only 25.

With hundreds of boats bearing Cubans sailing toward Florida, the United States faced a difficult problem. A new law, the Refugee Act of 1980, aimed to limit the number of refugees from the political and economic turmoil that gripped parts of Asia and Latin America. The law then limited the number of refugees from any one nation to 50,000 a year. Only if there were "grave humanitarian reasons" would more people be allowed in. Did the flood of people out of Cuba qualify to be admitted under the new law?

While the U.S. government was deciding the answer to this question, it placed the thousands of new exiles in hastily organized temporary quarters. The government put more than 125,000 Cubans in holding stations along the Florida coast.

In the spring of 1980, Castro allowed thousands of Cubans to flee the nation from the port of Mariel. This crowded freighter brought hundreds of Cubans to a new home in the United States.

The exiles were not eligible for federal aid normally extended to refugees. For more than three months, the exiles depended upon state and private agencies for care.

The burden fell heaviest upon Miami. The first of the new Cuban exiles arrived in late April. By mid-May, many thousands of people were packed under the bleachers in the Orange Bowl, a football stadium in Miami. Others camped in tents on public lands below Interstate Highway 95. Often their only belongings consisted of a pillow, a blanket, and the clothes on their back. These were the only items Cuban officials had allowed the exiles to take.

Because Cuba boasted that it had emptied its prisons and mental hospitals, the people who had left from Mariel got a bad name. Actually, fewer than 20 percent of them had spent any time in prison. The percentage dropped much lower when Castro's political prisoners were taken out of the count. Eventually, the United States granted refugee status—and aid—to all but 2,746 exiles.

Meeting a New Challenge. The Cubans of the Mariel Boatlift differed in many ways from the earlier waves of Cuban exiles. The exiles of the 1960s had been largely middle-class professionals, with strong ties to their Cuban-Spanish heritage. The Mariels were mostly working-class people. An estimated 71 percent worked at blue-collar trades. In addition, many Mariels reflected the African ancestry of a large percentage of Cuba's population.

Many Cuban Americans helped those from the boatlift by working in the city's refugee program. Centro Mater, for example, took in children at little or no charge so that parents could find work. Federal aid programs also helped. In some cases, these programs helped the new arrivals to move to other cities. Many moved to the industrial area of northern New Jersey.

Some members of the Mariel Boatlift achieved great success. Eduardo Suárez, for example, won 13 Emmy Awards for his work as operations manager of Channel 51, one of Miami's Spanish-language stations. Other Mariels took jobs in sugar mills, on farms, or in Miami's garment district.

Tourists and Rafters. Since 1980, Cubans have continued to land on U.S. shores. They have not arrived in huge clusters as in the Mariel Boatlift. Rather, the newest immigrants have formed a slow, steady stream. Perhaps 30,000 have entered on tourist visas and refused to go home. Others travel on rafts they have built from inner tubes of tires and the branches of mangrove trees. On one weekend in May 1991, the Coast Guard picked up more than 600 such rafters.

Since 1991, many Cubans have arrived aboard Flight 8506 from Havana. Flight 8506 left twice a day from José Martí Airport for Miami. Cubans who met certain requirements and whose U.S. relatives paid the nearly $1,000 in travel and visa fees could go on the chartered flights. They might stay a few weeks or a few months. Some never returned to Cuba.

Question Mark for the Future. The charter flights reflect changing world conditions. With the breakup of the Soviet Union in 1991, Cuba lost its biggest economic backer. The U.S. economic **embargo,** or ban on imported goods, imposed on Cuba in 1960, soon after the Cuban revolution, remained in effect. This embargo, in part, resulted in Cubans not having enough food. Shortages exist in nearly everything from gasoline to clothing.

In both Cuba and in Cuban American communities in the United States, people look with uncertainty toward the future. With Castro almost age 70, they wonder, What next? A popular saying for more than 30 years among Cuban exiles, has been "Next year in Havana." The saying sums up the hopes of many exiles that one day they will return to Cuba.

If conditions in Cuba change, how many Cuban Americans would actually return to Cuba after living in the United States for three decades? According to a survey by Spanish-language TV station WSCV in Miami, only 40 percent of those 34 years old or younger say they would return to Cuba. In contrast, more than 51 percent of those surveyed over the age of 41 claim they would go back.

Taking Another Look

1. What events led to the Mariel Boatlift from Cuba?

2. What were some effects of the Mariel Boatlift on Miami?

3. **Critical Thinking** Imagine you are a 25-year-old Cuban American who had come to the United States in 1980 during the Mariel Boatlift. Would you choose to return to Cuba to live if conditions on the island changed? Explain your answer.

SNAPSHOT OF THE TIMES

1962	The United States imposes an economic embargo on Cuba.
1968	Centro Mater founded in Miami.
1978	First Calle Ocho Festival takes place.
1980	Mariel Boatlift brings thousands of Cubans to the United States.
1985	Cuban American Xavier Suárez becomes mayor of Miami.
1991	Flight 8506 offers passage from Havana to Miami.

2 A STRONG CUBAN AMERICAN PRESENCE

◆ What distinguishes the Cuban American community in the 1990s?

Ana María Escagedo was one of the first children to attend the Centro Mater. Today she is a successful lawyer in Miami. Some of her earliest memories are of life in North Miami. "At home, we ate Cuban food, listened to Cuban music, and spoke Spanish. Today, we still speak Spanish at my parent's house." But when she became a teenager, some changes occurred. "I listened to rock-and-roll on the radio, while my parents listened to Latin music." When she started dating, her parents sent along a chaperone to supervise her behavior and that of her boyfriend. That was what they would have done in Cuba. "I didn't like that at all," said Ana María, laughing.

In her work as a lawyer in Miami, Ana María Escagedo's ability to speak both Spanish and English is a great asset. "Our clients come from all over the Spanish-speaking world," she noted.

What is it like to be among the first generation of Cuban Americans to grow up in the United States? "Great!" she exclaimed. "We have the chance to pick the best of both cultures."

Diversity and Success. More than one million Cuban Americans live in the United States today. They are the third-largest Spanish-speaking group in the nation. Their backgrounds and experiences vary greatly. Their occupations range from factory workers to wealthy business owners.

Today, slightly less than 30 percent of all Cuban Americans are lawyers, doctors, engineers, university professors, school administrators and teachers, and businesspeople. The majority work at blue-collar trades. They have jobs as service workers, farmers, machine operators, and craftworkers. Ties among Cuban Americans remain strong. Most Cuban American blue-collar workers have jobs in companies or agricultural businesses owned or managed by Cuban Americans.

Among Latino groups, Cuban Americans lead the way in income. In 1990, Cuban American families earned an average yearly income of $31,400. This figure was only slightly less than the $32,270 average yearly income of non-Latino white families.

In addition, more than 83 percent of all Cuban Americans aged 25 to 34 had graduated from high school. Within that same age group, over 24 percent had also completed four or more years of college.

The Second Havana. Like other Latino groups, Cuban Americans live in nearly every state of the Union. Union City, New Jersey, boasts the second-largest population of Cuban Americans in the nation after Miami. The more than 100,000 Cuban Americans there have brought new life to the neighborhoods in which they live. Cuban food stores, bakeries, and coffee shops line the streets.

But Miami continues to be the capital of Cuban America. Cuban Americans affectionately call the city "the second Havana." Today, more than 600,000 Cuban Americans—over 50 percent of all Cuban Americans, live in Dade County, where Miami is located. Since 1970, more Cuban Americans have moved into the Miami area than have moved out of it. This contrasts sharply with Puerto Ricans and Mexican Americans. They tend to spread out across the nation.

Cuban Americans have turned Miami into a Latin American boomtown. More than 250 **multinationals,** or companies with business operations in more than one nation, have opened headquarters there. Miami is located on the edge of the Caribbean basin. That and the city's strong Latino atmosphere have led Latin American business leaders to invest more than one billion dollars a year in the city.

From Refugees to Citizens. Since the failed Bay of Pigs invasion (see Chapter 21), more and more Cubans have become U.S. citizens. Cuban American voters have flexed their political muscle in recent years. They have sent the first Cuban Americans to Congress (see Chapter 30). In 1985, voters in Miami elected Xavier Suárez as the first Cuban American mayor of a major U.S. city.

Arriving in the United States from Cuba at the age of 18, Roberto C. Goizueta rose in the business world. Starting as a chemist, he became the chief executive and chairman of the Coca-Cola Company.

Xavier Suárez was born in Las Villas, Cuba, in 1949. He came to the United States in 1961 at age 12. His family settled in Washington, D.C., where he attended high school. Upon graduation, he went on to Villanova University and Harvard Law School. Suárez soon moved to Miami, where he set up a law practice in Little Havana. Suárez took in so many free legal cases that he became known as the "people's lawyer." In 1985, he won election as the "people's mayor."

Today, Suárez focuses on helping Miami adjust to the tremendous economic and cultural changes in the city. "It's hard to predict when we'll reach adulthood," he joked. But he has little doubt about the direction in which Miami is headed. "We already are the largest Spanish-speaking city in our nation," said Suárez.

A Center of Latino Culture. The heart of the Spanish-speaking culture in Miami is Calle Ocho (KAH-yeh OH-choh), or Eighth Street, in Little Havana. Here Cuban restaurants serve up heaping dishes of traditional Cuban foods such as *picadillo con arroz y huevos* (ground meat with rice and eggs). Newsstands are filled with newspapers and magazines written in Spanish. Older men play dominoes for hours in Antonio Macéo Park while they drink cups of thick Cuban coffee. Here and there, anti-Castro slogans and drawings streak the walls of buildings.

Yet, despite the strong Cuban presence, Calle Ocho is changing. Today, immigrants from all over Latin America head to Miami to start new lives in the United States.

Today, Calle Ocho is like Miami itself. It is a mix of Latino cultures. Perhaps one of the greatest contributions of Cuban Americans has been to open the doors of Miami to people from all over Latin America. In the 30 years in which Cuban

Businesswoman Cari Domínguez, left, takes the oath as director of the U.S. Office of Federal Contract Compliance in 1990. Looking on are husband Alberto, son Jason, and then Secretary of Labor Elizabeth Dole.

Older Cuban American men enjoy an afternoon in Antonio Maceo Park on Calle Ocho in Miami's "Little Havana." While they play, the men enjoy drinking traditional thick, black Cuban coffee.

Americans have made the city their home, they have helped turn Miami into what they proudly call the "Gateway of Latin America."

Taking Another Look

1. How has speaking both Spanish and English benefited Ana María Escagedo?

2. How have Cuban Americans helped increase the United States' contact with Latin America?

3. **Critical Thinking** Suppose you are a business owner from a Latin American country. Why might you consider locating your headquarters in Miami?

LOOKING AHEAD

Since the huge immigration of Cubans to the United States that began in the late 1960s, the Cuban American community has shown more diversity. Settling into Miami, Union City, and several other cities, Cuban Americans have formed stable communities that are a mix of Cuban and U.S. traditions.

Since 1980, the number of Latino immigrants to the United States from Central America and the Dominican Republic has risen sharply. In the past decade, immigrants from these regions have passed Cubans as the largest group of refugees seeking economic or political shelter in the United States.

THE CALLE OCHO FESTIVAL

Each March, more than one million people pour into Southwest Eighth Street to take part in the nation's largest block party. In what is known as the Calle Ocho Festival, people dance the samba or the cha-cha along 23 blocks of Little Havana.

The festival first started in 1978, when Cuban community leaders searched for a way to celebrate the beginning of the Catholic religious season known as Lent. The organizers expected fewer than 2,000 people to attend. But more than 100,000 showed up. Today, this Cuban festival rivals the famous Mardi Gras in New Orleans and Carneval in Rio de Janeiro, Brazil.

Because of the diversity of the Latino culture of Miami, the festival now forms part of a week-long celebration known as Carnaval Miami. The festival offers parades and marathon races. A dozen cooks use huge wooden oars to stir up the world's largest dish of *paella*—450 pounds of rice, chicken, lobster, and mussels. In the evenings, Latino recording artists such as Celia Cruz or Gloria Estefan and the Miami Sound Machine entertain the crowds.

The Calle Ocho Festival shows the strength of Cuban culture in Miami. Instead of being assimilated, or absorbed, into U.S. society, Cuban Americans have added what Gloria Estefan calls "our own ethnic flavor" to the nation.

CLOSE UP: Chapter 27

The Who, What, Where of History

1. **What** is Centro Mater?
2. **What** were the provisions of the Refugee Act of 1980?
3. **Where** did the huge 1980 boatlift of Cuban refugees begin?
4. **Where** did most Mariels settle?
5. **Who** is Eduardo Suárez?
6. **What** is Flight 8506?
7. **Where** is the second-largest Cuban American community located?
8. **What** are multinationals?
9. **Who** is Xavier Suárez?
10. **Where** is Calle Ocho?

Making the Connection

1. What was the connection between the Refugee Act of 1980 and the Mariel Boatlift?
2. What was the connection between the breakup of the Soviet Union and economic conditions in Cuba?
3. Explain the connection between the location of many multinational corporations in Miami, Miami's large Latino population, and the location of the city.

Time Check

1. In what year did the Mariel Boatlift take place?
2. How long has the United States had an economic embargo against Cuba?

What Would You Have Done?

1. Imagine that you are a Cuban American living in Miami in 1980. You have just heard of Castro's decision to

open the port of Mariel. Would you take part in the boatlift? Why or why not?

2. Suppose you are a Cuban American who has lived in the United States for more than 30 years. You have just learned that Castro has fallen from power. Would you return to Cuba? Why or why not?

Thinking and Writing About History

1. Write an editorial for a Miami paper that disputes the claim that all Mariels are prisoners. Support your editorial with specific examples from the chapter.

2. Write a skit in which a Cuban exile from 1959 and a Mariel from 1980 describe their differing experiences. Use information from this chapter and from Chapter 21 to write your skit.

Building Skills: Generalizing from a Primary Source

As you may recall from earlier lessons, a generalization is a broad statement that summarizes facts or data. The bar graph below offers data on the student population at Centro Mater in 1993. This bar graph tells you something about the Latino population in Little Havana. Study this bar graph and then answer the questions that follow.

1. Which group makes up the largest percentage of children at Centro Mater?

2. How many students from South America attend Centro Mater?

3. Based on the bar graph's figures, form a generalization about the largest groups of children at Centro Mater.

4. When Centro Mater was first formed, nearly all the children were Cuban. Form a generalization about how the nationalities of the children at Centro Mater have changed between the years 1968 and 1993.

Express Yourself!

Choose two or three classmates to work with. Reread the Focus On on page 356 about the Calle Ocho Festival. Then, design a poster advertising the Calle Ocho Festival. Draw pictures of events and activities that people might expect to find at the festival. Display your poster in class.

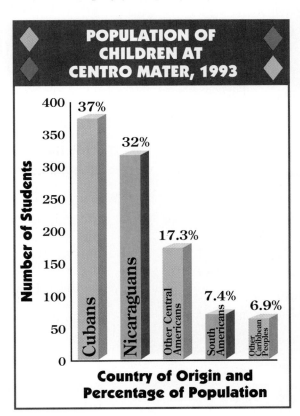

POPULATION OF CHILDREN AT CENTRO MATER, 1993

Number of Students

Cubans 37%
Nicaraguans 32%
Other Central Americans 17.3%
South Americans 7.4%
Other Caribbean Peoples 6.9%

Country of Origin and Percentage of Population

Nobel Prize winner Rigoberta Menchú of Guatemala told the world of human rights abuses committed during her country's civil war. The war caused thousands of Guatemalans to emigrate to the United States.

CHAPTER

28

Central Americans and Dominicans Today

(1980–Present)

SECTIONS

1 Leaving Central America

2 A Growing Central American Presence

3 Dominicans in the United States

THINKING ABOUT THE CHAPTER

How have Central Americans and Dominicans attempted to build new lives in the United States?

In 1982, 22-year-old Rigoberta Menchú told audiences around the world a story of violence against the Maya people of Guatemala, her native land. In appearance after appearance, crowds sat and listened carefully as Rigoberta described the torture and death of her brother, father, and mother. "I narrate my life," explained Rigoberta, "because I know my people cannot tell their story; but it's no different than mine. I am not the only orphan."

In 1992, Rigoberta Menchú won the Nobel Peace Prize for her outspoken work for "social justice . . . based on respect for the rights of indigenous [native] peoples." By that time, hundreds of thousands of people had fled Guatemala and other nations in Central America to the United States.

Joining them were thousands of others, who sought greater economic opportunities than they could find in their Caribbean homeland, the Dominican Republic. This chapter tells their stories.

1 LEAVING CENTRAL AMERICA

◆ Why did many Central Americans seek
◆ shelter in the United States in the 1980s and 1990s?

In the 1980s, the expression *la Violencia,* "the Violence," became part of the daily conversation of many Central Americans. Guatemalans had long used that expression to describe the internal struggles that began in their country in the 1950s. By the 1980s, the words also applied to events in El Salvador and Nicaragua.

An Ongoing Struggle. Guatemala's troubles were deep rooted. In that nation, descendants of the ancient Maya, who speak their own languages, made up more than half the population. Yet most of the land belonged to Spanish-speaking Guatemalans known as *ladinos* (lah-DEE-nohs).

Most political power rested in the hands of a few large *ladino* and U.S. landowners. Hopes for peaceful land reform ended with the U.S.-backed 1954 coup, which overthrew the elected Guatemalan government (see Chapter 23.) Many Maya and some *ladinos* opposed the coup. These people challenged the military government in a guerrilla war.

To crush the guerrillas, the military lashed out at the Maya. From 1978 to 1985, the army destroyed some 400 Maya communities. Tens of thousands of Maya died at the hands of death squads. To escape, some 150,000 Maya headed north, for Mexico. Thousands of refugees made their way even farther north, to the United States. There, the Maya struggled to build new lives in California and Florida.

Civil War in Nicaragua. As violence engulfed Guatemala, warfare ripped Nicaragua apart. The Sandinistas had come to power there in 1979 (see page 255). But the United States feared that the Sandinistas would build another Communist dictatorship, like Castro's in Cuba. So the U.S. government gave military and financial aid to Nicaraguans who opposed the Sandinistas. The Contras, as they were known, waged a fight to overthrow the Sandinista government. From 1982 to 1990 thousands of Nicaraguans died as a result of this war.

Caught between the warring factions, tens of thousands of Nicaraguans fled to the United States. Explained an 8-year-old refugee named María, "We came to the United States because my mom didn't want to see any more people die. She was tired of crying."

War in El Salvador. In the 1980s, fighting continued to cost many lives in still another Central American country, El Salvador. In 1984, after a long civil war (see Chapter 23), a constitutional government was set up. But the situation in the country did not improve. Promised land reforms never took place. Military death squads still murdered political opponents.

The United States poured aid into El Salvador to support right-wing governments. But human rights abuses by the government continued. These abuses kept alive popular support for the guerrillas who fought the government. By the end of the 1980s, the number of refugees from El Salvador matched the number fleeing from Guatemala to the United States.

1979 Sandinistas rise to power in Nicaragua.

1980s Civil war in Guatemala, El Salvador, and Nicaragua causes many from these countries to immigrate to the United States.

Economic conditions in the Dominican Republic lead to high immigration to the United States.

1982 The U.S. Supreme Court rules that children of undocumented immigrants may attend school.

1990 Nicaraguans elect a non-Sandinista government.

1992 Guatemalan Rigoberta Menchú wins the Nobel Peace Prize.

New Policies. As the 1980s drew to a close, pressure increased on the United States to end its aid to governments charged with abusing the human rights of their citizens. Within the United States, one of the groups that opposed U.S. policy in Central America was the Sanctuary Movement, made up of some 300 church organizations. The movement defied U.S. immigration laws by helping hundreds of Central American refugees find shelter in the United States.

In 1990, a decade of revolution in Nicaragua ended with the election of a new, non-Sandinista government. Changes also came to war-torn Guatemala and El Salvador. In the early 1990s, newly elected presidents of these countries opened talks with guerrillas. Even so, after more than 20 years of violence, Central Americans wondered if peace had come

for good. Rather than face continued uncertainty, more Central Americans chose to emigrate to the United States.

Taking Another Look

1. Why did many refugees flee Central America in the 1980s?

2. How did the Sanctuary Movement protest U.S. policies in Central America?

3. **Critical Thinking** Do you think the United States is responsible in part for the conditions that led many Central Americans to emigrate from their homeland? Explain.

2 A GROWING CENTRAL AMERICAN PRESENCE

◆ Where have large communities of Central Americans developed in the United States?

During the Contra war, thousands of Nicaraguans came to the United States. By late 1988, hundreds of Nicaraguans without U.S. immigration papers were crossing the U.S. border each week. Many of them believed the United States would accept them as refugees because they were fleeing from a country with a Communist government.

Instead, U.S. President Ronald Reagan announced that flight from "a Communist regime" did not guarantee a person automatic entry into the United States as a refugee. Thousands of Nicaraguans found themselves crowded into holding centers and facing possible deportation. The United States gave entry papers only to those few individuals and families whom it judged to be refugees according to an official, narrow meaning of that term.

In Miami, Florida, Nicaraguan and Cuban exiles march together to express their hopes concerning U.S. policy in Latin America. How did Cuban Americans help newly arrived Nicaraguans settle in the United States?

Little Managua. The plight of the Nicaraguan refugees electrified the Cuban community of Miami. Many in that community recalled their own flight from Castro's Cuba. Volunteers took to the phones to raise money to help the refugees. The Cuban-born Miami city manager, César Odio (OH-dee-oh), opened a temporary shelter for refugees at the Bobby Maduro Stadium.

By the 1990s, Miami had the largest population of Nicaraguans in the United States. Many new arrivals moved into a neighborhood that became known as Little Managua, named for the capital of Nicaragua. Like earlier Cuban refugees, the Nicaraguans struggled to adapt to life in the United States.

First, there was the matter of language. Miami high school senior Jerry Nicaragua explained:

When you first come here, English sounds like a bunch of noise. You can't understand anything. I learned English in a year. But I was afraid to speak because of my pronunciation. Luckily, in Miami many people speak Spanish.

Then, there was the importance of having the necessary immigration papers. Migrants needed these papers in order to be able to work legally. However, the wait for official papers might take years. Thousands of undocumented Central Americans lived in fear of deportation. But undocumented people did have one bit of good fortune in 1982. In that year, the U.S. Supreme Court ruled, in the case of *Plyer* v. *Doe,* that children of all immigrants, whether documented or undocumented, had a right to attend public school.

South Central Los Angeles. No other city in the United States felt the impact of Central American immigration more keenly than Los Angeles, California. Some even nicknamed it "the Central American capital of the United States." In 1990, Los Angeles was home to more than a half million Central Americans—about 14 percent of the city's total population. That count included more than 250,000 Salvadorans and 125,000 Guatemalans.

Most Central Americans lived in Pico-Union, a section of South Central Los Angeles. As newcomers to the United States, Central Americans in Pico-Union faced many hardships. The change was especially difficult for the Maya from Guatemala. The move from rural villages to a huge modern city left many of these refugees frightened and confused.

Agencies such as the Central American Refugee Center (CARECEN) tried to help the refugees in their resettlement. But problems remain. As one CARECEN official said, "Central Americans still face an incredible amount of poverty and a lack of jobs for unskilled workers."

Raising Hopes. To help solve those problems, human rights groups such as El Rescate (el res-KAH-teh), The Rescue, work to make things easier for immigrants from Central America. El Rescate's director, Oscar Andrade (ahn-DRAH-deh), explained, "We challenge our people to go to school, to own their own business, to excel."

The new arrivals also drew inspiration from Central Americans who had already succeeded in the United States. When a reporter asked one Guatemalan teenager to name one famous Central American, he quickly answered, "That's easy. Rubén Blades."

Born in Panama City, in 1948, **Rubén Blades** (BLAH-des) spent most of his early life in Panama. When he came to the United States, it was to study law. In 1985, Blades earned a law degree from Harvard University.

But it is not as a lawyer that most people know Blades. It is as an actor, a singer, and a composer of salsa music. Blades has used his talent to win two Grammy Awards for his recordings—and to promote social causes important to Latinos.

Central Americans continued to enter the United States during the 1990s. In 1992 alone, nearly 44,000 Guatemalans were granted legal entry to the United States. So were nearly 7,000 Salvadorans. Joining them was another large group of immmigrants. These people were from the Dominican Republic.

Taking Another Look

1. Why did many Nicaraguan refugees settle in Miami?

2. What problems have many recent Central American refugees faced?

3. **Critical Thinking** Why do you think many Latinos consider the ruling in *Plyer* v. *Doe* a historic decision?

3 DOMINICANS IN THE UNITED STATES

What is life like for Dominicans in the United States today?

As early as 5:30 A.M., Dominicans begin to line up outside the U.S. consulate in

A Dominican artist decorated this city handball court with figures of musicians that seem to be in motion—perhaps in rhythm to the merengue. Why have Dominicans emigrated to the United States in recent years?

Santo Domingo, the Dominican capital. They wait patiently as the rising sun heats the pavement. The Dominicans are let into the consulate a few at a time. There, they go through the paperwork involved in getting a visa for entry to the United States. The lucky Dominicans whose applications are approved head home and get ready for the flight to New York. Many of the unlucky ones whose visa applications are rejected do not give up. For them, illegal immigration, often through Puerto Rico, is the answer.

Reasons for Immigration. The United States issues a maximum of 20,000 immigration visas a year to people from the Dominican Republic. Since 1980, Dominicans have filled that quota every year. In the 1990s, no other country in the world had a higher percentage of its population legally immigrating to the United States. Today, Dominicans are the seventh largest immigrant group in the nation and the largest foreign-born group in New York City. In the New York area alone, their numbers top 700,000.

One Dominican, Esmilda María Abreu (ah-BREH-oo), entered the United States at age 4. She came to live with her grandmother in New York City while her mother struggled to finish medical school in the Dominican Republic. Like many Dominicans and other Latinos who live in the United States, her grandmother supported two families—one in the United States and one on the island. Explained Abreu:

> My grandmother worked in a sweatshop making purses. She earned the minimum wage and didn't speak any English. We lived in a one bedroom apartment. Yet, she was supporting my mom in medical school in the Dominican Republic as well as two uncles, an aunt, and myself.

Like Esmilda's grandmother, most Dominicans came to the United States for its economic opportunities. The 30-year Trujillo dictatorship (see page 277) had bankrupted the nation. In 1979, a hurricane devastated the country. More than 2,000 people died and property damage was estimated at about $1 billion. In the late 1980s, the Dominican Republic staggered under a $4 billion foreign debt. Inflation grew at an annual rate of 60 percent. The rate of unemployment on the island reached 25 percent.

A Strong Work Force. Dominican immigrants had varied backgrounds. Unlike immigrants from other Latin American nations, only about a quarter of Dominicans came from rural areas. Most Dominicans came from the urban middle class. Almost all could read and write. An estimated 33 percent had some college education or knew a skilled trade. In the Dominican Republic, they either found themselves without a job or working at jobs that did not use their skills and training. So they brought their hopes and talents to the United States.

Once in the United States, finding a job was a problem for Dominican immigrants. Many of the Dominicans who found jobs did manual work in small factories and in restaurants. Many women worked in the nonunion garment factories of the city. Like the Cuban immigrants of several generations ago, some Dominicans labored in the city's small cigar-manufacturing industry.

When Dominicans did find work, often they were overqualified for the position. Nevertheless, even in such jobs, they earned more than the average Dominican salary of $40 a month.

Many continued their education in the United States. "Dominicans really value education," explained Esmilda Abreu. "They see it as an opportunity to get ahead." The Abreu family demonstrates that belief in education. Esmilda's mother finally became a surgeon. Most of her cousins have attended or will attend college, and Esmilda was working for a master's degree from Teachers College, Columbia University.

Washington Heights. Florida, New Jersey, and New York are where most Dominicans settled. But the largest single group by far can be found in New York City's Washington Heights. This is a densely packed neighborhood on the island of Manhattan. Dominicans call the neighborhood Quisqueya Heights. *Quisqueya* (kees-KEH-yah) is the Native American name for Hispaniola, the island that the Dominican Republic shares with Haiti.

In Quisqueya Heights, a slice of Dominican culture comes alive in New York City. Cars fuel up at *bombas,* or service stations. People buy Dominican specialties at dozens of *mami y papi bodegas*—mom-and-pop grocery stores. Restaurants such as Las Tres Marías serve up hearty Dominican dishes such as *sancocho* (sahn-KOH-choh), or plantain stew. Everywhere is the sound of merengue, the Dominican dance music.

Like many other older neighborhoods in big cities, Washington Heights has its problems. Jobs are not easy to find. Drugs and drug-related crime are a burden for the community. Many young people, discouraged by the difficulty of finding jobs, drop out of school and join gangs. Good, affordable housing is in short supply. Since many Dominicans are dark skinned, they are often the victims of double discrimination—because of color and because of national origin.

New Lives, Old Ties. Community organizations help immigrants adapt to life in the United States. They provide recre-

Esmilda Abreu, a Dominican, grew up in Washington Heights in New York City. Called "Quisqueya Heights" by the Dominicans who live there, the neighborhood offers a taste of Dominican culture in the United States.

ational facilities, day care for children, family counseling, and classes in English. For help in coping with their immigration problems, Dominicans can turn to the Northern Manhattan Coalition for Immigrant Rights. A Dominican medical center provides health services. A Dominican Small Business Association assists the 9,000 small businesses owned by Dominicans. Many of those businesses are *bodegas,* where the Dominicans spend $1 billion each year.

Dominicans in Washington Heights and elsewhere maintain strong ties to their homeland. In 1987 alone, Dominicans sent an estimated $800 million to family members on the island. But strong ties with the United States are also developing. For more and more families, migration to the United States that was intended to be temporary is becoming permanent. More and more Dominicans are becoming U.S. citizens, proud to be called Dominican Americans.

Taking Another Look

1. Why have many Dominicans come to the United States in recent years?

2. Where do most Dominicans in the United States live?

3. **Critical Thinking** Why do you think more and more Dominicans in the United States are becoming U.S. citizens?

LOOKING AHEAD

Civil war, terrorism, or economic uncertainty sent thousands of Central Americans and Dominicans to the United States in the 1980s and 1990s. Similar conditions in the 1960s and 1970s had brought the first waves of South American immigrants to the United States. In the 1980s, the numbers of South American immigrants continued to grow, making them another vital part of the nation's Latino population.

It was a hot day in July 1991. Nicaraguan Dennis Martínez wound up for the pitch. As the ball whizzed past the batter, the umpire yelled "Strike!" The crowd went wild. Never before had a Latino pitched a perfect major league game in the United States.

People in the United States may consider baseball their national pastime, but it has become a national passion in the Caribbean Basin as well. Each Latino group has its heroes. Puerto Ricans are proud of Roberto Clemente, while Cuban Americans idolize José Canseco (kahn-SEH-ko). But perhaps Dominicans are the most enthusiastic baseball fans of all.

In the Dominican Republic, the government has built three baseball stadiums. Each town has dozens of teams. San Pedro alone boasts more than 200 teams.

Dominicans have been recruited by many teams in the U.S. major leagues. Although they play all positions, Dominicans have a special hold on *mediocampista* (meh-dee-oh-kam-PEES-tah), or "shortstop." Tony Fernández, Rafael Santana, Julio Franco, and Alfredo Griffin are but a few of the famous Dominican *mediocampistas*.

In 1983, the first Dominican won a place in the Baseball Hall of Fame. That year, pitcher Juan Marichal (mah-ree-CHAHL) joined the ranks of the nation's baseball legends.

CLOSE UP: Chapter 28

The Who, What, Where of History

1. **Who** is Rigoberta Menchú?

2. **What** was *la Violencia?*

3. **What** was the Sanctuary Movement?

4. **Where** is Little Managua?

5. **What** was the decision in *Plyer* v. *Doe?*

6. **Where** is Pico-Union?

7. **What** is El Rescate?

8. **What** problems cause many Dominicans to immigrate to the United States?

Making the Connection

1. What was the connection between the *ladinos* and the Maya of Guatemala?

2. What is the connection between the Trujillo dictatorship and present-day economic troubles in the Dominican Republic?

Time Check

1. In what year did the Supreme Court rule in the case of *Plyer* v. *Doe*?

2. How many years passed between the time the Sandinistas came to power in Nicaragua and when elections were held there?

What Would You Have Done

1. Imagine that a member of the Sanctuary Movement has asked you to help shelter Central American undocumented refugees. You could be arrested for hiding them. Would you agree to help? Why or why not?

2. Suppose that you are a Dominican student and you are denied a visa to

the United States. Would you wait to apply again or risk a trip to Puerto Rico? Explain.

Thinking and Writing About History

1. Rigoberta Menchú won the Nobel Peace Prize for defending the cultural rights of Maya. Oscar Arias won the prize for winning a cease-fire in Nicaragua. Write an acceptance speech for one of these two figures.

2. Create a mock interview in which a Maya refugee describes the series of events that led him or her from Guatemala to Los Angeles. Include comments on hardships encountered in the United States.

Building Skills: Analyzing Oral History

Oral history is made up of the stories and personal accounts told by everyday people. By reading oral histories, you can catch a glimpse of events through the eyes of the people who actually experienced them.

To read an oral history, keep the following tips in mind. First, find out the identity of the speaker. Next, determine the topic under discussion. Ask yourself how the person's background may influence his or her point of view. As you read the oral history, note any facts or opinions that the speaker may offer. Based on this analysis, form a conclusion about what the oral history tells you about the topic or event. If possible, check your conclusion against other sources of information.

Below is part of the oral history of Francisco Ramírez, a Guatemalan refugee. It comes from a book called *New Americans: An Oral History* by Al Santoni. Read the passage and then answer the questions that follow.

Francisco: *We think of our country— we are Kanjobals. Maybe someday, if we save money, we can go back and build a house and live the last years of our life in the town where we were born. But we cannot go back now, because conditions in Guatemala remain unstable and dangerous.*

If the American government accepts us, I would like to stay here and become a citizen. . . .

I hope we can apply under the new Immigration Law [of 1986] because between 1985 and 1986 I worked picking citrus and planting tomatoes and peppers [in the United States].

At the nursery where I now work, we have the W-4 tax forms that prove I have been working. . . .

1. What is the identity of the speaker?

2. What topics concern him?

3. What facts or opinions does he use to support his point of view?

4. Based on this account, what can you conclude about the reasons many Guatemalans have moved to the United States?

Express Yourself!

With a group of students, make a bulletin board display about the people of Guatemala, Nicaragua, or El Salvador. Display pictures, newspaper articles, essays, or poems that describe the experiences of the people of one of these countries.

Uruguayan American schoolchildren celebrate their heritage in the Hispanic Day Parade in New York. Increased immigration from South America has added new diversity to the U.S. Latino population.

SECTIONS

1 The Lure of Freedom

2 Building New Lives

South Americans in the United States Today

(1980–Present)

THINKING ABOUT THE CHAPTER

What are the national origins of South Americans who live in the United States today?

Florencia Florentín Rivarola (ree-vah-ROH-lah) knows the hard life of *campesinos* (kahm-peh-SEE-nohs), or peasant farmers. She was one of ten children of a *campesino* family in Paraguay. Florencia worked in her family's fields at an early age. Florencia recalled: "I never played. I never even had one toy when I was little. My play was working."

Florencia's large family lived in a one-room house made of clay and straw. To bring in money, her father hired out his eight sons as workers. Finally, with so many mouths to feed, he sent Florencia to be raised by an aunt and uncle.

That decision brought Florencia to the city of San Lorenzo. Florencia spoke Guaraní (gwah-rah-NEE), a Native American language that was one of Paraguay's two official languages. At a public school, she learned to speak Spanish, the nation's other official language. Some people discouraged Florencia from attending school. Florencia explained, "If you're a girl, they don't want you to go to school past the third grade. But I never agreed with that. Never!"

Florencia stayed in school until the 11th grade. But then her aunt died, and Florencia's days in school seemed to be over. However, in 1982, a wealthy family asked her to come to the United States as a housekeeper and nanny. In exchange, they promised to send her to school and give her a chance to learn English.

Driven by a fierce desire to learn and the hope for a better life, Florencia accepted. At age 18, she headed to the United States on a tourist visa. This chapter tells the story of Florencia and others like her who make up the nation's growing South American population.

1 THE LURE OF FREEDOM

◆ Why have growing numbers of South
◆ Americans sought to build new lives in the United States?

The Paraguay that Florencia left had been ruled with an iron hand since 1954 by General Alfredo Stroessner (STRES-ner). "Nobody could say anything against the government," recalled Florencia. "If people even joked about the government, they might just disappear." She looked forward to the freedom of the United States.

A Spirit of Freedom. Florencia's new job took her to Miami, Florida. But her employers did not keep their promises. They did not let her attend school or provide her with English lessons. To make matters worse, they worked her almost to exhaustion.

In the Spanish-speaking world of Miami, Florencia gradually met other Latinas—from Spain, Cuba, and elsewhere. Slowly, Florencia built up the courage to challenge her employers to provide what they had promised her.

When she did, they fired her and gave her a one-way ticket back to Paraguay. But Florencia's Latina friends gave her a place to stay and helped her find work. Finally, a Cuban American friend got her a student visa. "I got what I always wanted," said Florencia. "I finally went to school to study English."

Florencia Florentín Rivarola discusses her plans to begin a computer training program. When she came to the United States from Paraguay, Florencia fought for the opportunity to go back to school and learn English.

1980 Rebel group, the Shining Path, attacks Lima, Peru.

1980s–1990s Inflation increases the cost of living in many Latin American countries.

1985–1990 Immigration from South America to the United States jumps 40 percent.

1989 Chile holds free elections.

1992 Venezuelan government suppresses coup.

1993 Abimael Guzmán, leader of the Shining Path, is captured by Peruvian authorities.

In November 1992, Florencia got her high school diploma. With pride, she said, "To come from the jungle as a *campesina* and to get a high school degree in a big city like Miami. That is quite something."

The Land of Promise. In the early 1900s, when immigrants from Europe were pouring into the United States, people called the nation the Land of Promise. Florencia's story shows that many immigrants from South America still think of the United States that way.

Florencia returned to Paraguay for a visit in late 1992. A coup had overthrown General Stroessner. Still, Florencia believed that conditions had not improved.

Poor people still had no rights. People could tell I no longer lived in Paraguay. Fear was no longer written across my face. The United States had done that for me—it removed the fear.

In the 1980s and 1990s, similar stories could be told by other arrivals from South America. Argentine-born Rodolfo Singer reported that conditions in his Argentina had settled down since "the dirty war" ended (see Chapter 23). "But you still have more freedom here," explained Rodolfo. "In the United States, you can say anything you want. I think they call it freedom of speech."

Continued Troubles. In the last decades of this century, immigration from South America has surged. Economic hard times have driven many South Americans to the United States. In the late 1970s and early 1980s, the cost of living in Bolivia skyrocketed by 350 percent. Even higher rates of **inflation,** or rising prices, hit Peru. In 1988, the rate of inflation there was an enormous 119 percent. A suitcase full of Peruvian money was needed to pay for a restaurant meal worth $50.

As standards of living dropped, political unrest increased. In 1980, a violent Communist group called *el Sendero Luminoso,* or the Shining Path, burst onto the scene in Peru. In what Peruvians call the Black Night, the rebels swarmed into Lima and rained gunfire and bombs on the capital. For the next 13 years, terrorist acts claimed some 25,000 lives. In 1992, Peru finally captured Abimael Guzmán, the mastermind behind the Shining Path movement. But many of his followers continued to fight.

Other nations had other problems. In Colombia, large illegal-drug organizations known as **cartels** rivaled the power of the government. Battles between the cartels shook Colombia in the 1980s. Many government officials who tried to bring cartel members to justice were gunned down. The government stepped up efforts to break the power of the "drug lords." However, they remained powerful.

Under the weight of a huge foreign debt, the economy of Peru collapsed in 1988. Thousands fled to the United States and settled in several major cities. These Peruvian musicians perform traditional folk music on the streets of New Orleans.

Growing Immigration. In the 1990s, South American nations made greater strides toward establishing democracies. In 1989, for example, Chile held its first free election in more than a decade. However, political instability still continued to be a problem for many of the nations in the region. In 1992, for example, a failed coup attempt rocked Venezuela, the continent's oldest democracy. Economic problems also persisted throughout the region. As a result, immigrants from South America continued to come to the United States.

Figures from the U.S. Census Bureau revealed that between 1985 and 1990, the number of immigrants from Central and South America had jumped by some 40 percent. Experts estimate that the number of first- and second-generation South Americans in the United States will top one million early in the next century. Together with other Latino groups, they are changing the face of the nation.

Taking Another Look

1. What were some of the reasons South Americans came to the United States in the 1980s?

2. What trend do experts predict for the United States' South American population?

3. **Critical Thinking** In what ways is the experience of Florencia Florentin Rivarola typical of the lives of other Latino immigrants to the United States?

2 BUILDING NEW LIVES
◆ How have South Americans made their
◆ mark on the United States?

In the summer of 1974, 43-year-old Bolivian-born Jaime Escalante (es-kah-LAHN-teh) studied a population map of Los Angeles. The map showed the city's many ethnic neighborhoods. Escalante's

371

eye settled on solidly Mexican American East Los Angeles. A few days later, he applied for a job to teach math at Garfield High School in East Los Angeles. Garfield was one of the toughest schools in the city.

Stand and Deliver. Escalante knew that teaching math at a school like Garfield would be a challenge. But he was determined to show that Latino students could not only learn basic algebra and geometry but also succeed in more advanced courses in mathematics.

In La Paz, Bolivia, **Jaime Escalante** had earned great respect as a high school math and science teacher. But Bolivia's unstable government and economy worried him and his wife, Fabiola. In 1964, they decided to go to the United States. Escalante vowed to one of his brothers, "I am going to succeed even if I have to start from zero."

In California, Escalante did indeed start at zero. When the state refused to accept his teaching credentials, he went back to school. First, he learned English. Then, he earned an engineering degree. High-paying job offers came his way. But Escalante took the job he loved most—teaching.

In 1982, Escalante came to national attention when 18 of his students passed the Advanced Placement calculus examination. In 1988, the Bolivian teacher and his Mexican American students won fame in the movie *Stand and Deliver*, a celebration of Latino talent.

"Raise Your Sights." Escalante urged his students, "Raise your sights." Many South Americans in the United States have accepted Escalante's challenge. As a group, they have been highly successful. Some 70 percent of South Americans in the United States between the ages of 25 and 35 are high school graduates. More than 20 percent hold college degrees. In the 1990s, South Americans in the United States rivaled Cuban Americans in terms of rates of employment and size of income.

There are many reasons for such success. One is the drive and ambition of new arrivals such as Florencia Florentín Rivarola of Paraguay. Another is the large number of South American immigrants who come from the middle class, such as Jaime Escalante and Rodolfo and Mónica Singer. Most of them have come armed with education and technical skills that give them a head start in the United States.

New Communities. While South Americans live throughout the United States, the largest populations are in major cities such as Los Angeles, Chicago, Miami, and New York. In South America, people have traditionally looked to the cities for opportunity. Many immigrants to the United States head for the cities here as well. Mónica Singer explained: "After growing up in Buenos Aires, the move to New York City was not so hard. Both cities are very cosmopolitan [made up of people from all parts of the world]."

South American neighborhoods have grown up in several major cities. In Chicago, for example, a community of Colombian *costeños* (kohs-TEH-nyohs) has taken root. *Costeños* are of mixed African, Native American, and Spanish ancestry. In Colombia, the *costeños* live apart from Colombians of less mixed

This travel agency in Jackson Heights, New York, serves the largest South American community in the United States. Many South American immigrants visit their home countries to keep in touch with their families and their heritage.

descent, a reflection of the class system that grew up under Spanish rule. That pattern continues in the United States. Instead of living in Miami, where a large number of Colombians have settled, the *costeños* head to Chicago.

Diversity in New York City. The biggest settlement of South Americans in the United States is in Jackson Heights, in the New York City borough of Queens. Walking through Jackson Heights is like attending a meeting of the Organization of American States. Here the voices of people from most Latin American nations can be heard. Each immigrant group speaks Spanish with a little different accent from the others. As Rodolfo Singer reported, "We don't always understand each other."

You can taste the diversity in the area's restaurants—Peruvian, Uruguayan, Argentine, Ecuadoran, and more. You can see it on the newsstands, which carry papers from cities such as Santiago, Bogotá, and Buenos Aires. This diversity promises to increase in the next century.

Taking Another Look

1. From what South American countries have people come to the United States in recent years?

2. In what ways is Jackson Heights a diversified community of South American immigrants?

3. **Critical Thinking** The 1990 U.S. census combined South Americans and Central Americans into one category. Why do you think treating them separately in the future may give a more accurate picture of the two groups?

LOOKING AHEAD

The South American community in the United States has contributed to the growing Latino influence in the United States. In the next century, experts predict that larger numbers of Latinos will increase that influence even more. As the 1990s close, their impact can already be felt on nearly all aspects of U.S. life.

Miami's Bay of Biscayne Boulevard offers visitors a view of many of Miami's famous sites. From the boulevard, tourists may admire the modern office buildings in the business district and the huge oceangoing cruise ships docked on the Atlantic side of Biscayne Bay. The beautiful houses that line the bay's cove are another popular attraction. A sight missed by many, however, is a series of parking areas along the boulevard.

These parking areas face south. They allow people a chance to gaze across the water toward Latin America—the homeland of much of Miami's population. At the end of each parking area is a bust of a famous figure from Latin American history. Most of the sculptures are gifts to the United States from Latin American nations.

Peruvians take special pride in a gift from Lima, the capital of Peru. It is a monument to the writer Inca Garcilaso de la Vega (1539–1616). The inscription on the monument underscores the historic ties between Peru and Florida. It says, in part:

To honor the writer of Peru and the Americas. Author of Florida del Inca *[Florida of the Inca]: 1605, the exciting historical tale of the expedition of discovery of the Spanish Captain Hernando de Soto to these southern lands of the United States.*

CLOSE UP: Chapter 29

The Who, What, Where of History

1. **What** is a *campesino*?
2. **Who** was General Alfredo Stroessner?
3. **What** is inflation?
4. **Where** is the Shining Path based?
5. **Who** is Jaime Escalante?
6. **Who** are the *costeños*?
7. **Where** is Jackson Heights?

Making the Connection

1. What is the connection between high inflation and political instability and an increase in South American immigration to the United States?
2. What is the connection between changing immigration patterns and the population of Jackson Heights?

Time Check

1. In what year did the Shining Path first appear?
2. In what year did Venezuela experience a coup?

What Would You Have Done?

1. Imagine that you are a South American who is thinking about emigrating to the United States. Write a list of the pros and cons to help you decide what to do. Then, use your list to make a decision.
2. Suppose you were a South American immigrant. Would you choose to settle in Jackson Heights or in some other part of the United States? Explain.

Thinking and Writing About History

1. Compose a letter that Florencia

Florentín Rivarola might have written to her parents about the United States.

2. Imagine that you have been asked to produce a television series about Jaime Escalante's work at Garfield High School. Work with two or three classmates to outline several episodes of the series.

Building Skills: Interpreting a News Story

Most of our daily information about the world comes in the form of news stories presented on radio, on television, and in newspapers. These news stories may be either *hard* or *soft*. A *hard news* story reports on a critical event or topic in a factual manner. A *soft news* story, also known as a feature, reports on subjects of broad human interest. It is meant to entertain as well as inform.

To guide your interpretation of a news story, keep in mind the six question words commonly used by reporters: *who, what, when, where, why,* and *how?* Not all these questions may be answered by a news story, but they will help you discover key facts and points of interest. The news story on this page appeared in the *New York Times* on April 4, 1993. Read the article and then answer the questions that follow.

Santiago, Chile — . . . According to Government and United Nations figures, 40 percent of Chile's 13 million people, or 5.2 million, were living in poverty in March 1990 when [President Patricio] Aylwin took office after 17 years of military government. United Nations officials estimate that 33 percent, or about 4.2 million, are now below the poverty line. In Chile, this is generally considered to be a monthly income of less than $200 a month for a family of four. . . .

To achieve its goals, the Government has used an aggressive policy of tax increases, heavy social spending, and free-market growth. . . .

The progress does not mean that Chile has vanquished [ended] poverty or that levels here are lower than in Latin American countries like Argentina, Uruguay, and Costa Rica, where the segment of the population in poverty ranges from 15 to 20 percent.

But since economists predict the economy will continue to expand rapidly and the Government has agreed to continue high levels of social spending, Chile could soon be among the countries with the lowest poverty rates on the continent.

1. *Where* was the article written?
2. *What* changes have occurred in Chile?
3. *When* did these changes first appear?
4. *Who* does the reporter say is responsible for the changes?
5. *Why* were these changes initiated?
6. *How* were the changes brought about?
7. Would you describe this as a *hard* or *soft* news story? Explain.

Express Yourself!

Interview friends or family members who have immigrated to the United States. Ask them to explain why they decided to leave their homelands. Then ask why they chose to come to the United States. Use the answers from your interview to write a paragraph about what you have learned.

WE'VE GOT SOME DIFFICULT DAYS AHEAD, BUT IT REALLY DOESN'T MATTER WITH ME NOW, BECAUSE I'VE BEEN TO THE MOUNTAIN TOP, AND I'VE SEEN THE PROMISED LAND, I MAY NOT GET THERE WITH YOU, BUT I WANT YOU TO KNOW THAT WE AS A PEOPLE WILL GET TO THE PROMISED LAND."

The Centro Mater Runners—trophies resting at their feet—take a break after a race. The running team, based in Miami, Florida, is made up of teenage Latinos who train hard to win.

CHAPTER 30

SECTIONS

1 Latinos in the 1990s

2 The Growing Reach of Latino Culture

Toward a New Century
(1990–2000)

THINKING ABOUT THE CHAPTER

How has the nation's growing Latino population affected life in the United States?

In 1983, Ralph García watched young people race around on the basketball court at the Centro Mater Daycare Center in Miami (see page 349). These kids would make great runners, thought the Cuban-born teacher. He decided to form a team called the Centro Mater Runners.

For six years, Ralph devoted himself to the runners. For Ralph, no sacrifice was too great to ensure his team's success. Parents of the runners could not afford racing shoes, so Ralph worked at two jobs to buy them.

The tough streets of Little Havana posed a more serious problem. "I lost the first group to the streets," recalls Ralph. "But I swore to myself it would never happen again."

Ralph refused to give up. He spent a great deal of time with the runners. He trained with them mornings and after school. Eventually, news of his team and their struggle spread. The Miami Runners' Club raised money through an "Adopt a Runner" program. Marathon runner Beth Thomas volunteered as a second coach. By 1990, Ralph's team was winning races.

Children must leave Centro Mater at age 14. But they do not leave Ralph. "I won't quit on my kids when they turn 14," says Ralph. "The ages from 14 to 20 are crucial years. So I stay with them as a coach and as a friend."

Today, Ralph's star runners come from all over Latin America. They include Milton Zuloaga (soo-loh-AH-gah) of Peru, Hanskabell Amaragos (ah-mah-RAH-gohs) of the Dominican Republic, and Eddie Morales of Guatemala. There are also three award-winning runners from Nicaragua—Johnny Soza and Douglas and Jerry Nicaragua.

"They're the greatest kids on this planet," says Ralph. "They've survived tremendous cultural shock to win—not only races, but at life itself!" Struggles and triumphs shape the lives of many Latinos today, as you will read in this chapter.

1 LATINOS IN THE 1990S
◆ What are some of the characteristics of
◆ the nation's Latino population?

In March 1991, the U.S. Census Bureau released the first findings from its 1990 survey. Among the changes in the U.S. population, one fact stood out. In the ten years since 1980, the Latino population had boomed.

A People on the Rise. From 1980 to 1990, the Latino population of the United States rose by 53 percent. In 1990, almost 1 person in 10 in the United States was a Latino. The census count of Latinos stood at more than 22.3 million.

Experts predicted that Latinos would outnumber African Americans by the year 2015. If this happens, Latinos will be the nation's largest minority ethnic group in the 21st century.

The 1990 census also revealed several other important facts about Latinos. First, Latinos are young. The average age of Latinos is 25 as compared to 35 for the rest of the population. The largest single group falls in the age range of 5 to 17. Second, although Latinos of Mexican origin still counted as the largest group in 1990, other groups increased in size. The Puerto Rican and Cuban populations grew strongly. So did the number of Central and South Americans. The categories used to count Latinos are shown in the pie graph on page 379.

Challenges for the Future. Figures from the 1990 census also revealed some of the challenges facing the Latino community today. One of the biggest issues is the dropout rate among Latino youth. Of every ten students attending high school, four will not graduate. In addition, about 36 percent of Latino children live in poverty. Most of these children live in households headed by a single parent, usually the mother.

Norma Aburto Rice, a counselor for the Chicano Family Center in Houston, Texas, sees a connection between these figures. Says Rice:

> Many children tell me, "I have to quit school and help my mother." I tell them, "But you don't have a lot of chances to stop being poor when you quit school." But it's hard trying to argue with poverty.

A PROFILE OF LATINOS TODAY

U.S. POPULATION 1980–1990

	1980	1990
U.S. Population	226,546,000	248,710,000
Latino Population	14,609,000	22,354,000

Source: United States Bureau of the Census

POPULATION PROJECTION 1980–2020

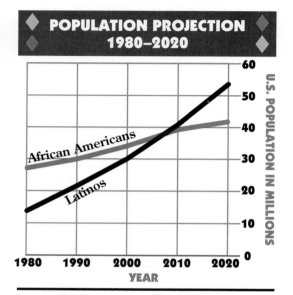

Source: *Time,* July 29, 1991

STATES WITH THE LARGEST LATINO POPULATIONS

State	Latino Population	Rank	Percentage in State	Percentage of U.S. Latinos
California	7,687,938	1	25.8	34.4
Texas	4,339,905	2	25.5	19.4
New York	2,214,026	3	12.3	9.9
Florida	1,574,143	4	12.2	7.0
Illinois	904,446	5	7.9	4.0
New Jersey	739,861	6	9.6	3.3
Arizona	688,338	7	18.8	3.1
New Mexico	579,224	8	38.2	2.6
Colorado	424,302	9	12.9	1.9

Sources: United States Decennial Census, 1990. United States Bureau of the Census, 1991.
U.S. Immigration and Naturalization Service, 1991.

◆ ◆ LATINOS BY ETHNIC GROUP ◆ ◆

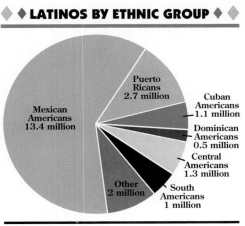

Puerto Ricans
2.7 million

Cuban Americans
1.1 million

Mexican Americans
13.4 million

Dominican Americans
0.5 million

Central Americans
1.3 million

South Americans
1 million

Other
2 million

Source: United States Bureau of the Census

AGE DISTRIBUTION OF LATINOS AND LATINAS

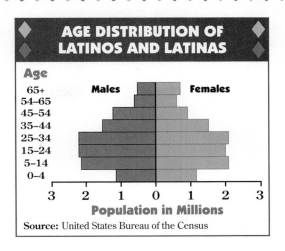

Source: United States Bureau of the Census

◆ ◆ SELECTED CHARACTERISTICS OF LATINO FAMILIES ◆ ◆

	Median Family Income	Percentage of Families Below Poverty Level	Percentage of Families Headed by Single Females	Percentage of Persons With Four Years of College or More
Latinos	$23,446	23.4	23.1	9.2
Non-Latinos	$35,183	9.2	16.0	22.2

Source: United States Bureau of the Census

◆ ◆ LATINOS AND LATINAS IN THE LABOR FORCE ◆ ◆

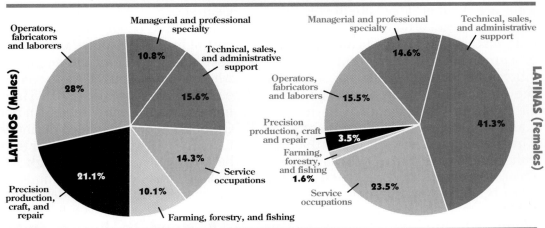

LATINOS (Males)

Operators, fabricators and laborers — 28%

Managerial and professional specialty — 10.8%

Technical, sales, and administrative support — 15.6%

Service occupations — 14.3%

Farming, forestry, and fishing — 10.1%

Precision production, craft, and repair — 21.1%

LATINAS (Females)

Managerial and professional specialty — 14.6%

Technical, sales, and administrative support — 41.3%

Operators, fabricators and laborers — 15.5%

Precision production, craft and repair — 3.5%

Farming, forestry, and fishing — 1.6%

Service occupations — 23.5%

Source: Current Population Reports, *The Hispanic Population of the United States*

379

Analyzing the data from the 1990 census took great effort. According to the census, the number of Latinos in the United States increased by 53 percent from 1980 to 1990. What effects might this increase have on Latinos?

Positive Signs. Other figures from the census show hope for the future. Poverty rates were highest for first-generation Latinos. This is especially true for Central American refugees who arrived in the 1980s. On the other hand, as one census official reports, "Most second- and third-generation Latinos are doing fine. They are about on a par with the record of other immigrant groups."

Proof that given an opportunity, Latinos as a group not only survive but even flourish can be found in California. Consider the Mexican American population there. In 1992, only 6 percent of Latinos in California received welfare payments. This percentage was far lower than for either Anglo or African American families. Over 40 percent of Latino households were headed by two parents, more than twice the rate for the rest of the California population. Further, in 94 percent of Latino households, at least one family member worked full time.

Poverty Revealed. However, poverty is still a problem for much of the Latino community. This came to national attention in 1992. That April, a Los Angeles jury acquitted four white police officers charged with beating Rodney King, an African American motorist (see page 324). Within hours, civil unrest began in South Central Los Angeles.

Fifty-three people were killed, and the cost of property damage was estimated at $800 million. One of the neighborhoods where unrest occurred was poverty-stricken Pico-Union (see page 361). This area is home to many Central American refugees. Of the 53 people who died during the disturbances, 19 were Latino. After the disturbances, police swept through the area looking for undocumented immigrants. As a result, 845 Latinos were deported.

A Need to Reach Out. Most Mexican Americans in the *barrios* of East Los Angeles stayed out of the disturbance.

Events afterward, however, involved growing numbers of Mexican Americans. The unrest revealed the depth of poverty faced by Central Americans. The search for undocumented migrants concerned Latino leaders such as Gloria Molina (see page 331). At meetings in the East Los Angeles *barrios,* Molina challenged Mexican Americans to reach out to Latinos from Central America. She said:

> At a time when we really needed to reach out there, we found that we were not as informed as we could have been. . . . All of us have a lot of work to do to learn about the changing demographics [nature of the people] of South Central Los Angeles.

Other Mexican American leaders backed Molina. María Salmón, a news editor at KVEA-Telemundo TV in Los Angeles, issued a challenge to Latinos: "Let's stop talking and fix things."

The Rebuilding Process. In 1993, a jury in federal court found two of the police officers involved in the beating incident guilty after a new trial. By this time, South Central Los Angeles had begun the difficult process of rebuilding. Amid the burned-out buildings, signs of hope stirred.

City officials began a jobs program to help relieve the poverty. Owners of the Grand Central Market contacted the "Jobs for a Future" program. They asked for volunteers to start a nonprofit tortilla company. Soon youths who had been involved in gangs appeared in the burned-out market area to lend a hand. They turned empty stalls into *tortillerías* (tohr-tee-yeh-REE-ahs), shops that sell tortillas.

In 1993, the New York Stock Exchange honored the youngsters at a dinner. Former rival gang members stood together and told the Wall Street executives how the program had affected their lives. One young man spoke for the others when he said, "I appreciate that when I wake up in the mornings I now have a job to come to." He added, "It was never like that before."

Latinos hope that there will be many such success stories. Using their large numbers to demand a greater voice in politics and government, Latino leaders like Gloria Molina seek to win the funding and pass the laws that will help prevent future Pico-Unions.

Taking Another Look

1. What did the 1990 census reveal about the nation's Latino population?

2. What challenges do Latinos face in the years ahead?

3. **Critical Thinking** What did the Los Angeles disturbances of 1992 show about the Latino community there?

2 THE GROWING REACH OF LATINO CULTURE

♦ How has a growing Latino population influenced life in the United States?

In 1989, the election campaign headquarters of Ileana Ros-Lehtinen (ROHS leh-TEEN-en) in Dade County, Florida, throbbed with the sounds of salsa. Celia Cruz, the "Queen of Salsa," put on a fiery show. Then, Cruz shouted a question to the crowd: "Who do the people want?" The crowd roared back: "Ros-Lehtinen!"

Excitement built as everyone waited to learn the results of a special election for the U.S. Congress. The county had not elected a woman in more than 50 years. There had never been a Latina in Congress. Nor had there ever been a Cuban American in either the House of Representatives or the Senate.

Around midnight, after the polls had closed, Celia Cruz stepped to the microphone. She shouted, *"¡Los Cubanos han ganando!"* ("The Cubans have won!") The victory gave meaning to the headline that had recently appeared in a New York City Spanish-language newspaper, *El Diario/La Prensa*: "It's Time to Pay Attention to Latinos."

A Political Voice. As the 1990s opened, Latino activists moved to organize Latino voters. To register Latinos, a group called *Hágase Contar* ("Make Yourself Count") took to the phones. In cities with large Latino populations, members explained the registration process in both Spanish and English. They urged people to take the time to put their names on the voting rolls. That way Latinos would be eligible to vote in the next election.

Latinos had made inroads in government since the days of *El Movimiento* in the 1960s and 1970s (see Chapter 22). Yet many Latinos were impatient with the slow pace of change. One Latino organizer complained, "We either get this nation's attention, or we continue being seen as a second-class minority group."

Many Latinos saw the 1992 election year as a test of Latino strength. After the 1990 census, many election districts had been redrawn. Thus, Latino votes would have more influence on the outcome of elections. In the 1992 elections, Latino voters helped send ten new Latinos to Congress. There they joined eight other Latino representatives. The new faces included two Latinas— Lucille Roybal-Allard (rohy-BAHL-ah-YAHRD) of California and Nydia Velázquez of New York.

Into the Cabinet. During the 1992 presidential campaign, Bill Clinton promised to appoint Latinos to the cabinet. He kept that promise. He selected former Denver mayor Federico Peña as Secretary of Transportation. For Housing and Urban Development (HUD), he chose his campaign advisor, Henry Cisneros.

Henry Cisneros included among his ancestors some of the first settlers of New Mexico. Other relatives had fled Mexico during the Mexican Revolution. Much of Cisneros's adult life had prepared him to take charge of HUD. In 1968, he graduated from Texas A & M University with a degree in city management. He later worked on the federal government's Model Cities Program.

In the 1980s, he served four terms as mayor of his native San Antonio. Cisneros led a drive to put more Latinos in decision-making positions in government, business, law, and other fields. He declared that only with this kind of clout could the Latino community win equal rights in U.S. society.

A Voice in Business. While Latino politicians rose in government, Latino business leaders began making their way into management positions of large corporations (see Gallery of Latino Entrepreneurs, pages 384–385). Yet the pace of progress to the very top ranks of large companies has been slow. A survey taken in 1992 showed that only 41 out of more than 7,000 directors of large corporations were Latinos. It is on a slightly lower level, the so-called middle-management level, where real progress has been made.

Similarly, great progress can be seen in the number of successful companies that Latinos have started. There is now a new and growing class of Latino **entrepreneurs,** people willing to risk money in businesses.

Most Latino entrepreneurs have built small businesses. By 1990, Latino-owned businesses numbered more than 422,000. Though they make up only 3 percent of all the companies in the United States, their numbers are growing. Between 1980 and 1990, for example, the number of Latino-owned businesses jumped by 70 percent. Those businesses included the Mexican *mercados* (mer-KAH-dohs), or grocery stores, of East Los Angeles. They also included the thousands of *bodegas* in the cities where Latinos had settled.

Contributions to Science. Growing numbers of Latinos are appearing in the nation's research laboratories and universities as well as in its businesses. These Latinos are making important contributions to science, technology, and education (see pages 386–387).

The U.S. space program, for example, is one area that has benefited from Latino contributions. Five Latino engineers—José Luis Gonzales, Rudy Barroza, Ramón Samaniego, Carlos Marshall, and Antonio Beltrán—helped the program get underway. These five engineering pioneers helped develop the first U.S. rockets in the 1950s.

A Cultural Voice. The growing influence of Latino life is all around us. Recently, a reporter asked President Clinton to name his favorite dish. Without hesitation he answered, "Enchiladas." This was just one sign of how Latino foods

GALLERY OF LATINO ENTREPRENEURS

Deborah Aguiar-Vélez (ah-GWEE-ahr VEH-les) (1955–)
New York-born Puerto Rican, Aguiar has won a reputation for
helping Latinas start businesses. Aguiar worked in the small-
business division of New Jersey's Department of Commerce.
She has served on the boards of the Hispanic Women's Task
Force and the Hispanic Leadership Opportunity Program. In
1990, the American Women in Economic Development
named Aguiar as the year's Outstanding Woman
Entrepreneur Advocate.

Carlos José Arboleya (ahr-boh-LEH-yah) (1929–)
Arboleya was a bank president in Cuba. He fled his native
country during the Castro revolution. In the United States, the
former banker took a job as a clerk in a shoe factory. Today, he
is one of Miami's leading domestic and international bankers.
His many awards for humanitarian work include the 1988
American Red Cross Man of the Year Award.

Nancy E. Archuleta (ahr-choo-LEH-tah) In 1985, Archuleta
founded her own company. Archuleta, who is of Mexican
American and Native American ancestry, has turned
MEVATEC into the nation's fastest-growing Latino-owned
business. It supplies high-tech materials for the nation's airforce and provides engineering services for the Defense
Department. In 1993, MEVATEC was nominated for an award
as one of the nation's leading small businesses.

Oscar de la Renta (1932–) Born in the Dominican
Republic, de la Renta has helped change the fashion tastes of
the world. As one of the world's top clothing designers, he is
well known from New York to Paris to Hong Kong. In 1982,
the talented designer opened *La Casa del Niño,* or The Home
of the Child, in the Dominican Republic. The non-profit shelter provides education and health care for the nation's poverty-stricken children.

Roberto C. Goizueta (1931–) Goizueta came to the United States from Cuba at age 18. By age 50, he had become the chief executive officer of the Coca-Cola Company. Goizueta was the first Latino to take charge of a major U.S. firm. Aside from running the company, Goizueta found time for community service. In 1984, he won the Herbert Hoover Humanitarian Award of the Boys Clubs of America. In 1986, he won the Ellis Island Medal of Honor.

Luis Nogales (noh-GAH-les) (1943–) The son of Mexican American farmworkers, Nogales grew up following the harvests. He later became involved in the Chicano movement. After winning a law degree at Stanford University, Nogales went to work in the media. He became president of the Spanish-language television network Univision. He also served on the board of the Mexican American Legal Defense Fund (MALDEF), working to advance the rights of Latinos.

Katherine Ortega (1934–) In 1983, Ortega followed Romana Banuelos (bah-NWEH-lohs) to become the second Latina to serve as Treasurer of the United States. Ortega is the daughter of a Mexican American blacksmith. In college, she studied business and economics. Ortega has worked for both the federal government and private businesses. Today, she is a member of the boards of directors of several major corporations.

Joseph A. Unanue (oo-NAHN-weh) (1925–) The Puerto Rican-born founder of Goya Foods, Inc. has turned his company into the nation's largest privately owned Latino enterprise. In 1993, Goya was rated one of the top 100 companies in providing economic opportunities for Latinos. Said Unanue: "This company owes so much to the [Latino] community, we must reach out to provide support in any way we can."

GALLERY OF LATINO SCIENTISTS

Luis Walter Alvarez (1911–1988) Alvarez, a Mexican American physicist born in California, has done pioneering work in his field. In 1986, Alvarez achieved one of the greatest honors granted to scientists—he won the Nobel Prize in physics. He has also won such outstanding awards as the Einstein Medal and National Medal of Science.

Angeles Alvariño de Leira (ahl-vah-REE-nyoh) (1916–) Born in El Ferrol, Spain, Alvariño has lived in the United States since 1957. Her work in oceanography, or the study of the ocean, and marine biology has won her a number of Fulbright and National Science Foundation awards. Today, she works at the National Marine Fisheries at La Jolla, California. There, Alvariño does the work she loves best—studying new species of sea life.

Teresa Bernárdez (behr-NAHR-des) (1931–) Bernárdez earned a medical degree from the University of Buenos Aires. She left her native Argentina in the 1960s to study psychiatry in the United States. She went on to become a professor of psychiatry at such schools as the University of Michigan and Radcliffe College. Bernárdez's research on women's health has won her many awards, including the Peace Award from the Pawlowski Foundation.

Graciela Candelas (kahn-DEH-lahs) (1922–) Candelas began her career in molecular biology in her native Puerto Rico. She later went on to study in the mainland United States. Today, Candelas lives and teaches in Puerto Rico. Because the University of Puerto Rico participates in exchange programs, Candelas regularly teaches at mainland institutions. In 1985, the Puerto Rican Institute in New York honored Candelas with its Special Science Award.

Francisco Dallmeier (1953–　) Dallmeier, a wildlife biologist, specializes in the conservation of earth's natural resources. A Venezuelan, he has worked for the Smithsonian Institution in Washington, D.C., since 1986. Although he calls the United States his home, he regularly travels to Bolivia, Brazil, Peru, Ecuador, Guatemala, Panama, Puerto Rico, and the Virgin Islands to train groups in ways to preserve the environment of the Americas.

José Méndez (1921–　) In 1947, Méndez graduated from the Universidad de San Carlos in Guatemala City. The young scientist went on to earn advanced degrees in physiology and nutrition in the United States. Today, Méndez teaches at Pennsylvania State University. He also participates in nutritional training programs in developing countries around the world. His dream is to stamp out world hunger.

Víctor Pérez-Méndez (1923–　) Born in Guatemala City, Guatemala, Pérez received college degrees from Hebrew University in Jerusalem, Israel, and Columbia University in New York City. Today, Pérez is one of the leading nuclear physicists in the United States. His many accomplishments include heading the physics department at the University of California at San Francisco and publishing more than 300 ground-breaking research papers.

Pedro Antonio Sánchez (1940–　) Born in Havana, Cuba, Sánchez has become one of the leading agronomists, or specialists in farm production, in the Americas. His work focuses on easing poverty through an end to deforestation and over-farming. His work has taken him all over South America and to Africa. For his outstanding service, the government of Peru awarded Sánchez the *Orden de Meríto Agrícola,* the Agricultural Order of Merit.

1980–1990 Latino population in the United States rises by 53 percent.

The number of Latino-owned businesses rises 70 percent.

1989 Ileana Ros-Lehtinen becomes the first female Cuban American to win election to Congress.

1992 Jury acquits four police officers charged in the beating of Rodney King sparking riots; 19 Latinos die in the riots and 845 are deported.

1993 President Clinton appoints Federico Peña and Henry Cisneros to top Cabinet positions.

have caught on with the general U.S. population. Tortillas now outsell bagels, English muffins, and pita bread. Salsa outsells ketchup. At baseball games, sports fans of all backgrounds order nachos as often as they order popcorn.

The United States has become more Latino in other ways as well. People's everyday conversations are sprinkled with Spanish words. "Bring it to me *pronto*." ("fast"). "*Adios, amigo*." ("Goodbye, friend."). "See you *mañana*." ("tomorrow"). "*¿Qué pasa?*" ("What's happening?") These are but a few of the hundreds of Spanish words that have slipped into the English language.

If you look and listen carefully, you will find signs and sounds of Latino influence almost everywhere. Check video stores for films with popular Latino actors and actresses such as Anthony Quinn, Edward James Olmos, Raul Julia, Andy Garcia, Elizabeth Peña, and Rosie Pérez.

Turn on the TV and you will see news people such as Jackie Nespral and Gisele Fernández. Cable television carries Spanish networks such as Univision or Telemundo.

Sort through CD racks in music stores and you will find recording artists such as Los Lobos, Gloria Estefan, and Barrio Boyzz. Check magazine stands and bookstores for titles with a Latino flavor.

Giving Back. The paths Latinos have followed in the United States are many. No one life is typical. But the story of Manuel Sotomayor (soh-toh-mah-YOR) gives a hint of the range of Latino experiences. His mother, Beatrice Hernández, came to San Francisco from Mexico at the turn of the century. In 1917, Beatrice married Mexican migrant Manuel Sotomayor. The following year, she gave birth to a son. In Mexican tradition, the child was given the same name as his father.

Young Manuel's father later went to seek his fortune in the boomtown of Mexicali. He never returned. Beatrice, however, inspired her son with a will to succeed. Manuel overcame the barriers of poverty to graduate from Harvard Business School. He became a management consultant whose work led him to Spain, Venezuela, and Mexico.

Manuel's travels gave him a renewed awareness of his heritage. On one trip to Mexico, he visited his mother's hometown of Mazatlán. In the cathedral, he searched for and found her birth certificate. He stills cherishes the memory.

Today, at age 75, Manuel serves as an advocate for disabled people such as his daughter Phyllis. He sits on advisory boards for several California counties. He

The sign declares "Guatemalans in New York," as the Latino musicians play for the crowd. Proud of their heritage, Latinos continue to enrich U.S. culture.

is also a member of a multicultural advisory committee for the state's program on disabilities. Manuel sums up his experience in these words:

> I'm a U.S. citizen from a Spanish-speaking background. I've benefited greatly from the system. But not all Spanish-speaking people have. I have a responsibility as a citizen to help other Spanish-speaking people. One of my first steps is to help . . . disabled people who speak Spanish. By being a voice for the . . . disabled, I can now say to myself: "So, Manuel, now you know why you were born."

Manuel Sotomayor's story is one of hard work. It also shows his appreciation of his Latino heritage and his desire to serve both the United States and the Latino community. These have been—and continue to be—-the keys to the Latino experience in U.S. history.

Taking Another Look

1. What political gains have Latinos made in the closing years of this century?

2. What gains in the business world have Latinos made in the last decade?

3. **Critical Thinking** What does the story of Manuel Sotomayor tell you about the Latino experience in the United States?

LOOKING AHEAD

This chapter marks the end of this book. However, it is not the end of the story of Latinos. Latinos will remain an important influence on the culture of the United States to which they have already contributed so much. Latinos will continue to cope with, and triumph over, difficulties. Finally, all the people of the United States will benefit from the determination and accomplishments of Latinos.

In 1992, a new star made her television debut in more than 80 different countries. A fluffy blue bilingual puppet, Rosita appears regularly on the children's show *Sesame Street*.

Rosita speaks both Spanish and English. She also experiences many of the barriers commonly encountered by Latino children. The spunky puppet shows children how to handle these problems in a positive way. She also gives non-Latino children a look at Latino culture.

Rosita's creator is Mexican puppeteer Carmen Osbahr. Osbahr explained: "Rosita is proud of being able to speak two languages."

Rosita reflects the large number of Spanish-speaking families in the United States today. A 1993 poll shows that nearly 50 percent of Latino families speak Spanish at home. But surveys also show that each group has its own expressions, accents, and sometimes its own rules of grammar. Rosita, for example, speaks with the Mexican accent of her creator. Noted one *Sesame Street* writer, "We're teaching Rosita some Puerto Rican and Cuban phrases."

Spanish words have been creeping into the English language for centuries. However, Rosita is helping non-Latino children learn even more Spanish expressions. A phrase Rosita uses is *"Se Habla Español"* ("Spanish Is Spoken Here").

CLOSE UP: Chapter 30

The Who, What, Where of History

1. **What** is the largest Latino group in the nation?
2. **Where** is Pico-Union?
3. **What** effect did the civil unrest that shook Los Angeles in 1992 have on the Latino community there?
4. **Who** is Ileana Ros-Lehtinen?
5. **Who** were the two Latinas elected to Congress in 1992?
6. **Who** is Henry Cisneros?
7. **What** are entrepreneurs?

Making the Connection

1. What was the connection between immigration trends of the 1980s and the results of the 1990 census?
2. What is the connection between the size of the Latino population and increased Latino political power?
3. What is the connection between the growth of the Latino population and recent changes in U.S. culture?

Time Check

1. During which decade did the Latino population rise by 53 percent?
2. In what year did Ileana Ros-Lehtinen win election to Congress?

What Would You Have Done?

1. Suppose that you are a Latino living in Pico-Union in 1993. What actions would you suggest to your community to help rebuild the area?

2. Suppose that you belonged to *Hágase Contar*. What reasons would you give Latinos to register to vote? If possible, present your reasons in Spanish and English.

Thinking and Writing About History

1. Imagine that you are a member of the Centro Mater Runners. Design a poster urging businesses to support a trip to the New York Marathon.

2. Write an article for your local newspaper with the following title: "Latino Influence is Here to Stay."

3. With several classmates, prepare a display showing evidence of the Latino influence on U.S. culture.

Building Skills: Identifying Trends

Through a study of history, you can identify certain patterns or *trends*. By spotting trends, you can make predictions about the future. Predictions based on the available facts help individuals, businesses, and governments plan ahead.

The table displayed on this page shows changes in the Latino population from 1950 to 2010. Use the information in the table to answer the questions below.

1. What information is shown in each column on the table?

2. (a) What percent of the U.S. population was Latino in 1970? (b) In 1990?

3. How does the table predict the Latino population will change from 1990 to 2000?

4. (a) How many Latinos lived in the United States in 1960? (b) In 1980?

5. Which of the following best describes Latino population trends from 1950 to 1990: steadily decreasing, steadily increasing, or little change?

6. Do you predict that the influence of the Latino population on U.S. culture will increase or decrease in the years ahead? What information in the table supports your answer?

LATINO POPULATION IN THE UNITED STATES 1950–2010

Year	Number (in thousands)	Percent of U.S. Population	Percent Change (Since Previous Decade)
1950	4,039	2.6	43.5
1960	6,346	3.5	57.2
1970	9,616	4.7	51.5
1980	14,608	6.4	51.9
1990	22,354	9.0	53.0
2000	30,271	10.9	35.4
2010	38,574	12.9	27.4

Sources: United States Bureau of the Census. Passel and Edmondston, "Immigration and Race: Recent Trends inImmigration to the United States," "The Future Immigrant Population of the United States," and "Immigration and Immigrant Generations in Population Projections."

Express Yourself!

Use an outline map of the world or use paper to trace the map of the world on pages 394–395. Ask your family or friends to list the places they have lived and to tell you when they lived there. On your map of the world, label all the places on your list. Also, write the dates when they lived in these places.

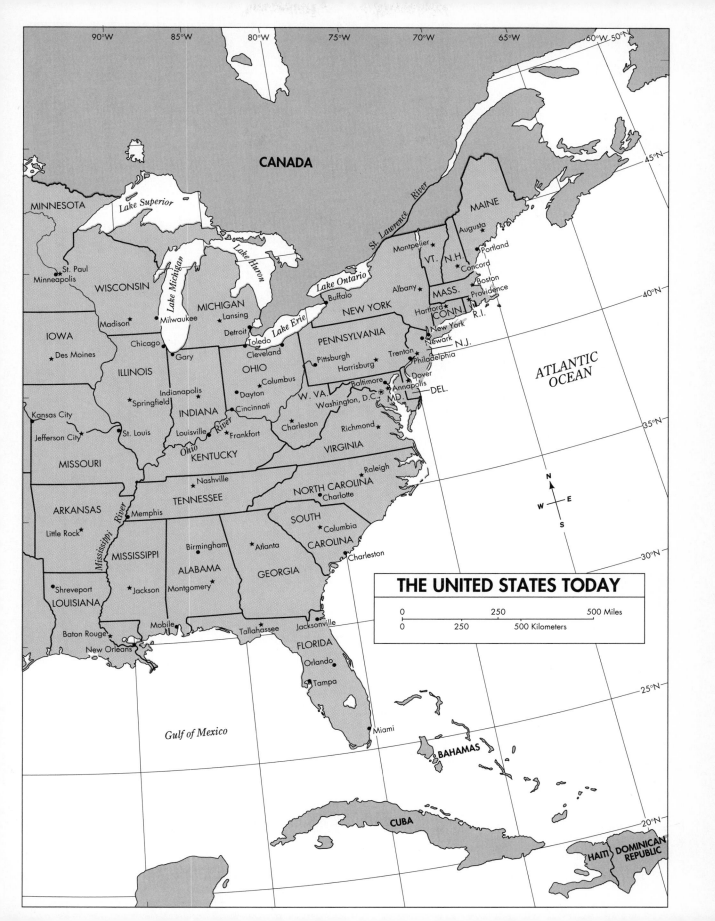

90°W · 85°W · 80°W · 75°W · 70°W · 65°W · 60°W · 50°N

CANADA

MINNESOTA

Lake Superior

St. Paul
Minneapolis

WISCONSIN

Lake Michigan

Lake Huron

MICHIGAN

Madison
Milwaukee · Lansing

IOWA

Des Moines

Chicago
Gary

ILLINOIS

Indianapolis
Springfield

INDIANA

Detroit
Toledo · Lake Erie
Cleveland

OHIO

Dayton
Columbus

Cincinnati

St. Lawrence River

MAINE
Augusta

Montpelier
VT. · N.H · Portland
Concord

Lake Ontario
Buffalo

Albany · Boston
Providence
MASS.
Hartford
CONN. · R.I.

NEW YORK

PENNSYLVANIA

Pittsburgh
Harrisburg · Trenton
Philadelphia
New York
Newark
N.J.

Dover

Baltimore
Annapolis
Washington, D.C.
MD. · DEL.

**ATLANTIC
OCEAN**

Kansas City

Jefferson City

MISSOURI

St. Louis

Louisville
Frankfort

Ohio River

KENTUCKY

W. VA.
Charleston

Richmond

VIRGINIA

35°N

40°N

Nashville

TENNESSEE

Raleigh

NORTH CAROLINA
Charlotte

ARKANSAS

Memphis

Mississippi River

Little Rock

SOUTH
Columbia
CAROLINA

Charleston

30°N

N
W · E
S

Birmingham

MISSISSIPPI

ALABAMA

Atlanta

GEORGIA

Shreveport

LOUISIANA

Jackson · Montgomery

THE UNITED STATES TODAY

0 — 250 — 500 Miles
0 — 250 — 500 Kilometers

Baton Rouge

New Orleans

Mobile

Tallahassee

Jacksonville

FLORIDA

Orlando

Tampa

Gulf of Mexico

Miami

25°N

BAHAMAS

20°N

CUBA

HAITI · DOMINICAN
REPUBLIC

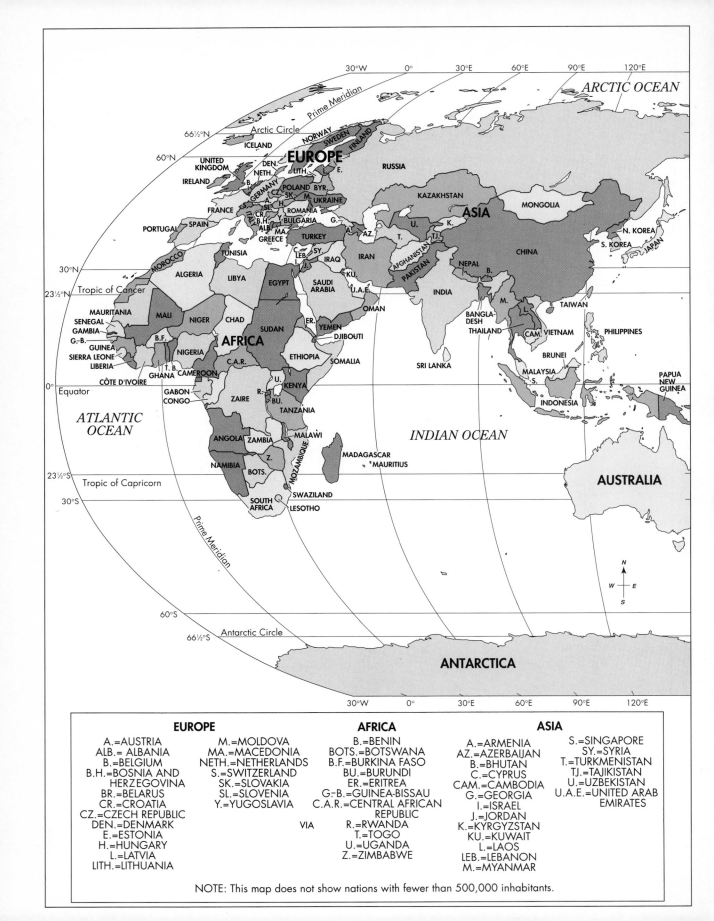

ARCTIC OCEAN

30°W · 0° · 30°E · 60°E · 90°E · 120°E

Prime Meridian

Arctic Circle
66½°N
60°N

NORWAY
SWEDEN
FINLAND
ICELAND

UNITED
KINGDOM
IRELAND

EUROPE

DEN.
NETH.
LITH.
E.
L.

RUSSIA

GERMANY
POLAND
BYR.
SK.
M.
UKRAINE

FRANCE

A.
S.
SL.
CZ.
H.
CR.
B.H.
Y.
ROMANIA
BULGARIA

KAZAKHSTAN

MONGOLIA

ASIA

N. KOREA
S. KOREA
JAPAN

PORTUGAL
SPAIN

ALB.
MA.
GREECE

TURKEY

G.
A.
AZ.
T.

U.
K.
TJ.

CHINA

30°N

MOROCCO

TUNISIA

C.
LEB.
SY.
I.
IRAQ

IRAN

AFGHANISTAN
PAKISTAN

NEPAL
B.

TAIWAN

23½°N   Tropic of Cancer

ALGERIA

LIBYA

EGYPT

SAUDI
ARABIA

KU.

U.A.E.

INDIA

BANGLA-
DESH

M.

MAURITANIA
SENEGAL
GAMBIA
G.-B.
GUINEA
SIERRA LEONE
LIBERIA
CÔTE D'IVOIRE

MALI

NIGER

CHAD

B.F.

NIGERIA

AFRICA

SUDAN

ER.
YEMEN
DJIBOUTI

OMAN

THAILAND

CAM.
VIETNAM
L.

PHILIPPINES

BRUNEI

C.A.R.

ETHIOPIA

SOMALIA

SRI LANKA

MALAYSIA
S.

PAPUA
NEW
GUINEA

0°   Equator

GHANA
T. B.
CAMEROON

GABON
CONGO

ZAIRE

U.
R.
BU.
KENYA

TANZANIA

INDIAN OCEAN

INDONESIA

ATLANTIC
OCEAN

ANGOLA

ZAMBIA

MALAWI

Z.
MOZAMBIQUE

MADAGASCAR
MAURITIUS

AUSTRALIA

23½°S   Tropic of Capricorn

NAMIBIA

BOTS.

30°S

SOUTH
AFRICA

SWAZILAND
LESOTHO

Prime Meridian

N
W   E
S

60°S

66½°S   Antarctic Circle

ANTARCTICA

30°W · 0° · 30°E · 60°E · 90°E · 120°E

EUROPE

A.= AUSTRIA
ALB.= ALBANIA
B.= BELGIUM
B.H.= BOSNIA AND
HERZEGOVINA
BR.= BELARUS
CR.= CROATIA
CZ.= CZECH REPUBLIC
DEN.= DENMARK
E.= ESTONIA
H.= HUNGARY
L.= LATVIA
LITH.= LITHUANIA

M.= MOLDOVA
MA.= MACEDONIA
NETH.= NETHERLANDS
S.= SWITZERLAND
SK.= SLOVAKIA
SL.= SLOVENIA
Y.= YUGOSLAVIA

AFRICA

B.= BENIN
BOTS.= BOTSWANA
B.F.= BURKINA FASO
BU.= BURUNDI
ER.= ERITREA
G.-B.= GUINEA-BISSAU
C.A.R.= CENTRAL AFRICAN
REPUBLIC
R.= RWANDA
T.= TOGO
U.= UGANDA
Z.= ZIMBABWE

VIA

ASIA

A.= ARMENIA
AZ.= AZERBAIJAN
B.= BHUTAN
C.= CYPRUS
CAM.= CAMBODIA
G.= GEORGIA
I.= ISRAEL
J.= JORDAN
K.= KYRGYZSTAN
KU.= KUWAIT
L.= LAOS
LEB.= LEBANON
M.= MYANMAR

S.= SINGAPORE
SY.= SYRIA
T.= TURKMENISTAN
TJ.= TAJIKISTAN
U.= UZBEKISTAN
U.A.E.= UNITED ARAB
EMIRATES

NOTE: This map does not show nations with fewer than 500,000 inhabitants.

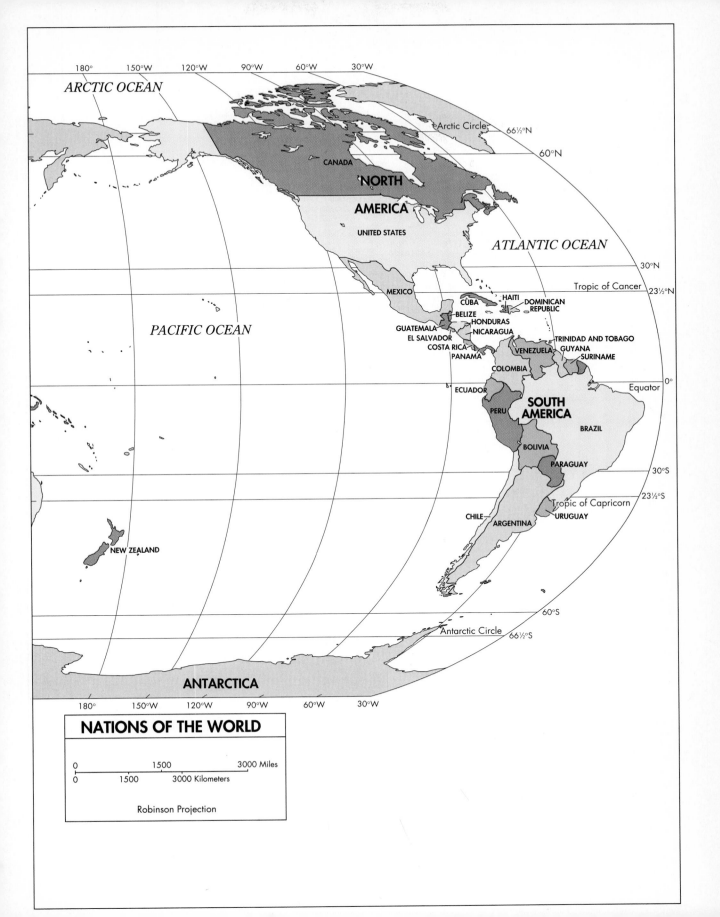

ARCTIC OCEAN

180°   150°W   120°W   90°W   60°W   30°W

Arctic Circle   66½°N

60°N

CANADA

NORTH

AMERICA

UNITED STATES

ATLANTIC OCEAN

30°N

Tropic of Cancer   23½°N

MEXICO

CUBA   HAITI
DOMINICAN
REPUBLIC
BELIZE
HONDURAS
GUATEMALA   NICARAGUA
EL SALVADOR
COSTA RICA
PANAMA

PACIFIC OCEAN

TRINIDAD AND TOBAGO
VENEZUELA   GUYANA
SURINAME
COLOMBIA

ECUADOR

0°
Equator

PERU   SOUTH
AMERICA

BRAZIL

BOLIVIA

PARAGUAY

30°S

23½°S
Tropic of Capricorn

CHILE   URUGUAY
ARGENTINA

NEW ZEALAND

60°S

Antarctic Circle   66½°S

ANTARCTICA

180°   150°W   120°W   90°W   60°W   30°W

NATIONS OF THE WORLD

0   1500   3000 Miles

0   1500   3000 Kilometers

Robinson Projection

LATIN AMERICA

Note: The capital cities of some island countries are shown in parentheses.

San Diego
El Paso
UNITED STATES
New Orleans
Miami
Gulf of Mexico
Nassau
BAHAMAS
Havana
CUBA
DOMINICAN REPUBLIC
Puerto Rico (U.S.)
Virgin Islands (U.S. & U.K.)
MEXICO
Kingston
HAITI
San Juan
ANTIGUA & BARBUDA (St. John's)
Mexico City
BELIZE
Belmopan
JAMAICA
Port-au-Prince
Santo Domingo
DOMINICA (Roseau)
HONDURAS
ST. LUCIA (Castries)
Guadeloupe (Fr.)
GUATEMALA
Tegucigalpa
Caribbean Sea
BARBADOS (Bridgetown)
Guatemala City
Managua
Martinique (Fr.)
ST. VINCENT & THE GRENADINES (Kingstown)
San Salvador
EL SALVADOR
NICARAGUA
GRENADA (St. George's)
COSTA RICA
Caracas
TRINIDAD & TOBAGO (Port-of-Spain)
San José
Panama City
Georgetown
PANAMA
VENEZUELA
Paramaribo
Panama Canal
GUYANA
Cayenne
Magdalena R.
Orinoco R.
French Guiana (Fr.)
Bogotá
SURINAME
COLOMBIA

ATLANTIC OCEAN

Tropic of Cancer
20°N
0° Equator

Quito
ECUADOR
Galápagos Islands (Ecuador)
Amazon R.

PERU
Lima
BRAZIL
São Francisco R.

PACIFIC OCEAN

La Paz
Brasília
BOLIVIA
Sucre
Paraguay R.
20°S
Tropic of Capricorn
PARAGUAY
Asunción
Paraná R.

N
W · E
S

CHILE
ARGENTINA
Santiago
Buenos Aires
URUGUAY
Montevideo
Río de la Plata

40°S

Falkland Islands (U.K.)

0   400   800 Miles
0   400   800 Kilometers

120°W   100°W   80°W   60°W   40°W   20°W

PRONUNCIATION GUIDE FOR SPANISH WORDS AND TERMS

This pronunciation guide will help you to pronounce the Spanish words and terms that appear in *The Latino Experience in U.S. History*. Pronunciations appear in parentheses. Hyphens are used to divide the syllables of words. The syllable that is being stressed, or emphasized, appears in capital letters. Other syllables are in lowercase letters.

Vowel Sound	Symbol	Example
a	ah	pata (PAH-tah)
ai, ay	eye	baile (BEYE-lay)
au	ow	causa (KOW-sah)
e in a syllable that ends with a vowel	eh	me (meh)
e in a syllable that ends with a consonant	e	comer (coh-MER)
ei, eu, ey	ay	reina (RAY-nah)
i	ee	filo (FEE-loh)
o	oh	como (COH-moh)
oi, oy	oi	oiga (OI-gah)
u	oo	luna (LOO-nah)
ua	wa	guapo (GWAH-poh)
ue	weh	buena (BWEH-nah)
ui	wee	buitre (BWEE-treh)

Consonant Sound	Symbol	Example
c before a, o, u	k	casa (KAH-sah)
c before e, i	s	cebolla (se-BOH-yah)
ch	ch	mucho (MOO-choh)
g before e, i	h, gh	gitana (hee-TAH-nah)
g (other)	g	haga (AH-gah)
h	(silent)	honor (oh-NOHR)
j	h	jota (HOH-tah)
ll	y	llora (YOH-rah)
ñ	ny	doña (DOH-nyah)
q	k	que (kay)
rr	rr	carro (KAH-rroh)
s	s	beso (BAY-soh)
x	ks	exacto (ek-SAHK-toh)
y in a word	y	mayo (MAH-yoh)
y alone (as a translation of "and")	ee	
z	s	zapato (sah-PAH-toh)

GLOSSARY

This glossary defines important terms used in this book. The page on which a term first appears is given in parentheses at the end of the definition.

abolitionist   person who worked for an end to slavery in the United States in the 1800s (106)

acto   (AHK-toh) a fast-moving play (287)

adelantados   (ah-del-ahn-TAH-dohs) governors (15)

adobe   (uh-DOH-bee) sunbaked brick made of clay and straw (5)

affirmative action   policy designed to compensate for past discrimination in hiring practices and education and to increase opportunities for minorities and women (321)

aliancistas   (ah-lee-ahn-SEES-tahs) members of the *Alianza,* a Latino group formed during the 1960s that asked the U.S. and Mexican governments to reconsider the ownership of old land grants (289)

aliens   citizens of another country (334)

amnesty   general pardon (174)

annex   add onto a territory or nation (107)

armada   a huge fleet (9)

autonomismo   (ow-toh-noh-MEES-moh) self-government (257)

autonomy   self-government (185)

barrio   (BAHRR-ee-oh) a section of a city where there are large numbers of Latinos (207)

bilingual   the ability to communicate in two languages (265)

blockade   the use of ground troops or warships to prevent the passage of persons or supplies to the area or territory of an enemy (274)

blockading   closing off (156)

boycott   organized refusal to buy or use a particular product or service in order to achieve certain aims (286)

braceros   (brah-SEH-rohs) contract laborers (199)

budget deficit   when the government spends more money than it takes in (321)

caciques   (kuh-SEEKS) Tabascan chiefs (25)

campesino   (kahm-peh-SEE-noh) a peasant farmer (368)

cartel   a large illegal-drug organization (370)

caudillos   (kow-DEE-yohs) military strongmen (109)

centralism   a concept of government in which power is concentrated in the national government (113)

Chicano   (chee-KAH-noh) a term developed during the 1960s to mean Mexican American and to express pride in being Mexican American (252)

Christianity   religion based on the teachings of Jesus (13)

civil disobedience   disobeying laws one considers to be unjust (289)

Cold War   war of words between the former Soviet Union and the United States after World War II (249)

colony   settlement of people living in a land outside their home country, but under the power of the home country (8)

Columbian Exchange   the exchange of items among people of different cultures during the 1500s (39)

commonwealth   a self-governing nation with political and economic ties to another country or nation (257)

communes   farms jointly owned and worked by formerly landless peasants (271)

Compromise of 1850   agreement under which Congress admitted California to the Union as a free state, left the slavery question in other former Mexican lands up to the settlers, and passed the Fugitive Slave Law (109)

Confederacy   government set up by the southern states when they seceded from the United States in 1860 (143)

congregaciones   (kohn-greh-gahs-YOHN-es) communities or settlements formed during the 1500s by Spanish priests who won permission to resettle Native Americans (38)

conquistadors   (kahn-KEES-tuh-dors) Spanish conquerors sent to the Americas in the 16th century (9)

Contras   (KOHN-trahs) groups of rebels who fought a guerrilla war against the Sandinista government in Nicaragua (299)

convoy system   a method whereby warships

accompany merchant or treasure ships to protect them from raiders (48)

coup (KOO) a sudden and usually violent overthrow of a government (297)

coyote name used for people who guide migrants without the necessary immigration papers across the border from Mexico to the United States (332)

criollos (kree-OH-yohs) people born of Spanish parents in the Americas (42)

Crusades a series of religious wars launched by European Christians aimed at winning back the Holy Land (modern-day Israel) (7)

cultural diffusion the spread of cultures across global regions (40)

cultural imperialism the act of destroying the culture of a people and replacing it with another culture (187)

culture way of life of a people including their skills, beliefs, customs, and arts (3)

death squad term used to describe bands of military thugs who murder anyone suspected of opposing the government in some Latin American countries (298)

Declaration of Independence a document issued by British colonists in North America in 1776 declaring the colonists' independence from Great Britain and their intent to found a new nation (68)

deportation the act of being expelled from a country (284)

descamisados (des-kah-mee-SAH-dohs) "shirtless ones"; the name given to urban workers in Argentina during the 1940s (253)

emancipation the act of freeing a person from slavery (73)

embargo a ban on imported goods (351)

empresarios (em-preh-SAHR-yohs) agents hired by the Spanish government to recruit settlers for Texas (101)

encomendero (en-koh-men-DEH-roh) owner of an *encomienda* (16)

encomienda (en-koh-mee-EN-dah) a portion of land granted by the Spanish government in the Americas. The *encomienda* system allowed the owner the right to use the labor of Native Americans who lived on the land. (16)

entradas (en-TRAH-dahs) expeditions (55)

entrepreneur a person who organizes, manages, and risks money in a business venture (383)

españoles (es-pahn-YOH-les) Spaniards (96)

excommunicate to deny religious rites (111)

Fair Employment Practices Committee committee set up by Franklin D. Roosevelt that aimed at ending discrimination in war industries (239)

federalism the idea that the central government shares its power with the states (113)

federal system a way of organizing government so that powers are shared between the states and the central government (69)

Fifteenth Amendment an amendment to the U.S. Constitution granting African American males the right to vote (143)

Foraker Act an act passed by the U.S. Congress in 1900 that placed Puerto Rico under the control of the U.S. government (186)

Fourteenth Amendment an amendment to the U.S. Constitution granting African Americans citizenship with equal rights under the law (143)

friars priests who were members of a Roman Catholic religious group (37)

fugitive a runaway (109)

Gadsden Purchase territory, consisting of parts of present-day southern New Mexico and Arizona, that was purchased from Mexico by the United States for $10 million in 1853; (108)

gaucho (GOW-choh) cowboy (111)

genízaro (hen-EE-sah-roh) a term used in New Mexico during the 1800s for a Native American who no longer lived among his or her own people or who had been captured and then freed (96)

GI Bill of Rights a series of laws passed to provide benefits to veterans to help them return to civilian life (239)

glaciers (GLAY-shuhrs) massive sheets of ice (3)

Great Depression worldwide economic slowdown of the 1930s (198)

guerrilla war   warfare conducted in small battles by small units of soldiers (177)

gunboat diplomacy   a diplomacy that Theodore Roosevelt had used to get the right to build the Panama Canal (196)

hacienda   (ah-SYEN-dah) a huge country estate (42)

hidalgo   (ee-DAHL-goh) a gentlemen (13)

home rule   self-government (186)

huelga   (WEL-gah) a strike (284)

human rights   the basic rights of people as human beings (298)

Immigration Act of 1924   U.S. law that set permanent quotas on immigration from outside the Western Hemisphere and banned the immigration of Asians (225)

indentured servant   a person who agrees to work for a certain length of time in return for passage to a colony (67)

indocumentados   (een-doh-koo-men-TAH-dohs) undocumented workers (326)

inflation   an economic condition under which prices of goods and services rise rapidly (370)

Iran-Contra scandal   scandal that uncovered that the U.S. government had secretly sold arms to Iran, despite the U.S ban on such sales (323)

Islam   a religion based on the teachings of Muhammad (7)

isolationism   a foreign policy that calls for avoiding alliances with other nations (198)

jíbaro   (HEE-bah-roh) one who worked on a sugar or tobacco plantation (187)

Jim Crow laws   system of laws put into effect after 1877 in the South that discriminated against African Americans and provided for segregated public facilities (143)

Jones Act   a law passed in 1917 granting U.S. citizenship to all Puerto Ricans who wanted it (186)

junta   (HOON-tuh) a ruling council (255)

kivas   (KEE-vuhs) underground chambers where Pueblo people performed religious ceremonies (5)

La Causa   (lah KOW-sah) The Cause; the movement begun in the 1960s by César Chávez and migrant farmworkers to form a union to win better wages and civil rights (284)

la familia   the family (331)

la huelga   see *huelga* (231)

Ladino   a language that combines elements of Spanish, Portuguese, and Hebrew   (280)

latifundia   (lah-tee-FOON-dee-ah) a large commercial farm (271)

lector   (lek-TOHR) a reader hired by cigar workers to read to them as they worked (165)

legislature   a lawmaking body (67)

Louisiana Purchase   French territory, stretching from the Mississippi River to the Rocky Mountains, purchased by the United States from Napoleon in 1803 (70)

mador   (MAH-dohr) a male Native American who was responsible for making sure that Christian converts attended religious services (62)

maestra   (mah-ES-trah) a female chaperone (62)

maquiladoras   (mah-kee-lah-DOH-rahs) assembly plants (334)

martial law   a state of emergency under which a country is controlled by the military (177)

mass production   ways of making huge quantities of goods cheaply and quickly   (144)

materialism   a love of money and wealth (175)

McCarthyism   the practice of charging people with political disloyalty on the basis of little or no evidence (250)

mesas   flat tablelands on the tops of cliffs (5)

mestizos   (mes-TEE-sohs) people of mixed Spanish and Native American ancestry (42)

Mexican Cession   lands that Mexico turned over to the United States after the Mexican American War in 1848 (108)

Middle Passage   passage across the Atlantic Ocean from West Africa to the Americas that was the route of the African slave trade (19)

migrant workers   seasonal farmworkers who travel across regions in order to find work (209)

migration   act of moving from one country or region to another (often in a group) (3)

Minuteman   Patriot of the American Revolution who was ready to fight at a minute's notice (68)

mission   a settlement devoted to spreading Christianity (38)

Missouri Compromise   agreement made in 1820 by which Missouri was admitted to the Union as a slave state, Maine was admitted as a free state, and the Louisiana Territory was divided into slave and free parts (106)

Monroe Doctrine   a U.S. foreign policy, announced in 1823, that warned European powers not to interfere in the Western Hemisphere (71)

Mountain Men   rugged fur trappers and traders who helped open the lands beyond the Mississippi in the early 1800s (106)

mulatto   (muh-LAHT-oh) a person who has one parent of European and one of African descent (42)

multinationals   companies with business operations in more than one nation (353)

mural   a wall painting depicting a scene or scenes (314)

Muslim   a person who practices the religion of Islam (8)

mustang   a wild horse (60)

mutualista   (moo-twah-LEES-tah) a mutual aid society established by Mexican Americans to help new immigrants adjust to life in the United States (217)

nationalism   pride in one's country (111)

nationalization   a policy whereby the government takes control of privately owned industries or companies (200)

naval stores   products used in the maintenance of ships, for example, tar, pitch, and turpentine (86)

neutral   not taking sides in a conflict (75)

New Deal   a package of political, economic, and social policies and practices established by President Franklin D. Roosevelt in the 1930s (199)

nomad   person who wanders from place to place to hunt and gather food (3)

nuevomexicano   (NWEH-voh-meh-hee-KAH-noh) a Spanish-speaking settler in New Mexico (95)

nuyorican   (noo-yoh-REE-kahn) a second-generation Puerto Rican who is born and raised on the mainland of the United States (306)

Open Door policy   policy under which no nation that wanted to invest in China could be kept from doing so (146)

Operation Bootstrap   program instituted in Puerto Rico during the 1950s to stimulate its economy (260)

pachucas   (pah-CHOO-kahs) Mexican American women who socialized with zoot-suiters (243)

pachucos   (pah-CHOO-kohs) Mexican American men who adopted the zoot-suit style (243)

Parliament   the lawmaking body in Great Britain (67)

partido **system**   (pahr-TEE-doh) a system under which a villager agreed to take care of a *rico's* flock of sheep in exchange for a share of the newborn animals (96)

Patriot   colonist who favored the independence of the 13 colonies from Great Britain (75)

patrones   (pah-TROHN-es) people who governed their communities and cared for the people (95)

peninsulares   (peh-neen-soo-LAH-res) in Spanish colonies, people who had been born in Spain and were therefore at the top of colonial society (42)

peon   a person forced to work for a colonial employer until his or her debts to the employer were paid (42)

peonage   a system of labor under which Native Americans were forced by their debts to continue working for colonists (42)

per capita income   average annual income per person (271)

pharaohs   (FAIR-ohs) Egyptian rulers (6)

Platt Amendment   an amendment to the Cuban constitution of 1901 that gave the United States certain rights in Cuba (189)

poblano   (poh-BLAH-noh) a civilian settler from New Spain (62)

political exile   a person who leaves a country for political reasons (272)

popular sovereignty   principle that the people who lived in a territory should decide whether or not to allow slavery there (109)

porteño   (pohr-TEH-nyoh) person who lives in the city of Buenos Aires (111)

poverty line   an officially defined level of income below which a family cannot afford its basic needs (262)

presidio   (prih-SEED-ee-oh) a fort (14)

privateer   owner of private ships that served as

warships, or the ships themselves (49)

Progressives   a group of reformers from the early 1900s who tried to make government more responsive to workers (195)

protectorate   a country that is technically independent but is really controlled by a stronger power (189)

public works program   program established by President Franklin D. Roosevelt to put people back to work during the Great Depression (199)

pueblos   the Spanish name given to Native Americans who lived in adobe houses in the Americas (5)

pyramid   (PIHR-uh-mihd) a huge building with a square base and sloping triangular sides (3)

ranchero   (rahn-CHEH-roh) an owner of a ranch (81)

rancho   (RAHN-choh) a small farm (57)

recession   an economic downturn (324)

Reconstruction   the period from 1865 to 1877 during which former Confederate states rejoined the Union (143)

Redcoat   name for a British soldier during the American Revolution (68)

Red scare   a period during which a fear of communism swept the United States (250)

referendum   a popular vote of the people (344)

refugee   a person forced to leave his or her homeland due to war or persecution (274)

repatriate   to send back or return a person to his or her homeland (228)

reservations   places where Native Americans lived who had been forced from their homelands onto land no one else wanted (145)

rico   (REE-koh) a wealthy individual (96)

Roosevelt Corollary   a U.S. policy, announced in 1904, that the United States would act as an "international police power" to prevent foreign nations from interfering in the Western Hemisphere (197)

Sandinistas   revolutionaries who had opposed the U.S. occupation of Nicaragua in the 1930s (255)

santero   (sahn-TEH-roh) a carver of wooden statues of saints (95)

sea dog   an English sailor who attacked Spanish ships in the Caribbean (9)

secede   to withdraw (152)

seceded   withdrew or separated (143)

secularize   removal of religious ownership or control (98)

segregate   to separate, usually according to race (143)

segregation   a policy of separation, usually according to race (251)

slavery   practice of owning human beings as property, or the condition of being enslaved (7)

social bandit   an outlaw who claims to be acting on behalf of an oppressed group (138)

Spanish Borderlands   name given to the northern lands of New Spain (54)

squatters   illegal settlers (136)

subsist   to live on (3)

superpowers   nations with the strongest military power and the greatest political and economic influence (249)

surplus   extra; more than needed (3)

tallow   substance made from the fat of animals and used to make candles and soap (98)

tariff   a tax (174)

tejano   (teh-HAH-noh) a Mexican settler in Texas (100)

Thirteenth Amendment   the amendment to the U.S. Constitution that freed enslaved African Americans (143)

title   ownership (135)

tribute   a payment that one people or nation is forced to pay to another (4)

U.S. Constitution   the body of laws under which the United States operates (69)

underground   name given to secret antigovernment movements (268)

vaquero   (vah-KEH-roh) a cattleherder (60)

vassal   a subject of the Aztec (27)

viceroy   a royal representative (41)

yellow journalism   exaggerated and sometimes untrue reporting of news events (179)

zoot suit   a suit that had an oversize jacket with wide lapels and padded shoulders, high-waisted baggy pants that narrowed to a snug fit at the cuffs, and a broad-brimmed hat (243)

SOURCES

Sources for quotations are given by page number (in parentheses) and in the order in which the quotations appear on each page.

UNIT 1

BIG PICTURE

(3) Michael C. Meyer and William L. Sherman, *The Course of Mexican History* (New York: Oxford, 1987) p. 111.

CHAPTER 1

(11) Paolo Emilio Taviani, *Columbus the Great Adventure* (New York: Orion, 1991), p. 83.   (11) Robert H. Fuson, *The Log of Christopher Columbus* (Maine: International Marine, 1987), p. 73.   (11) Kirkpatrick Sale, *The Conquest of Paradise* (New York: Plume, 1990), p. 61.   (11) Kirkpatrick Sale, *The Conquest of Paradise* (New York: Plume, 1990), p. 62.   (12) Robert H. Fuson, *The Log of Christopher Columbus* (Maine: International Marine, 1987), p. 76.   (12) Robert H. Fuson, *The Log of Christopher Columbus* (Maine: International Marine, 1987), p. 79.   (12) Kirkpatrick Sale, *The Conquest of Paradise* (New York: Plume, 1990), p. 92.   (12) Robert H. Fuson, *The Log of Christopher Columbus* (Maine: International Marine, 1987), p. 84.   (12) Kirkpatrick Sale, *The Conquest of Paradise* (New York: Plume, 1990), p. 103.   (13) Kirkpatrick Sale, *The Conquest of Paradise* (New York: Plume, 1990), p. 124.   (14) Kirkpatrick Sale, *The Conquest of Paradise* (New York: Plume, 1990), p. 139.   (14) Michele de Cuneo, quoted in Kirkpatrick Sale, *The Conquest of Paradise* (New York: Plume, 1990), p. 138.   (14) Paolo Emilio Taviani, *Columbus the Great Adventure* (New York: Orion, 1991), p. 181.   (17) Fray Antonio de Montesinos, quoted in Alastair Reed, *Reflections, Writing for Columbus* (New York: New York, 1992) p. 66.   (17) Daniel Boorstin, *The Discoverers* (New York: Random House, 1983), p. 631.   (18) Las Casas, quoted in Eric Williams, *From Columbus to Castro: A History of the Caribbean 1492–1969* (New York: Vintage, 1970) p. 37.   (18) Spanish king, quoted in Eric Williams, *From Columbus to Castro: A History of the Caribbean 1492–1969* (New York: Vintage, 1970) p. 42.   (19) Spanish writer, quoted in Eric Williams, *From Columbus to Castro: A History of the Caribbean 1492–1969* (New York: Vintage, 1970) p. 45.

CHAPTER 2

(23) John A. Crow, *The Epic of Latin America* (California: University of California, 1980) p. 73.   (23) Ferdinand Columbus, quoted in "La Ruta Maya," *National Geographic,* Oct. 1989.   (24) Fray Juan Díaz, quoted in "The Mysterious Maya," *National Geographic,* October 1989.   (25) Miguel Leon-Portilla, *The Broken Spears* (Boston: Beacon, 1962) p. 17.   (26) Miguel Leon-Portilla, *The Broken Spears* (Boston: Beacon, 1962) p. 25.   (26) Miguel Leon-Portilla, *The Broken Spears* (Boston: Beacon, 1962) p. 26.   (26) John A. Crow, *The Epic of Latin America* (California: University of California, 1980) p. 76.   (27) John A. Crow, *The Epic of Latin America* (California: University of California, 1980) p. 76.   (28) Bernal Díaz, quoted in John M. Cohen, *The Conquest of New Spain* (New York: Penguin, 1963) p. 214.   (29) Díaz, quoted in A.P. Maudslay, *Discovery and Conquest of Mexico 1517–1521* (New York: Buccaneer, 1986) p. 215.   (29) Ronald Wright, *Stolen Continents* (New York: Houghton Mifflin, 1992) p. 26.   (31) Miguel Leon-Portilla, *The Broken Spears* (Boston: Beacon, 1962) p. 93.

CHAPTER 3

(35) Jonathan Kandell, *La Capital* (New York: Owl Book, 1988) p. 126.   (36) Jonathan Kandell, *La Capital* (New York: Owl Book, 1988) pp. 129–130.   (37) Selden Rodman, *A Short History of Mexico* (New York: Stein and Day, 1982) p. 38.   (37) Ronald Wright, *Stolen Continents* (New York: Houghton Mifflin, 1992) p. 147.   (38) Vasco de Quiroga, quoted in John Crow, *The Epic of Latin America* (California: University of California, 1980) p. 193.   (38–39) Jonathan Kandell, *La Capital* (New York: Owl Book, 1988) p. 152.   (42) Jonathan Kandell, *La Capital* (New York: Owl Book, 1988) p. 157.   (44) John Bierhorst, *The Mythology of Mexico and Central America* (New York: William Morrow and Co., 1990) p. 86.   (45) Jonathan Kandell, *La Capital* (New York: Owl Book, 1988) p. 158.

CHAPTER 4

(49) Arturo Morales Carrión, *Puerto Rico: A Political and Cultural History* (New York: Norton, 1983) pp. 13–14.

CHAPTER 5

(56) Oñate, quoted in David J. Weber, *The Spanish Frontier in North America* (New Haven: Yale University, 1992) p. 81.   (58) Ramón, quoted in David J. Weber, *The Spanish Frontier in North America* (New Haven: Yale University, 1992) p. 161.   (61) Serra, quoted in John A. Schultz, *Spain's Colonial Outpost* (San Fransico: Boyd and Fraser, 1985) p. 33.   (62) Crespi, quoted in John A. Schultz, *Spain's Colonial Outpost* (San Fransico: Boyd and Fraser, 1985) p. 35.

UNIT 2

THE BIG PICTURE

(69) Pablo Vizcardo, quoted in Salvadorde Madariaga, *The Fall of the Spanish American Empire* (New York: Collier Books) p. 261.

CHAPTER 6

(74) Page Smith, *A New Age Now Begins: A People's History of the American Revolution* (New York: Penguin, 1984) p. 582.

CHAPTER 7

(85) David J. Weber, *The Spanish Frontier in North America* (New Haven: Yale University, 1992) p. 271.   (85) David J. Weber, *The Spanish Frontier in North America* (New Haven: Yale University, 1992) p. 280.   (90) Ronald Syme, *Bolívar the Liberator* (New York: William Morrow and Co., 1968) p. 135.

CHAPTER 8

(97) Ignacio Rodríguez Galván, J. Lloyd Read, *Mexican Historical Novel, 1826–1910* (New York: Instituto de las Españas, 1939).   (97) Michael C. Meyer and William L. Sherman, *The Course of Mexican History* (New York: Oxford University, 1987) p. 367.   (99) Mariano Vallejo, quoted in Time-Life Books, *The Spanish West* (Virginia: Time-Life, 1976) pp. 187–88.

UNIT 3

THE BIG PICTURE

(105) David S. Weber, *Foreigners in Their Native Land: Historical Roots of the Mexican Americans* (New Mexico: University of New Mexico, 1973) p. 104.   (105) Michael Aaron, *Sarmiento's Travels in the U.S.*

in 1847 (New Jersey: Princeton University Press, 1970) p. 120.   (105) Michael Aaron, *Sarmiento's Travels in the U.S. in 1847* (New Jersey: Princeton University Press, 1970) p. 133.   (105) Michael Aaron, *Sarmiento's Travels in the U.S. in 1847* (New Jersey: Princeton University Press, 1970) pp. 132–133.   (105) Sarmiento, quoted in Michael Aaron, *Sarmiento's Travels in the U.S. in 1847* (New Jersey: Princeton University Press, 1970) p. 304.   (106) Sarmiento, quoted in Michael Aaron, *Sarmiento's Travels in the U.S. in 1847* (New Jersey: Princeton University Press, 1970) p. 304.   (106) Sarmiento, quoted in Michael Aaron, *Sarmiento's Travels in the U.S. in 1847* (New Jersey: Princeton University Press, 1970) p. 169.   (109) Michael C. Meyer and William L. Sherman, *The Course of Mexican History* (New York: Oxford University, 1987) p. 314.

CHAPTER 9

(112) José Sánchez, quoted in David J. Weber, *Mexican Frontier, 1821–1846: The American Southwest Under Mexico* (New Mexico: University of New Mexico, 1982) p. 170.   (113) Mier y Terán, quoted in David J. Weber, *Mexican Frontier, 1821–1846: The American Southwest Under Mexico* (New Mexico: University of New Mexico, 1982) p. 170.   (114) Mier y Terán, quoted in David J. Weber, *Mexican Frontier, 1821–1846: The American Southwest Under Mexico* (New Mexico: University of New Mexico, 1982) p. 170.   (114) Lucas Alamán, quoted in David J. Weber, *Mexican Frontier, 1821–1846: The American Southwest Under Mexico* (New Mexico: University of New Mexico, 1982) p. 170.   (116) David J. Weber, *Mexican Frontier, 1821–1846: The American Southwest Under Mexico* (New Mexico: University of New Mexico, 1982) p. 251.   (116) Ramón Ruiz, *Truimphs and Tragedies* (New York: W.W. Norton, 1992) p. 209.   (116) Juan Almonte, quoted in David J. Weber, *Mexican Frontier, 1821–1846: The American Southwest Under Mexico* (New Mexico: University of New Mexico, 1982) p. 247.   (118) David J. Weber, *Mexican Frontier, 1821–1846: The American Southwest Under Mexico* (New Mexico: University of New Mexico, 1982) p. 178.

CHAPTER 10

(124) Thomas A. Bailey, *A Diplomatic History of the American People* (New York: Appleton-Century-Crofts, 1969) p. 255.   (125) General Arista, quoted in Time-Life Books, *The Spanish West* (Alexandria: Time-Life Books, 1976) p. 199.   (127) Time-Life Books, *The Spanish West* (Alexandria: Time-Life Books, 1976) p.

225.   (128) Livie Isauro Duran and H. Russell Bernard, *Treaty of Guadalupe Hidalgo* (New York: Macmillan, 1973) p. 203.

CHAPTER 11

(133) Carey McWilliams, *North from Mexico: The Spanish-Speaking People of the United States* (New York: Greenwood Press, 1968) p. 105.   (136) Luis Valdez and Stan Steiner, *Aztlan: An Anthology of Mexican American Literature* (New York: Alfred A. Knopf, 1972) pp. 103–104.   (137) Cortina, quoted in Luis Valdez and Stan Steiner, *Aztlan: An Anthology of Mexican American Literature* (New York: Alfred A. Knopf, 1972) p. 115.

UNIT 4

THE BIG PICTURE

(143) José Martí, quoted in Hugh Thomas, *Cuba, The Pursuit of Freedom* (New York: Harper and Row, 1971) p. 311.

CHAPTER 12

(150) Loreta Janeta Velazquez, *Blows of the Hammer* (Indianapolis: Bobbs-Merill, 1955) p. 295.   (151) Loreta Janeta Velazquez, *Blows of the Hammer* (Indianapolis: Bobbs-Merill, 1955) p. 297.   (153) Alvin M. Josephy, Jr., *The Civil War in the American West* (New York: Alfred A. Knopf, 1991) p. 80.   (156) Robert Ely, quoted in *Amercian Heritage,* vol. xix, (American Heritage Pub., 1968) pp. 109–110.   (156) U.S. Naval Institute, *David Glasgow Farragut; Our First Admiral* (Annapolis: U.S. Naval Institute, 1943) p. 142.

CHAPTER 13

(160) José Rivero Muñiz, "Tampa at the Close of the Nineteenth Century" *Florida Historical Quarterly* (April, 1963) p. 337.   (161) Gary R. Mormino and George E. Pozzetta, *The Immigrant World of Ybor City* (University of Illinois Press, 1987) p. 66.   (163) Virginia E. Sánchez Korrol, *From Colonia to Community: The History of Puerto Ricans in New York City, 1917–1948* (Westport: Greenwood Press, 1983) p. 40.   (164) José Rivero Muñiz, "Tampa at the Close of the Nineteenth Century" *Florida Historical Quarterly* (April, 1963) p. 447.   (165) Gerald E. Poyo, *With All and for the Good of All* (Duke University Press, 1989) p. 56.   (167) James O'Brien, quoted in Robert J. Rosenbaum, *Mexicano Resistance in the Southwest* (Austin: University of Texas Press, 1981) p. 119.   (168) Robert W. Larson, *New Mexico's Quest for Statehood (1846-1912)* (University of New Mexico Press, 1968) p. 303.   (168) Robert W. Larson, *New Mexico's Quest for Statehood (1846–1912)* (University of New Mexico Press, 1968) p. 281.   (169) Robert W. Larson, *New Mexico's Quest for Statehood (1846–1912)* (University of New Mexico Press, 1968) p. 279.

CHAPTER 14

(173–74) Deborah Bachrach, *The Spanish-American War* (California: Lucent Books, 1991) pp. 15–16. (176) Martí, quoted in Ann L. Henderson and Gary R. Mormino, *Spanish Pathways in Florida: 1492–1992* (Florida: Pineapple Press, 1991) p. 244.   (177) Albert Marrin, *The Spanish-American War* (New York: Macmillan, 1991) p. 14.   (178) William J. Calhoun, quoted in Albert Marrin, *The Spanish-American War* (New York: Macmillan, 1991) p. 17.   (179) Donald Barr Chidsey, *The Spanish-American War* (New York: Crown, 1971) p. 52.   (181) Rubén Darío, quoted in Hugh Thomas, *Cuba, The Pursuit of Freedom* (New York: Harper and Row, 1971) p. 417.

CHAPTER 15

(185) Davis, quoted in Deborah Bachrach, *The Spanish-American War* (California: Lucent Books, 1991) p. 87.   (185) Kal Wagenheim, *Puerto Rico, A Profile* (New York: Praeger, 1970) p. 63.   (186) Luis Muñoz Rivera, quoted in Denis J. Hauptly, *Puerto Rico, An Unfinished Story* (New York: Atheneum, 1991) p. 85.   (187) Kal Wagenheim, *Puerto Rico: A Profile* (New York: Praeger, 1970) p. 70.   (187) Raymond Carr, *Puerto Rico: A Colonial Experiment* (New York: New York University Press, 1984) p. 57. (190) Hugh Thomas, *Cuba, The Pursuit of Freedom* (New York: Harper and Row, 1971) p. 501.   (191) Hugh Thomas, *Cuba, The Pursuit of Freedom* (New York: Harper and Row, 1971) p. 539.

UNIT 5

THE BIG PICTURE

(195–6) Federico López, quoted in Albert Camarillo, *Chicanos in a Changing Society* (Harvard University Press, 1979) p. 156. (197) Manuel Ugarte, quoted in Thomas E. Skidmore and Peter H. Smith, *Modern Latin America* (New York: Oxford University, 1984) p. 328.

CHAPTER 16

(207) Pablo Mares, quoted in Manuel Gamio, *The Mexican Immigrant* (New York: Arno, 1969) p. 3. (207) Albert Camarillo, *Chicanos in California* (San Francisco: Boyd and Fraser, 1984) p. 331. (207) L.H. Gann and Peter J. Duignan, *The Hispanics in the United States: A History* (Boulder, Colorado: Westview, 1986) p. 441. (210) José Orozco, quoted in *Mexico, Splendors of Thirty Centuries* (New York: The Metropolitan Museum of Art, 1990) p. 591.

CHAPTER 17

(214) Albert Camarillo, *Chicanos in California* (Boyd and Fraser, 1984) p. 35. (217) Ernesto Galarza, quoted in Albert Camarillo, *Chicanos in California* (Boyd and Fraser, 1984) p. 36. (217) Albert Camarillo, *Chicanos in a Changing Society* (Harvard University Press, 1979) p. 148. (217) Elías Sepúlveda, quoted in Manuel Gamio, *The Mexican Immigrant* (Illinois: University of Chicago Press, 1931) p. 270. (217) Carlos Almanzán, quoted in Albert Camarillo, *Chicanos in California* (San Francisco: Boyd and Fraser, 1984) p. 39. (221) Department of Defense, "Registration 1918" (U.S. Government Printing Office, 1990) p. 26.

CHAPTER 18

(224) Ernesto Galarza, *Barrio Boy* (University of Notre Dame Press, 1971) p. 265. (227) Rodolfo Acuña, *Occupied America: The Chicano's Struggle Toward Liberation* (San Francisco, Canfield, 1972) p. 189. (228) Carey McWilliams, *North from Mexico: The Spanish-Speaking People of the United States* (New York: Greenwood Press, 1968) p. 193. (229) Luisa Moreno, quoted in Richard White, *Its Your Misfortune and None of My Own: A History of the American West* (University of Oklahoma Press, 1991) p. 471. (229) Ernesto Galarza, *Barrio Boy* (University of Notre Dame Press, 1971) p. 265. (231) Mark Reisler, *By the Sweat of Their Brow: Mexican Immigrant Labor in the United States, 1900–1940* (Westport, Connecticut: Greenwood Press, 1976) pp. 236–237.

CHAPTER 19

(242) L.H. Gann and Peter J. Duignan, *The Hispanics in the United States: A History* (Boulder, Colorado: Westview, 1986) (244) Carey McWilliams, *North from Mexico: The Spanish-Speaking People of the United States* (New York: Greenwood Press, 1968) p. 249.

UNIT 6

THE BIG PICTURE

(249) César Chávez, quoted in Peter Matthiessen, *Sal Si Puedes: César Chávez and the New American Revolution* (New York: Random House, 1969), p. 126.

CHAPTER 20

(257) Luis Cancel interview, March 3, 1993. (258) *Puerto Rico: A Brief Introduction* (Puerto Rico: Puerto Rico Economic Development Administration, 1990) p. 12. (258) Lolita Lebrón, quoted in Auturo Morales Carrión, *Puerto Rico: A Political and Cultural History* (New York: W.W. Norton, 1983) p. 293. (260) interview with a recent arrival at an unemployment office, March 3, 1993. (262) Luis Cancel interview. (262) Richard Rivera, quoted in Edward Mapp, *Puerto Rican Perspectives* (New Jersey: Scarecrow, 1974) p. 39. (262) C. Wright Mills, *The Puerto Rican Journey: New York's Newest Immigrants* (Russell, 1967) p. 26. (263) Julio Marzán, *Inventing a Word* "Ten con ten" (Columbia University Press, 1980) p. 20. (265) Belpré, quoted in *The Art of Writing for Children* (New Jersey Archives—N.Y. Public Library) p. 32. (265) Belpré, quoted in Lillian Lopez, *Puerto Rican Perspectives* (New Jersey: Scarecrow, 1974) p. 88.

CHAPTER 21

(268) Marta and Enrique Gutiérrez interview, March 11, 1993. (269) Marta Gutiérrez interview. (270) Peter Winn, *America* (New York: Pantheon, 1992) pp. 504, 505, 507. (273) Ana María Escagedo interview, March 11, 1993. (275) Miguel Seco interview, March 11, 1993. (276) María Escagedo interview.

CHAPTER 22

(282) César Chávez, quoted in Peter Matthiessen, *Sal Si Puedes: César Chávez and the New American Revolution* (New York: Random House, 1969), pp. 44–45. (283) César Chávez, quoted in Peter Matthiessen, *Sal Si Puedes: César Chávez and the New American Revolution* (New York: Random House, 1969) p. 46. (283) John Gregory Dunne, Delano (New York: Farrar, Straus, and Giroux, 1967) p. 71. (283) John Gregory Dunne, Delano (New York: Farrar, Straus, and Giroux, 1967) p. 72. (283) César Chávez, quoted in Peter Matthiessen, *Sal Si Puedes: César Chávez and the New American Revolution* (New York: Random House, 1969) p. 52. (283–84) César Chávez, quoted in Mark Day, *Forty Acres: César Chávez and the Farm Workers* (New York: Praeger,

1971) p. 9. (286) Mark Day, *Forty Acres: César Chávez and the Farm Workers* (New York: Praeger, 1971) p. 48. (283) Peter Matthiessen, *Sal Si Puedes: César Chávez and the New American Revolution* (New York: Random House, 1969) p. 52. (284) Peter Matthiessen, *Sal Si Puedes: César Chávez and the New American Revolution* (New York: Random House, 1969) p. 59. (285) César Chávez, quoted in John R. Howard, *Awakening Minorities: Continuity and Change* (Transaction Pub., 1983) p. 99. (288) Luis Valdez, quoted in Roger Hammer, *Hispanic America: Freeing the Free, Honoring Heroes* (Place in the Woods, 1984) p. 29. (288) Rubén Salazar, *Who is a Chicano? And What is it the Chicanos Want?* (Los Angeles Times, February 6, 1970). (294) Sara Evans, *Born for Liberty: A History of Women in America* (New York: Free Press, 1989) p. 273.

CHAPTER 23

(296) Sylvia Jordan interview, April 6, 1993. (297) Jordan interview. (298) Jordan interview. (299) Mónica Hernando interview, April 6, 1993. (299) Rodolfo Singer interview, April 6, 1993. (302) *Hispanic,* April, 1993.

CHAPTER 24

(304–5) Antonio Martorell interview, April 13, 1993. (305) Celia Vice, quoted in Edward Mapp, *Puerto Rican Perspective* (New Jersey: Scarecrow, 1974) p. 146. (307) Lourdes Casal, quoted in Nicolás Kanellos, *Biographical Dictionary of Hispanic Literature in the United States* (Westport: Greenwood Press, 1989) p. 53. (307) José Bedia, quoted in *Newsweek,* (November 30, 1992) p. 78. (314) Arnulfo D. Trejo, *The Chicanos, As We See Ourselves* "I Am Joaquín" (University of Arizona Press, 1979) p. 189. (318) "Arte Publico Press" *Poets and Writers* (March/April 1993) p. 44.

UNIT 7

THE BIG PICTURE

(321) Ricardo Aguilar Melantzón, quoted in Marilyn P. Davies, *Mexican Voices/American Dreams* (New York: Henry Holt, and Company), pp. 416–418.

CHAPTER 25

(328) Aurora Castillo, quoted in "L.A. Moms Fight Back" (*The Progressive,* August 1992) p. 3. (331) (*Newsweek,* May 20, 1991) p. 44. (331) Carlos

Fuentes, quoted in "Mirror of the Other" (*New Republic,* March 30, 1992) pp. 408–411. (332) "Maria Hinojosa, reporter for National Public Radio" (*New Yorker,* September 7, 1992). (334) Al Santoli, *New Americans* (New York: Ballantine Books, 1988) p. 285.

CHAPTER 26

(341) Mark Kurlansky, *A Continent of Islands* (Massachusetts: Addison-Wesley, 1992) p. 233. (341) José Rivera, quoted in Peter Winn, *America* (New York: Pantheon, 1992) p. 581.

CHAPTER 27

(349) Pedro Reboredo, quoted in Al Santoli, *New Americans* (New York: Ballantine Books, 1988) p. 382. (352) Ana María Escagedo interview, March 15, 1993. (354) *National Geographic,* January 1992.

CHAPTER 28

(358) *Facts on File,* October 1992. (359) María interview, April 20, 1993. (361) Jerry Nicaragua interview, April 20, 1993. (362) Carlos Vaquerano, *Hispanic,* April, 1993, p. 28. (362) *U.S. News and World Report,* May 25, 1992, p. 41. (363) Esmilda Maria Abreu interview, April 20, 1993.

CHAPTER 29

(368) Florencia Florentín Rivarola interview, April 7, 1993. (369) Florencia Florentín Rivarola interview. (370) Rodolfo Singer interview, April 7, 1993. (372) Monica Singer interview, April 7, 1993. (373) R. Singer interview.

CHAPTER 30

(376–77) Ralph García interview, April 29, 1993. (377) *U.S.A. Today,* August 27, 1991. (380) *U.S. News and World Report,* August 20, 1991, p. 31. (380) *New York Times,* May 11, 1992. (381) *Hispanic,* April, 1993, p. 30. (381) *Fortune,* May 17, 1993, p. 108. (381–82) Celia Cruz, quoted in Alex Stepick, *Report on the Americas,* September, 1992, pp. 39–45. (382) Alex Stepick, *Report on the Americas,* September, 1992, p. 18. (382) *Newsweek,* April 9, 1990, p. 20. (389) Manuel Sotomayor interview, April 29, 1993.

INDEX

Note: Pages in **boldface** indicate photographs, maps, charts, and graphs; pages in *italics* indicate incorporated biographies and galleries.

A

abolition
  in Texas, 114–115
  in Cuba, 174
abolitionists, 106
Abreu, Esmilda María, 363–364
Aburto Rice, Norma, 377
Acapulco, 41
Acoma pueblo, 56
acto, 287
Adams-Onís Treaty, 87
Adams, Quincy, 71
adelantados, 15
adobe, 5
affirmative action, 321
African Americans, 143, 144, 198, 239, 340, 377
  Civil Rights Movement (1941–1968), 251–252, 285, 286, 292
  discrimination, 220, 261
  Los Angeles (1992), 324
  population in U.S., 321
African-Caribbean, 306, 307
African Cubans, 190
African empires, 7
African West Indians, 196
Africans, 3, 6–7, 12. *See also* Slavery
  in British colonies, 67
Afro-Caribbean music, 316
Agrarian Reform Law (Cuba), 271
Aguiar-Vélez, Deborah, *384*
Aguila Blanca, 184
Aguilar Melantzón, Ricardo, 321
Ahearn, John, 342
Alamo, The, 60, 117–118
Alegría, Fernando, *301*
Algarín, Miguel, 306
aliancistas, 289
Alianza Federal de Pueblos Libres, (Federal Land Grant Alliance) 289
aliens, 334
Allende, Salvador, 254–255
Alliance for Progress, 254
Almanzán, Carlos, 217
Almonte, Juan, 117
Alta California, 61

Alvarado, Pedro de, 29–30, 36
Alvarez, Julia, *308*
Alvarez, Luis Walter, *386*
Alvariño de Leira, Angeles, *386*
Amaragos, Hanskabell, 377
American Federation of Labor (AFL), 231
  and Congress of Industrial Organizations (AFL-CIO), 283, 287
American G.I. Forum, 239
American Legion, 239
American Revolution, 68–70
  Spanish involvement in, 75–**78**
American Yellow Fever Commission, 188
Americas
  settlement of, **4–5**
Americas Review (journal), 318
Amigos del Tango, 302
amnesty, 174, 334
  Countries of Origin of Applicants for, 1986–1988, **334**
Anasazi, 5
Andrade, Oscar, 362
Angelina (the translator), *59*
Anglo American settlers, 77, 87
  influence in California, 133–135
  in New Mexico, 166–167
  in Texas, 101, 112–116
annex, 107
Anza, Juan Bautista de, 62
Apache, 5, 58, 60, 89
Apodaca, Jerry, 292
Appalachians, 75
Aquilar, Jerónimo de, 25
Arab, 8
Arbenz Guzman, Jacobo, 253, 297
Arboleya, Carlos José, *384*
Archuleta, Nancy E., *384*
Arévalo, Juan José, 297
Argentina, 90, 111, 148, 201, 253, 299–300, 325, 326
  immigrants to U.S., 300
Arias, Oscar, 326
Arista, Mariano, 125–126
Arizona, 128, 215, 218, 291, 292
  statehood, 168–169
Arkansas, 227
Arlington National Cemetery, 236
Armijo, Manuel, *96–97*, 123
Arnaz, Desi, 251, 315, 317
Arrau, Claudio, 251
Arroyo, Martina, *312*
Arte Público, 314, 318

Asians, 321, 322
ASPIRA, **264**
Atrévete, 341
Austin, Moses, 101
Austin, Stephen F., 101, 113, 115–117
Austria-Hungary, 197
autonomismo, 257
autonomy, 185
Áviles, Arthur, 346
Aztec, 4
  conquest of, 25–31
Aztlan, 32

B

Baca, Judith, *310*
Bacco, Julio, *312*
Baez, Joan, *312*
Balaguer, Joaquín, 278
Ballad of Gregorio Cortéz, The (movie), 246
Ballet Concierto de Puerto Rico, 346
balloons, use in war, **157**
Baja California, 61
Barkley, David, 215
Barletta, Naomi Lockwood, 382
barrio(s), 207–208, 216–217, 342
Barrio Boyzz, 388
Barroza, Rudy, 383
baseball, 366
Basque(s), 161, 234
Bataan Death March (1942), 237
Batista, Fulgencio, 254, 268–271
Baton Rouge, Louisiana, 78–79
Bay of Biscayne Boulevard (Miami), 374
Bay of Pigs (1961), 254, 272–**273**, 353
Bear Flag Republic, 126. *See also* California
Bedia, José, 307
Belaúnde Terry, Fernando, 254
Belpré, Pura, 264–265
Beltrán, Antonio, 383
Benavente, Fray Toribio de, 38
Benavides, Santos, 154
Berkeley (University of California at), 282, 301
Bernádez, Teresa, *386*
Bethlehem Steel, 220
bilingual, 265
Bilingual Education Act (1960), 292

Blades, Rubén, *362*
blockade, 274
blockading, 156
Bobo, Willie, 316
bodegas, 164, 256, 342
Bogotá, 90
Bolívar, Simón, 72, 90, 92, 173
Bolivia, 148, 325, 370
bombas, 316, 339
Bonaparte, Napoleon, 72
Border Jumpers, 336
Border Patrol, 225, 332
Bosch, Juan, 278
Bouchard, Hipólito, 89
Boyacá, 90
boycott, 286
bracero(s), 199, 240–242, **241**, 283
    as strikebreakers, 284
bracero program, 240, 284
Brazil, 201, 326, **327**
bridge countries, 274
Brigade 2506, 272
Briones de Miranda, Juana, 94
Bronze Star, 238
Brown Berets, 291
Brown v. *Board of Education*, 251
budget deficit, 321, 324
Buena Vista, Battle of (1847), 127
Buenos Aires, Argentina, 111, 299
Bush, George, 324
business interests, U.S.
    in Cuba, 188, 190, 269, 271, 324
    in Latin American, 198
    in Mexico, 327, 334–335
    in Puerto Rico, 260
Bustamante, Anastasio, 109

C

Cabeza de Vaca, Alvar Nuñez, 55
Cabrillo, Juan Rodríquez, 61
Caddo, 59
Calexico, Mexico, 283
Calhoun, William J., 178
California, 61, 88–89, 108–109, 291
    admission to Union, 133
    constitution of, 134–135
    Gold Rush, 132–**134**
    Great Central Valley, 283
    Great Depression, 227–229
    Mexican immigrants, 215–217
    possession by U.S., 126, 128
    the "Spanish state," 161
    ties with Great Britain, 99
    under Mexican rule, 98-99
   californio(s), 98, 126, 126–129, 132–135

Calle Ocho (Miami), 354, 356
Camarioca boatlift (1965), 274, **276**
Camden, New Jersey, 263
Camino Real, el, 57
campesinos, 368
Canada, 327, 335
Canal Zone, 196
Cancel, James, 266, 339
Cancel, Luis and Verania, 256–257, **261**, 262, 266, 340
Candelas, Graciela, *387*
Canseco, José, 366
Cárdenas, Lázaro, 200
Caribbean, 49–**50**
    during the 1960s and 1970s, **273**
Carlos III (King of Spain), 76
Carlos V (King of Spain), 41
Carnaval Miami, 356
Carnegie, Andrew, 144
Carranza, Venustiano, 204
Carrasco, Barbara, *310*
cartels, 370
Carter, Jimmy, 253, 255
Casal, Lourdes, 307
Casals, Pablo, *312*
casitas, 341
Castañeda, Carlos E., 239–*240*
Castillo Armas, Carlos, 297
Castillo, Aurora, 328
Castillo de San Marcos, 51
Castro, Fidel, 182, 254, 268–275, 298, 349–351
Castro, Raúl (of Arizona), 292
Castro, Raúl (of Cuba), 270–271
cattle
    in California, 98–99
   cattle drives, **78**, 113
    origins of, 80–81
caudillos, 109, 113, 253
Cavazos, Lauro, Jr., 321
Celso Barbosa, José, 261
Central America, 109, 149, 255, 297–299, 326, 358–362. *See also* El Salvador, Guatemala, Nicaragua
    conflict in, **300**
Central American Refugee Center (CARECEN), 362
Central American refugees, 380
Central Intelligence Agency (CIA), 253, 272, 297
centralism, 113
Centro Mater
    Daycare Center, 349, 352, 376–377
    Population of Children in 1993, **357**
    Runners, 376

Cervera y Topete, Pascual, 180
Céspedes, Carlos de, 173
cha-cha, 316
Chamorro, Violeta, 326
Chang-Diaz, Franklin, 158
Chapultepec, 127–128
Chaves, Manuel, **152**, *153*–154
Chávez, César, **248**, 252, **282**–287, 289, 291, 294
Chávez, Denise, 314
Chávez, Dennis, 232
Chávez, Helen, 283, 286
Chávez, Manuel, 284
Chicago, Illinois, 208, 219–220, 244, 260, 263, 276, 339
Chicana Service Action Center, 294
Chicano Art: Resistance and Affirmation, 1965–1985 (CARA), *310*
Chicano Family Center (Houston), 377
Chicano movement, 289–292. *See also El Movimiento*
Chicano Renaissance, 314
Chicano Youth Liberation Conference, 290
Chicanos(as), 217, 252–253, 288
    artists and writers, 314
Chile, 148, 254, 300, 325, 371
Chivington, John M., 153
Christianity
    in Americas, 37–38
cigar makers, 162–166
Cinco de Mayo, 226
Cisneros, Henry, **320**, 330, *383*
Cisneros, Sandra, *308*
civil disobedience, 289
civil rights laws, 251
Civilian Conservation Corps (CCC), 199
Clemente, Roberto, *317,* 366
Cleveland, Ohio, 219, 339
Clinton, Bill, 324–325, 383
Club Mexicano Independencia (CMI), 222
clubs, 163
Cold War, 249, 274, 297, 323–324
Colón, Miriam, 342
colonias, 216–217
colonization of the Americas, 8–9
Colorado, 128, 291
Columbia, 196, **298**, 300, 325, 370
    immigrants to U.S., 322, 372–373
Columbian Exchange, the, 39–41
Columbus, Christopher, 8, 10–11
    as governor, 14,16

exploration of Caribbean, 12–15
Columbus Day Celebration, 21
Columbus, New Mexico, 205
Comanche, 81, 124, 100
Comisión Femenil Mexicana Nacional, 294
commonwealth, 257
communes, 271
communism
    in Central America, 298, 323, 359
    in Cuba, 271
Communist(s), 249–250, 278
    Vietnamese, 252
Communist China, 249
Community Service Organization (CSO), 283, 285
Como, Puerto Rico, 184
Compromise of 1850, 109
***Confederación de Uniones de Campesinos y Obreros Mexicanos* (CUCOM) [Confederation of Unions of Mexican Farm Workers and Laborers],** 232
***Confederación de Uniones Obreras Mexicanas* (CUOM) [Confederation of Mexican Workers],** 231
Confederacy, the, 143
    and Latinos, 151–154
    attack of New Mexico, 153–154
congregaciones, 38
***Congreso de Pueblos de Habla Expañol, El,* (The Congress of Spanish-speaking Peoples),** 233
Congressional Medal of Honor, 213
    awarded to Mexican Americans, 238, 242
conquistadors, 9, 15, 161
Contras, 299, 323
convoy system, 48
Coolidge, Calvin, 187
Cordero, Rafael, 261
Córdoba, Argentina, 299
Corea, Chick, 316
Coronado, Vasquez de, 55–56
Coronel, Don Antonio, 132
corrido(s), 221
Cortés, Hernán, 9, 22–31, 34–35.
    See also Aztec, conquest of
Cortina, Juan Nepomuceno, *139*
Cós, General Martín Perfecto de, 117
Costa Rica, 149, 326
costeños, 372

cotton, 107, 101
Council of Spanish-Speaking People (Philadelphia), 338
Council of the Indies, 71
coup, 297
coyote, 332
Coyote, New Mexico, 289
Cozumel, 25
Crespi, Juan, 61–62
criollos, 42, 72, 73, 88
Crystal City, Texas, 290
Crockett, Davy, 118
Crusades, 7–8
Cruz, Antonio, 117
Cruz Azul Mexicana, 226
Cruz, Celia, *313,* 381–382
Cruz, Juana Ines de la, *41. See also* Sor Juana
***Cruzada Para la Justicia, La,* (The Crusade for Justice),** 290
Cuauhtémoc, *31*
Cuba, 15, 91, 349–351
    constitution, 189
    economy of, 174, 188, 190–191, 324
    end of Spanish rule, 148, 180
    independence, **189**
    political corruption, 190
    rebellion against Spain, 146, 157
    revolution, 249, 254, 269–272, 280
    struggle for independence, 172–179
    U.S. invasion of, 272–273
    U.S. military in, 180–181, 188–190, 197
Cuban(s)
    exiles, 272, 351
    in Florida, 160–161, 164–166
    immigrants to U.S., 164
    in Miami, 52, 272, 274–277, 280
    music, 315
    refugees, **248,** 274–**275**
Cuban Americans, 176, 276, 348–355, 361. *See also* Miami
    artists and writers, 307
    voters, 353, 381–382
Cuban Liberal party, 190
Cuban Missile Crisis (1962), 272–274
Cuban Revolutionary Army, 157
Cuban-Spanish-American War (1898), 146, 162, 179–**180**, 188, 192
Cubria, Mercedes, *274*
cultural diffusion, 40
cultural imperialism, 187

D

Dade County, Florida, 276, 353, 381

Dallmeier, Francisco, *386*
Darío, Rubén, 181
Davis, Richard Harding, 184–185
de la Cruz, Jesse López, 294
de la Renta, Oscar, *384*
death squads, 298, 359
Declaration of Independence (1776), 68, 70
Del Rio, Texas, 290
Delano, California, 283, 285–286, 288
Democratic National Convention (1968), 252
Democratic Party, 290
Denver, Colorado, 289
deportation, 228, 284
descamisados, 253
desparecidos, 300
Detroit, Michigan, 219, 244
Dewey, George, 180
Di Giorgio Fruit Corporation, 284, 286, 287
Día de la Patria, el, 163
Díaz, Bernal, 28
Díaz, Porfirio, 147–148, 202–204
disease
    as aid to conquest, 15, 31
    and Native Americans, 38
Distinquished Service Cross, 213, 215, 237
Distinquished Service Medal, 238
Dominican Republic, 146, 197, 254, 269, 277–278, 363–364, 366
Dominican Small Business Association, 365
Dominicans, 277–279
    baseball players, 366
    immigrants to U.S., 254, 278, 322, 340, 362–365
Domínguez, Cari, **354**
Domínguez, Manuel, 137
draft law (1914), 213
Drake, Sir Francis, 49
Duarte, José Napoleon, 326

E

Ecuador, 90, 325
East Harlem, 342
East Los Angeles, 328, 331, 380–381
Egyptian civilization, 7
Eisenhower, Dwight D., 297
***El Brillante* market,** **216**
***El Bronx Remembered* (Mohr),** *309*
El Caney, 179
***El Carroferril* (song),** 138
El Castillo de San Felipe del

Morro. *See* El Morro
El Clamor Público, 138, 140
"el desierto muerto," 124
El Diario/La Prensa, 140, 382
El Gallo, 290
El Morro, 192, 257
El Movimiento, 289, 310
  writers of, 314
El Paso-Juárez Trolley Company, 336
El Paso, Texas, 229, 332, 334, 336
El Rescate, 362
El Salvador, 149, 255, 297–299, 326, 359–360
  immigrants to U.S., 322, 359, 362
El Teatro Campesino, 287, 316
El Yara, 164
Elizabeth II (Queen of Spain), 156
Ely, Robert, 156
embargo, 351
emancipation, 73
Emergency Quota Act of 1921, 225
empresarios, 101, 116, 136
En el Norte (Barletta), 382
encomienda(s), 16–17
  laws ending, 36, 42
England
  colonies of, 8–9, 49–51
  war with Spain, 49
English on Wheels, 292
entradas, 55
entreprenuers, 383
Escagedo, Ana María, 273, 276, 352
Escalante, Jaime, 371–*372*
españoles, 96
Esparaza, Gregorio, 117–118
estadistas unidos, 259. *See also*
  New Progressive Party
Estado Libre Asociado de Puerto Rico (Free Associated State of Puerto Rico), 257. *See also* Puerto Rico
Estefan, Gloria, 356, 388
Esteves, Sandra María, 306
Europeans, 7–8
  and Mexican Americans, 220
  and Native Americans, 11
  as settlers in Carribean, 15–16
excommunicate, 111

F

Fair Employment Practices Committee (FEPC), 239–240
Farabundo Martí, Agustín, 299
Farabundo Martí National Liberation Front (FMLN), 299

farmworkers, 197, 199, 208–209, 215. *See also* Mexican immigrants; migrant farmworkers
  during Great Depression, 227–223
  Filipino, 285
  labor organizations, 225, 230–232, 283–287
Farragut, David, 155–156
Farragut, Jorge, 155
Fatio, Francis Philip, 86
Febres, George, *310*
federalism, 113
Felipe (King of Spain), 47–48
Ferdinand (King of Spain), 8
Fernández Cavada, Federico, 157–158
Fernández, Gisele, 388
Fernández, Roberto, 307, *308*
Fernández, Tony, 366
15th Amendment, 14
5307th Composite Group, 238
Finlay, Carlos Juan, *188*
Flight 8506, 351
Flores, Francisca, 294
Flores Magón, Ricardo and Enrique, 203
Florida, 47–48, 77, 85. *See also* Spanish Florida
Foraker Act (1900), 186, 213
Foraker, Joseph B., 186
Foreign Miners' Tax of 1850, 135
Fort Bute, 78
Fort Caroline, 47
Fort Pitt, 74, 77
Fort Texas, 124–125
14th Amendment, 143
France
  colonies of, 8–9, 47, 48
  Invasion of Mexico, 147
  World War II, 199
Franciscans, 37–38
Franco, Julio, 366
Frei, Eduardo, 254
French and Indian War (1754-1763), 67, 68, 75
French Croix de Guerre, 213, 214, 215
French Revolution, 72, 85
friars, 37
Fuentes, Carlos, 331

G

Gabaldón, Guy "Gabby," 237–238
Gadsen Purchase (1853), 108, 128
Galarza, Ernesto, 217, 224
Gálvez, Bernardo de, 73, 75–81, *76*, 85

Gálvez, José de, 61
Garcia, Andy, 388
García, Calixto, 179
García, Macario, 242
García, Ralph, 376-377
Garcilaso de la Vega, Inca, 374
Garduno, Adolfo, 237
Garfield High School, 372
Garrido, Juan, *15*
Gary, Indiana, 219
Garza, Jesús, 206
Garza, Juan, 242
gauchos, 111
genízaros, 96
Germany, 197, 199, 212–213
Gettysburg, Battle of (1863), 154, 157
GI Bill of Rights (1945), 239
Gibson, George, 74–75
glaciers, 3
Glorieta Pass, Battle at (1862), 152, 153–154
Goizueta, Roberto C., **353**, *385*
gold, search for, 23–24
Gold Star, **238**
Goldemberg, Isaac, *308*
Goliad, 118
Gómez, José Miguel, 190
Gómez, Máximo, 173, 177–178
Gonzales, Celedonio, 307
Gonzales, Manuel S., 237
Gonzales, Rodolfo "Corky," 289–291, **290**, 314
González, José Luis, 305, 383
González, Verania, 256–257
Good Neighbor Policy, 201
Gorbachev, Mikhail, 324
Gorras Blancas, las, 167
Gran Columbia, Republic of, 72–73, **89**, 90
Grand Central Market (Los Angeles), 381
Grande, Rutilio, 298–299
Grant, Ulysses S., 156
Great Britain
  colonies, 67–69
  and Latin America, 111, 148
  and Spain, 75
  War of 1812, 70
  World War I, 197
  World War II, 199
Great Depression (1929–1941), **198**–199
  effect on Latinos, 227–230
  in Latin America, 201
"great migration, the" (1950s), 260, 339

Great Society program, 252
Great Wall of Los Angeles, The,
   310, **315**
Greneda, 323
Griffin, Alfredo, 366
Grijalva, Juan de, 24
Grito de Lares, 162, 164
Guanahaní, 12
Guantánamo Bay, 182, 189, 274
Guaraní, 368`
Guatemala, 149, 253, 255, 296–298,
   325, 327, 358–359
Guatemalan
   exiles, 253
   refugees in U.S., 298
guerrilla war, 177
Guevara, Ernesto "Che," 254,
   270–271
gunboat diplomacy, 196
Gutierres Díaz, Abelardo, 165
Gutiérrez de Lara, Bernardo, 88
Gutiérrez, Horacio, *313*
Gutiérrez, José Angel, 290–**291,**
   330
Gutiérrez, Juana, 328–329
Gutiérrez, Luis, 341
Gutiérrez, Marta and Enrique,
   268–269, 271–272
Guzmán, Abimael, 370
Guzmán Fernandez, Antonio, 278
Guzmán, Nuño de, 55

H

haciendas, 42
Hágase Contrar, 382
Haiti, 85, 91, 197, 277
   immigrants to U.S., 322, 340
Harlington, Texas, 227
Hartford, Connecticut, 339
Havana, Cuba, 269–271, 349, 351
Hawaii, 161, 339
Hearst, William Randolph, 179
Henry, Patrick, 76
Hernández, Beatrice, 388
Hernández Cruz, Victor, 306
Hernández   de   Córdova,
   Francisco, 23–24
Hernando, Mónica, 299
Hidalgo y Castilla, Father Miguel,
   72, 88
hidalgos, 13
Hijuelos, Oscar, 307
Hinojosa, María, 331
Hinojosa, Rolando, 314
Hispanic Day Parade (New York
   City), **368**
Hispaniola, 12, 14, 15–16, 277

Hispano, 218
Hitler, Adolf, 199
Hohokam, 4
home rule, 186
Honduras, 149, 297
Hoover, Herbert, 228
Hopi, 5
Hornitos, California, 133
Hostos Community College, 305
House on Mango Street, The
   (Cisneros), *308*
How the García Girls Lost
   Their Accents (Alvarez), *308*
huelga, 231, 284–286
Huerta, Dolores, *286,* 294
Huerta, Victoriano, 204–205
human rights, 298, 359–360
Hussein, Saddam, 324

I

I Am Joaquín/Yo Soy Joaquín
   (Gonzales), 314
"I Love Lucy" (TV), 315
Idaho, 161, 234
Iglesias, Santiago, 187
illegal immigrants, **240, 284,**
   322–323, 332–334, 361
Immigration Act of 1924, 225
Immigration and Naturalization
   Service (INS), 332
Immigration Reform and Control
   Act of 1986, 323, 326, 332
immigrants, to U.S., 144–145,
   160–166, 195. *See also* Cubans,
   Dominicans, Mexicans, Puerto
   Ricans, Spanish
   and education, 372
   demand for, 215
   discrimination against, 145, 198
   population, 371
   poverty, 340, 380
Imperial Valley (California), 215
Inca, 4, 9
indentured servants, 67
independentistas, 258, 343–344.
   See also Puerto Rican Independence
   Party
Indian, **10,** 12
Indiana University, 318
indocumentados, 326, 332–333
inflation, 370
Influence of Sea Power Upon
   History, The (Mahan), 146
Instituto de Cultura Puerto-
   rriqueña (Institute of Puerto
   Rican Culture), 304–305
Insua, Alberto, *310*

Insurrectos, 173
Iran, 253
Iran-Contra scandal, 323
Iraq, 324
Isabella (Queen of Spain), 8, 14, 16
isolationism, 198
Italy, 199
Itliong, Larry, 285
Iturbide, Agustín de, 109

J

Jackson, Andrew, 118
Jackson Heights, 373
Japanese, 231
   World War II, 199, 236–237
Jefferson, Thomas, 70
Jémez Feast, 64
Jews, Latino, 280
jíbaros, 187, 260, 305
   music, **343**
Jim Crow laws, 143
Johnson, Lyndon B., 251, 278, 290,
   292
Jones Act (1917), 186–187, 213
Jones, Bill T., 346
Jordan, Sylvia, 296–297
Juan Bobo, 264
Juárez, Benito, 111, **147**
Juárez, Mexico, 229, 336
Julia, Raul, 316, 388
junta, 255

K

Kanellos, Nicolás, 318
Kearny, General Stephen W.,
   126–127
Kennedy, Ethel, 286
Kennedy, John F., 252, 254, 272,
   274, 290
Kennedy, Robert F., 252, **282,**
   286–287
Kent State University, 253
Kettle Hill, 179–180
King, Dr. Martin Luther, Jr., 251,
   252, 286, 290
Kino, Fray Eusebio, 54–55, 62
Kit Carson National Forest, 289
kivas, 5
Kuwait, 324

L

La Bamba (movie) *309*
La Capital, 41. *See also* Mexico City
La Carreta (The Oxcart)
   (Marqués) 305
La Carreta Made a U-Turn
   (Laviera), 306

La Causa, 284–25, 287–**288,** 331
La Cuarenta, 277
La Democracia, 186
la familia, 331
La Florida, 47–48. *See also* Florida
La Frontera, 333
La Isabella, 14, 15
la migra, 332–333
La Navidad, 13–14
La Opinión, 140
La Placita del Río Bonito, 170
La Raza Unida (The United People), 290–291, 330
La salamandra rosada (Vallbona), *309*
La vida es un especial (Fernández), *308*
labor unions, 240
Ladino, 280
ladinos, 359
Lakota, 3
Land Act of **1851,** 136
land grants, 135–136
L'Archeveque, Sostenes, 139
Larazolo, Octaviano A., 168, *218*
Laredo, Texas, 124, 240
Las Casas, Bartolomé de, 17, 18
Las Mujeres Muralistas, 314
latifundia, 271, 297
Latin America, 147–148, 200–201, **396**
  after World War II, 253–255
  democracy in, 325–326
  and Great Depression, 201
  heroes, 374
  independence from Mexico, 72–73, **90,** 91
  influence on U.S. culture, 316
  relations with Great Britain, 148
  U.S. intervention in, 196–197, 200–201, 253–255, 278
  World War I, 200
  World War II, 201
Latin Jazz (Suárez), *307*
Latinas, 294, 382
Latino(s)
  ancestors of, 6–7
  artists and writers, *308–313,* 318, 327
  California laws discriminating against, 135
  changes in the lives of, 1920s and 1930s, **235**
  civil rights, 226–227, 232, 285, 287. *See also* La Causa
  economic status, 380
  entrepreneurs, 382, *384–385*

immigrants to U.S., 251
influence on U.S. culture, 317–318, 383, 388
Jews, 280
job discrimination, 239
in NASA's space program, 158
and the New Deal, 229
population in U.S., 293, 321, **325,** 377, **378–379, 391**
scientists, 383, *386–387*
in the U.S. Civil War, 150–157
veterans of World War II, 239
in Vietnam, 291
voters, 382–387
in World War I, 212–214
in World War II, 236–239
Laviera, Tato, 306
League of United Latin American Citizens (LULAC), 227
Lebrón, Lolita, 258
lector, **164,** 165–166
Legion of Merit, 238
legislature, 67
Letter to Spanish Americans (Vizcardo y Guzmán), 84–85
Levitt, William J., 343
Levittown, Puerto Rico, 343
Libby Life (Cavada), 157
Libby Prison, Richmond, **157**
Liga Mexicana de Fútbol, La, 332
Liga Protectiva Mexicana, La, (The Mexican Protective League), 227
Lincoln, Abraham, 143, 156
Literatura chilena en el exilio, (Chilean Literature in Exile), 301
Little Havana, 276, 307, 348, 354, 356
Little Managua, 361
Lôme, Enrique Dupey de, 179
Longoria, Félix, 236-237, 239
Lopez, George, 102
Lopez, José, 102
López, Lillian, 265
López, Ricardo, 219
Lopez, Yolanda M., *310*
Los Angeles, 62–63, 130, 233, 276, 301, 339
  antiwar demonstrations, 253, 291
  Central American immigrants, 362
  civil unrest of 1992, 324, 380-381
  deportations, 229
  Latino population, 331
  Mexicans in, 208, 217, 329, 331
  South Americans in, 371–372

  zoot-suit riots, 244
Los Four, 314
Los Lobos, **316,** 388
Los Tigres del Norte, 332
Louisiana, 86–87
Louisiana Purchase (1803), 70, 87
L'Ouverture, Toussaint, 91
Lucero, Nicolás, 214
Lugo, Don Vincente, 130
Luna, Maximiliano, 180
Luna y Arellano, Tristán de, 47

M

Macéo, Antonio, **142,** 173, **177**
Machado y Morales, Gerardo, 190, 269
Madero, Francisco I., 202–204
mador, 62
maestra, 62
Magee, Augustus, 88
Mahan, Alfred Thayer, 146
Maine, U.S.S. (battleship), 178–179
maize, 44
Male, Belkis Cuza, *309*
Malintzin, 25. *See also* Maria, Doña
Malta, Elígio Carbonell, 160–161
Malvestiti, Abel, 302
mambo, 315
Mambo Kings Play Songs of Love, The (Hijuelos), 307
Manila Bay (Philippines), 180
maquiladora(s), 334–**335**
Mares, Pablo, 207
Margarita Miranda, Sister, 348
Maria, Doña, 26, 29
Marichal, Juan, 366
Mariel boatlift, 307, 349–351, **350**
Mariels, 351
Marqués, René, 305
Marshall, Carlos, 383
Marshall Plan, 249
Martí, José, 172–177, **175,** 181
martial law, **177–178**
Martínez, Dennis, 366
Martínez, José P., 238
Martínez, Vilma, 294
Martorell, Antonio, 304–**306,** *311*
mass production, 144
Matamoros, Mexico, 122, 124–125
materialism, 175
Maximilian, Ferdinand, 147
Maya, 3–4, 23–25, 36, 43, 362
  in Guatemala, 358–359
Mayagüez, Puerto Rico, 339, 344, 345
McCarthy, Joseph, 250
McCarthyism, 250

McKinley, William, 178–179
Medal of Honor, 215, 238. *See also* Congressional Medal of Honor
Medellín, Octavio, *311*
Menchaca, Joseph Félix, 81
Menchú, Rigoberta, 327, 358
Méndez, José, *387*
Mendoza, Don Antonio de, 55
Menéndez de Avilés, Pedro, *48*
Menocal, Mario García, 190
merengue, 316, 339
Mesilla, New Mexico, **94**
mestizos, 42, 62
Mexican American Legal Defense and Education Fund (MALDEF), 292, 334
Mexican Americans, 133, 328–335. *See also* Latinos; Los Angeles; migrant farmworkers
in California, 134–136
discrimination against, 135, 137–138, 145, 209, 213, 220, 236
gangs, 242–244, **243**
and labor organizations, 218, 225, 252
in Midwest, 208, 218–220
in New Mexico, 133–134, 228
in New York, 331–332
in Northeast, 220
organizations, 226
outlaws, 138–139
prejudice, 220, 242
population in U.S., 335
strikes, 213, 218, 231–232
voters, 290–291, 330, 331
wage discrimination, 229, 284
women, 239
in World War I, 213–215, 221
in World War II, 236–238
Mexican Cession, 108
Mexican Independence Day (September 16), 285
Mexican immigrants to U.S., 203, 206–209, 214–218, 225–226, 321, 332–334
deportation, 228–**229**
Mexican Revolution, **88**, 200, 203–206, 215
artists of, 210
and Mexican Migration to U.S., **208**
U.S. interest in, 204–205
Mexico, 123, 200, 203, 325. *See also* Republic of Mexico
constitution of 1824, 109; of 1836, 110; of 1857, 111; of 1917, 205–206

economy of, 326–327
Northern Frontier, 1822, **108**
and Texas, 107, 110, 113–119
war with U.S. (1846–1848), 107–108, 111, 124–128, **125**
World War II, 237
Mexico City, **28**, 35–36, 40–41, 109, 203
Miami, Florida, 272, 301
Cuban population, 274–277, 348–356
Guatemalans in, 296–297
and Latin America, 354–355
Nicaraguans in, 361
Middle Passage, 19
Mier y Terán, Manuel de, 112, 114
migrant farmworkers, 227, 230–231, 252
strikes, 284–286
unionization of, 282–287
migrant workers, 209
migration, 3
Miles, Nelson A., 180, 184
Minutemen, 68
Miranda, Francisco de, 84
Miró, Esteban, 86–87
Mission Espíritu Santo, 80
Mission Trail, El Paso, 336
missions, 38, 54–59, 61–63
in California, 61–62, **63**, 98
locations of, **57**
Mississippi River, 75–76
fight for, 78–79
Spanish closure of, 87
Mississippians, 6
Missouri Compromise (1820), 106
Mobile, Alabama, 79
Mobile Bay, Battle of (1864), 156
Mogollon, 4
Mohr, Nicholasa, 306, *309*
mojados, 240–241
Molina, Gloria, *331*, 381
Monroe Doctrine, 71, 146, 197
Monroe, James, 71
Montecuhzoma, 25–30
Monterey, California, 89
Monterrey, Mexico, 330
Montesinos, Fray Antonio de, 17, 46
Montoya, Joseph, 291–292
Morales, Eddie, 377
Moreno, Antonio, 139
Moreno, Luisa, 228, *232*
Moreno, Rita, 316
Mothers of East Los Angeles (META), **328**–329, 331

Motolinía. *See* Benavente, Fray Toribio de
Mound Builders, 5
Mountain Men, 106
mulattoes, 42
multinationals, 353
Muñoz Marín, Luis, *257*–260, 343
Muñoz Rivera, Luis, *186*
Muñoz, Victoria, **344**
mural(s), 210, 314, **320**
Murieta, Joaquín, 139
Museo del Barrio, El, 305–**306**, 342
Muslims, 8
mustangs, 60
mutualistas, 217, 222, 226, 232

N

Nacogdoches, Texas, 81, 88
Nahuatl, 25, 43
Napoleon III, 147
Narváez, Pánfilo de, 47, 55
National Chicano Moratorium, 291
National Farm Workers Association (NFWA), 284–287, 294
National Guard, 252–253, 289
National Road, 105
nationalism, 111
nationalization, 200
Nations of the World, **394**
Native Americans, **6**. *See also* slavery
allies of Spanish, 78
and British colonists, 67
conversion to Christianity, 13, 38, 56
and Cortés, 25
discrimination against, 145–146
in New Spain, 42–43
origins of, 3
of U.S. Southwest, 5
Navajos, 5
naval stores, 86
Navarro, José Antonio, 118, 120
Navy Commendation Medal, 238
Nespral, Jackie, 388
Nevada, 128
New Deal, 199
New Granada, 90
New Mexico, 56, 88–89, 237
consitutional convention, 168–**169**
land ownership in, 136
Mexican Americans in, 218, 229, 291–292
seizure by U.S., 126
statehood, 168–169, 218
under Mexican rule, 94–98

under U.S. rule, 133–136
and the U.S. Civil War, **152**–154,
New Orleans, Louisiana, 75–**77,**
82
capture of, 156
New Progressive Party (PNP),
258, 344
New Spain, 35–36, 41–43
New York City, 162–164, 220, 276,
301
Mexican Americans, 331–332
Puerto Rican artists, 305–306
Puerto Ricans, 260
South Americans in, 373
New York Journal, 179
New York Public Library, 265
New York Stock Exchange, 381
New York World, 179
Newark, New Jersey, 260, 276, 339
Nicaragua, 149, 197, 200, 254, 299,
323, 326, 359
immigrants to U.S., 322, 360–361
Nicaragua, Douglas, 377
Nicaragua, Jerry, 361, 377
Nicaraguan National Guard, 200
Nilda (Mohr), *309*
Niña, 11–12
Nixon, Richard M., 252–253
Nobel Peace Prize, 326, 327, 358
Noche en vela (Vallbona) *309*
noche triste, la, 30–31
Nogales, Arizona, 217
Nogales, Luis, *385*
nomads, 3
Noriega, Manuel, 324
North American Free Trade
Agreement (NAFTA), 327, 335
North Atlantic Treaty Organization
(NATO), 249
North Korea, 249
Northern Manhattan Coalition for
Immigrant Rights, 365
Northwest Territory, 70
Nueces River, 123–124, **125**
Nuestra Señora de Dolores
Mission, 55
nuevomexicanos, 94–97, 128–129,
166–169, **167**
Nuyorican Poets Cafe, 306
nuyoricans, 306, 340, 343

O

Obregón, Alvaro, 206
Ochuse, Florida, 47
October Crisis. *See* Cuban Missile
Crisis
Office of the Commonwealth of

Puerto Rico, 263, 341
Oklahoma, 227
Olmos, Edward James, 246, 316, 388
Olvera, Don Augustín, 130
Oñate, Juan de, 56–57
Open Door policy, 146
Operation Bootstrap, 260
Operation Desert Storm, 324
Orden de Hijos de América, La,
(The Order of the Sons of
America), 227
Ordinances of Governances, 48
Oregon, 106–107
Organization of American States
(OAS), 249
Orozco, José Clemente, 210, 314
Ortega, Daniel, 326
Ortega, Katherine, *385*
Ortíz Cofer, Judith, 306
Osbahr, Carmen, 390
Ovando, Nicolás de, 16, 23

P

pachucos, 242–244, 246
Pact of Zanjón, 174
Padilla, Heberto, 307, *309*
Palatka, Florida, 155
Palés Matos, Luis, 263
Palma, Tomás Estrada, 189
Panama, 196, 324
Panama Canal, 195–196
Pan-American Union, 200
Pantoja, Antonia, 262–264
Paraguay, 368–369
Parliament, 67–68
Parris, Daysi, 277–278
Partido del Pueblo, el, 167
Partido Popular Democrático
(PPD), 257–258
Partido Revolucionario Institu-
cional (PRI), 325
partido system, 96–97
patriots, 75
patrones, 95
Paz, Octavio, 327
Pedroso, Pauline, *176–177*
Pearl Harbor, 236–237
Pelli, César, *311*
Peña, Elizabeth, 388
Peña, Federico, 383
peninsulares, 42, 72, 73
Pennsylvania, 220
Pennsylvania Railroad, 220
Pensacola, Florida, 47, 79–80
peonage, 42
per capita income, 271
Peralta, Pedro de, 57

Peralta, Vincente, 135–136
Pérez, Javier, 326
Pérez, Manuel, 238
Pérez-Méndez, Victor, *387*
Pérez, Pedro, *311*
Pérez, Rosie, 388
Perón, Evita, 253
Perón, Juan, 253
Pershing, John J., 206
Persian Gulf War (1990), 324
Peru, 90, 148, 254, 325, 349, 370
Peruvian
musicians, 371
writers, 374
Philadephia, Pennsylvania, 260,
339
Philip II (King of Spain), 56
Philippines, 237
Pico, Andrés, 127
Pico-Union, 362, 380–381
Pima peoples, 54
Piñero, Jesús T., 257
Piñero, Miguel, 306
Pinochet, Augusto, 255
Pinta, 11–12
Pinzón, Martín Alonso, 11, 36
Pittsburgh Pirates, 317
Pizarro, Francisco, 9, 36
Platt Amendment, 189–190, 269
plenas, 316, 341–342
Plyer v. *Doe,* 361
poblanos, 62
political exiles, 272
Polk, James K., 124–125
Pollock, Oliver, 76, 78
Ponce de León, Juan, 15, 47
Popé, 58
Popular Democratic Party (PPD),
344
popular sovereignty, 109
porteños, 111
Porter, David, 155
Portolá, Gaspar de, 61
poverty line, 262, 340
presidio, 14
privateers, 49
Profecia de Guatimoc (Rodri-
quez-Galvan), 97
Progressives, 195
protectorate, 189
Protestant Church, 256, 266
protesters
antiwar, 252–253, 291
Public Law 600, 258. *See also*
Puerto Rico, Constitution Act
public works program, 199
Pueblo de Los Angeles, 130. *See*

also Los Angeles
pueblos, 5, 55
Puente, Tito ("El Rey"), *313*
Puerto Rican(s), 338–324
  artists and writers, 304–306, 342
  civil rights in U.S., 292–293
  culture, 305–306
  dance, 346
  in New York, 162–164, 251, 256–257, 260–265, 293, 339
  in New York City and on the Mainland, **262**
  Population Distribution, **340**
  population in U.S., 340
  post-WWII migration to U.S., 256–265, **262**
  U.S. citizenship, 186–187, 213, 257
  voters, 341
  in World War I, 213
  in World War II, 237, 239
Puerto Rican Family Institute, 263
Puerto Rican Forum, 263
Puerto Rican Heritage Publications, 305
Puerto Rican Independence Party (PIP), 258
Puerto Rican Merchants Association, 262
Puerto Rican Traveling Theater, 342
Puerto Rico, 15, 19, 49, 91, 343–345
  Constitution Act (1950), 258
  constitution of, 258
  end of Spanish rule, 148
  environment, 344–345
  government of, 185–188
  independence movement, 163
  political parties, 343–344
  rebellion against Spain, 162
  self-government, 257–260
  statehood, 259, 344
  under U.S. rule, 186–188
  U.S. invasion of, 180, 184–186
puertorriqueños, 260
Pulitzer, Joseph, 179
Pulitzer Prize, 307
Purple Heart, 213, 215

Q

Quetzalcoatl, 26. *See also* Cortes; Motecuhzoma
Quiche Indians, 327
Quinn, Anthony, 388
Quintanilla, Selena, 329
Quiroga, Vasco de, 38
Quisqueya Heights, 364

R

racism, 261, 278
railroads, 143–144, 166
  Mexican workers, 225, 240
Ramírez, Francisco, P., 140
Ramón, Diego, 58–59
rancheros, 81
ranchos, 57
  California, 98–99
Reagan, Ronald, 321–324, 360
Reboredo, Pedro, 349
recession, 324
Reconstruction, 143
Recovering the Hispanic Literary Heritage of the United States, 318
Red scare, 250
Redcoats, 68
Reed, Walter, 188
referendum, 344
refugee, 274
Refugee Act of 1980, 349
Registro de 1918, 221
repatriados, 229
repatriate, 228
Republic of San Joaquín, 289
Republic of Texas, 118. *See also* Texas
  recognition by U.S., 123
  relations with Mexico, 122–125
Republicans, 143
reservations, 145–146
resistance
  to Spanish conquest, 13, 15
  by pueblos, 57–58
ricos, 96
Rio Grande, 58, 108, 332
  border of Texas, 123–124, 128
Rivarola, Florencia Florentín, 368–370, **369,** 372
Rivera, Diego, 210, 314
Rivera, Richard, 262
Rivero, Horacio, 238
Roaring Twenties, 198, 221
Rockefeller Foundation, 318
Rockefeller, John D., 144
Rodríguez, Bermejo, 11
Rodríguez, Cleto, 238
Rodríguez Galván, Ignacio, 97
Rodríguez, Gerard, 238
Roman Catholic
  Church, 206, 298–299
  priests, 37
  religion, 266, 275
  religious conversions, 25
Romero, Oscar, 299
Ronstadt, Linda, 316
Roosevelt Corollary, 197

Roosevelt, Franklin D., 199, 200–201, 229, 239
Roosevelt, Theodore, 146, 179–180, 196–197
Rosas, Manuel de, 111
Rosenberg, Julius and Ethel, 250
Rosita (of "Sesame Street"), 390
Ros-Lehtinen, Ileana, 381
Ross, Fred, 282–283, 286
Rossello, Pedro, 344
Rough Rider Regiment, 179–180, 188
Royal Chicano Airforce, 314
Roybal-Allard, Lucille, 294, 382
Ruiz, Francisco, 118

S

Sacramento, California, 286
St. Augustine, Florida, 46 48, 50, 84–**85**
St. Croix, U.S. Virgin Islands, 12–13
St. Denis, Louis, 59
St. Louis, Missouri, 203, 219
Saipan, 238
Sal Si Puedes, 282
Salazar, Rubén, 253, 288, 291
Salinas, California, 219
Salmón, María, 381
salsa, 316, 339, 342, 381
Saltillo, Mexico 115
Samaniego, Ramón, 383
Sampson, William T., 179
San Antonio, Texas 60, 88, 115–118, **137,** 203, 227, 232,
  Mexican Americans in, 329–331
San Antonio de Béjar, 81
San Antonio Light, 329
San Diego, California, 61, 333
San Francisco, California, 62
San Gabriel, New Mexico, 56
San Jacinto, Battle of (1836), 118–119
San Jose State (University), 282
San José y San Miguel de Aguayo Mission, 229
San Juan Bautista, 58
San Juan Capistrano, 89
San Juan Hill, 179
San Juan, Puerto Rico, 192, 256, 260, 345
San Martín, José de, 90
San Miguel, Lolita, 346
San Pasqual, Battle of (1846–1847), 126
San Salvador, 12, 299. *See also* Guanahaní

San Telmo, 299
Sánchez, Félix, **214**
Sánchez, José, 112
Sánchez, Lola, 154–155
Sánchez, Luis Rafel, 305
Sánchez, Pedro Antonio, *387*
Sanctuary Movement, 360
Sandista Front for National Liberation (FSLN), 299
Sandinistas, 255, 299, 323
Sandino, Augusto César, 200, 255, 299
Santa Anna, Antonio López de, 109–110, *114*–118, 127
Santa Barbara, California, 89, 209 222
Santa Fe Battalion, 237
Santa Fe, New Mexico, 38, 57–58
Santa María, 11–12
Santamaría, Mongo, 316
Santana, Carlos, *313*
Santana, Rafael, 366
santero, 95, 102
Santiago, Chile, 301
Santiago, Cuba, **149,** 179–180
Santo Domingo, 16–17, 19, 277, 363
Sarmiento, Domingo Faustus, 105, 111
Scott, General Winfield, 127–128
Scribner's Magazine, 185
Se Habla Español, 390
secede(d), 143, 152
Seco, Miguel, 275–276
secularized, 98
segregation, 143, 251
Seguín, Juan, 117–120
Sendero Luminoso, el, *See* Shining Path
Sepúlveda, Dolores, 132
Sepúlveda, Elías, 217
Serna, Marcelino, 212–213
Serra, Fray Junípero, 61–62
"Sesame Street" (TV), 390
Shafter, William R., 179
Shining Path, the, 370
Sibley, Henry Hopkins, 153
Sierra Maestra (mountains), 270
Silent Majority, 252
Silver Star, 238
silver trade, 40–41
Singer, Rodolfo, 299–300, 302, 372
Siqueiros, David, 210
slave trade, 7
  beginnings of, 18–19
slavery, 7
  abolition of, 92
  and Africans, 17–19, 40

in British colonies, 67
in Cuba and Puerto Rico, 91, 174
in Haiti, 91
and Native Americans, 12, 14, 18, 55
in Texas, 101, 114–115, 118
under U.S. Consitution, 70
Slidell, John, 124
social bandits, 138–139
Social Security, 199
socialism, 297
Somoza, (family), 255, 299
Sonora, Mexico, 133
Sor Juana, 40–42
Soto, Gary, 314
Soto, Hernando de, 47
Soto, Pedro Juan, 305
Sotomayor, Manuel, 388–389
South America
  independence from Spain, 72, 89–91
South American
  immigrants to U.S., 300–301, 368–373
South Bronx, 256–257, 341, 343
South Bronx Project, 265
South Central Los Angeles. *See* Los Angeles
South Korea, 249
Southern Pecan Shelling Company, 232–**233**
Soviet Union, 249–250, 323–324
  and Cuba, 254, 273–274
Soza, Johnny, 377
Spain
  colonies, 8–9, 47
  and Cuban refugees, 272, 274, 275
  and Portugal, 10, **90**
  treaty with U.S., 85
  war against Britain, 77–80
  war against U.S. *See* Cuban-Spanish-American War
Spanish
  aid in American Revolution, 75–**78**
  Armada, **9,** 49
  Borderlands, 54–55, 58
  colonies in 1763, 71
  colonists and American Revolution, 69
  conquest of Americas, 12–17
  contributions in the American Revolution, **78**
  empire in the Americas (1600), **14**
  exploration, 5, 11, **14**
  Florida, 71, 80, 85, 87
  harbor defenses in the Caribbean, 1695, **53**
  immigrants, 161–162

Louisiana, 75
  rule in Latin America, end of, 148
Spanish Settlements
  in California, **63**
  in Florida and the Caribbean, **50**
  in the Southwest, **57**
Spanish-speaking people, 289
  immigrants to U.S., 161–166, 233
  prejudice against, 261
Spanish Speaking People's Division (of the U.S. State Department's Office of Inter-American Affairs), 244–245
squatters, 136
Stand and Deliver (movie), 246, 372
Stanford University, 282
Strawberry Strike, 231
Stroessner, Alfredo, 369–370
Suárez, Eduardo, 349, 351
Suárez Escagedo, Lucía, 348
Suárez, Virgil, 307
Suárez, Xavier, 353–*354*
sugar, 18–19
  in Cuba, 188, 190–**191,** 271
  trade in Caribbean, **18,** 91
Sugarland, Texas, 242
superpowers, 249

T

Tabasco, Mexico, 25
tabaqueros, 162. *See also* cigar makers
Taino, 11–12,14–16, 192
tallow, 98-99
Tampa, Florida, 160–161, 165
tango, the, 302
Tango Argentino (play), 302
tariff, 174
Taylor, General Zachary, 124, 126–127
Tecumseh, U.S.S. (battleship), 156
tejano(s), 100–101, 113, 115–119, 128
  music, 329–330
Tejeda, Frank, 330
Telemundo, 388
Temple Emanu-El (Miami), 280
Ten Years' War, 173–174. *See also* Cuba.
Tennessee (battleship), 156
Tenochtitlán, 25, 27–31, 34–35
Texas, 58–60, 80–81, 87, 227, 237
  annexation of, 107–108, 124
  Chicano movement, 290
  fight for, 88
  and Great Britain, 124
  independence from Mexico,

116–119, 122
land ownership in, 136
Mexican workers, 240–241
and New Mexico, 123–124, 152–153
revolt, 1835–1836, **119**
settlement of, 100–101
under Mexican rule, 112–116
and U.S. Civil War, 152–154
Thomas, Beth, 377
Thomas, Piri, 306
Three Rivers, Texas, 236
Tijerina, Reies López, 289
title, 135
Tlatelolco, 29
Torres, Rigoberto, 342
Trabajadores Unidos (United Workers), 218
Travis, William B., 116–117
Treaty of Guadalupe Hidalgo (1848), 108, 128, 135, 168
Treaty of Paris (1783), 69, 81
Trujillo, Rafael, 254, 269, 277–278, 363
Truman, Harry S., 257

U

Ugarte, Manuel, 197
Unanue, Joseph A., *385*
underground, 268
Unidos Contra EL SIDA (United Against AIDS), 341
Union City, New Jersey, 352
Unión de Trabajadores del Valle Imperial, La, (The Union of Workers of the Imperial Valley), 231
United Farm Workers (UFW), 252, 287, 314
United Fruit Company, 149, 253, 297
United Nations, 326
United Provinces of Central America, 149. *See also* Central America
United States of America, 69, **392**. *See also* American Revolution
acquisition of Guam, the Philippines, Puerto Rico, Wake, 180
acquisition of Spanish and Mexican lands, **129**
annexation of Texas, 108, 124
and Central America, 297–299, 323–324
Civil War, 143
Constitution of, 69–70
and Cuba, 173–174, 178–181, 188–190, 254, 272–274

and Dominican Republic, 278
and El Salvador, 359
expansion of, 105–109, 119, 146
and Guatemala, 297
industrialization, 161
invasion of Mexico, 127–128, 205
and Latin America, 146, 148–149, 196–197, 324
and Nicaragua, 359
settlers from, 107
slavery in, 105–106, **108**
war with Mexico (1846–1848), 107–108, 111, **125**
war with Spain. *See* Cuban-Spanish-American War
World War I, 197
World War II, 199, 201
U.S. Central Intelligence Agency. *See* Central Intelligence Agency
U.S. Congress, 179, 186, 341, 381–382
U.S. Counter Intelligence, 274
U.S. House of Representatives, 258, 341
U.S. Immigration Service, 228
Universidad Boricua, 264
University of Houston, 318
University of Texas, 239
Univision, 388
Unzaga, Luis de, 75
Uruguay, 300, 325
Utah, 128

V

Valázquez, Loreta Janeta, 150–152, **151**
Valdéz, Luis, 246, 287–288, *309,* 316
Valentino, Rudolph, 302
Vallbona, Rima de, *309*
Valle, Pedro del, 238
Vallejo, Manuel, 126
Vallejo, Mariano Guadalupe, 98–**99**
Valley of Mexico, 28
vaqueros, 60, 81
Vargas, Diego de, 58
Vásquez, Tiburcio, 139
vassals, 27
Vázquez de Ayllón, Lucas, 46
Vega, Bernardo, 163
Vega, Ed, 306
Velázquez, Diego, 23–24
Velázquez, Nydia, *341,* 382
Venceremos, 271, 290
Venezuela, 90, 146, 325, 326, 371
Veracruz, Mexico, 27, 38, 110, 127
seizure by U.S., 205

Vicario, Leona, *88*
Vice, Celia, 305
Vicksburg, Mississippi, 156
Victory Medal, 213, 215
Vietnam War, 252, 291
Villa, Francisco "Pancho," 204– 205
Villalobos, Gregorio, 38
Violencia, la, 359
Viruet, Lida, 339, 340, 344–345
Vizcardo y Guzmán, Juan Bautista, 84

W

Wagner Act (1935), 230
war factories, 239
War of 1812, 70–71, 156
War of the North American Invasion (1846–1848), 200
War of the Pacific (1879–1883), 148
Washington, D.C., 264
Washinton Heights, 364–365
Watergate, 253
Western Europe, 249, 326
Weyler, Valeriano, 177–178
Willing, James, 77
Wilson, Woodrow, 197, 204, 213
Women's Army Corps., 236, 274
Wood, Leonard, 188
World War I, 197, 200, 212–215
Honor Roll, **215**
World War II, 199, 236–239
Honor Roll, **238**
and Latin America, 201
Wounded Knee (1890), 146
Wyoming, 128

Y

Yabucoa, Puerto Rico, 341
Ybarra-Frausto, Tomás, 318
Ybor, Vicente Martínez, *165*
yellow fever, 188
yellow journalism, 179
Young Lords, 292–**293**
Yucatán Peninsula, *24*

Z

Zapata, Emiliano, *205*
Zavala, Lorenzo de, 116, 118–119
Zéspedes, Vicente Manuel de, 85–86
Zimmermann, Arthur, 200
zoot suit, 242–243
Zoot Suit (play) 246, *309*
Zoot-Suit riots, 244–**245**
Zuloaga, Milton, 377
Zuñi, 55